COLLINS
COBUILD

ENGLISH
USAGE

D0012257

THE UNIVERSITY
OF BIRMINGHAM

COLLINS
COBUILD

HarperCollins*Publishers*

HarperCollins Publishers
77-85 Fulham Palace Road
London W6 8JB

COBUILD is a trademark of William Collins Sons & Co Ltd

ISBN 0 00 370258 8 Paperback

Computer typeset by Promenade Graphics, Cheltenham
Printed and bound in Great Britain by Caledonian International
Book Manufacturing Ltd, Glasgow, G64

www.cobuild.collins.co.uk

Editorial team

Editor in Chief	John Sinclair
Editorial Director	Gwyneth Fox
Senior Editors	Elizabeth Manning John Todd
Assistant Editor	Ann Hewings
Editorial assistance	Ramesh Krishnamurthy Alyson McGee Christina Rammell Keith Stuart
Computer Officer	Zoe James
Secretary	Sue Crawley

HarperCollins Publishers
Annette Capel, Lorna Heaslip, Douglas Williamson

We would like to thank Mona Baker for her useful comments on the text, Louise Ravelli for assistance on the grammar entries, and Paul Laurent for checking American usage. We would also like to thank the people who suggested points to include in the book, in particular Maksymilian Baranowski, Abkarovits Endre, Francisco Gomes de Matos, Yuan Kele, Wolf Paprotté, and Martin Warren.

Introduction

I am very pleased to introduce an important addition to the COBUILD range of English Reference books. For the first time, a usage book has been compiled from a large and representative corpus of English texts – the Bank of English. Usage has long been a rather mysterious feature of language – partly a kind of 'good manners' with language and partly a set of notes on individual words. Neither a grammar nor a dictionary, a usage book seemed to fall in between them, with no proper place for it in language study.

COBUILD has changed all that. Our compilers are able to find out how people actually use language, by studying millions of words. The statements in this book are based on this study, and are supported by actual examples, not invented ones. Usage becomes the centre of language patterning, not a footnote to it.

When the COBUILD project was first set up in 1980, there were three books mentioned. One, a radical new dictionary, was the main aim, but it was thought at the time that two other books would make up a fairly comprehensive set of information about English. These were a grammar and a usage book.

The Dictionary was published in 1987, and the Grammar in 1990. This Usage Book completes the trio. Nearly everything a person needs to know about English should be found in one of these three books.

Usage is the vital detail of language, involving aspects of grammar, meaning, idiom, variety and purpose. It concentrates on the individuality of expression, and most of its statements concern the way words are arranged to express a particular meaning or to do a particular job. There is no generality in most of the statements in this book, because usage deals with all the things that are not covered by the generalities.

Grammar properly deals with broad general statements, like the distinction between count and uncount nouns, or transitive and intransitive verbs. Each of these divides into sub-classes and sub-sub-classes and so on until eventually we get down to the unusual behaviour of just one or two words. The point of grammar is now lost, and the detailed patterns of usage can be set out individually.

There is no strict dividing line, and many grammars for teaching are heavily biased towards usage. It is, after all, the usage end of grammar that learners most need. However powerful the generalities, learners are eventually measured by the actual words and phrases they use, and so they are probably more concerned about the precise points of usage than the abstract notions of countability or transitivity.

In this book, we provide a number of entries on grammatical categories in order to link the facts of usage with the broader issues of grammar. Beyond this level the reader must turn to the Collins Cobuild English Grammar for fuller treatment.

A traditional dictionary does not give much usage information, though some modern dictionaries, like the COBUILD range, show a lot through the choice of typical real examples. Dictionaries of idioms come close to usage, but the special meaning that we associate with an idiom is not usually a feature of a usage statement.

More and more nowadays, reference books are trying to help a user produce competent language. Previously they were mainly useful for understanding language. The pressure is on to provide guidance about every detail of usage. Native speakers of English have had usage books for many years, and language professionals like journalists have long had style books and compendiums of usage. Everyone needs a reference book of this kind, and the non-native user of English is no exception. This Usage Book is suitable for students from intermediate to advanced level, and for teachers of English.

The Entries

A large number of the entries are short notes on individual words and phrases. Two words may be easily confused, like 'comprehensive' and 'comprehensible'. One word may require another, for example 'afford' requires 'can', 'could', or 'be able to'. Where American and British usage are different, this is pointed out, so that you do not eat chips when you want crisps, or buy pants when you want trousers. A careful distinction is made between 'disabled', 'handicapped', 'crippled' and other words to which some people are very sensitive.

All the entries are in strict alphabetical order, with cross references. Some entries are longer, because of the special nature of the words. There are also a number of long entries on important usage topics such as **Invitations** and **Punctuation**. In these entries a large number of points are gathered together and presented so that the whole entry can be consulted, or just one or two of the points. There are frequent side headings to help users find a particular point, so that the entry can be used for quick reference.

One feature of COBUILD is that we try to list all the words or phrases that are used in the same way, rather than just giving one or two examples. The lists are very helpful for language production, for example those in the grammar entry on **Complements** give information on what verbs take what sort of complements.

The Examples

Above all, COBUILD rests its authority on actual examples. Thousands of real extracts from the growing Bank of English are used to demonstrate the usage points, and each of them is chosen as an appropriate model, so that it can be confidently followed. The English that people invent to illustrate a point is not part of their real communication and may be quite misleading.

If you are fluent in a language you cannot always bring to mind all the details of your actual usage, because it is below your conscious awareness. Hence you may not be able to produce an example that is really reliable.

At COBUILD there is no problem, except to select the very best from a huge range of real examples. These examples are not just 'based on' a corpus but are actual citations from a corpus. During the compilation of this Usage Book, the corpus has grown from 20,000,000 to 150,000,000 words, and we hope to convince users that real examples are the only reliable evidence of usage.

A usage book can be improved by comments from the users, and I always make a plea for feedback, because it helps us very much to design books which are helpful guides to the language.

John Sinclair
Editor-in-Chief, COBUILD
Professor of Modern English Language
University of Birmingham

The Bank of English

Since 1980 COBUILD has been gathering real language for its files. Each document or transcript is carefully indexed and put into a form suitable for the COBUILD computers to handle. The start of the Nineties prompted a big new effort to collect over two hundred million words. At the time of writing, this total is likely to be achieved before the end of 1992 – and we will need more and more to keep our information up to date.

This corpus is called the Bank of English, and it is a unique resource that powers all the COBUILD publications. The texts are carefully selected; although 200,000,000 words sounds a lot, there is so much now available from computer typesetting that a lot of skill is needed to make the corpus a faithful record of current English. Hundreds of tape recordings are made and carefully transcribed so that the spoken language is well represented, and all sorts of small-scale documents, local publications, letters etc. are gathered to balance the big output of the newspaper presses.

We are most grateful to the large number of contributors who have generously allowed their language to be used as a source of our knowledge, understanding and exemplification.

John Sinclair
Editor-in-Chief, COBUILD

Guide to the Usage

The aim of this book is to help learners of English to use individual words correctly and to choose the right words and structures for the meaning they want to convey. Each entry is based on the latest evidence in the Cobuild corpus, so that both learners and teachers will find the book useful as an authoritative reference on how English is actually used today. A priority has been to make it clear which words and structures are used in conversation, and which should only be used in writing. Differences between British and American usage are also clearly indicated.

For ease of access, entries are arranged alphabetically. When information about the use of a word, or additional relevant information, is to be found in an entry under another headword, a cross-reference is given.

There are various types of entry, as explained below.

Entries for individual words

The entries for individual words explain how to use the word, for example by saying which preposition should be used after the word, or whether you should use a 'to'-infinitive or an '-ing' form after it. This book deals with words which are known to cause problems for learners. For extra clarity, we often explicitly mention what learners should not say as well as what they should say. These comments should be useful for learners who are drawing false parallels between their own language and English, or between different words in English.

desire

A **desire** is a feeling that you want something or want to do something. You usually talk about a **desire for** something or a **desire to do** something.

...a tremendous desire for liberty.
Stephanie felt a strong desire for coffee.
He had not the slightest desire to go on holiday.

Note that you do not talk about a 'desire for doing' something.

When drawing the learner's attention to a way in which a word or expression cannot be used, we give the word or expression that should be used instead, if there is one.

accept

If you **accept** someone's advice or suggestion, you decide to do what they advise or suggest.

If she accepts the advice, she feels happier.
I knew that they would accept my proposal.

However, you do not say that you 'accept to do' what someone suggests. You say that you **agree to do** it.

The princess agreed to go on television.
She agreed to let us use her flat while she was away.

Entries for easily confused words

If two words are sometimes confused with each other, both words are given in the entry heading. For example, the entry headed **intelligent - intellectual** explains the differences between 'intelligent' and 'intellectual'.

Some entries explain the difference between words which are similar in form but have different meanings.

effective - efficient

Something that is **effective** produces the results that it is intended to produce.

...effective street lighting.
...an effective mosquito repellent.

A person, machine, or organization that is **efficient** does a job well and successfully, without wasting time or energy.

You need a very efficient production manager.
Engines and cars can be made more efficient.

human - humane

Human /hjuːmən/ means 'relating to people'.

...the human body.
...human relationships.

Humane /hjuːmeɪn/ means 'showing kindness and sympathy, especially in preventing or reducing suffering'.

...a humane plea for mercy and compassion.
...the most humane method of killing badgers.

Other entries distinguish between words which have a similar basic meaning but are used in slightly different ways.

called - named

You use **called** or **named** when you are giving the name of someone or something. **Named** is less common than **called,** and is not usually used in conversation.

Did you know a boy called Desmond?
We pass through a town called Monmouth.
Anna had a boyfriend named Shorty.

You can use **called** either after a noun or after 'be'.

Komis asked me to appear in a play called Katerina.
The book was called The Goalkeeper's Revenge.

You only use **named** immediately after a noun.

The victim was an 18-year-old girl named Marinetta Jirkowski.

There are also entries which point out differences between British and American usage, where these might cause confusion.

post - mail

The public service by which letters and parcels are collected and delivered is usually called the **post** in British English and the **mail** in American English. **Mail** is also sometimes used in British English, for example in the name 'Royal Mail'.

There is a cheque for you in the <u>post.</u>
Winners will be notified by <u>post.</u>
Your reply must have been lost in the <u>mail.</u>

British speakers usually refer to the letters and parcels delivered to them on a particular occasion as their **post.** American speakers refer to these letters and parcels as their **mail.** Some British speakers also talk about their **mail.**

They read their bosses' <u>post.</u>
I started to read my <u>mail.</u>

Entries dealing with groups of words

In some entries, larger groups of words which have a similar basic meaning but different shades of meaning are explained. For example, in the entry at **beautiful** there is an explanation of the differences between the following words: attractive, beautiful, good-looking, gorgeous, handsome, pretty, stunning. These entries have a vocabulary building function and could be exploited especially with more advanced students.

The following entries deal with larger groups of words:

beautiful	dignified	new	stubborn
cook	fat	obedient	thin
crippled	forceful	old	tools
curious	madness	proud	unusual
damage	mean	retarded	work

Some entries contain graded lists of words – that is, lists of words which indicate different degrees of something. For example, the entry at **happy - sad** shows a range of adjectives that are used to indicate how happy or sad someone is:

▶ ecstatic, elated, euphoric
▶ joyful, radiant, jubilant
▶ happy, cheerful, jolly
▶ light-hearted
▶ contented, fulfilled
▶ dissatisfied, moody, discontented
▶ sad, unhappy, depressed, gloomy, glum, dejected, despondent, dispirited
▶ miserable, wretched

Words indicating roughly the same degree are on the same line, preceded by a black arrow. The words on each line are then arranged in order of frequency. So, for example, 'ecstatic' is commoner than 'elated', and 'elated' is commoner than 'euphoric'.

The following entries contain graded lists:

happy - sad
like - dislike
pleased - disappointed
small - large

There are also the following graded lists of adverbials in the entry at **Adverbials**:

adverbials of frequency (never - always)
duration (briefly - always)
degree (little - enormously)
extent (partly - completely)
probability (conceivably - definitely)

There is a graded list of adverbs of degree used in front of adjectives in the entry at **Adverbs.**

Topic entries

Some entries in this book deal with topics of various kinds. They tell you about the words, structures, and expressions that you use when you are talking about a particular kind of thing, such as age or money, or when you are in a particular kind of situation, for example when you are saying goodbye or thank you. Some of the topic entries tell you about particular groups of words that have a common characteristic or use, for example abbreviations or words that are used to refer to groups. There are also entries on punctuation and spelling.

This book contains the following topic entries:

Abbreviations
Addressing someone
Advising someone
Age
Agreeing and disagreeing
Apologizing
Asking for repetition
Capital letters
Complimenting and congratulating someone
Criticizing someone
Days and dates
Fixed pairs
Greetings and goodbyes
Groups of things, animals, and people
'-ic' and '-ical' words
Intentions
Introducing yourself and other people
Invitations
Letter writing
Male and female
Meals
Measurements
Money

Names and titles
Nationality words
Numbers and fractions
Offers
Opinions
Permission
Pieces and amounts
Places
Possession and other relationships
Punctuation
Reactions
Replies
Requests, orders, and instructions
Spelling
Suggestions
Telephoning
Thanking someone
Time
Transport
Warning someone
Words with alternative spellings
Words with the same pronunciation
Words with two pronunciations

Grammar entries

The grammar entries in this book contain basic grammatical information, together with information on particularly difficult grammatical points. There is also a Glossary of grammatical terms on pages xii - xviii, which acts as an index to the grammar entries.

This book contains the following grammar entries:

Adjectives
Adverbials
Adverbs
Auxiliaries
Broad negatives
Clauses
Comparative and superlative adjectives
Comparative and superlative adverbs
Comparison
Complements
Conjunctions
Continuous tenses
Contractions
Determiners
'-ed' adjectives
Ellipsis
The Future
Imperatives
Infinitives
'-ing' adjectives

'-ing' forms
Inversion
Irregular verbs
Linking adverbials
'-ly' words
Modals
Modifiers
Noun groups
Noun modifiers
Nouns
Objects
The Passive
The Past
Past participles
Phrasal verbs
Plural forms of nouns
Possessive determiners
Prepositions
The Present
Pronouns

Qualifiers
Quantity
Questions
Question tags
Relative clauses
Reporting
Sentences
Singular and plural
Split infinitives
Subjects
The Subjunctive
Subordinate clauses
Tenses
'That'-clauses
'To'-infinitive clauses
Verbless clauses
Verbs
'Wh'-clauses
'Wh'-words

More detailed grammatical information on all these topics can be found in the Collins Cobuild English Grammar.

Left Column headings

Many entries have headings in a column to the left of the text which draw attention to the particular use or structure that is being dealt with, or to a word that is being contrasted with another word.

The label WARNING is used to draw the learner's attention to a potential error or area of confusion.

Register information

We have tried to make it clear which words and expressions are used in conversation and which are used mainly in writing. For example, 'accustomed to' and 'used to' have the same meaning, but people do not usually use 'accustomed to' in conversation. Words and expressions used in conversation are often also used in pieces written in an informal, conversational style, such as letters to friends and non-serious articles in magazines. Similarly, words and expressions used in writing are also often used in formal speech, for example news broadcasts and lectures.

When a word, expression, or structure occurs only in novels and written descriptions of events, we say that it occurs only 'in stories'. For example, 'dress' is used to mean 'put on your clothes' in stories, but in conversation you would say 'get dressed'. Words described as 'literary', such as the verb 'desire' and the adjective 'infamous', are used in poetical writing and passionate speeches.

In entries dealing with topics such as **Apologizing** and **Invitations**, we sometimes make a distinction between formal and informal ways of saying something. People use informal expressions when speaking to friends and relatives. They use formal expressions when speaking to people they do not know well or when they are in a formal situation such as a meeting. Formal expressions tend to be used especially by older people.

If we say that a word or expression is not used 'in modern English', we mean that you may come across it in a book written some time ago, but it would not sound natural in writing today, and should definitely not be used in conversation. For example, in modern English 'have' is used with words referring to meals, not 'take'. If a word is described as 'old-fashioned', it occurs in old books and may still be used by older people today, but is becoming uncommon.

If we say that a word or expression is not used 'in standard English', we mean that speakers of some varieties of English use it, but it would be regarded as incorrect by most people.

A word that is described as 'neutral' is used simply to indicate that someone or something has a particular quality. A word that is 'complimentary' or 'shows approval' indicates also that you admire the person you are describing. A word that is 'uncomplimentary' or 'shows disapproval' indicates that you disapprove of the person or do not find them attractive.

Glossary of grammatical terms

abstract noun a noun such as 'joy', 'size', or 'language' which refers to a quality, idea, or experience rather than something which is physical or concrete. Compare with **concrete noun**. See entry at **Nouns**.

active voice verb groups such as 'gives', 'took', or 'has made', where the subject is the person or thing doing the action or responsible for it. EG *The storm destroyed dozens of trees.* Compare with **passive voice**.

adjectival clause another name for **relative clause**.

adjective a word used to tell you more about a thing, such as its appearance, colour, size, or type. EG *...a pretty blue dress.* See entry at **Adjectives**.

adjunct another name for **adverbial**.

adverb a word such as 'quickly' or 'now' that gives information about the circumstances or nature of an event or state. See entries at **Adverbials** and **Adverbs**. Types of adverbs include:

adverb of degree an adverb which indicates the degree or intensity of an action or quality. EG *I enjoyed it enormously... She felt extremely tired.*

adverb of duration an adverb which indicates how long something lasts. EG *He smiled briefly.*

adverb of frequency an adverb which indicates how often something happens. EG *I sometimes regret it.*

adverb of manner an adverb which indicates the way in which something happens or is done. EG *She watched him carefully.*

adverb of place an adverb which gives information about position or direction. EG *Come here.*

adverb of time an adverb which gives information about when something happens. EG *I saw her yesterday.*

adverbial a word or phrase which gives information about the circumstances or nature of an event or state. EG *She laughed nervously... No birds or animals came near the body.* Also called 'adjunct'. See also **sentence adverbial**, and entry at **Adverbials**.

adverbial clause a subordinate clause which gives more information about the event described in the main clause. See entry at **Subordinate clauses**.

adverb phrase two adverbs used together. EG *She spoke very quietly.*

affirmative another name for **positive**.

affix a letter or group of letters that is added to the beginning or end of a word to make a different word. EG *anti-communist, harmless.* See also **suffix** and **prefix**.

agent the person who performs an action.

agreement another name for **concord**.

apostrophe s an ending ('s) added to a noun to indicate possession. EG *...Harriet's daughter... ...the professor's husband... ...the Managing Director's*

secretary. See entry at **'s**.

apposition the placing of a noun group after a noun or pronoun in order to identify someone or something or give more information about them. EG *...my daughter Emily.*

article see **definite article**, **indefinite article**.

aspect the use of verb forms to show whether an action is still continuing, is repeated, or is finished.

attributive used to describe adjectives such as 'classical', 'outdoor', and 'woollen' that are normally only used in front of a noun. When any adjective is used in front of a noun, you can say that it is used attributively. Compare with **predicative**.

auxiliary one of the verbs 'be', 'have', and 'do' when they are used with a main verb to form tenses, negatives, questions, and so on. Also called 'auxiliary verb'. **Modals** are also auxiliary verbs. See entries at **Auxiliaries** and **Modals**.

bare infinitive the infinitive of a verb without 'to'. EG *Let me think.*

base form the form of a verb which has no letters added to the end and is not a past form, for example 'walk', 'go', 'have', 'be'. The base form is the form you look up in a dictionary.

broad negative one of a small group of adverbs, including 'barely' and 'seldom', which are used to make a statement almost negative. EG *I barely knew her.* See entry at **Broad negatives**.

cardinal number a number used for counting, such as 'one', 'nineteen', or 'a hundred'. See entry at **Numbers and fractions**.

case the use of different forms of nouns or pronouns in order to show whether they are the subject or object of a clause, or whether they are possessive. EG *I/me, who/whom, Mary/Mary's.*

classifying adjective an adjective such as 'Indian', 'wooden', or 'mental' which is used to identify something as being of a particular type. These adjectives do not have comparatives or superlatives. Compare with **qualitative adjective**. See entry at **Adjectives**.

clause a group of words containing a verb. See also **main clause** and **subordinate clause**, and entry at **Clauses**.

cleft sentence a sentence in which emphasis is given to either the subject or the object by using a structure beginning with 'it', 'what', or 'all'. EG *It's a hammer we need... What we need is a hammer.*

collective noun a noun such as 'committee', 'team', or 'family' that refers to a group of people or things. See entry at **Nouns**.

colour adjective an adjective such as 'red', 'blue', or 'scarlet' which indicates what colour something is. See entry at **Adjectives**.

common noun a noun such as 'sailor', 'computer',

or 'glass' which is used to refer to a kind of person, thing, or substance. Compare with **proper noun.**

comparative an adjective or adverb with '-er' on the end or 'more' in front of it, for example 'friendlier', 'more important', and 'more carefully'. See entries at **Comparative and superlative adjectives** and **Comparative and superlative adverbs.**

complement a noun group or adjective which comes after a link verb such as 'be', and gives more information about the subject of the clause. EG *She is a teacher... She is tired.* See entry at **Complements.** See also **object complement.**

complex sentence a sentence consisting of a main clause and a subordinate clause. EG *She wasn't thinking very quickly because she was tired.* See entry at **Clauses.**

compound a combination of two or more words that function as a single unit. For example, 'self-centred' and 'free-and-easy' are compound adjectives, 'bus stop' and 'state of affairs' are compound nouns, and 'dry-clean' and 'roller-skate' are compound verbs.

compound sentence a sentence consisting of two or more main clauses linked by a coordinating conjunction. EG *They picked her up and took her into the house.* See entry at **Clauses.**

concessive clause a subordinate clause, usually introduced by 'although', 'though', or 'while', which contrasts with a main clause. EG *Although I like her, I find her hard to talk to.* See entry at **Subordinate clauses.**

concord the matching relationship between the forms of different words being used to refer to or talk about a person, thing, or group, which show whether you are talking about one person or thing, or more than one. EG *I look/She looks... This book is mine/These books are mine... ...one bell/three bells.* Also called 'agreement'. See entry at **Singular and plural.**

concrete noun a noun such as 'table', 'dress', or 'flower' which refers to something you can touch or see. Compare with **abstract noun.** See entry at **Nouns.**

conditional clause a subordinate clause usually starting with 'if' or 'unless'. The event described in the main clause depends on the condition described in the subordinate clause. EG *If it rains, we'll go to the cinema... They would be rich if they had taken my advice.* See entry at **Subordinate clauses.**

conjunction a word which links two clauses, groups, or words. There are two kinds of conjunction - **coordinating conjunctions,** which link parts of a sentence which are the same grammatical type ('and', 'but', 'or'), and **subordinating conjunctions,** which begin subordinate clauses ('although', 'because', 'when'). See entry at **Conjunctions.**

continuous tense a tense which contains a form of the verb 'be' and a present participle. EG *She was laughing... They had been playing badminton.* Also called 'progressive tense'. See entries at **Tenses** and **Continuous tenses.**

contraction a shortened form such as 'aren't' or 'she's', in which an auxiliary verb and 'not', or a

subject and an auxiliary verb, are joined together and function as one word. See entry at **Contractions.**

contrast clause another name for **concessive clause.**

coordinating conjunction see conjunction.

coordination the linking of words or groups of words which are of the same grammatical type, or the linking of clauses which are of equal importance. See entry at **Conjunctions.**

copula the verb 'be', when used with a complement. In this book, the term **link verb** is used for 'be' and for other verbs used with complements.

count noun a noun such as 'dog', 'lemon', or 'foot' which has a singular form and a plural form. See entry at **Nouns.**

declarative mood A clause in the declarative mood has the subject followed by the verb. Most statements are in the declarative mood. EG *I saw him yesterday.* Also called 'indicative mood'.

defective verb a verb which does not have all the inflected forms that regular verbs have. For example, all modals are defective verbs.

defining relative clause a relative clause which identifies the person or thing that is being talked about. EG *I wrote down everything that she said.* Compare with **non-defining relative clause.** See entry at **Relative clauses.**

definite article the determiner 'the'.

delexical verb a verb which has very little meaning in itself but is combined with an object to describe an action. 'Give', 'have', and 'take' are commonly used as delexical verbs. EG *She gave a small cry... I've had a bath.* See entry at **Verbs.**

demonstrative one of the words 'this', 'that', 'these', and 'those'. They are used as determiners and pronouns. EG *...this woman... ...that tree... This is fun... That looks interesting.* See entries at **that - those** and **this - these.**

dependent clause another name for **subordinate clause.**

determiner one of a group of words including 'the', 'a', 'some', and 'my' which are used at the beginning of a noun group. See entry at **Determiners.**

direct object a noun group referring to the person or thing directly affected by an action, in an active clause. EG *She wrote her name... I shut the windows.* Compare with **indirect object.** See entry at **Objects.**

direct speech speech reported in the words actually spoken by someone, without any changes in tense, person, and so on. See entry at **Reporting.**

disjunct another name for **sentence adverbial.**

ditransitive verb a verb such as 'give', 'take', or 'sell' which can have both an indirect and a direct object. EG *She gave me a kiss.* See entry at **Verbs.**

dynamic verb a verb such as 'run', 'fight', or 'sing' which can be used in continuous tenses. Compare with **stative verb.** See entry at **Continuous tenses.**

'-ed' adjectives an adjective ending in '-ed'. EG *I was amazed.* See entry at **'-ed' adjectives.**

'-ed' form another name for **past participle.**

ellipsis the leaving out of words when they are

obvious from the context. See entry at **Ellipsis.**

emphasizing adjective an adjective such as 'complete', 'utter', or 'total' which stresses how strongly you feel about something. EG *I feel a complete fool.* See entry at **Adjectives.**

emphasizing adverb an adverb which adds emphasis to a verb or adjective. EG *I simply can't do it... I was absolutely amazed.* See entries at **Adverbials** and **Adverbs.**

ergative verb a verb which can be used either transitively to focus on the person who performs an action, or intransitively to focus on the thing affected by the action. EG *He had boiled a kettle... The kettle had boiled.* See entry at **Verbs.**

exclamation a sound, word, or sentence which is spoken suddenly and loudly in order to express surprise, anger, and so on. EG *Oh God!* See entry at **Reactions.**

finite A finite verb group shows person, tense, or mood. A finite clause contains a finite verb group. EG *He loves gardening... You can borrow that pen if you want to.* Compare with **non-finite.**

first person see **person.**

focusing adverb an adverb such as 'only', 'mainly', or 'especially' which indicates the most relevant thing or the only relevant thing involved in something. See entry at **Adverbials.**

fronting a structure in which you put something which is not the subject of a clause at the beginning of the clause. EG *Lovely hair she had.*

general determiner a determiner such as 'a' or 'some' which is used when you are talking about people or things in a general or indefinite way. See entries at **Determiners** and **Quantity.**

gender the grammatical difference between masculine and feminine words such as 'he' and 'she'. See entry at **Male and female.**

genitive the possessive form of a noun, for example 'man's' or 'men's'. See entry at **'s.**

gerund an '-ing' form used as a noun. See entry at **'-ing' forms.**

gradable A gradable adjective can be used with a word such as 'very' or in a comparative or superlative form, in order to indicate that a person or thing has more or less of a quality. **Qualitative adjectives** such as 'big' and 'good' are gradable.

group noun another name for **collective noun.**

headword the main word of a noun group. EG *...a soft downy cushion with tassels.*

identifying relative clause another name for **defining relative clause.**

idiom a group of words such as 'kick the bucket' or 'new broom' which has a special meaning that cannot be understood by taking the meaning of each individual word.

'if'-clause a conditional clause or reported question beginning with 'if'.

imperative A clause in the imperative mood has the base form of the verb without a subject. It is the mood used especially for giving commands, orders, and instructions. It is also used for making offers and suggestions. EG *Come here... Take two tablets every four hours... Enjoy yourself.* See entry at **Imperatives.**

impersonal 'it' 'It' is called an impersonal subject when it is used to introduce or comment on a fact, or when it is used in a cleft structure. EG *It's raining... It was you who asked.* See entry at **it.**

indefinite article the determiners 'a' and 'an'.

indefinite place adverb a small group of adverbs including 'anywhere' and 'somewhere' which are used to indicate location or destination in a general or vague way. See entry at **Places.**

indefinite pronoun a small group of pronouns including 'someone' and 'anything' which are used to refer to a person or thing in a general or vague way. See entry at **Pronouns.**

indicative mood another name for **declarative mood.**

indirect object a second object which is used with a transitive verb to indicate who benefits from an action, or receives something as a result of it. EG *She gave me a rose.* See entry at **Verbs.**

indirect question another name for **reported question.**

indirect speech another name for **reported speech.**

infinitive the base form of a verb, for example 'go', 'have', or 'jump'. It is often used with 'to' in front of it. See entries at **Infinitives** and **'To'-infinitive clauses.**

inflection the variation in the form of a verb, noun, pronoun, or adjective to show differences in tense, number, case, and degree. EG *come, came; cat, cats; small, smaller, smallest.*

'-ing' adjective an adjective which has the same form as the '-ing' form of a verb. EG *...a smiling face.* See entry at **'-ing' adjectives.**

'-ing' clause a clause beginning with an '-ing' form. EG *Realising that something was wrong, I stopped.* See entry at **'-ing' forms.**

'-ing' form a verb form ending in '-ing' which is used, for example, to form continuous verb tenses. Also called 'present participle'. See entries at **'-ing' forms** and **'-ing' adjectives.**

'-ing' noun a noun such as 'swimming' or 'acting' which has the same form as the '-ing' form of a verb. See entry at **'-ing' forms.**

intensifier a submodifier such as 'very' or 'exceptionally' which is used to reinforce an adjective and make it more emphatic.

interjection another name for **exclamation.**

interrogative adverb one of the adverbs 'how', 'when', 'where', and 'why' when they are used to ask questions. EG *How do you know that?* See entries at **Questions** and **Reporting.**

interrogative mood A clause in the interrogative mood has part or all of the verb group in front of the subject. Most questions are in the interrogative mood. EG *Is it still raining?* See entry at **Questions.**

interrogative pronoun one of the pronouns 'who', 'whose', 'whom', 'what', and 'which' when they are used to ask questions. EG *Who did you talk to?* See entries at **Questions** and **Reporting.**

intransitive verb a verb which is used to talk about an action or event that only involves the subject and so does not have an object. EG *She arrived... I was yawning.* See entry at **Verbs.**

inversion changing the word order in a sentence,

especially changing the order of the subject and the verb. See entry at **Inversion**.

irregular having inflected forms which are not formed in the usual way. See entries at **Comparative and superlative adjectives**, **Comparative and superlative adverbs**, **Irregular verbs**, and **Plural forms of nouns**.

lexical verb another name for **main verb**.

linking adverbial a sentence adverbial such as 'moreover' or 'besides' which is used to introduce a related comment or reinforce what you are saying. Also called 'linking adjunct'. See entry at **Linking adverbials**.

link verb a verb such as 'be', 'become', 'seem', or 'appear' which links the subject and complement of a clause. See entries at **Complements** and **Verbs**.

'-ly' words words ending in 'ly', such as adverbs of manner. See entry at **'-ly' words**.

main clause a clause which is not dependent on, or is not part of, another clause. See entry at **Clauses**.

main verb a verb which is not an auxiliary or modal. Also called 'lexical verb'.

manner clause a subordinate clause, usually introduced with 'as', 'like', or 'the way', which describes the way in which something is done. EG *She talks like her mother used to.* See entry at **Subordinate clauses**.

mass noun a noun which is usually an uncount noun, but which can be used as a count noun when it refers to quantities or types of something. EG *...two sugars... ...cough medicines*. Some people call all uncount nouns mass nouns. See entry at **Nouns**.

measurement noun a noun such as 'metre' or 'pound' which refers to a unit of measurement. See entry at **Measurements**.

modal a verb such as 'can', 'might', or 'will' which is used with the base form of another verb to express possibility, requests, offers, suggestions, and so on. Also called 'modal auxiliary' or 'modal verb'. See entry at **Modals**.

modifier a word or group of words describing a person or thing which comes in front of a noun. EG *...a beautiful sunny day... ...a psychology conference*. See entry at **Modifiers**.

mood The mood of a clause is the type of structure it has which indicates whether it is basically a statement, command, or question. See **declarative mood**, **imperative mood**, and **interrogative mood**. See also **subjunctive**.

negative A negative clause uses a word such as 'not', 'never', or 'no-one' to indicate the absence or opposite of something, or to say that something is not the case. EG *She did not reply... I'll never forget.* Compare with **positive**. See entries at **not, no, none, no-one, nothing, nowhere**, and **never**.

negative word a word such as 'not', 'never', or 'no-one' which makes a clause negative.

nominal group another name for **noun group**.

nominal relative clause a clause beginning with a 'wh'-word which functions as a noun group. EG *I wrote down what she said*.

non-defining relative clause a relative clause which gives more information about someone or something, but which is not needed to identify them. EG *That's Mary, who was at university with me.* Compare with **defining relative clause**. See entry at **Relative clauses**.

non-finite A non-finite verb group is an infinitive, a participle, or a verb group beginning with a participle, which cannot be the only verb group in a sentence. A non-finite clause is based on a non-finite verb group. See entries at **'To'-infinitive clauses**, **'-ing' forms**, and **Past participles**.

noun a word such as 'woman', 'guilt', or 'Harry' which refers to a person or thing. See entry at **Nouns**.

noun clause another name for **nominal relative clause**.

noun group a group of words which acts as the subject, complement, or object of a clause, or as the object of a preposition. Also called 'nominal group' or 'noun phrase'. See entry at **Noun groups**.

noun phrase another name for **noun group**.

noun modifier a noun used in front of another noun, as if it were an adjective. EG *...a car door... ...a steel works*. See entry at **Noun modifiers**.

number the way in which differences between singular and plural are shown. EG *flower/flowers, that/those*. See entry at **Singular and plural**. See also **cardinal number** and **ordinal number**.

object a noun group which refers to a person or thing, other than the subject, which is involved in or affected by an action. See also **direct object** and **indirect object**. Prepositions are also followed by objects. See entry at **Objects**.

object complement an adjective or noun group which gives more information about the object of a clause, for example what the object becomes or is thought to be. EG *It made me tired... They consider him an embarrassment.* See entry at **Complements**.

object pronoun a personal pronoun which is used as the object of a verb or preposition. The object pronouns are 'me', 'us', 'you', 'him', 'her', 'it', and 'them'. See entry at **Pronouns**.

ordinal number a word such as 'first', 'tenth', or 'hundredth' that is used to indicate where something comes in a sequence. See entry at **Numbers and fractions**.

participle a verb form used for making different tenses. See **past participle** and **'-ing' form**.

particle an adverb or preposition such as 'out' or 'on' which combines with verbs to form phrasal verbs.

partitive a word such as 'pint', 'loaf', or 'portion' which is used before 'of' to indicate an amount. See entry at **Quantity**.

passive voice verb forms such as 'was given', 'were taken', 'had been made', where the subject is the person or thing that is affected by the action. EG *Dozens of trees were destroyed.* Compare with **active voice**. See entry at **The Passive**.

past form the form of a verb, often ending in '-ed', which is used for the simple past tense.

past participle a verb form such as 'disappointed', 'broken', or 'watched' which is used, for example, to form perfect tenses and passives. Also called '-ed' form, especially when used as an adjective. See entries at **Past participles** and **'-ed' adjectives**.

perfect tense a tense made with the auxiliary 'have' and a past participle. EG *I have met him... We had won.*

person a term used to refer to the three categories of people who are involved in something that is said. They are called the first person (the person who is speaking or writing), the second person (the person who is being addressed), and the third person (the people or things that are being talked about).

personal pronoun one of a group of words, including 'I', 'you', 'me', and 'they', which are used to refer to people or things whose identity is clear. See entry at **Pronouns**.

phase a structure in which you use two verbs in a clause in order to talk about two processes or events that are closely linked. EG *She helped to clean the house... They remember buying the tickets.* See entries at **Infinitives**, **'-ing' forms**, and **'To'-infinitive clauses.**

phrasal verb a combination of a verb and an adverb or preposition, or a verb, an adverb and a preposition, which together have a single meaning, for example 'back down', 'look after', and 'look forward to'. See entry at **Phrasal verbs.**

phrase a group of words which is not a complete clause. Also another name for **idiom**.

place clause a subordinate clause which is used to talk about the location of something. EG *I left it where it fell*. See entry at **Subordinate clauses**.

plural the form of a count noun or verb which is used to refer to or talk about more than one person or thing. EG *Puppies chew everything... The women were outside*. Compare with **singular**. See entry at **Singular and plural**.

plural noun a noun such as 'clothes', 'scissors', or 'vermin' which has only used a plural form. See entry at **Nouns**.

positive A positive clause is one that does not contain a negative word. Compare with **negative**.

possessive a possessive determiner or a noun with 's added to it, which shows who or what something belongs to or is associated with. EG *...your bicycle... ...Jerry's house*. See entries at **Possession and other relationships** and **'s**.

possessive determiner one of the words 'my', 'your', 'his', 'her', 'its', 'our', and 'their', which show who or what something belongs to or is connected with. Also called 'possessive adjective'. See entry at **Possessive determiners**.

possessive pronoun one of the words 'mine', 'yours', 'hers', 'his', 'ours', and 'theirs'. See entry at **Pronouns**.

postdeterminer one of a small group of adjectives which can be used after a determiner and in front of any other adjectives to make a reference clear and precise. EG *...the following brief description*. See entry at **Adjectives**.

predeterminer a word which comes in front of a determiner but is still part of the noun group. EG *...all the boys... ...double the trouble... ...such a mess*.

predicate what is said about the subject of a clause.

predicative used to describe adjectives such as 'alive', 'asleep', and 'sure' that are normally only used after a link verb such as 'be'. When any

adjective is used after a link verb, you can say that it is used predicatively. Compare with **attributive**.

prefix a letter or group of letters added to the beginning of a word in order to make a new word. EG *semi-circular*. Compare with **affix** and **suffix**.

premodifier another name for **modifier**.

preposition a word such as 'by', 'with', or 'from' which combines with a noun group or an '-ing' form to form an adverbial. See entry at **Prepositions**.

prepositional phrase a structure consisting of a preposition and its object. EG *...on the table... ...by the sea*.

prepositional verb a verb that is always or usually followed by a preposition. See entries at **Phrasal verbs** and **Verbs**.

present participle another name for **'-ing' form**.

progressive tense another name for **continuous tense**.

pronoun a word such as 'it', 'you', or 'none' which you use when you do not need or want to use a noun to refer to someone or something. See entry at **Pronouns**.

proper noun a noun such as 'Nigel', 'Edinburgh', or 'Christmas' which refers to a particular person, place, institution, and so on. Compare with **common noun**. See entry at **Nouns**.

purpose clause a subordinate clause, usually introduced by 'in order to', 'to', 'so that', or 'so', which indicates the purpose of an action. EG *I came here in order to ask you out to dinner*. See entry at **Subordinate clauses**.

qualifier a word or group of words describing a person or thing which comes after a noun or pronoun. EG *...a book with a blue cover... ...the shop on the corner*. See entry at **Qualifiers**.

qualitative adjective an adjective such as 'funny', 'intelligent', or 'small' which is used to indicate a quality, and which is gradable. Compare with **classifying adjective**. See entry at **Adjectives**.

quantifier a phrase ending in 'of', such as 'some of' or 'a lot of', which allows you to refer to a quantity of something without being precise about the exact amount. See entry at **Quantity**.

question a structure which typically has a verb in front of the subject and which is used to ask someone about something. EG *Have you lost something?... When did she leave?* Also called 'interrogative'. See entry at **Questions**.

question tag a structure consisting of an auxiliary verb followed by a pronoun, which is used at the end of a **tag question**. EG *She's quiet, isn't she?*

quote the part of a quote structure which indicates what someone has said using the words they themselves used. EG *I said 'Why not come along too?'*

quote structure a structure containing a reporting clause and a quote. EG *She said 'I'll be late.'* Compare with **report structure**. See entry at **Reporting**.

reason clause a subordinate clause, usually introduced by 'because', 'since', or 'as', which gives the reason for something. EG *Since you're here, we'll start*. See entry at **Subordinate clauses**.

reciprocal pronoun 'each other' and 'one another',

which are used to show that what one person does to another, the other does to them. EG *They loved each other.*

reciprocal verb a verb which describes an action which involves two people doing the same thing to each other. EG *They met in the street.*

reflexive pronoun a pronoun such as 'myself' or 'themselves' which is used as the object of a verb when the person affected by an action is the same as the person doing it. See entry at **Pronouns**.

reflexive verb a verb which is typically used with a reflexive pronoun. EG *Can you amuse yourself until dinner?* See entry at **Verbs**.

regular verb a verb that has four forms and follows the normal rules. See entry at **Verbs**.

relative clause a subordinate clause which gives more information about someone or something mentioned in the main clause. See also **defining relative clause** and **non-defining relative clause**, and entry at **Relative clauses**.

relative pronoun a word such as 'who' or 'which' that is used to introduce a relative clause. EG *...the girl who was carrying the bag.*

reported clause the part of a report structure which indicates what someone has said. EG *She said that I couldn't see her.*

reported question a question which is reported using a report structure rather than the exact words used by the speaker. Also called 'indirect question'. See entry at **Reporting**.

reported speech speech which is reported using a report structure rather than the exact words used by the speaker. Also called 'indirect speech'.

reporting clause a clause which contains a reporting verb, which is used to introduce what someone said. EG *They asked if I could come.*

reporting verb a verb such as 'suggest', 'say', or 'wonder' which is used with a quote or a reported clause.

report structure a structure containing a reporting clause and a reported clause. EG *She told me she'd be late.* Compare with **quote structure**. See entry at **Reporting**.

result clause a subordinate clause introduced by 'so', 'so that', or 'such that' which gives the result of something. EG *The house was severely damaged, so that it is now uninhabitable.* See entries at **'so'** and **'such'**.

rhetorical question a question which you use in order to make a comment rather than to obtain information. Rhetorical questions can end in an exclamation mark or a question mark. EG *Wouldn't it be awful with no Christmas!... Oh, isn't it silly?*

second person see person.

semi-modal one of the verbs 'dare', 'need', and 'used to', which sometimes behave like modals.

sentence a complete group of words which expresses a statement, question, command, or exclamation. See entry at **Sentences**.

sentence adverbial an adverbial which applies to the whole clause, rather than to just a part of it. EG *Fortunately, he wasn't seriously injured.* Also called 'sentence adjunct'. See entry at **Opinions**.

's' form the base form of a verb with 's' on the end,

used in the simple present tense. EG *She likes reading.*

simple tense a tense in which no auxiliary is used. EG *I waited... She sang.*

singular the form of a count noun or verb which is used to refer to or talk about one person or thing. EG *A growing puppy needs milk... That woman is my mother.* Compare with **plural**. See entry at **Singular and plural**.

singular noun a noun such as 'sun', 'look', or 'manner' which is typically used in the singular form. See entry at **Nouns**.

specific determiner a determiner such as 'the', 'that', or 'my' which is used when referring to someone or something that has already been mentioned or whose identity is obvious. See entry at **Determiners**.

split infinitive a 'to'-infinitive which has the 'to' separated from the base form by an adverbial or other phrase. EG *...to boldly go where no man has gone before.* See entry at **Split infinitives**.

stative verb a verb such as 'be', 'know', or 'own' which is not usually used in continuous tenses. Compare with **dynamic verb**. See entry at **Continuous tenses**.

strong verb another name for **irregular verb**.

subject the noun group in a clause that refers to the main person or thing you are talking about. In a statement, the subject comes before the verb. EG *We were going shopping... He was murdered.* See entry at **Subjects**.

subject pronoun a personal pronoun which is used as the subject of a clause. The subject pronouns are 'I', 'we', 'you', 'he', 'she', 'it', and 'they'. See entry at **Pronouns**.

subjunctive a mood which is used in some subordinate clauses. See entry at **The Subjunctive**.

submodifier an adverb which is used in front of an adjective or another adverb in order to strengthen or weaken its meaning. EG *...very interesting... ...quite quickly.*

subordinate clause a clause which must be used with a main clause. See entry at **Subordinate clauses**.

suffix a letter or group of letters added to the end of a word in order to make a different word, tense, case, or word class. EG *slowly, childish.* Compare with **affix** and **prefix**.

superlative an adjective or adverb with '-est' on the end or 'most' in front of it, for example 'thinnest', 'quickest', and 'most wisely'. See entries at **Comparative and superlative adjectives** and **Comparative and superlative adverbs**.

tag a clause consisting of a pronoun and an auxiliary, which is added to a reply. EG *'Do you like it?' — 'Yes, I do.'* See also **question tag**.

tag question a statement to which a **question tag** (an auxiliary verb and a pronoun) has been added. EG *She's quiet, isn't she?*

tense the form of a verb group which shows whether you are referring to the past, present, or future. See entries at **Tenses** and **The Future**, **The Past** and **The Present**.

future 'will' or 'shall' with the base form of the verb, used to refer to future events. EG *She will come tomorrow.*

future continuous 'will' or 'shall' with 'be' and a present participle, used to refer to future situations. EG *She will be going soon.*

future perfect 'will' or 'shall' with 'have' and a past participle, used to refer to future situations. EG *I shall have finished by tomorrow.*

future perfect continuous 'will' or 'shall' with 'have been' and a present participle, used to refer to future situations. EG *I will have been walking for three hours by then.*

simple past the past form of a verb, used to refer to past events and situations. EG *They waited.*

past continuous 'was' or 'were' with a present participle, used to refer to past situations. EG *They were worrying about it yesterday.*

past perfect 'had' with a past participle, used to refer to past situations. EG *She had finished.* Also called 'pluperfect'.

past perfect continuous 'had been' with a present participle, used to refer to past situations. EG *He had been waiting for hours.*

simple present the base form and the 's' form, usually used to refer to present events and situations. EG *I like bananas... My sister hates them.*

present continuous the simple present of 'be' with a present participle, used to refer to present situations. EG *Things are improving.*

present perfect 'have' or 'has' with a past participle, used to refer to past situations which still exist or past events that affect the present. EG *She has loved him for ten years.*

present perfect continuous 'have been' or 'has been' with a present participle, used to refer to past situations which still exist. EG *We have been sitting here for hours.*

'that'-clause a clause starting with 'that' which is used mainly when reporting what someone said. EG *She said that she'd wash up for me.* 'That' can be omitted when the clause is used after a reporting verb. See entry at **'That'-clauses.**

third person see **person.**

time clause a subordinate clause which indicates the time of an event. EG *I'll phone you when I get back.* See entry at **Subordinate clauses.**

title a word such as 'Mrs', 'Lord', or 'Queen' which is used before a person's name and shows their position or status. See entry at **Names and titles.**

'to'-infinitive the base form of a verb preceded by 'to', for example 'to go', 'to have', 'to jump'.

'to'-infinitive clause a subordinate clause based on a 'to'-infinitive. EG *I wanted to see you.* See entry at **'To'-infinitive clauses.**

transitive verb a verb which is used to talk about an action or event that involves more than one person or thing, and therefore is followed by an object. EG *She's wasting her money.* See entry at **Verbs.**

uncount noun a noun such as 'money', 'furniture', or 'intelligence' which refers to a general kind of thing rather than to an individual item, and so has only one form. Also called 'uncountable noun'. See entry at **Nouns.**

verb a word such as 'sing', 'spill', or 'die' which is used with a subject to say what someone or something does, or what happens to them. See entry at **Verbs.**

verbal noun an '-ing' form used as a noun. See entry at **'-ing' forms.**

verb group a main verb, or a combination of one or more auxiliaries or modals and a main verb. EG *I'll show them... She's been sick.*

verbless clause a group of words that has the same function as a main clause or a subordinate clause but does not contain a verb. EG *What about some lunch? I stood with my hands behind my back.* See entry at **Verbless clauses.**

vocative a word such as 'darling' or 'madam' used when speaking to someone, as if it were their name. See entry at **Addressing someone.**

'wh'-clause a clause starting with a 'wh'-word. See entries at **'Wh'-clauses** and **Reporting.**

'whether'-clause a clause beginning with 'whether' that is used to report a 'yes/no'-question. EG *I asked her whether she'd seen him.* See entry at **Reporting.**

'wh'-question a question which expects an answer mentioning a particular person, thing, place, amount, and so on, rather than just 'yes' or 'no'. EG *What did you buy?* Compare with **'yes/no'-question.** See entry at **Questions.**

'wh'-word one of a group of words starting with 'wh', such as 'what', 'when' and 'who', which are used in 'wh'-questions. 'How' is also called a 'wh'-word because it behaves like the other 'wh'-words. See entry at **'Wh'-words.**

'yes/no'-question a question which can be answered simply with either 'yes' or 'no'. EG *Are you married?* Compare with **'wh'-question.** See entry at **Questions.**

Pronunciation Guide

Vowel sounds

ɑː	heart, start, calm
æ	act, mass, lap
aɪ	dive, cry, mind
aɪə	fire, tyre, buyer
aʊ	out, down, loud
aʊə	flour, tower, sour
e	met, lend, pen
eɪ	say, main, weight
eə	fair, care, wear
ɪ	fit, win, list
iː	feed, me, beat
ɪə	near, beard, clear
ɒ	lot, lost, spot
əʊ	note, phone, coat
ɔː	more, cord, claw
ɔɪ	boy, coin, joint
ʊ	could, stood, hood
uː	you, use, choose
ʊə	lure, pure, cure
ɜː	turn, third, word
ʌ	but, fund, must
ə	the weak vowel in butter, about, forgotten
i	the weak vowel in very
u	the first weak vowel in tuition

Consonant sounds

b	bed, rub
d	done, red
f	fit, if
g	good, dog
h	hat
j	yellow
k	king, pick
l	lip, bill
m	mat, ram
n	not, tin
p	pay, lip
r	run
s	soon, bus
t	talk, bet
v	van, love
w	win
x	loch
z	zoo, buzz
ʃ	ship, wish
ʒ	measure
ŋ	sing
tʃ	cheap, witch
θ	thin, myth
ð	then, loathe
dʒ	joy, bridge

Stress is shown by underlining the vowel in the stressed syllable, as in 'accept /əksept/'

Letters

These are vowel letters:

a   e   i   o   u

These are consonant letters:

b   c   d   f   g   h   j   k   l   m   n   p   q   r   s   t   v   w   x   y   z

The letter y is sometimes used as a vowel, for example in 'shy' and 'myth'.

Corpus Acknowledgements

In writing this book, we have used data from the Bank of English, a collection of modern written and spoken texts. This includes The Times and The Sunday Times, provided by Times Newspapers Ltd, and data provided by the BBC World Service and National Public Radio of Washington. We would also like to thank the following people and organizations for their permission for the use of copyright material:

Associated Business Programmes Ltd for: *The Next 200 Years* by Herman Kahn with William Brown and Leon Martel first published in Great Britain by Associated Business Programmes Ltd 1977 © Hudson Institute 1976. David Attenborough and William Collins Sons & Co Ltd for: *Life on Earth* by David Attenborough first published by William Collins Sons & Co Ltd 1979 © David Attenborough Productions Ltd 1979. James Baldwin for: *The Fire Next Time* by James Baldwin published in Great Britain by Michael Joseph Ltd 1963 © James Baldwin 1963. B T Batsford Ltd for: *Witchcraft in England* by Christina Hole first published by B T Batsford Ltd 1945 © Christina Hole 1945. Michael Billington for: 'Lust at First Sight' by Michael Billington in the *Illustrated London News* July 1981 and 'Truffaut's Tolerance' by Michael Billington in the *Illustrated London News* August 1981. Birmingham International Council For Overseas Students' Aid for: BICOSA Information Leaflets 1981. Basil Blackwell Publishers Ltd for: *Breaking the Mould? The Birth and Prospects of the Social Democratic Party* by Ian Bradley first published by Martin Robertson & Co Ltd 1981 © Ian Bradley 1981. *Seeing Green (The Politics of Ecology Explained)* by Jonathon Porritt first published by Basil Blackwell Publisher Ltd 1984 © Jonathon Porritt 1984. Blond & Briggs Ltd for: *Small is Beautiful* by E F Schumacher first published in Great Britain by Blond & Briggs Ltd 1973 © E F Schumacher 1973. The Bodley Head Ltd for: *The Americans (Letters from America 1969-1979)* by Alistair Cooke first published by Bodley Head Ltd 1979 © Alistair Cooke 1979. *Baby and Child Care* by Dr Benjamin Spock published in Great Britain by The Bodley Head Ltd 1955 © Benjamin Spock MD 1945, 1946, 1957, 1968, 1976, 1979. *What's Wrong With The Modern World?* by Michael Shanks first published by The Bodley Head Ltd 1978 © Michael Shanks 1978. *Future Shock* by Alvin Toffler first published in Great Britain by The Bodley Head Ltd 1970 © Alvin Toffler 1970. *Zen and the Art of Motorcycle Maintenance* by Robert M Pirsig first published in Great Britain by The Bodley Head Ltd 1974 © Robert M Pirsig 1974. *Marnie* by Winston Graham first published by the Bodley Head Ltd 1961 © Winston Graham 1961. *You Can Get There From Here* by Shirley MacLaine first published in Great Britain by The Bodley Head Ltd 1975 © Shirley MacLaine 1975. *It's An Odd Thing, But ...* by Paul Jennings first published by Max Reinhardt Ltd 1971 © Paul Jennings 1971. *King of the Castle (Choice and Responsibility in the Modern World)* by Gai Eaton first published by the Bodley Head Ltd 1977 © Gai Eaton 1977. *Revolutionaries in Modern Britain* by Peter Shipley first published by The Bodley Head Ltd 1976 © Peter Shipley 1976. *The Prerogative of the Harlot (Press Barons and Power)* by Hugh Cudlipp first published by The Bodley Head Ltd 1980 © Hugh Cudlipp 1980. *But What About The Children (A Working Parents' Guide to Child Care)* by Judith Hann first published by The Bodley Head Ltd 1976 © Judith Hann 1976. *Learning to Read* by Margaret Meek first published by The Bodley Head Ltd 1982 © Margaret Meek 1982. Bolt & Watson for: *Two is Lonely* by Lynne Reid Banks first published by Chatto & Windus 1974 © Lynne Reid Banks 1974. The British and Foreign Bible Society with William Collins Sons & Co Ltd for: *Good News Bible (with Deuterocanonical Books/Apocrypha)* first published by The British and Foreign Bible Society with William Collins Sons & Co Ltd 1979 © American Bible Society: Old Testament 1976, Deuterocanonical Books/Apocrypha 1979, New Testament 1966, 1971, 1976 © Maps, British and Foreign Bible Society 1976, 1979. The British Council for: *How to Live in Britain (The British Council's Guide for Overseas Students and Visitors)* first published by The British Council 1952 © The British Council 1984. Mrs R Bronowski for: *The Ascent of Man* by J Bronowski published by Book Club Associates by arrangement with The British Broadcasting Corporation 1977 © J Bronowski 1973. Alison Busby for: *The Death of Trees* by Nigel Dudley first published by Pluto Press Ltd 1985 © Nigel Dudley 1985. Tony Buzan for: *Make The Most of your Mind* by Tony Buzan first published by Colt Books Ltd 1977 © Tony Buzan 1977. Campbell Thomson & McLaughlin Ltd for: *Ring of Bright Water* by Gavin Maxwell first published by Longmans Green & Co 1960, published in Penguin Books Ltd 1976 © The Estate of Gavin Maxwell 1960. Jonathan Cape Ltd for: *Manwatching (A Field Guide to Human Behaviour)* by Desmond Morris first published in Great Britain by Jonathan Cape Ltd 1977 © Text, Desmond Morris 1977 © Compilation, Elsevier Publishing Projects SA, Lausanne, and Jonathan Cape Ltd, London 1977. *Tracks* by Robyn Davidson first published by Jonathan Cape Ltd 1980 © Robyn Davidson 1980. *In the Name of Love* by Jill Tweedie first published by Jonathan Cape Ltd 1979 © Jill Tweedie 1979. *The Use of Lateral Thinking* by Edward de Bono first published by Jonathan Cape 1967 © Edward de Bono 1967. *Trout Fishing in America* by Richard Brautigan first published in Great Britain by Jonathan Cape Ltd 1970 © Richard Brautigan 1967. *The Pendulum Years: Britain and the Sixties* by Bernard Levin first published by Jonathan Cape Ltd 1970 © Bernard Levin 1970. *The Summer Before The Dark* by Doris Lessing first published in Great Britain by Jonathan Cape Ltd 1973 © Doris Lessing 1973. *The Boston Strangler* by Gerold Frank first published in Great Britain by Jonathan Cape Ltd 1967 © Gerold Frank 1966. *I'm OK - You're OK* by Thomas A Harris MD first published in Great Britain as The Book of Choice by Jonathan Cape Ltd 1970 © Thomas A Harris MD, 1967, 1968, 1969. *The Vivisector* by Patrick White first published by Jonathan Cape Ltd 1970 © Patrick White 1970. *The Future of Socialism* by Anthony Crosland first published by Jonathan Cape Ltd 1956 © C A R Crosland 1963. *Funeral in Berlin* by Len Deighton first published by Jonathan Cape Ltd 1964 © Len Deighton 1964. Chatto & Windus Ltd for: *A Postillion Struck by Lightning* by Dirk Bogarde first published by Chatto & Windus Ltd 1977 © Dirk Bogarde 1977. *Nuns and Soldiers* by Iris Murdoch published by Chatto & Windus Ltd 1980 © Iris Murdoch 1980. *Wounded Knee (An Indian History of the American West)* by Dee Brown published by Chatto & Windus Ltd 1978 © Dee Brown 1970. *The Virgin in the Garden* by A S Byatt published by Chatto & Windus Ltd 1978 © A S Byatt 1978. *A Story Like The Wind* by Laurens van der Post published by Clarke Irwin & Co Ltd in association with The Hogarth Press Ltd 1972 © Laurens van der Post 1972. *Brave New World* by Aldous Huxley published by Chatto & Windus Ltd 1932 © Aldous Huxley and Mrs Laura Huxley 1932, 1960. *The Reivers* By William Faulkner first published by Chatto & Windus Ltd 1962 © William Faulkner 1962. *Cider With Rosie* by Laurie Lee published by The Hogarth Press 1959 © Laurie Lee 1959 *The Tenants* by Bernard Malamud first published in Great Britain by Chatto & Windus Ltd 1972 © Bernard Malamud 1971. *Kinflicks* by Lisa Alther first published in Great Britain by Chatto & Windus Ltd 1976 © Lisa Alther 1975. William Collins Sons & Co Ltd for: *The Companion Guide to London* by David Piper published by William Collins Sons & Co Ltd 1964 © David Piper 1964. *The Bedside Guardian 29* edited by W L Webb published by William Collins & Sons Ltd 1980 © Guardian Newspapers Ltd 1980. *Bear Island* by Alistair MacLean first published by William Collins Sons & Co Ltd 1971 © Alistair MacLean 1971. *Inequality in Britain: Freedom, Welfare and the State* by Frank Field first published by Fontana Paperbacks 1981 © Frank Field 1981. *Social Mobility* by Anthony Heath first published by Fontana Paperbacks 1981©Anthony Heath 1981. *Yours Faithfully* by Gerald Priestland first published by Fount Paperbacks 1979 © British Broadcasting Corporation 1977, 1978. *Power Without Responsibility: The Press and Broadcasting in Britain* by James Curran and Jean Seaton first published by Fontana Paperbacks 1981 © James Curran and Jean Seaton 1981. *The Times Cookery Book* by Katie Stewart first published by William Collins Sons & Co Ltd 1972 © Times Newspapers Ltd. *Friends from the Forest* by Joy Adamson by Collins and Harvill Press 1981 © Elsa Limited 1981. *The Media Mob* by Barry Fantoni and George Melly first published by William Collins Sons & Co Ltd 1980 © Text, George Melly 1980 © Illustrations, Barry Fantoni 1980. *Shalom (a collection of Australian and Jewish Stories)* compiled by Nancy Keesing first published by William Collins Publishers Pty Ltd 1978 © William Collins Sons &Co Ltd 1978. *The Bedside Guardian 31* edited by W L Webb first published by William Collins Sons & Co Ltd 1982 © Guardian Newspapers Ltd 1982. *The Bedside Guardian 32* edited by W L Webb first published by William Collins Sons & Co Ltd 1983 © Guardian Newspapers Ltd 1983. *Design for the Real World* by Victor Papanek first published in Great Britain by Thames & Hudson Ltd 1972 © Victor Papanek 1971. *Food For Free* by Richard Mabey first published by William Collins Sons & Co Ltd 1972 © Richard Mabey 1972. *Unended Quest* by Karl Popper (first published as Autobiography of Karl Popper in The Philosophy of Karl Popper in The Library of Philosophers edited by Paul Arthur Schlipp by the Open Court Publishing Co 1974) published by Fontana Paperbacks 1976 © The Library of Living Philosophers Inc 1974 © Karl R Popper 1976. *My Mother My Self* by Nancy Friday first published in Great Britain by Fontana Paperbacks 1979 © Nancy Friday 1977. *The Captain's Diary* by Bob Willis first published by Willow Books/William Collins Sons & Co Ltd 1984 © Bob Willis and Alan Lee 1984 © New Zealand Scorecards, Bill Frindall 1984. *The Bodywork Book* by Esme Newton-Dunn first published in Great Britain by Willow Books/William Collins Sons & Co Ltd 1982 © TVS Ltd/Esme Newton-Dunn 1982. *Collins' Encyclopaedia of Fishing in The British Isles* edited by Michael Prichard first published by William Collins Sons & Co Ltd 1976 © William Collins Sons & Co Ltd 1976. *The AAA Runner's Guide* edited by Heather Thomas first published by William Collins Sons & Co Ltd 1983 © Sackville Design Group Ltd 1983. *Heroes and Contemporaries* by David Gower with Derek Hodgson first published by William Collins Sons & Co Ltd 1983 © David Gower Promotions Ltd 1983. *The Berlin Memorandum* by Adam Hall first published by William Collins Sons & Co Ltd 1965 © Jonquil Trevor 1965. *Arlott on Cricket: His Writings on the Game* edited by David Rayvern Allen first published by William Collins (Willow Books) 1984 © John Arlott 1984. *A Woman in Custody* by Audrey Peckham first published by Fontana Paperbacks 1985 © Audrey Peckham 1985. *Play Golf with Peter Alliss* by Peter Alliss published by the British Broadcasting Corporation 1977 © Peter Alliss and Renton Laidlaw 1977. Curtis Brown Ltd for: *The Pearl* by John Steinbeck first published by William Heinemann Ltd 1948 © John Steinbeck 1948. *An Unfinished History of the World* by Hugh Thomas first published in Great Britain by Hamish Hamilton Ltd 1979 © Hugh Thomas 1979, 1981. *The Winter of our Discontent* by John Steinbeck first published in Great Britain by William Heinemann Ltd 1961 © John Steinbeck 1961. *Burr* by Gore Vidal first published in Great Britain by William Heinemann Ltd 1974 © Gore Vidal 1974. *Doctor on the Job* by Richard Gordon first published by William Heinemann Ltd 1976 © Richard Gordon Ltd 1976. Andre Deutsch Ltd for: *How to be an Alien* by George Mikes first published by Andre Deutsch Ltd 1946 © George Mikes and Nicholas Bentley 1946. *Jaws* by Peter Benchley first published in Great Britain by Andre Deutsch Ltd 1974 © Peter Benchley 1974. *A Bend in the River* by V S Naipaul first published by Andre Deutsch Ltd 1979 © V S Naipaul 1979. *Couples* by John Updike first published by Andre Deutsch Ltd 1968 © John Updike 1968. *Games People Play* by Eric Berne published in Great Britain by Andre Deutsch Ltd 1966 © Eric Berne 1964. *The Age of Uncertainty* by John Kenneth Galbraith first published by The British Broadcasting Corporation and Andre Deutsch Ltd 1977 © John Kenneth Galbraith 1977. The Economist Newspaper Ltd for: *The Economist* (9-15 May 1981 and 22-28 August 1981) © published by The Economist Newspaper Ltd 1981. Faber & Faber Ltd for: *Lord of the Flies* by William Golding first published by Faber & Faber Ltd 1954 © William Golding 1954. *The Complete*

Book of Self-Sufficiency by John Seymour first published in Great Britain by Faber & Faber Ltd 1976 © Text, John Seymour 1976, 1977 © Dorling Kindersley Ltd 1976, 1977. *Conversations with Igor Stravinsky* by Igor Stravinsky and Robert Craft first published by Faber & Faber Ltd 1959 © Igor Stravinsky 1958,1959. John Farquharson Ltd for: *The Moon's A Balloon* by David Niven published in Great Britain by Hamish Hamilton Ltd 1971 © David Niven 1971. John Gaselee for: 'Going it Alone' by John Gaselee in the *Illustrated London News* July 1981 and 'The Other Car's Fault' by John Gaselee in the *Illustrated London News* August 1981. Glidrose Publications Ltd for: *The Man with the Golden Gun* by Ian Fleming first published by Jonathan Cape Ltd © Glidrose Productions Ltd 1965. Victor Gollancz Ltd for: *The Next Horizon* by Chris Bonnington published by Victor Gollancz Ltd 1976 © Chris Bonnington 1973. *Summerhill: A Radical Approach to Education* by A S Neill first published by Victor Gollancz Ltd 1962 © A S Neill 1926, 1932, 1937, 1953, 1961 (US permission by Hart Publishing Inc). *Lucky Jim* by Kingsley Amis first published by Victor Gollancz Ltd 1954 © Kingsley Amis 1953. *The Mighty Micro (The Impact of the Computer Revolution)* by Christopher Evans first published by Victor Gollancz Ltd 1979 © Christopher Evans 1979. *The Longest Day* by Cornelius Ryan published by Victor Gollancz Ltd 1960 © Cornelius Ryan 1959. *Asking for Trouble (Autobiography of a Banned Journalist)* by Donald Woods published by Victor Gollancz Ltd 1980 © Donald Woods 1980. *The Turin Shroud* by Ian Wilson first published in Great Britain by Victor Gollancz Ltd 1978 © Ian Wilson 1978. *Murdo and Other Stories* by Iain Crichton Smith published by Victor Gollancz Ltd 1981 © Iain Crichton Smith 1981. *The Class Struggle in Parliament* by Eric S Heffer published by Victor Gollancz Ltd 1973 © Eric S Heffer 1973. *A Presumption of Innocence (The Amazing Case of Patrick Meehan)* by Ludovic Kennedy published by Victor Gollancz Ltd 1976 © Ludovic Kennedy 1976. *The Treasure of Sainte Foy* by MacDonald Harris published by Victor Gollancz Ltd 1980 © MacDonald Harris 1980. *A Long Way to Shiloh* by Lionel Davidson first published by Victor Gollancz Ltd 1966 © Lionel Davidson 1966. *Education After School* by Tyrrell Burgess first published by Victor Gollancz Ltd 1977 © Tyrrell Burgess 1977. *The View From Serendip* by Arthur C Clarke published by Victor Gollancz Ltd 1978 © Arthur C Clarke 1967, 1968, 1970, 1972, 1974, 1976, 1977. *On Wings of Song* by Thomas M Disch published by Victor Gollancz Ltd 1979 © Thomas M Disch 1979. *The World of Violence* by Colin Wilson published by Victor Gollancz Ltd 1963 © Colin Wilson 1963. *The Lightning Tree* by Joan Aiken published by Victor Gollancz Ltd 1980 © Joan Aiken Enterprises 1980. *Russia's Political Hospitals* by Sidney Bloch and Peter Reddaway published by Victor Gollancz Ltd 1977 © Sidney Bloch and Peter Reddaway 1977. *Unholy Loves* by Joyce Carol Oates first published in Great Britain by Victor Gollancz Ltd 1980 © Joyce Carol Oates 1979. *Consenting Adults (or The Duchess will be Furious)* by Peter De Vries published by Victor Gollancz Ltd 1981 © Peter De Vries 1980. *The Passion of New Eve* by Angela Carter published by Victor Gollancz Ltd 1977 © Angela Carter 1977. Gower Publishing Co Ltd for: *Solar Prospects (The Potential for Renewable Energy)* by Michael Flood first published in Great Britain by Wildwood House Ltd in association with Friends of the Earth Ltd 1983 © Michael Flood. *Voiceless Victims* by Rebecca Hall first published in Great Britain by Wildwood House Ltd 1984 © Rebecca Hall 1984. Graham Greene and Laurence Pollinger Ltd for: *The Human Factor* by Graham Greene first published by The Bodley Head Ltd 1978 © Graham Greene 1978. Syndication Manager, The Guardian, for: *The Guardian* (12 May 1981, 7 September 1981 and 15 September 1981) © published by Guardian Newspapers Ltd 1981. Hamlyn for: *How to Play Rugby* by David Norrie published by The Hamlyn Publishing Group Ltd 1981 © The Hamlyn Publishing Group Ltd 1981. *How to Play Badminton* by Pat Davies first published by The Hamlyn Publishing Group Ltd 1979 © The Hamlyn Publishing Group Ltd 1979. Margaret Hanbury for: *Crisis and Conservation: Conflict in the British Countryside* by Charlie Pye-Smith and Chris Rose first published by Pelican/Penguin Books Ltd 1984 © Charlie Pye-Smith and Chris Rose 1984. Paul Harrison for: *Inside the Third World* by Paul Harrison first published in Great Britain by The Harvester Press Ltd 1980 © Paul Harrison 1979. A M Heath & Co Ltd for: *Rembrandt's Hat* by Bernard Malamud published by Chatto & Windus Ltd 1982 © Bernard Malamud 1968, 1972, 1973. William Heinemann Ltd for: *It's an Old Country* by J B Priestley first published in Great Britain by William Heinemann Ltd 1967 © J B Priestley 1967. Heinemann Educational Books Ltd and Gower Publishing Co Ltd for: *The Environmental Crisis (A Handbook for all Friends of the Earth)* edited by Des Wilson first published by Heinemann Educational Books Ltd 1984 © Foreword, David Bellamy 1984 © Individual Chapters, the Author of the Chapter 1984 © In the selection and all other matters Des Wilson 1984. The Controller, Her Majesty's Stationery Office, for: Department of Health and Social Security leaflets published by Her Majesty's Stationery Office 1981 © The Crown. David Higham Associates Ltd for: 'Two Peruvian Projects' by E R Chamberlain in the *Illustrated London News* September 1981. *Akenfield: Portrait of an English Village* by Ronald Blythe first published by Allen Lane, Penguin Books Ltd 1969 © Ronald Blythe 1969. *The Far Pavillions* by M M Kaye first published by Allen Lane/Penguin Books Ltd 1978 © M M Kaye 1978. *Staying On* by Paul Scott first published by William Heinemann Ltd 1977 © Paul Scott 1977. *Let Sleeping Vets Lie* by James Herriot first published by Michael Joseph Ltd 1973 © James Herriot 1973. *The Midwich Cuckoos* by John Wyndham first published in Great Britain by Michael Joseph Ltd 1957 © The Estate of John Wyndham 1957. *The Girl in a Swing* by Richard Adams first published in Great Britain by Allen Lane in Penguin Books Ltd 1980 © Richard Adams 1980. Dr K B Hindley for: 'Hot Spots of the Deep' by Dr K B Hindley in the *Illustrated London News July* 1981. Hodder and Stoughton Ltd for: *Supernature* by Lyall Watson first published by Hodder & Stoughton Ltd 1973 © Lyall Watson 1973. *Tinker Tailor Soldier Spy* by John Le Carre first published by Hodder & Stoughton Ltd 1974 © Le Carre Productions 1974. The Editor, Homes and Gardens, for: *Homes and Gardens* (October 1981) (Number 4 Volume 63) © published by IPC Magazines Ltd 1981. Hughes Massie Ltd for: *Elephants Can Remember* by Agatha Christie first published by William Collins Sons & Co Ltd 1972 © Agatha Christie Mallowan. Hutchinson Publishing Group Ltd for: *An Autobiography* by Angela Davis published in Great Britain by Hutchinson & Co Publishers Ltd by arrangement with Bantam Books Inc 1975 © Angela Davis 1974. *The Day of the Jackal* by Frederick Forsyth published in Great Britian by Hutchinson & Co Publishers Ltd 1971 © Frederick Forsyth 1971. *Roots* by Alex Haley first published in Great Britain by Hutchinson & Co Publishers Ltd 1977 © Alex Haley 1976. *The Climate of Treason* by Andrew Boyle first published by Hutchinson & Co Publishers Ltd 1979 © Andrew Boyle 1979. *The Collapsing Universe: The Story of Black Holes* by Isaac Asimov first published by Hutchinson & Co Publishers Ltd 1977 © Isaac Asimov. *XPD* by Len Deighton published by Book Club Associates by arrangement with Hutchinson & Co Publishers Ltd 1981 © Len Deighton 1981. *Show Jumping with Harvey Smith* by Harvey Smith first published by Stanley Paul & Co Ltd 1979 © Tyne-Tees Television Ltd, A Member of the Trident Group 1979. *2001: A Space Odyssey by* Arthur C Clarke first published by Hutchinson & Co Publishers Ltd 1968 © Arthur C Clarke and Polaris Productions Inc 1968 © Epilogue material, Serendip BV 1982, 1983. The Illustrated London News and Sketch Ltd for: *The Illustrated London News* (July 1981, August 1981 and September 1981) © published by the Illustrated London News and Sketch Ltd 1981. The Editor, International Herald Tribune, for: *International Herald Tribune* (25-26 July 1981) © published by International Herald Tribune with The New York Times and The Washington Post 1981. Michael Joseph Ltd for: *Chronicles of Fairacre: Village School* by Miss Read first published in Great Britain by Michael Joseph Ltd 1964 © Miss Read 1955, 1964. *Fire Fox* by Craig Thomas first published in Great Britain by Michael Joseph Ltd 1977 © Craig Thomas 1977. William Kimber & Co Ltd for: *Exodus* by Leon Uris originally published in Great Britain by Alan Wingate Ltd 1959 © Leon Uris 1958. Kogan Page Ltd for: *How to Save the World (Strategy for World Conservation)* by Robert Allen first published by Kogan Page Ltd 1980 © IUCN-UNEP-WWF 1980. Marketing Department, Lloyds Bank PLC, for: *Lloyds Bank Leaflets* (1981) © published by Lloyds Bank PLC 1981. Macmillan Publishers Ltd for: *Appropriate Technology: Technology with a Human Face* by P D Dunn first published by the Macmillan Press Ltd 1978 © P D Dunn 1978. John Murray Publishers Ltd for: *A Backward Place* by Ruth Prawer Jhabvala first published by John Murray Publishers Ltd 1965 © R Prawer Jhabvala 1965. *Food For All The Family* by Magnus Pyke first published by John Murray Publishers Ltd 1980 © Magnus Pyke 1980. *Simple Movement* by Laura Mitchell and Barbara Dale first published by John Murray Publishers Ltd 1980 © Laura Mitchell and Barbara Dale 1980. *Civilisation: A Personal View* by Kenneth Clark first published by the British Broadcasting Corporation and John Murray Publishers Ltd 1969 © Kenneth Clark 1969. The Editor, National Geographic, for: *National Geographic* January, February and March (1980) © published by The National Geographic Society 1979, 1980. The National Magazine Co Ltd for: *Cosmopolitan* (May 1981 and July 1981) © published by the National Magazine Co Ltd 1981. Neilson Leisure Group Ltd for: *NAT Holidays' 'Caravans and Tents in the Sun'* (Summer 1983) holiday brochure. Newsweek Inc for: *Newsweek* (11 May 1981, 27 July 1981 and August 1981) © published by Newsweek Inc 1981. The Associate Editor, Now!, for: *Now!* (14-20 November 1980) © published by Cavenham Communications Ltd 1980. Harold Ober Associates Inc for: *The Boys from Brazil* by Ira Levin first published by Michael Joseph Ltd 1976 © Ira Levin 1976. Edna O'Brien and A M Heath & Co Ltd for: *August is a Wicked Month* by Edna O'Brien first published by Jonathan Cape Ltd 1965 © Edna O'Brien 1965. Pan Books Ltd for: *Dispatches* by Michael Herr first published in Great Britain by Pan Books Ltd 1978 © Michael Herr 1968, 1969, 1970, 1977. *Health and Safety at Work* by Dave Eva and Ron Oswald first published by Pan Books Ltd 1981 © Dave Eva, Ron Oswald and the Workers' Educational Association 1981. *Democracy at Work* by Patrick Burns and Mel Doyle first published by Pan Books Ltd 1981 © Patrick Burns,Mel Doyle and the Workers' Educational Association 1981. *Diet for Life (A Cookbook for Arthritics)* by Mary Laver and Margaret Smith first published by Pan Books Ltd 1981 © Mary Laver and Margaret Smith 1981. Penguin Books Ltd for: *Inside the Company: CIA Diary* by Philip Agee first published in Allen Lane/Penguin Books Ltd 1975 © Philip Agee 1975. Penguin Books Ltd and Spare Ribs Ltd for: *Spare Rib Reader* edited by Marsha Rowe first published in Penguin Books Ltd 1982 © Spare Ribs Ltd 1982. A D Peters & Co Ltd for: 'The Dark Side of Israel' by Norman Moss in Illustrated London News July 1981, 'Aftermath of Osirak' by Norman Moss in the *Illustrated London News* August 1981 and 'Turning Point for Poland' by Norman Moss in the *Illustrated London News* September 1981. 'Recent Fiction' by Sally Emerson in the *Illustrated London News* July 1981, August 1981 and September 1981. *The Complete Upmanship* by Stephen Potter first published in Great Britain by Rupert Hart-Davis Ltd 1970 © Stephen Potter. Elaine Pollard for: Personal Letters 1981 donated by Elaine Pollard. Laurence Pollinger Ltd for: *A Glastonbury Romance* by John Cowper Powys first published by MacDonald & Co Ltd 1933. Murray Pollinger for: *Kiss Kiss* by Roald Dahl published in Great Britain by Michael Joseph Ltd 1960 © Roald Dahl 1962. *Can You Avoid Cancer?* by Peter Goodwin first published by the British Broadcasting Corporation 1984 © Peter Goodwin 1984. Preston Travel Ltd for: Preston Sunroutes 'Camping and Self-Catering' (April to October 1983) holiday brochure. Punch Publications Ltd for: *Punch* (6 May 1981, 29 July 1981, 12 August 1981, 26 August 1981 and 9 September 1981) © published by Punch Publications Ltd 1981. Radala and associates for: *The Naked Civil Servant* by Quentin Crisp first published by Jonathan Cape Ltd 1968 © Quentin Crisp 1968. The Rainbird Publishing Group Ltd for: *The Making of Mankind* by Richard E Leakey first published in Great Britain by Michael Joseph Ltd 1981 © Sherma BV 1981. Robson Books Ltd for: *The Punch Book of Short Stories 3* selected by Alan Coren first published in Great Britain by Robson Books Ltd in association with Punch Publications Ltd 1981 © Robson Books Ltd 1981.*The Best of Robert Morley* by Robert Morley first published in Great Britain by Robson Books Ltd 1981 © Robert Morley 1981. Deborah Rogers Ltd for: 'Picasso's Late Works' by Edward Lucie-Smith in the *Illustrated London News* July 1981, 'David Jones at the Tate' by Edward Lucie-Smith in the *Illustrated London News* August 1981 and 'Further Light on Spanish Painting' by Edward Lucie-Smith in the *Illustrated London News* September 1981. *The Godfather* by Mario Puzo first published in Great Britain by William Heinemann Ltd 1969 © Mario Puzo 1969. Routledge & Kegan Paul Ltd for: *How To Pass Examinations* by John Erasmus first published by Oriel Press Ltd 1967 © Oriel Press Ltd 1980. *Daisy, Daisy* by Christian Miller first published by Routledge & Kegan Paul Ltd 1980 © Christian Miller 1980. *The National Front* by Nigel Fielding first published by Routledge & Kegan Paul Ltd 1981 © Nigel Fielding 1981. *The Myth of Home Ownership* by Jim Kemeny first published by Routledge & Kegan Paul Ltd 1980 © J Kemeny 1981. *Absent With Cause (Lessons of Truancy)* by Roger White first published by Routledge & Kegan Paul Ltd 1980 © Roger White 1980. *The Powers of Evil (in Western Religion, Magic and Folk Belief)* by Richard Cavendish first published by Routledge & Kegan Paul Ltd 1975 © Richard Cavendish 1975. *Crime and Personality* by H J

Corpus Acknowledgements

Eysenck first published by Routledge & Kegan Paul Ltd 1964 © H J Eysenck 1964, 1977. Martin Secker & Warburg Ltd for: *Changing Places* by David Lodge first published in England by Martin Secker & Warburg Ltd 1975 © David Lodge 1975. *The History Man* by Malcolm Bradbury first published by Martin Secker & Warburg 1975 © Malcolm Bradbury 1975. *Humboldt's Gift* by Saul Bellow first published in England by The Alison Press/Martin Secker & Warburg Ltd 1975 © Saul Bellow 1973, 1974, 1975. *Wilt* by Tom Sharpe first published in England by Martin Secker & Warburg Ltd 1976 © Tom Sharpe 1976. *The Last Days of America* by Paul E Erdman first published in England by Martin Secker & Warburg Ltd 1981 © Paul E Erdman 1981. *Autumn Manoeuvres* by Melvyn Bragg first published in England by Martin Secker & Warburg Ltd 1978 © Melvyn Bragg 1978. *The Act of Being* by Charles Marowitz first published in England by Martin Secker & Warburg Ltd 1978 © Charles Marowitz 1978. *As If By Magic* by Angus Wilson first published in England by Martin Secker & Warburg Ltd 1973 © Angus Wilson 1973. *All the President's Men* by Carl Bernstein and Bob Woodward first published in England by Martin Secker & Warburg Ltd 1974 © Carl Bernstein and Bob Woodward 1974. *The Myth of the Nation and the Vision of Revolution* by J L Talmon first published by Martin Secker & Warburg Ltd 1981 © J L Talmon 1980. *Animal Farm* by George Orwell first published by Martin Secker & Warburg 1945 © Eric Blair 1945. Anthony Sheil Associates Ltd for: *Daniel Martin* by John Fowles first published in Great Britain by Jonathan Cape Ltd 1977 © J R Fowles Ltd 1977. *Love Story* by Erich Segal published by Hodder & Stoughton Ltd 1970 © Erich Segal 1970. Sidgwick & Jackson Ltd for: *The Third World War* by General Sir John Hackett and others first published in Great Britain by Sidgwick & Jackson Ltd 1978 © General Sir John Hackett 1978. *Superwoman* by Shirley Conran first published by Sidgwick & Jackson Ltd 1975 © Shirley Conran 1975, 1977. *An Actor and His Time* by John Gielgud first published in Great Britain by Sidgwick & Jackson Ltd 1979 © John Gielgud, John Miller and John Powell 1979 © Biographical Notes, John Miller 1979. Simon & Schuster for: *Our Bodies Ourselves (A Health Book by and for Women)* by the Boston Women's Health Book Collective (British Edition by Angela Phillips and Jill Rakusen) published in Allen Lane and Penguin Books Ltd 1978 © The Boston Women's Health Collective Inc 1971, 1973, 1976 © Material for British Edition, Angela Phillips and Jill Rakusen 1978. Souvenir Press Ltd for: *The Bermuda Triangle* by Charles Berlitz (An Incredible Saga of Unexplained Disappearances) first published in Great Britain by Souvenir Press Ltd 1975 © Charles Berlitz 1974. Souvenir Press Ltd and Michael Joseph Ltd for: *Airport* by Arthur Hailey first published in Great Britain by Michael Joseph Ltd in association with Souvenir Press Ltd 1968 © Arthur Hailey Ltd 1968. Sunmed Holidays Ltd for: 'Go Greek' (Summer 1983) holiday brochure. Maurice Temple Smith Ltd for: *Friends of the Earth Pollution Guide* by Brian Price published by Maurice Temple Smith Ltd 1983 © Brian Price 1983. Maurice Temple Smith and Gower Publishing Co Ltd for: *Working the Land (A New Plan for a Healthy Agriculture)* by Charlie Pye-Smith and Richard North first published by Maurice Temple Smith Ltd 1984 © Charlie Pye-Smith and Richard North 1984. Times Newspapers Ltd for: *The Sunday Times Magazine* (13 January 1980, 20 January 1980 and 11 May 1980) © published by Times Newspapers Ltd 1981. *The Times* (7 September 1981) © published by Times Newspapers Ltd 1981. Twenty's Holidays for: 'The Best 18-33 Holidays' (Winter 1982/83) holiday brochure. University of Birmingham for: Living in Birmingham (1984) © published by The University of Birmingham 1984. Birmingham University Overseas Student Guide © The University of Birmingham. Working with Industry and Commerce © published by The University of Birmingham 1984. University of Birmingham Prospectus (June 1985) © published by The University of Birmingham 1985. University of Birmingham Library Guide © published by The University of Birmingham. University of Birmingham Institute of Research and Development (1984) © published by the University of Birmingham 1984. Biological Sciences at The University of Birmingham (1985) © published by The University of Birmingham 1985. History at the University of Birmingham (1985) © published by the University of Birmingham 1985. Faculty of Arts Handbook (1984-85) © published by The University of Birmingham 1984. Virago Press Ltd for: *Benefits* by Zoe Fairbairns published by Virago Press Ltd 1979 © Zoe Fairbairns 1979. *Simple Steps to Public Life* by Pamela Anderson, Mary Stott and Fay Weldon published in Great Britain by Virago Press Ltd 1980 © Action Opportunities 1980. *Tell Me A Riddle* by Tillie Olsen published by Virago Press Ltd 1980 © this edition Tillie Olsen 1980. A P Watt (& Sons) Ltd for: *The Glittering Prizes* by Frederic Raphael first published in Great Britain by Penguin Books Ltd 1976 © Volatic Ltd 1976. *Then and Now* by W Somerset Maugham first published by William Heinemann Ltd 1946 © W Somerset Maugham 1946. *The Language of Clothes* by Alison Lurie published by William Heinemann Ltd 1981 © Alison Lurie 1981. 'Herschel Commemorative' by Patrick Moore in the *Illustrated London News* July 1981. 'The Outermost Giant' by Patrick Moore in the *Illustrated London News* August 1981. 'Cosmic Bombardment' by Patrick Moore in the *Illustrated London News* September 1981. Weidenfeld & Nicolson Ltd for: 'The Miraculous Toy' by Susan Briggs in the *Illustrated London News* August 1981. *The Needle's Eye* by Margaret Drabble first published by Weidenfeld & Nicolson Ltd 1972 © Margaret Drabble 1972. *Success Without Tears: A Woman's Guide to the Top* by Rachel Nelson first published in Great Britain by Weidenfeld & Nicolson Ltd 1979 © Rachel Nelson 1979. *Education in the Modern World* by John Vaizey published by Weidenfeld & Nicolson Ltd 1967 © John Vaizey 1967. *Rich Man, Poor Man* by Irwin Shaw first published in Great Britain by Weidenfeld & Nicolson Ltd 1970 © Irwin Shaw 1969, 1970. *Lolita* by Vladimir Nabokov first published in Great Britain by Weidenfeld & Nicolson Ltd 1959 © Vladimir Nabokov 1955, 1959, 1968, © G P Putnam's Sons 1963 © McGraw-Hill International Inc 1971. *The Third World* by Peter Worsley first published by Weidenfeld & Nicolson Ltd 1964 © Peter Worsley 1964, 1967. *Portrait of a Marriage* by Nigel Nicolson published by Weidenfeld & Nicolson Ltd 1973 © Nigel Nicolson 1973. *The Dogs Bark: Public People and Private Places* by Truman Capote first published in Great Britain by Weidenfeld & Nicolson Ltd 1974 © Truman Capote 1974. *Great Planning Disasters* by Peter Hall first published in Great Britain by George Weidenfeld & Nicolson Ltd 1980 © Peter Hall 1980. The Writers and Readers Publishing Co-operative Ltd for: *Working with Words, Literacy Beyond School* by Jane Mace published by The Writers and Readers Publishing Co-operative Ltd 1979 © Jane Mace 1979. *The Alienated: Growing Old Today* by Gladys Elder OAP published by The Writers and Readers Publishing Co-operative Ltd 1977 © Text, The Estate of Gladys Elder 1977 © Photographs, Mike Abrahams 1977. *Beyond the Crisis in Art* by Peter Fuller published by The Writers and Readers Publishing Cooperative Ltd 1980 © Peter Fuller 1980. *The War and Peace Book* by Dave Noble published by The Writers and Readers Publishing Co-operative Ltd 1977 © Dave Noble 1977. *Tony Benn: A Political Biography* by Robert Jenkins first published by The Writers and Readers Publishing Co-operative Ltd 1980 © Robert Jenkins 1980. *Nuclear Power for Beginners* by Stephen Croall and Kaianders Sempler first published by The Writers and Readers Publishing Co-operative Ltd 1978 © Text, Stephen Croall 1978, 1980 © Illustrations Kaianders Sempler 1978, 1980. Yale University Press for: *Life in the English Country House: A Social and Architectural History* by Mark Girouard published by Yale University Press Ltd, London 1978 © Yale University 1978. The British Broadcasting Corporation for transcripts of radio transmissions of 'Kaleidoscope', 'Any Questions', 'Money Box' and 'Arts and Africa' 1981 and 1982. The British Broadcasting Corporation and Mrs Shirley Williams for transcripts of television interviews with Mrs Shirley Williams 1979. Dr B L Smith, School of Mathematics and Physical Sciences, University of Sussex for programmes on Current Affairs, Science and The Arts originally broadcast on Radio Sussex 1979 and 1980 © B L Smith. The following people in the University of Birmingham: Professor J McH Sinclair, Department of English, for his tapes of informal conversation (personal collection). Mr R Wallace, formerly Department of Accounting and Finance, and Ms D Houghton, Department of English, for transcripts of his accountancy lectures. Dr B K Gazey, Department of Electrical Engineering and Dr M Montgomery, University of Strathclyde, Department of English, for a transcript of Dr Gazey's lecture. Dr L W Poel, Department of Plant Biology, and Dr M Montgomery, University of Strathclyde, Department of English, for a transcript of Dr Poel's lecture. Professor J G Hawkes, formerly Department of Plant Biology, for recordings of his lectures. Dr M S Snaith, Department of Transportation for recordings of his lectures. Dr M P Hoey, Department of English, and Dr M Cooper, The British Council, for a recording of their discussion on discourse analysis. Ms A Renouf, Department of English, for recordings of job and academic interviews 1977. Mr R H Hubbard, formerly a B Phil (Ed) student, Faculty of Education, for his research recordings of expressions of uncertainty 1978-79. Mr A E Hare, formerly a B Phil (Ed) student, Faculty of Education, for his transcripts of telephone conversations 1978. Dr A Tsui, formerly Department of English, for her recordings of informal conversation. Mr J Couperthwaite, formerly Department of English, for a recording of informal conversation 1981. Ms C Emmott, M Litt student, Department of English, for a recording of informal conversation 1981. Mrs B T Atkins for the transcript of an account of a dream 1981. The British Council for 'Authentic Materials Numbers 1-28' 1981. Professor M Hammerton and Mr K Coghill, Department of Psychology, University of Newcastle-upon-Tyne, for tape recordings of their lectures 1981. Mr G P Graveson, formerly research student, University of Newcastle, for his recordings of teacher discussion 1977. Mr W R Jones, formerly research student, University of Southampton, for his recordings of classroom talk. Mr Ian Fisher, formerly BA student, Newcastle Polytechnic, for his transcripts of interviews on local history 1981. Dr N Coupland, formerly PhD student, Department of English, UWIST, for his transcripts of travel agency talk 1981. Professor D B Bromley, Department of Psychology, University of Liverpool, for his transcript of a research recording. Mr Brian Lawrence, formerly of Saffron Walden County High School, for a tape of his talk on 'The British Education System' 1979.

Every effort has been made to trace the copyright holders, but if any have been inadvertently overlooked the publishers will be pleased to make the necessary acknowledgments at the first opportunity.

A

a - an

You use **a** and **an** when you are talking about a person or thing for the first time. **A** and **an** are called the **indefinite article.** You only use **a** and **an** with singular count nouns. The second time you refer to the same person or thing, you use **the.**

She picked up a book.
The book was lying on the table.

After weeks of looking we eventually bought a house.
The house was in a small village.

You can describe someone or something using **a** or **an** with an adjective and a noun, or with a noun and a qualifier.

His brother was a sensitive child.
He seemed a worried man.
The information was contained in an article on biology.
I chose a picture that reminded me of my own country.

Note that you do not omit **a** or **an** in front of a noun when the noun refers to someone's profession or job. For example, you say 'He is **an** architect'. You do not say 'He is architect'.

He became a schoolteacher.
She is a model and an artist.

'a' or 'an'? You use **a** in front of words beginning with consonant sounds and **an** in front of words beginning with vowel sounds.

Then I saw a big car parked nearby.
...an empty house.

You use **an** in front of words beginning with 'h' when the 'h' is not pronounced. For example, you say '**an honest** man'. You do not say 'a honest man'.

...in less than an hour.
...an honest answer.

An is used in front of the following words beginning with 'h':

heir	honest	honourable
heiress	honorary	hour
heirloom	honour	hourly

You use **a** in front of words beginning with 'u' when the 'u' is pronounced /ju:/ (like 'you'). For example, you say '**a unique** occasion'. You do not say 'an unique occasion'.

He was a University of London law student.

They could elect a union member.

A is used in front of the following words:

ubiquitous	unilateral	universe	use	utensil
unanimous	unilateralist	university	used	uterus
unicorn	union	uranium	useful	utilitarian
unification	unique	urinal	useless	utility
uniform	unisex	urinary	user	utopian
uniformed	unit	urine	usual	
uniformity	united	usable	usually	
unifying	universal	usage	usurper	

You use **an** in front of an abbreviation when the letters are pronounced separately and the first letter begins with a vowel sound.

Benn resigned from the Government, though remaining an MP.
There has been an SOS out for you for three days.

'a' meaning 'one'   **A** and **an** are used to mean 'one' in front of some numbers and units of measurement. See entries at **Numbers and fractions** and **Measurements**.

Abbreviations

An **abbreviation** is a shortened form of a word, compound, or phrase, made by leaving out some of the letters or by using only the first letter of each word. For example, 'g' is an abbreviation for 'gram' in an expression of weight such as '25g', and 'BBC' is an abbreviation for 'British Broadcasting Corporation'. Some abbreviations are more commonly used than the full form.

You have to follow the accepted way of abbreviating, although with certain words there can be more than one way. For example, you can use either 'cont.' or 'contd.' as an abbreviation for 'continued'.

In general, if a word begins with a capital letter, its abbreviation also begins with a capital letter. For example, the title 'Captain' is written with a capital letter when used in front of a name, so the abbreviation 'Capt' is also written with a capital letter.

There are five basic types of abbreviation.

abbreviating   The first three types are used for abbreviating a single word.
one word
● The first type consists of the first letter of the word. When read aloud, the abbreviation is usually pronounced like the full word.

m = metre
p. = page
F = Fahrenheit
N = North

● The second type consists of the first few letters of the word. When read aloud, the abbreviation is usually pronounced like the full word.

cont. = continued
usu. = usually
vol. = volume
Brit. = British
Hon. = Honourable
Thurs. = Thursday

● The third type consists of the word with several letters missed out. When read aloud, the abbreviation is pronounced like the full word.

asst. = assistant
dept. = department
jct = junction
km = kilometre
tbsp. = tablespoonful
Sgt = sergeant

Note that the abbreviations for 'headquarters', 'television', and 'tuberculosis' are of this type but consist of capital letters: 'HQ', 'TV', and 'TB'. You say each letter separately. In the case of some units of measurement, the second letter is a capital. For example, the abbreviation for 'kilowatt' or 'kilowatts' is 'kW'.

abbreviating more than one word
The fourth and fifth types of abbreviation are used for abbreviating a compound noun or a phrase.

● The fourth type consists of the first letter of each word. You usually say each letter separately, with the main stress on the last letter.

MP = Member of Parliament
CD = compact disc
HRH = His/Her Royal Highness
USA = United States of America
VIP = very important person
rpm = revolutions per minute

The choice of 'a' or 'an' before an abbreviation of this type depends on the pronunciation of the first letter of the abbreviation. For example, you say 'an MP' not 'a MP' because the pronunciation of 'M' begins with a vowel sound: /em/.

Note that abbreviations of compound nouns usually consist of capital letters even when the full words do not begin with capital letters. However, abbreviations of phrases usually consist of small letters.

A few abbreviations of this type also include the second letter of one of the words, which is not written as a capital. For example, the abbreviation for 'Bachelor of Science' (someone who has a science degree) is 'BSc'.

● The fifth type of abbreviation uses the first letter of each word to form a new word. This type of abbreviation is called an **acronym**. You pronounce an acronym as a word, rather than saying each letter.

BASIC /beisik/ = Beginner's All-purpose Symbolic Instruction Code
OPEC /əupek/ = Organization of Petroleum-Exporting Countries
TEFL /tefl/ = teaching English as a foreign language

Most acronyms consist of capital letters. When an acronym is written with small letters, for example 'laser' (= light amplification by stimulated emission of radiation), it is regarded as an ordinary word.

full stops with abbreviations
You can put a full stop at the end of the first three types of abbreviation, or after each letter of the fourth kind of abbreviation.

b. = born
Apr. = April
St. = Saint
D.J. = disc jockey

However, people often do not put in full stops nowadays, especially between capital letters. Full stops are less commonly put at the end of abbreviations in British writing than in American writing.

BA = Bachelor of Arts
CBI = Confederation of British Industry
Mr = Mister

Full stops are not usually used when writing abbreviations that are pronounced as words.

NATO /ˈneɪtəʊ/ = North Atlantic Treaty Organization
AIDS /eɪdz/ = acquired immune deficiency syndrome

plurals of abbreviations If you want to make an abbreviation plural, you usually add a small 's' to the singular abbreviation.

hr, hrs
MP, MPs
UFO, UFOs

WARNING With words which refer to units of measurement, you usually use the same abbreviation for the singular and the plural. For example, 'ml' is the abbreviation for both 'millilitre' and 'millilitres'.

The plural of 'p' (= page) is 'pp', and the plural of 'St' (= Saint) is 'SS'.

a bit

See entry at **bit**.

able

See entry at **can - could - be able to**.

about

You use **about** when you mention what someone is saying, writing, or thinking.

It was wonderful to hear Brian talking about John.
I'll have to think about that.

You can say that a book is **about** a particular subject or that it is **on** that subject.

They suggested that I should write a book about window dressing.
...the author of a book on Chinese regional cookery.

The author is writing a book about the Outer Hebrides.
...Anthony Daniels' book on Guatemala.

You can also use **about** to say what a novel or play deals with. You do not use 'on'.

...a nail-biting novel about a sinister teenage secret society.
...a Norwegian story about a king who has seven sons.

'about to' If you are **about to do** something, you are going to do it soon.

You are about to cross the River Jordan.
I was about to go home.

You do not use an '-ing' form in sentences like these. You do not say, for example, 'You are about crossing the River Jordan'.

above

If an amount or measurement is **above** a particular level, it is greater than that level.

...children above the age of 5.
...applicants aged 15 and above.
...a degree above absolute zero.

WARNING You do not use **above** in front of a number when you are talking about a quantity or number of things or people. For example, you do not say 'She had above thirty pairs of shoes'. You say 'She had **over** thirty pairs of shoes' or 'She had **more than** thirty pairs of shoes'.

They paid out <u>over</u> 3 million pounds.
He saw <u>more than</u> 800 children, dying of starvation.

For more information about approximate numbers, see entry at **Measurements.**

absent

If someone is **absent from** a meeting, ceremony, or place, they are not there.

She was <u>absent from</u> the committee.
The Security Police discovered I was <u>absent from</u> my house.

Note that you use **from** after 'absent' in sentences like these. You do not use 'at'.

If it is clear what meeting, ceremony, or place you are talking about, you can simply say that someone is **absent**.

The Mongolian delegate to the assembly was <u>absent</u>.

Absent is a fairly formal word. In conversation, you say that someone is **not at** a meeting, ceremony, or place, or that they are **not there**.

She <u>wasn't at</u> Molly's wedding.
The boy <u>wasn't at</u> home at the time of the tragedy.
At the time when she most needed me I <u>wasn't there</u>.

accept

If you **accept** something that you have been offered, you agree to take it.

Müller <u>accepted</u> a glass of port.

advice and suggestions
If you **accept** someone's advice or suggestion, you decide to do what they advise or suggest.

If she <u>accepts</u> the advice, she feels happier.
I knew that they would <u>accept</u> my proposal.

However, you do not say that you 'accept to do' what someone suggests. You say that you **agree to do** it.

The princess <u>agreed to go</u> on television.
She <u>agreed to let</u> us use her flat while she was away.

situations and people
If you **accept** a difficult or unpleasant situation, you recognize that it cannot be changed.

…unwillingness to <u>accept</u> bad working conditions.
The astronaut <u>accepts</u> danger as being part of the job.

However, you do not say that you 'cannot accept' a person you strongly dislike. You say that you **cannot stand** them or **cannot bear** them.

She said she <u>couldn't stand</u> him.
I <u>can't bear</u> the sight of him.

'except'
Do not confuse **accept** /əksept/ with **except** /ɪksept/. **Except** is a preposition or conjunction, used to introduce the only thing or person that a statement does not apply to.

All the boys <u>except</u> Piggy started to giggle.

See entry at **except.**

acceptable

You say that something is **acceptable** when it is satisfactory, or when people do not object to it.

To my relief he found the article acceptable.
In war killing is acceptable.

'willing' You do not say that someone is 'acceptable' to do something. You say that they are **willing** to do it.

Ed was quite willing to let us help him.
Would you be willing to go to Berkhamsted?

accommodation

Accommodation is a room or rooms to stay, work, or live in. In British English, **accommodation** is an uncount noun. You do not talk about 'accommodations' or 'an accommodation'.

There is a shortage of accommodation.
...student accommodation.
The centre provides accommodation for 5,360 civil servants.

Speakers of American English sometimes talk about **accommodations.**

Their feelings of suspense were centred around room accommodations.

accompany

If you **accompany** someone somewhere, you go there with them. **Accompany** is a fairly formal word.

She asked me to accompany her to the church.

In conversation, you say **go with** or **come with.**

I went with my friends to see what it looked like.
He wished Ellen had come with him.

However, there is no passive form of **go with** or **come with.** If you want to use a passive form, you must use **accompany.**

He was accompanied by Clare Boothe Luce, his second wife.
She came out of the house accompanied by Mrs Jones.

accord

If you do something **of** your **own accord,** you do it freely and because you want to do it.

She knew they would leave of their own accord.

WARNING You must use 'own' in sentences like these. You do not say, for example, 'She had gone of her accord'.

You also do not say that someone does something 'on' their own accord.

according to

If you say that something is the case **according to** a particular person, book, or document, you mean that you got the information from that person, book, or document.

According to Dr Santos, the cause of death was drowning.
The road was forty miles long according to my map.

You do not usually use **according to** in conversation. Instead of saying 'According to George, the roads are very slippery this morning', you say 'George **says** the roads are very slippery this morning'.

Arnold says they do this in Essex as well.
The notice says his dog cannot go without a lead.

'in my opinion'   You also never say 'according to me' or 'according to us'. If you want to emphasize that what you are saying is your own opinion, you say '**In my opinion...**' or '**In our opinion...**'.

In my opinion we face a national emergency.
At the height of the season the temple gets crowded, and in our opinion it's best to visit it in the evening.

For more information on expressing opinions, see entry at **Opinions**.

WARNING   You do not use **according to** and **opinion** together. You do not say, for example, 'According to the bishop's opinion, the public has a right to know'. You say '**The bishop's opinion is that** the public has a right to know'.

Aristotle's opinion is that dialectic comes before everything else.
The general opinion is that French wines are the best.

accuse - charge

'accuse'   If you **accuse** someone **of** doing something wrong, you say that they did it.

He accused them of drinking beer while driving.
He is accused of killing ten young women.

Note that you do not say that you accuse someone 'for' doing something wrong.

'charge'   When the police **charge** someone **with** committing a crime, they formally accuse them of it.

He was arrested and charged with committing a variety of offences.

accustomed to

If you are **accustomed to** something, you have become familiar with it and you no longer find it strange. **Accustomed to** usually comes after verbs such as 'be', 'become', 'get', or 'grow'.

It did not get lighter but I became accustomed to the dark.
I am not accustomed to being interrupted.

Note that you do not say that someone is 'accustomed with' something.

'used to'   In conversation, you do not usually say that someone is 'accustomed to' something. You say that they are **used to** it. **Used to** usually comes after 'be' or 'get'.

Pilots are used to the mid-afternoon switch from one runway to the other.
I was beginning to get used to the old iron bed.

You can say that someone is **accustomed to doing** something or **used to doing** something.

The bank president is accustomed to working in the Elysée Palace.
We are used to queueing.

You do not say that someone is 'accustomed to do' something or 'used to do' something.

If you **accustom yourself to** something different, you accept it and become familiar with it.

He sat very still, trying to accustom himself to the darkness.

acronyms

See entry at **Abbreviations**.

actual

You use **actual** to emphasize that the place, object, or person you are talking about is the real or genuine one.

The predicted results and the <u>actual</u> results are very different.
The interpretation bore no relation to the <u>actual</u> words spoken.

WARNING   You only use **actual** in front of a noun. You do not say that something 'is actual'.

'current' and 'present'   You do not use 'actual' to describe something which is happening, being done, or being used at the present time. Instead you use **current** or **present**.

Whether all those measures would see Boston through its <u>current</u> crisis remained doubtful.
…the power and potential danger of the armed forces in the <u>present</u> situation.

actually

You use **actually** when you are saying what the truth is about something, in contrast to other things that might have been said or thought.

This load had <u>actually</u> been dispatched three months previously.
<u>Actually</u>, I didn't come here just to help you with the party.
'Mr Hooper is a schoolteacher.'—'A university lecturer, <u>actually</u>.'

You also use **actually** when you are mentioning something that is very surprising. You put **actually** in front of the surprising part of what you are saying.

I was <u>actually</u> cruel sometimes.
The real value of oil has <u>actually been falling</u> in the last two years.

WARNING   You do not use **actually** to emphasize that something is happening now, rather than in the past or future. Instead you use **presently, at present,** or **right now**. See entries at **presently** and **now**.

Addressing someone

When you talk to someone, you sometimes use their name. You can sometimes use their title, if they have one. Sometimes you use a word that shows how you feel about them, for example 'darling' or 'idiot'. Words used to address people are called **vocatives.**

Vocatives are not as common in English as in some other languages. They are less common in British English than in American English.

position of vocatives   If you use a vocative, you usually use it at the end of a sentence.

I told you he was okay, <u>Phil</u>.
Where are you staying, <u>Mr Swallow</u>?
Yes, <u>George</u>.

When you want to get someone's attention, you use a vocative at the beginning of a sentence.

John, how long have you been at the university?
Dad, why have you got that suit on?

A vocative can also be used between clauses or after the first group of words in a clause. People often do this to emphasize the importance of what they are saying.

I must remind you, Mrs Babcock, that I did warn you of possible repercussions from failure to take your medication.
Don't you think, John, it would be wiser to wait?

writing vocatives When you are writing speech down, you separate a vocative from words in front of it or after it using a comma.

Don't leave me, Jenny.
John, do you think that there are dangers associated with this policy?

addressing someone you do not know If you want to say something to someone you do not know, for example in the street or in a shop, you do not usually use a vocative at all. You say 'Excuse me' if you need to attract their attention. For more information about the use of 'Excuse me', see entry at **Apologizing.**

WARNING In modern English, the titles 'Mr', 'Mrs', 'Miss', and 'Ms' are only used in front of names. You should not use them on their own to address people you do not know, nor should you use 'gentleman' or 'lady'. You should not use 'sir' or 'madam' either; these words are normally only used by people who work in shops to address customers politely.

It is usually considered old-fashioned to use a word that indicates the person's job, such as 'officer' (to a policeman). However, 'doctor' and 'nurse' can be used.

Is he all right, doctor?

Some people use 'you' to address someone whose name they do not know, but this is very impolite.

addressing someone you know If you know the surname of the person you are talking to, you can address them using their title (usually 'Mr', 'Mrs', or 'Miss') and surname. This is fairly formal.

Thank you, Mr Jones.
Goodbye, Dr Kirk.

Titles showing a person's rank can be used without a surname after them.

I'm sure you have nothing to worry about, Professor.
Good evening, Captain.
Is that clear, Sergeant?

'Mr' and 'Madam' are sometimes used in front of the titles 'President', 'Chairman', 'Chairwoman', and 'Chairperson'.

No, Mr President.

See entry at **Names and titles** for information on titles that are used with names.

WARNING People do not usually address other people using their first name and surname. The only people who use this form of address are presenters of radio and television programmes talking to their guests.

If you know someone well, you can address them using their first name. However, people do not usually do this in the course of an ordinary conversation, unless they want to make it clear who they are talking to.

What do you think, John?
Shut up, Simon!

It's not a joke, Angela.

Short, informal forms of people's names, such as 'Jenny' and 'Mike', are sometimes used as vocatives. However, you should not use a form like this unless you are sure that the person does not object to it.

addressing relatives People address their parents and grandparents using a noun that shows their relationship to them.

Someone's got to do it, mum.
Sorry, Grandma.

The following list shows the commonest nouns that people use to address their parents and grandparents:

mother: Mum, Mummy, Mother
father: Dad, Daddy
grandmother: Gran, Grannie, Grandma, Nan, Nanna
grandfather: Grandad, Grandpa

'Aunt' and 'Uncle' are also used as vocatives, usually in front of the person's first name. The more informal word 'Auntie' (or 'Aunty') can be used on its own.

This is Ginny, Aunt Bernice.
Goodbye, Uncle Harry.
I'm sorry, Auntie Jane.
Hello, auntie.

WARNING Nouns indicating other family relationships, such as 'daughter', 'brother', and 'cousin' are not used as vocatives.

addressing a group of people If you want to address a group of people formally, for example at a meeting, you say 'ladies and gentlemen' (or 'ladies' or 'gentlemen', if the group is not mixed).

Good evening, ladies and gentlemen.

If you want to address a group of people informally, you can use 'everyone' or 'everybody', although it is not necessary to use any vocative.

I'm so terribly sorry, everybody.

If you want to address a group of children or young people, you can use 'kids'. You can use 'boys' or 'girls' if the group is not mixed.

Come and say 'How do you do?' to our guest, kids.
Give Mr Hooper a chance, boys.
Girls, a really bad thing has come up.

The use of 'children' as a vocative is formal.

vocatives showing dislike People show dislike, contempt, or impatience using nouns and combinations of nouns and adjectives as vocatives, usually with 'you' in front of them.

No, you fool, the other way.
Shut your big mouth, you stupid idiot.
Give it to me, you silly girl.

vocatives showing affection Vocatives showing affection are usually used by themselves.

Goodbye, darling.
Come on, love.

WARNING Some people use 'my' or the person's name in front of affectionate vocatives, but this usually sounds old-fashioned or humorous.

We've got to go, my dear.
Oh Harold darling, why did he die?

other vocatives   People who are serving in shops, or providing a service to the public, sometimes politely call male customers or clients 'sir' and female ones 'madam'.

A liqueur of any kind, sir?
'Thank you very much.'—'You're welcome, madam.'

A number of words, such as 'love', 'dear', and 'mate', are used by people in informal situations to address other people, including people they do not know. These vocatives are often characteristic of a region or a social group, or both.

She'll be all right, mate.
Trust me, kid.

WARNING   You are advised not to use any of these vocatives, because they would sound inappropriate from someone who is not a native speaker from a particular region.

GRAMMAR # Adjectives

An **adjective** is a word that is used to describe someone or something or give information about them.

form   The form of an adjective does not change: the same form is used for singular and plural, for subject and object, and for male and female.

We were looking for a good place to camp.
Good places to fish were hard to find.

qualitative   **Qualitative adjectives** are adjectives that indicate that someone or
adjectives   something has a particular quality. For example, 'sad', 'pretty', 'happy', and 'wise' are qualitative adjectives.

...a sad story.
...a small child.

Qualitative adjectives are **gradable.** This means that the person or thing referred to can have more or less of the quality mentioned. The usual way of indicating the amount of a quality that something or someone has is by using **submodifiers** such as 'very' and 'rather'. See entry at **Adverbs.**

...an extremely narrow road.
...a very pretty girl.
...a rather clumsy person.

classifying   **Classifying adjectives** are adjectives that are used to indicate that
adjectives   something is of a particular type. For example, if you say 'financial help', you are using the adjective 'financial' to classify the noun 'help'. There are many different kinds of help: 'financial help' is one of them.

...my daily shower.
...Victorian houses.
...civil engineering.

colour adjectives   **Colour adjectives** are used to indicate what colour something is.

...a small blue car.
Her eyes are green.

To specify a colour more precisely, a word such as 'light', 'pale', 'dark', or 'bright' is put in front of the adjective.

...light brown hair.
...a bright green suit.
...a dark blue dress.

Colour words can be used as uncount nouns, and the main colour words can be used as count nouns.

The snow shadows had turned a deep blue.
They blended in so well with the khaki and reds of the landscape.

emphasizing **Emphasizing adjectives** are used in front of a noun to emphasize your
adjectives description of something or the degree of something.

He made me feel like a complete idiot.
Some of it was absolute rubbish.

The following adjectives are emphasizing adjectives:

absolute	outright	pure	total
complete	perfect	real	true
entire	positive	sheer	utter

specifying There is a small group of adjectives, sometimes called **postdeterminers**,
adjectives which you use to indicate precisely what you are referring to. These
adjectives come after a determiner and in front of any other adjectives.

...the following brief description.
He wore his usual old white coat.

They also come in front of numbers.

What has gone wrong during the last ten years?

The following adjectives are used in this way:

additional	first	next	past	same
certain	following	only	present	specific
chief	further	opposite	previous	usual
entire	last	other	principal	whole
existing	main	particular	remaining	

adjectives with A large number of adjectives end in '-ed' or '-ing'. See entries at **'-ed'**
special endings **adjectives** and **'-ing' adjectives**.

For information on adjectives ending in '-ic' and '-ical', see entry at **'-ic'**
and '-ical' words.

For information on adjectives ending in '-ly', see entry at **'-ly' words**.

compound **Compound adjectives** are made up of two or more words, usually written
adjectives with hyphens between them. They may be qualitative, classifying, or
colour adjectives.

I was in a light-hearted mood.
Olivia was driving a long, low-slung, bottle-green car.
...a good-looking girl.
...a part-time job.

comparative and **Comparative adjectives** are used to say that something has more of a
superlative quality than something else. **Superlative adjectives** are used to say that
adjectives something has more of a quality than anything else of its kind. Only
qualitative adjectives and a few colour adjectives have superlatives. See
entry at **Comparative and superlative adjectives**.

position of adjectives
Most adjectives can be used in front of nouns to give more information about something that is mentioned.

She bought a loaf of white bread.
There was no clear evidence.

WARNING
Adjectives cannot usually be used after a determiner without being followed by either a noun or 'one'. You cannot say, for example, 'He showed me all of them, but I preferred the green'. You have to say 'He showed me all of them, but I preferred the green one'. See entry at **one**.

For information on the use of 'the' with an adjective to refer to a group of people, as in 'the rich', see entry at **the.**

Most adjectives can also be used after a link verb such as 'be', 'become', or 'feel'.

The room was large and square.
I felt angry.
Nobody seemed amused.

Some adjectives are normally used only after link verbs, not in front of nouns, when used with a particular meaning. For example, you can say 'She was alone' but you cannot say 'an alone girl'.

The following adjectives are only used after link verbs:

afraid	asleep	glad	sorry
alive	aware	ill	sure
alone	content	ready	well

Instead of using these adjectives in front of a noun, you can sometimes use an alternative word or expression. For example, instead of 'the afraid child' you can say 'the frightened child'.

See also separate entries at these words.

coordination of adjectives
When two adjectives are used as the complement of a link verb, a conjunction (usually 'and') is used to link them. With three or more adjectives, the last two are linked with a conjunction, and commas are put after the others.

The day was hot and dusty.
The house was old, damp and smelly.

When more than one adjective is used in front of a noun, the adjectives are not usually separated by 'and'. You do not normally say 'a short, fat and old man'. For more information on how to link adjectives, see entry at **and.**

order of adjectives
When more than one adjective is used in front of a noun, the usual order is as follows:

qualitative adjective – colour adjective – classifying adjective

...a little white wooden house.
...rapid technological advance.
...a large circular pool of water.
...a necklace of blue Venetian beads.

However, non-gradable adjectives indicating shape, such as 'circular' and 'rectangular', often come in front of colour adjectives, even though they are classifying adjectives.

...the rectangular grey stones.
...the circular yellow patch on the lawn.

order of qualitative adjectives

The order of qualitative adjectives is normally as follows:

opinions – size – quality – age – shape

We shall have a nice big garden with two apple trees.
It had beautiful thick fur.
...big, shiny beetles.
He had long curly red hair.
She put on her dirty old fur coat.

Note that when you refer to 'a nice big garden' or 'a lovely big garden', you usually mean that the garden is nice because it is big, not nice in some other way. For more information, see entry at **nice.**

order of classifying adjectives

If there is more than one classifying adjective in front of a noun, the normal order is:

age – shape – nationality – material

...a medieval French village.
...a rectangular plastic box.
...an Italian silk jacket.

Other types of classifying adjective usually come after a nationality adjective.

...the Chinese artistic tradition.
...the American political system.

comparatives and superlatives

Comparatives and superlatives normally come in front of all other adjectives in a noun group.

Some of the better English actors have gone to live in Hollywood.
These are the highest monthly figures on record.

noun modifiers

When a noun group contains both an adjective and a **noun modifier** (a noun used in front of another noun), the adjective is placed in front of the noun modifier.

He works in the French film industry.
He receives a large weekly cash payment.

adjectives after a noun

You do not usually put adjectives after nouns. However, there are some exceptions, which are explained below.

You can put an adjective after a noun if the adjective is followed by a prepositional phrase or a 'to'-infinitive clause.

...a warning to people eager for a quick cure.
...the sort of weapons likely to be deployed against it.

The adjectives 'alive' and 'awake' can be put after a noun which is preceded by a superlative, an adverb, or 'first', 'last', 'only', 'every', or 'any'.

Is Phil Morgan the only man alive who knows all the words to that song?
She sat at the window, until she was the last person awake.

A few formal adjectives are only used after a noun:

designate	incarnate
elect	manqué

...British Rail's <u>chairman designate</u>, Mr Robert Reid.
She was now the <u>president elect</u>.

adjectives before or after a noun

A few adjectives can be used in front of or after a noun without any change of meaning:

affected	required
available	suggested

Newspapers were the only <u>available</u> source of information.
...the number of teachers <u>available</u>.

A few adjectives can be used in front of or after a noun which is preceded by a superlative or 'first', 'last', 'only', 'every', or 'any':

free	necessary	possible	visible
imaginable	open	vacant	

...the best <u>possible</u> environment.
I said you'd assist him in every way <u>possible</u>.

A few adjectives have a different meaning depending on whether they come in front of a noun or after it. For example, 'the concerned mother' describes a mother who is worried, but 'the mother concerned' simply refers to a mother who has been mentioned.

...the approval of interested and <u>concerned</u> parents.
The idea needs to come from the <u>individuals concerned</u>.

The following adjectives have different meanings in different positions:

concerned	present	responsible
involved	proper	

For more information, see separate entries at these words.

adjectives after measurements

Some adjectives that describe size can come after a noun group consisting of a number or determiner and a noun that indicates the unit of measurement.

He was about <u>six feet tall</u>.
The island is only <u>29 miles long</u>.

The following adjectives can be used like this:

deep	long	thick
high	tall	wide

See entry at **Measurements**.

'Old' is used after noun groups in a similar way. See entry at **Age**.

adjectives with prepositions and other structures

Some adjectives are usually followed by a particular preposition, a 'to'-infinitive, or a 'that'-clause, because otherwise their meaning would be unclear or incomplete. For example, you cannot simply say that someone is 'accustomed'. You have to say that they are 'accustomed to' something.

He seemed to be becoming <u>accustomed to</u> my presence.
They are very <u>fond of</u> each other.
The sky is <u>filled with</u> clouds.

The following lists show adjectives which must be followed by a preposition when used immediately after a link verb.

accustomed to	conducive to	prone to	resistant to
allergic to	devoted to	proportional to	subject to
attributable to	impervious to	proportionate to	subservient to
attuned to	injurious to	reconciled to	susceptible to
averse to	integral to	resigned to	unaccustomed to

aware of	desirous of	illustrative of	reminiscent of
bereft of	devoid of	incapable of	representative of
capable of	fond of	indicative of	
characteristic of	heedless of	mindful of	

unhampered by	rooted in	conversant with	tinged with
descended from	steeped in	filled with	
inherent in	swathed in	fraught with	
lacking in	contingent on	riddled with	

In some cases, there is a choice between two prepositions.

We are in no way immune from this danger.
He was curiously immune to teasing.

The following adjectives are usually or always used immediately after a link verb and can be followed by the prepositions indicated:

burdened by/with	inclined to/towards	parallel to/with
dependent on/upon	incumbent on/upon	reliant on/upon
immune from/to	intent on/upon	stricken by/with

Many adjectives can be followed by a preposition. If you are not sure which preposition to use after a particular adjective, look at the entry for the adjective in this book.

For lists of adjectives followed by a 'to'-infinitive clause or a 'that'-clause, see entries at **'To'-infinitive clauses** and **'That'-clauses**.

adjuncts

An **adjunct** is the same as an **adverbial**. See entry at **Adverbials**.

adverbial clauses

An **adverbial clause** is a subordinate clause which gives more information about the main clause. See entry at **Subordinate clauses**.

GRAMMAR # Adverbials

Adverbials are words or phrases which give information about when, how, where, or in what circumstances something happens. An adverbial can be an adverb, a group of words whose main word is an adverb, or a prepositional phrase. A few noun groups can also be used as adverbials.

The main types of adverbials indicate manner, aspect, opinion, place, time, frequency, duration, degree, extent, emphasis, focus, and probability. These are explained below, and then information is given on the position of adverbials in a clause.

For information on adverbials such as 'moreover', 'however', and 'next', which are used to indicate connections between clauses, see entry at **Linking adverbials.**

manner   **Adverbials of manner** are used to describe the way in which something happens or is done.

They looked anxiously at each other.
He did not play well enough to win.
She listened with great patience as he told his story.
I'm going to handle this my way.

Most adverbs of manner are formed by adding '**-ly**' to an adjective. For example, the adverbs 'quietly' and 'badly' are formed by adding '-ly' to the adjectives 'quiet' and 'bad'. See entry at '**-ly' words.**

I didn't play badly.
He reported accurately what they had said.

Some adverbs of manner have the same form as adjectives and have similar meanings.

I've always been interested in fast cars.
The driver was driving too fast.

These are the ones most commonly used:

direct	late	right	straight
fast	loud	slow	tight
hard	quick	solo	wrong

The adverb of manner related to the adjective 'good' is 'well'.

He is a good dancer.
He dances well.

Note that 'well' can also be an adjective describing someone's health.

'How are you?'—'I am very well, thank you.'

aspect   Not all adverbs ending in '-ly' are adverbs of manner. You use '-ly' adverbs formed from classifying adjectives to make it clear what aspect of something you are talking about. For example, if you want to say that something is important in the field of politics or from a political point of view, you can say that it is 'politically important'.

It would have been politically damaging for him to retreat.
We had a very bad year last year financially.

Here is a list of the most common of these adverbs:

biologically	geographically	politically	statistically
commercially	intellectually	psychologically	technically
economically	logically	racially	visually
emotionally	morally	scientifically	
financially	outwardly	socially	

'Speaking' is sometimes added to these adverbs. For example, 'technically speaking' can be used to mean 'from a technical point of view'.

He's not a doctor, technically speaking.

He and Malcolm decided that, <u>racially speaking</u>, anyway, they were in complete agreement.

opinion
Other '-ly' adverbs are used to indicate your reaction to, or your opinion of, the fact or event you are talking about. These are sometimes called **sentence adverbs.**

<u>Surprisingly,</u> most of my help came from the technicians.
<u>Luckily,</u> I had seen the play before so I knew what it was about.

For a list of these adverbs, see entry at **Opinions.**

For information about other small groups of '-ly' adverbs, see entry at **'-ly' words.**

WARNING
Some '-ly' adverbs have a different meaning from adjectives to which they seem to be related. For example, 'hardly' has a different meaning from 'hard'.

This has been a long <u>hard</u> day.
Her bedroom was so small she could <u>hardly</u> move in it.

For more information, see entries at **awful - awfully, bare - barely, hard - hardly, late - lately, scarce - scarcely, short - shortly,** and **terrible - terribly.**

place
Adverbials of place are used to say where something happens or where something goes.

A plane flew <u>overhead</u>.
The children were playing <u>in the park</u>.
No birds or animals came <u>near the body</u>.

For information on adverbials of place, see entries at **Places** or at the individual adverbs and prepositions.

time
Adverbials of time are used to say when something happens.

She will be here <u>soon</u>.
He was born <u>on 3 April 1925</u>.
Come and see me <u>next week</u>.

For information on adverbials of time, see entries at **Days and dates** and **Time,** or at the individual words.

frequency
Adverbials of frequency are used to say how often something happens.

We <u>often</u> swam in the sea.
She <u>never</u> comes to my parties.
The group met <u>once a week</u>.

Here is a list of adverbials of frequency, arranged from 'least often' to 'most often':

► never
► rarely, seldom, hardly ever, not much, infrequently
► occasionally, periodically, intermittently, sporadically, from time to time, now and then
► sometimes
► often, frequently, regularly, a lot
► usually, generally, normally
► nearly always
► always, all the time, constantly, continually

'Regularly' and 'periodically' indicate that something happens at fairly regular intervals. 'Intermittently' and 'sporadically' indicate that something happens at irregular intervals.

duration   **Adverbials of duration** are used to say how long something takes or lasts.

> *She glanced <u>briefly</u> at Lucas.*
> *We were married <u>for fifteen years.</u>*

Here is a list of adverbials of duration, arranged from 'least long' to 'longest':

- ► briefly
- ► temporarily
- ► long
- ► indefinitely
- ► always, permanently, forever

Note that 'long' is normally used only in questions and negative sentences.

> *Have you known her <u>long?</u>*
> *I can't stay <u>long.</u>*

degree   **Adverbials of degree** are used to indicate the degree or intensity of a state or action.

> *I still enjoy it <u>a great deal.</u>*
> *I enjoyed the <u>course immensely.</u>*
> *They had suffered <u>severely.</u>*

The following adverbials of degree are used with verbs. They are arranged from 'very low degree' to 'very high degree'.

- ► little
- ► a bit, a little, slightly
- ► significantly, noticeably
- ► rather, fairly, quite, somewhat, sufficiently, adequately, moderately
- ► very much, a lot, a great deal, really, heavily, greatly, strongly, considerably, extensively, badly, dearly, deeply, hard, soundly, well
- ► remarkably, enormously, intensely, profoundly, immensely, tremendously, hugely, severely, radically, drastically

Note that 'quite' can also be used to indicate completeness or to emphasize a verb. See entry at **quite.**

Some of these adverbials are used with only one verb or with a restricted set of verbs, as shown in the examples below.

> *We <u>love him dearly.</u>*
> *I should <u>dearly like</u> to meet her.*
> *The corn ration was <u>drastically reduced.</u>*
> *Our attitude to the land itself must be <u>radically changed.</u>*
> *He protested that he had not touched it, but was disbelieved and <u>soundly beaten.</u>*

For information on the use of adverbs of degree in front of adjectives and other adverbs, see section at **submodifiers** in entry at **Adverbs.**

extent   **Adverbials of extent** are used to indicate the extent to which something happens or is true.

> *The city had been <u>totally</u> destroyed.*
> *The tightness in my chest had <u>almost</u> disappeared.*
> *The Labour Party was <u>largely</u> created by the trade unions.*

The following adverbials of extent are used with verbs. They are arranged from 'smallest extent' to 'greatest extent'.

- ► partly, partially
- ► largely

- ▶ almost, nearly, practically, virtually
- ▶ completely, entirely, totally, quite, fully, perfectly, altogether, utterly

emphasis **Emphasizing adverbs** add emphasis to the action described by a verb.

I quite agree.
I simply adore this flat.

The following adverbs are used to add emphasis:

absolutely	just	quite	simply
certainly	positively	really	

Some emphasizing adverbs are used to emphasize adjectives. See entry at **Adverbs**.

focus You can use **focusing adverbs** to indicate the main thing involved in a situation.

I'm particularly interested in classical music.
We want especially to thank the numerous friends who encouraged us.

The following adverbs can be used like this:

chiefly	mostly	predominantly	specially
especially	notably	primarily	specifically
mainly	particularly	principally	

Some focusing adverbs can be used to emphasize that only one thing is involved in what you are saying.

This is solely a matter of money.
It's a large canvas covered with just one colour.

The following adverbs can be used like this:

alone	just	purely	solely
exclusively	only	simply	

The adverbs of extent 'largely', 'partly', and 'entirely' can be used to focus on additional information.

The house was cheap partly because it was falling down.

Adverbs of frequency such as 'usually' and 'often' can also be used like this.

They often fought each other, usually as a result of arguments over money.

probability **Adverbials of probability** are used to indicate how certain you are about something.

I definitely saw her yesterday.
The driver probably knows the quickest route.

The following adverbials are used to indicate probability or certainty. They are arranged from 'least certain' to 'most certain'.

- ▶ conceivably
- ▶ possibly
- ▶ perhaps, maybe
- ▶ hopefully
- ▶ probably
- ▶ presumably

▶ almost certainly
▶ no doubt, doubtless
▶ definitely

position:
manner,
place, time

Adverbials of manner, place, and time usually come after the main verb. If the verb has an object, the adverbial comes after the object.

She sang beautifully.
Thomas made his decision immediately.

If more than one of these adverbials is used in a clause, the usual order is manner, then place, then time.

They were sitting quite happily in the car.
She spoke very well at the village hall last night.

If the object of the verb is a long one, the adverbial is sometimes put in front of it.

He could picture all too easily the consequences of being found by the owners.
Later I discovered in a shop in Monmouth a weekly magazine about horse-riding.

You can also put an adverb of manner in front of the main verb.

He carefully wrapped each component in several layers of foam rubber.
Dixon swiftly decided to back down.
He silently counted four, then put the receiver down.

Adverbs of manner are rarely put in front of the verb if the verb would then be the last word in the clause. For example, you would say, 'She listened carefully'. You would not say 'She carefully listened'. However, sentences such as 'Smith gladly obliged', where the adverb describes the attitude of the subject, are possible in stories and formal speech.

I gladly gave in.
His uncle readily agreed.
Amanda reluctantly desisted.

If the verb group contains one or more auxiliaries, you can put the adverb of manner in front of the main verb or after the first auxiliary, especially if that auxiliary is a modal.

I felt that the historical background had been very carefully researched.
She had carefully measured out his dose of medicine.
They were all quietly smiling.
Still, Brody thought, one death would probably be quickly forgotten.
Provided you are known to us, arrangements can quickly be made to reimburse you.
They might easily have been taken for brothers.
They told me that today you lost out on the NATO contract that you had so desperately been counting on.

Note that adverbs which indicate how well something is done go after the object of the verb if there is one. If there is no object, they go after the verb.

Teddy did everything perfectly.
I didn't play badly.
You played well.

If the verb is passive, the adverb can also go in front of the verb, after any auxiliaries.

I had been well conditioned by the world in which I grew up.

In the sharp blacks and whites from the midday sun Bond was well camouflaged.

Most adverbs of manner which do not end in '-ly', for example 'hard' and 'loud', are only used after verbs or the objects of verbs.

You work too hard.

The exception is 'fast', which is also used in front of the present participles of verbs in continuous tenses.

We are fast becoming a nation fed entirely on canned and processed food.

If the adverbial is a prepositional phrase, it is usually put at the end of the clause, not in front of the verb. For example, you say 'He looked at her in a strange way'. You do not say 'He in a strange way looked at her'.

One consequence is that the horse's incisor teeth become worn down in an unusual way.
He had been brought up through each level in the proper manner.
It just fell out by accident.

putting the adverbial first

In stories and descriptive accounts, adverbials of manner are sometimes put at the beginning of a sentence. This position gives the adverbial more emphasis.

Gently I took hold of Mary's wrists to ease her arms away.
Slowly people began to desert the campaign.
With a sigh, he rose and walked away.

Similarly, adverbials of time and duration are often placed first in accounts of events.

At eight o'clock I went down for my breakfast.
In 1937 he retired.
For years I'd had to hide what I was thinking.

Adverbials of place are often put first when describing a scene or telling a story, or when contrasting what happens in one place with what happens in another.

In the kitchen there was a message for him from his son.
In Paris there was a massive wave of student riots.
At the very top of the steps was a bust of Shakespeare on a pedestal.
She rang the bell for Sylvia. In came a girl she had not seen before.

Note that in the last two examples, inversion occurs: that is, the verb is put in front of the subject. Inversion does not occur when the subject is a pronoun.

Off they ran.

WARNING

You cannot use a pronoun and 'be' after an adverbial. For example, you cannot say 'At the top of the steps it was'.

When negative adverbials are put first, inversion occurs even when the subject is a pronoun.

Never have so few been commanded by so many.
On no account must they be let in.

See entry at **Inversion.**

Adverbials which indicate your opinion (sentence adverbials) are usually put first in a sentence. See entry at **Opinions.**

position: frequency, probability

Adverbials of frequency and probability are often put after the first auxiliary, if there is one, or in front of the main verb.

Landlords have usually been able to evade land reform.
Women are often encouraged to do the jobs that don't particularly interest men.

They can probably afford another one.
This sometimes led to trouble.

They can also be put first in a clause.

Sometimes people expect you to do more than is reasonable.
Presumably they'd brought him home and he'd invited them in.

They are put after the link verb 'be' when there is no auxiliary.

They are usually right.
He was definitely scared.

Note that adverbs of probability are put in front of negative contractions such as 'don't' and 'won't'.

They definitely don't want their girls breaking the rules.
He probably doesn't really want them at all.
It probably won't be that bad.

'Maybe' and 'perhaps' are usually put first in a clause.

Maybe I ought to go back there.
Perhaps they just wanted to warn us off.

position:
degree, extent

Some adverbs of degree and extent usually come in front of the main verb. If there are auxiliaries, they can come after the first auxiliary or in front of the main verb.

He almost crashed into a lorry.
She really enjoyed the party.
We quite liked her.
So far we have largely been looking at the new societies from the inside.
This finding has been largely ignored.

The following adverbs are used like this:

almost	nearly	really	virtually
largely	rather	quite	

Other adverbs of degree and extent can come in front of the main verb, after the main verb, or after the object (if there is one).

Mr Brooke strongly criticized the Bank of England.
I disagree completely with John Taylor.
That argument doesn't convince me totally.
They agreed that nuclear weapons should be totally prohibited.
This conclusion has been heavily criticized by Robert Maze.

The following adverbs are used like this:

badly	heavily	severely
completely	little	strongly
greatly	seriously	totally

Some adverbials of degree are always or nearly always used after a verb or the object of a verb.

The audience enjoyed it hugely.
I missed you terribly.
Annual budgets varied tremendously.

The following adverbials are used like this:

a bit	a lot	immensely	terribly
a great deal	hard	moderately	tremendously
a little	hugely	remarkably	

Adverbs

position:
emphasizing
Emphasizing adverbs usually come after the subject, after an auxiliary, or after 'be'.

I absolutely agree.
I would just hate to have a daughter like her.
That kind of money is simply not available.

Note that they are put in front of negative contractions such as 'don't' and 'won't'.

It just can't be done.
That simply isn't true.

position:
focusing
Focusing adverbs are generally put after the first auxiliary or in front of the main verb, or in front of the words you are focusing on.

Up to now, the law has mainly had a negative role in this area.
This at least told him what he chiefly wanted to know.
I survive mainly by pleasing others.

If the verb is 'be', the focusing adverb is put after 'be' if there is no auxiliary.

Economic development is primarily a question of getting more work done.

The focusing adverbs 'alone' and 'only' can be put in other positions in a clause. For more information, see entries at **alone** and **only**.

WARNING
You do not usually use an adverbial to separate a verb from its object. You do not say, for example, 'I like very much English'. You say 'I like English very much'.

GRAMMAR **Adverbs**

An adverb is a word that gives information about how, when, where, or in what circumstances something happens. For example, 'quickly', 'well', 'now', and 'here' are adverbs.

Sit there quietly, and listen to this music.
Everything we used was bought locally.

For full information on the different types of adverbs used to give information about events and situations, see entry at **Adverbials**.

submodifiers
Some **adverbs of degree** can be used in front of adjectives and other adverbs. When adverbs of degree are used in this way they are called **submodifiers**.

...a rather clumsy person.
...an extremely disappointed young man.

He prepared his speech very carefully.
We were able to hear everything pretty clearly.

Submodifiers which are used in front of an adjective to reinforce it and make it more emphatic are sometimes called **intensifiers**.

They're awfully brave.
The other girls were dreadfully dull.

The following adverbs are intensifiers:

awfully	extremely	horribly	remarkably
dreadfully	greatly	incredibly	terribly
exceptionally	highly	really	very

Note that 'greatly' is only used in front of adjectives ending in '-ed' and the adjectives 'different' and 'superior'.

He was not greatly surprised to learn that she had left.

The following submodifiers indicate a small or moderate degree of a quality. They are arranged from 'low degree' to 'higher degree'.

▶ faintly
▶ a bit, a little, slightly
▶ rather, quite, fairly, somewhat, relatively, moderately
▶ reasonably
▶ pretty

Note that 'quite' can also be used to emphasize adjectives. See entry at **quite.**

'A bit' and 'a little' can only be used in front of an adjective when the adjective is being used after a verb such as 'be'. You cannot use them with an adjective that is in front of a noun. For example, you say 'It was a bit unpleasant', but you do not say 'It was a bit unpleasant experience'. For more information, see entries at **bit** and **little - a little.**

You use emphasizing adverbs to modify adjectives such as 'astonishing', 'furious', and 'wonderful' which indicate an extreme degree of a quality.

...a quite astonishing ignorance of human nature.
I think he's absolutely wonderful.

The following emphasizing adverbs are used in front of adjectives:

absolutely	entirely	simply
altogether	perfectly	totally
completely	quite	utterly

'Purely' is used in front of classifying adjectives and noun group complements to indicate that something is of only one kind. It is not used in front of qualitative adjectives.

The action had been purely instinctive.
...something that appears at first glimpse to be a purely local issue.

adding to a description In writing, adverbs formed from qualitative adjectives can be used in front of an adjective to add to a description of someone or something. For example, if someone is confident and cool, you can describe them as 'coolly confident'.

...her nervously polite manner.
...these proudly individual characters.

advice - advise

'advice' Advice /ədvaɪs/ is a noun. If you give someone **advice,** you tell them what you think they should do.

One woman went to a psychiatrist for advice.
She promised to follow his advice.

Advice is an uncount noun. You do not talk about 'advices' or 'an advice'. However, you can talk about **a piece of advice.**

His final piece of advice was that the councils should not become too institutionalized.
Could I give you one last piece of advice?

Advise /ədvaɪz/ is a verb. If you **advise** someone to do something, you say that you think they should do it.

He advised her to see her own doctor.
He advised me not to buy it.

You do not use **advise** without an object. You do not say, for example, 'He advised to leave as quickly as possible'. If you do not want to say who is receiving the advice, you say '**His advice was** to leave as quickly as possible'.

John's advice was to wait until the date of the hearing.

Advising someone

There are many ways of giving someone advice.

In conversation, or in informal writing such as letters to friends, you can use 'I should', 'I would', or 'I'd'.

I have someone here for you. I should come and pick him up straight away.
I would try to restrain him gently by saying 'It isn't polite.'
I'd buy tins of one vegetable rather than mixtures.

People often emphasize these expressions with 'if I were you'.

If I were you, I'd just take the black one.
I should let it go if I were you.

You can also say 'You ought to...' or 'You should...'. People often say 'I think' first, in order not to sound too forceful.

You should explain this to him at the outset.
If you don't like your neighbours, I think you should start trying to get on with them.
I think maybe you ought to try a different approach.

You can indicate to someone which course of action or choice is likely to be most successful by using the informal expression 'Your best bet is...' or '...is your best bet'.

Well, your best bet is to go to Thomas Cook in the High Street.
I think Boston's going to be your best bet.

firm advice   If you want to give advice firmly, especially if you are in a position of authority, you can say 'You'd better...'. This way of giving advice can also be used as a kind way of telling someone to do something that will benefit them.

You'd better write it down.
You'd better get a job.
Perhaps you'd better listen to him.
I think you'd better go in and have a sit down.

When you are talking to someone you know well, you can use an imperative form. However, you should not use an imperative to give advice in any other situation.

That's one of the nicest girls I've met for a long time. Make sure you don't lose her.
Take no notice of him, Mr Swallow.
'We have nothing about this from our Department,' he said. 'Well, phone your Minister,' I said.

People sometimes add 'and' followed by a good consequence of taking the advice, or 'or' followed by a bad consequence. These structures are similar in meaning to conditional sentences.

Stick with me and you'll be okay.
Now hold onto the chain, or you'll hurt yourself.

Note that 'and' and 'or' are also used like this in threats.

Just try — and you'll have a real fight on your hands.
Drop that gun! Drop it or I'll kill you!

Imperative forms are also used by experts to give advice: see the section on **professional advice** later in this entry.

serious advice　A more formal and serious way of giving advice is to say 'I advise you to...'.

'What shall I do about it?'—'I advise you to consult a doctor, Mrs Smedley.'
If you have never used explosives I strongly advise you to get somebody who has used them to come and help you the first time.

A very strong way of giving advice is to say 'You must...'.

You must tell the pupils what it is you want to do, so that they feel involved.
You must maintain absolute control of the shot at all times.

professional advice　There are other ways of giving advice which are used mainly in books, articles, and broadcasts.

One common way is to use an imperative form.

If you are left with a nasty burnt mess in your saucepans, try soaking them overnight in lukewarm water and detergent.
Clean one room at a time.
Choose an activity that really fits in with your way of life.
If you don't have a freezer, keep bread in a dry, cool, well-ventilated bin.
Make sure you get out all weed roots and grass.

Another way of advising that is used mainly in writing and broadcasting is to say 'It's a good idea to...'.

It's a good idea to spread your savings between several building societies.
It's a good idea to get a local estate agent to come and value your house.

Another expression that is used is 'My advice is...' or 'My advice would be...'. Again, this is used especially by professionals or experts, who have knowledge on which to base their advice.

If you are thinking of going out to practise when it is blowing a gale, my advice is: stay at home.
My advice would always be: find out what the local people consider good to eat in your locality and eat that.

The expression 'A word of advice' is sometimes used to introduce a piece of advice.

A word of advice — never be put off by those who suggest that practising is somehow un-British.

suggestions and warnings　See also entry at **Suggestions.** For information on how to advise someone not to do something, see entry at **Warning someone.**

---

advocate

See entry at **lawyer.**

affect - effect

'affect' Affect /əfekt/ is a verb. To **affect** someone or something means to change or influence them in some way.

...the ways in which computers can affect our lives.
The disease affected Jane's lungs.

'effect' Effect /ɪfekt/ is usually used as a noun. An **effect** is a change or event which occurs because something else has happened.

...the effect of noise on people in the factories.
This has the effect of separating students from teachers.

You can say that something **has a** particular **effect on** something else.

Improvement in water supply can have a dramatic effect on health.
Interest rates and mortgage rates are having a significant effect on Conservative support.

Effect is sometimes used as a verb. If you **effect** something that you are trying to achieve, you succeed in achieving it. This is a formal use.

Production was halted until repairs could be effected.

afford

If you **can afford** something, you have enough money to buy it.

...families who can afford cars.
Do you think one day we'll be able to afford a new sofa?

Afford is almost always used with 'can', 'could', or 'be able'. You do not say that someone 'affords' something.

The amount of money that someone **can afford** is the amount they are able to spend on something.

It's more than I can afford.
They paid a thousand usually, sometimes more if they could afford it.

You say that someone **can afford to have** something or **can afford to do** something.

...a situation where everybody can afford to have a car.
I can't afford to rent this flat.
Work out how much you can afford to pay each of them.

You do not say that someone 'can afford having' something or 'can afford doing' something.

You do not use a passive form of **afford.** You do not say that something 'can be afforded'. Instead you say that **people can afford** it.

Nobody buys second-hand binoculars any more. People can afford new ones now.

afloat

If someone or something is **afloat,** they are floating on water rather than sinking.

By kicking constantly he could stay afloat.
Her hooped skirt kept her afloat and saved her.

You do not use **afloat** in front of a noun.

afraid - frightened

If you are **afraid** of someone or something, you feel fear because you think they may harm you.

They were afraid of you.
The guards were so afraid that they trembled.

You can also say that you are **frightened** of someone or something. **Frightened** has the same meaning as 'afraid'.

You're frightened of Alice.
Everyone here is frightened of the volcano.

If you are unwilling to do something because you think it might be harmful or dangerous, you can say that you are **afraid to do** it or **frightened to do** it.

He was afraid to advance any farther.
What is the use of freedom if people are frightened to go out?

Afraid is only used after verbs such as 'be' and 'feel'. You do not use it in front of a noun. You do not talk, for example, about 'an afraid child'. However, you can talk about 'a **frightened** child'.

He was not going to act like a frightened kid.

You do not usually use a modifier with **afraid**. You do not say, for example, 'I was a bit afraid'. If you want to talk about degrees of fear, you usually use **frightened.**

He was still very frightened.
I am just a little bit frightened.
I was too frightened to ask what was going on.

another meaning of 'afraid'   **Afraid** has another meaning. You use it to say that you are worried that something unpleasant might happen and you want to avoid it. When you use **afraid** like this, it is usually followed by a report clause.

She was afraid that I might be embarrassed.

You can also say that you are **afraid of doing** something. For example, instead of saying 'I was afraid that I might get lost', you can say 'I was **afraid of getting** lost'.

She was afraid of being late for school.
He was terribly afraid of offending anyone.

'I'm afraid...'   You use **'I'm afraid...'**, **'I'm afraid so'**, and **'I'm afraid not'** to express regret in a polite way. **'I'm afraid so'** means 'yes'. **'I'm afraid not'** means 'no'.

I'm afraid I can't agree.
'I hear she's leaving. Is that right?'—'I'm afraid so.'
'Can you come round this evening?'—'I'm afraid not.'

after - afterwards

'after' used as a preposition   If something happens **after** a particular time or event, it happens during the period that follows that time or event.

Dan came in just after midnight.
We'll hear about everything after dinner.

You can say that someone does something **after doing** something else.

After completing The Open Society, I sent it to America for publication.
Frank Brown was released from prison after serving three years.

'after' used as an adverb	You can also use **after** as an adverb, but only in expressions like 'soon after', 'shortly after', and 'not long after'.

Douglas came round to see me, and soon after I met him again at a friend's.
Shortly after Fania called me.
Not long after she started dragging the go-cart down the narrow streets.

'afterwards'	Instead of 'after', you can use another adverb, **afterwards**. There is no difference in meaning.

She died soon afterwards.
Shortly afterwards her marriage broke up.
Her husband lost his fortune in the Wall Street crash and died not long afterwards.

'afterward'	**Afterward** is also sometimes used, especially in American English.

I left soon afterward.
Shortly afterward, he made a trip from L.A. to San Jose.

WARNING
You do not use **after** as an adverb on its own. You do not say, for example, 'I met him after'. You say 'I met him **afterwards**' or 'I met him **later**'.

Somebody will hear you and may repeat it afterwards.
You'd better give him a ring later.

In standard English, you do not use **after** when mentioning a specific period of time. You do not say, for example, 'I met him a month after'. You say 'I met him a month **afterwards** or 'I met him a month **later**'.

That was actually done about eight months afterwards.
I returned some three or four weeks later.

WARNING
You do not say that someone is 'after' a particular age. You say that they are **over** that age.

She was well over fifty.

You do not use **after** to say that something is at the back of something else. The word you use is **behind**.

There were two boys sitting behind me.

after all

You use **after all** when you are mentioning an additional point which confirms or supports what you have just said.

After all, we don't intend to put him on trial.
It had to be recognized, after all, that I was still a schoolboy.

You also use **after all** to say that something is the case or may be the case in spite of what had previously been thought.

Perhaps it isn't such a bad village after all.
Can it be that these people are actually sincere after all?

WARNING
You do not use **after all** when you want to introduce a final point, question, or topic. Instead you use **finally** or **lastly**.

Finally I want to say something about the heat pump.
Finally, Carol, are you encouraged by the direction education is taking?
Lastly I would like to ask about your future plans.

afternoon

The **afternoon** is the part of each day which begins at noon or lunchtime and ends at about six o'clock.

the present day	You refer to the afternoon of the present day as **this afternoon**.

I rang Pat this afternoon.
Can I take it with me this afternoon?

You refer to the afternoon of the previous day as **yesterday afternoon**.

We circulated printed copies to other London newspapers yesterday afternoon.

You refer to the afternoon of the next day as **tomorrow afternoon**.

I'll be home tomorrow afternoon.

single events in the past	If you want to say that something happened during a particular afternoon in the past, you use **on**.

Olivia Davenport was due on Friday afternoon.
The box was delivered on the afternoon before my departure.

If you have been describing what happened during a particular day, you can then say that something happened **that afternoon** or **in the afternoon**.

That afternoon I walked into Ironstone.
I left Walsall in the afternoon and went by bus and train to Nottingham.
Friends were coming in the afternoon to take me to a game.

If you are talking about a day in the past and you want to mention that something had happened during the afternoon of the day before, you say that it had happened **the previous afternoon**.

He had spoken to me the previous afternoon.

If you want to say that something happened during the afternoon of the next day, you say that it happened **the following afternoon**.

I arrived at the village the following afternoon.

In stories, if you want to say that something happened during an afternoon in the past, without saying which afternoon, you say that it happened **one afternoon**.

One afternoon as I sat working in my office I heard a knock at the door.

You can also say, for example, that something happened **one November afternoon** or **on a November afternoon**.

He told me his story one cold March afternoon.
I visited it on a warm May afternoon.

talking about the future	If you want to say that something will happen during a particular afternoon in the future, you use **on**.

The semi-finals will be on Wednesday afternoon.

If you are already talking about a day in the future, you can say that something will happen **in the afternoon**.

We will arrive at Pisa early in the morning, then in the afternoon we will go on to Florence.

If you are talking about a day in the future and you want to say that something will happen during the afternoon of the next day, you say that it will happen **the following afternoon**.

We could run him in either the race at Lingfield or the Derby trial the following afternoon.

regular events	If something happens or happened regularly every afternoon, you say that it happens or happened **in the afternoon** or **in the afternoons**.

In the afternoon we go for a drive.
He is usually busy in the afternoons.

In the afternoon he would take a nap.

I went to the bookstore in the afternoons.

If you want to say that something happens regularly once a week during a particular afternoon, you use **on** followed by the name of a day of the week and **afternoons.**

The estate is going to be opened to the public on Sunday afternoons.
On Saturday afternoons she used to serve behind the counter.

exact times   If you have mentioned an exact time and you want to make it clear that you are talking about the afternoon rather than the early morning, you add **in the afternoon.**

We arrived at three in the afternoon.

afterwards

See entry at **after - afterwards.**

Age

asking about   When you want to ask about the age of a person or thing, you use **How old**
age   and the verb 'be'.

'How old are you?'—'Thirteen.'
'How old is he?'—'About sixty-five.'
'How old's your house?'—'I think it was built about 1950.'

indicating   There are several ways in which you can say how old someone or
someone's age   something is. You can be exact, or you can be less precise and indicate their approximate age.

exact age   When you want to say how old someone is, you use the verb 'be' followed by a number.

I was nineteen, and he was twenty-one.
I'm only 63.

You can put 'years old' after the number if you want to be more emphatic.

She is twenty-five years old.
I am forty years old.

You can also put 'years of age' after the number, but this is more formal and is more usual in written English.

He is 28 years of age.

WARNING   You never use 'have' to talk about age. For example, you do not say 'He has thirteen years'. You say 'He is thirteen' or 'He is thirteen years old'.

When you are mentioning someone, you can indicate their exact age using 'of' or 'aged' after the noun which refers to them, followed by a number.

...a man of thirty.
...two little boys aged nine and eleven.

You can also mention someone's age using a compound adjective in front of a noun. For example, you can refer to a 'five-year-old' boy. Note that the noun referring to the period of time, such as 'year', is always singular, even though it comes after a number. The compound adjective is usually hyphenated.

...a twenty-two-year-old student.

...a five-month-old baby.

You can also refer to someone using a compound noun such as 'ten-year-old'.

All the six-year-olds are taught by one teacher.
...Melvin Kalkhoven, a tall, thin thirty-five-year-old.

approximate age

If you are not sure exactly how old someone is, or you do not want to state their exact age, you can use the verb 'be' followed by 'about', 'almost', 'nearly', 'over', or 'under', and a number.

I think he's about 60.
He must be nearly thirty.
She was only a little over forty years old.
There weren't enough people who were under 25.

You can also use 'above the age of' or 'below the age of' followed by a number. This is more formal.

55 percent of them were below the age of twenty-one.

You can indicate that someone's age is between 20 and 29 by saying 'He's in his twenties' or 'She's in her twenties'. You can use 'thirties', 'forties', and so on in the same way. Young people aged 13 to 19 are said to be 'in their teens'. Note that you use 'in' and a possessive determiner in these structures.

He was in his sixties.
I didn't mature till I was in my forties.
...when I was in my teens.

You can use 'early', 'mid-', 'middle', or 'late' to indicate approximately where someone's age comes in a particular ten-year period (or eight-year period in the case of 'teens').

Jane is only in her early forties.
She was in her mid-twenties.
He was then in his late seventies.

You can put most of the above structures after a noun such as 'man' or 'woman' to indicate someone's approximate age.

...help for ladies over 65.
She had four children under the age of five.
...a woman in her early thirties.

You cannot, however, use 'about', 'almost', or 'nearly' immediately after a noun. For example, you cannot say 'a man about 60'. You say 'a man of about 60'.

You can refer to a group of people whose age is more or less than a particular number using a compound noun which consists of 'over' or 'under' followed by the plural form of the number.

The over-sixties do not want to be turned out of their homes.
Schooling for the under-fives should be expanded.

similar ages

If you want to indicate that someone's age is similar to someone else's, you can use the verb 'be' followed by expressions such as 'my age', 'his own age', and 'her parents' age'.

I wasn't allowed to do that when I was her age.
I'm thinking now of senior management who might be your or my age.
He guessed the policeman was about his own age.

To indicate the age of a person you are mentioning, you can use these expressions after the noun which refers to the person, or after the noun and 'of'.

I just happen to know a bit more literature than most girls my age.
It's easy to make friends because you're with people of your own age.

age when
something
happens

There are several ways of indicating how old someone was when something happened.

You can use a clause beginning with 'when'.

I left school when I was thirteen.
Even when I was a child I was frightened of her.

You can use 'at the age of' or 'at', followed by a number showing the person's age.

She had finished college at the age of 20.
All they want to do is leave school at sixteen and get a job.

'Aged' followed by a number is also used, mainly in writing, especially when talking about someone's death.

Her husband died three days ago, aged only forty-five.

A structure with an ordinal is sometimes used in writing, especially to emphasize that someone did something when they were old. For example, instead of saying that someone did something 'at the age of 79', you can say that they did it 'in their eightieth year'.

He died in 1951, in his eighty-ninth year.

'As' is used with a noun group such as 'a girl' or 'a young man' to indicate that someone did something when they were young. This structure occurs mainly in writing.

She suffered from bronchitis as a child.
As teenagers we used to stroll round London during lunchtime.

If you want to indicate that someone does something before they reach a particular age, you can say that they do it, for example, 'before the age of four' or 'by the age of four'.

He maintained that children are not ready to read before the age of six.
It set out the things he wanted to achieve by the age of 31.

If you want to indicate that someone does something after they reach a particular age, you can say that they do it, for example, 'after the age of four'.

One trouble is that the first baby in some families gets more fussing over than is good for him, especially after the age of 6 months.

indicating the
age of a thing

If you want to say how old something is, you use the verb 'be' followed by a number, followed by 'years old'.

It's at least a thousand million years old.
The house was about thirty years old.

Note that you cannot just use 'be' and a number, as you can when stating the age of a person. You cannot say, for example, 'The house was about thirty'.

The usual way of indicating the age of something you are mentioning is to use a compound adjective in front of the noun referring to it. For example, you can refer to a 'thirty-year-old' house. As with compound adjectives indicating the age of a person, the noun 'year' is always singular and the adjective is usually hyphenated.

...Mr Watt's rattling, ten-year-old car.
...a violation of a six-year-old agreement.

You can also use a number, especially a large number, and 'years old' after a noun referring to a thing.

...rocks 200 million years old.

You can indicate the approximate age of something by using an adjective indicating the period in history in which it existed or was made.

...a splendid Victorian building.
...a medieval castle.

You can indicate the century when something existed or was made by using a modifier consisting of an ordinal number and 'century'.

...a sixth-century church.
...life in fifth-century Athens.

aged

This word is pronounced in two different ways. For information on **aged** /eɪdʒd/, see entry at **Age**. For information on **aged** /eɪdʒɪd/, see entry at **old**.

aggressive

See entry at **forceful**.

ago

You usually use **ago** to say how long it is since something happened. For example, if something happened five years **ago**, it is now five years since it happened.

We met two years ago.
We got married about a year ago.

When you are talking about an event in the past, you use the simple past tense with **ago**. For example, you say 'He **died** four years ago'. You do not say 'He has died four years ago'.

All that stuff disappeared thirty years ago.
I did it just a moment ago.

You only use **ago** when you are talking about a period of time measured back from the present. If you are talking about a period measured back from some earlier time, you use **before** or **previously**.

The centre had been opened some years before.
Three years previously I had been admitted to the Royal Canadian Hospital, Taplow.

WARNING You do not use **ago** and 'since' together. You do not say, for example, 'It is three years ago since it happened'. You say 'It happened **three years ago**' or '**It is three years since** it happened'.

He died two years ago.
It is two weeks now since I wrote to you.

You also do not say that something has been happening 'since three years ago'. You say that it has been happening **for three years**.

I have lived here for nearly twenty years.

I have known you <u>for a long time.</u>
I haven't smoked <u>for fifteen years.</u>

See entries at **for** and **since**.

agree

'agree with' If you **agree with** someone about something, you both have the same opinion about it.

You <u>agreed with</u> me that we could rule out Watson.

If you **agree with** an action or suggestion, you approve of it.

I <u>agree with</u> what they are doing.

Note that you do not say that you 'agree' an action or suggestion or 'are agreed with' it.

'agree to' If you **agree to** something that is suggested or proposed, you say that you will allow it to happen or be done.

He <u>had agreed to</u> the use of force.

However, you do not say that someone 'agrees to' an invitation. You say that they **accept** it.

He readily <u>accepted</u> our invitation to speak about his case.

If you **agree to do** something that you have been asked to do, you say that you will do it.

She <u>agreed to let</u> us use her flat.
She finally <u>agreed to come</u> to the club on Wednesday.

Note that you do not say that you 'agree doing' something.

'agree on' If people reach a decision together about something, you can say that they **agree on** it.

The government had still to <u>agree on</u> the provisions of the Bill.

'agree that' You can say what their decision is using **agree** and a 'that'-clause.

They <u>agreed that</u> all existing sanctions should be maintained.

The passive form '**It was agreed that...**' is often used.

It <u>was agreed that</u> something had to be done.

'be agreed' When a decision is made, you can say that the people making it **are agreed.** This is a formal use.

Are we <u>agreed</u>, gentlemen?

Agreeing and disagreeing

This entry first explains how to ask someone whether they agree with you or not, and then explains different ways of showing agreement and disagreement.

asking for agreement You can ask someone if they agree with your opinion of something or someone by using a question tag. When you do this, you usually expect them to agree with you.

That's an extremely interesting point, <u>isn't it?</u>
It was really good, <u>wasn't it</u>, Andy?

Note that people sometimes use question tags like this and carry on talking because they think a reply is unnecessary.

You can also use a question tag to ask someone if they agree that something is a fact.

Property in France is quite expensive, isn't it?
That's right, isn't it?
You don't have a television, do you?

You can also indicate that you want someone to express agreement by using a negative 'yes/no'-question, or by saying a statement as if it were a question.

Wasn't it marvellous?
So there's no way you could go back to work?
He's got a scholarship?

You can use the tag 'don't you?' after a clause in which you say that you like or dislike something, or think it is good or bad. The pronoun 'you' is stressed.

I adore it, don't you?
I think this is one of the best things, don't you?

In formal situations, people sometimes use expressions such as 'Don't you agree...?' and 'Would you agree...?'

Don't you agree with me that it is rather an impossible thing to do after all this time?
Would you agree with that analysis?

expressing agreement

When you want to indicate that you agree with someone or something, the simplest way is to say 'yes'. People often say something further, especially in more formal discussions.

'It depends where you live.'—'Yes.'
'It's quite a nice school, isn't it?'—'Yes, it's well decorated and there's a nice atmosphere there.'
'You also give out information about courses for English teachers, don't you?'—'Yes; and I also talk to teachers about courses.'

You can add an appropriate tag such as 'I do' or 'it is' to 'Yes'. This tag is often followed by a question tag.

'That's fantastic!'—'Yes, it is, isn't it?'
'I was really rude to you at that party.'—'Yes, you were. But I deserved it.'

You can also just add a question tag to 'Yes', or use a question tag by itself. You do not expect a reply.

'He's a completely changed man.'—'Yes, isn't he?'
'What a lovely evening!'—'Isn't it?'

People often make the sound 'Mm' instead of saying 'Yes'.

'Strange, isn't it?'—'Mm.'

WARNING

If you want to express agreement with a negative statement, you say 'No', not 'Yes'.

'She's not an easy person to live with.'—'No.'
'I don't think it's as good now.'—'No, it isn't really.'
'That's not very healthy, is it?'—'No.'

You can also express agreement using expressions such as 'That's right', 'That's true', or 'True', when agreeing that something is a fact. You say 'That's true' or 'True' when you think a good point has been made.

'*Most teenagers are perfectly all right.*'—'*That's right, yes.*'
'*You don't have to be poor to be lonely.*'—'*That's true.*'
'*I'll have more to spend then.*'—'*Yes, that's true.*'
'*They're a long way away.*'—'*True.*'

People sometimes say 'Sure' when accepting what someone has said in a discussion.

'*You can earn some money as well.*'—'*Sure, sure, you can make quite a bit.*'

The expression 'I agree' is quite formal.

'*It's a catastrophe.*'—'*I agree.*'

When someone has made a statement about what they like or think, you can indicate that you share their opinion by saying 'So do I' or 'I do too'.

'*I find that amazing.*'—'*So do I.*'
'*I like baked beans.*'—'*Yes, I do too.*'

When you want to indicate that you share someone's negative opinion, you can say 'Nor do I', 'Neither do I', or 'I don't either'.

'*I don't like him.*'—'*Nor do I.*'
'*Oh, I don't mind where I go as long as it's a break.*'—'*No, I don't either.*'

strong agreement
You can show strong agreement by using expressions such as the ones shown in the examples below. Most of these sound rather formal. 'Absolutely' and 'Exactly' are less formal.

'*I thought June Barry's performance was the performance of the evening.*'—'*Absolutely. I thought she was wonderful.*'
'*It's good practice and it's good fun.*'—'*Exactly.*'
'*I feel I ought to give her a hand.*'—'*Oh, quite, quite.*'
'*I must do something, though.*'—'*Yes, I quite agree.*'
'*There's far too much attention being paid to these hoodlums.*'—'*Yes, I couldn't agree more.*'
'*The public showed that by the way it voted in the General Election.*'—'*That's quite true.*'
'*We reckon that this is what he would have wanted us to do.*'—'*I think you're absolutely right.*'

You can show that you agree strongly with someone's description of something by repeating the adjective they have used and using 'very' in front of it. You usually use 'indeed' after the adjective.

'*It was very tragic, wasn't it.*'—'*Very tragic indeed.*'
'*The pacing in all these performances is subtle, isn't it?*'—'*Oh, very subtle indeed.*'

partial agreement
If you agree with someone, but not entirely or with reluctance, you can reply 'I suppose so'.

'*I must have a job.*'—'*Yes, I suppose so.*'
'*That's the way to save lives, and save ourselves a lot of trouble.*'—'*I suppose so.*'

If you are replying to a negative statement, you say 'I suppose not'.

'*Some of these places haven't changed a bit.*'—'*I suppose not.*'

expressing ignorance or uncertainty
If you do not know enough to agree or disagree with a statement, you say 'I don't know'.

'*He was the first four-minute miler, wasn't he?*'—'*Perhaps. I don't know.*'

If you are not sure of a particular fact, you say 'I'm not sure'.

'*He was world champion one year, wasn't he?*'—'*I'm not sure.*'
'*Oh, that'd be nice, wouldn't it?*'—'*I'm not sure.*'

expressing disagreement

Rather than simply expressing complete disagreement, people usually try to disagree politely using expressions which soften the contradictory opinion they are giving. 'I don't think so' and 'Not really' are the commonest of these expressions.

'You'll change your mind one day.'—'Well, I don't think so. But I won't argue with you.'
'It was a lot of money in those days.'—'Well, not really.'

The expressions shown below are also used.

'Don't you know Latin?'—'Of course he does.'—'Actually, no, I don't know it very well.'
'It might be – well, someone she'd met by accident.'—'Oh, do you really think so, Julia?'
'It's a dog's life being a singer. And you have to mix with scum.'—'I don't know about that.'
'It's all over now, anyway.'—'No, I'm afraid I can't agree with you there.'

People often say 'Yes' or 'I see what you mean', to indicate partial agreement, and then go on to mention a point of disagreement, introduced by 'but'.

'You've just said yourself that you got fed up with it after a time.'—'Yes, but only after three weeks.'
'It's a very clever film.'—'Yes, perhaps, but I didn't like it.'
'They ruined the whole thing.'—'I see what you mean, but they didn't know.'

strong disagreement

The following examples show stronger ways of expressing disagreement. You should be very careful when using them, in order to avoid offending people.

'That's very funny.'—'No it isn't.'
'It might be a couple of years.'—'No! Surely not as long as that!'
'He killed himself.'—'That's not right. I'm sure that's not right. Tell me what happened.'
'You were the one who wanted to buy it.'—'I'm sorry, dear, but you're wrong.'

The expressions shown in the following examples are more formal.

'University education does divide families in a way.'—'I can't go along with that.'
'There would be less of the guilt which characterized societies of earlier generations.'—'Well, I think I would take issue with that.'
'When it comes to the state of this country, he should keep his mouth shut.'—'I wholly and totally disagree.'

In formal situations, you can use 'With respect...' to make your disagreement seem more polite.

'We ought to be asking the teachers some tough questions.'—'With respect, Mr Graveson, you should be asking pupils some questions as well, shouldn't you?'

When people are angry, they use very strong, impolite words and expressions to disagree.

'He's absolutely right.'—'Oh, come off it! He doesn't know what he's talking about.'
'They'll be killed.'—'Nonsense.'
'He wants it, and I suppose he has a right to it.'—'Rubbish.'
'You're ashamed of me.'—'Don't talk rubbish.'
'He said you plotted to get him removed.'—'That's ridiculous!'

'He's very good at his job, isn't he?'—'You must be joking! He's absolutely useless!'

With people you know well, you can use expressions like these in a casual, light-hearted way.

aim

Someone's **aim** is what they intend to achieve.

His aim is to have 100 agencies established.
It is our aim in the Asian Games to give every nation the chance to raise its flag at a medal ceremony.

You can say that someone does something **with the aim of achieving** a particular result.

They had left before dawn with the aim of getting a grandstand seat.
They hurled themselves on to the rearmost carriages with the probable aim of liberating the prisoners.

You do not say that someone does something 'with the aim to achieve' a result.

alight

If something is **alight,** it is burning.

The fire was safely alight.
A candle was alight on the chest of drawers.

To **set** something **alight** means to cause it to start burning.

…paraffin that had been poured on the ground and set alight.

WARNING   You do not use **alight** in front of a noun. You do not say, for example, 'People rushed out of the alight building'. You say 'People rushed out of the **burning** building'.

alike

If two or more things or people look **alike,** there seems to be no difference between them.

They all looked alike to me.

If two or more things or people are **very alike** or **very much alike,** they are very similar.

We are a close family and very alike.
Monty and Jeremy were very much alike.

If two or more things are **exactly alike,** there is no difference between them.

No two proteins are exactly alike.

WARNING   You do not use **alike** in front of a noun. You do not say, for example, 'They wore alike hats' or 'They wore exactly alike hats'. You say 'They wore **similar** hats' or 'They wore **identical** hats'.

The twins insist on wearing similar clothes.
…two women in identical pinafores.

alive

If you say that a person or animal is **alive,** you mean they are not dead.

I think his father is still alive.
She knew the seal was alive.

You never use **alive** in front of a noun. Instead you use **living** to talk about people, or **live** /laɪv/ to talk about animals.

I have no living relatives.
There are many problems in transporting live animals.

Alive can also be used after words like 'very' and 'so' to say that someone enjoys life and is full of energy.

Young people are so alive and exciting.
Floyd felt more alive than he had for years.

all

used as a determiner

You use **all** immediately in front of the plural form of a noun to talk about every thing or person of a particular kind.

All dogs are nasty, smelly brutes.
All pupils will be expected to learn how to use information technology.

You can use **all** immediately in front of an uncount noun when you are making a general statement about something.

All crime is some kind of revolutionary activity.

When you use **all** in front of the plural form of a noun, you use a plural form of a verb after it.

All boys like to eat.

When you use **all** in front of an uncount noun, you use a singular form of a verb after it.

All pollution is simply an unused resource.

used with other determiners

If you want to say something about every thing or person in a group, you use **all,** followed by 'the', 'these', 'those', or a possessive determiner, followed by the plural form of a noun.

All the cloths were lying flat on the bench.
All the girls think it's great.
He has done all these things.
She likes all those children so much.
All my friends must have known.

If you want to say something about the whole of a particular thing, you use **all,** followed by 'the', 'this', 'that', or a possessive determiner, followed by an uncount noun or the singular form of a count noun.

They lugged all the stuff into the hall.
She was around all the time.
Had all this strife been necessary?
I want to thank the people of New York for all their help.

You can put **of** between **all** and a determiner. This use is more common in American English than in British English.

All of the defendants were proved guilty.
All of these religions are closely bound to particular cultures.
All of my stuff was in order.

It will probably never be possible to establish the exact truth about all of their activities.

used in front of pronouns

You can use **all** or **all of** in front of the pronouns 'this', 'that', 'these', and 'those'.

Oh dear, what are we going to do about all this?
…the agony all of this must have caused.

Were you really interested in all that?
Maybe all of that is true, but that's not what the narrative is about.

I got all these for two quid.
I think probably all of these would show up better on a better slide.

However, in front of personal pronouns you must use **all of.** You do not use 'all'.

Drink it, all of you.
It would be impossible to list all of it in one programme.

You do not use 'we' or 'they' after **all of.** Instead you use **us** or **them.**

All of us eat starches to a greater or lesser extent.
All of them were taken on a guided tour of the State Bedrooms.

used after the subject

All can also be used after the subject of a clause. For example, instead of saying 'All our friends came', you can say 'Our friends **all** came'. When there is no auxiliary, **all** goes in front of the verb, unless the verb is 'be'.

Their names all began with S.
We all felt a bit guilty.

If the verb is 'be', **all** goes after 'be'.

They were all asleep.
This is all new to me.

If there is an auxiliary, you put **all** after it.

It will all be over soon.
We don't all have your advantages.

If there is more than one auxiliary, you put **all** after the first one.

The bedroom dresser drawers had all been pulled open.

All can also come after the direct or indirect object of a verb when this object is a personal pronoun.

We treat them all as if they were china.
I really do hate you all.

used as a pronoun

All can itself be used as a pronoun with the meaning 'everything' or 'the only thing'. It is often used like this in front of a relative clause.

It was the result of all that had happened previously.
All I did was wash the little girl's ears.
All I've got is a number.

All is sometimes used as the subject of a sentence to refer to every person in a group. This is a rather formal use.

All were sitting as before.
All were agreed that the consensus had broken down.

WARNING

You do not use a noun group beginning with **all** as the subject of a negative sentence. You do not say, for example, 'All the children are not noisy'. Instead you use **none** or **not all.** However, there is a difference in meaning. '**None** of the children are noisy' means 'Not one of the children is noisy'. '**Not all** of the children are noisy' means 'Some of the children are not noisy'.

After **none** you can use either a singular or plural form of a verb.

None of these suggestions is very helpful.
None of us were allowed to go.

When you use **not all** with the plural form of a noun, you use a plural form of a verb after it.

Not all hippies are devoid of these values.
Not all the houses we get offered have central heating.

When you use **not all** with an uncount noun or the singular form of a count noun, you use a singular form of a verb after it.

Not all British industry is delighted.

'both'   Do not confuse **all** with **both**. You use **all** when you are talking about three or more things. You use **both** when you are talking about just two things. See entry at **both**.

'every'   **Every** has a similar meaning to **all**. '**Every** teacher was consulted' means the same as '**All** the teachers were consulted'.

However, there is a difference between **all** and **every** when you use them with expressions of time. For example, if you spend **all day** doing something, you spend the whole of one day doing it. If you do something **every day,** you keep doing it each day.

We can stay here and drink wine all night.
These trolleys journeyed up and down all day.
She told me that she came that way every day.
...a dozen places like it were advertised every evening in the local paper.

'whole'   **Whole** and **the whole of** also have a similar meaning to **all**. For example, '**the whole** building' and '**the whole of** the building' both mean the same as 'all the building'.

However, **all** and **whole** have different meanings in front of the plural form of a noun. If you say '**All** the buildings have been destroyed', you mean that every building has been destroyed. If you say '**Whole** buildings have been destroyed', you mean that some buildings have been destroyed completely.

I've taken all my sulphur pills.
...all the cooking utensils.
This established new balances of power for whole regions.
There were whole speeches I did not understand.

allow - permit - let

Allow, permit, and **let** are all used to say that someone is given permission to do something, or is not prevented from doing something. **Permit** is a formal word.

'allow' and   **Allow** and **permit** are followed by an object and a 'to'-infinitive clause.
'permit'
He agreed to allow me to take the course.
Her father would not permit her to eat sweets.

You can say that people **are not allowed to** do something or **are not permitted to** do something.

Visitors were not allowed to walk about unescorted.
Customers are not permitted to converse with the artistes.

You can also say that something **is not allowed** or that it **is not permitted**.

Running was not allowed in the school.
Spiked bowling boots are not permitted on the matting.

'let'   **Let** is followed by an object and an infinitive without 'to'.

Let me go to the party on Saturday. I won't be late.

You do not use **let** in any passive constructions.

'enable'   Do not confuse any of these words with **enable**. To **enable** someone to do something means to give them the opportunity to do it. It does not mean to give them permission to do it.

Contraception enables women to plan their families.
This would enable me to go to Canada.

all right

If you say that something is **all right,** you mean that it is satisfactory or acceptable.

Is everything all right, sir?

All right is the usual spelling. **Alright** is sometimes used, but many people think this spelling is incorrect.

almost - nearly

used to modify adjectives and noun groups   **Almost** and **nearly** both mean 'not completely' or 'not quite'. They are usually used in front of adjectives or noun groups.

The hay was almost ready for cutting.
We're nearly ready now.

I spent almost a month in China.
He spent nearly five years in the Leningrad special hospital.

It was made of wood like almost all the houses.
She liked doing nearly all the things we liked doing.

used to modify verbs   **Almost** and **nearly** can also be used with verbs. If there is no auxiliary, you put **almost** or **nearly** in front of the verb.

Fanny almost fainted.
We almost ran over some little animal.
Dad nearly died after being bitten by a button-spider.
I nearly smashed the phone in fury.

If there is an auxiliary, you put **almost** or **nearly** after the auxiliary.

Arthur had almost forgotten the poisoned cakes.
Some have almost reached International Master level.
He had nearly fallen flat on his face.
Dougal had nearly run out of food.

If there is more than one auxiliary, you put **almost** or **nearly** after the first one.

I've nearly been drowned in it three times.

For a graded list of words which are used with verbs to indicate extent, see section on **extent** in entry at **Adverbials**.

used to modify adverbials   **Almost** and **nearly** can also be used in front of some time adverbials such as 'every morning' and 'every day', and in front of some place adverbials such as 'there' and 'home'.

We took to going out almost every evening.
I used to ride nearly every day.

We are almost there.
I think we are nearly there.

However, **nearly** is hardly ever used in front of adverbs ending in '-ly'. You should use **almost** in front of these adverbs.

She said it almost crossly.
'What can I say now?' he asked, almost angrily.
Your boss is almost certainly there.

used with 'like' You can say that one thing is **almost like** another.

It made me feel almost like a hostess.

You do not usually say that one thing is 'nearly like' another.

used with time expressions You can use **almost** or **nearly** in front of time expressions. If it is **almost** or **nearly** a particular time, it will be that time soon.

It was almost 10 p.m.
It's almost supper-time.
By now it was nearly five past ten.

Note that you only use **almost** or **nearly** like this after 'be'. You do not say, for example, 'They arrived at almost five o'clock'. Instead you say '**It was almost** five o'clock **when** they arrived'.

It was nearly nine o'clock when Simon made his appearance.
It was almost dark when Kunta, feeling very awkward, finally approached some of the boys.

used with negatives You can use **almost** in front of negative words such as 'never', 'no', 'none', 'no-one', 'nothing', and 'nowhere'.

A handbag was considered personal and almost never looked into.
There is almost no leadership at all.
I sold a picture by reducing the price to almost nothing.

You cannot use **nearly** in front of negative words like these.

However, you can use **nearly** after 'not' to emphasize a negative statement. For example, instead of saying 'The room is not big enough', you can say 'The room is **not nearly** big enough'.

It's not nearly so nice.
We don't do nearly enough to help.
I haven't done nearly as much as I would like.

You cannot use **almost** after 'not' like this.

adding modifiers You can use 'very' or 'so' in front of **nearly**.

We were very nearly at the end of our journey.
Now they were very nearly men.
...the American who so nearly won the Open Championship in 1970.
...the family that had challenged the Corleone power, and had so nearly succeeded.

In conversation, you can also use 'pretty' in front of **nearly**.

I came across a paragraph about a girl I'd pretty nearly forgotten.
'Do you know that thirty miles is eight hours solid marching?'—'Is it?'—'Pretty nearly.'

You cannot use 'very', 'so', or 'pretty' in front of **almost**.

alone

If you are **alone,** you are not with any other people.

I wanted to be alone.
Barbara spent most of her time alone in the flat.

WARNING

You do not use **alone** in front of a noun. For example, you do not talk about 'an alone woman'. Instead, you say 'a woman **on her own**'.

You find this quite often with people on their own.

'lonely'

Do not confuse **alone** with **lonely.** If you are **lonely,** you are unhappy because you do not have any friends or anyone to talk to. **Lonely** is used either in front of a noun or after a verb like 'be' or 'feel'.

He had befriended a lonely little boy.
She must be very lonely here.

another
meaning of
'alone'

Alone has another meaning. You use it immediately after a noun or pronoun to say that something is true about only one person or thing. For example, if you **alone** know something, you are the only person who knows it.

Simon alone knew the truth.
Pride alone prevented her from giving up.

along

You use **along** to indicate that someone or something moves or occurs in or next to something long and narrow such as a road or a river.

Tim walked along Ebury Street.
...the trees all along Bear Creek.
The current passes along this wire here.

WARNING

You do not use **along** to describe movement from one side of an area to another. For example, you do not talk about going 'along' a desert. Instead you use **through** or **across.**

...hitch-hiking through Arizona.
...the walk through the Alpine meadows.
He wandered across Hyde Park.

When someone or something goes into a hole and comes out the other side, you do not say that they go 'along' the hole. You say that they go **through** it.

...scrambling through the hole.

a lot

See entry at **lot.**

aloud - loudly

'aloud'

If you say something **aloud,** you say it so that other people can hear you.

In no previous war could men say aloud what was on their minds.

If you read **aloud** a piece of writing, you say the words so that people can hear what has been written.

She read aloud to us from the newspaper.

'loudly'

If you do something **loudly,** you make a lot of noise when you do it.

The audience laughed loudly.

already

referring to
an action

You use **already** to say that something has happened before now, or that it has happened sooner than expected. When referring to an action, speakers of British English use a perfect tense with **already**. They put **already** after 'have', 'has', or 'had', or at the end of a clause.

We've already agreed to wait.
He had already invited Dougal Haston.
I've had tea already, thank you.
I can't stop him working – he's cleared half the site already.

Some speakers of American English use the simple past tense instead of the present perfect tense. For example, instead of saying 'I have already met him', they say 'I **already** met him' or 'I met him **already**'.

You already woke up the kids.
I told you already – he's the professor.

referring to
a situation

Already is also used to say that a situation exists at an earlier time than expected. If there is no auxiliary, you put **already** in front of the verb, unless the verb is 'be'.

They already exercise considerable influence in all western countries.
By the middle of June the Campaign already had more than 1000 members.

If the verb is 'be', you put **already** after it.

It was already dark.
Satellites are already beyond absolute human control.
By the time he got home, Julie was already in bed.

If there is an auxiliary, you put **already** after the auxiliary.

Computers are already considered by many skilled players to be more satisfactory competitors than humans.

If there is more than one auxiliary, you put **already** after the first one.

Portable computers can already be plugged into TV sets.

If you want to emphasize that a situation exists at an earlier time than expected, you can put **already** at the beginning of a sentence.

Already the French expansion has begun to taper off.
Already a bud on one of the roses was on the point of blooming.

'all ready'

Do not confuse **already** with **all ready**. **All ready** is a simple combination of **all**, meaning 'completely', and **ready**.

Your tea's all ready for you.

alright

See entry at **all right**.

also - too - as well

You use **also, too,** or **as well** when you are giving more information about something.

'also'

Also is usually used in front of a verb. If there is no auxiliary, you put **also** immediately in front of the verb, unless the verb is 'be'.

I also began to be interested in cricket.
They also helped out.

If the verb is 'be', you put **also** after it.

I was also an American.
Knowledge, which is in many ways our blessing, is also our curse.

If there is an auxiliary, you put **also** after the auxiliary.

The leisure centre has also proved uneconomic.
The basic symptoms of the illness were also described on the card.

If there is more than one auxiliary, you put **also** after the first one.

We'll also be hearing about the work of Una Woodruff.
If that light blows, then every other light on the circuit will also have gone.

Also is sometimes put at the beginning of a clause.

I thought it was the perfect answer. Also, Tony and I had never done a historical subject.

Note that you never put **also** at the end of a clause.

'too' You usually put **too** at the end of a clause.

Now the problem affects middle-class children, too.
It was a pretty play, and very sad too.

In conversation, **too** is used after a word or phrase when you are making a brief comment on something that has just been said.

'His father kicked him out of the house.'—'Quite right, too.'
'They've finished mending the road.'—'About time, too!'

Too is sometimes put after the first word group in a clause.

I wondered whether I too would become one of its victims.
Physically, too, the peoples of the world are incredibly mixed.

However, the position of **too** can make a difference to the meaning of a sentence. 'I am an American **too**' can mean either 'Like the person just mentioned, I am an American' or 'Besides having the other qualities just mentioned, I am an American'. However, 'I **too** am an American' can only mean 'Like the person just mentioned, I am an American'.

He was playing well, too.
Now we have the financial backing too.
Nerissa, too, felt miserable.
Macdonald, too, was alarmed by the violence.

WARNING You do not put **too** immediately after a link verb or an auxiliary. You do not say, for example, 'I am too an American'. You also do not put **too** at the beginning of a sentence.

For information on other uses of this word, see entry at **too**.

'as well' **As well** always goes at the end of a clause.

Filter coffee is definitely better for your health than boiled coffee. And it tastes nicer as well.
They will have a rough year next year as well.

negatives You do not usually use **also, too,** or **as well** in negative clauses. You do not say, for example, 'I'm not hungry and she's not hungry too'. You say 'I'm not hungry and she's not hungry **either**'. You can also say 'I'm not hungry and **neither is she**' or 'I'm not hungry and **nor is she**'.

Teddy Boylan wasn't at the ceremony, either.
I didn't call America either.
It wasn't the only danger, either.
'I don't normally drink at lunch.'—'Neither do I.'
'No thank you, I don't smoke.'—'Nor do I.'

alternate - alternative

'alternate'
Alternate actions, events, or processes keep happening regularly after each other.

...the alternate contraction and relaxation of muscles.

If something happens on **alternate** days, it happens on one day, then does not happen on the next day, then happens again on the day after it, and so on. Things can also happen in **alternate** weeks, months, or years.

We saw each other on alternate Sunday nights.
The two courses are available in alternate years.

'alternative'
You use **alternative** to describe something that can be used, had, or done instead of something else.

But still people try to find alternative explanations.
There is, however, an alternative approach.

Alternative can also be used as a noun. An **alternative** to something is something else that you can have or do instead.

Economists have great difficulty imagining alternatives to communism and capitalism.
A magistrate offered them a Domestic Education course as an alternative to prison.
There is no alternative to permanent storage.

You can also say that someone has two or more **alternatives**, meaning that they have two or more courses of action to choose from.

If a man is threatened with attack, he has five alternatives: he can fight, flee, hide, summon help, or try to appease his attacker.

Note that it used to be considered incorrect to talk about more than two alternatives.

alternately - alternatively

'alternately'
You use **alternately** to say that two actions or processes keep happening regularly after each other.

Each piece of material is washed alternately in soft water and coconut oil.
The little girl had alternately sulked and made scenes.

'alternatively'
You use **alternatively** to give a different explanation from one that has just been mentioned, or to suggest a different course of action.

Or alternatively was he short of cash because he had never been to the Rosses' house at all?
Alternatively, you can use household bleach.

although - though

used as
conjunctions
You use **although** or **though** to introduce a subordinate clause in which you mention something which contrasts with what you are saying in the main clause. **Though** is not used in very formal English.

It was not for myself that I wanted the old piano, although I could play a little.
It wasn't entirely my decision, though I think that generally I agree with it.

You can put 'even' in front of **though** for emphasis.

She wore a fur coat, even though it was a very hot day.

Note that you do not put 'even' in front of **although**.

| WARNING | When a sentence begins with **although** or **though**, you do not use 'but' or 'yet' to introduce the main clause. You do not say, for example, 'Although he was late, yet he stopped to buy a sandwich'. You say 'Although he was late, **he stopped** to buy a sandwich'. |

Although he was English, he spoke fluent and rapid French.
Though he hadn't stopped working all day, he wasn't tired.

You also do not use **although** or **though** in front of a noun group. You do not say, for example, 'Although his hard work, he failed his exam'. You say '**In spite of** his hard work, he failed his exam' or '**Despite** his hard work, he failed his exam'.

In spite of poor health, my father was always cheerful.
Despite her forcefulness, Cindy was uncertain what to do next.

When a clause beginning with **though** ends with a complement, you can bring the complement forward to the beginning of the clause. For example, instead of saying 'Though he was tired, he insisted on coming to the meeting', you can say '**Tired though he was**, he insisted on coming to the meeting'.

Tempting though it may be to follow this point through, it is not really relevant and we had better move on.
I had to accept the fact, improbable though it was.
Astute business man though he was, Philip was capable at times of extreme recklessness.

When a clause beginning with **though** ends with an adverb, you can often put the adverb at the beginning of a clause.

Some members of the staff couldn't handle Murray's condition, hard though they tried.

However, when a clause beginning with **although** ends with a complement or adverb, you cannot move the complement or adverb to the beginning of the clause.

| 'though' used as an adverb | **Though** is sometimes used as an adverb. You use it when you are making a statement which contrasts with what you have just said. You usually put **though** after the first word group in the sentence. In conversation, you can also put **though** at the end of a sentence. |

Barrington, though, was soon into his stride.
Gradually, though, it all came together.
For Newcastle, though, it was the climax of a hectic year.
I can't stay. I'll have a coffee though.

Note that **although** is never used as an adverb.

altogether

Altogether means 'completely'.

The noise had stopped altogether.
...an altogether different kind of support.

For a graded list of words used to indicate extent, see section on **extent** in entry at **Adverbials**.

You also use **altogether** to show that an amount is a total.

You will get £340 a week altogether.

'all together' Do not confuse **altogether** with **all together**. You use **all together** to say that a group of people or things are together or do something together, and that none of them is missing.

It had been so long since we were all together – at home, secure, sheltered.

always

If something **always** happens in particular circumstances, it is certain to happen in those circumstances. If something has **always** been the case, there has never been a time when it was not the case.

When **always** has one of these meanings, it is used with a verb in a non-continuous tense. If there is no auxiliary, **always** goes in front of the verb, unless the verb is 'be'.

Talking to Harold always cheered her up.
A man always remembers his first love.

If the verb is 'be', you usually put **always** after it.

She was always in a hurry.
There is always someone to lift the baby up.

If there is an auxiliary, you usually put **always** after it.

I've always been very careful.
He's always been so kind to us all.

If there is more than one auxiliary, you usually put **always** after the first one.

Zoe has always been allowed to choose what she wanted to eat.

If you say that something is **always** happening, you mean that it happens often and repeatedly and that this is annoying or surprising. When you use **always** like this, you use it with a verb in a continuous tense.

Uncle Harold was always fussing and worrying.
The bed was always collapsing.

WARNING You do not use **always** in comparisons, negative sentences, or questions to mean 'at any time in the past' or 'at any time in the future'. Instead you use **ever**. For example, you do not say 'They got on better than always before'. You say 'They got on better than **ever** before'.

...the biggest shooting star they had ever seen.
Neither of us would ever again get a job in films.
How will they ever be able to serve a boss?

For a graded list of words used to indicate frequency, see section on **frequency** in entry at **Adverbials**.

a.m.

See entry at **Time**.

among

If you are **among** a group of people or things, you are surrounded by them.

James wandered among his guests.
Among his baggage was a medicine chest.

You do not say that you are 'among' two people or things. You say that you are **between** them.

Myra and Barbara sat in the back, the baby between them.
She put the cigarette between her lips.
The island is midway between São Paulo and Porto Alegre.

dividing You can say that something is divided **among** or **between** a group of people. There is no difference in meaning.

...his estate, which he divided among his brothers and sisters.
Different scenes from the play are divided between five couples.

differences You do not use **among** when you are talking about differences. You do not say, for example, 'I couldn't see any difference among the three chairs'. You say 'I couldn't see any difference **between** the three chairs'.

There was an important difference between the political analysts and the military ones.
A good 'seeing' computer of the late 1970s could tell the difference between a cup, a saucer, a spoon, and a teapot.

For more information about **between**, see entry at **between**.

amount

An **amount** of something is how much of it you have, need, or get.

...the amount of salt lost in sweat.
I was horrified by the amount of work I had to do.

You can talk about a 'large amount' or a 'small amount'.

Use only a small amount of water at first.
The army gave out only small amounts of food.
There is no proof that larger amounts will prevent more colds.

However, you do not talk about a 'big amount' or a 'little amount'.

When you use **amount** in the plural, you use a plural verb with it. For example, you say 'Large amounts of money **were** wasted'. You do not say 'Large amounts of money was wasted'.

Increasing amounts of force are necessary.
Very large amounts of money are required.

WARNING You do not talk about an 'amount' of things or people. For example, you do not say 'There was an amount of chairs in the room'. You say 'There **were a number** of chairs in the room'. When you use **number** like this, you use a plural verb with it.

A number of European countries became involved in an arms race.
There are a great number of African novelists.

an

See entry at **a - an**.

and

And can be used to link noun groups, adjectives, adverbs, verbs, or clauses.

linking When you are talking about two things or people, you put **and** between two
noun groups noun groups.

I'll give you a nice cup of tea and a ginger biscuit.
...a friendship between a boy and a girl.

When you are linking more than two noun groups, you usually only put **and** in front of the last one.

The small canoes were taking such things as dried indigo, cotton, beeswax, and hides to the big canoes.
The local authorities list the extra houses, roads, parks and old people's homes that will have to be provided.

linking adjectives You put **and** between two adjectives when they come after verbs such as 'be', 'seem', and 'feel'.

The room was large and square.
The bed felt cold and hard.

When there are more than two adjectives after one of these verbs, you usually only put **and** in front of the last one.

We felt hot, tired, and thirsty.
The child is generally outgoing, happy and busy.

When you use two or more adjectives in front of a noun, you do not usually put **and** between them.

...a beautiful pink suit.
...rapid technological advance.

However, if the adjectives are colour adjectives, you must use **and.**

...a black and white swimming suit.

Similarly, if you are using adjectives which classify a noun in a similar way, you use **and.**

...a social and educational dilemma.

You also use **and** when you put adjectives in front of a plural noun in order to talk about groups of things which have different or opposite qualities.

Both large and small firms deal with each other regularly.
...European and American traditions.

WARNING You do not use **and** to link adjectives when you want them to contrast with each other. For example, you do not say 'He was fat and agile'. You say 'He was fat **but** agile'.

We are poor but happy.
...a small but comfortable hotel.

linking adverbs You can use **and** to link adverbs.

Mary was breathing quietly and evenly.
They walk up and down, smiling.

linking verbs You use **and** to link verbs when you are talking about actions performed by the same person, thing, or group.

I shouted and hooted at them.
They just sat and chatted.

If you want to say that someone does something repeatedly or for a long time, you can use **and** after a verb, and then repeat the verb.

They laughed and laughed.
Isaacs didn't give up. He tried and tried.

In conversation, you can sometimes use **and** after 'try' or 'wait' instead of using a 'to'-infinitive clause. For example, instead of saying 'I'll try to get a newspaper', you say 'I'll try **and** get a newspaper'. Note that in sentences like these you are describing one action, not two.

I'll try and answer the question.
I prefer to wait and see how things go.

You only use **and** like this when you are using the future tense of 'try' or 'wait', or when you are using the infinitive or imperative form.

If you **go and** do something or **come and** do something, you move from one place to another in order to do it.

I'll go and see him in the morning.
She would come and hold his hand.

In conversation, if you say that someone **has gone and** done something, you are expressing annoyance at something foolish that they have done.

That idiot Antonio has gone and locked our door.

linking clauses **And** is often used to link clauses.

I came here in 1972 and I have lived here ever since.

When you are giving advice or a warning, you can use **and** to say what will happen if something is done. For example, instead of saying 'If you go by train, you'll get there quicker', you can say 'Go by train **and** you'll get there quicker'.

Do as you're told and you'll be all right.
You put me out here and you'll lose your job tomorrow.

You do not normally put **and** at the beginning of a sentence, but you can sometimes do so when you are writing down what someone said, or writing in a conversational style.

Send him ahead to warn Eric. And close that door.
I didn't mean to scare you. And I'm sorry I'm late.

omitting repeated words When you are linking verb groups which would contain the same auxiliary, you do not need to repeat the auxiliary.

Having washed and changed, Scylla went out on to the verandah.

Similarly, when you are linking nouns which would have the same adjective, preposition, or determiner in front of them, you do not need to repeat the adjective, preposition, or determiner.

...the young men and women of England.
My mother and father worked hard.

'both' for emphasis When you link two word groups using **and,** you can emphasize that what you are saying applies to both word groups by putting **both** in front of the first word group. See entry at **both**.

negative sentences You do not normally use **and** to link groups of words in negative sentences. For example, you do not say 'She never reads and listens to stories'. You say 'She never reads **or** listens to stories'.

He was not exciting or good looking.

See entry at **or**.

However, you use **and** when you are talking about the possibility of two actions occurring at the same time. For example, you say 'I can't think **and** talk at the same time'. You also use **and** if two noun groups occur so frequently together that they are regarded as a single item. For example, 'knife' and 'fork' are always joined by **and** even in negative sentences such as 'I haven't got my knife **and** fork'.

Unions haven't taken health and safety as seriously as they might have done.

When two noun groups are regarded as a single item like this, they almost always occur in a fixed order. For example, you talk about your **knife and**

fork, not your 'fork and knife'. For a list of pairs of words of this kind, see entry at **Fixed pairs.**

anniversary

An **anniversary** is a date which is remembered or celebrated because a special event happened on that date in a previous year.

November 7th was the anniversary of the Bolshevik Revolution.
...the celebrations of the 250th anniversary of the birth of Josef Haydn.

'birthday' Note that you do not refer to the anniversary of the date when you were born as your 'anniversary'. You call it your **birthday.**

On my twelfth birthday I received a letter from my father.
It was 10 December, my daughter's birthday.

announcement - advertisement

'announcement' An **announcement** is a public statement giving information about something.

The government made a public announcement about the progress of the talks.
The announcement gave details of small increases in taxes.

'advertisement' An **advertisement** is an item in a newspaper or on television which tries to persuade you to buy something, or which gives you information about an event or job vacancy.

...an advertisement for Black and White whisky.
...an advertisement for an assistant cashier.

another

used to mean **Another** thing or person of a particular kind means one more thing or
'one more' person of that kind. **Another** is usually followed by a singular count noun.

Could I have another cup of coffee?
He opened another shop last month.

You can use **another** with 'few' or a number in front of a plural count noun.

Within another few minutes reports of attacks began to come in.
The woman lived for another ten days.

WARNING You do not use **another** immediately in front of a plural count noun or an uncount noun. You do not say, for example, 'Another men came into the room'. You say '**More** men came into the room'.

More officers will be brought in as and when circumstances dictate.
We need more information.

used to mean **Another** thing or person also means a different thing or person from the
'different' one you have been talking about.

It all happened in another country.
He mentioned the work of another colleague, John Lyons.

Some other is sometimes used with a similar meaning.

I will have to think of some other way of getting across to Europe.
They talked about some other guy they knew.

WARNING As with the previous meaning, you do not use **another** in front of a plural count noun or an uncount noun. You do not say, for example, 'They arrange things better in another countries'. You say 'They arrange things better in **other** countries'.

Other people must have thought like this.
...toys, paints, books and other equipment.

used as a pronoun

Another is sometimes used as a pronoun.

I saw one girl whispering to another.

answer

used as a verb

When you **answer** someone who has asked you a question, you say something back to them. You can either say that someone **answers** a person or that they **answer** a question.

I didn't know how to answer her.
I tried my best to answer her questions.

Note that you do not 'answer to' someone who has asked you a question, or 'answer to' their question.

used as a noun

An **answer** is something that you say to someone when they have asked you a question.

'Is there anyone here?' I asked. There was no answer.

An **answer to** a problem is a possible solution to it.

At first is seemed like the answer to all my problems.

Note that you do not talk about an 'answer for' a problem.

anti-social

Anti-social behaviour is harmful or annoying to other people.

...the growing use of the computer by anti-social elements as a weapon of crime.
Don't let your children develop an anti-social habit such as bullying.

'unsociable'

People who do not like the company of other people are sometimes described as **anti-social**, but the usual word used to describe such people is **unsociable.**

She was an awkward and unsociable girl.

anxious

If you are **anxious** about someone or something, you are worried about them.

I was quite anxious about George.

If you are **anxious to do** something, you want very much to do it.

Mother and father were most anxious to be correct.
He seemed anxious to go.

Note that you do not say that someone is 'anxious for doing' something.

If you are **anxious for** something, you want to have it, or you want it to happen.

...civil servants anxious for promotion.
He was anxious for real negotiations.

If you are **anxious that** something should happen, you want it to happen very much.

Lyons was most anxious that this should happen.
He was anxious that Holbein should paint pictures of his English friends.

Note that when you use a 'that'-clause after **anxious**, you usually use 'should' in it.

'nervous' Do not confuse **anxious** with **nervous**. If you are **nervous**, you are rather frightened about something that you are going to do or experience.

I began to get nervous about crossing roads.
Both actors were exceedingly nervous on the day of the performance.

any

You use **any** to say that something is true about each thing or person of a particular type, about each member of a group, or about each part of something.

You use **any** in front of a singular count noun to talk about each thing or person of a particular type.

Any big container will do.
...things that any man might do under pressure.

You use **any** in front of a plural count noun to talk about all things or people of a particular type.

One must beware of any forecasts about fuel supplies.
The patients know their rights like any other consumers.

You use **any** in front of an uncount noun to talk about an amount of something.

Throw any vegetable matter to the pig.

When you use **any** in front of a singular count noun or an uncount noun, you use a singular form of a verb with it.

Any book that attracts children as much as this has to be taken seriously.
While any poverty remains, it must have the first priority.

When you use **any** in front of a plural count noun, you use a plural form of a verb with it.

Before any decisions are made, ministers are carrying out a full enquiry.

'any of' You use **any of** in front of a plural noun group beginning with 'the', 'these', 'those', or a possessive to talk about each thing or person belonging to a particular group.

It was more expensive than any of the other magazines.
Any of the local boatmen will take you to the caves.
Milk in any of these forms is just as nutritious as when it comes straight from the cow.
Current rates can be obtained on request at any of our branches.

You can use either a plural or singular form of a verb with **any of** and a plural noun group. The singular form is more formal.

Find out if any of his colleagues were at the party.
There is no sign that any of these limits has yet been reached.

You use **any of** in front of a singular noun group beginning with 'the', 'this', 'that', or a possessive to talk about each part of something.

I'm not going to give you any of the land.
I feel horribly guilty taking up any of your precious time.

You can also use **any of** in front of the pronouns 'this', 'that', 'these', 'those', 'it', 'us', 'you', or 'them'.

Has any of this been helpful?
I don't believe any of it.
She might have been wearing any of them.

Note that you do not use **any** without 'of' in front of these pronouns.

You can use either a plural or singular form of a verb with **any of** and the pronouns 'these', 'those', 'us', 'you', and 'them'.

We would hotly contest the idea that any of us were middle class.
I don't think any of us wants that.

used in questions and negatives

Any is used, especially after 'have', in questions and negative sentences.

Do you have any facts to back up all this?
He said he hadn't any feelings about his own childhood.

For more information about this use, see entry at **some**.

used as a pronoun

Any can also be used as a pronoun.

Discuss it with your female colleagues, if you have any.
The meeting was different from any that had gone before.

anybody

See entry at **anyone - anybody**.

any more

If you want to say that something that happened in the past does not happen now, you say that it does not happen **any more**. You can also say that something is not the case **any more**. **Any more** usually comes at the end of a clause.

There was no noise any more.
He can't hurt us any more.
People just do not care any more.

Note that you do not say that something does not happen 'no more'.

Any more is sometimes spelled **anymore** in American English.

The land isn't valuable anymore.

'no longer'

Instead of saying that something 'does not happen any more', you can say that it **no longer happens**. This is a fairly formal use. You put **no longer** in front of the verb, unless the verb is 'be'.

We no longer feed infants in this way.
Their clothing no longer gave effective protection against the heat.

If the verb is 'be', you put **no longer** after it.

She was no longer cross with Tusker.

If you use a modal, you put **no longer** between the modal and the main verb.

They can no longer gather food for themselves.
Ralph could no longer make himself heard.

In writing, **no longer** is sometimes put at the beginning of a clause, followed by an auxiliary or modal or 'be', and then the subject.

No longer were they isolated from each other.
No longer can boys and girls pick up their skills from their mothers and fathers.

You do not use **no longer** like this in conversation.

'any longer'   Instead of saying that something 'does not happen any more' or 'no longer happens', you can say that it **does not happen any longer.** This use is less common. **Any longer** goes at the end of a clause.

She could not doubt it any longer.

anyone - anybody

You use **anyone** or **anybody** to talk about people in general, or about each person of a particular kind. There is no difference in meaning between **anyone** and **anybody.**

Anyone can miss a plane.
Anybody can go there.

If anyone asks where you are, I'll say you've just gone out.
If anybody wants me for anything, tell them I'll be back soon.

used in   **Anyone** and **anybody** are very commonly used in questions and negative
questions and sentences.
negatives
Was there anyone behind you?
There wasn't anyone there.

For more information about this use, see entry at **someone - somebody.**

'any one'   Do not confuse **anyone** with **any one.** You use **any one** to emphasize that you are referring to only one of something.

That was more money than he had seen at any one time in all his twenty-one years.

anyplace

See entry at **anywhere.**

anything

You use **anything** to talk about a thing or event which might exist or happen, or about each thing or event of a particular kind.

The situation is very tense; anything might happen.
'Do you like beer?'—'I like anything alcoholic.'

used in   **Anything** is very commonly used in questions and negative sentences.
questions and
negatives *Why do we have to show him anything?*
I did not say anything.

For more information about this use, see entry at **something.**

any time

If you can do something **any time** or **at any time,** you can do it whenever you want to.

If you'd like to give it a try, just come any time.
They can leave at any time.

When you use **any time** without 'at', you can spell it **anytime.**

I could have left anytime.
We'll be hearing from him anytime now.

If you want to say that something can be done whenever a particular thing is needed, you can use **any time** with a 'that'-clause, usually without 'that'.

Any time you need him, let me know.
Any time the bees want a queen to hatch out of the egg, they can do it.

Any time is also used in negative sentences to mean 'some time'.

We mustn't waste any time in Athens.
I haven't had any time to learn how to use it properly.

When you use **any time** to mean 'some time', you do not spell it 'anytime'.

anyway

You use **anyway** when you are adding a remark to something you have just said. Usually the remark is something you have just thought of, and makes your previous statement seem less important or relevant.

We ought to spend less on the defence missiles, which I reckon are pretty useless anyway.
I decided to postpone the idea of doing a course, and anyway I got accepted by the Council.

'any way' — Do not confuse **anyway** with **any way**. **Any way** usually occurs in the phrase **in any way,** which means 'in any respect' or 'by any means'.

He never threatened her in any way.
I am not connected in any way with the medical profession.
If I can help her in any way, you have only to speak to me.

anywhere

Anywhere means in any place, or in any part of a particular place.

It is better to have it in the kitchen than anywhere else.
They are the oldest rock paintings anywhere in North America.

'anyplace' — Some speakers of American English say **anyplace** instead of 'anywhere'.

The fact is we're afraid to go anyplace alone.
Airports were more closely watched than anyplace else.

used in questions and negatives — **Anywhere** is very commonly used in questions and negative statements.

Is there an ashtray anywhere?
I decided not to go anywhere.

For more information about this use, see entry at **somewhere.**

apart

If two people are **apart**, they are not in each other's company.

They could not bear to be apart.

Note that you do not use **apart** in front of a noun.

'apart from' — You use **apart from** when you mention an exception to a statement that you are making.

Apart from Ann, the car was empty.
She had no money, apart from the five pounds that Christopher had given her.

When **apart** is used in sentences like these, it must be followed by 'from' and not by any other preposition.

apartment

See entry at **flat - apartment.**

apologize

If you **apologize to** someone, you say you are sorry.

Afterwards George apologized to him personally.

Note that **apologize** must be followed by 'to' in sentences like these. You do not say that you 'apologize' someone.

If you **apologize for** something you have done, or **apologize for** something someone else has done, you say you are sorry about it.

Later, Bred apologized to Savchenko for the conduct of a few members of the company.

Apologizing

There are several ways of apologizing and accepting apologies. You apologize when you have upset someone or caused trouble for them in some way.

The commonest way of apologizing is to say 'Sorry' or 'I'm sorry'. When using 'I'm sorry', you can use adverbs such as 'very', 'so', 'terribly', and 'extremely' to be more emphatic.

'Stop that, please. You're giving me a headache.'—'Sorry.'
Sorry I'm late.
I'm sorry about this morning.
I'm sorry if I've distressed you by asking all this.
I'm very sorry, but these are vital.
I'm so sorry to keep on coughing.
I'm terribly sorry – we shouldn't have left.

Some people use 'awfully' to modify 'sorry' but this sounds rather formal or old-fashioned.

I'm awfully sorry to give you this trouble at a time like this.

When apologizing for accidentally doing something, for example stepping on someone's foot, some people say 'I beg your pardon' or 'I do beg your pardon' instead of 'Sorry'. This is rather old-fashioned.

As she backed away from the door, she bumped into someone behind her. 'I beg your pardon,' she said.

Speakers of American English say 'Excuse me'.

interrupting, approaching, or leaving someone

You use 'Excuse me' to apologize politely to someone when you are disturbing or interrupting them, or when you want to get past them. This is also the expression to use when you want to speak to a stranger.

Excuse me for disturbing you at home.
Excuse me butting in.
Excuse me, but is there a fairly cheap restaurant near here?
Excuse me, do you mind if I move your bag slightly?

The expression 'Pardon me' is used by some speakers of American English.

Pardon me, Sergeant, I wonder if you'd do me a favour?

When you are disturbing or interrupting someone, you can also say 'I'm sorry to disturb you' or 'I'm sorry to interrupt'.

I'm sorry to disturb you again but we need some more details on this fellow Wilt.
Sorry to interrupt, but I've some forms to fill in.

You also say 'Excuse me' when you have to leave someone for a short time in order to do something.

Excuse me. I have to make a telephone call.
Will you excuse me a second?

doing something embarrassing

You can use 'Excuse me' or 'I beg your pardon' to apologize when you have done something slightly embarrassing or impolite, such as burping, hiccupping, or sneezing.

saying something wrong

You say 'I beg your pardon' to apologize for making a mistake in what you are saying, or for using the wrong word. You can also say 'sorry'.

It is treated in a sentence as a noun – I beg your pardon – as an adjective.
It's in the southeast, sorry, southwest corner of the USA.

formal apologies

When you want to apologize in a formal way, you can say explicitly 'I apologize'.

I apologize for my late arrival.
How silly of me. I do apologize.
I really must apologize for bothering you with this.

Another formal expression, used especially in writing, is 'Please accept my apologies'.

Please accept my apologies for this unfortunate incident.

Some people say 'Forgive me'.

Forgive me, Mr Turner. I am a little disorganized this morning.

You can use 'forgive' in polite expressions like 'Forgive me' and 'Forgive my ignorance' to reduce the directness of what you are saying, and to apologize in a mild way for saying something that might seem rude or silly.

Look, forgive me, but I thought we were going to talk about my book.
Forgive my ignorance, but who is Jane Fonda?

apologies on notices

'Regret' is often used in public notices and formal announcements.

London Transport regrets any inconvenience caused by these repairs.
The notice said: 'Dr.Beamish has a cold and regrets he cannot meet his classes today.'

accepting an apology

To accept an apology, you normally use a short fixed expression such as 'That's okay', 'That's all right', 'Forget it', 'Don't worry about it', or 'It doesn't matter'.

'I'm sorry.'—'It's perfectly all right.'
'I'm sorry about this, sir.'—'That's all right. Don't let it happen again.'
'I apologize for my outburst just now.'—'Forget it.'
She spilt his drink and said 'I'm sorry.' 'Don't worry about it,' he said, 'no harm done.'
'I'm sorry to ring at this late hour.'—'I'm still up. It doesn't matter.'

WARNING

Some words and expressions that are used to apologize are also used to ask someone to repeat something that they just said. See entry at **Asking for repetition.**

apostrophe

See entry at **Punctuation.**

appeal

In British English, if someone **appeals against** a legal decision or sentence, they formally ask a court to change the decision or reduce the sentence.

He appealed against the five year sentence he had been given.

Speakers of American English do not use 'against' after **appeal**. They say that someone **appeals** a decision.

Casey's lawyer said he was appealing the interim decision.

appear

When something **appears,** it moves into a position where you can see it.

A glow of light appeared over the sea.

You also use **appear** to say that something becomes available for people to read or buy.

His second novel appeared under the title 'Getting By'.
It was about the time that video recorders first appeared in the shops.

When you are mentioning the date or period when something became available, you often use **there.** For example, instead of saying 'In the 1960s a new type of car appeared', you say 'In the 1960s **there appeared** a new type of car'.

In the same year there appeared a book which can be quoted as the supreme example of anti-poetic rationalism.
As early as the mid-twenties there appeared on the market chairs, tables and stools designed by Wijdveldt.

Note that in sentences like these you must use 'there'. You do not say, for example, 'In the 1960s appeared a new type of car'.

'appear to'   If something **appears to** be the case, it seems to be the case. Similarly, if something **appears to** be a particular thing, it seems to be that thing. **Appear to** is more formal than 'seem to'.

I don't appear to have written down his name.
Their offer appears to be the most attractive.

apply

If you **apply** to have something or do something, you write asking formally to be allowed to have it or do it.

I've applied for another job.
The repatriation process has now been going on for some time, but only about 30,000 - 40,000 have applied to go back.

Apply has another meaning. If you **apply** something to a surface, you put it onto the surface or rub it into it. This is a formal use of **apply**, which usually occurs only in written instructions.

Apply a little liquid wax polish.

In conversation and in most kinds of writing, you do not say that you **apply** something. You say that you **put** it **on, rub** it **on, rub** it **in,** or **spread** it **on.**

...the cream that she put on to soothe her sunburn.
Try a little methylated spirit rubbed on with a soft cloth.
Rub in linseed oil to darken it.

appreciate

If you **appreciate** something that someone has done for you, you are grateful to them because of it.

Thanks. I really appreciate your help.
We would much appreciate guidance from an expert.

You can use **appreciate** with 'it' and an 'if'-clause to say politely that you would like someone to do something. For example, you can say 'I would **appreciate it if** you would deal with this matter urgently'.

I would appreciate it if you could bring all that happened into the open.

Note that you must use 'it' in sentences like these. You do not say, for example, 'I would appreciate if you would deal with this matter urgently'.

approach

If you **approach** something, you get nearer to it.

He approached the front door.
Footsteps approached the cell in the darkness.

Note that **approach** is not followed by 'to'. You do not say, for example, 'He approached to the front door'.

approve

If you **approve of** someone or something, you have a good opinion of them.

His mother had not approved of Julie.
Steve approved of the whole affair.

Note that you do not say that you 'approve to' someone or something.

If someone in authority **approves** a plan or idea, they formally agree to it and say that it can happen.

The White House approved the exercise.
The directors quickly approved the new deal.

Note that for this meaning of **approve** you do not use 'of'.

arise - rise

Both **arise** and **rise** are irregular verbs. The other forms of 'arise' are **arises, arising, arose, arisen**. The other forms of 'rise' are **rises, rising, rose, risen**.

When an opportunity, problem, or new state of affairs **arises,** it begins to exist. This is the most common meaning of **arise**.

He promised to help Rufus if the occasion arose.
A serious problem has arisen.

When something **rises,** it moves upwards.

Clouds of birds rose from the tree-tops.

When someone who is sitting **rises,** they stand up. You can also use **rise** to say that someone gets out of bed in the morning. See entry at **rise - raise**.

armchair

See entry at **chair - armchair**.

army

An **army** is a large organized group of people who are armed and trained to fight. After **army** you can use either a singular or plural form of a verb.

The army is in a high state of readiness.
The army are clearing up quite a bit of the land.

around

Around has the same meaning as 'round', when 'round' is used as a preposition or an adverb. **Around** is more common in American English than in British English.

She was wearing a scarf round her head.
He had a towel wrapped around his head.

The earth moves round the sun.
The satellite has passed once more around the earth.

Think of what's happening politically round the world.
...the growth of vigilante societies around the country.

He swung round and faced the window.
The large lady turned around in a huff.

You can also use **around** instead of 'round' as the second part of some phrasal verbs.

Don't wait for April to come round before planning your vegetable garden.
...when the new academic year came around in the autumn.

Irving got round the problem in a novel way.
An impasse has developed and I don't know how to get around it.

In conversation, **around** and **round about** are sometimes used to mean 'approximately'.

He owns around 200 acres.
I've been here for round about ten years.

Note that you do not use 'round' like this.

arrival

When someone arrives at a place, you can talk about their **arrival** there. This is a rather formal use.

His arrival was hardly noticed.
A week after her arrival, we had a General School Meeting.

If you want to say that something happens immediately after someone arrives at a place, you can use a phrase beginning with 'on'. For example, you can say '**On his arrival** in London, he went straight to Oxford Street'.

...the store of roubles that Ivan had given him on his arrival.
The British Council will book temporary hotel accommodation on your arrival in London.

The possessive determiner is often omitted. For example, instead of saying 'on their arrival', you can just say **on arrival.**

The principal guests were greeted on arrival by the Lord Mayor of London.
On arrival at the fairground, the elephant seemed to recognise its 'home'.

Note that you must use **on,** not 'at', in sentences like these. You do not say, for example, 'At his arrival in London, he went straight to Oxford Street'.

arrive - reach

You use **arrive** or **reach** to say that someone comes to a place at the end of a journey.

I'll tell Professor Hogan you've arrived.
He reached Bath in the late afternoon.

'arrive'   You usually say that someone **arrives at** a place.

...by the time we arrived at Victoria Station.
...from the moment he had arrived at the Harlowes' bungalow.

However, you say that someone **arrives in** a country or city.

He had arrived in France slightly ahead of schedule.
The American Ambassador to Mexico arrived in Quito today.

WARNING   You never say that someone 'arrives to' a place.

You also do not say that someone 'arrives at home' or 'arrives in home'. You say that they **arrive home**.

We arrived home and I carried my suitcases up the stairs behind her.

You do not use a preposition after **arrive** in front of 'here', 'there', 'somewhere', or 'anywhere'.

I arrived here yesterday.
When we arrived there, we went to the garage.
Plans are deliberately indefinite, more to travel than to arrive anywhere.

'reach'   **Reach** always takes a direct object. You do not say that someone 'reaches at' a place or that they 'have just reached'.

It was dark by the time I reached their house.

another   **Arrive at** and **reach** can both be used to say that someone eventually
meaning   makes a decision or finds the answer to something.

It took us several hours to arrive at a decision.
They were unable to reach a decision.

I had arrived at a conclusion on the basis of the only facts then available to me.
The commission could not reach a conclusion because of inadequate data.

'come to'   **Come to** can be used in a similar way.

Kwezi thought for a while, then seemed to come to a decision.
I came to the conclusion that I didn't really fancy civil engineering.

arrogant

See entry at **proud**.

articles

For information on the **indefinite article**, see entry at **a - an**. For information on the **definite article**, see entry at **the**.

as

used in time   If something happens **as** something else happens, it happens while the
clauses   other thing is happening.

She wept bitterly as she told her story.

You also use **as** to say that something is done whenever something happens.

Parts are replaced as they grow old.

Note that you do not use **as** simply to mean 'at the time that'. For example, you do not say 'As I started work here, the pay was £2 an hour'. You say '**When** I started work here, the pay was £2 an hour'. See entry at **when**.

used to mean 'because'

As is often used to mean 'because' or 'since'.

She bought herself an iron as she felt she couldn't keep borrowing Anne's.
As he had been up since 4 a.m. he was no doubt now very tired.

See entry at **because.**

used with adjectives

You can use **as** in front of an adjective to say how someone or something is regarded or described.

He regarded them as snobbish.
They regarded manual work as degrading.
Officials described him as brilliant.

used in prepositional phrases

You can also use **as** in prepositional phrases to say how someone or something is regarded, described, treated, or used.

He was regarded as something of a troublemaker.
She was classified as a third category invalid.
I treated business as a game.
I wanted to use him as an agent.

You can also use **as** in prepositional phrases to say what role or function someone or something has.

He worked as a clerk.
He served as Kennedy's ambassador to India.
Bleach removes colour and acts as an antiseptic and deodoriser.

used in comparisons

In writing, **as** is sometimes used to compare one action to another.

He looked over his shoulder as Jack had done.
She pushed him, as she had pushed her son.

Like and **the way** are used in a similar way. See entry at **like - as - the way.**

You can also use **as** in front of some prepositional phrases, especially at the beginning of a sentence. For example, instead of saying 'She took a holiday in April, as she had done in previous years', you can say '**As in previous years,** she took a holiday in April'.

As in previous elections, Benn was to coordinate broadcasting.

When you have just made a statement, you can use **as** as a conjunction to indicate that the statement also applies to another person, thing, or group. After **as** you use 'be', 'have', an auxiliary, or a modal, then the subject.

Edmund Burke liked that term, as did the authors of America's Federalist Papers.

WARNING

You do not usually use **as** in front of a noun group when you are comparing one thing or person to another. You do not say, for example, 'She sang as a bird'. You say 'She sang **like** a bird'.

He swam like a fish.
I am a worker like him.
Children, like animals, are noisy at meal times.

However, you can make a comparison using **as,** an adjective or adverb, and another **as.** For example, you can say 'You're just **as bad as** your sister'. For more information about this use, see entry at **as ... as.**

You do not use **as** after comparative adjectives. You do not say, for example, 'The trees are taller as the church'. You say 'The trees are taller **than** the church'.

She was much older than me.
I am happier than I have ever been.

as ... as

When you are comparing one person or thing to another, you can use **as** followed by an adjective or adverb followed by another **as.**

You're just as bad as your sister.
...huge ponds as big as tennis courts.
The meal was as awful as the conversation.
She wanted to talk to someone as badly as I did.

After these expressions, you can use either a noun group and a verb, or a noun group on its own.

You're as old as I am.
...some man as old as Father.

François understood the difficulties as well as he did.
I can't remember it as well as you.

If you use a personal pronoun on its own, it must be an object pronoun such as 'me' or 'him'. It used to be considered correct to use a subject pronoun such as 'I' or 'he', but this now sounds very old-fashioned.

Jane was not as clever as him.

If you use a personal pronoun and a verb, you must use a subject pronoun.

The teacher is just as sensitive as they are.
...somebody who's as bad at it as I am.

using modifiers You can put words and expressions such as 'almost', 'just', and 'at least' in front of **as ... as** structures.

I could see almost as well at night as I could in sunlight.
It is just as bad to overfeed pets as it is to underfeed them.
He may be at least as unpopular as the President.

used with negatives You can also use **as ... as** structures in various kinds of negative sentence.

They aren't as clever as they appear to be.
I don't notice things as well as I used to.
You've never been as late as this without telephoning.
There is no one as dangerous as an idealist with a machine gun.

So is sometimes used instead of the first 'as', but this use is not common.

The young otter is not so handsome as the old one is.
I had seldom seen him looking so pleased with himself as he was now.

used to describe size or extent You can use expressions such as 'twice', 'three times', or 'one fifth' in front of **as ... as** structures. You do this when you are indicating the size or extent of something by comparing it to something else.

...volcanoes twice as high as Everest.
This animal is three times as popular with girls as with boys.
Water is eight hundred times as dense as air.

using just one 'as' If it is quite clear what you are comparing someone or something to, you can omit the second **as** and the following noun group or clause.

A megaphone would be as good.
This fish is twice as big.

ashamed - embarrassed

'ashamed' If you are **ashamed,** you feel guilty because you believe you have done something wrong or unacceptable.

She had behaved badly and was ashamed.
They were ashamed to tell their people how they had been cheated.

You say that someone is **ashamed of** something.

He felt ashamed of his selfishness.
It's nothing to be ashamed of.

'embarrassed' If you are **embarrassed,** you are upset because you think something makes you seem foolish.

The Belgian looked embarrassed.
She had been too embarrassed to ask her friends.

You say that someone is **embarrassed by** something or **embarrassed about** it.

He seemed embarrassed by his brother's outburst.
I felt really embarrassed about it.

Note that you do not say that someone is 'embarrassed of' something.

as if

You can use **as if** or **as though** at the beginning of a clause when you are describing how someone or something looks, or how someone behaves.

The furniture looked as though it had come out of somebody's attic.
He lunged towards me as if he expected me to aim a gun at him.

using 'were' Many people think it is incorrect to use 'was' in clauses of this type. They say you should use **were** instead.

He looked at me as if I were mad.
She remembered it all as if it were yesterday.

However, in conversation people usually use **was.**

The secretary spoke as though it was some kind of password.
He gave his orders as if this was only another training exercise.

You can use **was** or **were** in conversation, but in formal writing you should use **were.**

'like' Some people say **like** instead of 'as if' or 'as though'.

He looked like he felt sorry for me.
There he stands pumping his silly neck up and down just like it was a piston.

This use is generally regarded as incorrect.

ask

You say that someone **asks** a question.

He started asking Diana a lot of questions.

Note that you do not say that someone 'says' a question.

reporting questions You also use **ask** when you are reporting questions. After **ask** you usually use a noun group and an 'if'-clause or 'wh'-clause.

When you report a question to which the answer is 'yes' or 'no', you usually use **ask** with an 'if'-clause.

She asked him if his parents spoke French.

Someone asked me if the work was going well.

You can also use a clause beginning with 'whether'.

I asked Professor Bailey whether he agreed.

When you report a question to which the answer is not 'yes' or 'no', you usually use **ask** with a 'wh'-clause.

I asked him what he wanted.
He asked me where I was going.

WARNING In the 'wh'-clause, the subject and the verb do not change places. You do not say, for example, 'He asked me when was the train leaving'. You say 'He asked me when **the train was** leaving'.

You can say that someone **asks** someone else their name or their age.

He asked me my name.

You can say that someone **asks** someone else the time.

Whenever the butler came by, she asked him the time.

You can also say that someone **asks** someone else's opinion about something.

I was asked my opinion about the new car.

You do not need to say who a question is addressed to if this is already clear from the context.

A young man asked if we were students.
She asked why he was so silent.
I asked how they liked the film.

WARNING You never use 'to' when mentioning who a question is addressed to. You do not say, for example, 'He asked to me my name'.

direct reporting You can use **ask** when reporting directly what someone says.

'How many languages can you speak?' he asked.
'Have you met him?' I asked.

reporting requests You also use **ask** when you are reporting requests. When someone says that they want to be given something, you report this using **ask** and 'for'. For example, if a man says 'Can I have a bunch of roses?', you report this as 'He **asked for** a bunch of roses'.

Carl asked for Bavarian cream.
An Italian came in and asked for a loaf of white bread.

When someone says that they want to speak to another person, for example on the telephone, you say that they **ask for** that person.

He rang the office and asked for Cynthia.
He lifted the telephone and asked for the Prime Minister's private office.

When someone tells another person that they want them to do something, you report this using **ask** and either a 'to'-infinitive clause or an 'if'-clause.

He asked her to marry him.
He was asked to leave.
Five or six years ago her sister asked me if I would paint her.
I asked him if he would mind not smoking.

Asking for repetition

You ask someone to repeat what they have said when you have not heard them or when you have not understood them. You can also ask someone to repeat what they have said when you feel that what they have said is surprising or impolite.

asking informally

In an informal situation, you usually ask someone to repeat what they have said using a short fixed expression such as 'Sorry?', 'I'm sorry?, or 'Pardon?'

'Have you seen the health guide book anywhere?'—'Sorry?'—'Seen the health guide book?'
'Well, what about it?'—'I'm sorry?'—'What about it?'
'How old is she?'—'Pardon?'—'I said how old is she?'

Some people say 'Come again?'

'It's on Monday.'—'Come again?'—'Monday.'

In American English, 'Excuse me?' is generally used. Some people say 'Pardon me?'

'You do see him once in a while, don't you?'—'Excuse me?'—'I thought you saw him sometimes.'

Some people use 'What?', 'You what?', or 'Eh?' to ask someone to repeat something, but these expressions are impolite.

'Do you want another coffee?'—'What?'—'Do you want another coffee?'
'Well, I still have a cheque book.'—'Eh?'—'I said I still have a cheque book.'

You can use a 'wh'-word to check part of what someone has said.

'Can I speak to Nikki, please?'—'Who?'—'Nikki.'
'We've got a special offer in April for Majorca.'—'For where?'—'Majorca.'
'I don't like the tinkling.'—'The what?'—'The tinkling.'

If you think you heard what someone said but are not sure, or are surprised, you can repeat it, or repeat part of it, making it sound like a question.

'I just told her that rain's good for her complexion.'—'Rain?'
'I have a message for you?'—'A message?'

You add 'again' to the end of a question when you are asking someone to repeat something that they told you a little while ago and which you have forgotten.

What's his name again?
Where are we going again?

asking more formally

When talking to someone you do not know well, for example on the phone, you use longer expressions such as 'Sorry, what did you say?', 'I'm sorry, I didn't quite catch that', 'I'm sorry, I didn't hear what you said', 'I'm sorry, would you mind repeating that again?', and 'Would you repeat that, please?'

'What about tomorrow at three?'—'Sorry, what did you say?'—'I said, What about meeting tomorrow at three?'
Would you repeat that, I didn't quite catch it.

The expressions 'Beg your pardon?' and 'I beg your pardon?' are sometimes used, but they are fairly formal and old-fashioned.

'Did he listen to you?'—*'Beg your pardon?'*—*'Did he listen to you?'*
'Did they have a dog?'—*'I beg your pardon?'*—*'I said did they have a dog?'*

Note that 'I beg your pardon?' (but not 'Beg your pardon?') is also used to indicate that you find what someone says surprising or offensive. The word 'beg' is stressed.

'Where the devil did you get her?'—*'I beg your pardon?'*

asleep

See entry at **sleep - asleep**.

as long as

used in conditionals

You can use **as long as** to say that one thing is true only if another thing is true. For example, if you say 'We should catch the plane **as long as** the bus doesn't break down', you mean 'If the bus doesn't break down, we should catch the plane'. Note that you use a simple tense after **as long as**.

You can look as long as you don't touch.
We were all right as long as we kept our heads down.

duration

You also use **as long as** to say that something lasts for a long period of time, or for as much time as possible.

Any stomach-ache that persists for as long as one hour should be seen by a doctor.
Everyone holds off buying as long as they can.
She hesitated as long as she dared.

WARNING

You do not use **as long as** when you are talking about distances. You do not say, for example, 'I followed him as long as the bridge'. You say 'I followed him **as far as** the bridge'.

assertive

See entry at **forceful**.

assignment - homework

'assignment'

An **assignment** is a task that someone is given to do, usually as part of their job.

My first major assignment as a reporter was to cover a large-scale riot.

An **assignment** is also a piece of academic work given to students.

The course has heavy reading assignments.
Such a student would go to his first class, get his first assignment and probably do it out of habit.

In American English, an **assignment** is also a piece of work given to schoolchildren to do at home.

'homework'

In British English, work given to schoolchildren to do at home is called **homework**.

He never did any homework.

WARNING

Homework is an uncount noun. You do not talk about 'homeworks' or 'a homework'. Note that pupils **do** homework. They do not 'make' homework.

assist

If you **assist** someone, you help them. **Assist** is a fairly formal word.

We may be able to assist with the tuition fees.
He was asked to assist in keeping the hotel under surveillance.

In very old-fashioned English, to **assist** at an event or occasion means to be there when it happens. In modern English, you do not use **assist** like this. You say that someone **is present** at an event or occasion.

He had been present at the dance.
Howard insisted on being present.

as soon as

As soon as is a conjunction. You use **as soon as** to say that something will happen immediately after something else has happened.

As soon as we get the tickets we'll send them to you.

Note that you usually use the simple present tense after **as soon as.** You do not use a future tense. You do not say, for example, 'I will call you as soon as I will get back to my room'. You say 'I will call you as soon as I **get** back to my room'.

Ask him to come in, will you, as soon as he arrives.
We're getting married just as soon as her divorce comes through.

When you are talking about the past, you use the simple past tense after **as soon as.**

As soon as she got out of bed the telephone stopped ringing.

assume

See entry at **suppose - assume.**

assure - ensure - insure

'assure'   If you **assure** someone that something is true or will happen, you tell them that it is definitely true or will definitely happen, often in order to make them less worried.

Please assure Matthew that my house is not about to slide into the sea.

'ensure'   In British English, to **ensure** that something happens means to make certain that it happens.

His reputation was enough to ensure that he was always welcome.

'insure'   In American English, this word is usually spelled **insure.**

I shall try to insure that your stay is a pleasant one.

Insure has another meaning. In both British and American English, if you **insure** your property, you pay money to a company so that if the property is lost, stolen, or damaged, the company will pay you a sum of money.

Insure your baggage before you leave home.

as though

See entry at **as if.**

as usual

See entry at **usual - usually.**

as well

See entry at **also - too - as well**.

as well as

linking
noun groups

If you say that something is true of one person or thing **as well as** another, you are emphasizing that it is true not only of the second person or thing but also of the first one.

Women, as well as men, have a fundamental right to work.

linking
adjectives

You can also use **as well as** to link adjectives. When you do this, you are emphasizing that something has not only the second quality you mention but also the first one.

It has symbolic as well as economic significance.

linking
clauses

You can use **as well as** in a similar way to link clauses. However, the second clause must be a non-finite clause beginning with an '-ing' form.

She was an individual as well as being the airport manager's wife.
She negotiates the licences as well as ordering the equipment.

WARNING

You do not use a finite clause after **as well as.** You do not say, for example, 'She negotiates the licences as well as she orders the equipment'.

at

place or position

At is used to talk about the position of something, or about the place where something happens.

There was a staircase at the end of the hallway.
He said I was to be at a certain place in the Kaiserstrasse at 3 p.m.

You often use **at** to mean 'next to' or 'beside'.

The boat was anchored at Westminster Bridge.
Captain Imrie stopped me at the door.

You say that someone sits **at** a table or desk, for example when they are eating or writing.

She was sitting at the dressing table.
I was sitting at my desk reading.

If you want to mention the building where something exists or where something happens, you usually use **at.**

...the exhibition of David Jones' work at the Tate Gallery.
Dr Campbell told of his examination of Meehan at Ayr Police Station on July 15th.
I saw George Garforth at the Club.
He lived at 14 Burnbank Gardens, Glasgow.

In British English, you say that someone is **at** school or **at** university.

He had done some acting at school.
After a year at university, Benn joined the RAF.
He was just starting his final year at University College, London.

Speakers of American English usually say that someone is **in** school.

She had played Rosalind in High School.

See entry at **school - university**.

You say that someone stops **at** a particular place during a journey.

We pulled in for lunch at a roadhouse.
We docked at Panama.

You say that something happens **at** a meeting, ceremony, or party.

He made his remarks at a press conference.
The whole village were out at a funeral.
At parties they gulped your gin as if they had just been released from prison.
He had a fight at a high school dance.

time   **At** is also used to say when something happens.

You use **at** when you are mentioning a precise time.

At 2.30 a.m. he returned.
He had picked up Irene at 4.30 a.m.

If you want to know the precise time when something happened or will happen, you can say '**At what time...?**' but people usually say '**What time...?**'

What time did you get back to London?
What time does the boat leave?
'We are having a party on the beach.'—'What time?'—'At nine.'

You can say that something happened or will happen '**at** dawn', '**at** dusk', or '**at** night'.

She had come in at dawn.
It was ten o'clock at night.

However, you say that something happened or will happen '**in the** morning', '**in the** afternoon', or '**in the** evening'.

If something happens **at** a meal time, it happens while the meal is being eaten.

At dinner we had another in our series of conversations.
He told her at lunch that he couldn't take her to the game tomorrow.

You say that something happens **at** Christmas or **at** Easter.

She sends a card at Christmas.
What will happen to me at Easter?

However, you say that something happens **on** a particular day during Christmas or Easter.

I expect they even play cricket on Christmas Day.
On Easter Monday I headed for a hotel called the Europejski.

In British English, **at** is used with 'weekend'.

Relatives are relied on to provide food at the weekend and during holidays.

American speakers usually use **over** with 'weekend'.

The Museum threw a party over the weekend.

at first

See entry at **first - firstly**.

athletics - athletic

'athletics'   **Athletics** consists of sports such as running, the high jump, and the javelin.

He has retired from active athletics.

Athletics is an uncount noun. You use a singular form of a verb with it.

Athletics was developing rapidly.

'athletic'   **Athletic** is an adjective. It can mean 'relating to athletics'.

...athletic trophies.

However, when you use **athletic** to describe a person, you mean that they are fit, healthy, and active. You do not mean that they take part in athletics.

...athletic young men.

at last

See entry at **last - lastly**.

at present

See entry at **presently**.

attempt

See entry at **try - attempt**.

attendant

An **attendant** is someone whose job is to help people in a place such as a filling station or museum.

She stopped the car and told the attendant to fill it up.

You do not refer to someone who works in a shop selling goods to customers as an 'attendant'. A person like this is called a **shop assistant** in British English and a **sales clerk** in American English.

'Do you know, I've never worn trousers,' she said to the shop assistant.
...a sales clerk at the Soul Shack record store.

attention

If you give something your **attention,** you look at it, listen to it, or think about it carefully.

When he felt he had their attention, he began.
He switched his attention back to his magazine.

You can also say that someone **pays attention to** something.

You must pay attention to his eyes.
There's far too much attention being paid to these hooligans.

Note that you do not say that someone 'pays attention at' something.

attorney

See entry at **lawyer**.

attractive

See entry at **beautiful**.

audience

You refer to all the people who are watching or listening to a play, concert, film, or television play as the **audience.** You can use either a singular or plural form of a verb with **audience.**

The audience was not offered a printed text.
The television audience were able to hear some of the comments.

You can also use **audience** to refer to the people who read a particular writer's books or hear about someone's ideas.

...the need for intellectuals to communicate their ideas to a wider audience.

aural - oral

'aural'   **Aural** means 'relating to your ears and your sense of hearing'. **Aural** is pronounced /ˈɔːrəl/ or /ˈaʊrəl/.

I have used written and aural material.

'oral'   **Oral** means 'relating to your mouth'. It also describes things that involve speaking rather than writing. **Oral** is pronounced /ˈɔːrəl/.

...an oral test in German.

Both **aural** and **oral** are fairly formal words. They are used mainly to talk about teaching methods and examinations.

autumn

In British English, **autumn** or **the autumn** is the season between summer and winter.

Saturday was the first day of autumn.
She had waited throughout the autumn.

If you want to say that something happens every year during this season, you say that it happens **in autumn** or **in the autumn.**

In autumn the hard berries turn a delicate orange.
Winter wheat grows quite fast in the autumn.

Note that you do not say that something happens 'in the autumns'.

In American English, autumn is referred to as **the fall.**

In the fall we are going to England.

GRAMMAR   # Auxiliaries

An **auxiliary** or **auxiliary verb** is a verb that is used with a main verb to form a verb group. The auxiliaries 'be' and 'have' are used to form tenses. 'Be' is also used to form passive verb groups. The auxiliary 'do' is most commonly used in questions and negative clauses.

I am feeling reckless tonight.
They have been looking for you.

Thirteen people were killed.
Did you see him?
I do not remember her.

See entries at **Tenses, Questions,** and **not.** See entry at **do** for the use of 'do' to emphasize or focus on an action.

You put the auxiliaries you want to use in the following order: 'have' (for perfect tenses), 'be' (for continuous tenses), 'be' (for passive tenses).

Twenty-eight flights have been cancelled.
Three broad strategies are being adopted.

WARNING   You do not use the auxiliary 'do' in combination with other auxiliaries.

Auxiliaries are often used without a main verb when the verb has already been used.

I didn't want to go but a friend of mine did.
'Have you been there before?'—'Yes, I have.'

See entries at **Ellipsis** and **Replies.**

The different forms of the auxiliaries 'be', 'have', and 'do' are shown in the following table.

	be	have	do
Simple present:			
with 'I'	am	have	do
with 'you', 'we', 'they' and plural noun groups	are		
with 'he', 'she', 'it' and singular noun groups	is	has	does
Simple past:			
with 'I', 'he', 'she', 'it' and singular noun groups	was	had	did
with 'you', 'we', 'they' and plural noun groups	were		
Participles:			
present participle	being	having	doing
past participle	been	had	done

modals   **Modals,** such as 'can', 'should', 'might', and 'may', are also auxiliary verbs. You put them in front of all other auxiliaries.

The law will be changed.
She must have been dozing.

For more information, see entry at **Modals.**

contractions   For information on the contracted forms of auxiliaries, see entry at **Contractions.**

avoid

If you **avoid** something, you take action to prevent it from happening to you.

...a book on how to avoid a heart attack.
...techniques that will avoid mistakes.

If you **avoid doing** something, you make sure that you do not do it.

Thomas turned his head, trying to avoid breathing in the smoke.
You must avoid giving any unnecessary information.

Note that you do not say that you 'avoid to do' something.

If you cannot control or change the way you behave, you do not say that you 'can't avoid' it. You say that you **can't help** it or that you **can't help yourself.**

It was so crowded, I couldn't help leaning on him a little.
You know what his temper's like, he just can't help himself.

If someone does not allow you to do what you want to do, you do not say that they 'avoid' you doing it. You say that they **prevent** you **from** doing it.

My only idea was to prevent him from speaking.

await

If you **await** something, you expect it to come or happen, and you are often not intending to take some action until it comes or happens.

Daisy had remained behind to await her return.
I shall await the appointment of the tribunal which will clear my name.
We must await the results of field studies yet to come.

Await is a fairly common word in formal writing, but you do not usually use it in conversation. Instead you use **wait for**, often followed by an object and a 'to'-infinitive. For example, instead of saying 'I awaited her reply', you say 'I **waited for her to reply**'.

I waited for Kate to return.
They just waited for me to die.

awake

Awake, wake, awaken, waken, and wake up can all be used as intransitive verbs to say that someone becomes conscious again after being asleep. They can also be used as transitive verbs to say that someone makes you conscious when you have been asleep.

Awake and **wake** are irregular verbs. Their past tenses are **awoke** and **woke**, and their past participles are **awoken** and **woken.**

'awake' and
'wake'
Awake and wake are fairly common in writing, especially as intransitive verbs.

I awoke from a deep sleep.
I sometimes wake at four in the morning.

'awaken' and
'waken'
Awaken and waken are old-fashioned or literary words. They are usually used as transitive verbs.

She was awakened by a loud bang.
When she was asleep nothing wakened her.

'wake up'
In ordinary conversation, you use **wake up.**

...young babies waking up at night and crying.
Ralph, wake up!
They went back to sleep but I woke them up again.

other meanings
You can say that something **awakens** your interest or feelings.

My first visit to a theatre awakened an interest which never left me.
I can only hope to awaken some enthusiasm for my subject.

If you **wake up to** a problem or a dangerous situation, you become aware of it.

The Church must wake up to the financial problems of the clergy.
The West began to wake up to the danger it faced.

'awake' used as
an adjective

Awake can also be used as an adjective. If someone is **awake**, they are not asleep.

An hour later he was still awake.
Lynn stayed awake for a long time.

Awake is usually used after verbs like 'be', 'stay', 'keep', and 'lie', but it can also be used with verbs like 'shake' and 'prod' to say that someone wakes someone else up.

You would have to shake her awake.
Wendy would nudge me awake.

Awake is sometimes used after a noun.

She was the last person awake.
He was walking more like a somnambulist than a person fully awake.

WARNING

You never use **awake** in front of a noun.

You do not say that someone is 'very awake'. You say that they are **wide awake** or **fully awake.**

He was wide awake by the time we reached my flat.
She rose, still not quite fully awake.

award

See entry at **reward - award.**

aware

'aware of'

If you are **aware of** something, you are conscious of it, or you know that it exists.

Ralph was aware of the heat for the first time that day.
People became aware of American jazz.

'familiar with'

If you know or understand something well, you do not say you are 'aware of' it. You say you are **familiar with** it.

I am of course familiar with your work.
...to become familiar with affairs of state.

awful - awfully

'awful'

The adjective **awful** is used in two ways:

In conversation, you use it to say that something is very unpleasant or of very poor quality.

Isn't the weather awful?
Gas smells awful.
The road is awful; narrow and bumpy.

In writing or conversation, you also use **awful** to say that something is very shocking or distressing.

...an account of that awful war.
My husband had an awful death.

'awfully'

The adverb **awfully** is used in a completely different way. It is used in front of an adjective to emphasize that someone or something has a quality to a great extent.

You're an awfully kind person, Dr Marlowe.
I'm awfully sorry.

It's getting <u>awfully</u> dark.

Note that **awfully** is only used in conversation, and is a rather old-fashioned word.

awhile - a while

'awhile' Awhile is an adverb used after a verb. It means 'for a short period of time'.

I may have to stay there <u>awhile</u>.
Can't you just wait <u>awhile</u>?

'a while' A while is an indefinite period of time. You can say that someone does something **for a while** or **after a while**.

For a while it looked as if it might work.
Henze settled on Ischia <u>for a while</u>.
<u>After a while</u>, we drove off.

You can use adjectives such as 'short', 'little', or 'long' in front of **while**.

I'm going to have to leave you on your own for <u>a short while</u>.
...a book that I read <u>a little while</u> ago.

B

back

used with an intransitive verb You use **back** with an intransitive verb to say that someone returns to a place where they were before.

In six weeks we've got to go <u>back</u> to West Africa.
I went <u>back</u> to the kitchen.
I'll come <u>back</u> after dinner.

'be back' In conversation, instead of saying that someone will 'come back', you often say that they will **be back**.

I imagine he'll <u>be back</u> for lunch.
The boys'll <u>be back</u> from chapel any minute.

WARNING You never use **back** with the verb 'return'. You do not say, for example, 'He returned back to his office'. You say 'He **returned** to his office'.

I <u>returned</u> from the Middle East in 1956.

used with a transitive verb You use **back** with a transitive verb to say that someone or something is taken or sent to a place where they were before. **Back** usually goes after the direct object.

We brought <u>Dolly back</u>.
He took <u>the tray back</u>.

When the direct object is a pronoun, **back** always goes after it.

I brought <u>him back</u> to my room.

She put it back on the shelf.

However, when the direct object is a long noun group, or a noun group followed by a relative clause, you put **back** in front of the noun group.

He recently sent back his rented television set.
He put back the silk sock which had fallen out of the drawer.
He went to the market and brought back fresh food which he cooked at home.

returning to a former state

Back can also be used to say that someone or something returns to a state they were in before.

He went back to sleep.
...a £30 million plant which will turn all the waste back into sulphuric acid.

used as a noun

Back is also used as a noun. Your **back** is the part of your body from your neck to your waist that is on the opposite side to your chest and stomach.

We lay on our backs under the ash tree.
She tapped him on the back.

The **back** of an object is the side or part that is towards the rear or farthest from the front.

They trooped down some steps at the back of the building.
Keep some long-life milk at the back of your refrigerator.

The **back** of a door is the side which faces into a room or cupboard.

Pin your food list on the back of the larder door.

The **back** of a piece of paper is the side which has no writing on, or the side which you look at second.

Sign on the back of the prescription form.

Note that you do not talk about the 'back side' of a door or piece of paper.

backwards

If you move or look **backwards,** you move or look in the direction your back is facing.

The hummingbird can fly backwards.
He overbalanced and stepped backwards onto a coffee cup.
The little creature swivels its head through 180 degrees to look directly backwards over its shoulder blades.

If you do something **backwards,** you do it the opposite way to the usual way.

Listen to the tape backwards.

Note that **backwards** is only used as an adverb.

'backward'

Speakers of American English usually say **backward** instead of 'backwards'.

The snout hit Hooper in the chest and knocked him backward.

In both British and American English, **backward** is used as an adjective. A **backward** movement or look is one in which someone or something moves or looks backwards.

She took a backward step.
Without a backward glance, he walked away.

When **backward** is an adjective, it can only be used in front of a noun.

For another meaning of **backward,** see entry at **retarded.**

back yard

See entry at **yard**.

bad - badly

'bad'   Something that is **bad** is unpleasant, harmful, or undesirable.

I have some very bad news.
Candy is bad for your teeth.
The weather was bad.

The comparative and superlative forms of 'bad' are **worse** and **worst**.

Her marks are getting worse and worse.
...the worst thing which ever happened to me.

WARNING   You never use the forms 'badder' and 'baddest'.

'badly'   You do not use **bad** as an adverb. You do not say, for example, 'The Conservatives did bad in the elections'. You say 'The Conservatives did **badly** in the elections'.

I cut myself badly.
The room was so badly lit I couldn't see what I was doing.

When **badly** is used like this, its comparative and superlative forms are **worse** and **worst**.

Some people ski worse than others.
...the worst affected areas.

Badly has another meaning which is quite different. If you need or want something **badly,** you need or want it very much.

We need the money badly.
I want you so badly.
I am badly in need of advice.

For this meaning of **badly,** you do not use the comparative and superlative forms 'worse' and 'worst'. Instead you use the forms **more badly** and **most badly.**

She wanted him more badly than ever.
This is the area that most badly needs the relationship.

Many other words and expressions can be used in a similar way to this meaning of **badly.** For a graded list, see section on **degree** in entry at **Adverbials**.

bag

A **bag** is a container made of paper or plastic which is used to carry things.

...a bag of sugar.
...a plastic bag full of sticky labels.

Note that **a bag of** something can refer either to a bag and its contents, or just to the contents.

When he went to bed he put a bag of salt beside his head.
He ate a whole bag of sweets.

A **bag** is also a container with handles or a strap, which you use to carry things such as shopping.

He was carrying a red shopping bag.

You can refer to a woman's handbag as her **bag.**

She opened her bag and took out a handkerchief.

In American English, pieces of luggage are usually referred to as **bags.** Some British speakers also use **bags** with this meaning.

The porter took her bags.

Most British speakers refer to a large piece of luggage as a **case** or **suitcase.**

The three cases were in the boot.
She arrived dragging and bumping her heavy suitcase.

baggage

See entry at **luggage - baggage.**

bake

See entry at **cook.**

band

A **band** is a narrow strip of material such as cloth or metal which is joined at the ends so that it can be fitted tightly round something.

...a panama hat with a red band.
A man with a black band around his arm stood alone.
Her hair was in a pony tail secured with a rubber band.

'tape' You do not refer to the magnetic strips on which sounds are recorded as 'bands'. You call them **tapes.**

Do you want to put on a tape?
His manager persuaded him to make a tape of the song.

bank

The **bank** of a river or lake is the ground at its edge.

...the river bank.
Leaving her mask and flippers on the bank, she plunged straight into the pool.

A **bank** is also a place where you can keep your money in an account.

You should ask your bank for a loan.

'bench' and Note that you do not refer to a long, narrow seat in a park or garden as a
'seat' 'bank'. You call it a **bench** or a **seat.**

Rudolf sat on the bench and waited.
She sat on a seat on the promenade.

banknote

A **banknote** is a piece of paper money.

Some of the banknotes were unbelievably dirty.

'note' In British English, a banknote is usually referred to as a **note.**

He handed me a ten pound note.

'bill' In American English, a banknote is usually referred to as a **bill.**

He took out a five dollar bill.

For another meaning of **bill,** see entry at **bill - check.**

bar

In American English, a place where you can buy and drink alcoholic drinks is called a **bar.**

Leaving Rita in a bar, I made for the town library.

In British English, a place like this is called a **pub.**

We used to go drinking in a pub called the Soldier's Arms.

See entry at **pub.**

In British English, the rooms in a pub where people drink are called the **bars.** In a hotel, club, or theatre, the place where you can buy and drink alcoholic drinks is also called a **bar.**

...the terrace bar of the Continental Hotel.

bare - barely

'bare'   **Bare** is an adjective. If something is **bare,** it has no covering.

The doctor stood uneasily on the bare floor.
He put his hand on my bare leg.

'barely'   **Barely** is an adverb. It has a totally different meaning from **bare.** You use **barely** to say that something is only just true or possible.

He was so drunk he could barely stand.
The otter was barely two months old.

WARNING   You do not use 'not' with **barely.** You do not say, for example, 'The temperature was not barely above freezing'. You say 'The temperature was **barely** above freezing'.

If you use an auxiliary or modal with **barely,** you put the auxiliary or modal first. You say, for example, 'He **can barely** read'. You do not say 'He barely can read'.

The story of this star had barely begun.
He could barely get his words out.

Barely is sometimes used in longer structures to say that one thing happened immediately after another. For example, you can say 'We had **barely** started the meal when Jane arrived'.

The ship had barely cleared the harbour when an Italian customs cutter raced after her.
I had barely said my name before he had led me to the interview room.

Note that you use **when** or **before** after **barely.** You do not use 'than'. You do not say, for example, 'We had barely started the meal than Jane arrived'.

barrister

See entry at **lawyer.**

bass - base

These words are both pronounced /beɪs/.

'bass'   A **bass** is a male singer who can sing very low notes.

...from the piping choirboys to the sonorous bass.

A **bass** saxophone, guitar, or other musical instrument is one that has a lower range of notes than other instruments of its kind.

The girl vocalist had been joined by the lead and bass guitars.

'base'   The **base** of something is its lowest edge or part.

> *...the switch on the lamp base.*
> *Birds have a large oil-gland near the base of their tail.*

bath - bathe

'bath'   In British English, a **bath** /bɑːθ/ is a long rectangular container which you fill with water and sit in while you wash your body.

> *The bathroom had two basins, a huge bath and more towels than I had ever seen.*

In American English, a container like this is called a **bathtub** or a **tub.**

> *I spent hours in the warmth of the bathtub.*
> *I lowered myself deeper into the tub.*

If you **bath** someone, you wash them in a bath.

> *She will show you how to bath the baby.*
> *We bathed and dried Sandy together.*

You do not say that people **bath** themselves. British speakers say that someone **has a bath.**

> *I'm going to have a bath.*

'bathe'   American speakers say that someone **takes a bath** or, more formally, that they **bathe** /beɪð/.

> *I took a bath, my second that day.*
> *After golf I would return to my apartment to bathe and change.*

Bathe is not used with this meaning in British English. In British English, when someone **bathes,** they swim or play in a lake or river or in the sea.

> *It is dangerous to bathe in the sea here.*

This use of **bathe** is now rather old-fashioned. In modern English, you usually say that someone **goes swimming** or **goes for a swim.** American speakers sometimes say that someone **takes a swim.**

> *She's going for a swim.*
> *I went down to the ocean and took a swim.*

In both British and American English, if you **bathe** a cut or wound, you wash it.

> *He bathed the cuts on her feet.*
> *She had watched her mother bathe his face and bandage his hands.*

Note that 'bath' and 'bathe' both have the present participle **bathing** and the past tense and past participle **bathed.** However, **bathing** and **bathed** are pronounced /bɑːθɪŋ/ and /bɑːθt/ when they relate to 'bath', and /beɪðɪŋ/ and /beɪðd/ when they relate to 'bathe'.

be

Be is the most common verb in English. It is used in many different ways.

The present tense forms of 'be' are **am, are,** and **is,** and the past tense forms are **was** and **were. Be** is used as both an **auxiliary** and a main verb.

> *...a problem which is getting worse.*
> *It was about four o'clock.*

See entry at **Auxiliaries.**

'Am', 'is', and 'are' are not usually pronounced in full. When you write down what someone says, you usually represent 'am' and 'is' using **'m** and **'s**.

I'm sorry,' I said.
'But it's not possible,' Lili said.
'Okay,' he said. 'Your brother's going to take you to Grafton.'

You can also represent 'are' using **'re,** but only after a pronoun.

'We're winning,' he said.

You can also use the forms **'m, 's** and **'re** when you are writing in a conversational style.

See entry at **Contractions.**

used as an auxiliary

Be is used as an auxiliary to form continuous tenses and passives.

She was watching us.
Several apartment buildings were destroyed.

See entry at **Tenses.**

In conversation, **get** is often used to form passives. See entry at **get.**

used as a main verb

You use **be** as a main verb when you are describing things or people or giving information about them. After **be,** you use a **complement.** A complement is either an adjective or a noun group.

We were very happy.
He is now a teenager.

See entry at **Complements.**

indicating someone's job

When **be** is followed by a noun group indicating a unique job or position within an organization, you do not have to put 'the' in front of the noun.

At one time you wanted to be President.

Note that **make** is sometimes used instead of 'be' to say how successful someone is in a particular job or role. For example, instead of saying 'He will be a good president', you can say 'He will **make** a good president'.

indicating age and cost

You can talk about a person's age by using **be** followed by a number.

Rose Gibson is twenty-seven.

You can also use **be** to say how much something costs.

How much is it?
It's five pounds.

For further information, see entries at **Age** and **Money.**

with prepositional phrases

You can use many kinds of prepositional phrase after **be.**

He was still in a state of shock.
I'm from Dortmund originally.
...people who are under pressure.

with 'to'-infinitives

You sometimes use 'to'-infinitive clauses after **be.**

After dinner they were to go to a movie.
Who is to question him?

For further information, see entry at **'To'-infinitive clauses.**

in questions and negative clauses

When you use **be** as a main verb in questions and negative clauses, you do not use the auxiliary 'do'.

Are you O.K?
Is she Rick's sister?
I was not surprised.
It was not an easy task.

in continuous tenses	**Be** is not usually used as a main verb in continuous tenses. However, you can use it in continuous tenses to describe someone's behaviour at a particular time.

You're being very silly.

'be' and 'become'	Do not confuse **be** with **become**. **Be** is used to indicate that someone or something has a particular quality or nature, or is in a particular situation. **Become** is used to indicate that someone or something changes in some way.

Before he became Mayor he had been a tram driver.
It was not until 1845 that Texas became part of the U.S.A.

See entry at **become**.

after 'there'	**Be** is often used after 'there' to indicate the existence or occurrence of something.

There is a rear bathroom with a panelled bath.
There are other possibilities.
There was a brief silence.

WARNING	You cannot use **be** without 'there' to indicate that something exists or happens. You cannot say, for example, 'Another explanation is' or 'Another explanation must be'. You must say '**There is** another explanation' or '**There must be** another explanation'. See entry at **there**.

after 'it'	**Be** is often used after 'it' to describe something such as an experience, or to comment on a situation.

It was very quiet in the hut.
It was awkward keeping my news from Ted.
It's strange you should come today.

See entry at **it**.

'have been'	If you have visited a place and have now come back from it, British speakers say that you **have been** there.

I have been to Santander many times.

See entry at **go**.

be able to

See entry at **can - could - be able to**.

beach - shore - coast

'beach'	A **beach** is an area of sand or pebbles next to the sea or a lake. You can relax or play on a beach, or use it as a place to swim from.

He wandered off along the beach.

'shore'	The **shore** of a sea, lake, or wide river is the land along its edge. The **shore** can be smooth and sandy or very rocky.

...the waves breaking against the shore.

'coast'	The **coast** is the border between the land and the sea, or the part of a country that is next to the sea.

He landed on the coast of South Carolina.
...the industrial cities of the coast.

bear

Bear is one of several verbs which can be used to talk about people experiencing unpleasant situations. The other forms of 'bear' are **bears, bore, borne.**

You use **bear** in positive sentences when you are talking about a very unpleasant situation. Typically, you talk about someone **bearing** pain or hardship, meaning that they accept it in a brave way.

It was painful, of course, but he bore it.
Peter bore this with a sort of humble patience.

'endure'　**Endure** is used in a similar way.

You must be ready to endure hardships and even death.

'can't bear'　**Bear** is often used in negative sentences. If you say that you cannot **bear** something or someone, you mean that they are so annoying or irritating that you do not want to be involved with them in any way.

I couldn't bear staying in the same town as that man.
I can't bear him!

'can't stand'　**Stand** is used in a similar way.

He kept on nagging and I couldn't stand it any longer.
She said she couldn't stand him.

'tolerate' and 'put up with'　If you **tolerate** or **put up with** something, you accept it, although you do not like it or approve of it.

...the tendency to tolerate extremes of human behaviour.
The local people have to put up with gaping tourists.

bear - bare

These words are both pronounced /beə/.

'bear'　**Bear** is used as a noun or a verb.

A **bear** is a large, strong wild animal with thick fur and sharp claws.

The bear reared on its hind legs.

If you **bear** a difficult situation, you accept it and are able to deal with it.

This disaster was more than some of them could bear.

See entry at **bear.**

To **bear** something also means to carry or support it. This is a fairly formal use.

His ankle now felt strong enough to bear his weight.

'bare'　**Bare** is usually used as an adjective. Something that is **bare** has no covering.

...her bare feet.
The walls were bare.

See entry at **bare - barely.**

beat

If you **beat** someone or something, you hit them several times very hard.

His stepfather used to beat him.

The past tense of 'beat' is **beat,** not 'beated'. The past participle is **beaten.**

The rain beat against the window.

Helmuth had been <u>beaten</u> severely by the gamekeeper.

If you **beat** someone in a game, you defeat them.

Arsenal <u>beat</u> Oxford United 5-1.

beautiful

The following words can all be used to describe someone who is nice to look at:

attractive	good-looking	handsome	stunning
beautiful	gorgeous	pretty	

Attractive, good-looking, and **gorgeous** are commonly used to describe both women and men.

...a remarkably <u>attractive</u> girl.
You're still an <u>attractive</u> man.

She was a <u>good-looking</u> woman of fifty, with naturally red cheeks and a Scots accent.
He was a very <u>good-looking</u> lad with a fine physique.

She's <u>gorgeous</u>.
...this <u>gorgeous</u> young hunk of male flesh.

Attractive and **gorgeous** are also used to describe young children, but **good-looking** is not.

She had grown into a chubby <u>attractive</u> child, with a mop of auburn curls like her mother's.

Handsome is used more often to describe men than women. It is used to describe any man who has regular, pleasant features. However, it is only used to describe women when their features are large and regular rather than small and delicate.

He was a tall, dark, and undeniably <u>handsome</u> man.
In the 1930's the ideal woman was classically <u>handsome</u> rather than childishly pretty.

Beautiful and **pretty** are generally used to describe women and children rather than men. Only very young boys are described as **pretty,** not older boys, because this word implies a delicate, feminine appearance.

...a <u>beautiful</u> young girl with long hair.
Our mother was laughing and looking <u>pretty</u> and happy.
'Such a <u>pretty</u> baby,' clucked Mrs Morrison.

You can also describe a woman as **stunning**, especially when she has made herself look particularly attractive or is wearing very attractive clothes.

Though her features were strong, she was not unattractive and might have been quite <u>stunning</u> had she taken even a mild interest in clothes.

degree of beauty If you say that someone is **beautiful,** you are implying that they are nicer to look at than if you said they were **attractive, good-looking, handsome,** or **pretty.** If you say that someone is **gorgeous** or **stunning,** you mean that they are extremely nice to look at.

WARNING You can describe someone's appearance by saying that they 'look nice' or 'look wonderful', but if you call someone 'a nice man' or 'a wonderful woman', or say that they 'are nice' or 'are wonderful', you are describing their character, not their appearance. Similarly, 'lovely' is more often used to describe someone's character than their appearance.

because

You use **because** when you are giving the reason for something.

If someone asks a question beginning with 'Why?', you can reply using **because.**

'Why shouldn't I come?'—'Because you're too busy.'

If you have said that something is the case and you want to say why it is the case, you usually add a reason clause beginning with **because.**

I couldn't see Helen's expression, because her head was turned.
Rudolph's father did the shopping, because, he said, his wife was extravagant.

'as' and 'since'   In writing, the reason clause is sometimes put first, and **as** or **since** is used instead of 'because'.

As the gorilla is so big and powerful, it has no real enemies.
Since evaporated milk is about twice the strength of fresh milk, you always dilute it with at least an equal amount of water.

WARNING   When you use **as** or **since** at the beginning of a sentence, you do not put an expression such as 'that is why' at the beginning of the second clause. You do not say, for example, 'As you have been very ill yourself, that is why you will understand how I feel'. You simply say 'As you have been very ill yourself, **you will understand** how I feel'.

If you want to say that there is a special reason for something, you can use words like 'especially' or 'particularly' in front of **as** or **since.** When you do this, you put the reason clause after the main clause.

I was frightened when I went to bed, especially as my room was so far up.
It was nice to have someone to talk to, particularly as it looked as if I was going to be there all night.

'for'   In stories, **for** is sometimes used instead of 'because'. This is an old-fashioned use.

This was where he spent a great deal of his free time for he had nowhere else to go.
His two older sisters slept downstairs, for they had to be up first.

'because of'   Sometimes you use a noun group instead of a clause when you are mentioning the reason for something. When you do this, you put **because of** in front of the noun group.

President Gorbachov's visit was postponed because of the earthquake in Armenia.
Because of the heat, the front door was open.

become

When something or someone **becomes** a particular thing, they start being that thing.

When you feed a current through the coil, it becomes a magnet.
Anybody can become a qualified teacher.

The past tense of 'become' is **became,** not 'becomed'.

We became good friends at once.
The smell became stronger and stronger.

The past participle is **become.**

Would you say that life has become a lot easier for you?

The notion had become very popular in the United States.

When **become** is followed by a singular noun group, the noun group usually begins with a determiner.

Portugal became a colonial power.
I became a construction engineer.
...the aristocratic young man who becomes his friend.

However, when the noun group refers to a unique job or position within an organization, the determiner can be omitted.

In 1960 he became Ambassador to Hungary.
He went on to become head of one of the company's largest divisions.

The following words can be used to mean 'become'. Note that these words can only be followed by an adjective. You do not use a noun group after them.

'get'   **Get** is very often used to mean 'become'. In conversation, you usually say **get** rather than 'become'.

It was getting dark.
She began to get suspicious.
If things get any worse, you'll have to come home.

'grow'   In written English, **grow** is sometimes used to mean 'become'. You use **grow** to say that someone or something gradually changes to a particular state or condition.

Some of her ministers are growing impatient.
The sun grew so hot that they were forced to stop working.

'come'   **Come** can be used with 'loose' or 'unstuck' to say that something gradually becomes loose or unstuck.

Waterproof sheets should be pinned or tied down at all corners so that they will not come loose.
Some of the posters came unstuck.

If a dream, wish, or prediction **comes true,** it actually happens.

My wish had come true.

'go' and 'turn'   Sometimes you use **go** or **turn** to mean 'become'. If you want to say that something becomes a different colour, you use **go** or **turn.**

Her hair was going grey.
The grass had turned brown.

If you want to say that a person's face suddenly changes colour, you use **go** or **turn.** For example, you say that someone **goes** or **turns** pale.

Ralph went crimson.
He turned bright red.
Colonel Williams gaped, then flushed, then went absolutely white.

Note that you do not say that someone 'gets pale' or 'becomes pale'.

If you want to say that someone feels a sudden change in their body, you use **go.**

I went numb.
He went cold all over.
Their mouths went dry.

You use **go** to say that something suddenly becomes slack or limp.

The rope went slack.

He went as limp as an armful of wet laundry.

If you want to say that someone becomes blind or deaf, you usually use **go.**

She was bedridden and going blind.

If you want to say that someone becomes mad, or starts behaving as if they are mad, you use **go.**

His sister went insane.
He went raving mad.
Uncle Nick went wild with excitement.

There are also several expressions in which **go** is used to mean 'become'. For example, you say that a plan or scheme 'goes wrong' or 'goes awry', that a telephone 'goes dead', or that someone's mind 'goes blank'.

In some expressions, **go** is used to say that a person or organization changes their legal status. For example, you say that someone 'goes bankrupt', that a company 'goes public', or that a school 'goes comprehensive'.

before

indicating time
If something happens **before** a time or event, it happens earlier than that time or event.

We arrived just before two o'clock.
It was just before Christmas.
Before the First World War, farmers used to use horses instead of tractors.

You also use **before** when you are talking about the past and you want to refer to an earlier period of time. For example, if you are describing events that took place in 1986, you refer to 1985 as 'the year **before**'.

The two had met in Bonn the weekend before.
The quarrel of the night before seemed forgotten.

You use **before last** to refer to a period of time that came before the last one of its kind. For example, if today is Wednesday 18th September, you refer to Friday 13th September as 'last Friday', and Friday 6th September as 'the Friday **before last**'.

We met them on a camping holiday the year before last.
'When did he arrive?'—'The afternoon before last.'

indicating position
Before is sometimes used to mean 'in front of'. This is a formal or old-fashioned use.

He stood before the panelled door leading to the cellar.
The tea had been set before them.

When someone has to appear in a court of law, you can say that they are brought **before** the judge or magistrate.

All three had been taken before a magistrate.

When a proposal is being considered by a parliament, you can say that it is **before** the parliament.

...the Legal Services Bill now before Parliament.

You also use **before** or **in front of** when you are talking about the order in which things appear in speech or writing. For example, if you are describing the spelling of the word 'friend', you can say that the letter 'i' comes **before** or **in front of** the letter 'e'.

If the verb is 'be', 'certainly' can come either <u>before</u> or after the verb.
You can put 'both' immediately <u>in front of</u> a single noun group when it
refers to two people or things.

begin

See entry at **start - begin - commence.**

behaviour

Someone's **behaviour** is the way they behave.

I had been puzzled by his <u>behaviour</u>.
...the obstinate <u>behaviour</u> of a small child.

Note that **behaviour** is an uncount noun. You do not talk about 'behaviours'
or 'a behaviour'.

Note also that the American spelling of this word is **behavior.**

behind

used as a preposition

If you are **behind** something, you are near the part of it that is considered
to be its back.

They parked the motorcycle <u>behind</u> some bushes.
Just <u>behind</u> the cottage was a sort of shed.

WARNING

You do not use 'of' after **behind.** You do not say, for example, 'They parked
the motorcycle behind of some bushes'.

used as an adverb

Behind can also be used as an adverb.

The sun was almost directly <u>behind</u>.
I walked on <u>behind</u>, kicking up the dead leaves.

believe

If you **believe** a person or **believe** what they say, you accept that what they
say is true.

He knew I didn't <u>believe him</u>.
It all sounded so straightforward that I <u>believed it</u> myself.
Don't <u>believe a word he says</u>.

If you **believe** that something is the case, you think that it is the case.

I <u>believe</u> some of those lakes are over a hundred feet deep.
China makes you <u>believe</u> that everything is possible.

Instead of saying that you 'believe that something is not' the case, you
usually say that you **don't believe that it is** the case.

He <u>didn't believe that was the reason</u>.
I just <u>don't believe that Allen or you had anything to do with Stryker's</u>
<u>death</u>.

Believe can be followed by an object and a 'to'-infinitive. For example,
instead of saying 'I believed that she was clever', you can say 'I **believed
her to be** clever'. This is a rather formal use.

I <u>believed him to be</u> right.
He still <u>believed himself to be</u> a failure.

Similarly, you can say either that **it is believed that** something is the case, or that something **is believed to** be the case. For example, you can say 'It **is believed that** the building is 700 years old' or 'The building **is believed to** be 700 years old'.

It is believed that two prisoners have escaped.
The automobile is widely believed to have changed our cities.
...drugs which were believed to expand the consciousness.

WARNING   **Believe** is not used in continuous tenses, even when you are talking about something which is happening now. You do not say, for example, 'I am believing you'. You say 'I **believe** you'.

I believe you have to look at the positive side of things.
I believe that these findings should be fairly presented to your readers.

If someone asks you if something is the case, you can say 'I **believe so**'.

'Is it to rent?'—'I believe so.'

Note that when you are asked if something is the case, you do not say 'I believe it'.

'believe in'   If you **believe in** God or in such things as ghosts or Father Christmas, you think that they exist. If you **believe in** such things as miracles, you think that they happen.

I don't believe in ghosts.
Only 29 per cent of the population believe in a personal God.

If you **believe in** an idea or policy, you are in favour of it because you think it is good or right, or will have the desired result.

Socialists believe in liberty.
You don't really believe in freedom.

belong

If something **belongs to** you, you own it or it is yours.

Everything you see here belongs to me.
You can't take the cart home because it belongs to Harry.

When **belong** is used with this meaning, it must be followed by 'to'. You do not say, for example, 'This bag belongs me'. You say 'This bag **belongs to** me'.

WARNING   **Belong** is not used in continuous tenses. You do not say, for example, 'This money is belonging to my sister'. You say 'This money **belongs to** my sister'.

The flat belongs to a man called Jimmy Roland.
One of the rooms belongs to my niece, Judy.

another meaning of 'belong'   You can also use **belong** to say where someone or something ought to be. After **belong** you use an adverbial such as 'here', 'over there', or 'in the next room'.

I don't belong here, mother. I'm not like you.
The plates don't belong in that cupboard.

below

See entry at **under - below - beneath**.

beneath

See entry at **under - below - beneath**.

beside - besides

'beside'   If one thing is **beside** another, it is next to it or at the side of it.

Beside the shed was a huge wire birdcage.
I sat down beside my wife.

'besides'
used as a
preposition   **Besides** means 'in addition to' or 'as well as'.

What languages do you know besides Arabic and English?
The farm possessed three horses besides Clover.
Then you can make something else besides bombs?

'besides' used to
link clauses   You can use **besides** to introduce a non-finite clause beginning with an '-ing' form. For example, you can say 'He writes novels and poems, **besides working** for the BBC'. Note that you do not say 'He writes novels and poems besides he works for the BBC'.

Education must sow the seeds of wisdom, besides implanting knowledge and skills.
Besides being good company, he was always ready to have a go at anything.

'besides' used
as an adverb   **Besides** can also mean 'in addition to the thing just mentioned'.

He needed so much else besides.

You can also use **besides** when you are making an additional point or giving an additional reason which you think is important.

Would these figures prove anything? And besides, who keeps such statistics?

best

Best is the superlative form of both 'good' and 'well'. See entry at **good - well**.

If you **do your best**, you try as hard as you can to achieve something. See entry at **do**.

bet

If you **bet** on a future event, you make an agreement with someone which means that you receive money if you are right about what happens, and lose money if you are wrong. The past tense and past participle of 'bet' is **bet**, not 'betted'.

He bet me a hundred pounds that I wouldn't get through.

better

Better is the comparative form of both 'good' and 'well'. You do not say that something is 'more good' or is done 'more well'. You say that it is **better** or is done **better**.

The results were better than expected.
Milk is much better for you than lemonade.

Some people can ski better than others.
We are better housed than ever before.

You can use words such as 'even', 'far', 'a lot', and 'much' in front of **better**.

This wise old gentleman knew him even better than Annette did.

I decided that it would be <u>far better</u> just to wait.
I like it <u>a lot better</u> than asparagus.
I always <u>feel much better</u> after it.

another
meaning of
'better'

Better is also used to say that someone has recovered from an illness or injury.

Her cold was <u>better</u>.
I hope you'll be <u>better</u> soon.

'had better'

If you say that someone **had better** do something, you mean that they ought to do it. **Had better** is always followed by an infinitive without 'to'.

I <u>had better</u> introduce myself.
I'<u>d better</u> go.

WARNING

In standard English, you must use **had** in sentences like these. You do not say 'I better introduce myself' or 'I better go'.

In negative sentences, 'not' goes after **had better**.

I'<u>d better not</u> let her go.

WARNING

In standard English, you do not say that someone 'hadn't better' do something.

'better still'

You use **better still** when you are mentioning something you have just thought of which is an improvement on something else that has been mentioned.

How about some Bach to begin with? Or, <u>better still</u>, Vivaldi?
<u>Better still</u>, we can compare the earnings of both single and married men and women.

'rather'

You do not use **better** on its own when you are correcting a mistake you have made, or when you think of a more appropriate word than one you have just used. You do not say, for example, 'Suddenly there stood before him, or better above him, a gigantic woman'. You say 'Suddenly there stood before him, or **rather** above him, a gigantic woman'.

One picture speaks volumes. Or <u>rather</u> lies volumes.

between

describing
position

If something is **between** two things, it has one of the things on one side of it and the other thing on the other side of it.

The revolver lay <u>between</u> the two bodies.
The island of Santa Catarina is roughly midway <u>between</u> São Paulo and Porto Alegre.

You can also say that someone puts something **between** two things.

She put the cigarette <u>between</u> her lips and lit it.

WARNING

You do not usually say that something is **between** several things. You say that it is **among** them. See entry at **among**.

differences

You talk about a difference **between** two things or people.

I asked him whether there was much difference <u>between</u> British and European law.

choosing

When someone makes a choice, you say that they choose **between** two things or people.

It was difficult to choose <u>between</u> Hobson and the other British finalist, Peter Donohoe.

You say that someone chooses between one thing or person **and** another.

They must choose between home-ownership <u>and</u> furnished renting.

beware

If you tell someone to **beware** of a person or thing, you are warning them that the person or thing may harm them.

Beware of the dog.
I would beware of companies which depend on one product only.

Beware is only used as an imperative or infinitive. It does not have any other forms such as 'bewares', 'bewaring', or 'bewared'.

bid

If you **bid** for something that is being sold, you offer to pay a particular amount of money for it. When **bid** has this meaning, its past tense and past participle is **bid**.

He bid a quarter of a million pounds for the portrait.

People used to use **bid** with expressions like 'good day' and 'farewell'. This use still occurs sometimes in stories. When **bid** has this meaning, its past tense is either **bid** or **bade** and its past participle is either **bid** or **bidden.**

The old woman brought him his coffee and shyly bid him a goodbye.
We bade her farewell.

Tom had bid her a good evening.
We had bidden them good night.

'say' In modern English, you use **say** instead of 'bid' in sentences like these.

I said good evening to them.
Gertrude had already had her supper and had said good night to Guy.

However, when you use **say,** the indirect object goes after the direct object. You do not say 'I said them good evening'.

big - large - great

Big, large, and **great** are used to talk about size. They can all be used in front of count nouns, but only **great** can be used in front of uncount nouns.

describing objects **Big, large,** and **great** can all be used to describe objects. **Big** is the word you usually use in conversation. **Large** is more formal. **Great** is used in stories to indicate that something is very impressive because of its size.

'Where?'—'Over there, by that big tree.'
A leopard frequently retreats to a large tree when it has made a kill.
A great tree had fallen across one corner.

describing amounts You use **large** or **great** to describe amounts.

She made a very large amount of money.
...drugs taken in large quantities.
Young people consume great quantities of chips.

You do not use 'big' to describe amounts.

describing feelings When you are describing feelings or reactions, you usually use **great.**

I was full of great expectations.
To my great astonishment she started to tell me about how she had first seen him.

When 'surprise' is a count noun, you can use either **big** or **great** in front of it.

The fact that the Government's policy does not make sense should not come as a big surprise.

It comes as a great surprise to me that the Department is about to issue a document concerning archaeology.

You do not use 'large' to describe feelings or reactions.

talking about qualities

When you are talking about qualities, you use **great**.

...little girls who may or may not turn into adults of great beauty.
The book brought back those early days of the war with great clarity.

You do not use 'big' or 'large' to talk about qualities.

describing problems

When you are describing a problem or danger, you use **big** or **great**.

The biggest problem at the moment is unemployment.
The greater the threat, the less tolerance there can be.

You do not usually use 'large' to describe a problem or danger.

indicating importance

Great is also used to say that a person or place is important or famous.

...one of the greatest engineers of this century.
...the great cities of the Rhineland.

used with other adjectives

In conversation, you can use **great** and **big** together, or you can use either **great** or **big** with another adjective of size. You do this to emphasize the size of something. When you use **great** and **big** together, you always put **great** first.

...a great big gaping hole.
...somewhere out there in the big wide world.
...an enormous great grin.

You do not use adjectives of size together like this in formal writing.

For a list of adjectives which are used to describe how large or small something is, see entry at **small - large**.

WARNING

You can say that someone is in **great** pain, but you do not usually use **big**, **large**, or **great** to describe an illness. Instead you use adjectives such as **bad**, **terrible**, or **severe**.

The child has a bad cold with fever.
Neither of us had any sign of the terrible headaches that some people get.
The child is then likely to develop a severe anaemia.

bill - check

In British English, a **bill** is a piece of paper showing how much money you owe for a meal in a restaurant.

Two women at the next table paid their bill and walked out.

In American English, a piece of paper like this is called a **check**.

He waved to a waiter and got the check.

For another meaning of **check**, see entry at **cheque - check**.

In American English, a **bill** is a piece of paper money. See entry at **banknote**.

billfold

See entry at **wallet**.

billion

A **billion** is a thousand million, or 1,000,000,000.

In January 1977, there were 4 billion people in the world.

In Britain, some people use **billion** to refer to a million million, or 1,000,000,000,000.

bit

'a bit'   **A bit** means 'to a small extent or degree'.

The balance sheet is a bit like an end-of-term school report.
He was a bit deaf.
The bunch of poppies was getting a bit droopy.
You're doing it a bit better now.
Tonight he has been a bit naughty.

Note that you cannot use **a bit** with an adjective when the adjective is in front of a noun. You do not say, for example, 'He was a bit deaf man'.

Many other words and expressions can be used in a similar way to **a bit.** For graded lists, see section on **degree** in entry at **Adverbials** and section on **submodifiers** in entry at **Adverbs.**

'a bit of'   In conversation, you can use **a bit of** in front of 'a' and a noun. You do this to make a statement seem less extreme.

Our room was a bit of a mess too.
This question comes as a bit of a shock at first.

'a bit' with   You can add **a bit** at the end of a negative statement to make it more
negatives   strongly negative.

I don't like this a bit.
She hadn't changed a bit.

'not a bit'   You can use **not a bit** in front of an adjective to emphasize that someone or something does not have a particular quality. For example, if you say you are **not a bit** hungry, you mean you are not hungry at all.

They're not a bit interested.
I've found everyone so friendly, but not a bit inquisitive.

'for a bit'   **For a bit** means 'for a short period of time'.

She was silent for a bit.
Why can't we stay here for a bit?

Bit is also the past tense of 'bite'. See entry at **bite.**

bite

When a person or animal **bites** something, they use their teeth to cut into it or through it. The past tense of 'bite' is **bit,** not 'bited'. The past participle is **bitten.**

My dog bit me.
You are quite liable to get bitten by an eel.

blame

If you **blame** someone for something bad that has happened, you say or think that they are responsible for it.

The rest of the family blamed her for indirectly causing Sonny's death.
I was blamed for the theft.

'to blame'   If someone is **to blame** for something bad that has happened, they are responsible for it.

It was a terrible failure for which I knew I was partly to blame.
Mr Walters is not to blame for Mr Warrender's humiliation.
Huge budget deficits were partly to blame for the high levels of interest rates.

'fault'
You do not say that something is someone's 'blame'. You say that it is their **fault.**

It's not my fault.
This was all Jack's fault.
It's all the fault of a girl called Sarah.

'at fault'
If someone is **at fault,** they have made a mistake which has undesirable consequences.

We failed to explain that to the public and we are at fault in that.

Note that you do not say that someone is 'in fault'.

blind

Blind can be used as an adjective, a verb, or a noun.

used as an
adjective
If someone is **blind,** they cannot see, because there is something wrong with their eyes.

He is ninety-four years of age and he is blind, deaf, and bad-tempered.

Note that you do not say that 'someone's eyes are blind'.

used as a verb
If something **blinds** you, it makes you blind.

The acid went on her face and blinded her.

If something **blinds** you to a situation, it prevents you from being aware of it. This is the most common use of the verb **blind.**

We have to beware that missionary zeal doesn't blind us to the realities here.

used as a noun
You can refer to all the blind people in a country as **the blind.**

What do you think of the help that's given to the blind?

A **blind** is a wide roll of cloth or paper which you can pull down over a window in order to keep the light out, or to prevent people from looking in.

She slammed the window shut and pulled the blind.

In American English, a device like this is sometimes called a **shade** or **window shade.**

blow up

See entries at **explode** and **inflate.**

board

If you **board** a bus, train, plane, or ship, you get on it or into it.

Griffiths took a taxi to the Town station and boarded a train there.
Decker boarded another ship, the Panama.

'on board'
When you are **on board** a bus, train, plane, or ship, you are on it or in it.

He ran out of the bar, not stopping until he was on board a city bus.
The scarf belonged to somebody on board the Scarborough.

WARNING
You do not use 'of' after **on board.** You do not say, for example, 'It belonged to somebody on board of the Scarborough'.

boat - ship

'boat'
A **boat** is a small vessel for travelling on water, especially one that carries only a few people.

John took me down the river in the old boat.
...a fishing boat.

'ship' A larger vessel is usually referred to as a **ship**.

The ship was due to sail the following morning.

However, in conversation large passenger ships which travel short distances are sometimes called **boats**.

She was getting off at Hamburg to take the boat to Stockholm.

WARNING When you are describing the way in which someone travels, you do not say that they travel 'by the boat' or 'by the ship'. You say that they travel **by boat** or **by ship**.

We are going by boat.
They were sent home by ship.

bog

See entry at **marsh - bog - swamp**.

bonnet - hood

In British English, the metal cover over the engine of a car is called the **bonnet**. In American English, it is called the **hood**.

I unlocked the boot and laid the tools on the bonnet.
...the raised hood, under which I had bent to watch the mechanic at work.

other meanings Both **bonnet** and **hood** have other meanings:

A baby's **bonnet** is a hat which ties under the baby's chin.

A **hood** is part of a coat, jacket, or cloak which you can pull up over your head to protect you from bad weather.

boot - trunk

In British English, the **boot** of a car is the space at the back or front where you put luggage or other things. In American English, this part of a car is called the **trunk**.

Is the boot open?
Each car had been carrying a large supply of gasoline in the trunk.

other meanings Both **boot** and **trunk** have other meanings:

A **boot** is a kind of heavy shoe.

A **trunk** is a large case or box with strong, rigid sides.

The **trunk** of a tree is the large main stem from which the branches grow.

border

The **border** between two countries is the dividing line between them.

They crossed the border into Mexico.
...the German-Polish border.

'frontier' You refer to a border as a **frontier** when it is guarded and separates countries which have different political systems or are in dispute about something.

The distance to the frontier is no more than 15 kilometres.
...India's frontier problems.

You talk about one country's border or frontier **with** another.

...the steel mesh and barbed wire fence that marks the <u>border with</u> mainland China.
Spain reopened its <u>frontier with</u> Gibraltar.

'boundary' The **boundary** of an area of land is its outer edge. You can talk about the **boundary** of a region or local administrative area.

You have to stay within your county <u>boundary.</u>
...the <u>boundary</u> of the Snowdonia National Park.

WARNING You do not talk about the 'boundary' of a country. Instead you talk about its **borders.**

...the <u>borders</u> of Turkey.
Meanwhile, along Afghanistan's <u>borders,</u> matters are no less confused.

bore

Bore is a verb, and it is also the past tense of the verb 'bear'. See entry at **bear.**

If something or someone **bores** you, you do not find them interesting, and you do not want to concern yourself with them any longer.

His brand of conservatism <u>bores</u> many of his countrymen.
There had been a time when they enjoyed his company, but now he <u>bored</u> them.

'bored' You can say that you are **bored with** something or someone.

Tom was <u>bored with</u> the film.
They never seem to get <u>bored with</u> each other.

'boring' Do not confuse **bored** with **boring**. If you say that something is **boring**, you mean that it bores you.

Was it a <u>boring</u> journey?
...all those <u>boring</u> evenings with people I never wanted to see.

born - borne

Both these words are pronounced /bɔːn/.

'born' When a baby **is born,** it comes out of its mother's body at the beginning of its life.

They are given names when they <u>are born.</u>

You often say that a person **was born** at a particular time or in a particular place.

Caro <u>was born</u> on April 10th.
Mary <u>was born</u> in Glasgow in 1899.

WARNING You do not say that someone 'has been born' at a particular time or in a particular place.

'borne' If something **is borne** somewhere, it is carried there. **Borne** is the past participle of the verb 'bear'.

The image of the Virgin <u>was borne</u> into the piazza on a high litter.

borrow - lend

If you **borrow** something that belongs to someone else, you take it, with or without their permission, intending to return it.

Could I <u>borrow</u> your car?
I <u>have borrowed</u> my father's wire-cutters from the tool shed.

If you **lend** something you own to someone else, you allow them to have it or use it for a period of time.

I often lend her money.
One of the grandest paintings in England has been lent to the National Gallery.

Note that you do not normally talk about borrowing or lending things that cannot move. You do not say, for example, 'Can I borrow your garage next week?' You say 'Can I **use** your garage next week?'

He wants to use the phone.

Similarly, you do not usually say 'He lent me his office'. You say 'He **let me use** his office'.

She brought them thermoses of coffee and let them use her bath.

bosom

See entry at **breast**.

both

When you link two word groups using 'and', you can put **both** in front of the first word group for emphasis. For example, if you want to emphasize that what you are saying applies to each of two things or people, you put **both** in front of the first of two noun groups.

By that time both Robin and Drew were overseas.
Both she and Dixon were completely safe.
Both Islam and Hinduism are world religions.
They feel both anxiety and joy.

Similarly you can put **both** in front of the first of two adjectives, verb groups, or adverbials.

Herbs are both beautiful and useful.
These headlines both mystified and infuriated him.
What is shattered, I suspect, is morale, both at the front and at home.

The word group after **both** should be of the same type as the word group after 'and'. For example, you say 'I told **both** Richard **and** George'. You do not say 'I both told Richard and George'.

used with one noun group

You can put **both** immediately in front of a single noun group when it refers to two people or things. For example, you can say '**Both boys** were Hungarian'. You can also say '**Both the boys** were Hungarian' or '**Both of the boys** were Hungarian'. There is no difference in meaning.

...the assassination of both Kennedy brothers.
Both the kings under whom he served had financial difficulties.
Both of the diplomats blushed when the company thanked them.

WARNING

Note that you do not say 'Both of boys were Hungarian' or 'The both boys were Hungarian'. You also do not use 'two' after **both**. You do not say 'Both the two boys were Hungarian'.

You can use either **both** or **both of** in front of noun groups beginning with 'these', 'those', or a possessive determiner.

The answer to both these questions is 'yes'.
Both of these houses were described by Aubrey.

I've got both their addresses.
Both of their homes are built near the sea.

used in front of pronouns	You can also use **both** or **both of** in front of the pronouns 'these' and 'those'.

Both these are almost impossible to calculate in financial terms.
Both of these are at the southeastern corner of the Square.

However, in front of personal pronouns you must use **both of**.

This plan of yours is certain to lead to unhappiness for both of you.
Luca was too strong for both of them.

You do not use 'we' or 'they' after **both of**. Instead you use 'us' or 'them'.

Both of us went to Balliol College, Oxford.
Both of them were admitted to Michael's house by one of the bodyguards.

used after the subject	**Both** can also be used after the subject of a sentence. For example, instead of saying 'Both my sisters came', you can say 'My sisters **both** came'. When there is no auxiliary, **both** goes in front of the verb, unless the verb is 'be'.

They both got into the boat.
We both love dancing.
Tony and Nigel both laughed noisily.

If the verb is 'be', **both** goes after 'be'.

They were both schoolteachers.
We were both there.

If there is an auxiliary, you put **both** after it.

Shearson Lehman and James Capel have both expressed an interest.
They have both had a good sleep.
Mark, we're both talking rubbish.

If there is more than one auxiliary, you put **both** after the first one.

They shall both be put to death.

Both can also come after a personal pronoun when the pronoun is the direct or indirect object of the verb.

The commissioners looked curiously at them both.
Mrs Bond is coming over to see us both next week.

negative sentences	You do not usually use **both** in negative sentences. For example, you do not say 'Both his students were not there'. You say '**Neither of** his students was there'. See entry at **neither**.

Similarly, you do not say 'I didn't see both of them'. You say 'I didn't see **either of** them'. See entry at **either**.

used as a pronoun	**Both** can also be used as a pronoun.

A child should be receiving either meat or eggs daily, preferably both.
Both were desperately in love with Violet.

WARNING	You do not use **both** to talk about more than two things or people. Instead you use **all**. See entry at **all**.

bottom

Your **bottom** is the part of your body that you sit on. You can use **bottom** in conversation and in most kinds of writing.

Her bottom was pressed firmly against the wall.

'buttocks'	In formal writing, you refer to this part of your body as your **buttocks**.

...the muscles on his shoulders and buttocks.

'bum' and 'butt'   In conversation, some British speakers say **bum** instead of 'bottom', and some American speakers say **butt**. It is best to avoid both these words as many people think they are impolite.

boundary

See entry at **border**.

box-car

See entry at **carriage**.

brackets

See entry at **Punctuation**.

brake

See entry at **break - brake**.

brand

A **brand** of a product is the version made by one particular manufacturer. You usually use **brand** to talk about foods, or about other products which do not last for a long time.

There used to be so many different brands of tea.
The cheapest detergents are Surf and Tide, which should sell at 20 per cent cheaper than other brands.

Do not confuse **brand** with **make**. You use **make** to talk about products such as machines or cars, which last for a long time. See entry at **make**.

break - brake

These words are both pronounced /breɪk/.

'break'   If you **break** something, you damage it badly, usually by hitting it or dropping it so that it divides into two or more pieces.

I tried to break the porthole, but with no success.
She will spank her child for breaking a cup.

The past tense of 'break' is **broke,** not 'breaked'. The past participle is **broken**.

She stepped backwards onto a cup, which broke into several pieces.
He has broken a window with a ball.

See entry at **broken**.

Note that several other words can be used with a similar meaning to **break**. See entry at **damage**.

'brake'   A **brake** is a device on a vehicle which makes it slow down or stop.

He took his foot off the brake.

Brake is also used as a verb. When a vehicle or its driver **brakes,** the driver makes the vehicle slow down or stop by using the brake or brakes.

The taxi braked to a halt.

breakfast

Your **breakfast** is your first meal of the day. You eat it in the morning, just after you get up.

They had hard-boiled eggs for breakfast.
I open the mail immediately after breakfast.

See entry at **Meals**.

breast

A woman's **breasts** are the two soft, round pieces of flesh on her chest that can produce milk to feed a baby.

...a beggar girl with a baby at her breast.
...women with small breasts.

'bust' A woman's breasts can be referred to as her **bust,** especially when you are talking about their size. Note that **bust** refers to both breasts together. You do not talk about a woman's 'busts'.

She has a very large bust.

Bust is also used to talk about the measurement around the top part of a woman's body at the level of her breasts.

'Bust 34' means that the garment is a size 12.

'bosom' A woman's breasts can also be referred to as her **bosom** /bʊzəm/. This is an old-fashioned or literary word.

...hugging the cat to her bosom.

breathe - breath

'breathe' **Breathe** /briːð/ is a verb. When people or animals **breathe,** they take air into their lungs and let it out again.

It was difficult for him to breathe.
I stood by the window and breathed deeply.

'breath' **Breath** /breθ/ is a noun. Your **breath** is the air which you take into your lungs and let out again when you breathe.

Piggy let out his breath with a gasp.
Jenny paused for breath.

briefly

See section on **duration** in entry at **Adverbials**.

bring - take - fetch

'bring' If you **bring** someone or something with you when you come to a place, you have them with you.

He would have to bring Judy with him.
Please bring your calculator to every lesson.

The past tense and past participle of 'bring' is **brought.**

My secretary brought my mail to the house.
I've brought you a present.

If you ask someone to **bring** you something, you are asking them to carry or move it to the place where you are.

Bring me a glass of Dubonnet.

You do not say that you 'bring' a small child to bed. You say that you **put** the child to bed.

A baby may learn to resist being <u>put to bed</u> by furious crying.
Most parents change the nappies before they <u>put</u> the child back <u>to bed</u>.

'take' If you **take** someone or something to a place, you carry or drive them there.

It's his turn to <u>take</u> the children to school.

If you **take** someone or something with you when you go to a place, you have them with you.

She gave me some books to <u>take</u> home.
Don't forget to <u>take</u> your umbrella.

'fetch' If you **fetch** something, you go to the place where it is and return with it to the place where you were before.

I don't want you to <u>fetch</u> anything for me.
I went and <u>fetched</u> another glass.

bring up

When you **bring up** a child, you look after it until it is grown up, and you try to give it particular beliefs and attitudes.

Tony <u>was brought up</u> strictly.
The great majority of them <u>have been brought up</u> in working-class homes.

You can use adverbs such as 'well' or 'badly' in front of **brought up.** If you say that a young person is **well brought up,** you mean that their behaviour shows that they were taught how to behave properly when they were a child.

She's a <u>nicely brought up</u> girl, anyone can see that.
She was a good, <u>properly brought up</u> young woman.

'raise' In American English, **raise** can be used to mean 'bring up'.

Henry and his wife May <u>have raised</u> ten children.
Paul came to America when he was two years old and <u>was raised</u> as a ranch kid in Oregon.

Note that Americans do not say that someone is 'well raised'.

'educate' Do not confuse **bring up** or **raise** with **educate**. To **educate** a child means to teach it various subjects, usually at school.

Many more schools are needed to <u>educate</u> the young.
He was sent home as being impossible to <u>educate</u>.

Britain - British - Briton

Britain or **Great Britain** consists of England, Scotland, and Wales. The **United Kingdom** consists of England, Scotland, Wales, and Northern Ireland. The **British Isles** refers to Britain, Ireland, and all the smaller islands around the coast.

The nationality of someone from the United Kingdom is **British,** although some people prefer to call themselves **English, Scottish, Welsh,** or **Northern Irish.** It is incorrect and may cause offence to call all British people 'English'.

In writing, an individual British person can be referred to as a **Briton.**

The youth, a 17-year-old <u>Briton,</u> was searched and arrested.

You can refer to all the people who come from Britain as **the British.**

The British are very good at sympathy.
The British have always been a freedom-loving race.

The British can also be used to refer to a group of British people, for example the British representatives at an international conference.

The British have made these negotiations more complicated.
The British had come up with a bold and dangerous solution.

For more information on talking about nationality, see entry at **Nationality words.**

broad

See entry at **wide - broad.**

GRAMMAR ## Broad negatives

A **broad negative** is one of a small group of words which are used to make a statement almost negative.

We were scarcely able to move.
Fathers and sons very seldom now go together to football matches.

The five broad negatives are:

barely	rarely	seldom
hardly	scarcely	

The position of broad negatives within a clause is similar to that of 'never'. See entry at **never.**

with 'any' words   If you want to say that there is very little of something, you can use a broad negative with 'any' or with a word which begins with 'any-'.

There is rarely any difficulty in finding enough food.
Hardly anybody came.

'almost'   Instead of using a broad negative, you can use 'almost' followed by a negative word such as 'no' or 'never'. For example, 'There was almost no food left' means the same as 'There was hardly any food left'.

They've almost no money for anything.
Men almost never begin conversations.

For information on other uses of 'almost', see entry at **almost - nearly.**

tag questions   If you make a **tag question** out of a statement that contains a broad negative, the tag at the end of the statement is normally positive, as it is with other negatives.

She's hardly the right person for the job, is she?
You seldom see that sort of thing these days, do you?

For more information on the meanings and use of some of these broad negatives, see entries at **bare - barely, hard - hardly, scarce - scarcely,** and **seldom.**

broken

Broken is the past participle of the verb 'break'.

He has broken a window with a ball.

Broken is also used as an adjective. A **broken** object has split into pieces or has cracked, for example because it has been hit or dropped.

He sweeps away the broken glass under the window.
...a heap of broken dinner plates.
The doctor came in, holding a broken door latch.

If a machine or device is not functioning because there is something wrong with it, you do not usually say that it 'is broken'. You say that it **does not work** or **is not working.**

One of the lamps didn't work.
Chris sits beside him with sweaters on because the heater doesn't work.
The traffic lights weren't working properly.

bruise

See entry at **damage**.

bum

See entry at **bottom**.

burgle - burglarize

In British English, if you **are burgled** or if your house **is burgled,** someone breaks into your house and steals things.

Gesher had recently been burgled.

American speakers usually say that a house **is burglarized.**

Her home had been burglarized.

burst

When something **bursts** or when you **burst** it, it suddenly splits open, and air or some other substance comes out. The past tense and past participle of 'burst' is **burst,** not 'bursted'.

As he braked, a tyre burst.

If you **burst** into tears, you suddenly begin to cry.

When the news was broken to Meehan he burst into tears.

Note that you do not say that someone 'bursts in tears'.

WARNING

Do not confuse **burst** with **bust.** If you **bust** something, you break or damage it so badly that it cannot be used. See entry at **bust.**

bus - coach

A **bus** is a large motor vehicle which carries passengers by road from one place to another. In Britain, a comfortable bus that carries passengers on long journeys is called a **coach**. In America, vehicles for long journeys are usually called **buses.**

I'm waiting for the bus back to town.
The coach leaves Cardiff at twenty to eight.

In the far horizon a silvery Greyhound <u>bus</u> appears.

If you are on a bus or coach journey, you say that you are travelling or going **by bus** or **by coach.**

I don't often travel <u>by bus.</u>
It is cheaper to travel to London <u>by coach</u> than by train.

Note that you do not say that you are travelling 'by a bus' or 'by the coach'.

When someone enters a bus or coach at the beginning of their journey, you usually say that they **get on** it.

When I <u>get on</u> a bus and I see an advert, I read it.

When someone leaves a bus or coach at the end of their journey, you usually say that they **get off** it.

A man of his description was seen <u>getting off</u> a bus near the scene of the murder.

Note that you do not say that someone 'goes into' a bus or coach, or 'goes out of' it.

business

used as an uncount noun

Business is work relating to the production, buying, and selling of goods or services.

There are good profits to be made in the hotel <u>business.</u>
Are you in San Francisco for <u>business</u> or pleasure?

There are a number of other nouns which refer to activities which people are paid to do. For more information on these words, see entry at **work.**

WARNING

You do not refer to a discussion connected with business as 'a business'. You do not say, for example, 'We've got a business to see to'. You say 'We've got **some business** to see to'.

I was sent up here to do <u>some business</u> with someone.
We've still got <u>some business</u> to do. Do you mind just sitting?

used as a count noun

A **business** is a company, shop, or organization which produces and sells goods or provides a service.

He set up a small travel <u>business.</u>

bust

Bust can be used as a verb, an adjective, or a noun. The past tense and past participle of the verb is either **bust** or **busted.**

used as a verb

If you **bust** something, you break or damage it so badly that it cannot be used. Note that you only use **bust** with this meaning in conversation. You do not use it in formal writing.

She found out about Jack <u>busting</u> the double-bass.

used as an adjective

In conversation, if you say that something is **bust,** you mean that it is broken or very badly damaged.

That clock's been <u>bust</u> for weeks.

If a company **goes bust,** it loses so much money that it is forced to close down. You do not use this expression in formal English.

We know they <u>went bust</u> in 1954.

used as a noun	A woman's **bust** is her breasts. See entry at **breast**.

but

You use **but** to introduce something which contrasts with what you have just said.

used to link clauses	**But** is usually used to link clauses.

It was a long walk but it was worth it.
I try and see it their way, but I can't.

You do not normally put **but** at the beginning of a sentence, but you can do so when you are replying to someone, or writing in a conversational style.

'Somebody wants you on the telephone.'—'But nobody knows I'm here.'
I always thought that. But then I'm probably wrong.

used to link adjectives or adverbs	You can also use **but** to link adjectives or adverbs which contrast with each other.

...a small but comfortable hotel.
We are poor but happy.
Quickly but silently she darted out of the cell.

used with negative words to mean 'only'	**But** is sometimes used after negative words such as 'nothing', 'no-one', 'nowhere', or 'none'. A negative word followed by **but** means 'only'. For example, 'We have **nothing but** carrots' means 'We only have carrots'.

I've got nothing but idle visions.
Like me, she speaks in nothing but precise scientific terms.
I heard no-one but his uncles.

used to mean 'except'	**But** is also used after 'all' and after words beginning with 'every-' or 'any-'. When **but** is used after one of these words, it means 'except'. For example, 'He enjoyed everything **but** maths' means 'He enjoyed everything **except** maths'.

Thomas Hardy spent all but a few years in his native Dorset.
He ate everything but the beetroot.
There would be no time for anything but work.
Could anyone but Balmain have done it?

'but for'	**But for** is sometimes used to introduce the only factor that prevents something from happening. This use only occurs in writing.

The figure would have been higher but for delays in the delivery of the planes.

'but one'	**But** is also used in the phrases **last but one** and **next but one.** If you say that something is the **last but one** in a series, you mean that it is the one before the final one.

It'd be the last job but one.
This is what you were asked to do in the last but one quiz.

If you say that something is the **next but one** in a series, you mean that it is the one after the next one.

When a line ends in a word like 'plum', we repeat the syllable in the next line but one.

butt

See entry at **bottom**.

buttocks

See entry at **bottom**.

buy

When you **buy** something, you obtain it by paying money for it. The past tense and past participle of 'buy' is **bought,** not 'buyed'.

I'm going to buy everything that I need in good time.
Never buy anything white that must be dry-cleaned.
Many people have their cars bought for them by the firm they work for.

If you pay for a drink that is drunk by someone else, you say that you **buy** them the drink.

Let me buy you a drink.

Note that you do not say that you 'pay' someone a drink.

by

used in passives

By is most often used in passive sentences. If something is done or caused **by** a person or thing, that person or thing does it or causes it.

He was brought up by an aunt.
The defending champion, John Pritchard, was beaten by Chris Boardman.
This view has been challenged by a number of workers.
I was startled by his anger.
His best friend was killed by a grenade.

When an '-ed' word is used like an adjective to describe a state rather than an action, it is not always followed by **by.** Some '-ed' words are followed by 'with' or 'in'.

The room was filled with pleasant furniture.
The railings were decorated with thousands of bouquets.
The walls of her flat are covered in dirt.

used with time expressions

If something happens **by** a particular time, it happens at or before that time.

He can cook the tea and be out by seven o'clock.
By 1940 the number had grown to 185 million.
I arrived a mile outside the town by mid-afternoon.

Note that **by** can only be used with this meaning as a preposition. You do not use it as a conjunction. You do not say, for example, 'By I had finished my lunch, we had to start off again'. You say '**By the time** I had finished my lunch, we had to start off again'.

By the time I went to bed, I was absolutely exhausted.

used to describe position

You can use **by** to say that someone or something is at the side of a person or object.

I sat by her bed.
There were lines of parked cars by each kerb.

Next to is used in a similar way.

She went and sat next to him.
There was a bowl of goldfish next to the bed.

WARNING

You do not use **by** with the names of towns or cities. You do not say, for example, 'I was by Coventry when I ran out of petrol'. You say 'I was **near** Coventry when I ran out of petrol'.

...on a country road near Belfast.
Mandela was born near Elliotdale.

saying how something is done	**By** can be used with various nouns to say how something is done. You do not usually put a determiner in front of the noun.

The money will be paid by cheque.
We heard from them by phone.
I always go by bus.

However, if you want to say that something is done using a particular object or tool, you often use **with,** rather than 'by'. **With** is followed by a determiner.

Clean mirrors with a mop.
He brushed back his hair with his hand.

After 'watch', 'look', or 'see' you usually use **through** followed by a determiner.

He's looking at them through a magnifying glass.

You can use **by** with an '-ing' form to say how something is achieved.

They were making a living by selling souvenirs to the tourists.
He then tries to solve his problems by accusing me of being corrupt.

by far

See entry at **very.**

C

cab

See entry at **taxi - cab.**

cabin - cabinet

'cabin' A **cabin** is a small room on a boat or ship, or an area within a plane.

I made my way along the passageway until I came to Captain Imrie's cabin.
...the First Class cabin.

'cabinet' A **cabinet** is a cupboard used for storing things such as medicines or papers, or for displaying ornaments.

...a glass cabinet with Chinese things in it.

café - coffee

'café' A **café** /kæfeɪ/ is a place where you can buy drinks and light meals or snacks. In Britain, **cafés** do not sell alcoholic drinks. **Café** is often spelled **cafe.**

...a waiter from a nearby café.
Inside the cafe it was dark and cool.

'coffee'   **Coffee** /kɒfi/ is a hot drink.

...*a cup of* coffee.

call

attracting   If you **call** something, you say it in a loud voice, usually because you are
attention   trying to attract someone's attention.

'Edward!' she called. 'Edward! Lunch is ready!'
I could hear a voice calling my name.
'Here's your drink,' Boylan called to him.

telephoning   If you **call** a person or place, you telephone them.

Call me when you get home.
Grechko called the office and complained.

When you use **call** like this, it is not followed by 'to'. You do not say, for
example, 'I called to him at his London flat'. You say 'I **called** him at his
London flat'.

visiting   If someone **calls on** you, or if they **call,** they make a short visit in order to
see you or deliver something. **Call** is not used like this in American
English.

He had called on Seery at his London home.
Goodnight. Do call again.
The postman calls about 7 o'clock every morning.

You can also say that someone **pays a call on** you or **pays** you **a call.** These
expressions are used in both British and American English.

We went to pay a call on some people I used to know.
Off you go in the morning and pay him a call.

called - named

You use **called** or **named** when you are giving the name of someone or
something. **Named** is less common than **called,** and is not usually used in
conversation.

Did you know a boy called Desmond?
We pass through a town called Monmouth.
Anna had a boyfriend named Shorty.

You can use **called** either after a noun or after 'be'.

Komis asked me to appear in a play called Katerina.
The book was called The Goalkeeper's Revenge.

You only use **named** immediately after a noun.

The victim was an 18-year-old girl named Marinetta Jirkowski.

camp bed

See entry at **cot - crib - camp bed.**

can - could - be able to

These words are used to talk about ability, awareness, and the possibility
of something being the case. They are also used to say that someone has
permission to do something. These uses are dealt with separately in this
entry.

can - could - be able to

Can and **could** are called **modals**. See entry at **Modals**.

Both **can** and **could** are followed by an infinitive without 'to'.

Some people can ski better than others.
I could work for twelve hours a day.

negative forms The negative form of 'can' is **cannot** or **can't**. **Cannot** is never written 'can not'. The negative form of 'could' is **could not** or **couldn't**. To form the negative of 'be able to', you either put 'not' or another negative word in front of 'able', or you use the expression **be unable to**.

Many elderly people cannot afford telephones.
My wife can't sew.
It was so black you could not see a hand in front of your face.
They couldn't sleep.
We were not able to give any answers.
We were unable to afford the entrance fee.

ability: Can, **could,** and **be able to** are all used to talk about a person's ability to
the present do something.

You use **can** or **be able to** to talk about ability in the present. **Be able to** is more formal than **can**.

You can all read and write.
The goliath frog is able to jump three metres or so.
…people who are unable to appreciate new ideas.

Could is also used to talk about ability in the present, but it has a special meaning. If you say that someone **could** do something, you mean that they have the ability to do it, but they do not in fact do it.

We could do a great deal more in this country to educate people.

ability: You use **could** or a past form of **be able to** to talk about ability in the past.
the past
He could run faster than anyone else.
A lot of them couldn't read or write.
I wasn't able to do these quizzes.

If you say that someone **was able to** do something, you usually mean that they had the ability to do it and they did it. **Could** does not have this meaning.

After treatment he was able to return to work.
The farmers were able to pay the new wages.

If you want to say that someone had the ability to do something but did not in fact do it, you say that they **could have done** it.

You could have given it all to me.
You could have been a little bit tidier.

If you want to say that someone did not do something because they did not have the ability to do it, you say that they **could not have done** it.

I couldn't have gone with you, because I was in London at the time.

If you want to say that someone had the ability to do something in the past, although they do not now have this ability, you say that they **used to be able to** do it.

I used to be able to make it happen.
You used to be able to see the house from here.

ability: You use a future form of **be able to** to talk about ability in the future.
the future
I shall be able to answer that question tomorrow.

ability: report structures	**Could** is often used in report structures. For example, if a man says 'I can speak Arabic', you usually report this as 'He said he **could** speak Arabic'.
	Ferguson said I could ask for a transfer if after six months I still don't like it.
ability: 'be able to' after other verbs	**Be able to** is sometimes used after modals such as 'might' or 'should', and after verbs such as 'want', 'hope', or 'expect'.
	I might be able to help you. *You may be able to get extra money.* *You should be able to feel this.* *She would not be able to drive to inland cities alone here.* *You're foolish to expect to be able to do that.*
	You do not use **can** or **could** after any other verbs.
'being able to'	You can use an '-ing' form of **be able to**.
	...the satisfaction of being able to do the job.
	There is no '-ing' form of **can** or **could**.
awareness	**Can** and **could** are used with verbs such as 'see', 'hear', and 'smell' to say that someone is or was aware of something through one of their senses.
	I can smell gas. *I can't see her.* *I could see a few stars in the sky.*
	Note that this is the most common way of expressing awareness through one of your senses. For example, if you become aware of a phone ringing, you say 'I **can hear** a phone ringing'. You do not say 'I hear a phone ringing'.
possibility: the present and the future	**Could** and **can** are used to talk about possibility in the present or future.
	You use **could** to say that there is a possibility that something is or will be the case.
	Don't eat it. It could be a toadstool. *There could be something in the blood.* *300,000 jobs could be lost.*
	Might and **may** can be used in a similar way.
	It might be a trap. *Kathy's career may be ruined.*
	See entry at **might - may**.
WARNING	You do not use **could not** to say that there is a possibility that something is not the case. Instead you use **might not** or **may not**.
	It might not be possible. *It may not be easy.*
	If you want to say that it is impossible that something is the case, you use **cannot** or **could not**.
	Kissinger cannot know what the situation is in the country. *You can't talk to the dead.* *It couldn't possibly be poison.*
	You use **can** to say that something is sometimes possible.
	Such shifts in opinion can sometimes have a snowball effect.

possibility: the past	You use **could have** to say that there is a possibility that something was the case in the past.

He could have been doing research on his own.

Might have and **may have** can be used in a similar way.

The teacher might have known the local policeman.
It may have been a dead bird.

You also use **could have** to say that there was a possibility of something being the case in the past, although it was not in fact the case.

It could have been worse.
I could have escaped sentence by inventing a false name for my informant.

WARNING	You do not use **could not have** to say that there is a possibility that something was not the case. Instead you use **might not have** or **may not have**.

She mightn't have known what the bottle contained.

If you want to say that it is impossible that something was the case, you use **could not have.**

I couldn't have known that in a few weeks I would lose control too.
The man couldn't have thought at all.

permission	**Can** and **could** are used to say that someone is allowed to do something.

You can take out money at any branch of your own bank.
He could come and build in my wood.

Cannot and **could not** are used to say that someone is or was forbidden to do something.

You can't bring outsiders into a place like this.
'May I speak to Mr Jordache, please?'—'No, you can't.'
Standish could not have questioned the man; outside a Customs enclosure a Customs officer had no right to interrogate anyone.

See also entry at **Permission**.

cancel

See entry at **delay - cancel - postpone**.

candy

See entry at **sweets - candy**.

cannot

See entry at **can - could - be able to**.

Capital letters

obligatory capital letter	You must use a capital letter for the first word of a sentence or a piece of direct speech. See entry at **Punctuation**.

You must also start the following words and word groups with a capital letter:

● names of people, organizations, books, films, and plays (except for short, common words like 'of', 'the', and 'and')

...Miss Helen Perkins, head of management development at Price Waterhouse.
...their new film, 'Three Men and a Little Lady'.
Troilus and Coriolanus are the greatest political plays that Shakespeare wrote.

Note that you spell even short, common words with a capital letter when they come at the beginning of the title of a book, film, or play.

...his new book, 'A Future for Socialism'.

● names of places

Dempster was born in India in 1941.
The strongest gust was recorded at Berry Head, Brixham, Devon.

● names of days, months, and festivals

The trial continues on Monday.
It was mid-December and she was going home for Christmas.

● nouns referring to people of a particular nationality

The Germans and the French move more of their freight by rail, water or pipe than the British.
I had to interview two authors — one an American, one an Indian.

● names of people used to refer to art, music, and literature created by them

In those days you could buy a Picasso for £300.
I listened to Mozart.
I stayed in the dressing-room until lunchtime, reading my latest Jeffrey Archer.

● nouns referring to products produced by a particular company

I bought a second-hand Volkswagen.
...a cleansing powder which contains bleach (such as Vim).

● titles used in front of someone's name

There has been no statement so far from President Bush.
The tower was built by King Henry II in the 12th century.

● adjectives indicating nationality or place

...a French poet.
...the Californian earthquake.

● adjectives indicating that something is associated with or resembles a particular person

...his favourite Shakespearean sonnet.
...in Victorian times.
He loved being the centre of attention and dropped easily into Tarzanesque poses.

'I' The personal pronoun 'I' is always written as a capital letter.

I thought I was alone.

WARNING The words 'me', 'my', 'mine', and 'myself' are not written with a capital letter, unless they come at the beginning of a sentence.

optional capital letter You can use either a small letter or a capital letter at the beginning of

● words referring to directions such as 'North' and 'South'

We shall be safe in the north.
The home-ownership rate in the South East of England is higher than in the North.

- words referring to decades

Adult literacy work became in the <u>seventies</u> a kind of call for emergency troops.
Most of it was done in the <u>Seventies</u>.

- names of seasons

I planted it last <u>autumn</u>.
In the <u>Autumn</u> of 1948 Caroline returned to the United States.

- titles of people (especially when used to refer to a type of person)

...the great <u>prime ministers</u> of the past.
...one of the greatest <u>Prime Ministers</u> who ever held office.

...portraits of the <u>president</u>.
...the brother of the <u>President</u>.

referring to God Some people write 'he', 'him', and 'his' with a capital letter when they are referring to God or Jesus.

Some said they saw the Son of God; others did not see <u>Him</u>.

---

car

See entry at **carriage**.

card - cart - chart

'card' A **card** is a piece of stiff paper with information on.

Put all the details on the <u>card</u>.
...a membership <u>card</u>.

A **card** is also a piece of stiff paper folded in half with a picture and a message printed on it, which you send someone on a special occasion.

...a birthday <u>card</u>.
They used to send me a <u>card</u> at Christmas time.

You can also refer to a postcard as a **card**.

Send us a <u>card</u> so we'll know where you are.

'cart' A **cart** is a vehicle with wheels, used to carry goods along roads or tracks and usually pulled by a horse or other animal.

...a <u>cart</u> loaded with hay.

'chart' A **chart** is a diagram, picture, or graph which makes information easy to understand.

...large <u>charts</u> illustrating world poverty.

A **chart** is also a map of the sea near a coast.

He had no <u>charts</u> for these waters.

care

If you **care** about something, you feel that it is very important or interesting and you are concerned about it.

...people who <u>care</u> about the environment.
We teased him because all he <u>cared</u> about was birds.

I'm too old to care what I look like.

If you do not **care** about something, it does not matter to you.

She couldn't care less what they thought.
Who cares where she is?

'care for'   If you **care for** people or animals, you look after them.

You must learn how to care for children.
With so many new animals to care for, larger premises were needed.

If you **do not care for** something, you do not like it. This is a rather old-fashioned use.

I didn't much care for the way he looked at me.

If you ask someone if they **would care for** something, you are asking them if they would like to have it or do it. This is also a rather old-fashioned use.

Would you care for a cup of tea?

'take care'   To **take care of** someone or something or **take good care of** them means to look after them.

It is certainly normal for a mother to want to take care of her own baby.
He takes good care of my goats.

Note that you do not say that someone 'takes care about' someone else or 'takes a good care of' them.

If you **take care of** a task or situation, you deal with it.

There was business to be taken care of.
If you'd prefer, they can take care of their own breakfast.

You also use **take care** when you are telling someone to be careful about something.

Take care what you tell him.
Take great care not to spill the mixture.

Take care and **take care of yourself** are also ways of saying goodbye.

'Night, night, Mr Beamish,' called Chloe. 'Take care.'

careful - careless - carefree

'careful'   If you are **careful**, you do something with a lot of attention.

She told me to be careful with the lawnmower.
He had to be careful about what he said.
This law will encourage more careful driving.

'careless'   If you are **careless**, you do things badly because you are not giving them enough attention. **Careless** is the opposite of **careful**.

I had been careless and let him wander off on his own.
We are rather careless about the way we cook.

'carefree'   Someone who is **carefree** has no worries and can therefore enjoy life.

She had been lively and carefree.
...his normally carefree attitude.

carnival

See entry at **fair - carnival**.

carousel

See entry at **roundabout**.

carriage

Carriage is one of several nouns which are used to refer to vehicles pulled by railway engines.

In British English, a **carriage** is one of the separate sections of a train that carries passengers.

The man left his seat by the window and crossed the carriage to where I was sitting.

'car'   In American English, these sections are called **cars**.

In British English, **car** used to be part of the name of some special kinds of railway carriage. For example, a carriage might be called a 'dining car', a 'restaurant car', or a 'sleeping car'. These terms are no longer used officially, but people still use them in conversation.

'truck' and 'wagon'   In British English, a **truck** or **wagon** is an open vehicle used for carrying goods on a railway.

...a long truck loaded with bricks.
...selling the use of railway wagons under his personal control.

'box-car'   In American English, vehicles like these are usually called **box-cars**.

Note that a **truck** is also a large motor vehicle used for transporting goods by road. See entry at **lorry - truck**.

carry - take

Carry and **take** are usually used to say that someone moves a person or thing from one place to another.

He picked up his suitcase and carried it into the bedroom.
My father carried us on his shoulders.
She gave me some books to take home.
It's his turn to take the children to school.

transport   You can also say that a ship, train, or lorry **is carrying** goods of a particular kind. Similarly you can say that a plane, ship, train, or bus **is carrying** passengers.

...tankers carrying Iranian crude oil.
...the Pakistani airliner carrying 145 passengers and crew.
...dozens of trains carrying commuters to work.

Take can be used in a similar way, but only if you say where someone or something is being taken to. You can say, for example, 'The ship **was taking** crude oil **to Rotterdam**', but you cannot just say 'The ship was taking crude oil'.

He was aboard an aircraft which took cereal, drugs and cooking oil to Aweil yesterday.

You can say that a small vehicle such as a car **takes** you somewhere.

The taxi took him back to Victoria.

Note that you do not say that a small vehicle 'carries' you somewhere.

cart

See entry at **card - cart - chart**.

case

'in case'
You use **in case** or **just in case** to say that someone has something or does something because a particular thing might happen.

I've got the key in case we want to go inside.
We tend not to go too far from the office, just in case there should be a bomb scare that would prevent us getting back.

WARNING
After **in case** or **just in case,** you use a simple tense or 'should'. You do not use 'will' or 'shall'.

You do not use **in case** or **just in case** to say that something will happen as a result of something else happening. You do not say, for example, 'I will go in case he asks me'. You say 'I will go **if** he asks me'.

He qualifies this year if he gets through his exams.

'in that case'
You say **in that case** or **in which case** to refer to a situation which has just been mentioned and to introduce a statement or suggestion that is a consequence of it.

'The bar is closed,' the waiter said. 'In that case,' McFee said, 'allow me to invite you back to my flat for a drink.'
I greatly enjoy these meetings unless I have to make a speech, in which case I'm in a state of dreadful anxiety.

'in this respect'
You do not use 'in this case' to refer to a particular aspect of something. For example, you do not say 'Most of my friends lost their jobs, but I was very lucky in this case'. You say 'Most of my friends lost their jobs, but I was very lucky **in this respect**'.

We must be careful not to kill the market with over-exposure and the new tournament could be a problem in this respect.
Creating a number of partially competitive units is unrealistic. The proposals for primary health care are particularly flawed in this respect.

cast

If you **cast** a glance in a particular direction, you glance in that direction.

Carmody casts an uneasy glance at Howard.
Out came Napoleon, casting haughty glances from side to side.

The verb **cast** has several other meanings. Note that for all its meanings its past tense and past participle is **cast,** not 'casted'.

He cast a quick glance at his friend.
He cast his mind back over the day.
He had cast doubt on our traditional beliefs.
Will had cast his vote for the President.

casualty

See entry at **victim.**

cause

used as a noun
The **cause of** an event is the thing that makes it happen.

Nobody knew the cause of the explosion.
Disease or illness is not a cause of this type of mental slowness.

Note that you use **of,** not 'for', after **cause.**

You do not use 'because of' or 'due to' with **cause.** You do not say, for example, 'The cause of the fire was probably due to a dropped cigarette'. You say 'The cause of the fire **was** probably a dropped cigarette'.

The main cause of the complacency about future energy supplies was undoubtedly the emergence of nuclear energy.
The cause of the symptoms appears to be inability to digest gluten.

used as a verb To **cause** something means to make it happen.

We have a good idea what causes an earthquake.
Does smoking cause cancer?

You can say that something **causes someone to do** something.

...a blow to the head which had caused him to lose consciousness.
It had caused her to be distrustful of people.

You do not say that something 'causes that someone does' something.

cereal - serial

These words are both pronounced /sɪəriəl/.

'cereal' A **cereal** is a plant such as wheat, maize, or rice that produces grain.

Wheat may have been the first cereal to be cultivated.

Some kinds of food made from grain are also called **cereals.** In many countries, these foods are eaten with milk at breakfast time.

...a box of cereal.
...a new breakfast cereal.

'serial' A **serial** is a story which is divided into several parts. The parts are broadcast at different times on television or radio, or printed in different editions of a magazine.

The novel has recently been dramatized as a television serial.

certain - sure

having no doubts If you are **certain** or **sure** about something, you have no doubts about it.

He felt certain that she would disapprove.
I'm sure she's right.

Note that **certain** and **sure** cannot be used with this meaning in front of a noun.

definite truths If it is **certain** that something is true, it is definitely true. If it is **certain** that something will happen, it will definitely happen.

It is certain that he did not ask for the original of the portrait.
It seemed certain that the satellite had burned up completely on re-entering the earth's atmosphere.
It is certain that they will have some spectacular successes.
It seems certain that they will both have to stay in prison for the rest of their lives.

Note that you do not say that it is 'sure' that something is true or will happen.

Instead of saying that it is certain that someone or something will do something, you can say that they **are certain to do** it or **are sure to do** it.

I'm waiting for Cynthia. She's certain to be late.
The growth in demand is certain to drive up the price.

These fears <u>are sure to go away</u> as the baby gets older.
The telephone stopped ringing. 'It's <u>sure to ring</u> again,' Sarah said.

Instead of saying that it is certain that someone will be able to do something, you often say that they **can be certain of** doing it or **can be sure of** doing it.

Anyone <u>could be virtually certain of</u> boarding.
He <u>could be sure of</u> taking his men unawares.
You <u>can always be sure of</u> controlling one thing — the strength with which you hit the ball.

You do not use words such as 'very' or 'extremely' in front of **certain** or **sure**. If you want to emphasize that someone has no doubts or that something is true, you use words such as 'absolutely' and 'completely'.

We are not yet <u>absolutely certain</u> that this report is true.
Whether it was directed at Eddie or me, I couldn't be <u>completely certain</u>.
Can you be <u>absolutely sure</u> that a murder has been committed?
She felt <u>completely sure</u> that she was pregnant.

certainly

Certainly is used to emphasize statements. You often use **certainly** when you are agreeing with something that has been said or confirming that something is true.

It <u>certainly</u> looks wonderful, doesn't it?
Ellie was <u>certainly</u> a student at the university but I'm not sure about her brother.

position in sentence
    Certainly is usually used to modify verbs. If there is no auxiliary, you put **certainly** in front of the verb, unless the verb is 'be'.

The letters <u>certainly added</u> fuel to the flames of her love for Tom.
It <u>certainly gave</u> some of her visitors a fright.

If the verb is 'be', **certainly** can go either in front of it or after it. It usually goes after it.

It <u>was certainly</u> acceptable to Bach and Mozart.
The so-called electronic brains <u>are certainly</u> the most spectacular.
That <u>certainly isn't</u> true.

If there is an auxiliary, you usually put **certainly** after the auxiliary.

...a large building that <u>would certainly be</u> empty and available.
They <u>can certainly be</u> quite big enough for a diver to put his foot into.
He decided he'<u>d certainly proved</u> his point.

If there is more than one auxiliary, you usually put **certainly** after the first one. **Certainly** can also go in front of the first auxiliary.

He <u>will certainly be</u> able to offer you advice.
They <u>would certainly have been accused</u> of cowardice.
The roadway <u>certainly could be widened</u>.

If you use an auxiliary without a main verb, you put **certainly** in front of the auxiliary.

'I don't know whether I've succeeded or not.'—'Oh, you <u>certainly have</u>.'
'Do you think this was a film that needed making?'—'Yes, I <u>certainly do</u>.'

You can also put **certainly** at the beginning of a sentence.

The stock markets fear a further rise in interest rates. <u>Certainly</u>, the City thinks the government acted too late.

For many years union representatives have found themselves battling with employers. _Certainly,_ there will be many such struggles in the future.
Certainly it was not the act of a sane man.

'almost certainly'

If you think that something is the case, but you are not quite sure about it, you can say that it is **almost certainly** the case.

There will _almost certainly_ be a lady personnel officer.
I am _almost certainly_ being watched.

Note that you never put 'nearly' in front of **certainly.**

Many other words can be used to say how certain you are about something. For a graded list, see section on **probability** in entry at **Adverbials.**

'certainly not'

You say **certainly not** when you want to say 'no' in a strong way, usually in answer to a question.

'Had you forgotten?'—'_Certainly not._'
'Leave me alone, please.'—'_Certainly not._ You agreed to finish it and we are relying on you.'

chair - armchair

A **chair** is a piece of furniture for one person to sit on, with a support for the person's back. When a chair is a very simple one, you say that someone sits **on** it.

Anne was sitting _on an upright chair._
Sit _on this chair,_ please.

When a chair is a comfortable one, you usually say that someone sits **in** it.

He leaned back _in his chair_ and looked out of the window.

An **armchair** is a comfortable chair with a support on each side for your arms. You always say that someone sits **in** an armchair.

He was sitting quietly _in his armchair,_ smoking a pipe and reading the paper.

chairman

The **chairman** is the person who is in charge of a meeting or debate.

The vicar, full of apologies, took his seat as _chairman._

The head of an organization is often referred to as its **chairman.**

...Sir John Hill, _chairman_ of the Atomic Energy Authority.

'chairwoman'

In the past, **chairman** was used to refer to both men and women, but it is now not often used to refer to a woman. The woman in charge of a meeting or organization is sometimes referred to as the **chairwoman.**

Margaret Downes Is this year's _chairwoman_ of the Irish Institute.

'chairperson' and 'chair'

The person in charge of a meeting or organization is also sometimes referred to as the **chairperson** or **chair.** These words can be used to refer to either a man or a woman.

...Ruth Michaels, _chairperson_ of the Women Returners' Network.
You should address your remarks to the _chair._

chance

If it is possible that something will happen, you can say that there is **a chance that it will happen** or **a chance of it happening.**

There was _a chance that the Republic would withdraw the rest of its troops._

...when there was a chance of the bridge being built.

If something is fairly likely to happen, you can say that there is **a good chance** that it will happen.

There was a good chance that I would be killed.
We've got a good chance of winning.

If something is unlikely to happen, you can say that there is **little chance** that it will happen. If you are sure that it will not happen, you can say that there is **no chance** that it will happen.

There's little chance that the situation will improve.
There's no chance of going home.

If someone is able to do something on a particular occasion, you can say that they have **the chance to do** it.

You will be given the chance to ask questions.
The study recommends that every young person should have the chance to take part in adventurous outdoor activity.

'chances'
You can talk about someone's **chances of doing** something. For example, if someone will probably achieve something, you can say that their **chances of achieving** it are good.

What are your chances of becoming a director?
Single women have relatively equal chances of achieving white-collar work.

Note that you do not talk about someone's 'chances to achieve' something.

'by chance'
If something happens **by chance**, it was not planned.

Many years later he met her by chance at a dinner party.

'luck'
Note that if you say that something happens 'by chance', you are not saying whether it is a good thing or a bad thing. If something good happens without being planned, you refer to it as **luck**, not 'chance'.

I couldn't believe my luck.
How can we ever be rescued except by luck?

charge

See entry at **accuse - charge**.

chart

See entry at **card - cart - chart**.

cheap - cheaply

'cheap' as an adjective
Cheap goods or services cost less than other goods or services of the same type.

...cheap red wine.
...cheap plastic buckets.
A solid fuel cooker is cheap to run.

'cheap' as an adverb
In conversation, **cheap** can also be used as an adverb, but only with verbs which refer to the buying, selling, or hiring of things.

I thought you got it very cheap.
You can hire boots pretty cheap.

'cheaply' With other verbs, the adverb you use is **cheaply**.

You can play golf comparatively cheaply.
In fact you can travel just as cheaply by British Airways.

'low' You do not say that things such as wages, costs, or payments are 'cheap'. You say that they are **low.**

If your family has a low income, you can apply for a student grant.
...tasty meals at a fairly low cost.

check

See entries at **cheque - check** and **bill - check.**

checkroom

See entry at **cloakroom - checkroom.**

cheerful

See entry at **glad.**

cheers - cheerio

'cheers' British and American people often say **cheers** to each other just before drinking an alcoholic drink.

I took Captain Imrie's chair, poured myself a small drink and said 'Cheers!'
Cheers, Helen. Drink up.

Some British people also say **cheers** instead of 'thank you' or 'goodbye'.

'Here you are.'—'Oh, cheers. Thanks.'
'Thanks for ringing.'—'OK, cheers.'—'Bye bye.'—'Cheers.'

'cheerio' **Cheerio** is a more common way of saying goodbye. It is used mainly in British English.

I'll give Brigadier Sutherland your regards. Cheerio.

chef - chief

'chef' A **chef** /ʃef/ is a cook in a hotel or restaurant.

Her recipe was passed on to the chef.
...a chef trained at Maxim's to produce rich and imaginative menus.

'chief' The **chief** /tʃiːf/ of a group or organization is its leader.

...the current CIA chief.
...Jean Ducret, chief of the Presidential Security Corps.

chemist

In British English, a **chemist** is a person who is qualified to prepare and sell drugs and medicines.

...the pills the chemist had given him.

'pharmacist' In American English, someone like this is usually called a **pharmacist**.

The boy was eighteen, the son of the pharmacist at the Amity Pharmacy.

another meaning of 'chemist' In both British and American English, a **chemist** is also a person who studies chemistry or who does work connected with chemical research.

...a research chemist.

chemist's - drugstore

'chemist's' In Britain, a **chemist's** or **chemist** is a shop where you can buy medicine, cosmetics, and some household items.

I found her buying bottles of vitamin tablets at the chemist's.
He bought the perfume at the chemist in St James's Arcade.

'drugstore' In the United States, a shop where you can buy medicine and cosmetics is called a **drugstore**. In drugstores, you can also buy simple meals and snacks.

'pharmacy' A chemist's or drugstore can be referred to formally as a **pharmacy**.

cheque - check

'cheque' In British English, a **cheque** is a printed form on which you write an amount of money and say who it is to be paid to. Your bank then pays the money to that person from your account.

Ellen gave the landlady a cheque for £80.

'check' In American English, this word is spelled **check**.

They sent me a check for $520.

In American English, a **check** is also a piece of paper showing how much money you owe for a meal in a restaurant.

He waved to a waiter and got the check.

In British English, a piece of paper like this is called a **bill**.

chicken - hen - chick

'chicken' A **chicken** is a bird which is kept on a farm for its eggs or meat.

She loved to chase the chickens.

Chicken is the meat of a chicken.

There was fried chicken and mashed potatoes for dinner.

'hen' A **hen** is a female chicken, although people often refer to a group of chickens of both sexes as **hens**.

'chick' A **chick** is a baby bird of any kind.

The mother birds stay together while they are feeding the chicks.

chief

See entry at **chef - chief**.

childish - childlike

'childish' You say that someone is **childish** if you think they are behaving in a silly or immature way.

He can be extremely understanding and kind one minute, and completely unreasonable and childish the next.
...his bad jokes, his childish pride in his latest gadgets.

'childlike' You describe someone's voice or appearance as **childlike** when it seems like that of a child.

Her voice was fresh and childlike.
She looked at me with her big, childlike eyes.

chips

In British English, **chips** are long, thin pieces of potato fried in oil. Pieces of potato like these are called **fries** or **french fries** in American English.

...fish and chips.
They go out to a place near the Capitol for a steak and fries.

In American English, **chips** or **potato chips** are very thin slices of potato that have been fried until they are hard and crunchy. Pieces of potato like these are called **crisps** in British English.

...a bag of potato chips.
...a packet of crisps.

choose

When you **choose** someone or something from a group of people or things, you decide which one you want.

Why did he choose these particular places?

The past tense of 'choose' is **chose**, not 'choosed'. The past participle is **chosen**.

I chose a yellow dress.
A few weeks ago you were chosen as the new Bishop of Jarrow.

'pick' and **Pick** and **select** have very similar meanings to **choose**. **Select** is more
'select' formal than **choose** or **pick**, and is not usually used in conversation.

Next time let's pick somebody who can fight.
They select books that seem to them important.

'choose to' If someone **chooses to do** something, they do it because they want to or because they feel it is right.

Some women choose to manage on their own.
She did not choose to sit at the back.
The way we choose to bring up children is vitally important.

You do not say that someone 'picks to do' something or 'selects to do' something.

chord - cord

These words are both pronounced /kɔːd/.

'chord' A **chord** is a number of musical notes played or sung together to produce a pleasant sound.

He played some random chords.

'cord' **Cord** is strong, thick string. A **cord** is a piece of this string.

She tied a cord around her box.

A **cord** is also a length of wire covered with plastic which connects a piece of electrical equipment to an electricity supply.

Christian name - first name

'Christian name' In British English, a person's **Christian name** is the name given to them when they were born or when they were christened. Many people have two or more Christian names. Christian names come in front of a person's surname.

Do all your students call you by your Christian name?
'You remember their mother's Christian name?'—'Margaret, I think.'

'first name'
In American English, **Christian name** is not used. American speakers talk about a person's **first name**. British people who are not Christians also use **first name.**

At some point in the conversation Boon had begun calling Philip by his <u>first name</u>.

'forename'
On official forms, you are usually asked to write your surname and your **first name** or **forename. Forename** is only ever used in writing.

'given name'
In American English, **given name** is sometimes used instead of 'first name' or 'forename'.

For more information about names, see entry at **Names and titles.**

church

A **church** is a building in which Christians hold religious services.

The <u>church</u> has two entrances.
...St Clement's <u>Church,</u> Sandwich.

You use **church** immediately after a preposition when you are talking about a religious service held in a church. For example, if someone goes to a service in a church, you say that they go **to church.**

In the morning all the peasants went <u>to church.</u>
People had heard what had happened <u>at church.</u>
Will we see you <u>in church</u> tomorrow?
I saw him <u>after church</u> one morning.

A **Church** is one of the groups of people within the Christian religion, for example Catholics or Methodists. You can refer to all the people and officials who belong to one of these groups as **the Church.**

<u>The Church</u> should indeed speak on the matter.
Surely <u>the Church</u> ought always to support peaceful change and reconciliation.

cinema

See entry at **film.**

class

A **class** is a group of pupils or students who are taught together.

If <u>classes</u> were smaller, children would learn more.
I had forty students in my <u>class.</u>

'form'
In many British schools and in some American private schools, **form** is used instead of 'class'. **Form** is used especially with a number to refer to a particular class or age group.

...the fifth <u>form.</u>
She's in <u>Form</u> 5.

'grade'
A **grade** in an American school is similar to a **form** in a British school.

...a boy in the second <u>grade.</u>

classic - classical

'classic' used as an adjective
A **classic** example of something has all the features or characteristics which you expect something of its kind to have.

This statement was a <u>classic</u> illustration of British politeness.
London is the <u>classic</u> example of the scattered city.

Classic is also used to describe films or books which are judged to be of outstanding quality.

...one of the classic works of the Hollywood cinema.
...Brenan's classic analysis of Spanish history.

'classic' used as a noun   A **classic** is a book which is well-known and thought to be of a high literary standard.

We had all the standard classics at home.

Classics is the study of the ancient Greek and Roman civilizations, especially their languages, literature, and philosophy.

She obtained a first class degree in Classics.

'classical'   **Classical** music is music written by composers such as Mozart and Beethoven. Music of this kind is often complex in form, and is considered by many people to have lasting value.

I spend a lot of time reading and listening to classical music.
...classical pianists.

Classical is also used to refer to things connected with ancient Greek or Roman civilization.

...classical mythology.
Truffles have been savoured as a delicacy since classical times.

GRAMMAR **Clauses**

A **clause** is a group of words containing a verb. A **simple sentence** has one clause.

I waited.
She married a young engineer.

main clauses   A **compound sentence** has two or more **main clauses** – that is, clauses which refer to two separate actions or situations which are equally important. Clauses in compound sentences are joined with **conjunctions** such as 'and', 'but', and 'or'.

He met Jane at the station and went shopping.
I wanted to go but I felt too ill.
You can come now or you can meet us there later.

Note that the subject of the second clause can be omitted if it is the same as that of the first clause.

subordinate clauses   A **complex sentence** contains a **subordinate clause** and at least one main clause. A subordinate clause gives more information about a main clause, and is introduced by a conjunction such as 'because', 'if', 'that', or a 'wh'-word. Subordinate clauses can come in front of, after, or inside the main clause.

When he stopped, no one said anything.
They were going by car because it was more comfortable.
I said that I should like to come.
The man who came into the room was small.

See entries at **Subordinate clauses** and **Relative clauses.** For more information on 'that'-clauses and 'wh'-clauses used after reporting verbs, see entry at **Reporting.**

non-finite clauses   A **non-finite clause** is a subordinate clause which is based on a participle or an infinitive.

Quite often while talking to you they'd stand on one foot.
He pranced about feeling very important indeed.
I wanted to talk to her.

See entries at **'-ing' forms**, **Past participles**, and **'To'-infinitive clauses**.

client

See entry at **customer - client**.

cloakroom - checkroom

A **cloakroom** is a room where you leave your hat and coat, especially in a place of entertainment. In American English, a room like this is sometimes called a **checkroom**.

In British English, **cloakroom** is also a polite word for a toilet. See entry at **toilet**.

In American English, a **checkroom** is also a place where luggage can be left for a short time, especially at a railway station.

close - closed - shut

If you **close** /kləʊz/ something such as a door, you move it so that it covers or fills a hole or gap.

He opened the door and closed it behind him.

You can also say that you **shut** something such as a door. There is no difference in meaning. The past tense and past participle of 'shut' is **shut**, not 'shutted'.

I shut the door quietly.

Both **closed** and **shut** can be used as adjectives.

All the other downstairs rooms are dark and the shutters are closed.
The windows were all shut.

However, only **closed** can be used in front of a noun. You can talk about a **closed** window, but not a 'shut' window.

He listened to her voice coming faintly through the closed door.

You can use either **close** or **shut** to say that work or business stops for a short time in a shop or public building.

Many libraries close on Saturdays at 1 p.m.
What time do the shops shut?

You can say that a road, border, or airport **is closed**.

The border with Hong Kong was closed just as my wife and daughters reached there.

You do not say that a road, border, or airport 'is shut'.

Close is sometimes used to say that something is brought to an end.

He spoke as though he wanted to close the conversation.
The case is closed.

You do not use **shut** with this meaning.

WARNING
Do not confuse the verb **close** with the adjective **close** /kləʊs/. If something is **close** to something else, it is near to it. See entry at **near - close**.

closet

See entry at **cupboard**.

clothes - clothing - cloth

'clothes'   Clothes /kləʊðz/ are things you wear, such as shirts, trousers, dresses, and coats.

I took off all my clothes.

There is no singular form of **clothes.** You cannot, for example, talk about 'a clothe'. In formal English, you can talk about a **garment,** a **piece of clothing,** or an **article of clothing,** but in ordinary conversation, you usually name the piece of clothing you are talking about.

'clothing'   Clothing /kləʊðɪŋ/ is the clothes people wear. **Clothing** is an uncount noun. You do not talk about 'clothings' or 'a clothing'.

He takes off his wet clothing.
All masters had to provide their slaves with food, clothing, and a house.

'cloth'   Cloth /klɒθ/ is fabric such as wool or cotton which is used for making such things as clothes.

...strips of cotton cloth.
The women were weavers of cloth.

Note that when **cloth** is used like this, it is an uncount noun.

A **cloth** is a piece of fabric used for cleaning or dusting. Note that the plural form of 'cloth' is **cloths,** not 'clothes'.

Clean with a soft cloth dipped in warm soapy water.
Don't leave damp cloths in a cupboard.

coach

See entry at **bus - coach.**

coast

See entry at **beach - shore - coast.**

coat

A **coat** is a piece of clothing with long sleeves which you wear over your other clothes, especially in order to keep warm.

She was wearing a heavy tweed coat.
Get your coats on.

You only use **coat** to refer to a piece of clothing which is worn outdoors. Knitted clothes which cover the upper part of your body and which you can wear indoors are called 'cardigans', 'jumpers', or 'sweaters'.

coffee

See entry at **café - coffee.**

collaborate - co-operate

'collaborate'   When people **collaborate** on a project, they work together in order to produce something. For example, two writers can **collaborate** to produce a single piece of writing.

Anthony and I are collaborating on a paper for the conference.
The film was directed by Carl Jones, who collaborated with Rudy de Luca in writing it.

'co-operate' When people **co-operate,** they help each other.

...an example of the way in which human beings can co-operate for the common good.

If you **co-operate** with someone who asks for your help, you help them.

The editors agreed to co-operate.
I couldn't get the RAF to co-operate.

The spelling **cooperate** is sometimes used.

They are willing to cooperate in the training of medical personnel.

college

A **college** is an institution where students study after they have left school.

Computer Studies is one of the many courses at the local technical college.
...the Royal College of Music.

You use **college** immediately after a preposition when you are talking about someone's attendance at a college. For example, you say that someone is **at college.**

He hardly knew Andrew at college.
He says you need the money for college.
What do you plan to do after college?

colon

See entry at **Punctuation.**

colour

When you are describing the colour of something, you do not normally use the word **colour.** You do not say, for example, 'He wore a green colour tie'. You say 'He wore a **green** tie'.

She had blonde hair and green eyes.
...a bright yellow hat.

However, you sometimes use the word **colour** when you are asking about the colour of something, or when you are describing a colour in an indirect way.

What colour was the bird?
The paint was the colour of grass.

Note that in sentences like these you use **be,** not 'have'. You do not say 'What colour has the bird?' or 'The paint has the colour of grass'.

You also use the word **colour** when you are using more unusual colour words. For example, you can say that something is **a bluish-green colour.**

Both cubs were a silvery-grey colour.
There was the sea, a glittering cream colour.

You can also say, for example, that something is **bluish-green in colour.**

The leaves are rough and grey-green in colour.
The shells are pale brown to grey-blue in colour.

You can also add the suffix **-coloured** to the name of a colour.

...the cloudberry, an amber-coloured blackberry.

He selected one of his most expensive cream-coloured suits.

Note that the American spellings of 'colour' and '-coloured' are **color** and **-colored**.

come

You use **come** to talk about movement towards the place where you are, or towards a place where you have been or will be.

Come and look.
The joiner didn't come to put it back.
You must come and see me about it.

The past tense of 'come' is **came**. The past participle is **come**.

The children came along the beach towards me.
A ship had just come in from Turkey.

'come' or 'go'? When you are talking about movement away from the place where you are, you use **go,** not 'come'. You also use **go** when you are describing movement which is neither towards you nor away from you. For more information on talking about movement, see entry at **go.**

Note that you use 'here' with **come** and 'there' with **go.**

Elizabeth, come over here.
I still go there all the time.

If you invite someone to accompany you somewhere, you usually use **come,** not 'go'.

Will you come with me to the hospital?

In some situations, you can use **come** or **go** to show indirectly whether you will be in a place that you are referring to. For example, if you say 'Are you **going** to John's party?', you are not indicating whether you yourself are going to the party. However, if you say 'Are you **coming** to John's party?', you are showing that you will definitely be there.

'come' When you are saying what happened to someone else, for example in a
in stories story, you use **come** to talk about movement towards that person.

She looked up when they came into the room.
He thought he'd have another drink before the train came.

In stories, if someone **comes to** a place, they arrive there.

She eventually came to the town of Peconic.

'come and' You use **come and** with another verb to say that someone visits you or moves towards you in order to do something.

Come and see me whenever you feel depressed.
She would come and hold his hand.

used to mean **Come** is sometimes used to mean 'become'.
'become'
After a few taps the cover came loose.
Remember that some dreams come true.

See entry at **become.**

come from

If you **come from** a particular place, you were born there, or it is your home.

'Where do you come from?'—'India.'
I come from Zambia.

Note that you do not use a continuous tense in sentences like these. You do not say, for example, 'Where are you coming from?' or 'I am coming from Zambia'.

come to

See entry at **arrive - reach**.

come with

See entry at **accompany**.

comic - comical

When people or things seem amusing or absurd, you can describe them as **comic** or **comical**.

Everything began to appear strange and comic.
There is something slightly comical about him.

Comic is also used to describe things which are intended to be funny. When **comic** has this meaning, you only use it in front of a noun.

He likes wearing comic hats.
He did comic tricks like hiding in a tree and falling out of it.

Comic appears with this meaning in several compounds, such as 'comic opera', 'comic strip', and 'comic relief'.

Comical is not usually used to describe things which are intended to be funny.

comma

See entry at **Punctuation**.

commence

See entry at **start - begin - commence**.

comment - commentary

'comment' A **comment** is something you say which expresses your opinion of something.

People in the town started making rude comments.
It is unnecessary for me to add any comment.

'commentary' A **commentary** is a description of an event that is broadcast on radio or television while the event is taking place.

We gathered round the radio to hear the commentary.
...a commentary on the Cheltenham Gold Cup.

committee

A **committee** is a group of people who represent a larger group or organization and who make decisions or plans on behalf of that group or organization.

A special committee has been set up.

You can use either a singular or plural form of a verb after **committee**.

Since 1963 the Committee has struggled, unable to shake off its weaknesses.
The National Executive Committee have their travelling expenses paid.

common

If something is **common,** it is found in large numbers or it happens often.

The rhesus is one of the commonest monkeys in India.
In some parts of the world it is common to see people with a swelling of the neck called goitre.

You do not use a 'that'-clause after **common.** You do not say, for example, 'It is quite common that motorists fall asleep while driving'. You say 'It is quite common **for motorists to fall asleep** while driving'.

It is common for a child to become deaf after even a moderate ear infection.
It is quite common for dogs to be poisoned in this way.

company

A **company** is a business organization that makes money by selling goods or services.

He is a geologist employed by an oil company.

You can use either a singular or plural form of a verb after **company.**

The company has taken on 1600 more highly-paid staff.
The insurance company have approved the burglarproofing.

GRAMMAR **Comparative and superlative adjectives**

comparative adjectives **Comparative adjectives** are used to indicate that something has more of a quality than something else, or more than it used to have. The comparative of an adjective is formed by adding '-er', as in 'smaller', or by putting 'more' in front of the adjective, as in 'more interesting'.

...the battle for safer and healthier working environments.
Current diesel engines are more efficient than petrol engines in terms of miles per gallon.

superlative adjectives **Superlative adjectives** are used to indicate that something has more of a quality than anything else of its kind, or more than anything else in a particular group or place. The superlative of an adjective is formed by adding '-est', as in 'smallest', or by putting 'most' in front of the adjective, as in 'most interesting'. Superlatives are usually preceded by 'the'.

...the oldest building in the city.
A house or a self-contained flat is the most suitable type of accommodation for a family.

WARNING In conversation, people often use a superlative rather than a comparative when they are comparing just two things. For example, someone might say 'The train is quickest' rather than 'The train is quicker' when comparing a train service with a bus service. However, you should not use a superlative like this in formal writing.

forming comparative and superlative adjectives

The choice between adding '-er' and '-est' or using 'more' and 'most' usually depends on the number of syllables in the adjective.

With one-syllable adjectives, you usually add '-er' and '-est' to the end of the adjective.

tall – taller – tallest
quick – quicker – quickest

If the adjective ends in a single vowel letter and a single consonant letter, you double the consonant letter (unless the consonant is 'w').

big – bigger – biggest
fat – fatter – fattest

If the adjective ends in 'e', you remove the 'e'.

rare – rarer – rarest
wide – wider – widest

'Dry' usually has the comparative 'drier' and the superlative 'driest'. However, with the other one-syllable adjectives ending in 'y' ('shy', 'sly', and 'spry'), you do not change the 'y' to 'i' before adding '-er' and '-est'.

two syllables

You also add '-er' and '-est' to two-syllable adjectives ending in 'y', such as 'angry', 'dirty', and 'silly'. You change the 'y' to 'i'.

happy – happier – happiest
easy – easier – easiest

Other two-syllable adjectives usually have comparatives and superlatives formed with 'more' and 'most'. However, 'clever' and 'quiet' have comparatives and superlatives formed by adding '-er' and '-est'.

Some two-syllable adjectives have both kinds of comparative and superlative.

I can think of many pleasanter subjects.
It was more pleasant here than in the lecture room.

Exposure to sunlight is one of the commonest causes of cancer.
...five hundred of the most common words.

Here is a list of common adjectives which have both kinds of comparative and superlative:

common	handsome	narrow	polite	simple
cruel	likely	obscure	remote	stupid
gentle	mature	pleasant	shallow	subtle

'Bitter' has the superlative form 'bitterest' as well as 'most bitter'. 'Tender' has the superlative form 'tenderest' as well as 'most tender'.

three or more syllables

Adjectives which have three or more syllables usually have comparatives and superlatives with 'more' and 'most'.

dangerous – more dangerous – most dangerous
ridiculous – more ridiculous – most ridiculous

However, this does not apply to three-syllable adjectives formed by adding 'un-' to the beginning of other adjectives, for example 'unhappy' and 'unlucky'. These adjectives have comparatives and superlatives formed by adding '-er' and '-est' as well as ones formed by using 'more' and 'most'.

He felt crosser and unhappier than ever.
He may be more unhappy seeing you occasionally.

Comparative and superlative adjectives

<table>
<tr><td>irregular forms</td><td>A few common adjectives have irregular comparative and superlative forms.</td></tr>
</table>

good — better — best
bad — worse — worst
far — farther/further — farthest/furthest
old — older/elder — oldest/eldest

See entries at **farther - further** and **elder** for more information on the forms of 'far' and 'old'.

'little'   There is no comparative or superlative of 'little' in standard English. To make a comparison, 'smaller' and 'smallest' are used.

'ill'   'Ill' does not have a comparative or superlative form. When you want to use a comparative, you use 'worse'.

Each day Kunta felt a little worse.

colour adjectives   Usually only qualitative adjectives have comparatives and superlatives, but a few basic colour adjectives also have these forms.

His face was redder than usual.
...some of the greenest scenery in America.

compound adjectives   The comparatives and superlatives of compound adjectives are usually formed by putting 'more' and 'most' in front of the adjective.

nerve-racking — more nerve-racking — most nerve-racking

Some compound adjectives have as their first part adjectives or adverbs with single-word comparatives and superlatives. The comparatives and superlatives of these compounds sometimes use these single-word forms, rather than 'more' and 'most'.

good-looking — better-looking — best-looking
well-known — better-known — best-known

The following compound adjectives have comparatives or superlatives using single-word forms:

good-looking	long-standing	well-behaved	well-off
high-paid	low-paid	well-dressed	
long-lasting	short-lived	well-known	

another use of 'most'   'Most' can also be used in front of some adjectives to mean 'very'.

This book was most interesting.
My grandfather was a most extraordinary man.

See entry at **most**.

'more or less'   The expression 'more or less' is used in front of adjectives (and other words) to indicate that something is almost the case. It does not indicate a comparison.

The basic federal organization remained more or less intact.
I had gradually become more or less immune to feeling of every kind.

using comparatives   Comparatives can be used in front of nouns or as complements after link verbs.

Their demands for a bigger defence budget were refused.
To the brighter, more advanced child, they will be challenging.

Be more careful next time.
His breath became quieter.

Comparatives normally come in front of all other adjectives in a noun group.

Some of the <u>better</u> English actors have gone to live in Hollywood.

comparatives with 'than' Comparatives are often followed by 'than' and a noun group or clause, to specify the other thing involved in the comparison.

My brother is younger <u>than me.</u>
I was a better writer <u>than he was.</u>
I would have done a better job <u>than he did.</u>

linked comparatives You can indicate that the amount of one quality or thing is linked to the amount of another quality or thing by using two comparatives preceded by 'the'.

<u>The larger</u> the organization, <u>the less</u> scope there is for decision.
<u>The earlier</u> you detect a problem, <u>the easier</u> it is to cure.

Note that you can use comparative adjectives or adverbs in this structure. You can also use the comparative determiners and pronouns 'more', 'less', and 'fewer'.

using superlatives Superlatives can be used in front of nouns, or as complements after link verbs.

He was the <u>cleverest</u> man I ever knew.
Now we come to the <u>most important</u> thing.

He was the <u>youngest.</u>
The sergeant was the <u>tallest.</u>

Superlatives normally come in front of all other adjectives in a noun group.

These are the <u>highest</u> monthly figures on record.

You usually put 'the' in front of a superlative. However, 'the' is omitted after a link verb when the comparison does not involve a group of things. It is also sometimes omitted in conversation or informal writing when comparing a group of things.

Beef is <u>nicest</u> slightly underdone.
Wool and cotton blankets are generally <u>cheapest.</u>

WARNING You cannot omit 'the' when the superlative is followed by a structure indicating what group of things you are comparing. For example, you cannot say 'Amanda was youngest of our group'. You must say 'Amanda was the youngest of our group'.

You can use possessive determiners and nouns with 's instead of 'the' in front of a superlative.

...the <u>school's</u> most famous headmaster.
...<u>my</u> newest assistant.

Note that this is not usually done when the superlative is used after a link verb.

indicating group or place You can use a superlative on its own if it is clear what is being compared. However, if you need to indicate the group or place involved, you use:

● a prepositional phrase, normally beginning with 'of' for a group or 'in' for a place

Henry was the biggest <u>of them.</u>
These cakes are probably the best <u>in the world.</u>
...one of the worst deserts <u>in Australia.</u>

● a relative clause

It's the best I'm likely to get.
The visiting room was the worst I had seen.
That's the most convincing answer that you've given me.

● an adjective ending in '-ible' or '-able'

...the longest possible gap.
...the most beautiful scenery imaginable.

'of all' If you want to emphasize that something has more of a quality than anything else of its kind or in its group, you can use 'of all' after a superlative adjective.

The third requirement is the most important of all.
We are unlikely yet to have discovered the oldest fossils of all.

with ordinal numbers **Ordinal numbers,** such as 'second', are used with superlatives to say that something has more of a quality than nearly all other things of its kind or in its group. For example, if you say that a mountain is 'the second highest mountain in the world', you mean that it is higher than any other mountain except the highest one.

...Mobil, the second biggest industrial company in the United States.
It is Japan's third largest city.

comparison with 'less' and 'least' To indicate that something does not have as much of a quality as something else or as it had before, you can use 'less' in front of an adjective. See entry at **less.**

The cliffs here were less high.
As the days went by, Sita became less anxious.

To indicate that something has less of a quality than anything else or less than anything in a particular group or place, you use 'least' in front of an adjective.

This is the least popular branch of medicine.

GRAMMAR **Comparative and superlative adverbs**

Comparative and superlative adverbs are used to say how something happens or is done compared with how it happened or was done on a different occasion. They are also used to say how something is done by one person or thing compared with how it is done by someone or something else.

forming comparative and superlative adverbs The comparative of an adverb is usually formed by putting 'more' in front of the adverb.

He began to speak more quickly.
The people needed business skills so that they could manage themselves more effectively.

The superlative of an adverb is usually formed by putting 'most' in front of the adverb.

You are likely to have bills which can most easily be paid by post.
The country most severely affected was Holland.

single-word forms Some very common adverbs have comparatives and superlatives that are single words and are not formed using 'more' and 'most'.

The comparative and superlative forms of 'well' are 'better' and 'best'.

...when I got to know him better.
Why don't you go back to doing what you do best?

The usual comparative and superlative forms of 'badly' are 'worse' and 'worst'.

Socially, my wife fares <u>worse</u> than I do.
Those in the poorest groups are <u>worst</u> hit.

However, 'badly' has a special meaning for which the comparative and superlative are 'more badly' and 'most badly'. This is explained in the entry at **bad - badly**.

Adverbs which have the same form as adjectives have the same comparatives and superlatives as the adjectives.

This would enable claims to be dealt with <u>faster</u>.
They worked <u>harder</u>, they were more honest.
The person who sang <u>loudest</u> took the rest of us with him.

The following words have the same comparative and superlative forms whether they are used as adverbs or adjectives:

close	far	long	near	straight
deep	fast	loud	quick	tight
early	hard	low	slow	wide

The adverb 'late' has the comparative form 'later', and the adverb 'soon' has the comparative form 'sooner'. The superlative forms 'latest' and 'soonest' are hardly ever used.

'the' with superlatives

It is possible to use 'the' with single-word superlative adverbs, but this use is not common.

The old people work <u>the hardest</u>.

---

compare

When you **compare** things, you consider them and discover their differences or similarities.

It's interesting to <u>compare</u> the two prospectuses.

When **compare** has this meaning, you can use either 'with' or 'to' after it. For example, you can say 'It's interesting to compare the new prospectus **with** the old one' or 'It's interesting to compare the new prospectus **to** the old one'.

...studies <u>comparing</u> Russian children <u>with</u> those in Britain.
I haven't got anything to <u>compare</u> it <u>to</u>.

Note that this use of 'to' used to be considered incorrect.

Compare has another meaning. You use it to say that one person or thing is said to be like another one.

As an essayist he <u>is compared</u> frequently <u>to</u> Paine and Hazlitt.
A dominant idea can <u>be compared to</u> a river that has cut deep into the landscape.

When you use **compare** like this, you must use 'to' after it. You do not use 'with'.

Comparison

You can use **comparative adjectives** or **comparative adverbs** to say that something has more of a quality than something else, or more than it used to have.

The climbing became more difficult.
I thought I could deal with it better than Ivan.

See entries at **Comparative and superlative adjectives** and **Comparative and superlative adverbs**.

It is also possible to make comparisons using words and structures which indicate that something is the same as something else or is done in the same way.

Once she returned to Woodland, life went on very much as before.
You're just as bad as your sister.
He looked like an actor.
Their life expectancy is about the same as ours.

For more information about these uses, see entries at **as, as … as, like - as - the way,** and **same - similar.**

complain

'complain about'   If you **complain about** something, you say that it is wrong or unsatisfactory.

Mothers complained about the lack of play space.
She never complained about the weather.

Note that you do not use 'over' or 'on' after **complain**. You do not say, for example, 'Mothers complained over the lack of play space' or 'She never complained on the weather'.

'complain of'   You can also say that someone **complains of** something. However, if you **complain of** something, you are usually drawing someone's attention to it, as well as saying that it is wrong or unsatisfactory.

Women complain of pressure on them to get jobs.
Rioters in both countries complained of police brutality.

If you **complain of** a pain, you say that you have it.

He complained of pain in the chest.

complement - compliment

These words can both be used as verbs or nouns. When they are used as verbs, they are pronounced /ˈkɒmplɪment/. When they are used as nouns, they are pronounced /ˈkɒmplɪmənt/.

'complement'   If one thing **complements** another, they increase each other's good qualities when they are brought together.

Crisp pastry complements the juicy fruit of an apple pie.
Current advances in hardware development nicely complement British software skills.

A **complement** is an adjective or noun group which comes after a link verb such as 'be'. See entry at **Complements.**

'compliment' If you **compliment** someone, you tell them that you admire something that they have or something that they have done.

He complimented Morris on his new car.
She is to be complimented for handling the situation so well.

A **compliment** is something that you do or say to someone to show your admiration for them.

She took his acceptance as a great compliment.

You say that you **pay** someone a compliment.

He knew that he had just been paid a great compliment.

GRAMMAR # Complements

A **complement** is an adjective or noun group which comes after a **link verb** such as 'be', and gives more information about the subject of the clause.

The children seemed frightened.
He is a geologist.

There are also complements which describe the object of a clause: see the section below on **object complements**.

adjectives as complements **Adjectives** can be used as complements after the following link verbs:

appear	feel	keep	remain	stay
be	get	look	seem	taste
become	go	pass	smell	turn
come	grow	prove	sound	

We were very happy.
The other child looked neglected.
Their hall was larger than his whole flat.

WARNING You do not use an adverb after a link verb. For example, you say 'We felt very happy', not 'We felt very happily'.

'Come', 'go', and 'turn' are used with a restricted range of adjectives. For more information on this, and on the use of 'get' and 'grow', see entry at **become**.

noun groups as complements **Noun groups** can be used as complements after the following link verbs:

be	constitute	look	remain	sound
become	feel	make	represent	
comprise	form	prove	seem	

He always seemed a controlled sort of man.
He'll make a good president.
I feel a bit of a fraud.

Note that when you are saying what someone's job is, you use 'a' or 'an'. You do not just use the noun. For example, you say 'She's **a journalist**'. You do not say 'She's journalist'.

pronouns as complements **Pronouns** are sometimes used as complements to indicate identity or to describe something.

It's me again.
This one is yours.
You're someone who does what she wants.

Complements

'to'-infinitive clauses For information on the use of 'to'-infinitives after complements, as in 'It's an easy mistake to make', see entry at **'To'-infinitive clauses.**

other verbs with complements A small number of verbs which refer to actions can be followed by complements. For example, instead of saying 'He returned. He had not been harmed', you can say 'He returned unharmed'.

George stood motionless for at least a minute.
I used to lie awake watching the rain seep through the roof.
He died young.

The following verbs can be used with a complement like this:

be born	escape	return	survive
die	hang	sit	
emerge	lie	stand	

object complements Some transitive verbs have a complement after their object when they are used with a particular meaning. This complement describes the object, and is often called the **object complement.**

The following transitive verbs are used with an adjective as object complement:

believe	eat	label	presume	serve
call	find	leave	pronounce	term
certify	hold	like	prove	think
consider	judge	make	reckon	want
declare	keep	prefer	render	

Willie's jokes made her uneasy.
He had proved them all wrong.
Do you want it white or black?

Some verbs are used with a very restricted range of object complements:

to drive someone crazy/mad	to plane something flat/smooth
to burn someone alive	to rub something dry/smooth
to get someone drunk/pregnant	to send someone mad
to knock someone unconscious	to shoot someone dead
to paint something red, blue, etc	to sweep something clean
to pat something dry	to turn something white, black, etc
to pick something clean	to wipe something clean/dry

She painted her eyelids deep blue.
He wiped the bottle dry with a dishcloth.

The following transitive verbs are used with a noun group as object complement:

appoint	consider	elect	label	prove
believe	crown	find	make	reckon
brand	declare	hold	presume	term
call	designate	judge	proclaim	think

They consider him an embarrassment.
In 1910 Asquith made him a junior minister.

The following transitive verbs are used with a name as object complement:

call	dub	nickname
christen	name	

Everyone called her Molly.

complete

Complete is usually used as an adjective. For some of its meanings, you can use words like 'more' and 'very' in front of it.

used to mean 'as great as possible'

You usually use **complete** to say that something is as great in degree, extent, or amount as possible.

You need a complete change of diet.
They were in complete agreement.

When **complete** has this meaning, you do not use words like 'more' or 'very' in front of it.

used to talk about contents

Complete is also used to say that something contains all the parts that it should contain.

I have a complete medical kit.
This is not a complete list.

When two things do not contain all the parts that they should contain but one thing has more parts than the other, you can say that the first thing is **more complete** than the second one.

For a more complete picture of David's progress we must depend on his own assessment.

Similarly, if something does not contain all the parts that it should contain but contains more parts than anything else of its kind, you can say that it is the **most complete** thing of its kind.

...the most complete skeleton so far unearthed from that period.

used to mean 'thorough'

Complete is sometimes used to mean 'thorough'. When **complete** has this meaning, you can use words like 'very' and 'more' in front of it.

She followed her mother's very complete instructions on how to organize a funeral.
You ought to have a more complete check-up if you are really thinking of going abroad.

used to mean 'finished'

Complete is also used to say that something such as a task or new building has been finished.

The harvesting of groundnuts was complete.
...blocks of luxury flats, complete but half-empty.

When **complete** has this meaning, you do not use words like 'more' or 'very' in front of it.

completely

See section on **extent** in entry at **Adverbials**.

compliment

See entry at **complement - compliment**.

Complimenting and congratulating someone

clothes and appearance If you know someone quite well, or are talking to someone in an informal situation, you can compliment them on their clothes or appearance using an expression such as 'That's a nice coat', 'What a lovely dress', or 'I like your jacket'.

That's a nice dress.
That's a smart jacket you're wearing.
What a pretty dress.
I like your haircut.
I love your shoes. Are they new?

You can also say something like 'You look nice' or 'You're looking very smart today'. If you want to be more emphatic, you can use adjectives such as 'great' or 'terrific'.

You're looking very glamorous.
You look terrific.

You can also compliment someone on their appearance by saying that what they are wearing suits them.

I love you in that dress, it really suits you.

In Britain, men (especially older men) do not often comment on each other's appearance.

meals You can compliment someone on a meal by saying something like 'This is delicious' during the meal or 'That was delicious' after the meal.

This is delicious, Ginny.
He took a bite of meat, chewed it, savoured it, and said, 'Fantastic!'
Mm, that was lovely.

skills You can compliment someone on doing something skilfully or well using an exclamation.

What a marvellous memory you've got!
Oh, that's true. Yes, what a good answer!
'Look – there's a boat.'—'Oh yes – well spotted!'

A teacher might praise a pupil who has given a correct answer by saying 'Good'.

'What sort of soil do they prefer?'—'Acid soil.'—'Good.'

achievements You can say 'Congratulations' to someone to congratulate them on achieving something.

Well, congratulations, Ginny. You've done it.
Congratulations to all three winners.

Note that you can also say 'Congratulations' to someone when something nice has happened to them.

'I'm being discharged tomorrow.'—'That is good news. Congratulations.'
'Congratulations,' the doctor said. 'You have a son.'

For other ways of expressing your reaction to good news, see the section on **expressing pleasure** in the entry at **Reactions**.

There are several more formal ways of congratulating someone.

I must congratulate you on your new job.
Let me offer you my congratulations on your success.

Let me be the first to congratulate you on a wise decision, Mr Dorf.
May I congratulate you again on your excellent performance.
I'd like to congratulate you on your stand. You have courage and integrity.
Very good. I congratulate you. A beautiful piece of work.

You can congratulate someone informally by saying 'Well done'.

I then attached the syringe and injected 10 cc of the stuff. 'Well done,'
said the vet.

accepting
compliments
and
congratulations You can accept compliments with several different expressions.

Oh, thanks!
It's very nice of you to say so.
I'm glad you think so.

If someone compliments you on something you are wearing, you can also
say something like 'It is nice, isn't it?'

'I do like your dress.'—'Yes, it is nice, isn't it?'

You can also respond by saying how old it is, or how or where you got it.

'That's a nice blouse.'—'Have you not seen this before? I've had it for
years.'
'That's a nice piece of jewellery.'—'Yeah, my ex-husband bought it for me.'

If someone compliments you on your skill, you can say something modest
that implies that what you did was not very difficult or skilful.

Oh, there's nothing to it.
'Terrific job.'—'Well, I don't know about that.'

When someone congratulates you, you usually say 'Thanks' or 'Thank you'.

'I hear your voice is back as good as ever and you've got all your old fans
back. Congratulations.'—'Thanks.'

---

composed

See entry at **comprise**.

comprehensible - comprehensive

'comprehensible' If something is **comprehensible**, you can understand it.

The object is to make our research readable and comprehensible.
...language comprehensible only to the legal mind.

'comprehensive' If something is **comprehensive**, it is complete and includes everything that
is important.

...a comprehensive list of all the items in stock.
Linda received comprehensive training after joining the firm.

comprehension - understanding

'comprehension' Both **comprehension** and **understanding** can be used to talk about
someone's ability to understand something.

He noted Bond's apparent lack of comprehension.
The problems of solar navigation seem beyond comprehension.
A very narrow subject would have become too highly technical for general
understanding.

'understanding'
If you have an **understanding** of something, you have some knowledge of it, or you know how it works or what it means.

I doubt whether he had any real understanding of Shakespeare.
The job requires an understanding of Spanish.

Note that you cannot use **comprehension** with this meaning.

Understanding has another meaning. If there is **understanding** between people, they are friendly towards each other and trust each other.

What we need is greater understanding between management and workers.

comprehensive

See entry at **comprehensible - comprehensive**.

comprise

You say that something **comprises** particular things when you are mentioning all its parts.

The village's social facilities comprised one public toilet and two telephones.

'be composed of' and 'consist of'
You can also say that something **is composed of** or **consists of** particular things. There is no difference in meaning.

The book is composed of essays written over the last twenty years.
The committee consists of scientists and engineers.

Some people say that something 'is comprised of' particular things, but this is generally thought to be incorrect.

WARNING
You do not use a passive form of **consist of**. You do not say, for example, 'The committee is consisted of scientists and engineers'.

'constitute'
Constitute works in the opposite way to the verbs just mentioned. You say that the parts of something **constitute** the whole.

These 75,000 men constituted the whole strength of the Dutch Army.

You can also say that a number of things **constitute** a fraction of a whole.

Conifers constitute about a third of the world's forests.

'make up'
Make up can be used in either an active or passive form. In its active form, it has the same meaning as **constitute**.

Women now make up two-fifths of the British labour force.

In its passive form, it is followed by 'of' and has the same meaning as **be composed of**.

All substances are made up of molecules.
Nearly half the Congress is made up of lawyers.

WARNING
You do not use a continuous form of any of these verbs. You do not say, for example, 'The committee is consisting of scientists and engineers'.

conceited

See entry at **proud**.

concentrate

If you **concentrate** on something, you give special attention to it, rather than to other things.

Concentrate on your driving.
He believed governments should concentrate more on education.

You can say that someone **is concentrating** on something.

They are concentrating on saving life.
In 'Sociobiology', I was concentrating on ants, birds, and baboons.

Note that you do not say that someone 'is concentrated' on something.

When something **is concentrated** in a place, it is all in that place, rather than being spread around in several places.

Modern industry has been concentrated in a few large urban centres.

concerned

used after a link verb
The adjective **concerned** is usually used after a link verb such as 'be'.

If you **are concerned about** something, you are worried about it.

He was concerned about the level of unemployment.
We were concerned about our environment and were beginning to get organized.

If a book, speech, or piece of information **is concerned with** a subject, it deals with it.

This chapter is concerned with changes that are likely to take place.

Note that you do not say that a book, speech, or piece of information 'is concerned about' a subject.

used after a noun
Concerned can also be used immediately after a noun. You use it to refer to people or things involved in a situation that you have just mentioned.

We've spoken to the lecturers concerned.
Some of the chemicals concerned can cause cancer.

Concerned is often used with this meaning after the pronouns 'all', 'everyone', and 'everybody'.

It was a perfect arrangement for all concerned.
This was something of a relief to everyone concerned.

concerto

A **concerto** /kənʃɜːtəʊ/ is a piece of classical music written for one or more solo instruments and an orchestra.

...Beethoven's Violin Concerto.

'concert'
Note that you do not call a performance of music given by musicians a 'concerto'. You call it a **concert** /kɒnsət/.

She had gone to the concert that evening.

condominium

See entry at **flat - apartment**.

confidant - confident

'confidant'
Confidant /kɒnfɪdænt/ is a noun. A **confidant** is a person who you discuss your private problems and worries with. You use the spelling **confidante** when the person is a woman.

...Colonel House, a friend and confidant of President Woodrow Wilson.
She became her father's only confidante.

'confident' **Confident** /ˈkɒnfɪdənt/ is an adjective. If you are **confident** about something, you are certain that it will happen in the way you want.

He said he was very confident that the scheme would be successful.
I feel confident about the future of British music.

People who are **confident** are sure of their own abilities.

... a witty, young and confident lawyer.
His manner is more confident these days.

conform

If you **conform,** you behave in the way that you are expected to behave.

You must be prepared to conform.

You also use **conform** to say that something is what is wanted or required. When you use **conform** like this, you use either 'to' or 'with' after it.

Such a change would not conform to the present wishes of the great majority of people.
Every home should have a fire extinguisher which conforms with British Standards.

GRAMMAR **Conjunctions**

A **conjunction** is a word which links two clauses, groups, or words. There are two kinds of conjunction: coordinating conjunctions and subordinating conjunctions.

coordinating conjunctions **Coordinating conjunctions** link clauses, groups, or words of the same grammatical type, for example two main clauses or two adjectives.

The most common coordinating conjunctions are:

and	nor	then
but	or	yet

Anna had to go into town and she wanted to go to Bride Street.
I asked if I could borrow her bicycle but she refused.
Her manner was hurried yet painstakingly courteous.

'Nor', 'then', and 'yet' can be used after 'and'. 'Nor' and 'then' can be used after 'but'.

Eric moaned something and then lay still.
It is a simple game and yet interesting enough to be played with skill.
Institutions of learning are not taxed but nor are they much respected.

When coordinating conjunctions are used to link clauses that have the same subject, the subject is not usually repeated in the second clause.

She was born in Budapest and raised in Manhattan.
He didn't yell or scream.
When she saw Morris she went pale, then blushed.

For more detailed information, see entries at **and, but, nor,** and **or.**

subordinating conjunctions **Subordinating conjunctions** introduce **subordinate clauses.** A subordinating conjunction does not have to come between two clauses. It can introduce the first clause in a sentence.

He only kept thinking about it because there was nothing else to think about.

When the jar was full, he turned the water off.
Although she was eighteen, her mother didn't like her to stay out late.

For information on which conjunctions are used to introduce the various types of subordinate clause, see entry at **Subordinate clauses.**

---

conscious - consciousness - conscience - conscientious

'conscious' **Conscious** is an adjective. If you are **conscious** of something, you are aware of it.

She became conscious of Rudolph looking at her.
I was conscious that he had changed his tactics.

If you are **conscious,** you are awake, rather than asleep or unconscious.

The patient was fully conscious during the operation.

'consciousness' **Consciousness** is a noun. You can refer to your mind and thoughts as your **consciousness.**

We assume that the brain is the seat of consciousness and intelligence.
Doubts were starting to enter into my consciousness.

If you **lose consciousness,** you become unconscious. If you **regain consciousness** or **recover consciousness,** you become conscious again after being unconscious. These are fairly formal expressions.

He fell down and lost consciousness.
He began to regain consciousness just as Koch was leaving.
She died in hospital without recovering consciousness.

'conscience' **Conscience** is a noun. Your **conscience** is the part of your mind which tells you whether what you are doing is right or wrong.

My conscience told me to vote against the others.
Their consciences were troubled by stories of famine and war.

'conscientious' **Conscientious** is an adjective. Someone who is **conscientious** is very careful to do their work properly.

He was a very conscientious minister.
She seemed a conscientious, rather earnest young woman.

consider

If you **consider** something, you think about it carefully.

He had no time to consider the matter.
The American courts are currently considering claims by veterans of the Vietnam war.

You can say that someone **is considering doing** something in the future.

They were considering opening an office on the West Side of the city.
He was considering taking the bedside table downstairs.

Note that you do not say that someone 'is considering to do' something.

considerably

See section on **degree** in entry at **Adverbials.**

consist of

See entry at **comprise.**

constantly

See section on **frequency** in entry at **Adverbials.**

constitute

See entry at **comprise**.

consult

If you **consult** someone, you ask them for their opinion or advice.

If your baby is losing weight, you should consult your doctor promptly.
She wished to consult him about her future.
If you are renting from a private landlord, you should consult a solicitor to find out your exact position.

Some speakers of American English say **consult with** instead of 'consult'.

The Americans would have to consult with their allies about any military action in Europe.
He had flown backwards and forwards to Washington to consult with the President himself.

contemporary

See entry at **new**.

content

Content can be used as a noun, an adjective, or a verb. When it is used as a noun, it is pronounced /kɒntent/. When it is used as an adjective or verb, it is pronounced /kəntent/.

used as a plural noun
The **contents** of something such as a box or room are the things inside it.

...pouring out the contents of the bag.

Note that **contents** is a plural noun. You cannot talk about 'a content'.

The **contents** of something such as a document or tape are the things written in it or recorded on it.

He knew by heart the contents of the note.

used as an uncount noun
The **content** of something such as a speech, piece of writing, or television programme is the information it gives, or the ideas or opinions expressed in it.

I was disturbed by the content of some of the speeches.
BBC radio and television both now carry more current affairs content than does the popular press.

used as an adjective
If you are **content to do** something or are **content with** something, you are willing to do it, have it, or accept it.

A few teachers were content to pay the fines.
Children are not content with glib explanations.

If you are **content,** you are happy and satisfied. **Content** is not used with this meaning in front of a noun.

However hard up they were, they stayed content.
Not for years had she felt more content.

'contented'
You can also use **contented** to say that someone is happy and satisfied. **Contented** can be used in front of a noun or after a verb.

...firms with a loyal and contented labour force.
For ten years they lived like this and were perfectly contented.

Several other words can be used with a similar meaning to **content** or **contented**. For a list of these, see entry at **happy - sad**.

'content' used as a verb	If you **content yourself with** doing something, you are satisfied with it and do not try to do other things.

She didn't take part in the discussion, but contented herself with smoking cigarettes. |

continent

A **continent** is a very large area of land surrounded or almost surrounded by sea. A continent usually consists of several countries. Africa and Asia are continents.

...the South American continent.

'the Continent'	In Britain, when people talk about **the Continent,** they mean the mainland of Europe, especially central and southern Europe.

On the Continent, the tradition has been quite different.
Sea traffic between the United Kingdom and the Continent was halted. |

continual - continuous

Continual and **continuous** can both be used to describe things which continue to happen or exist without stopping.

...a continual movement of air.
...the necessity for continual change.
...a continuous loving relationship.

Continual can only be used in front of a noun. You do not use it after a verb.

Continuous can be used either in front of a noun or after a verb.

It is dangerous to circle the head round in one continuous movement.
The change was gradual and by no means steady and continuous.

If you are describing something undesirable which continues to happen or exist without stopping, it is better to use **continual** rather than **continuous**.

Life is a continual struggle.
It was sad to see her the victim of continual pain.

Continual can also be used to describe things which happen repeatedly.

He still smoked despite the continual warnings of his nurse.
Valenti's face was handsome though bloated by continual drinking.

It is usually regarded as incorrect to use **continuous** to describe things which happen repeatedly.

continually

See section on **frequency** in entry at **Adverbials**.

GRAMMAR ## Continuous tenses

A **continuous tense** contains a form of the verb 'be' and a present participle. Continuous tenses are used when talking about temporary situations at a particular point in time. See entry at **Tenses.**

dynamic verbs	Verbs which are used in continuous tenses are sometimes called **dynamic verbs.**

The video industry has been developing rapidly.
He'll be working nights next week. |

Contractions

Contractions

stative verbs There are a number of verbs which are not normally used in continuous tenses. Verbs of this kind are sometimes called **stative verbs.**

The verbs in the following list are not normally used in continuous tenses when they are used with their commonest or basic meaning.

admire	despise	include	owe	seem
adore	detest	interest	own	sound
appear	dislike	involve	please	stop
astonish	envy	keep	possess	suppose
be	exist	know	prefer	surprise
believe	fit	lack	reach	survive
belong to	forget	last	realize	suspect
concern	hate	like	recognize	understand
consist of	have	look like	remember	want
contain	hear	love	resemble	wish
deserve	imagine	matter	satisfy	
desire	impress	mean	see	

'be' 'Be' is not usually used as a main verb in continuous tenses. However, you use it in continuous tenses when you are describing someone's behaviour at a particular time.

You're being naughty.

'have' 'Have' is not used in continuous tenses to talk about possession. However, you can use it in continuous tenses to indicate that someone is doing something. See entry at **have.**

We were just having a philosophical discussion.

other verbs Some verbs have very specific senses in which they are not used in continuous tenses. For example, 'smell' is sometimes used in continuous tenses when it means 'to smell something deliberately', but not when it means 'to smell of something'.

She was smelling her bunch of flowers.
The air smelled sweet.

The following verbs are not used in continuous tenses when they have the meanings indicated:

depend (be related to)	smell (of something)	weigh (have weight)
feel (have an opinion)	taste (of something)	
measure (have length)	think (have an opinion)	

GRAMMAR **Contractions**

A **contraction** is a shortened form in which a subject and an auxiliary verb, or an auxiliary verb and 'not', are combined to form one word.

I'm getting desperate.
She wouldn't believe me.

You use contractions when you are writing down what someone says, or when you are writing in a conversational style, for example in letters to friends.

The contracted forms of 'be' are used when 'be' is a main verb as well as when it is an auxiliary. The contracted forms of 'have' are not usually used when 'have' is a main verb.

156

The following table shows contractions of personal pronouns and 'be', 'have', 'will', 'shall', and 'would'.

be—simple present		
I am	I'm	/aɪm/
you are	you're	/jɔ:/, /jʊə/
he is	he's	/hi:z/
she is	she's	/ʃi:z/
it is	it's	/ɪts/
we are	we're	/wɪə/
they are	they're	/ðeə/
Also: 's added to names, singular nouns, and 'wh'-words 'there's', 'here's', 'that's'		

have—simple present		
I have	I've	/aɪv/
you have	you've	/ju:v/
he has	he's	/hi:z/
she has	she's	/ʃi:z/
it has	it's	/ɪts/
we have	we've	/wi:v/
they have	they've	/ðeɪv/
Also: 's added to names, singular nouns, and 'wh'-words 'there's', 'there've' (not common), 'that's'		

have—simple past		
I had	I'd	/aɪd/
you had	you'd	/ju:d/
he had	he'd	/hi:d/
she had	she'd	/ʃi:d/
it had	it'd	/ɪtəd/
we had	we'd	/wi:d/
they had	they'd	/ðeɪd/
Also: 'there'd', 'who'd'		

will/shall		
I shall/will	I'll	/aɪl/
you will	you'll	/ju:l/
he will	he'll	/hi:l/
she will	she'll	/ʃi:l/
it will	it'll	/ɪtəl/
we shall/will	we'll	/wi:l/
they will	they'll	/ðeɪl/
Also: 'll added to names and nouns (in speech) 'there'll', 'who'll', 'what'll', 'that'll'		

would		
I would	I'd	/aɪd/
you would	you'd	/ju:d/
he would	he'd	/hi:d/
she would	she'd	/ʃi:d/
it would	it'd	/ɪtəd/
we would	we'd	/wi:d/
they would	they'd	/ðeɪd/
Also: 'there'd', 'who'd', 'that'd'		

Contractions

WARNING

You cannot use any of the above contractions at the end of a clause. You must use the full form instead. For example, you say 'I said I would', not 'I said I'd'.

negative contractions

The following table shows contractions of 'be', 'do', 'have', modals, and semi-modals with 'not'.

be		
are not	aren't	/ɑːnt/
is not	isn't	/ɪznt/
was not	wasn't	/wɒznt/
were not	weren't	/wɜːnt/

do		
do not	don't	/dəʊnt/
does not	doesn't	/dʌznt/
did not	didn't	/dɪdnt/

have		
have	haven't	/hævnt/
has	hasn't	/hæznt/

modals		
cannot	can't	/kɑːnt/
could not	couldn't	/kʊdnt/
might not	mightn't	/maɪtnt/
must not	mustn't	/mʌsnt/
ought not	oughtn't	/ɔːtnt/
shall not	shan't	/ʃɑːnt/
should not	shouldn't	/ʃʊdnt/
will not	won't	/wəʊnt/
would not	wouldn't	/wʊdnt/

semi-modals		
dare not	daren't	/deənt/
need not	needn't	/niːdnt/

WARNING

There is no contracted form of 'am not' in standard English. In conversation and informal writing, 'I'm not' is used. However, 'aren't I?' is used in questions and question tags.

Aren't I brave?
I'm right, aren't I?

In standard English, a pronoun followed by a negative contraction of a modal or 'have' is more commonly used than a contraction followed by 'not'. For example, 'I won't', 'I wouldn't', and 'I haven't' are more common than 'I'll not', 'I'd not', and 'I've not'.

However, in the case of 'be', both types of contraction are equally common. For example, 'you're not' and 'he's not' are used as commonly as 'you aren't' and 'he isn't'.

You aren't responsible.
You're not responsible.

modals and 'have'

The auxiliary 'have' is not usually pronounced in full after 'could', 'might', 'must', 'should', and 'would'. The contractions 'could've', 'might've', 'must've', 'should've', and 'would've' are occasionally used in writing when reporting a conversation.

I must've fallen asleep.

You should've come to see us.

contrary

'on the contrary'
You say **on the contrary** when you are contradicting a statement that has just been made.

'You'll get tired of it.'—'On the contrary. I shall enjoy it.'

You also use **on the contrary** to introduce a positive statement which confirms a negative statement that you have just made.

There was nothing ugly about her dress: on the contrary, it had a certain elegance.

'on the other hand'
You do not say 'on the contrary' when you are going to mention a situation that contrasts with one you have just described. You do not say, for example, 'I don't like living in the centre of the town. On the contrary, it's useful when you want to buy something'. You say 'I don't like living in the centre of the town. **On the other hand,** it's useful when you want to buy something'.

It's certainly hard work. But, on the other hand, a man who wishes to have a career has to make a great many sacrifices.

control

Control can be used as a verb or a noun.

used as a verb
If someone **controls** something such as a country or an organization, they have the power to take all the important decisions about the way it is run.

The Australian administration at that time controlled the island.
His family had controlled the Times for more than a century.

Note that when **control** is used as a verb, it is not followed by a preposition.

used as a noun
Control is also used as a noun to refer to the power that someone has in a country or organization. You say that someone has control **of** a country or organization, or control **over** it.

They bought control of a building company and a glass factory.
Political control over colonies also proved useful.

another meaning
Control is used in the names of the parts of an airport, sea terminal, or border crossing where your documents and luggage are officially checked to make sure that they are in order.

...passport and customs controls.

However, you do not use **control** as a verb to mean 'check' or 'inspect'. You do not say, for example, 'My luggage was controlled'. You say 'My luggage **was checked**' or 'My luggage **was inspected**'.

He offered me a cigar while the baggage was being checked.
The guard took his ID card and inspected it.

convince

If you **convince** someone of something, you make them believe it is true.

These experiences convinced me of the drug's harmful effects.
It took them a few days to convince me that it was possible.

Some American speakers use **convince** with a 'to'-infinitive to say that one person makes another person decide to do something, by giving them a good reason for doing it.

Lyon did his best to <u>convince</u> me to settle in Tennessee.
I hope you will help me <u>convince</u> my father to leave.

'persuade' Some British speakers also use **convince** in this way. However, this use is generally regarded as incorrect. Instead of using 'convince' in sentences like these, you should use **persuade.**

Marsha was trying to <u>persuade</u> Posy to change her mind.
They had no difficulty in <u>persuading</u> him to launch a new paper.

convinced

If you are **convinced** of something, you are sure that it is true or genuine.

I am <u>convinced</u> of your loyalty.
He was <u>convinced</u> that her mother was innocent.

You do not use words such as 'very' or 'extremely' in front of **convinced.** If you want to emphasize that someone has no doubts about something, you use words such as 'fully' or 'totally' in front of **convinced.**

To be <u>fully convinced</u> that reading is important, they have to find books they like.
I am <u>totally convinced</u> it was an accident.
He is <u>absolutely convinced</u> that the Reagan administration is thinking of using the bomb here.
Davidson Black was <u>firmly convinced</u> that primitive man would one day be found in China.

WARNING You do not use a 'to'-infinitive after **convinced.** You do not say, for example, 'He is convinced to have failed'. You say 'He is **convinced that he has** failed'.

cook

'cook'
used as a noun A **cook** is someone who cooks meals as their job.

Each house had a <u>cook</u> and an assistant <u>cook.</u>

You can also describe anyone's ability to cook by using **cook** with an adjective. For example, you can say that someone is **a good cook** or **a bad cook.**

Are you <u>a good cook?</u>
Appuhamy was <u>an excellent cook.</u>

'cook'
used as a verb If you **cook** a meal or a particular type of food, you prepare it for eating and then heat it, for example in an oven or saucepan.

As dawn broke we began to <u>cook</u> our breakfast.
We <u>cooked</u> the pie in the oven.

Note that **cook** is only used to talk about food, not drinks.

Several other verbs can be used to talk about the preparation of food and drinks:

'make' If you **make** a meal or a drink, you combine foods or drinks together to produce something different. Note that someone can **make** a meal without heating anything.

I <u>made</u> his breakfast.
I <u>have made</u> you a drink.

'prepare'	**Prepare** is used in two ways. If you **prepare** food, you clean or cut it so that it is ready to be used.

Prepare the vegetables. Peel and slice the celeriac, and then cut into fine strips.

To **prepare** a meal or drink means the same as to **make** it (see above). This is a fairly formal use.

'get'	If you **get** a meal, you prepare it or cook it. You can also say that someone **gets** a meal **ready**. If you **get** a drink, you either mix drinks together or pour a drink.

Then I'd get the tea ready.
I was downstairs getting the drinks.

'fix'	In American English, if you **fix** a meal or drink, you **make** it (see above).

Sometimes Jean would come in and fix breakfast for both of them.
Morris fixed himself a stiff drink.

There are many verbs which refer to different ways of cooking things:

'bake', 'roast'	When you **bake** or **roast** something, you cook it in an oven without liquid. You **bake** bread and cakes, but you **roast** meat. When you **roast** potatoes, you cook them in an oven in some fat. You can also **roast** a large piece of meat or a bird over a fire.

Note that you use **roast**, not 'roasted', to describe meat and potatoes that have been roasted.

...a traditional roast beef dinner.

'grill', 'toast'	When you **grill** or **toast** something, you cook it under or over strong heat. You **grill** meat and vegetables, but you **toast** slices of bread. Speakers of American English usually use **broil** rather than 'grill'.
'boil', 'poach', 'steam'	When you **boil** something, you cook it in boiling water. When you **poach** something, you cook it gently in shallow hot water. You can also **steam** something; that is, cook it in the steam rising from a pan of hot water.
'fry'	When you **fry** something, you cook it in hot fat or oil.
'casserole', 'stew', 'braise'	When you **casserole, stew,** or **braise** something, you cook it fairly slowly in a liquid or sauce.

cooker

A **cooker** is a metal oven and hot plate that you use for boiling, grilling, or roasting food.

The food was warming in a saucepan on the cooker.

Note that you do not refer to a person who cooks meals as a 'cooker'. You call them a **cook**. See entry at **cook**.

co-operate

See entry at **collaborate - co-operate**.

cord

See entry at **chord - cord**.

corn

In American English, **corn** is usually used to refer to the kernels of a particular type of maize, served as a vegetable. In British English, this vegetable is called **sweetcorn**.

In British English, **corn** is used to refer to any type of cereal plant growing in a particular area, for example wheat, barley, or maize.

corner

A **corner** is a place where two sides or edges of something meet.

...a television set in the corner of the room.

When two streets meet, you refer to each of the places where their edges meet as a **corner.**

There is a telephone box on the corner.

You usually say that something is **in** a corner. However, you use **on** when you are talking about the corner of a street.

Peel was working in the corner of a room.
...in one corner of the small, square playground.

...the garage on the corner of the street.
The drugstore was on the corner of the block.

corps - corpse

These words look similar but they are pronounced differently and have completely different meanings.

'corps'   A **corps** /kɔː/ is a group of people, often soldiers, who have been trained or organized for a particular purpose or task.

...the Royal Army Ordnance Corps.
...the diplomatic corps.

'corpse'   A **corpse** /kɔːps/ is a dead body.

At the edge of the woods he found the corpse of a young paratrooper.

cost

See entry at **price - cost.**

cot - crib - camp bed

In British English, a **cot** is a bed for a baby. A cot has high sides to prevent the baby from falling out. In American English, a bed like this is called a **crib.**

In American English, a **cot** is a narrow bed for an adult. It is made of canvas fitted over a frame, and you can fold it up. You take it with you when you go camping, or you use it as a spare bed at home. In British English, a bed like this is called a **camp bed.**

could

See entry at **can - could - be able to.**

council - counsel

'council'   Council /kaʊnsəl/ is a noun. A **council** is a group of people who run a local area such as a town, city, or county.

...Wiltshire County Council.

Some other groups of people who run organizations are also called **Councils.**

...the Arts Council.
...the British Council of Churches.

'counsel' Counsel /kaʊnsəl/ is usually used as a verb. If you **counsel** someone, you give them advice about their problems.

Part of her work is to counsel families when problems arise.

country

A **country** is one of the political areas which the world is divided into.

The level of unemployment in this country is too high.
Does this system apply in other European countries?

'the country' You refer to land which is away from towns and cities as **the country.**

We live in the country.
There was a big move of people away from the country to the towns.

WARNING When you use **country** like this, the only determiner you can use with it is 'the'. You do not say, for example, 'I like living in Paris, but my parents prefer to live in a country'.

couple

See entry at **pair - couple.**

course

A **course** is a series of lessons or lectures on a particular subject. It usually includes reading and written work that a student has to do. You say that someone takes a course **in** a subject.

The department also offers a course in Opera Studies.
...the Special Honours course in Latin.

Note that you do not say that someone takes a course 'of' a subject.

In British English, the people who are taking a course are referred to as the people **on** the course.

The other people on the course had the advantage that they could go into schools and see how their reading schemes were in fact working.

In American English, they are referred to as the people **in** the course.

How many are there in the course as a whole?

craft

A **craft** is an activity such as weaving, carving, or pottery that involves making things skilfully by hand, often in a traditional way. When **craft** has this meaning, its plural form is **crafts.**

It's a pity to see the old crafts dying out.

A **craft** is also a vehicle such as a boat, hovercraft, or submarine that carries people or things on or under water. When **craft** has this meaning, its plural form is **craft.**

There were eight destroyers and fifty smaller craft.

crazy

See entry at **madness.**

credible - credulous - creditable

'credible' If something is **credible,** it can be believed.

His latest statements are hardly credible.
This is not credible to anyone who has studied the facts.

Note that **credible** is most commonly used in negative sentences.

'credulous'
People who are **credulous** are always ready to believe what other people tell them, and are easily deceived.

Credulous women bought the mandrake root to promote conception.

'creditable'
A performance, achievement, or action that is **creditable** is of a reasonably high standard.

He polled a creditable 44.8 percent.
Their performance was even less creditable.

crib

See entry at **cot - crib - camp bed.**

crime

A **crime** is an illegal action for which a person can be punished by law. You usually say that someone **commits** a crime.

A crime has been committed.
The police had no evidence of him having committed any actual crime.

Note that you do not say that someone 'does' a crime or 'makes' a crime.

crippled

In the past, when someone had a physical condition that severely affected their life, people used to say that they were **crippled** or refer to them as **a cripple.** Nowadays, these words are avoided because they are thought to be offensive.

The adjectives **disabled, handicapped,** and **physically handicapped** are often used to describe people who have a condition of this kind. **Handicapped** and **physically handicapped** are used especially to describe someone who is born with the condition. You can also say that someone is **in a wheelchair,** if they are unable to walk.

The most sensitive ways of referring to people with a restricting physical condition are to call them **people with disabilities** or **people with special needs.**

Those who will gain the most are people with disabilities and their carers.
Employers are not prepared to pay for the training of young people with special needs.

crisps

See entry at **chips.**

criterion

A **criterion** is a standard by which you judge or evaluate something.

Profitability is the sole criterion for our policy.

The plural of 'criterion' is **criteria,** not 'criterions'.

The Commission did not apply the same criteria to advertising.

WARNING
Criteria is only used as a plural form. You do not talk about 'a criteria' or 'this criteria'.

critic - critical - critique

'critic' Critic /krɪtɪk/ is a noun. A **critic** is a person who writes reviews and expresses opinions in newspapers or on television about books, films, music, or art.

What did the New York critics have to say about the production?
...comments by a couple of television critics.

'critical' You do not use **critic** as an adjective. The adjective which means 'relating to the work of a critic' is **critical**. When **critical** has this meaning, you only use it in front of a noun.

I was planning a serious critical study of Shakespeare.

Critical has two other meanings. For both these meanings, **critical** can be used either in front of a noun or after a verb.

If you are **critical** of someone or something, you express disapproval of them.

Whole groups of nations adopted a more critical attitude towards apartheid.
He had long been critical of Conservative policy.

A **critical** time or situation is extremely important or serious.

This was a critical moment in his career.
The problem of food supplies is bound to be critical.

'critique' Critique /krɪtiːk/ is a noun. A **critique** is a written analysis and judgement of a situation or of a person's work. **Critique** is a formal word.

...an intelligent and incisive critique of our society.
In 1954, Golub published 'A Critique of Abstract Expressionism'.

'review' You do not refer to an item written in a newspaper by a critic as a 'critique'. You call it a **review.**

...a book review.
He hadn't even given the play a bad review.

Criticizing someone

People do not usually express criticism strongly unless they know the person they are criticizing well.

If you want to criticize someone for doing something badly, you can say something like 'That's not very good' or 'I think that's not quite right'.

What answer have you got? Oh dear. Thirty-three. That's not very good.
I think your answer's wrong.

A teacher might criticize a pupil's work by saying 'You can do better than this'.

stronger criticism If you want to criticize someone for doing something wrong or stupid, you can use a question beginning 'Why did you...?' or 'Why didn't you...?' Questions like this can be used to express great anger or distress, or merely exasperation.

Why did you send him? Why Ben?
Why did you lie to me?

Why did you do it?
Why didn't you tell me?

You can be more direct and say 'You shouldn't have...' or 'You should have...'.

You shouldn't have given him money.
You should have asked me.

Some people say 'How could you?' when they feel very strongly that someone has been thoughtless.

How could you? You knew I didn't want anyone to know!
How could you be so stupid?

very strong criticism There are other ways of expressing criticism which are even more direct or impolite. If you use expressions like the ones below, you will probably offend the other person.

That's no good.
That won't do.
This is wrong. These are all wrong.
You're hopeless.
'He told me he was going straight to you.'—'But he didn't.'—'You liar.'

---

critique

See entry at **critic - critical - critique.**

cry

Cry can be used as a verb or a noun. The other forms of the verb are **cries, crying, cried.** The plural of the noun is **cries.**

If you **cry**, tears come out of your eyes because you are unhappy, afraid, or in pain.

Helen began to cry.
Feed the baby as often as it cries.
They cried for their mothers.
We heard what sounded like a little girl crying.

In conversation, you can say that someone has a **cry.**

She felt a lot better after a good cry.

'weep' **Weep** means the same as **cry. Weep** is an old-fashioned word which is now used only in stories. The past tense and past participle of 'weep' is **wept,** not 'weeped'.

The girl was weeping as she kissed him goodbye.
James wept when he heard the news.

another meaning of 'cry' In a story, if someone **cries** something, they shout it.

'Come on!' he cried.
He cried out angrily, 'Get out of my house!'

A **cry** is something that someone shouts.

When she saw him she uttered a cry of surprise.
We heard cries of 'Help! Please help me!' coming from the river.

cup

A **cup** is a small, round container, usually with a handle, from which you drink hot drinks such as tea and coffee. When you are not holding a cup, you usually rest it on a **saucer**.

...a china cup.
John put his cup and saucer on the coffee table.

'glass'   You do not refer to a container made out of glass and used for cold drinks as a 'cup'. You call it a **glass**.

I put down my glass and stood up.
He poured Ellen a glass of wine.

cupboard

A **cupboard** is a piece of furniture with doors at the front and usually shelves inside.

'wardrobe'   A **wardrobe** is a tall cupboard, usually in a bedroom, which has space for hanging clothes.

'closet'   A cupboard or wardrobe is sometimes built into the wall of a room, rather than being a separate piece of furniture. In American English, a built-in cupboard or wardrobe is called a **closet**.

curb - kerb

'curb'   Curb can be used as a noun or a verb.

If you **curb** something, you control it and keep it within definite limits.

...proposals to curb the powers of the Home Secretary.
A man must decide either to curb his appetites or surrender to them.

You can say that someone imposes a **curb** on something.

This requires a curb on public spending.
In the sixties spending curbs were relaxed.

'kerb'   Curb is also the American spelling of the noun **kerb**. There is no difference in pronunciation. The **kerb** is the raised edge between a pavement and a road.

The taxi pulled into the kerb.
I pulled up at the curb.

curiosity

Curiosity is a desire to know about something and to learn as much as possible about it.

She looked at me, eyes wide open and full of curiosity.
She showed an insatiable curiosity about my past.

'out of curiosity'   You often say that someone does something **out of curiosity**.

Out of curiosity, I went down to the chapel on the first Sunday.

Note that you do not say that someone does something 'from curiosity'.

You can also say **out of curiosity** when you are asking a question. You do it to indicate that you are interested in the answer, but are not going to take any action as a result of knowing it.

They are definitely not for sale, but just out of curiosity, how much would he give?

curious

The following words can all be used to describe a person who is eager to find out about someone's life, or about an event or situation:

curious	interested	prying
inquisitive	nosy	

Curious is a neutral word, which does not show approval or disapproval.

Dominic was not <u>curious</u> about Tom's past and Tom didn't bother to tell him about the months on the road.

Interested is usually complimentary when it is used to talk about someone's interest in a person's life.

She put on a good show of looking <u>interested</u>.

Nosy and **prying** are used to show disapproval.

'Who is the girl you came in with?'—'Don't be so <u>nosy</u>.'
Computer-based records can easily be protected from <u>prying</u> eyes by simple systems of codes.

Note that **prying** is usually used with 'eyes'.

Inquisitive is sometimes used to show disapproval, but it can also be neutral or even complimentary.

Mr Courtney was surprised. 'A ring, you say?' He tried not to sound <u>inquisitive</u>.
Up close, he was a man with <u>inquisitive</u> sparkling eyes and a fresh, very down-to-earth smile.

another meaning of 'curious'

Curious can also be used to mean 'strange' or 'puzzling'.

A very <u>curious</u> incident now occurred.
He's a <u>curious</u> fellow.

Several other words can be used to mean 'strange' or 'puzzling'. For more information, see entry at **unusual**.

currant - current

These words are both pronounced /kʌrənt/.

'currant'

Currant is a noun. A **currant** is a small dried grape.

...dried fruits such as <u>currants</u>, raisins and dried apricots.

'current' used as a noun

Current can be used as a noun or an adjective.

A **current** is a steady and continuous flowing movement of some of the water in a river or lake, or in the sea.

The child had been swept out to sea by the <u>current</u>.

A **current** is also a steady flowing movement of air, or a flow of electricity through a wire or circuit.

A <u>current</u> of heated air rose all day from the mountain top.
There was a powerful electric <u>current</u> running through the wires.

'current' used as an adjective

Current is used to describe things which are happening or being used now, rather than at some time in the past or future.

Our <u>current</u> methods of production are far too expensive.

Several other words can be used with a similar meaning to **current**. For more information on these, see entry at **new**.

custom

See entry at **habit - custom**.

customer - client

'customer' A **customer** is someone who buys something, especially from a shop.

She's one of our regular customers.

'client' A **client** is a person or company that receives a service from a professional person or organization in return for payment.

...a solicitor and his client.

cut

If you **cut** something, you use something such as a knife or pair of scissors in order to remove a piece of it or damage it. The past tense and past participle of 'cut' is **cut,** not 'cutted'.

She cut the cake and gave me a piece.
...a few job adverts cut from the Times.

For information on words with a similar meaning, see entry at **damage**.

D

damage

Damage is one of several verbs which refer to ways of causing injury or harm.

Damage and **harm** are the most general verbs.

It is important for a child to learn that one should not damage someone else's property.
Too much detergent cannot harm a fabric, so long as it has been properly dissolved.

severe damage The following verbs refer to severe damage or harm of a general kind:

destroy	mutilate	ruin
devastate	pull apart	vandalize
mangle	ravage	wreck

The statue was destroyed.
Low-lying land is flooded and ruined.

Defile and **desecrate** are used to refer to damage done to something precious, pure, or sacred.

They began to find their places of worship desecrated with blood and mud.

damage to someone's body The following verbs refer to damage done to a person's body:

bruise	stab
injure	wound

Every year thousands of people are injured in accidents at work.
During the war he had been wounded in Africa.

Injure and **wound** are the most general terms, although **wound** is used mainly to refer to injuries caused in fighting. If someone **is bruised,** their skin is not broken but a purple mark appears. People **are stabbed** with something pointed, such as a knife.
See also entries at **injure** and **wound.**

spoiling The following verbs refer to acts which spoil the appearance or surface of something:

deface	mark	smudge
discolour	scar	spoil
disfigure	smear	stain

He was strongly cautioned against defacing the walls with obscenities.
When he untied the bundle in his kitchen, there were five oily guns staining the white cloth.

Deface, disfigure, mark, and **spoil** are the most general terms.

cutting The following verbs are used to refer to damage done with a knife, axe, or other sharp instrument:

cut	hack	nick	scratch	slice
chop	lacerate	pierce	sever	slit
gash	lop off	score	slash	

Their clothes were slashed to ribbons.
The wire had been neatly severed.

If you **cut, chop, hack, lop, slash,** or **slice** part of something **off,** you remove it.

Most of my hair had to be cut off.

Only **lop** has to be used with 'off'; you can use the other five verbs without 'off' to refer to damage that does not remove part of the object.

You can also **sever** part of something. **Sever** is a formal word.

One constable's hand was severed by a sword blow.

If you **score** or **scratch** something, you make a thin line in its surface. If you **nick** something, you make a small cut in it. The other verbs refer to bigger or deeper cuts.

dividing into pieces The following verbs refer to dividing something hard by force into two or more pieces, or dividing one part of it from another:

break	fracture	snap
chip	shatter	splinter
crack	smash	split

Doors and windows were smashed with sledgehammers.
The lorries cracked and ruined the roads.

If you **chip** or **splinter** something, you break a small piece of it off. If you **crack** something, a line appears where two parts of it are no longer joined. The other verbs refer to more serious damage.

You **tear, rip,** or **shred** cloth or paper.

She took the cheque and tore it into pieces.

A twig ripped a hole in my sleeve.

You **burst** something that is completely full of air or liquid, such as a balloon.

If you **crumble, crush,** or **pulverize** something, you press it so that it becomes a mass of small pieces.

I crumbled bread in my hands.
...after the rocks had been crushed, heated, and chemically processed.

changing the shape

The following verbs refer to acts which damage something by changing its shape:

bend	dent	squash
crumple	flatten	twist

He crumpled each picture and threw it on the floor.
The large bronze urns were dented beyond restoring.

Crush can also be used with this meaning when you are talking about cloth or paper.

Her dress had got crushed.

dare

The verb **dare** has two meanings.

main meaning

In its main meaning, it is normally used only in negative sentences and questions.

If you say that someone **daren't** do something, you mean that they do not have enough courage to do it.

I daren't ring Jeremy again.

If you are talking about the past, you say that someone **did not dare** do something or **didn't dare** do something. In formal writing, you can say that someone **dared not** do something.

She did not dare leave the path.
I didn't dare speak or move.
He dared not show that he was pleased.

A 'to'-infinitive is sometimes used after **did not dare.**

She did not dare to look at him.
He did not dare to walk to the village.

In other kinds of negative sentence, you can use an infinitive with or without 'to' after **dare.**

No one dares disturb him.
No other manager dared to compete.

In 'yes/no'-questions, you put the base form **dare** in front of the subject without using an auxiliary or modal. After the subject, you use an infinitive without 'to'.

Should she write to the girl? Dare she write?
Dare she go in?

Note that you use the base form whether you are talking about the present or the past.

In 'wh'-questions, you use a modal such as 'would' in front of **dare.** After **dare,** you can use either a 'to'-infinitive or an infinitive without 'to'.

Who *would dare to tell him?*
What bank *would dare offer such terms?*

'I dare say' You say **I dare say** or **I daresay** to indicate that you think that something is probably true.

It's worth a few pounds, I dare say, but no more.
Well, I daresay you've spent all your money by now.

Note that **I dare say** is a fixed phrase which cannot be varied. You do not say, for example, 'You dare say' or 'I dare to say'.

used as a In its other meaning, **dare** is used as a transitive verb. If you **dare**
transitive verb someone to do something dangerous, you challenge them to do it.

I dare you to spend the night in the graveyard.

data

Data is information, usually in the form of facts or statistics that can be analysed or used in further calculations.

Such tasks require the worker to process a large amount of data.
This will make the data easier to collect.

Data is usually regarded as an uncount noun and is used with a singular form of a verb.

The data was still being processed at the Census Office.
…whenever the data involves confrontation between nuclear powers.

People usually say **this data**, rather than 'these data'.

Processing this data only takes a moment.
He may be incapable of transferring this data correctly to a patient's records.

However, some people think these uses are incorrect. They say that **data** is the plural form of the noun 'datum', and should therefore be used with a plural form of a verb. They also say that you should talk about **these data**, not 'this data'.

He now denies that all knowledge comes from the senses at the moment the sense data are received.
For the most part these data are properly handled by conventional dualistic logic.

It is probably best in any kind of formal or scientific writing to use a plural form of a verb with **data** and to talk about **these data** rather than 'this data'. In other situations, you can use either form.

day

A **day** is one of the seven twenty-four hour periods in a week.

The attack occurred six days ago.
Can you go any day of the week? What about Monday?

You also use **day** to refer to the time when it is light and when people are awake and doing things. When **day** has this meaning, you can use it either as a count noun or an uncount noun.

The days were dry and the nights were cold.
…a typical working day.
They had waited three days and three nights for this opportunity.
The festivities would go on all day.
They hunt by day.

'today'   You refer to the actual day when you are speaking or writing as **today**.

I hope you're feeling better today.
I want to get to New York today.

Today is also used to refer to the present period in history.

Today we are threatened on all sides by financial and political crises.

'the other day'   You use **the other day** to indicate that something happened fairly recently.

I saw Davis the other day.
The other day, one of them asked me to tell him the main differences between reporting the America of today and the America of thirty years ago.

referring to a   If you want to refer to a particular day when an event happened or will
particular day   happen, you usually use a prepositional phrase beginning with **on**.

We didn't catch any fish on the first day.
On May Day we sat as honoured foreign guests in T'ien-an Men Square.
On the day after the race try to jog.

If you have already been talking about events that happened during a particular day, you can say that something else happened **that day**.

Geoff had appeared for lunch that day at Eden Gardens.
Then I took a bath, my second that day.
Later that day Mason was taken by police car from Barlinnie back to the High Court.

You can also say that something had happened **the day before** or **the previous day**.

The day before Kate had worn scarlet shorts for tennis.
My belongings had been taken from me the previous day.

You can also say that something happened **the next day** or **the following day**.

The next day the revolution broke out.
We were due to meet Hamish the following day.

When you have been talking about a particular day in the future, you can say that something will happen **the following day** or **the day after**.

Scotland's selectors will meet tomorrow evening and their team will be named the following day.
I could come the day after.

'every day'   If something happens regularly on each day, you say that it happens **every day**.

Every day I see Mr Davis.
Every day my newspaper tells me how dead our present religion is.

WARNING   Do not confuse **every day** with the adjective **everyday**. For an explanation of the differences, see entry at **everyday - every day**.

'these days'   You use **these days** when you are talking about things that are happening now, in contrast to things that happened in the past.

If you need medical help abroad these days, it can run into a small fortune.
Bob was drunk, as usual these days.

Nowadays is used in a similar way.

Kids nowadays are lazy.
Why don't we ever see Jim nowadays?

Days and dates

'in those days' You say **in those days** when you are describing a situation in the past which no longer exists.

Ice-cream in those days in Poland was considered to be a dangerous food. You yourself taught in the school in those days.

'one day' You use **one day** to say that something will happen at some indefinite time in the future.

Maybe he'll be Prime Minister one day.
Don't cry, Julie, I'll come back one day, I promise.

In stories, **one day** is used when a writer has just described a situation and is mentioning the first of a series of events.

One day a man called Cayley came in to pay his electricity bill.

other uses There are several ways in which **day** or **days** can be used to refer to a particular period in history.

In Shakespeare's day, women's parts were played by male actors.
She wrote in the early days of the republic.
In these days of vaccination measles and mumps are not so common as they used to be in my young days.
This is the main problem of the present day.

Note that when you use **day** or **days** like this in an adverbial, the preposition you use in the adverbial is always 'in'.

Days and dates

This entry tells you how to indicate the day, month, or year when something happens. Information on days, months, years, dates, seasons, decades, and centuries is given first, followed by information on which preposition to use. There is also information about other ways of talking about the date of an event.

For information on how to indicate the time or part of the day when something happens, see entry at **Time.**

days These are the days of the week:

Monday	Wednesday	Friday	Sunday
Tuesday	Thursday	Saturday	

Days of the week are always written with a capital letter. They are usually used without a determiner.

I'll send the cheque round on Monday.
Why didn't you come to the meeting on Wednesday?

However, if you are referring generally to any day with a particular name, you put 'a' in front of the day.

It is unlucky to cut your nails on a Friday.

If you want to say that something happened or will happen on a particular day of a particular week, especially when making a contrast with other days of that week, you put 'the' in front of the day.

He died on the Friday and was buried on the Sunday.
We'll come and see you on the Sunday.

See also the section on 'regular events' later in this entry.

Saturday and Sunday are often referred to as 'the weekend', and the other days as 'weekdays'.

I went down and fetched her back at the weekend.
The Tower is open 9.30 to 6.00 on weekdays.

Note that Saturday is sometimes considered to be a weekday.

When people say that something happens 'during the week', they mean that it happens on weekdays, not on Saturday or Sunday.

They used to spend the whole Sunday at chapel but most of them behaved shockingly during the week.

special days A few days in the year have special names, for example:

New Year's Day (1st January)
St Valentine's Day (14th February)
Good Friday (not fixed)
Easter Sunday (not fixed)
Easter Monday (not fixed)
Hallowe'en (31st October)
Christmas Eve (24th December)
Christmas Day (25th December)
Boxing Day (26th or 27th December)
New Year's Eve (31st December)

months These are the months of the year:

January	April	July	October
February	May	August	November
March	June	September	December

Months are always written with a capital letter.

I wanted to leave in September.

In a date, months can be represented by a number, as shown in the section on 'writing dates' later in this entry. January is represented by 1, February by 2, and so on.

You can use 'early', 'mid', and 'late' to specify part of a month. Note that you cannot use 'middle' like this, although you can use 'the middle of'.

I should very much like to come to California in late September or early October.
We must have five copies by mid February.
By the middle of June the Campaign already had more than 1000 members.

years You normally say a year in two parts. For example, '1970' is said as 'nineteen seventy', and '1820' is said as 'eighteen twenty'.

In the case of years ending in '00', you say the second part as 'hundred'. For example, '1900' is said as 'nineteen hundred'.

Note that people often write 'the year 2000', not just '2000'. They usually say 'the year two thousand'.

There are two ways of saying years ending in '01' to '09'. For example, '1901' can be said as 'nineteen oh one' or 'nineteen hundred and one'.

'AD' and 'BC' To be more specific, for example when talking about early history, 'AD' is added in front of a year or after it to show that it occurred a particular number of years after the time when Christ is believed to have been born.

The Chinese were printing by movable type in AD 1050.
The earliest record of an animal becoming extinct dates from about 800 AD.

'AD' is an abbreviation for the Latin expression 'anno Domini', which means 'in the year of our Lord'.

'BC' (meaning 'before Christ') is added after a year to show that it occurred before Christ is believed to have been born.

The figurine was found near a sandal dated at 6925 BC.

writing dates When writing a date, you use a number to indicate which day of the month you are talking about. There are several different ways of writing a date:

20 April
20th April
April 20
April 20th
the twentieth of April

If you want to give the year as well as the day and the month, you put it last.

I was born on December 15th, 1933.

You can write a date entirely in figures:

20/4/92
20.4.92

Note that Americans put the month in front of the day when writing the date in figures, so the date above would be written '4/20/92' or '4.20.92'.

Dates within a piece of writing are not usually written entirely in figures. However, this way of writing dates is often used for the date at the top of a letter, and for dates on forms.

saying dates You say the day as an ordinal number, even when it is written in figures as a cardinal number. Speakers of British English say 'the' in front of the number. For example, 'April 20' is said as 'April the twentieth'. Speakers of American English usually say 'April twentieth'.

When the month comes after the number, you use 'of' in front of the month. For example, '20 April' would be said as 'the twentieth of April'.

You can omit the month when it is clear which month you are referring to.

So Monday will be the seventeenth.
St Valentine's Day is on the fourteenth.

When you want to tell someone today's date, you use 'It's'.

'What's the date?'—'It's the twelfth.'

seasons These are the four seasons of the year:

spring	autumn
summer	winter

Seasons are sometimes written with a capital letter, but it is more usual to use a small letter.

I was supposed to go last summer.
I think it's nice to get away in the autumn.

In American English, 'fall' is used instead of 'autumn'.

They usually give a party in the fall and in the spring.

For information on using these words, see entries at **spring, summer, autumn,** and **winter.**

'Springtime', 'summertime', and 'wintertime' are also used to refer generally to particular times of year. Note that there is no word 'autumntime'.

decades and centuries

A decade is a period of ten years. A century is a period of a hundred years.

Decades are usually thought of as starting with a year ending in zero and finishing with a year ending in nine. For example, the decade from 1960 to 1969 is referred to as 'the 1960s'.

In the 1950s, synthetic hair was invented.
In the 1840s it was still possible for working-class newspapers to be profitable,

When you are talking about a decade in the twentieth century, you do not have to indicate the century. For example, you can refer to the 1920s as 'the 20s', 'the '20s', 'the twenties', or 'the Twenties'.

...the depression of the twenties and thirties.
Most of it was done in the Seventies.

WARNING

You cannot refer to the first or second decade of a century in the way described above. Instead you can say, for example, 'the early 1800s' or 'the early nineteenth century'.

Centuries are considered by many people to start with a year ending in 00 and finish with a year ending in 99. They are calculated from the birth of Christ and referred to using ordinals. For example, the years 1400-1499 are referred to as 'the fifteenth century', and we are currently in 'the twentieth century' (1900-1999). Centuries can also be written using figures, for example 'the 20th century'.

And then, in the eighteenth century, dawned the age of the French Salon.
That practice continued right through the 19th century.

Note that some people think that centuries start with a year ending in 01, so, for example, the twentieth century is 1901-2000.

You can, if necessary, indicate whether you are referring to a century before or after the birth of Christ using 'BC' or 'AD'.

The great age of Greek sport was the fifth century BC.

You can also refer to a century using the plural form of its first year. For example, you can refer to the eighteenth century as 'the 1700s' or 'the seventeen hundreds'.

The building goes back to the 1600s.
...furniture in the heavy style of the early eighteen hundreds.

part of a decade or century

You can use 'early', 'mid', and 'late' to specify part of a decade or century. Note that you cannot use 'middle' like this, although you can use 'the middle of'.

His most important writing was done in the late 1920s and early 1930s.
...the wars of the late nineteenth century.
In the mid 1970s forecasting techniques became more sophisticated.
The next major upset came in the middle of the nineteenth century.

using prepositions

You use particular prepositions when mentioning the day, date, or time of year of an event.

● You use 'at' with:

religious festivals: at Christmas, at Easter
short periods: at the weekend, at the beginning of March

● You use 'in' with:

months: in July, in December

seasons: in autumn, in the spring
long periods: in wartime, in the holidays
years: in 1985, in the year 2000
decades: in the thirties
centuries: in the nineteenth century

- You use 'on' with:

days: on Monday, on weekdays, on Christmas Day
dates: on the twentieth of July, on June 21st, on the twelfth

Note that American speakers sometimes omit 'on'.

Can you come Tuesday?

To indicate that something happened at some time in a particular period, or throughout a period, you can use 'during' or 'over'.

There were 1.4 million enquiries during 1988 and 1989 alone.
More than 1,800 government soldiers were killed in fighting over Christmas.

using other adverbials

You can indicate when something happens using the adverbs 'today', 'tomorrow', and 'yesterday'.

One of my children wrote to me today.

You can also use a noun group consisting of a word like 'last', 'this', or 'next' combined with a word like 'week', 'year', or 'month'. Note that you do not use prepositions with these time expressions.

They're coming next week.

See entries at **last - lastly, this - these,** and **next** for detailed information on the use of these expressions.

If you say that you did something 'the week before last', you mean that you did it in the week just before the week that has just passed.

Eileen was accompanying her father, to visit friends made on a camping trip the year before last in Spain.
I saw her the Tuesday before last.

If you say that something happened 'a week ago last Tuesday', you mean that it happened exactly one week before the previous Tuesday.

If you say that you will do something 'the week after next', you mean that you will do it in the week after the week that comes next.

He wants us to go the week after next.

If you say that something is going to happen 'Thursday week', you mean that it is going to happen exactly one week after the next Thursday.

'When is it to open?'—'Monday week.'

If you say that something will happen 'three weeks on Thursday', you mean that it will happen exactly three weeks after the next Thursday.

indefinite dates For information on how to indicate an indefinite date, see entry at **Time.**

modifying nouns If you want to indicate that you are referring to something that occurred or will occur on a particular day or in a particular period, you use 's after a noun group referring to that day or period.

How many of you were at Tuesday's lecture?
...yesterday's triumphs.
...next week's game.
...one of this century's most controversial leaders.

You can use the name of a day or period of the year as a modifier if you are referring to a type of thing.

Some of the people in the Tuesday class had already done a ten or twelve hour day.
I had summer clothes and winter clothes.
Ash had spent the Christmas holidays at Pelham Abbas.

When indicating what season a day occurs in, you use the name of the season as a noun modifier. You can also use 's with 'summer' and 'winter'.

...a clear spring morning.
...wet winter days.

...a summer's day.
...a cold winter's night.

qualifying   You can use adverbials indicating date as qualifiers.

The sudden death of his father on 17 November 1960 did not find him unprepared.

regular events   If something happens regularly, you can say that it happens 'every day', 'every week', and so on.

The nurse came in and washed him every day.
I used to go every Sunday.
Every week we sang 'Lord of the Dance'.

You can also use an adverb such as 'daily' or 'monthly'. This is more formal and less common.

It was suggested that we give each child an allowance yearly or monthly to cover all he or she spends.

If you want to say that something happens regularly on a particular day of the week, you can use 'on' and the plural form of the day instead of using 'every' and the singular form of the day. You do this when you are simply saying when something happens, rather than emphasizing that it is a regular event.

He went there on Mondays and Fridays.

If something happens at intervals of two days, two weeks, and so on, you can say that it happens 'every other day', 'every other week', and so on.

We wrote every other day.

A less common way of indicating an interval is to say that something happens 'on alternate days', 'in alternate weeks', and so on.

Just do some exercises on alternate days at first.

You can also indicate an interval by saying that something happens 'every two weeks', 'every three years', and so on.

World Veteran Championships are staged every two years.
...an antidote of serum renewed every six months.

You can also indicate that something happens regularly by saying that it happens, for example, 'once a week', 'once every six months', or 'twice a year'.

The group met once a week.
...in areas where it only rains once every five or ten years.
You only have a meal three times a day.

dead

used as an
adjective

Dead is usually used as an adjective. Someone who is **dead** is no longer living. You can use **dead** to talk about someone who has just died, or about someone who died a long time ago.

The dead peasant woman was lying in an open coffin.
He was shot dead in a gunfight.
He misses his dead sister in Maidenhead.

You can also say that animals or plants are **dead**.

The disease was caused by using protein from dead sheep in cattle feed.
Mary threw away the dead flowers.

WARNING

Do not confuse **dead** with **died**. **Died** is the past tense and past participle of the verb 'die'. You do not use **died** as an adjective.

used as a noun

You can refer to a group of people who have died as **the dead**.

Among the dead was a five-year-old girl.

deaf

If someone is **deaf**, they are unable to hear anything, or unable to hear very well.

She was deaf as well as short-sighted.
...a school for deaf children.

Note that you do not say that someone's 'ears are deaf'.

deal

'a great deal'
and
'a good deal'

A great deal or **a good deal** of something is a lot of it. **A great deal** is more common than **a good deal**.

There was a great deal of concern about energy shortages.
Monkeys and apes spend a great deal of time grooming one another's fur.
She drank a good deal of coffee with him in his office.

Note that these expressions can only be used with uncount nouns. You can talk, for example, about **a great deal of money,** but not about 'a great deal of apples'.

A great deal and **a good deal** can also be used as adverbials. If you do something **a great deal** or **a good deal**, you spend a lot of time doing it.

They talked a great deal.

For a graded list of similar adverbials, see section on **degree** in entry at **Adverbials**.

'deal with'

When you **deal with** a situation or problem, you do what is necessary to achieve the result you want.

They learned to deal with any sort of emergency.

The past tense and past participle of 'deal' is **dealt** /delt/, not 'dealed'.

When they had dealt with the fire, another crisis arose.

If a book, speech, or film **deals with** a particular subject, it is concerned with it.

The book deals with the pursuit of Rommel's army after El Alamein.
The film deals with a strange encounter between two soldiers.

'deal in'   If someone **deals in** a particular type of goods, they sell them.

He dealt in all domestic commodities.
The shop deals only in trousers.

definitely

See entry at **surely.**

delay - cancel - postpone

'delay'   If you **delay** doing something, you do it at a later time.

The government delayed granting passports to them until a week before their departure.
Try and persuade them to delay some of the changes.

If a plane, train, ship, or bus **is delayed,** it is prevented from leaving or arriving on time.

The coach was delayed for about five hours.
The flight has been delayed one hour, due to weather conditions.

'cancel' and   **Cancel** and **postpone** are used to talk about events that have been
'postpone'   arranged in advance.

To **cancel** an event means to decide officially that it will not take place.

The performances were cancelled because the leading man was ill.
The powerboat championships at Poole were cancelled yesterday because of poor weather.

To **postpone** an event means to arrange for it to take place at a later time than was originally planned.

The crew did not know that the invasion had been postponed.
Football games had to be postponed for a couple of days.

delighted

If you are **delighted,** you are very pleased and excited about something.

He was delighted with his achievement.
He was delighted to meet them again.

You do not use words such as 'very' or 'extremely' in front of **delighted.** If you want to say that someone is extremely pleased and excited, you can say that they are **absolutely delighted.**

They were absolutely delighted with François from the start.

You do not use words such as 'fairly', 'quite', or 'almost' in front of **delighted.**

For a graded list of words that indicate how pleased someone is, see entry at **pleased - disappointed.**

'delightful'   Do not confuse **delighted** with **delightful.** If you say that someone or something is **delightful,** you mean that they are very pleasant and attractive.

Her children really are delightful.
...a delightful room.

delusion

See entry at **illusion - delusion.**

demand

Demand is used as a noun or a verb.

used as a noun A **demand** for something is a firm request for it.

...his demands for stronger armed forces.

used as a verb If you **demand** something, you ask for it very forcefully.

They are demanding higher wages.
I demand to see a doctor.
She had been demanding that he visit her.

Note that when **demand** is used as a verb, you do not use 'for' after it.

demonstration

A **demonstration** is a public meeting or march in which people show their opposition to something or their support for something. You usually say that people **hold** or **stage** a demonstration.

Young men refusing military service held a demonstration.
The Anti-Apartheid Movement will be allowed to stage a demonstration.

You do not say that people 'make' a demonstration.

deny

If you **deny** an accusation or a claim, you say that it is not true.

The accused women denied all the charges brought against them.
He denied that he was involved.
Green denied doing anything illegal.

Note that **deny** must be followed by an object, a 'that'-clause, or an '-ing' form. You say, for example, 'He accused her of stealing, but she **denied it**'. You do not say 'He accused her of stealing but she denied'.

'say no' If someone answers 'no' to an ordinary question in which they are not accused of anything, you do not say that they 'deny' what they are asked. You do not say, for example, 'I asked him if the train had left, and he denied it'. You say 'I asked him if the train had left, and he **said no**'.

She asked if you'd been in and I said no.
I asked her whether we could have a party and she said no.

'refuse' If someone says that they will not do something, you do not say that they 'deny' it. You say that they **refuse to do** it or **refuse**.

Three employees were dismissed for refusing to join a union.
We asked them to play a game with us, but they refused.

depart

See entry at **leave**.

depend

'depend on' If you **depend on** someone or something or **depend upon** them, you need them in order to survive.

At college Julie had seemed to depend on Simon more and more.
We in the United Kingdom have depended heavily on coal both for industrial and domestic use.

The factories depend upon natural resources.

You also use **depend on** to say that something will only happen if something else is the case.

The success of the meeting depends largely on whether the chairman is efficient.

Depend is never used as an adjective. You do not say, for example, that someone or something is 'depend' on another person or thing. You say that they are **dependent** on that person or thing.

'depending on' You use **depending on** to say that something varies according to particular circumstances.

This training takes a variable time, depending on the chosen speciality.
There are, depending on the individual, a lot of different approaches.

'it depends' Sometimes people answer a question by saying 'It depends', rather than 'yes' or 'no'. They usually then explain under what circumstances something might happen or be the case.

'Won't you do any other subjects?'—'Well, it depends. I don't particularly want to do geology. Astronomy would be quite good, if I'm allowed to do it.'

dependent - dependant

used as an adjective If you are **dependent on** someone or something, you need them in order to survive.

At first, a patient may feel very dependent on the nurses.
...those who are entirely dependent for their welfare on the public services.
All competitively priced newspapers became dependent on advertising.

Note that you do not use any preposition except 'on' after **dependent**.

used as a noun In British English, your **dependants** are the people who you support financially, such as your children.

...shorter or more flexible working hours for people with dependants.

In American English, this noun is usually spelled **dependent**.

The statements provide evidence that you do not need to work to support yourself or your dependents.

descend

To **descend** means to move downwards to a lower level.

The valley becomes more exquisite as we descend.
The lift descended one floor.

Descend is a formal or literary word. When someone or something moves downwards to a lower level, you normally say that they **go down** or **come down**.

I want to go down in the cage and take some pictures.
He stood at the foot of the stairs calling for her to come down.

describe

The verb **describe** can be used either with a direct object or with a 'wh'-clause.

description

used with a direct object

When you **describe** someone or something, you say what they are like.

Can you describe your son?
Next he described a drive on a Saturday afternoon.

You can use **describe** with a direct object and an indirect object. The direct object goes first.

He described the murderer in detail to Detective Lieutenant Lipes.
She described the feeling to me.

used with a 'wh'-clause

Describe can be used in front of various kinds of 'wh'-clause.

The man described what he had seen.
He described how he escaped from prison.

You can use **describe** with an indirect object and a 'wh'-clause. The indirect object goes first.

I can't describe to you what it was like.
I found it difficult to describe to him what had happened in Patricia's house.

WARNING

When you use **describe** with an indirect object, you must put 'to' in front of the indirect object. You do not say, for example, 'I can't describe you what it was like'.

description

A **description of** someone or something is an account of what they are like.

They now had a description of Calthrop and a photograph of his head and shoulders.
...his description of army life in Northern Ireland.
...a detailed description of the house.

Note that you do not use any preposition except 'of' after **description**.

desert - dessert

'desert'

Desert is used as a noun or a verb. The noun and the verb are pronounced differently.

A **desert** /dezət/ is a large area of land where there is very little water or rain, no trees, and very few plants.

...the Sahara Desert.

When people or animals **desert** /dɪzɜ:t/ a place, they leave it, with the result that it becomes empty.

Even the butterflies deserted the open space.

If one person **deserts** another, they leave them and no longer help or support them.

She deserted her family and ran away with him.

If a member of the armed forces **deserts,** he or she leaves without permission and without intending to return.

I knew something was wrong when he deserted from the army a couple of years ago.

'dessert'

Dessert /dɪzɜ:t/ is sweet food served at the end of a meal.

For dessert there was ice cream.

desire

Desire can be used as a noun or a verb.

used as a noun	A **desire** is a feeling that you want something or want to do something. You usually talk about a **desire for** something or a **desire to do** something.

...a tremendous desire for liberty.
Stephanie felt a strong desire for coffee.
He had not the slightest desire to go on holiday.

Note that you never talk about a 'desire for doing' something.

used as a verb	If you **desire** something, you want it. This is a formal or literary use.

The government of the United States desires peace.
She wanted extreme weather. She desired tempests, mountains of snow.

Note that when **desire** is used as a verb, you do not use 'for' after it.

despite

See entry at **in spite of - despite**.

dessert

See entry at **desert - dessert**.

destroy

If you **destroy** something, you damage it so completely that it can no longer be used.

Several apartment buildings were destroyed by the bomb.
I destroyed the letter as soon as I had read it.

For information about other words that can be used to describe severe damage, see entry at **damage.**

'spoil' and 'ruin'	If someone or something prevents an experience from being enjoyable, you do not say that they 'destroy' the experience. You say that they **spoil** it or **ruin** it.

Go and welcome your guests. I hope I've not spoiled things.
The evening had been spoiled by Charles Boon and Mrs Zapp.

Back injury is an unpleasant complaint to suffer from. It's ruined many people's holidays.
The weather had completely ruined their day.

detail - details

'detail'	A **detail** is an individual feature or element of something.

I can still remember every single detail of that night.
He described it down to the smallest detail.

'details'	If you obtain **details** of something, you obtain information about it.

You can get details of nursery schools from the local authority.
A pamphlet with further details, describing the course, is available from the Arts Registry.

Note that you do not say that you obtain 'detail' of something.

deter

To **deter** someone **from doing** something means to prevent them from doing it or to persuade them not to do it.

During the war, a flood would not have deterred me from going there on foot.

This did not <u>deter</u> Ealing council <u>from passing</u> a motion commending the police for their 'courage and patience'.

Note that you do not say that something deters someone 'to do' something.

GRAMMAR # Determiners

A **determiner** is a word used in front of a noun to indicate whether you are referring to a specific thing or just to something of a particular type. There are two types of determiners: specific determiners and general determiners.

specific determiners

You use **specific determiners** when the person you are talking to will know which person or thing you are referring to. The specific determiners are:

- the **definite article:** 'the'

<u>The</u> man began to run towards <u>the</u> boy.

- **demonstratives:** 'this', 'that', 'these', 'those'

How much is it for <u>that</u> big box?
Young people don't like <u>these</u> operas.

- **possessive determiners:** 'my', 'your', 'his', 'her', 'its', 'our', 'their'

I'd been waiting a long time to park <u>my</u> car.
<u>Her</u> face was very red.

See entries at the individual words and at **Possessive determiners.**

general determiners

You use **general determiners** when you are mentioning people or things for the first time, or talking about them generally without saying exactly which ones you mean.

There was <u>a</u> man in the lift.
You can stop at <u>any</u> time you like.
There were <u>several</u> reasons for this.

The general determiners are:

a	another	enough	little	neither
a few	any	every	many	no
a little	both	few	more	other
all	each	fewer	most	several
an	either	less	much	some

For more information about general determiners, see entries at the individual words, and entry at **Quantity.**

related pronouns

Most words used as determiners are also used as pronouns.

<u>This</u> is a very complex issue.
Have you got <u>any</u> that I could borrow?
There is <u>enough</u> for all of us.

However, 'the', 'a', 'an', 'every', 'no', 'other', and the possessive determiners cannot be used as pronouns. You use 'one' as a pronoun instead of 'a' or 'an', 'each' instead of 'every', 'none' instead of 'no', and 'others' instead of 'other'.

Have you got <u>one</u>?
<u>Each</u> has a separate box and number.

There are <u>none</u> left.
Some stretches of road are more dangerous than <u>others</u>.

---

device - devise

'device' Device /dɪvaɪs/ is a noun. A **device** is an object that has been made or built for a particular purpose, such as recording or measuring something.

Firemen carry a little alarm <u>device</u> in their pocket.
...an electronic <u>device</u>.

For information on other words which are used to refer to useful objects, see entry at **tools.**

'devise' Devise /dɪvaɪz/ is a verb. If you **devise** a plan, system, or machine, you have the idea for it and you work it out or design it.

It had been necessary to <u>devise</u> a system of universal schooling.
Year by year we <u>devise</u> more precise instruments with which to observe the planets.

die

When a person, animal, or plant **dies**, they stop living. The other forms of **die** are **dies, dying, died.**

We thought we were going to <u>die</u>.
Every day people <u>were dying</u> there.
Blake <u>died</u> in January, aged 76.

When someone dies as a result of a disease or injury, you can say that they **die of** the disease or injury or **die from** it.

An old woman <u>dying of</u> cancer was taken into hospital.
His first wife <u>died from</u> cancer in 1971.

He <u>died of</u> a heart attack.
...a man who <u>died from</u> a suspected heart attack.

Many of the injured sailors <u>died of</u> their wounds.
Simon Martin <u>died from</u> brain injuries caused by blows to the head.

You do not use any preposition except 'of' or 'from' after **die** in sentences like these.

See also entry at **dead.**

die - dye

These words are both pronounced /daɪ/.

'die' Die is a verb. When a person, animal, or plant **dies**, they stop living. The other forms of 'die' are **dies, dying, died.** See entries at **die** and **dead.**

'dye' Dye is both a noun and a verb. If you **dye** something such as hair or cloth, you change its colour by soaking it in a coloured liquid. This liquid is called a **dye.** The other forms of the verb 'dye' are **dyes, dyeing, dyed.**

She mixed finely pounded indigo leaves to <u>dye</u> her cloth deep blue.
Dip them in a yellow <u>dye</u>.

differ

If two things are different from each other in some way, you can say that one thing **differs from** the other. **Differ** is a fairly formal word.

Schoolchildren's needs <u>differ from</u> those of adults.
How does it <u>differ from</u> what's happening in Poland?

The problems the Chinese face differ importantly from those facing Africa.

Note that you do not use any preposition except 'from' after **differ**.

difference

The **difference** between things is the way or ways in which they are not the same.

Is there much difference between British and European law?
There is an essential difference between computers and humans.
Look at their difference in size.

If something **makes a difference** to a situation, it changes it.

This insight into the causes of truancy certainly makes a difference to staff attitudes.
The fact that she considered herself engaged to Ashton made no difference to his feelings for her.

'distinction' If someone points out that two things are different, you do not say that they 'make a difference' between the things. You say that they **make a distinction** or **draw a distinction** between them.

It is important to make a distinction between claimants who are over retirement age and those who are not.
You seem to be making a careful distinction between being a Christian and being a member of a church.
He drew a distinction between the protection of privacy for private individuals and a similar protection offered to men and women who lived public lives.

different

If one thing is **different from** another, it is unlike the other thing in some way.

The meeting was different from any that had gone before.
Health is different from physical fitness.

Many British people say that one thing is **different to** another. **Different to** means the same as **different from**.

Work can be said to be different to a career.
Morgan's law books were different to theirs.

Note that some people object to this use. In conversation, you can use either **different from** or **different to**, but in writing it is better to use **different from**.

American speakers say that one thing is **different from** or **different than** another.

I love the English style of football. It's so different than ours.

WARNING You do not use 'different than' in British English.

'very different' If there is a great difference between two things, you can say that one thing is **very different** from the other.

They are in an enclosed community, which is very different from going to work for eight hours a day.

Note that you do not say that one thing is 'much different' from another.

If two things are quite similar, you can say that one thing is **not very different** from the other or **not much different** from the other.

I discovered that things were <u>not very different</u> from what I had seen in New York.
The food an old person needs is <u>not much different</u> from what anyone else requires.
Inflation during March was <u>not much different</u> from the annual rate that has prevailed for some time.

'no different'   If two things are alike, you can say that one thing is **no different** from the other.

The fields you could see from the bus window seemed <u>no different</u> from equivalent fields in Iowa.

Note that you do not say that one thing is 'not different' from another.

difficulty

A **difficulty** is something that prevents you from doing something easily.

There are a lot of <u>difficulties</u> that have to be overcome.
The main <u>difficulty</u> is a shortage of time.

'have difficulty'   If you **have difficulty doing** something or **have difficulty in doing** something, you are unable to do it easily.

He seemed to be <u>having difficulty balancing</u> his bricks.
I was <u>having difficulty breathing.</u>
She was a girl who <u>had</u> great <u>difficulty in learning</u> to read and write.

Note that you do not say that someone 'has difficulty to do' something.

dignified

The following words can all be used to describe someone who behaves in a calm, serious way:

dignified	po-faced	solemn
formal	pompous	staid
grave	self-important	stuffy

Dignified is a complimentary word.

Doctors were respected everywhere. They always looked clean and <u>dignified.</u>

Formal, grave, and **solemn** are neutral words, which do not show approval or disapproval.

'How is your mother?' Daintry asked with <u>formal</u> politeness.
...as she explains the concept of gross national product to her <u>solemn</u> students.

Staid is fairly uncomplimentary.

The others are a pretty <u>staid</u> lot.

Po-faced, pompous, self-important, and **stuffy** are used to show disapproval. **Po-faced** and **stuffy** are not used in formal writing.

There had been many occasions when he had felt like murdering that <u>pompous</u> old fool Mr Tilbery.
His irrepressible irreverence has frequently landed him in trouble with the <u>stuffy</u> and <u>self-important.</u>

dinner

In Britain, people usually call their main meal of the day **dinner.** Some people have this meal in the middle of the day, and others have it in the evening.

Tell him his dinner's in the oven.
I haven't had dinner yet.

'lunch'   People who call their evening meal 'dinner' usually refer to a meal eaten in the middle of the day as **lunch.**

What did you have for lunch?
I'm going out to lunch.

'luncheon'   **Luncheon** is a formal word for 'lunch'.

...a private luncheon at the Aldwych club.

See entry at **Meals.**

directly - direct

Directly is most commonly used to say that something does not involve an intermediate stage or action, or another person.

They denied having negotiated directly or indirectly with the terrorists.
They have their cash directly from the government.
I shall be writing to you directly in the next few days.

Instead of saying that you receive something 'directly' from someone, you can say that you receive it **direct** from them.

Other money comes direct from industry.
If it does emerge that you are out of pocket, you will be reimbursed direct.

Similarly, instead of saying that one person writes 'directly' to another, you can say that they write **direct** to them.

I should have written direct to the manager.

movement   **Directly** is also used to talk about movement. If you go **directly** to a place, you go there by the shortest possible route, without calling anywhere else.

I had expected to spend a few days in New York, then go directly to my place in Cardiff-by-the-Sea.

You can also say that someone goes **direct** to a place.

Why hadn't he gone direct to the lounge?

WARNING   If you can travel to a place by one plane, train, or bus, without changing to another plane, train, or bus, you do not say that you can go there 'directly'. You say that you can go there **direct.**

You can't go to Manchester direct. You have to change trains at Birmingham.

looking at something   If you look straight at a person or thing, you can say that you are looking **directly** at them.

She turned her head and looked directly at them.

position   If something is **directly** above, below, opposite, or in front of something else, it is exactly in that position.

The sun was almost directly overhead.
The cabin occupied by the Count and Antonio was directly opposite across a passageway.

<table>
<tr><td>saying when
something
happens</td><td>You can also use directly to say that something will happen very soon. This is a rather old-fashioned use.</td></tr>
</table>

She's in a meeting at the moment but she will be here directly.
We'll be up directly. Just take your own things with you.

If you say that you will do something **directly,** you mean that you will do it immediately. This is also a rather old-fashioned use.

I'll move back into my old room directly.
Harrowby asked me to show you to his room directly.

If something happens **directly after** something else, it happens immediately after it.

It's a good idea have a rest directly after lunch.
Honeysuckle should be pruned directly after flowering.

In British English (but not American English), **directly** is also used as a conjunction to say that one thing happens immediately after another.

Directly he heard the door close, he picked up the telephone.
Directly I saw the word Pankot it occurred to me that you must have known Colonel Layton and his family.

direct speech

For information on how to punctuate **direct speech,** see entry at **Punctuation.**

dirty

Something that is **dirty** has dust, mud, or stains on it and needs to be cleaned.

...dirty marks on the walls.

You can also say that a person is **dirty.**

The children were hot, dirty, and exhausted.

You do not use words such as 'completely' or 'absolutely' with **dirty.** If you want to emphasize that someone or something is covered in a lot of dirt, you say that they are **very dirty** or **really dirty.**

The mud squirted up into your long skirts and made them filthy. People got very dirty then.
Before washing soak really dirty blankets in the bath.

disabled

See entry at **crippled.**

disagree

If you **disagree with** a person, statement, or idea, you have a different opinion of what is true or correct.

I disagree completely with John Taylor.
I disagree with much of what he says.

Note that you do not use any preposition except 'with' when you are mentioning the person, statement, or idea that you disagree with.

You can say that you **disagree with** someone **about** something.

I disagree with them about cycle maintenance.

You can also say that two or more people **disagree about** something.

He and I disagree about it.
Historians disagree about the date at which these features ceased to exist.

'refuse' If someone indicates that they will not do something, you do not say that they 'disagree' to do it. You say that they **refuse** to do it.

Don't let a sleepy baby refuse to be put to bed.
The pupils had refused to go home for their lunch.

See entry at **refuse**.

disappear

If someone or something **disappears,** they go.or are taken to a place where they cannot be seen or cannot be found.

I saw him disappear round the corner.
She disappeared down the corridor.
Tools disappeared and were never found.
...a certain tin of fruit that disappeared from the school larder.

Note that you do not use **disappeared** as an adjective. If you cannot find something because it is not in its usual place, you do not say that it 'is disappeared'. You say that it **has disappeared.**

He discovered that a pint of milk had disappeared from the pantry.
By the time the examiners got to work, most of the records had disappeared.

disappointed

See entry at **pleased - disappointed**.

disc - disk

In British English, a **disc** is a flat circular object.

The metal is protected with a waxed cardboard disc.
Cut out a metal disc to fit inside it.

In American English, this word is spelled **disk.**

In both British and American English, a **disk** is also a flat circular plate which is used to store large amounts of information for use by a computer.

The disk is then slotted into a desktop PC.
The image data may be stored on disk.

discourage

To **discourage** someone **from doing** something means to make them less willing to do it.

She wants to discourage him from marrying the girl.
The rain discouraged us from going out.

Note that you do not say that you discourage someone 'to do' something.

discover

See entry at **find**.

discuss

If you **discuss** something with someone, you talk to them seriously about it.

She could not discuss his school work with him.
They discussed where Gertrude and Anne should go.
We discussed whether George should go with Chris.

Note that **discuss** is always followed by a direct object, a 'wh'-clause, or a 'whether'-clause. You cannot say, for example, 'I discussed with him' or 'They discussed'.

discussion

If you have a **discussion** with someone, you have a serious conversation with them.

My next discussion with him took place a year later.
After the lecture there was a discussion.

You say that you have a discussion **about** something or a discussion **on** something.

I had been involved in discussions about this with Ted and Frank.
We're having a discussion on leisure activities.

'argument'
You do not use **discussion** to refer to a disagreement between people, especially one that results in them shouting angrily at each other. This kind of disagreement is usually called an **argument.**

He and David had been drawn into a ferocious argument.
I said no, and we got into a big argument over it.

disease

See entry at **illness - disease.**

disinterested

You use **disinterested** to describe someone who is not involved in a situation and can therefore make fair decisions or judgements about it.

I'm a disinterested observer.

Some people also use **disinterested** to say that someone is not interested in something or someone.

Her mother had always been disinterested in her.

'uninterested'
However, this use is often regarded as incorrect. Instead of 'disinterested', it is better to say **uninterested.**

Lionel was uninterested in the house.
Etta appeared totally uninterested.

disk

See entry at **disc - disk.**

dislike

If you **dislike** someone or something, you find them unpleasant.

From what I know of him I dislike him intensely.
She disliked the theatre.

You can say that someone **dislikes doing** something.

I very much <u>dislike receiving</u> confidences from overwrought people.
I grew to <u>dislike working</u> for the cinema.

You do not say that someone 'dislikes to do' something.

For a graded list of words and expressions used to indicate how much someone likes or dislikes something, see entry at **like - dislike.**

dismount

If you **dismount** from a bicycle or horse, you get down from it so that you are standing next to it.

The police officer <u>dismounted</u> from his bicycle.
When she urged the donkey forward with her heel, it backed instead, so that she was forced to <u>dismount</u>.

'get off'   **Dismount** is a formal word. You normally say that someone **gets off** a bicycle or horse.

The wind got so strong that I could no longer bicycle against it; I <u>got off</u> and walked.
'To hell with love,' he muttered as he <u>got off</u> his horse.

dispose

If you **dispose of** something that you no longer want or need, you throw it away or give it to someone.

Miles of telex tape had to be <u>disposed of.</u>

Note that you must use 'of' after **dispose.** You do not say that someone 'disposes' something.

'get rid of'   **Dispose** is a fairly formal word. In conversation, you usually say that someone **gets rid of** something.

Now let's <u>get rid of</u> all this stuff.
There was a lot of rubbish to <u>be got rid of.</u>

disqualified

See entry at **unqualified - disqualified.**

dissatisfied

See entry at **unsatisfied - dissatisfied.**

distance

For information on ways of expressing distance, see entry at **Measurements.**

distasteful

See entry at **tasteless - distasteful.**

distinct - distinctive - distinguished

'distinct'   If one thing is **distinct** from another, there is an important difference between them.

Our interests were quite <u>distinct</u> from those of the workers.
...a tree related to but quite <u>distinct</u> from the European beech.

You describe something as **distinct** when it is clear and definite.

I have the distinct feeling that my friend did not realize what was happening.
A distinct improvement had come about in their social outlook.

'distinctive'   You use **distinctive** to describe things which have a special quality that makes them easy to recognize.

Irene had a very distinctive voice.

'distinguished'   A **distinguished** person is very successful, famous, or important.

His grandfather had been a distinguished professor at the University.
...rushing to meet the distinguished visitors.

distinction

See entry at **difference**.

distinguished

See entry at **distinct - distinctive - distinguished**.

disturb - disturbed

'disturb'   If you **disturb** someone, you interrupt what they are doing and cause them inconvenience.

If she's asleep, don't disturb her.
Sorry to disturb you, but can I use your telephone?

'disturbed'   The adjective **disturbed** usually has a different meaning. If someone is **disturbed,** they are very upset emotionally and need special care or treatment.

...emotionally disturbed youngsters.

disused - unused - misused

'disused'   A **disused** place or building is no longer used for its original purpose and is now empty.

The sculpture was stored in a disused lorry factory.

'unused'   Something that is **unused** has never been used.

A pile of unused fuel lay nearby.

'misused'   When something **is misused,** it is used in a wrong or careless way.

He wanted to prevent science from being misused.
In some cases pesticides are deliberately misused.

dive

If you **dive,** you jump head-first into water with your arms straight above your head.

He taught me to swim and dive and water-ski.

You also use **dive** to say that someone jumps or rushes in a particular direction.

You can dive off left into St James's Place.

In British English, the past tense for both senses of 'dive' is **dived**. In American English, it is usually **dove** /dəʊv/.

She dived into the water and swam away.
I dove right in after her.

We dived to the ground.
Many survivors, though dazed, immediately dove into the debris to free the injured.

do

Do is one of the most common verbs in English. Its other forms are **does, doing, did, done.** It can be used as an auxiliary or a main verb.

used as an auxiliary

For general information on the use of **do** as an auxiliary, see entry at **Auxiliaries.**

For information on **do** as an auxiliary in questions, see entries at **Questions** and **Question tags.**

For information on **do** as an auxiliary in negative clauses, see entries at **not** and **Imperatives.**

Do has two other special uses as an auxiliary:

used for emphasis

You can use it to emphasize a statement. The forms **do, does,** and **did** can all be used in this way.

I do feel sorry for Roger.
A little knowledge does seem to be a dangerous thing.
He did bring home a regular salary.

You can use **do** in front of an imperative when you are urging someone to do something or accept something.

Do help yourself.
Do have a chocolate biscuit.

used to focus on an action

You can also use **do** as an auxiliary to focus on an action performed by someone or something.

When you use **do** like this, you put **what** at the beginning of the sentence, followed by a noun or noun group and the auxiliary **do.** After **do,** you put **is** or **was** and an infinitive with or without 'to'.

For example, instead of saying 'Carolyn opened a bookshop', you can say **'What Carolyn did was to open** a bookshop' or **'What Carolyn did was open** a bookshop'.

What Stephen did was to interview a lot of old people.
What it does is draw out all the vitamins from the body.

You can use **all** instead of 'what' if you want to emphasize that just one thing is done and nothing else.

All he did was shake hands and wish me luck.
All she ever does is make jam.

used as a main verb

Do is used as a main verb to say that someone performs an action, activity, or task.

We did quite a lot of work yesterday.
I did all the usual things to raise money.
Every decade there is a census which is done in detail.

Do is often used with '-ing' nouns referring to jobs connected with the home, and with nouns referring generally to work.

He does all the shopping and I do the washing.
Have you done your homework yet?

The man who did the job had ten years' training.
He has to get up early and do a hard day's work.

In conversation, **do** is often used instead of more specific verbs. For example, if you **do your teeth,** you brush your teeth. If you **do the flowers,** you arrange some flowers.

Do I need to do my hair?
She had done her breakfast dishes.

WARNING   You do not normally use **do** when you are talking about creating or constructing something. Instead you use **make.**

I like making cakes.
Sheila makes all her own clothes.
An electric blender makes soups, purees and puddings in a few seconds.
Chimpanzees not only use tools but make them.

See entry at **make.**

'do your best'   If you **do your best,** you try as hard as you can to achieve something.

I'm sorry. I did my best.

After **do your best** you can use a 'to'-infinitive.

We do our best to make sure it's up-to-date information.
Everyone did their best to save the cattle.

Note that you do not say that someone 'makes their best'.

repeating 'do'   In questions and negative clauses, you often use **do** twice. You use it first as an auxiliary to form the question or negative verb group, and then repeat it as the main verb. The main verb is always in the infinitive form without 'to'.

What did she do all day when she wasn't working?
If this exercise hurts your back do not do it.

'do about'   You use 'about' after **do** in questions and negative clauses when you are talking about ways of dealing with a problem.

What do you do about children's education?
I'll see what I can do about this.
Really there is nothing we can do about it.

Note that you do not use any preposition except 'about' in clauses like these.

doubt

Doubt is used as a noun or a verb.

used as a noun   A **doubt** is a feeling of uncertainty about something.

Frank had no doubts about the outcome of the trial.
I had moments of doubt.

'no doubt'   You add **no doubt** to a statement to say that you are assuming that something is true, although you cannot really be certain about it.

As Jennifer has no doubt told you, we are leaving tomorrow.
During the night you'll no doubt be enjoying the carnival atmosphere.

If you say **there is no doubt that** something is true, you mean that it is certainly true.

There's no doubt that it's going to be difficult.
There was no doubt that he was in a highly excitable condition.

Note that you must use a 'that'-clause after **there is no doubt.** You cannot use an 'if'-clause or a 'whether'-clause.

Many other words and expressions can be used to say how certain you are about something. For a graded list, see section on **probability** in entry at **Adverbials.**

'without doubt' Another way of emphasizing that something is true is to add **without doubt** to a statement. This is a rather formal use.

Hugh Scanlon became without doubt one of the most powerful men in Britain.

used as a verb If you **doubt** whether something is true or possible, you think it is probably not true or possible.

I doubt whether it would have more than a limited appeal.
I doubt if Alan will meet her.

If someone says that something is the case, or asks you if something is the case, you can indicate that you think it is unlikely by saying '**I doubt it**'.

'I believe I know you.'—'I doubt it. I'm Frederica Potter.'
'Do your family know you're here?'—'I doubt it.'

Note that you do not say 'I doubt so'.

downstairs

If you go **downstairs** in a building, you go down a staircase towards the ground floor.

He went downstairs and into the kitchen.
His two older sisters slept downstairs, for they had to be up first.

Note that you do not use 'to', 'at', or 'in' in front of **downstairs.**

downwards

In British English, if you move or look **downwards,** you move or look towards the ground or the floor.

The helicopter darted downwards.
Gerran gazed downwards with an expression of perplexed distaste.

Downwards is only used as an adverb.

'downward' Speakers of American English usually say **downward** instead of 'downwards'.

The blood from the wound spread downward.
He kept his head on one side as he spoke, looking downward.

In both British and American English, **downward** is used as an adjective. A **downward** movement or look is one in which someone or something moves or looks downwards.

She made a bold downward stroke with the paintbrush.
...a downward glance.

When **downward** is an adjective, you can only use it in front of a noun.

dozen

You can refer to twelve things as **a dozen** things.

...a dozen eggs.
When he got there he found more than a dozen men having dinner.

Note that you use 'a' in front of **dozen.** You do not talk about 'dozen' things.

You can talk about larger numbers of things by putting a number in front of **dozen**. For example, you can refer to 48 things as **four dozen** things.

On the trolley were two dozen cups and saucers.
They had come in demanding three dozen chocolate chip cookies for a party.

Note that you use the singular form **dozen** after a number. You do not talk about 'two dozens cups and saucers'. You also do not use 'of' after **dozen**. You do not say 'two dozen of cups and saucers'.

'dozens' In conversation, you can use **dozens** to talk vaguely about a very large number of things. **Dozens** is followed by 'of' when it is used in front of a noun.

She's borrowed dozens of books.
There had been dozens of attempts at reform.

draught - draft

Draught and **draft** are both pronounced /drɑːft/.

used as nouns In British English, a **draught** is a current of air coming into a room or vehicle.

The draught from the window stirred the papers on her desk.
They used to open the windows and doors to create a draught.

In American English, this is spelled **draft**.

...a damp draft of musty air.

In British English, **draughts** is a game played by two people with round pieces on a board like a chessboard. This game is called **checkers** in American English.

In both British and American English, a **draft** of a letter, book, or speech is an early version of it.

...the change from the first draft to the final printed version.
He showed me the draft of an article he was writing.

'draft' used Draft can also be used as a verb. In both British and American English,
as a verb when people **are drafted** somewhere, they are moved there to do a particular job.

Extra staff were drafted from Paris to Rome.

In American English, if you **are drafted,** you are ordered to serve in one of the armed forces.

I was drafted into the navy.
He took a temporary job while he was waiting to be drafted.

dream

Dream can be used as a noun or a verb. The past tense and past participle of the verb is either **dreamed** /driːmd, dremt/ or **dreamt** /dremt/. Dreamt is not usually used in American English.

used as a noun A **dream** is an imaginary series of events that you experience in your mind while you are asleep.

In his dream he was sitting in a theatre watching a play.

You say that someone **has** a dream.

Last night I had a dream.

Sam has bad dreams because soon he will be going to prep school.

You do not usually say that someone 'dreams' a dream.

A **dream** is also an unlikely situation or event that you often think about because you would like it to happen.

My dream was to farm in the American style.
His dream of becoming President had come true.

used as a verb   When someone experiences imaginary events while they are asleep, you can say that they **dream** something happens or **dream that** something happens.

I dreamed Marnie was in trouble.
Daniel dreamed that he was back in Minneapolis.

You can also say that someone **dreams about** someone or something or **dreams of** them.

Last night I dreamed about you.
I dreamed of ants converging on us from the whole estate.

When someone thinks about a situation that they would like to happen, you can say that they **dream of having** something or **dream of doing** something.

He dreamed of having a car.
For over a century every small boy dreamed of becoming an engine driver.

You do not say that someone 'dreams to have' something or 'dreams to do' something.

dress

When someone **dresses**, they put on their clothes. This use of **dress** occurs mainly in stories.

When he had shaved and dressed, he went down to the kitchen.
Finally he dressed, choosing a thin silk polo-necked sweater.

In conversation, you do not usually say that someone 'dresses'. You say that they **get dressed.**

Please hurry up and get dressed, Morris.
I got dressed and went downstairs.

If you say that someone **dresses** in a particular way, you mean that they usually wear clothes of a particular type.

He still dressed like the bank manager he had been.
I really must try to make him change the way he dresses.

'dressed in'   If you want to describe someone's clothes on a particular occasion, you can say that they are **dressed in** something.

He was dressed in a black suit.
He saw people coming towards him dancing, dressed in colourful clothes and feathers.

When a person's clothes are all the same colour, you can say that they are **dressed in** that colour.

All the girls were dressed in white.

'dress up'   If you **dress up,** you put on different clothes so that you look smarter than usual. People **dress up** in order to go, for example, to a wedding or to an interview for a new job.

I can't be bothered to dress up this evening.

You can say that someone is **dressed up.**

I have never seen you dressed up. You look very beautiful.

If someone **dresses up as** someone else, they wear the kind of clothes that person usually wears.

My father dressed up as a tramp.

You only use **dress up** to say that someone puts on clothes which are not their usual clothes. If someone normally wears smart or attractive clothes, you do not say that they 'dress up well'. You say that they **dress well.**

They all had enough money to dress well and buy each other drinks.
We are told by advertisers and fashion experts that we must dress well and use cosmetics.

drink

Drink is used as a verb or a noun.

used as a transitive verb
When you **drink** a liquid, you take it into your mouth and swallow it. The past tense of 'drink' is **drank,** not 'drinked' or 'drunk'.

I drank some of my ginger beer.
We drank a bottle of whisky together.

The past participle is **drunk.**

He was aware that he had drunk too much whisky.

Drunk is also used as an adjective. See entry at **drunk - drunken.**

used as an intransitive verb
If you use **drink** without an object, you are usually referring to the drinking of alcohol.

I never drink alone.
You shouldn't drink and drive.
We ate and drank and talked and laughed.

If you say that someone **drinks,** you mean that they regularly drink too much alcohol.

Her mother drank, you know.
He paid someone to investigate Mr Williams and found he drank and brawled.

If you say that someone **does not drink,** you mean that they do not drink alcohol at all.

She said she didn't smoke or drink.

used as a count noun
A **drink** is an amount of liquid that you drink.

I asked her for a drink of water.
Lynne brought me a hot drink.

To **have a drink** means to spend some time, usually with other people, drinking alcoholic drinks.

I'm going to have a drink with some friends this evening.

Drinks usually refers to alcoholic drinks.

The drinks were served in the sitting room.
After a few drinks he would get his clarinet out.

used as an uncount noun
Drink is alcohol.

There was plenty of food and drink at the party.
We are trying to keep him away from drink.

drown

When someone **drowns,** they die because their head is under water and they cannot breathe. You can either say that someone **drowns** or that they **are drowned.** There is no difference in meaning.

She had fallen into the sea and drowned.
They jumped in the river and were drowned.

drugstore

See entry at **chemist's - drugstore.**

drunk - drunken

Drunk is the past participle of the verb 'drink'. See entry at **drink.**

'drunk' used as an adjective
Drunk is also an adjective. If someone is **drunk,** they have drunk too much alcohol and are not in complete control of their behaviour.

The colonel was so drunk that he could barely get his words out.
She was being driven home by an extremely drunk young man.

When someone drinks too much alcohol and loses control of their behaviour, you say that they **get drunk.**

He had decided that he was never going to get drunk again.
We all got happily drunk.

'drunken'
Drunken has the same meaning as 'drunk' but it is only used in front of a noun. You do not say that someone 'is drunken'.

...stiffer penalties for drunken drivers.
At about noon a mob of drunken Irish attacked the frigate.

You use **drunken** rather than 'drunk' to describe the behaviour of people who are drunk.

...a long drunken party.
I descended into a deep drunken sleep.

You also use **drunken** rather than 'drunk' to describe people who are often drunk.

Where will she go? Back to her drunken husband in Canada?

due to

If an event **is due to** something, it happens or exists as a direct result of it.

His death was due to natural causes.
My desire to act was due to Laurence Olivier's performance in 'Hamlet'.

Due to is sometimes used to introduce the reason for an undesirable situation.

Due to repairs, the garage will be closed next Saturday.
The flight has been delayed one hour, due to weather conditions.

This use is fairly common, but some people object to it. Instead of saying 'due to', you can say **owing to** or **because of.**

Owing to the heavy rainfall many of the roads were impassable.
I missed my flight owing to a traffic hold-up.
Because of the Fleetwood Mac concert at Maine Road, our scheduled midweek match with Manchester City has been put back a week.
Police closed the Strand because of smoke billowing over the road.

dull

If you say that something is **dull**, you mean that it is not interesting.

I thought the book dull and unoriginal.
It will be so dull here without you.

'blunt'   In modern English, if a knife is no longer sharp, you do not say that it is 'dull'. You say that it is **blunt**.

Scrape off as much as possible with a blunt knife.

during

You usually use **during** to say that something happens continuously or often from the beginning to the end of a period of time.

She heated the place during the winter with a huge wood furnace.
This was evident in the weekly column he wrote for the Guardian during 1963-1964.

In sentences like these, you can almost always use **in** instead of **during**. There is very little difference in meaning. When you use **during**, you are usually stressing the fact that something is continuous or repeated. See entry at **in**.

You can also use **during** to say that something happens while an activity takes place.

Fred had worked a great deal with her at Oxford during the war.
Ash was wondering angrily what they would think if a group of Indians behaved in a similar manner during a service at Westminster Abbey.

You can sometimes use **in** in sentences like these, but the meaning is not always the same. For example, 'What did you do **during** the war?' means 'What did you do while the war was taking place?', but 'What did you do **in** the war?' means 'What part did you play in the war?'

single events   Both **during** and **in** can be used to say that a single event happened at some point in the course of a period of time.

He had died during the night.
His father had died in the night.

She left Bengal during the late Spring of 1740.
Mr Tyrie left Hong Kong in June.

It is more common to use **in** in sentences like these. If you use **during**, you are usually emphasizing that you are not sure of the exact time when something happened.

WARNING   You do not use **during** to say how long something lasts. You do not say, for example, 'I went to Wales during two weeks'. You say 'I went to Wales **for** two weeks'. See entry at **for**.

duty

See entry at **obligation - duty**.

dye

See entry at **die - dye**.

E

each

used as a determiner
You use **each** in front of the singular form of a count noun to talk about every person or thing in a group. You use **each** rather than 'every' when you are thinking about the members of a group as individuals.

Each applicant has five choices.
They would rush out to meet each visitor.
Each country is subdivided into several districts.
Each seat was covered with a white lace cover.

'each of'
Instead of using **each**, you can sometimes use **each of**. For example, instead of saying 'Each soldier was given a new uniform', you can say '**Each of** the soldiers was given a new uniform'. **Each of** is followed by a determiner and the plural form of a count noun.

Each of the books has little bits of paper protruding from its pages.
Each of these phrases has a different meaning.
They inspected each of her appliances with care.

You also use **each of** in front of plural pronouns.

Each of us could be alone for most of the day.
They were all just sitting there, each of them thinking private thoughts.
We have statistics for each of these.

When you use **each of** in front of a plural noun or pronoun, you use a singular form of a verb after the noun or pronoun.

Each of these cases was carefully locked.
Each of us looks over the passenger lists.

WARNING

You never use **each** without 'of' in front of a plural noun or pronoun.

If you want to emphasize that something is true about every member of a group, you can say **each one of** instead of 'each of'.

This view of poverty influences each one of us.
An expert lecturer can make each one of his listeners feel that they are the object of his attention.

WARNING

You do not use words such as 'almost', 'nearly', or 'not' in front of **each**. You do not say, for example, 'Almost each house in the street is for sale'. You say 'Almost **every** house in the street is for sale'.

They show great skills in almost every aspect of school life.
Nearly every town has its own opera house.
Not every secretary wants to move up in the world.

You also do not use **each** or **each of** in a negative clause. You do not say, for example, 'Each boy did not enjoy football' or 'Each of the boys did not enjoy football'. You say '**None of** the boys enjoyed football'.

None of them are actually African.
None of these suggestions is very helpful.

See entry at **none**.

used after the subject
Each is sometimes used after the subject of a clause. For example, instead of saying 'Each of them received a new pair of boots', you can say '**They each** received a new pair of boots'. In constructions like these, the subject and the verb are always plural.

They each chose a word from the list.

We each have our private views about it.

This type of construction is often used to indicate that an amount relates to each member of a group separately and not to the whole group. For example, if you say 'Arsenal and Everton **each** scored two goals', you are indicating that four goals were scored altogether, not two.

Bolivia and Paraguay each have around 700,000 workers away from home.

When you are talking about an amount like this, you often put **each** at the end of the clause.

They cost eight pounds each.
All three groupings polled 32 per cent each.
...large aluminium cylinders, weighing several tons each.

used as a pronoun

Each can be used as a pronoun to mean 'each person' or 'each thing'.

Elliott and Cram are trying to forget their poor performances here on Saturday. Each is planning a series of races in the next month.
None of the earlier stages are self-sufficient. Each is a preparation for the next.
If there is more than one convenient hostel, you could spend a few nights at each.

Each one is sometimes used instead of **each**.

The canoes went skimming down the river with five or six women in each one.
Babies are individuals. This means each one needs to be closely watched.

referring back to 'each'

You usually use a singular pronoun such as 'he', 'she', 'him', or 'her' to refer back to an expression containing **each**.

Each boy said what he thought had happened.

However, when you are referring back to an expression such as 'each person' or 'each student' which does not indicate a specific sex, you usually use **they** or **them**.

There was to be a flat rate charge for each individual, irrespective of where they lived.

For a fuller discussion of these uses, see entry at **he - they**.

each other - one another

You use **each other** or **one another** when you are talking about actions or feelings that involve two or more people together in an identical way. For example, if Simon likes Louise and Louise likes Simon, you say that Simon and Louise like **each other** or like **one another**. **Each other** and **one another** are sometimes called **reciprocal pronouns**.

Each other and **one another** are usually used as the direct or indirect object of a verb.

We help each other a lot.
They sent each other gifts from time to time.
The birds greet one another or change places on the nest.

You can also use them as the object of a preposition.

Terry and Mark were jealous of each other.
They didn't dare to look at one another.

possessives

You can form possessives by adding **'s** to **each other** and **one another**.

I hope that you all enjoy each other's company.
Apes spend a great deal of time grooming one another's fur.

differences   There is very little difference in meaning between **each other** and **one another**. One another is fairly formal, and many people do not use it at all. Some people prefer to use **each other** when they are talking about two people or things, and **one another** when they are talking about more than two. However, it is not usual to make this distinction.

easily

See entry at **easy - easily**.

east

The **east** is the direction which you look towards in order to see the sun rise.

Ben noticed the first faint streaks of dawn in the east.
Sounds of war from the east grew closer.

An **east** wind blows from the east.

It has turned bitterly cold, with a cruel east wind.

The **east** of a place is the part that is towards the east.

...old people in the east of Glasgow.
...a plane which travelled on to the east of the continent.

East occurs in the names of some countries and regions.

...the former Portuguese colony of East Timor.
This beautiful flower grows in grassy places, mainly in East Anglia.
...tribes such as the Masai in East Africa.

'eastern'   However, you do not usually talk about the 'east' part of a country. You talk about the **eastern** part.

...the eastern part of Germany.

Similarly, you do not talk about 'east Europe' or 'east England'. You say **eastern** Europe or **eastern** England.

...the economies of Central and Eastern Europe.
...a scheduled early morning flight from Nancy in eastern France.
...the Eastern Mediterranean.

easterly

If something moves in an **easterly** direction, it moves towards the east.

The yacht was continuing in an easterly direction.

However, an **easterly** wind blows **from** the east.

There was an icy easterly wind blowing off the sea.

eastwards

If you move or look **eastwards,** you move or look towards the east.

...shipping making its way eastwards across the Atlantic.
I looked out through the window and could see eastwards as far as the distant horizon.

Eastwards is only used as an adverb.

'eastward'   In American English and old-fashioned British English, **eastward** is often used instead of 'eastwards'.

The two cousins hurried eastward against the sharp wind.
He walked back into the field, scanning eastward for dark figures.

In both British and American English, **eastward** is sometimes used as an adjective in front of a noun.

...an eastward movement.

easy - easily

'easy'   Something that is **easy** can be done or achieved without effort or difficulty.

Both sides had secured easy victories earlier in the day.
Competitions in the Spectator are never easy.

The comparative and superlative forms of 'easy' are **easier** and **easiest**.

This is much easier than it sounds.
This was in many ways the easiest stage.

You can say that **it is easy to do** something. For example, instead of saying 'Riding a camel is easy', you can say '**It is easy to ride** a camel'. You can also say 'A camel **is easy to ride**'.

It is easy to be world champions at a game hardly anybody else plays.
It is easy to blame the unrest on political agitation.
The house is easy to keep clean.
Their defences were ridiculously easy to penetrate.

'easily'   **Easy** is not used as an adverb, except in the expressions 'go easy', 'take it easy', and 'easier said than done'. If you want to say that something is done without difficulty, you say that it is done **easily**.

Put things in a place where you can find them quickly and easily.
Belgium easily beat Mexico 3-0.

The comparative and superlative forms of **easily** are **more easily** and **most easily.**

Milk is digested more easily when it is skimmed.
These are the foods that are most easily contaminated with poisonous bacteria.

economics

Economics is a noun. It usually refers to the study of the way in which money, industry, and trade are organized.

...the science of economics.
...a degree in economics.

When **economics** has this meaning, it is an uncount noun. You use a singular form of a verb with it.

Economics deals with man in his environment.

If you want to say that something relates to the subject of economics, you use **economics** in front of another noun.

...an economics degree.
...Hull University's economics department.

Note that you do not talk about an 'economic' degree or an 'economic' department.

The **economics** of an industry are the aspects of it which are concerned with making a profit.

...the economics of the timber trade.

When **economics** is used with this meaning, it is a plural noun. You use a plural form of a verb with it.

When this happens, the economics of the industry are dramatically affected.

'economy'   **Economy** is also a noun. The **economy** of a country or region is the system by which money, industry, and trade are organized there.

New England's economy is still largely based on manufacturing.
Unofficial strikes were damaging the British economy.

Economy is also careful spending or the careful use of things in order to save money.

His seaside home was small for reasons of economy.

'economies'   If you make **economies,** you try to save money by not spending it on unnecessary things.

It might be necessary to make a few economies.

'savings'   However, you do not refer to the money that someone has saved as their 'economies'. You refer to this money as their **savings.**

She drew out all her savings.

'economic'   **Economic** is an adjective. You use it to describe things connected with the organization of money and trade in a country or region. When **economic** has this meaning, you only use it in front of a noun. You do not use it after a verb.

...the problems of economic planning.
What has gone wrong with the economic system during the last ten years?

If you say that something is **economic,** you mean that it makes a profit, or does not result in money being lost. When **economic** has this meaning, it can go either in front of a noun or after a verb.

It is difficult to provide an economic public transport service.
We have to keep fares high enough to make it economic for the service to continue.

'economical'   **Economical** is also an adjective. It can be used to say that something is cheap to operate or use.

...the economical harnessing of atomic energy.
This system was extremely economical because it ran on half-price electricity.

You can also say that a person is **economical** when they do not spend much money. Several other words can be used with a similar meaning. For more information, see entry at **mean.**

GRAMMAR   **'-ed' adjectives**

A large number of adjectives end in '-ed'.

related to verbs   Many of them have the same form as the past participle of a transitive verb, and have a passive meaning. For example, a 'frightened' person is a person who has been frightened by something.

When I saw my face in the mirror, I was astonished at the change.
Soak dried fruit in water before cooking it.

Some past participles which do not end in '-ed' are also used as adjectives. They are sometimes called '-ed' adjectives.

It is a good idea to get at least two <u>written</u> estimates.
...searching for a <u>lost</u> ball.

A few '-ed' adjectives are related to intransitive verbs and have an active meaning. For example, an 'escaped' prisoner is a prisoner who has escaped.

The following '-ed' adjectives have an active meaning:

accumulated	escaped	fallen	swollen
dated	faded	retired	wilted

She is the daughter of a <u>retired</u> army officer.
...a tall woman with a <u>swollen</u> leg.

related to verbs but different in meaning
Some '-ed' adjectives are related to verbs in form, but have a different meaning from the usual meaning of the verb. For example, to 'attach' something to something else means to join or fasten it on, but a person who is 'attached' to someone or something is very fond of them.

The tiles <u>had been attached</u> with an inferior adhesive material and were already beginning to fall off.
'Oh, yes,' says Howard, 'I'm quite <u>attached</u> to Henry. I've known him for ages.'

The following adjectives have a different meaning from the usual or commonest meaning of the related verb:

advanced	disposed	marked
attached	disturbed	mixed
determined	guarded	noted

related to nouns
Many adjectives are formed by adding '-ed' to a noun. They indicate that a person or thing has the thing that the noun refers to. For example, a 'bearded' man has a beard.

The following adjectives are formed by adding '-ed' to a noun:

armoured	detailed	gloved	salaried	turbaned
barbed	flowered	hooded	skilled	veiled
beaded	freckled	pointed	spotted	walled
bearded	gifted	principled	striped	winged

The visitor was a <u>bearded</u> man with mean and unreliable eyes.
Every <u>skilled</u> adult reader takes all of this for granted.

not related to verbs or nouns
There are a few '-ed' adjectives that are not related to verbs or nouns in the ways described above. For example, the adjective 'antiquated' is not related to a verb, because there is no such verb as 'antiquate'.

The following adjectives are not directly related to verbs or nouns:

antiquated	beloved	crazed	rugged
ashamed	bloated	deceased	sophisticated
assorted	concerted	indebted	

It was not until the 1970s that a <u>concerted</u> effort was made to import the game of pool into Britain.

Without language, complex social systems and sophisticated technology would be impossible.

edit

If you **edit** a text, you examine it and make corrections to it so that it is suitable for publication.

I am indebted most particularly to Mrs Maria Jepps, who checked and edited the entire work.

'publish' Do not confuse **edit** with **publish**. When a company **publishes** a book or magazine, it prints copies of it, which are then sent to shops to be sold.

The Collins Cobuild English Language Dictionary was published in 1987.

educate

See entry at **bring up**.

effect

See entry at **affect - effect**.

effective - efficient

'effective' Something that is **effective** produces the results that it is intended to produce.

...effective street lighting.
...an effective mosquito repellent.

'efficient' A person, machine, or organization that is **efficient** does a job well and successfully, without wasting time or energy.

You need a very efficient production manager.
Engines and cars can be made more efficient.

effeminate

See entry at **female - feminine - effeminate**.

efficient

See entry at **effective - efficient**.

effort

If you **make an effort** to do something, you try hard to do it.

Daintry made one more effort to escape.
Little effort has been made to investigate this claim.

Note that you do not say that someone 'does an effort'.

either

used as a
determiner You use **either** in front of the singular form of a count noun to say that something is true about each of two people or things.

It's a mistake for either parent to ask children about what happened while they were visiting the other parent.
In either case, Robert would never succeed.

'either of'	Instead of using **either,** you can use **either of.** For example, instead of saying 'Either answer is correct', you can say '**Either of** the answers is correct'.

You could hear everything that was said in <u>either of the rooms</u>.
They didn't want <u>either of their children</u> to know about this.

You use **either of** in front of plural pronouns.

One speech by <u>either of them</u> would have ended his uncertainty.
He was better dressed than <u>either of us</u>.

WARNING	You do not use **either** without 'of' in front of a plural noun or pronoun.

Some people use a plural form of a verb after **either of** and a noun group. For example, instead of saying 'I don't think either of you is wrong', they say 'I don't think either of you **are** wrong'.

It's a wonder either of you <u>are</u> here to tell the tale.

This use is acceptable in conversation, but in formal writing you should always use a singular form of a verb after **either of.**

used as a
pronoun

Either can be used on its own as a pronoun. This is a fairly formal use.

<u>Either</u> is acceptable.
I was given two computer print-outs; my name was not on <u>either</u>.

used in negative
statements

You can use **either** or **either of** in a negative statement to emphasize that the statement applies to both of two things or people. For example, instead of saying about two people 'I don't like them', you can say 'I don't like **either of** them'.

She could not see <u>either</u> man.
There was no sound from <u>either of</u> the flats.
'Which one do you want?'—'I don't want <u>either</u>.'

used to mean
'each'

When you use **either** in front of 'side' or 'end', it can have the same meaning as 'each'. For example, 'There were trees on **either side** of the road' means 'There were trees on each side of the road'.

...a narrow road which had small houses built on <u>either side</u> of it.

If you say that two things are on **either side** of something, you mean that one thing is on one side of it and the other thing is on the other side.

The two ladies sat in large armchairs on <u>either side</u> of the stage.
...two small summerhouses at <u>either end</u> of the yew-tree walk.

used as an
adverb

When one negative statement follows another, you can put **either** at the end of the second one.

I can't play tennis and I can't play golf <u>either</u>.
'I haven't got that address.'—'No, I haven't got it <u>either</u>.'
'He's never been like this before.'—'He's never had that ghastly colour, <u>either</u>.'

For other ways of linking two negative statements, see entries at **neither** and **nor.**

either ... or

You use **either** and **or** when you are mentioning two alternatives and you want to indicate that no other alternatives are possible. You put **either** in front of the first alternative and **or** in front of the second one.

Recruits are interviewed by <u>either</u> Mrs Darby <u>or</u> Mr Bootle.
He must have concluded that I was <u>either</u> naïve <u>or</u> impudent.

I was expecting you either today or tomorrow.
People either leave or are promoted.
Either the government will have to give these people what they want immediately or it must take firm steps to end the strike.

In conversation, **either** is not always used immediately in front of the first alternative; it is sometimes used in front of a verb earlier in the sentence. For example, instead of saying 'I will ring you either today or tomorrow', people sometimes say 'I will **either** ring you today or tomorrow'.

I suppose you either find it funny or boring.
She would either have been Australian or South African.

This use is acceptable in conversation, but you should avoid it in formal writing.

used in negative statements   You use **either** and **or** in negative statements when you are emphasizing that a statement refers to both of two things or qualities. For example, instead of saying 'I haven't been to Paris or Rome', you can say 'I haven't been to **either** Paris **or** Rome'.

He was not the choice of either Dexter or the team manager.
Dr Kirk, you're not being either frank or fair.
This should not be disastrous either morally or politically.

See also entry at **neither ... nor**.

elder

'elder'   The **elder** of two people is the one who was born first.

Posy was the elder of the two.

If you have a sister or brother who was born before you, you can refer to them as your **elder** sister or brother.

He had none of his elder brother's charm.

'eldest'   The **eldest** of a group of people, especially the brothers and sisters in a family, is the one who was born first.

Gladys was the eldest of four children.
Her eldest son was killed in the First War.

'older' and 'oldest'   **Elder** and **eldest** are slightly formal, and many people do not use them at all. Instead of 'elder' and 'eldest' you can use **older** and **oldest**.

He's my older brother.
Six of their children were there, including the oldest, Luke.

You can use **older** and **oldest** in some ways in which you cannot use 'elder'. For example, you can use **older** after 'be', 'get', or 'grow', and in front of 'than'.

Try it when you are a little older.
We're all getting older.
As he grew older, his fascination with bees developed into an obsession.
Harriet was ten years older than I was.

You cannot use **elder** in any of these ways.

You can also use **older** and **oldest** to talk about things.

On older houses there may be guarantees for treatment against woodworm.
It is the oldest of London squares.
It claims to be the oldest insurance company in the world.

You cannot use **elder** or **eldest** to talk about things.

elderly

See entry at **old**.

elect

used as a verb

Elect is usually used as a verb. When people **elect** someone, they choose that person to represent them, by voting for them.

They met to elect a president.
Why should we elect him Mayor?
You could be elected as an MP.

WARNING

You only say that someone **is elected** when they are chosen by voting. If they are chosen in some other way, you use another word such as 'choose', 'select', or 'pick'. See entry at **choose.**

used as an adjective

Elect is sometimes added after words such as 'president' or 'governor' to indicate that someone has been appointed to a post but has not officially started to carry out their duties. When **elect** has this meaning, it is only used immediately after a noun.

...the President elect.
...the Archbishop of Canterbury elect.

WARNING

You do not use **elect** as an adjective simply to say that someone has been elected by voting. Instead you use **elected** in front of a noun.

...a democratically elected government.
The newly elected governor was trying to sack the college president.

electric - electrical

'electric'

You use **electric** in front of nouns to talk about particular machines or devices that use electricity.

...an electric motor.
I switched on the electric fire.

'electrical'

You use **electrical** when you are talking in a more general way about machines, devices, or systems which use or produce electricity. **Electrical** is typically used in front of nouns such as 'equipment', 'appliance', and 'component'.

...electrical appliances such as dishwashers and washing machines.
...electrical fittings.

You also use **electrical** to talk about people or organizations connected with the production of electricity or electrical goods.

...electrical engineers.
...the electrical and mechanical engineering industries.

elevator

See entry at **lift**.

GRAMMAR # Ellipsis

Ellipsis involves leaving out words which are obvious from the context. In many cases you use an auxiliary in place of a full verb group, or in place of a verb group and its object. For example, you say 'John won't like it but Rachel will' instead of 'John won't like it but Rachel will like it'.

They would stop it if they could.
I never did go to Stratford, although I probably should have.
...a topic which should have attracted far more attention from philosophers than it has.

A full clause would sound unnatural in these examples.

If you do not want to use a modal or the auxiliaries 'be' or 'have', you usually have to use 'do', 'does', or 'did'.

Do farmers still warrant a ministry all to themselves? I think they do.
I think we want it more than they do.

'be'　You do not, however, use the auxiliary 'do' to stand for the link verb 'be'. You just use a form of 'be'.

'I think you're right.'—'I'm sure I am.'

If the second verb group contains a modal, you usually put 'be' after the modal.

'He thought that the condition was hereditary in his case.'—'Well, it might be.'

However, this is not necessary if the first verb group contains a modal.

I'll be back as soon as I can.

'Be' is sometimes used after a modal in the second clause to contrast with another link verb such as 'seem', 'look', or 'sound'.

'It looks like tea to me.'—'Yes, it could be.'

With passives, 'be' is often, but not always, kept after a modal.

He argued that if tissues could be marketed, then anything could be.

'have' used as a main verb　When you are using 'have' as a main verb, for example to indicate possession, you can use a form of 'have' or a form of 'do' to refer back to it. American speakers usually use a form of 'do'.

She probably has a temperature — she certainly looks as if she has.
...since the Earth has a greater diameter than the Moon does.

Note that in the second example you do not need to use any verb after 'than'. You can just say 'since the Earth has a greater diameter than the Moon'.

'have' used as an auxiliary　When you use the auxiliary 'have' to stand for a perfect passive or continuous passive tense, you do not usually add 'been'. For example, you say, 'Have you been interviewed yet? I have.'

However, when 'have' is used in a similar way after a modal, 'been' cannot be omitted.

I'm sure it was repeated in the media. It must have been.
Priller noticed that they were not flying in tight formation as they should have been.

'to'-infinitive clauses　Instead of using a full 'to'-infinitive clause after a verb, you can just use 'to', if the action or state has already been mentioned.

Don't tell me if you don't want to.
At last he agreed to do what I asked him to.

'dare' and 'need'　You can omit a verb after 'dare' and 'need', but only when they are used in the negative.

'I don't mind telling you what I know.'—'You needn't. I'm not asking you to.'
'You must tell her the truth.'—'But, Neill, I daren't.'

'would rather'	Similarly, the verb is only omitted after 'would rather' when it is used in a negative clause or an 'if'-clause.

It's just that I'd rather not.
We could go to your place, if you'd rather.

'had better'	The verb is sometimes omitted after 'had better', even when it is used affirmatively.

'I can't tell you.'—'You'd better.'

However, you do not usually omit 'be'.

'He'll be out of town by nightfall.'—'He'd better be.'

in conversation	Ellipsis often occurs in conversation in replies and questions. See entries at **Agreeing and disagreeing, Questions, Reactions,** and **Replies.**
in coordinate clauses	Words are often left out of the second of two coordinate clauses, for example after 'and' or 'or'. See entry at **and.**

else

You use **else** after words such as 'someone', 'somewhere', or 'anything' to refer to another person, place, or thing, without saying which one.

...someone else's house.
Let's go somewhere else.
I had nothing else to do.

used with 'wh'-words	You can use **else** after most 'wh'-words. For example, if you ask '**What else** did they do?', you are asking what other things were done besides the things that have already been mentioned.

What else do I need to do?
Who else was there?
Why else would he be so willing to plead guilty?
Where else could they live in such comfort?
How else was I to explain what had happened?

Note that you do not use **else** after 'which'.

'little else' and 'much else'	**Else** is often used after 'little' and 'much'. If you say, for example, 'There was **little else** I could do', you mean that there were not many additional things that you could do.

There was little else he could say.
The firm had grown big by bothering about profits and very little else.
My excuse was that I had so much else to do.

'or else'	**Or else** is used as a conjunction with a similar meaning to 'or'. You use it to introduce the second of two possibilities.

I think I was at school, or else I was staying with a school friend during the vacation.
Either she was disappointed or else something had made her shy.

You also use **or else** when you are mentioning the undesirable results that will occur if someone does not do a particular thing.

You've got to be very careful or else you'll miss the turn-off into our drive.
It's important that your child should have a wide range of books or else he will confine his view of reading to the books in school.

embark

See entry at **go into.**

embarrassed

See entry at **ashamed - embarrassed**.

emigration - immigration - migration

'emigrate'   If you **emigrate**, you leave your own country and go to live permanently in another country.

He received permission to emigrate to Canada.
He had emigrated from Germany in the early 1920's.

'emigration'   You refer to the process by which people leave their own country in order to live somewhere else as **emigration**.

...new laws on emigration.
...the encouragement given to peasant emigration.

'emigrant'   People who emigrate are called **emigrants**.

Thousands of emigrants boarded Cunard ships for the New World.

'immigrant'   When emigrants arrive in the country where they intend to live, they are referred to as **immigrants**.

...a Russian immigrant.
A ship carrying 54 illegal immigrants sailed into the harbour yesterday.

'immigration'   You refer to the process by which people come to live in a country as **immigration**.

She asked for his views on immigration.
...immigration procedures.

'migrate'   When people **migrate**, they temporarily move to another place, usually a city or another country, in order to find work.

The only solution people can see is to migrate.
Millions have migrated to the cities.

'migration'   This process is called **migration**.

...mass migration into cities.
Migration for work is accelerating in the Third World.

'migrant'   People who migrate are called **migrants** or **migrant workers**.

...migrants looking for a place to live.
In South America alone there are three million migrant workers.

another meaning of 'migrate'   When birds or animals **migrate**, they move from one place to another at the same time each year.

Texas is the first landfall of most birds migrating north.
Every spring they migrate towards the coast.

employ

If you **employ** someone, you pay them to work for you.

The companies employ 7.5 million people between them.
He was employed as a research assistant.

If something **is employed** for a particular purpose, it is used for that purpose. You can say, for example, that a particular method or technique **is employed**.

A number of ingenious techniques are employed.

The methods employed are varied, depending on the material in question.

You can also say that a machine, tool, or weapon **is employed**.

Computers and electronic devices could be employed in a number of ways. What matters most is how the tools are employed.

'use'   However, **employ** is a formal word when it is used to talk about such things as methods or tools. You usually say that a method or tool **is used**.

This method has been extensively used in the United States.
These weapons are used against human targets.

employment

See entry at **work**.

enable

See entry at **allow - permit - let**.

end

When something **ends** or when you **end** it, it stops.

The current agreement ends on November 24.
He refused to end his nine-week-old hunger strike.

'end with'   If you **end with** something, it is the last of a series of things that you say, do, or perform.

He ended with an emphatic assertion that if the matter had been left to him, it would have been resolved long before.
Whatever the concert was, we always ended with 'Spread a Little Happiness'.

'end by'   If you **end by doing** something, it is the last of a series of things that you do.

I ended by saying that further instructions would be given to him later.
We talked of various things and he ended by playing me some Bach on the piano.

'end up'   **End up** is used in conversation to say what happens to someone at the end of a series of events. You can say that someone **ends up** in a particular place, that they **end up** with something, or that they **end up** doing something. You do not use **end up** in formal writing.

I had to change to another train and I ended up at Banbury, which is 20 miles away.
She was afraid to close the window and ended up with a cold.
We ended up taking a taxi there.

endure

See entry at **bear**.

energy - energetic

'energy'   **Energy** is the physical ability that someone has to do active things.

He has neither the time nor the energy to play with the children.
You must eat to give yourself energy.

'energetic' If someone has a lot of this ability, you say that they are **energetic**.

...three energetic little girls.
I have found you honest, loyal, and energetic.

You can also describe behaviour or activities as **energetic**.

...the boy who plays energetic games.

another meaning of 'energy' **Energy** is also the power which comes from fuels such as gas, coal, and oil.

...nuclear energy.
Supersonic flight is very expensive. It uses a lot of energy.

When you are talking about something connected with this power, you can use **energy** in front of a noun.

...warnings about an energy shortage.
Our energy problems are over.

Note that you do not use **energetic** with this meaning. You do not say, for example, 'Our energetic problems are over'.

engaged

When two people have agreed to marry each other, or have announced formally that they are going to be married, you can say that they are **engaged**.

They were not officially engaged.
...an engaged couple.

You can also say that each person is **engaged**.

I am getting on for twenty and I have become engaged.
As an engaged girl, she would be unable to accept invitations from other men.

You say that someone is **engaged to** the person they are going to marry.

Sonny was formally engaged to Sandra.

Note that you do not say that someone is 'engaged with' the person they are going to marry.

engine

See entry at **machine**.

engineer - engine driver

'engineer' An **engineer** is a skilled person who uses scientific knowledge to design and construct machinery, electrical devices, or roads and bridges.

...a brilliant young mining engineer.
He trained as an engineer and worked in industry and management until 1973.

An **engineer** is also a person who repairs mechanical or electrical devices.

The telephone engineer can't come until Wednesday.

In American English, a person who drives a train is also called an **engineer**.

An engineer pulled his freight train into a siding.

'engine driver'	In British English, a person who drives a train is called an **engine driver**.

Every little boy has an ambition to be an engine driver.

English

English is used as an adjective or a noun.

used as an adjective	**English** means 'belonging or relating to England, its people, or its language'.

My wife's English.
...an English pub.
...the English language.

English is sometimes used to mean 'belonging or relating to Great Britain'. However, it is better to avoid this use, as it may cause offence to people who come from Scotland, Wales, or Northern Ireland.

used as a noun	**English** is the language spoken in Britain, the United States, and many other countries.

Do you speak English?
Half the letter was in Swedish and half in English.

There are some differences between the way in which this language is spoken and written in Britain and the way in which it is spoken and written in the United States. Many of these differences are explained in this book. We often describe a word or expression as being used 'in British English' or 'in American English'.

English is also the study of the English language or English literature.

Karen obtained A levels in English, French, and Geography.
...an English lesson.

People who come from England are sometimes referred to as **the English**.

The English love privacy.
The English don't give up anything without a fight.

You can sometimes refer to a group of English people, for example supporters of the England football team, as **the English.**

The English have been allocated 4,800 tickets.
The English present that day were a few families scattered along the beach enjoying the sunshine.

'Englishman' and 'Englishwoman'	You do not refer to a single English person as an 'English'. You refer to them as an **Englishman** or an **Englishwoman**.

Not a single Englishman was arrested.
...a beautiful Englishwoman.

See also entry at **Britain - British - Briton**.

enjoy

If you **enjoy** something, you get pleasure and satisfaction from it.

I enjoyed the holiday enormously.
I've enjoyed every minute of it.

If you experience pleasure and satisfaction on a particular occasion, you can say that you **enjoyed yourself**.

Mr Van Buren asked me if I had enjoyed myself.
I've enjoyed myself very much.

People often say '**Enjoy yourself**' to someone who is going to a social occasion such as a party or a dance.

Enjoy yourself on Wednesday.

Enjoy is normally only used as a transitive or reflexive verb. You do not say 'I enjoyed'. However, some American speakers say 'Enjoy!', meaning 'Enjoy yourself'.

used with an '-ing' form

You can say that someone **enjoys doing** something or **enjoys being** something.

The jar was always stacked with cookies that she had enjoyed baking.
They enjoyed being in a large group.

Note that you do not say that someone 'enjoys to do' or 'enjoys to be' something.

enough

after adjectives and adverbs

You use **enough** after an adjective or adverb to say that someone or something has as much of a quality as is needed.

It's big enough.
We have a long enough list.
It seemed that Henry had not been careful enough.
I was not a good enough rider.
The student isn't trying hard enough.

If you want to say who the person or thing is acceptable to, you add a prepositional phrase beginning with 'for'.

That's good enough for me.
Will that be soon enough for you?
If you find that the white wine is not cold enough for you, ask for some ice to be put in it.

If you want to say that someone has as much of a quality as they need in order to do something, you add a 'to'-infinitive after **enough.**

The children are old enough to travel to school on their own.

You can also use a 'to'-infinitive after **enough** to say that something has as much of a quality as is needed for someone to be aware of it or to do something with it. Between **enough** and the 'to'-infinitive you put a prepositional phrase beginning with 'for'.

The bullets passed close enough for us to hear their whine.

Another way of saying that something has as much of a quality as is needed for something to be done with it is simply to add a 'to'-infinitive after **enough.** For example, instead of saying 'The boat was close enough for me to touch it', you can say 'The boat was **close enough to touch**'.

None of the crops was ripe enough to eat.
Some employers claim that women don't stay long enough to train.

WARNING

You do not use a 'that'-clause after **enough** when you are saying what is needed for something to be possible.

Enough is sometimes used after an adjective to confirm or emphasize that something or someone has a particular quality.

It's a common enough dilemma.

When you make a statement of this kind, you often add a second statement that contrasts with it.

She's likeable enough, but very ordinary.

used as a determiner	**Enough** is used in front of the plural form of a count noun to say that there are as many things or people as are needed.

There aren't enough neutrons for the reaction to be sustained.
I asked Professor Bailey whether there were enough women going into engineering.

You can also use **enough** in front of an uncount noun to say that there is as much of something as is needed.

We had enough room to store all the information.
He hasn't had enough exercise.

used after a noun	**Enough** is sometimes used after uncount nouns such as 'room', 'time', or 'food'. For example, you can say either 'There was **enough room** to park a car' or 'There was **room enough** to park a car'. There is no difference in meaning; however, it is more common to put **enough** in front of the noun.

There would never be room enough for everything.
He would have time enough to get to the milking sheds before dark.

'enough of'	You do not use **enough** immediately in front of a noun group beginning with a determiner, or in front of a pronoun. Instead you use **enough of**.

Just bring enough of the things your baby likes best.
There's not enough of them to go round.
They haven't had enough of it.

When you use **enough of** in front of a plural noun or pronoun, you use a plural form of a verb with it.

Eventually enough of these shapes were collected.
There were enough of them to form an identifiable group.

When you use **enough of** in front of a singular or uncount noun or a singular pronoun, you use a singular form of a verb with it.

There has always been enough of the colonial tradition to make it easy to evoke these responses.
There is enough of it for everybody.

used as a pronoun	**Enough** can be used on its own as a pronoun.

I've got enough to worry about.
Enough has been said about this already.

'not enough'	Note that you do not use **enough**, or **enough** and a noun, as the subject of a negative sentence. You do not say, for example, 'Enough people didn't come'. You say '**Not enough** people came'.

Not enough has been done to help them.
Not enough has been said, and I'm sure everyone realizes this.
Not enough attention is paid at the design stage of the machinery.

modifying adverbs	You can use adverbs such as 'nearly', 'almost', 'just', 'hardly', and 'quite' in front of **enough.**

This was nearly enough to lose them their chance of winning.
At present there is just enough to feed them.
There was hardly enough time to get the by-pass completed.

You can also use these adverbs in front of an expression consisting of an adjective and **enough.**

We are all nearly young enough to be mistaken for students.
Some of these creatures are just large enough to see with the naked eye.
...children who are hardly old enough to be out on their own.

<table>
<tr><td>used with
sentence
adverbs</td><td>You can use enough after sentence adverbs like 'interestingly' or 'strangely' to draw attention to a surprising quality in what you are saying.</td></tr>
</table>

Interestingly enough, this proportion has not increased.
I find myself strangely enough in agreement with John for a change.
Funnily enough, old people seem to love bingo.

enquire

See entry at **inquire - enquire**.

ensure

See entry at **assure - ensure - insure**.

enter

If you **enter** a room or building, you go into it.

Colonel Rolland entered a small cafe.

Enter can be used without an object.

They stopped talking as soon as they saw Brody enter.

'go into' and 'come into'
Enter is a rather formal word, and you do not usually use it in conversation. Instead you say that someone **goes into** or **comes into** a room or building.

He shut the street door behind me as I went in.
Boylan came silently into the room.

Note that you never say that someone 'enters' a car, train, ship, or plane. For more information, see entry at **go into**.

entirely

See section on **extent** in entry at **Adverbials**.

envious - enviable

'envious'
If you are **envious,** you wish you had something such as a possession, quality, or ability that someone else has.

We see them doing things we are not allowed to do, and are envious.
I tried hard not to be envious.

You say that you are **envious of** a person or **envious of** something that they have.

...a girl who is deeply envious of her brother.
They may be envious of your success.

'enviable'
You use **enviable** to describe a possession, quality, or ability that someone has, and that you wish you had yourself.

...enviable accommodation.
She learned to speak foreign languages with enviable fluency.

equally

You use **equally** in front of an adjective to say that a person or thing has as much of a quality as someone or something else that has been mentioned.

He was a superb pianist. Irene was equally brilliant.

Note that you do not use **equally** in front of 'as' when making a comparison. You do not say, for example, 'He is equally as tall as his brother'. You say 'He is **just as tall as** his brother'.

Severe sunburn is just as dangerous as a heat burn.
He was just as shocked as I was.

See entry at **as ... as**.

equipment

Equipment consists of the things you need for a particular activity.

...kitchen equipment.
...fire-fighting equipment.

Equipment is an uncount noun. You do not talk about 'equipments' or 'an equipment'. You can refer to a single item as a **piece of equipment.**

He knows how vitally important a piece of equipment your radio is.
The leader carried a number of pieces of equipment with him.

error

An **error** is a mistake.

The doctor committed an appalling error of judgement.
...errors in grammar.

You can say that something is done **in error**. This is a fairly formal use.

They had arrested him in error.
Another village had been wiped out in error.

In conversation, you usually say that something is done **by mistake**.

I opened the door into the library by mistake.

Note that you do not say that something is done 'by error'.

escape

The verb **escape** has several meanings. For some of these meanings, it is used as a transitive verb. For others, it is used as an intransitive verb.

used as a transitive verb If you **escape** a situation that is dangerous, unpleasant, or difficult, you succeed in avoiding it.

Many crossed the border to escape the carnage in their homeland.
He seemed to escape the loneliness of extreme old age.
Ralph walked in the rear, thankful to have escaped responsibility for a time.

If you cannot **escape** a feeling or belief, you cannot help having it.

One cannot escape the feeling that there is something missing.
It is difficult to escape the conclusion that they are actually intended for the black market.

used as an intransitive verb If you **escape from** a place where you are in danger, you succeed in leaving it.

Last year thousands escaped from the country in small boats.

If you **escape from** a place such as a prison, you get out of it and are free.

In 1966 the spy George Blake escaped from prison.
Even if he managed to escape, where would he run?

Note that you do not say that someone 'escapes' a prison or any other place.

If you **escape** when someone is trying to catch you, you avoid being caught.

The two other burglars were tipped off by a lookout and <u>escaped.</u>

'get away' **Get away** can be used with the same meaning.

George Watin <u>got away</u> and is presumed to be living in Spain.

especially - specially

used in front of adjectives These adverbs have a similar meaning when they are used in front of adjectives. For example, you can emphasize that something is very useful by saying that it is **especially** useful or **specially** useful.

He found his host <u>especially</u> irritating.
...a pub where the beer was <u>specially</u> good.

used in other positions When **especially** and **specially** are not used in front of adjectives, their meanings are different.

You use **especially** to indicate that what you are saying applies more to one thing or situation than to others.

He was kind to his staff, <u>especially</u> those who were sick or in trouble.
Double ovens are a good idea, <u>especially</u> if you are cooking several meals at once.

When **especially** relates to the subject of a sentence, you put it immediately after the subject.

Children's bones, <u>especially,</u> are very sensitive to radiation.

You use **specially** to say that something is done or made for a particular purpose.

They'd come down <u>specially</u>.
...a <u>specially</u> designed costume.
...strong beer <u>specially</u> brewed in Burton-on-Trent.

ethic - ethics - ethical

'ethic' A particular **ethic** is an idea or moral belief that influences the behaviour and attitudes of a group of people.

...the American '<u>frontier</u>' ethic of expansion and opportunity.
...the Protestant <u>work ethic.</u>

'ethics' **Ethics** are moral beliefs and rules about right and wrong. When you use **ethics** with this meaning, it is a plural noun. You use a plural form of a verb with it.

The basic <u>ethics</u> which any religion sets forward <u>are</u> more or less the same as those of any other religion.

Ethics is also the study of questions about what is morally right or wrong. When **ethics** has this meaning, it is an uncount noun. You use a singular form of a verb with it.

We are only too ready to believe that <u>ethics</u> <u>is</u> a field where thinking does no good.

'ethical' **Ethic** is never used as an adjective. The adjective that means 'relating to ethics' is **ethical**.

...an <u>ethical</u> problem.
He had no real <u>ethical</u> objection to drinking.

even

You use **even** to indicate that what you are saying is surprising. You put **even** in front of the surprising part of your statement.

Even Anthony enjoyed it.
She liked him even when she was quarrelling with him.
No one dared even to whisper.
I shall give the details to no one, not even to you.

However, **even** usually goes after an auxiliary or modal, not in front of it.

You didn't even enjoy it very much.
I couldn't even see the creek ahead.
They may even give you a lift in their van.

used with comparatives

You use **even** in front of a comparative to emphasize that someone or something has more of a quality than they had before. For example, you say 'The weather was bad yesterday, but it is **even worse** today'.

He became even more suspicious of me.
They were even more drunk than they had been when we hired them.

You also use **even** in front of a comparative to emphasize that someone or something has more of a quality than someone or something else. For example, you say 'The train is slow, but the bus is **even slower**'.

Barber had something even worse to tell me.
The identification of Tutankhamun's mother is even more difficult.

'even if' and 'even though'

Even if and **even though** are used to introduce subordinate clauses. You use **even if** to say that a possible situation would not prevent something from being true.

Even if you disagree with her, she's worth listening to.
I hope I can come back, even if it's only for a few weeks.

Even though has a similar meaning to 'although', but is more emphatic.

Gregory, Platt, and Lydon will play even though they are not fully fit.
I was always afraid of men, even though I had lots of boyfriends.

WARNING

If you begin a sentence with **even if** or **even though,** you do not put 'yet' or 'but' at the beginning of the main clause. You do not say, for example, 'Even if you disagree with her, yet she's worth listening to'.

However, you can use **still** in the main clause. This is a very common use.

Even though there are great savings to be made, the potential user still needs to be educated in the economics of the marketplace.
But even if they do change the system, they've still got an economic crisis on their hands.

'even so'

You use **even so** to emphasize that something is true in spite of what you have just said.

Their feathers are constantly shed and renewed. Even so they need constant care.
The flame rose, throwing pools of light on the ceiling. Even so, the kitchen remained mostly in shadow.

evening

The **evening** is the part of each day between the end of the afternoon and the time when you go to bed.

evening

<table>
<tr>
<td>the present day</td>
<td>You refer to the evening of the present day as this evening.</td>
</tr>
</table>

Come and have a drink with me <u>this evening</u>.
I came here <u>this evening</u> because I particularly wanted to be on my own.

You can refer to the evening of the previous day as **yesterday evening,** but it is more common to say **last night.**

'So you saw me in King Street <u>yesterday evening</u>?'—'Yes.'
I met your husband <u>last night</u>.
I've been thinking about what we said <u>last night</u>.

You refer to the evening of the next day as **tomorrow evening** or **tomorrow night.**

Gerald's giving a little party <u>tomorrow evening</u>.
Will you be home in time for dinner <u>tomorrow night</u>?

single events in the past

If you want to say that something happened during a particular evening in the past, you use **on.**

She telephoned Ida <u>on Tuesday evening</u>.
<u>On the evening</u> after the party, Dick went to see Roy.

If you have been describing what happened during a particular day, you can say that something happened **that evening** or **in the evening.**

<u>That evening</u> the children asked me to watch television with them.
He came back <u>in the evening</u>.

If you are talking about a day in the past and you want to mention that something had happened during the evening of the day before, you say that it had happened **the previous evening** or **the evening before.**

Duggan had registered <u>the previous evening</u> at a hotel.
Fanny picked up the grey shawl Bet had given her <u>the evening before</u>.

If you want to say that something happened during the evening of the next day, you say that it happened **the following evening.**

Mopani arrived at Hunter's Drift <u>the following evening</u>.
I told Patricia that I would take her to Cranthorpe <u>the following evening</u>.

In stories, if you want to say that something happened during an evening in the past, without saying which evening, you say that it happened **one evening.**

<u>One evening</u> the school showed a Lon Chaney film.
She had gone out <u>one evening</u> last summer, to sit on her front step.

You can also say, for example, that something happened **one April evening** or **on a Saturday evening.**

<u>One mild May evening</u> he asked me over to inspect it.
Mac picked me up <u>on a Friday evening</u>.

talking about the future

If you want to say that something will happen during a particular evening in the future, you use **on.**

The winning project will be announced <u>on Monday evening</u>.
I will write to her <u>on Sunday evening</u>.

If you are already talking about a day in the future, you can say that something will happen **in the evening.**

The school sports day will be on June 22 with prizegiving <u>in the evening</u>.

regular events

If something happens regularly every evening, you say that it happens **in the evening** or **in the evenings.**

A 2-year-old may keep climbing out of bed <u>in the evening</u> to rejoin the family.
<u>In the evening</u> I like to lay breakfast as this is one less job for the morning.

In the evenings she used to sit on the sofa in her long black trousers, smoking endless cigarettes.

However, if you want to say that something happens regularly once a week during a particular evening, you use **on** followed by the name of the day and **evenings.**

Am I no longer allowed to play chess on Monday evenings?
We would all gather there on Friday evenings.

exact times   If you have mentioned an exact time and you want to make it clear that you are talking about the evening rather than the morning, you add **in the evening.**

He arrived about six in the evening.

ever

Ever is used in negative sentences, questions, and comparisons to mean 'at any time in the past' or 'at any time in the future'.

No one's ever accused me of it.
I don't think I'll ever be homesick here.
Did he ever play football?
I'm happier than I've ever been.

'yet'   You do not use **ever** in questions or negative sentences to ask whether an expected event has happened, or to say that it has not happened so far. You do not say, for example, 'Has the taxi arrived ever?' or 'The taxi has not arrived ever'. The word you use is **yet.**

Have you had your lunch yet?
It isn't dark yet.

See entry at **yet.**

'always'   You do not use **ever** in positive sentences to say that there was never a time when something was not the case. You do not say, for example, 'I've ever been happy here'. The word you use is **always.**

She was always in a hurry.
Talking to Harold always cheered her up.

See entry at **always.**

'still'   You do not use **ever** to say that something is continuing to happen. You do not say, for example, 'When we left Lowestoft, it was ever raining'. The word you use is **still.**

Unemployment is still falling.
She still lives in London.
She was still beautiful.
I was still a schoolboy.

See entry at **still.**

'ever since'   If something has been the case **ever since** a particular time, it has been the case all the time from then until now.

'How long have you lived here?'—'Ever since I was married.'
We have been devoted friends ever since.

'ever so' and   In conversation, you can use **ever so** in front of an adjective to emphasize
'ever such'   the degree of something.

They are ever so kind.

If the adjective is part of a noun group, you use **ever such** instead of 'ever so'. **Ever such** always goes in front of 'a' or 'an'.

I had ever such a nice letter from her.

You do not use **ever so** or **ever such** in formal writing.

'ever' with
'wh'-words

Sometimes people use **ever** after a 'wh'-word at the beginning of a sentence. They do this to express surprise. For example, instead of saying 'Who told you that?', they say **'Who ever** told you that?'

Who ever would have thought that?
'I'm sorry. I'd rather not say.'—'Why ever not?'
How ever did you find me?

When these questions appear in writing, **what ever**, **where ever**, and **who ever** are sometimes written as single words: **whatever**, **wherever**, and **whoever**.

Whatever is the matter?
Wherever did you get this?
Whoever heard of a bishop resigning?

However, many people consider these forms to be incorrect, and it is better to write **what ever**, **where ever**, and **who ever** as two separate words. **How ever** and **why ever** are always written as two separate words.

every

You use **every** in front of the singular form of a count noun to indicate that you are referring to all the members of a group and not just some of them.

She spoke to every person at the party.
I agree with every word Peter says.
Every child would have milk every day.
This new wealth can be seen in every village.

'every' and 'all'

You can often use **every** or **all** with the same meaning. For example, **'Every** dog should be registered' means the same as **'All** dogs should be registered'.

However, **every** is followed by the singular form of a noun, whereas **all** is followed by the plural form.

Every child is entitled to be educated at the state's expense.
I was equally interested in all children.

See entry at **all**.

'each'

Instead of **every** or **all**, you sometimes use **each**. You use **each** when you are thinking about the members of a group as individuals.

Each customer has the choice of thirty colours.
Each meal will be served in a different room.

See entry at **each**.

referring back to
'every'

You usually use a singular pronoun such as 'he', 'she', 'him', or 'her' to refer back to an expression beginning with **every**.

Every businessman would do without advertising if he could.

However, when you are referring back to an expression such as 'every student' or 'every inhabitant' which does not indicate a specific sex, you usually use **they** or **them**.

Every passenger and crew member is the doctor's patient, and there's no escape from them.

For a fuller discussion of these uses, see entry at **he - they**.

used with **expressions** **of time**	You use **every** to indicate that something happens at regular intervals.

They met every day.
Every Monday Mr Whymper visited the farm.

Note that **every** and **all** do not have the same meaning when they are used with expressions of time. For example, if you do something **every morning**, you do it regularly each morning. If you do something **all morning**, you spend the whole of one morning doing it.

He used to walk into his club every afternoon at three o'clock.
Her voice was hoarse. 'You have a cold?'—'No. It's just from talking all afternoon.'

He had been running three miles every day.
That person has been following us all day.

'every other'   If something happens, for example, **every other** year or **every second** year, it happens one year, then does not happen the next year, then happens the year after that, and so on.

We only save enough money to take a real vacation every other year.
It seemed easier to shave every second day.

everybody

See entry at **everyone - everybody**.

everyday - every day

'everyday'   **Everyday** is an adjective. You use it to describe something which is normal and not exciting or unusual in any way.

People could resume a normal everyday life.
…things that were common and everyday to him but luxuries to them.

'every day'   **Every day** is an adverbial. If something happens **every day**, it happens regularly each day.

Shanti asked the same question every day.

everyone - everybody

You usually use **everyone** or **everybody** to refer to all the people in a particular group. There is no difference in meaning between **everyone** and **everybody**.

The police had ordered everyone out of the office.
There wasn't enough room for everybody.

You can also use **everyone** and **everybody** to talk about people in general.

Everyone has the right to freedom of expression.
Everybody has to die some day.

In conversation, **everyone** and **everybody** are sometimes used to mean 'a lot of people'.

…the war that everyone had said could never happen.
'Do you know him at all?'—'Everybody knows Lonnie.'

After **everyone** or **everybody** you use a singular form of a verb.

Everyone wants to find out what is going on.
Everybody is selling the same product.

referring back	When you are referring back to **everyone** or **everybody,** you usually use 'they', 'them', or 'their'.

Will everyone please carry on as best they can.
Everybody had to empty their purses.

For a discussion of these uses, see entry at **he - they.**

'every one'	Do not confuse **everyone** with **every one.** You use **every one** to emphasize that something is true about each one of the things or people you are mentioning.

He read every one of my scripts.
She turned her attention to her friends. Every one had had a good education.

everything

You use **everything** to refer to all the objects, actions, activities, or facts in a particular situation.

I don't agree with everything he says.
I will arrange everything.

After **everything** you use a singular form of a verb.

Usually everything is very informal.
Everything happens much more quickly.

Everything is always written as one word. You do not write 'every thing'.

everywhere

Everywhere is an adverb. If you say that something happens or exists **everywhere,** you mean that it happens or exists in all parts of a place or area.

Everywhere in Asia it is the same.
People everywhere are becoming aware of the problem.

You do not usually use a preposition in front of **everywhere.** You do not say, for example, 'He has been to everywhere'. You say 'He has been **everywhere**'.

However, you can use 'from' with **everywhere.**

They heard from everywhere the lovely clear voices of women singing.
...a strange light that seemed to come from everywhere at once.

evidence

Evidence is anything that you see, hear, or read which causes you to believe that something is true or has really happened.

We saw evidence everywhere that a real effort was being made to promote tourism.
There was no evidence of quarrels between them.

Evidence is an uncount noun. You do not talk about 'evidences' or 'an evidence'. However, you can talk about a **piece of evidence.**

The first piece of evidence comes from a major report from the National Institute of Economic and Social Research.
It was one of the strongest pieces of evidence in the Crown's case.

exam - examination

An **exam** or **examination** is an official test that you take part in to show your knowledge or ability in a particular subject. **Exam** is the word most commonly used. **Examination** is more formal and is used mainly in written English.

I was told the exam was difficult.
...a three-hour written examination.

When someone takes part in an exam, you say that they **take** it or **sit** it.

Many children want to take these exams.
After the third term we'll be sitting the exam.

In conversation, you can also say that someone 'does' an exam.

There is no set time to do this exam.

If someone is successful in an exam, you say that they **pass** it.

Larry passed university exams at sixteen.
They cannot hope to get the kind of job they want even if they pass all their exams.

WARNING

To **pass** an exam always means to succeed in it. It does not mean to take part in it.

If someone is unsuccessful in an exam, you say that they **fail** it.

He failed the written paper.
I passed the written part but then failed the oral section hopelessly.

You also say that someone **passes in** or **fails in** a particular subject.

I've been told that I'll probably pass in English and French.
I took it in case I should fail in one of the other subjects.

example

If something has the typical features of a particular kind of thing, you can say that it is an **example** of that kind of thing.

It's a very fine example of traditional architecture.
This is yet another example of the disregard of human values.

When someone mentions an example of a particular kind of thing, you say that they are **giving** an example of that kind of thing.

Could you give me an example?
Let me give you an example of a skill which is not taught in schools but which could be.

Note that you do not say that someone 'says' an example.

'for example' When you mention an example of something, you often say **for example**.

Japan, for example, has two languages.
There must be some discipline in the home. For example, I do not allow my daughter Zoe to play with my typewriter.

Note that you do not say 'by example'.

except

You use **except** to introduce the only thing, person, or group that your main statement does not apply to.

used with a noun group	You usually use **except** in front of a noun group.

Anything, <u>except water,</u> is likely to block a sink.
All the boys <u>except Peter</u> started to giggle.

You can use **except** in front of object pronouns such as 'me', 'him', or 'her', or in front of reflexive pronouns such as 'himself' or 'herself'.

There's nobody that I really trust, <u>except him.</u>
Audrey had allowed no one inside the room <u>except himself.</u>

However, you do not use **except** in front of subject pronouns. You do not say, for example, 'There's no one here except I'.

WARNING	Do not confuse **except** with **besides**. You use **except** when you mention something that a statement does not apply to. **Besides** means 'in addition to'.

What languages do you know <u>besides</u> Arabic and English?

See entry at **beside - besides**.

'but'	After 'all' or a word beginning with 'every-' or 'any-' you can use **but** instead of 'except'.

The great ship capsized, carrying her Admiral and <u>all but</u> a handful of her crew to the bottom.
It is no longer respectable to marry for <u>anything but</u> love.

used with a verb	You cannot use **except** immediately in front of a finite verb. You can, however, use it in front of a 'to'-infinitive.

He demanded nothing of her <u>except to be there.</u>
She seldom goes out <u>except to go to Mass.</u>

After 'do', you can use **except** in front of an infinitive without 'to'.

There was little I could <u>do except wait.</u>
She <u>did nothing except make</u> empty conversation.

used with a finite clause	You can use **except** in front of a finite clause, but only when the clause is introduced by 'when', 'while', 'where', 'what', or 'that'.

He no longer went out, <u>except when Jeannie forced him.</u>
I have every confidence in your wisdom <u>except where this sort of thing is concerned.</u>
I knew nothing about Judith <u>except what I'd heard at second hand.</u>
I can scarcely remember what we ate, <u>except that it was plentiful and simple.</u>

'except for'	You use **except for** in front of a noun group when you are mentioning something that prevents a statement from being completely true.

The classroom was silent, <u>except for the busy scratching of pens on paper.</u>
The room was very cold and, <u>except for Morris,</u> entirely empty.

WARNING	Do not confuse **except** /ɪksept/ with **accept** /əksept/. **Accept** is a verb. If you **accept** something that you have been offered, you agree to take it.

I protested that I couldn't <u>accept</u> as a present something she so clearly adored.

See entry at **accept**.

exception

An **exception** is something or someone that a general statement does not apply to.

The troops had the support of the local population, the <u>exception</u> being some environmentalist groups who protested at the noise.

Women, with a few exceptions, are not involved in politics.

When you are mentioning an exception, you often use the expression **with the exception of**.

We all went, with the exception of Otto, who complained of feeling unwell.
They are all, with the exception of one Swedish coin, of Portuguese origin.

'**no exception**' If you want to emphasize that a general statement applies to a particular person or thing, you can say that they are **no exception**.

We've mentioned elsewhere the joys of many Greek islands in springtime, and Paxos is no exception.
The Monday following an outing often brings some absentees from school, and today was no exception.

'**without exception**' If you want to emphasize that a statement applies to all the people or things in a group, you can say that it applies to all of them **without exception**.

Every country without exception is committed to economic growth.
Without exception all our youngsters wanted to leave school and start work.

exchange

When people **exchange** things, they give them to each other at the same time.

We exchanged addresses.
They exchanged glances.

If you **exchange** one thing **for** another, you give the first thing to someone and they give the second thing to you.

She exchanged the jewels for money.
Leather goods made in the camp were exchanged for bread and clothing.

excited

Excited is used to describe how a person feels when they are looking forward eagerly to an enjoyable or special event.

He was so excited he could hardly sleep.
There were hundreds of excited children to meet us.

You say that someone is **excited about** something.

I was wildly excited about everything.

You can say that someone is **excited about doing** something.

Kendra was especially excited about seeing him after so many years.

Note that when someone is looking forward to doing something, you do not say that they are 'excited to do' it.

'**exciting**' Do not confuse **excited** with **exciting**. You use **exciting** to describe something which is enjoyable, special, or unusual and which makes you feel excited.

Growing up in the heart of London was very exciting.
It did not seem a very exciting idea.

exclamation mark - exclamation point

In British English, the punctuation mark used as the end of an exclamation (!) is called an **exclamation mark**. In American English, it is called an **exclamation point**. See entry at **Punctuation**.

excuse

Excuse is used as a noun or a verb. When it is a noun, it is pronounced /ɪkˈskjuːs/. When it is a verb, it is pronounced /ɪkˈskjuːz/.

used as a noun   An **excuse** is a reason that you give in order to explain why something has been done, has not been done, or will not be done.

It might be used as an excuse for evading our responsibilities.
There is no excuse for this happening in a new building.

You say that someone **makes** an excuse.

I made an excuse and left.
You don't have to make any excuses to me.

You do not say that someone 'says' an excuse.

used as a verb   If someone **is excused** from doing something, they are officially allowed not to do it.

He is to be excused from duty for one year.
You can apply to be excused payment if your earnings are low.

In conversation, if you say you must **excuse** yourself or if you ask someone to **excuse** you, you are indicating politely that you must leave.

This is where I ought to excuse myself.
You'll have to excuse me; I ought to be saying goodnight.

If you **excuse** someone for something wrong they have done, you decide not to criticize them or be angry with them.

Such delays cannot be excused.

'forgive'   **Forgive** is used in a similar way. However, when you say that you **forgive** someone, you usually mean that you have already been angry with them or quarrelled with them. You cannot use **excuse** in this way.

I forgave him everything.

'apologize'   When people say they are sorry for something they have done, you do not say that they 'excuse themselves'. You say that they **apologize.**

In her first letter she had apologized for being so mean to Rudolph.

'excuse me'   People often say '**Excuse me**' as a way of apologizing. For more information, see entry at **Apologizing.**

exhausted - exhausting - exhaustive

'exhausted'   If you are **exhausted,** you are very tired indeed.

At the end of the day I felt exhausted.
All three men were hot, dirty and exhausted.

You do not use words such as 'rather' or 'very' in front of **exhausted.** You can, however, use words such as 'completely', 'absolutely', or 'utterly'.

'And how are you feeling?'—'Exhausted. Completely exhausted.'
The guest speaker looked absolutely exhausted.
Utterly exhausted, he fell into a deep sleep.

'exhausting'   If an activity is **exhausting,** it is very tiring.

...a difficult and exhausting job.
Carrying bags is exhausting.

'exhaustive'   An **exhaustive** study or description is thorough and complete.

He studied the problem in exhaustive detail.
For a more exhaustive treatment you should read Margaret Boden's 'Artificial Intelligence and Natural Man'.

exist

If something **exists,** it is actually present in the world.

National differences do seem to exist.
Tendencies towards sadistic behaviour exist in all human beings.
They walked through my bedroom as if I didn't exist.

When **exist** has this meaning, you do not use it in a continuous tense. You do not say, for example, 'Tendencies towards sadistic behaviour are existing in all human beings'.

You also use **exist** to say that someone manages to live under difficult conditions or with very little food or money.

How we are to exist out here I don't know.
She existed only on milk.

When **exist** has this meaning, it can be used in a continuous tense.

People were existing on a hundred grams of bread a day.

expect

If you **expect** that something will happen, you believe that it will happen.

I expect you'll be glad when I get on the bus this afternoon.
They expect that about 1,500 of the existing force will take up the chance to go to sea.

You can sometimes use a 'to'-infinitive after **expect** instead of a 'that'-clause. For example, instead of saying 'I expect Johnson will come to the meeting', you can say 'I **expect Johnson to come** to the meeting'. However, the meaning is not quite the same. If you say 'I expect Johnson will come to the meeting', you are expressing a simple belief. If you say 'I expect Johnson to come to the meeting', you are indicating that you want Johnson to come to the meeting and that you will be annoyed or disappointed if he does not come.

The horse is on tremendous form and I expect him to win.
Nobody expected the strike to succeed.
The talks are expected to last two or three days.

Instead of saying you 'expect something will not' happen, you usually say you **do not expect it will** happen or **do not expect it to** happen.

I don't expect it will be necessary.
I did not expect to find detectives waiting at home.
I did not expect to be acknowledged.

If you say that you **expect** something is the case, you mean that you are fairly confident that it is the case.

I expect they've gone.
I expect they even play cricket on Christmas Day.

Instead of saying you 'expect something is not' the case, you usually say you **do not expect it is** the case.

I do not expect such parties are given now.

If someone asks if something is the case, you can say '**I expect so**'.

'They're shut now, aren't they?'—'Oh gosh, are they?'—'I expect so, at this time.'
'Did you say anything when I first came up to you?'—'Well, I expect so, but how on earth can I remember now?'

Note that you do not say 'I expect it'.

If you **are expecting** someone or something, you believe that they are going to arrive or happen.

They were expecting Wendy and the children.
Rodin was expecting an important letter from France.
We are expecting rain.

Note that when **expect** is used like this, you do not use a preposition after it.

'wait for'   Do not confuse **expect** with **wait for.** If you **are waiting for** someone or something, you are remaining in the same place or delaying doing something until they arrive or happen.

Whisky was served while we waited for Vorster.
He sat on the bench and waited for his coffee.
We all have to wait for a kettle to boil.

See entry at **wait.**

expensive

If something is **expensive,** it costs a lot of money.

...expensive clothes.
'Vogue' was more expensive than the other magazines.

You do not say that the price of something is 'expensive'. You say that it is **high.**

The price is much too high.
This must result in consumers paying higher prices.

experience

If you have **experience** of something, you have seen it, done it, or felt it.

I had no military experience.
The new countries have no experience of democracy.

An **experience** is something that happens to you or something that you do.

Moving house can be a traumatic experience.

You say that someone **has** an experience.

I had a peculiar experience tonight.

You do not say that someone 'makes' an experience.

'experiment'   You do not use **experience** to refer to a scientific test which is carried out in order to discover or prove something. The word you use is **experiment.**

...experiments in physics.
You try it out in an experiment in a laboratory.

You usually say that someone **does** an experiment.

You don't really need to do an experiment.
It's like working out what's happening when you're doing an experiment.

You do not say that someone 'makes' an experiment.

explain

If you **explain** something, you give details about it so that it can be understood.

The Head should be able to explain the school's teaching policy.

You say that you explain something **to** someone.

Let me explain to you about Jackie.
It was explained to him that he would not be expected to enter the chapel.

Note that you must use 'to' in sentences like these. You do not say, for example, 'Let me explain you about Jackie'.

You can use **explain** with a 'that'-clause to say that someone tells someone else the reason for something.

I explained that I was trying to write a book.

explode

When a bomb **explodes,** it bursts loudly and with great force, often causing a lot of damage.

A bomb had exploded in the next street.

You can say that someone **explodes** a bomb.

They exploded a nuclear device.

'blow up'   However, if someone destroys a building with a bomb, you do not say that they **explode** the building. You say that they **blow** it **up.**

He was going to blow the place up.

extended - extensive

'extended'   You use **extended** to describe things which last longer than usual.

...extended news bulletins on TV.
...going home on extended leave.

'extensive'   If something is **extensive,** it covers a large area.

...an extensive Roman settlement in north-west England.

An **extensive** effect is very great.

Many buildings suffered extensive damage in the blast.

Extensive also means 'covering many details'.

We had fairly extensive discussions.

exterior - external

'exterior'   The **exterior** of a building or vehicle is the outside part of it.

The church is famous for its exterior.
You're supposed to keep your car exterior in good condition.

Exterior is often used as an adjective in front of a noun to refer to an outside part of a building or vehicle.

The aerial can be fixed to an exterior wall.
...the exterior bodywork.

'external'   **External** can be used in front of a noun to refer to an outside part of a building.

...external walls.
...external doorways.

External can be used in front of other nouns to refer to things which happen, come from, or exist outside a place or area of activity.

Death rates drop because of external factors.

They did it in response to external pressures.

You cannot use **exterior** in this way.

extreme

Extreme means 'very great in degree or intensity'.

He died in extreme poverty.
...extreme anxiety.
You must proceed with extreme caution.

Extreme opinions are unacceptably severe or unreasonable.

...extreme views.
He had written to Marcus Garvey rejecting his extreme black nationalism.

You do not use **extreme** in front of nouns that refer to events or changes. Instead you use adjectives such as 'major', 'great', or 'considerable'.

...the need for major expansion of the University.
This would give great encouragement to the freedom fighters.

F

fabric

Fabric is cloth or other material produced by weaving cotton, nylon, wool, silk, or other threads together.

A piece of white fabric was thrown out of the window.
...silks and other soft fabrics.

You do not use **fabric** to refer to a building where machines are used to make things. A building like this is usually called a **factory**. See entry at **factory**.

fact

A **fact** is an item of knowledge or information that is true.

It may help you to know the full facts of the case.
The report is several pages long and full of facts and figures.

WARNING

You never talk about 'true facts' or say, for example, 'These facts are true'.

'the fact that'

You can refer to a whole situation by using a clause beginning with **the fact that**.

The fact that quick results are unlikely is no excuse for delay.
The fact that the centre is overcrowded is the major issue with the local opponents.

Note that you must use 'that' in clauses like these. You do not say, for example, 'The fact quick results are unlikely is no excuse for delay'.

factory

A building where machines are used to make things is usually called a **factory**.

...a carpet factory.
...factories producing domestic electrical goods.

'works'   A place where things are made or where an industrial process takes place can also be called a **works**. A **works** can consist of several buildings and may include outdoor equipment and machinery.

...an old iron works.

After **works** you can use either a singular or plural form of a verb.

The sewage works was like a closed fort.
There is a good site for the fifth terminal, between the runways where the Perry Oak sludge works are now.

'mill'   A building where a particular material is made is often called a **mill**.

...a cotton mill.
...a steel mill.

'plant'   A building where chemicals are produced is called a chemical **plant**.

...the Rhone-Poulenc chemical plant in Dagenham.

A power station can also be referred to as a **plant**.

...the re-opening of a nuclear plant.

fair - carnival

'fair'   In British English, a **fair** is an event held in a park or field at which people pay to ride on various machines for amusement or try to win prizes in games.

'carnival'   In American English, an event like this is called a **carnival**.

In British English, a **carnival** is an outdoor public festival which is held every year in a particular place. During a carnival, music is played and people sometimes dance in the streets.

fair - fairly

'fair'   You say that behaviour or a decision is **fair** when it is reasonable, right, or just.

It wouldn't be fair to disturb the children's education at this stage.
Be fair, darling. It's not their fault.

'fairly'   You do not use **fair** as an adverb, except in the expression 'play fair'. If you want to say that something is done in a reasonable or just way, the word you use is **fairly**.

We want it to be fairly distributed.
He had not put the defence case fairly to the jury.

Fairly also means 'to quite a large degree'.

The information was fairly accurate.
I wrote the first part fairly quickly.

WARNING   You do not use **fairly** in front of a comparative form. You do not say, for example, 'The train is fairly quicker than the bus'. In conversation, you say 'The train is **a bit** quicker than the bus'.

Golf's a bit more expensive.
I began to understand her a bit better.

In writing, you use **rather** or **somewhat**.

Edberg is a rather better grass-court player than Kratzmann.
This appearance came somewhat earlier than originally planned.

Many other words and expressions can be used to indicate degree. For graded lists, see section on **degree** in entry at **Adverbials** and section on **submodifiers** in entry at **Adverbs**.

fair - fare

These words are both pronounced /feə/.

'fair'
Fair is used as an adjective or a noun. If something is **fair,** it is reasonable, right, or just. See entry at **fair - fairly.**

If someone is **fair** or has **fair** hair, they have light coloured hair.

My daughter has three children, and they're all fair.

A **fair** is an event held in a park or field for people's amusement. See entry at **fair - carnival.**

'fare'
Fare is used as a noun or a verb. Your **fare** is the money you pay for a journey by bus, taxi, train, boat, or plane.

Coach fares are cheaper than rail fares.

The **fare** at a restaurant is the food served there. This is an old-fashioned use.

Army kitchens serve better fare than some hotels.

Fare is used as a verb to say how well or badly someone is treated or how successful they are at something. This use occurs mainly in writing.

They fared badly in the 1978 elections.
How would an 8-stone boxer fare against a 14-stone boxer?

fall

Fall can be used as a verb or a noun.

used as a verb
You use **fall** as a verb to talk about a quick downward movement onto or towards the ground.

Drizzle was beginning to fall.
...when the leaves start to fall.

The past tense of 'fall' is **fell,** not 'falled'. The past participle is **fallen.**

The china fell from her hand and shattered.
...table napkins that had fallen to the floor.

WARNING
Fall is an intransitive verb. You cannot say that someone 'falls' something. You do not say, for example, 'She screamed and fell the tray'. You say 'She screamed and **dropped** the tray'.

He bumped into a chair and dropped his cigar.
Careful! Don't drop it!

Similarly, you do not say that someone 'falls' a person. You do not say, for example, 'He bumped into the old lady and fell her'. You say 'He bumped into the old lady and **knocked** her **down**' or 'He bumped into the old lady and **knocked** her **over**'.

I nearly knocked down a person at the bus stop.
I got knocked over by a car when I was six.

When someone who is standing or walking **falls,** they drop downwards so that they are kneeling or lying on the ground.

He tottered and fell full-length.
She lost her balance and would have fallen if she hadn't supported herself.

In conversation, you do not usually say that someone 'falls'. You say that they **fall down** or **fall over.**

He fell down in the mud.
He fell over backwards and lay as if struck by lightning.

You can also say that a tall object **falls down** or **falls over.**

The pile of hymn books fell down and scattered all over the floor.
A tree fell over in a storm.

used as a noun   **Fall** is also used as a noun. If you have a **fall,** you lose your balance and drop on to the ground, hurting yourself.

He read that his mother had had a bad fall.

In American English, the **fall** is the season between summer and winter.

In the fall, there is nowhere I would rather be than Vermont.

British speakers call this season **autumn.** See entry at **autumn.**

familiar

If someone or something is **familiar,** you recognize them because you have seen, heard, or experienced them before.

There was something familiar about him.
Gradually I began to recognize familiar faces.

'familiar to'   If something is **familiar to** you, you know it well.

My name was now familiar to millions of people.
The things Etta spoke of were familiar to Judy only from magazines.

'familiar with'   If you know or understand something well, you can say that you are **familiar with** it.

I am of course familiar with your work.
...statements which I am sure you are familiar with.

famous

If someone or something is **famous,** very many people know about them.

...a famous writer.
...the most famous Australian animal, the kangaroo.
...Sir Basil Blackwell, proprietor of the famous Oxford bookshop.

'well-known'   **Well-known** has a similar meaning to **famous.** However, a **well-known** person or thing is usually known to fewer people or in a smaller area than a **famous** one.

...a club run by Paul Ross, a well-known Lakeland climber.
...his two well-known books on modern art.

Well-known can be spelled with or without a hyphen. You usually spell it with a hyphen in front of a noun and without a hyphen after a verb.

I took him to a well-known doctor in Harley Street.
The building became very well known.

'notorious'   Someone or something that is **notorious** is well known for something that is bad or undesirable.

The area was notorious for murders.
...his notorious arrogance.

'infamous'   People and things are described as **infamous** when they are well known because they are connected with wicked or cruel behaviour.

Here the infamous Burr killed the noble Hamilton.
...the infamous Doctors' Plot of 1953.

Infamous is a rather literary word. Note that it is not the opposite of 'famous'.

far

distance   You use **how far** when you are asking about a distance.

How far is it to Charles City?
How far is Amity from here?
He asks us how far we have come.

However, you do not use **far** when you are stating a distance. You do not say, for example, that something is 10 kilometres 'far' from a place. You say that it is 10 kilometres **from** the place or 10 kilometres **away from** it.

The property was a mere fifty miles from the ocean.
I was about five miles away from some hills.

You use **far** in questions and negative sentences to mean 'a long distance'. For example, if you say that it is **not far** to a place, you mean that the place is not a long distance from where you are.

Do tell us more about it, Lee. Is it far?
It isn't far now.
I don't live far from here.

You do not use **far** like this in positive sentences. You do not say, for example, that a place is 'far'. You say that it is **far away** or **a long way away**.

The lightning was far away.
He is far away in Australia.
That's up in the Cairngorms, which is quite a long way away.

In modern English, **far** is not used in front of a noun. You do not, for example, talk about 'far hills'. Instead you use **distant** or **faraway**.

...a distant blue plain.
...the faraway sound of a waterfall.

degree or extent   You also use **far** in questions and negative sentences to talk about the degree or extent to which something happens.

How far have you got in developing this?
Prices will not come down very far.
None of us would trust them very far.

used as an intensifier   You use **far** in front of comparatives to say that something has very much more of a quality than something else. For example, if you say that one thing is **far bigger** than another, you mean that it is very much bigger than the other thing.

It is a far better picture than the other one.

The situation was far more dangerous than Woodward realized.

Far more in front of a noun means 'very much more' or 'very many more'.

He had to process far more information than before.
Professional training was provided in far more forms than in Europe.

You can also use **far** in front of 'too'. For example, if you say that something is **far too big,** you mean that it is very much bigger than it should be.

I was far too polite.
Managements are still being far too optimistic.

You can use **far** in front of 'too much' or 'too many'. For example, if you say that there is **far too much** of something, you mean that there is a very much greater quantity than is necessary or desirable.

Teachers are being bombarded with far too much new information.
Every middle-class child gets far too many toys.

See also entry at **farther - further.**

fare

See entry at **fair - fare.**

farther - further

Farther and **further** are both comparative forms of 'far'. **Farthest** and **furthest** are the superlative forms.

When you are talking about distance, you can use any of these forms.

Birds were able to find food by flying farther and farther.
He must have found a window open further along the balcony.
Gus was in the farthest corner of the room.
The sun is then at its furthest point to the south.

However, when you are talking about the degree or extent of something, you can only use **further** or **furthest.**

He needed to develop his reading further.
The furthest you can get on a farm is foreman, and you won't be this until it's nearly time to retire.

fascinated

If you are **fascinated by** something or **fascinated with** it, you find it very interesting.

I was fascinated by the idea that Ellen Terry and Gordon Craig were my near relations.
He became fascinated with their whole way of life.

You can also say that you are **fascinated by** a person.

At first Rita was fascinated by him.

You do not use words such as 'very' or 'extremely' in front of **fascinated.** If you find something very interesting indeed, you can say that you are **absolutely fascinated** or **deeply fascinated** by it.

Dr Shaw had been absolutely fascinated by a print on her wall.
He was deeply fascinated by war.

fast

Fast, quick, rapid, and **swift** are all used to say that something moves or happens with great speed. **Rapid** and **swift** are not usually used in conversation.

'fast'	**Fast** is used both as an adjective and an adverb. There is no adverb 'fastly'.

...fast communications.
I ran as fast as I could.

'quick' Quick is an adjective. You do not usually use it as an adverb. Instead you use the adverb **quickly**.

It is this muscle which gives us our quick, springing movements.
I walked quickly up the passage.

In conversation, you can use the comparative form **quicker** as an adverb.

I swam on a bit quicker.
Goats could ruin a farmer's field quicker than baboons.

In writing, you usually use **more quickly.**

He began to speak more quickly.

You can use the superlative form **quickest** as an adverb in speech or writing.

The child may cool off quickest if the parents go about their business.

'rapid' and 'swift' Rapid and swift are adjectives. The adverbs corresponding to them are **rapidly** and **swiftly**.

Jobs tend to be plentiful at a time of rapid economic growth.
They walked rapidly past the churchyard.

...darting in swift pursuit of its prey.
He walked swiftly towards home.

asking about speed Fast is the word you usually use when you are asking about the speed of something.

How fast is the fish swimming?
...looking out of the windows to see how fast we were going.

vehicles You use **fast** to say that a vehicle is capable of moving with great speed.

...a fast car.
...a fast train.

people You do not usually use **fast** to talk about people, but you can use it in front of words like 'driver' and 'runner' to say that someone drives quickly or is capable of running quickly.

Not being a fast runner, I was glad I had parked close to the hall.

changes When you are talking about the speed at which something changes, you usually use **rapid** or **swift**.

People are worried about the rapid and massive increase in military spending.
Swift change is a characteristic of decay, not of growth.

no delay Fast, quick, rapid, and swift are all used to say that something happens without any delay.

I only got a fast return on my investment once.
They are pressing for a quick resumption of arms negotiations.
...managers plagued by demands for rapid decisions.
The response was swift and intense.

short duration You can use **quick, rapid,** or **swift** to say that something lasts only a short time.

...a quick visit.
You are likely to make a rapid recovery.
...the swift descent from gentility to near-poverty.

fat

The following words can all be used to describe someone who has a lot of flesh on their body:

beefy	chunky	fleshy	podgy	stout
big	corpulent	gross	portly	thick-set
broad	cuddly	heavy	pudgy	tubby
bulky	dumpy	obese	solid	well-built
buxom	fat	overweight	squat	
chubby	flabby	plump	stocky	

Big, broad, bulky, chunky, corpulent, fleshy, heavy, plump, stocky, stout, and **thick-set** are fairly neutral words.

Stout prosperous men converged on the hotel.
...the portrait of a plump, dark girl, the Colonel's daughter.

You use **big** to describe someone who is tall and has quite a lot of flesh.

Zabeth was a big woman with a dark complexion.

You use **stocky** to describe someone who is fairly short and has quite a lot of flesh.

His friend was a stocky, bald man in his late forties.

Beefy, buxom, chubby, cuddly, portly, solid, tubby, and **well-built** are words that you use when you like the person you are describing and think their shape is quite attractive. **Beefy, cuddly,** and **tubby** are used in conversation.

His relatives were all solid, well-built people with dark or gray curly hair.

Buxom is used only to describe women.

...the buxom ladies in Rubens' paintings.

Chubby is used mainly of babies and children. **Portly** is used mainly of people who are middle-aged and rather dignified.

She had grown into a chubby attractive child, with a mop of auburn curls.
...a portly gentleman in his late fifties.

Dumpy, fat, flabby, gross, obese, overweight, podgy, pudgy, and **squat** are considered impolite and should not be used when speaking to the person you are describing, or to someone who knows and likes them.

He'll get fat, the way he eats.
He was a flabby, dough-faced, melancholy bachelor.
Laura was hugely overweight.

Obese and **overweight** are also used in more technical contexts.

Really obese children tend to grow up into obese men and women.
Overweight people run a slightly higher risk of cancer than people of average weight.

People who are **dumpy** or **squat** are both short and fat.

She was a little woman, and would probably, one day, be a dumpy one.

WARNING

Wide is used to describe things, not people.

...the wide staircase leading down to the hall.

However, it can be used to describe parts of the body.

Her features were coarse — a wide forehead, a large nose, prominent cheekbones.
She had a wide mouth that smiled a great deal.

fault

See entry at **blame**.

favourite

Your **favourite** thing or person of a particular type is the one you like most.

What is your favourite television programme?
I'm getting on to my favourite topic.

You never use 'most' with **favourite**. You do not say, for example, 'This is my most favourite book'. You say 'This is my **favourite** book'.

The American spelling of 'favourite' is **favorite**.

fear

Fear is used as a noun or a verb.

used as a noun   **Fear** is an unpleasant feeling that you have when you think you are in danger.

They huddled together, quaking with fear.
She was brought up with no fear of animals.

You do not say that someone 'feels fear'. You say that they **are afraid** or **are frightened**.

They were afraid of you. They knew you had killed many men.
Everyone here is frightened of the volcano.

See entry at **afraid - frightened**.

used as a verb   If you **fear** someone or something, you are afraid of them.

...a woman whom he disliked and feared.
He fears nothing.

Note that you do not use **fear** as a verb in conversation.

feel

Feel is a common verb which has several meanings. Its past tense and past participle is **felt**, not 'feeled'.

awareness   If you **can feel** something, you are aware of it because of your sense of touch, or you are aware of it in your body.

I can feel the heat of the sun on my face.
It's still alive. I can feel its heart.
I wonder if he can feel pain.

Note that you usually use **can** in sentences like these. You say, for example, 'I **can feel** a pain in my foot'. You do not say 'I feel a pain in my foot'. You also do not use a continuous tense. You do not say 'I am feeling a pain in my foot'.

If you want to say that someone was aware of something in the past, you use **felt** or **could feel**.

They felt the wind on their damp faces.
She could feel the gravel through the thin soles of her slippers.

However, if you want to say that someone suddenly became aware of something, you must use **felt**.

He felt a sting on his elbow.

You can use an '-ing' form after **felt** or **could feel** to indicate that someone was aware of something that was continuing to take place.

He felt moisture creeping through to his skin.
He could feel the warm blood pouring down his face.

You can use an infinitive without 'to' after **felt** to indicate that someone became aware of a single action.

She felt his hand pat hers.

touching   When you **feel** an object, you touch it deliberately in order to find out what it is like.

Eric felt his face. 'I'm all rough. Am I bleeding?'

impressions   The way something **feels** is the way it seems to you when you hold it or touch it.

His fork felt heavy.
How does it feel? Warm or cold?
It looks and feels like a normal fabric.

When you use **feel** like this, you do not use a continuous tense. You do not say, for example, 'His fork was feeling heavy'.

emotions and sensations   You can use **feel** with an adjective to say that someone is or was experiencing an emotion or sensation. When you use **feel** like this, you use either a simple tense or a continuous tense.

I feel lonely.
I'm feeling terrible.

She felt happy.
I was feeling hungry.

You can also use **feel** with a noun group to say that someone experiences an emotion or sensation. When you use **feel** with a noun group, you use a simple tense.

Mrs Oliver felt a sudden desire to burst out crying.

WARNING   When you use **feel** to say that someone experiences an emotion or sensation, you do not use a reflexive pronoun. You do not say, for example, 'I felt myself uncomfortable'. You say 'I **felt** uncomfortable'.

'feel like'   If you **feel like** a particular type of person or thing, you are aware of having some of the qualities or feelings of that person or thing.

I felt like a dwarf.
I feel like a hurt animal.

If you **feel like doing** something, you want to do it.

Whenever I felt like talking, they were ready to listen.
Are there days when you don't feel like writing?

In sentences like these, you can sometimes use a noun group instead of an '-ing' form. For example, instead of saying 'I feel like going for a walk', you can say 'I **feel like** a walk'.

I feel like a stroll.
Do you feel like a game?
I feel like a drink.

Note that you never say that you 'feel like to do' something.

beliefs   If you **feel** that something is the case or that something should be done, you believe it.

I feel I'm neglecting my duty.
He felt I was making a terrible mistake.
Does this make you feel we ought to become as independent as possible?

For emphasis, you can use 'strongly' or 'very strongly' after **feel**.

I feel very strongly that Sieglinde is a real person.

WARNING   You do not use a continuous tense of **feel** in sentences like these. You do not say, for example, 'I am feeling I ought to go'. You say 'I **feel** I ought to go'.

Instead of saying that you 'feel that something is not' the case, you can say that you **do not feel that it is** the case.

She did not feel that she was entitled to join this group.
He still did not feel that he could trust anyone.

female - feminine - effeminate

'female'   **Female** means 'relating to the sex that can have babies'. You can use **female** as an adjective to talk about either people or animals.

...pay claims from female employees.
A female toad may lay 20,000 eggs each season.

You can also use **female** as a noun, but only to talk about animals.

The male fertilizes the female's eggs.
He came upon a family of lions – a big male, a beautiful female, and two half grown cubs.

'feminine'   **Feminine** means 'typical of women, rather than men'.

...feminine handwriting.
...a good, calm, reasonable and deeply feminine woman.

You do not use **feminine** to talk about animals.

'effeminate'   **Effeminate** is only used to describe men and boys. People say that a man or boy is **effeminate** if he behaves, looks, or sounds like a woman or girl. It is best not to use this word, as many people find it offensive.

They find European men slightly effeminate.

fetch

See entry at **bring - take - fetch.**

few - a few

used in front of   **Few** and **a few** are both used in front of nouns, but they do not have the
nouns   same meaning.

You use **a few** simply to indicate that you are talking about a small number of people or things. When you use **few** without 'a', you are emphasizing that there are only a small number of people or things of a particular kind.

So, for example, if you say 'I have **a few** friends', you are simply saying that you have some friends. However, if you say 'I have **few** friends', you are saying that you do not have enough friends and are lonely.

A few children were playing in the road.
Few children will be able to cope with the long journeys.

They may have a few books on the shelf.
There were few books in Grandfather's study.

used as   **Few** and **a few** can be used in a similar way as pronouns.
pronouns
Each volunteer spent one night a week in the cathedral. A few spent two.
Many are invited but few are chosen.

'not many'   In conversation, people do not usually use **few** without 'a'. Instead they use **not many.** For example, instead of saying 'I have few friends', people usually say 'I **haven't got many** friends' or 'I **don't have many** friends'.

They haven't got many good players in their side.
I don't have many visitors.

You do not use **few** or **a few** when you are talking about a small amount of something. You do not say, for example, 'Would you like a few more milk in your tea?' You say 'Would you like **a little** more milk in your tea?' See entry at **little - a little.**

fewer

See entry at **less.**

fictional - fictitious

'fictional'   A **fictional** character, thing, or event occurs in a story, play, or film, and has never actually existed or happened.

I had to put myself into the position of lots of fictional characters.
...a musical about a fictional composer called Moony Shapiro.

Fictional also means 'relating to fiction and the telling of stories'.

...a clever fictional device.

'fictitious'   Something that is **fictitious** is false and is intended to deceive people.

They bought the materials under fictitious names.

film

A **film** consists of moving pictures shown on a screen, especially one shown to an audience in a building built for this purpose.

Have you seen the film Lawrence of Arabia?

Films are sometimes referred to as **pictures.** In America, films are often called **movies.**

We worked together in the last picture I made.
His last book was made into a movie.

When British people go to see a film, they say that they are going to the **cinema** or to the **pictures.** American speakers talk about going to the **movies.**

Everyone has gone to the cinema.
She went twice a week to the pictures.
Some friends and I were driving home from the movies.

In Britain, a building where films are shown is usually called a **cinema.** In America, it is called a **movie theater** or **movie house.**

finally

You can use **finally** to indicate that something is the last one in a series of things or events.

Trotsky lived in Turkey, France, Norway and finally Mexico.

You can also use **finally** to introduce a final point, ask a final question, or mention a final item.

Finally, Carol, are you encouraged by the direction education is taking?

When something happens that you have been waiting for or expecting for a long time, you can say that it **finally** happens. When you use **finally** like this, you put it in front of the verb, if there is no auxiliary.

When John finally arrived he said he had lost his way.
One of them stared at me for a long time and finally asked whether I was Angela Davis.

If there is an auxiliary, you put **finally** after it.

Parliament had finally legalized trade unions.

find

result of a search

If you **find** something you have been looking for, you see it or learn where it is.

The mill will not be easy to find.

The past tense and past participle of 'find' is **found,** not 'finded'.

I eventually found what I was looking for.
His body has not been found.

Note that when **find** has this meaning, you do not use 'out' after it.

'discover'

Discover is sometimes used instead of 'find'. **Discover** is a rather formal word.

They finally discovered the drawing room.

If you cannot see the thing you are looking for, you say that you **cannot find** it.

I think I'm lost — I can't find the bridge.

However, you do not say that you 'cannot discover' something.

noticing something

You can use **find** or **discover** to say that someone notices an object somewhere.

She found a drawing on her bed.
Look what I've found!
A bomb could well be discovered and that would ruin everything.

Come across has a similar meaning.

They came across something that looked like the skull of a large monkey.

obtaining information

If you **find, find out,** or **discover** that something is the case, you learn that it is the case.

The observers found that the same rules applied here.
We found out that she was wrong.
He has since discovered that his statement was wrong.

In clauses beginning with 'when', 'before', or 'as soon as', you can omit the object after **find out.** You cannot do this with **find** or **discover.**

When mother finds out, she'll divorce you.
You want it to end before anyone finds out.
As soon as I found out, I jumped into the car.

If you **find out** or **discover** some information that is difficult to obtain, you succeed in obtaining it.

Have you found out who killed my husband?

By the time we had discovered what had happened, the ants were attacking the entire collection.

You can also say that someone **finds out** facts that are easy to obtain.

I found out the train times.

You do not say that someone 'discovers' facts that are easy to obtain.

another meaning of 'discover' If you **discover** a place, substance, fact, or method which nobody knew about before, you are the first person to find it or know it.

Columbus discovered the largest island in the Caribbean.
Penicillin was discovered by Alexander Fleming.

another meaning of 'find' You can use **find** followed by 'it' and an adjective to say whether it is difficult or easy for someone to do something. For example, if you have difficulty doing something, you can say that you **find it difficult to do** it.

The 87 girls in the survey said they found it difficult to show how clever they were.
She found it impossible to believe that I meant it.

Note that you must use 'it' in sentences like these. You do not say, for example, 'She found impossible to believe that I meant it'.

fine - finely

Fine is usually used as an adjective, but in conversation you can also use it as an adverb. **Fine** has three main meanings.

used to mean 'very good' You can use it to say that something is very good or impressive.

Paul Scofield gave a fine performance.
From the top there is a fine view.

When you use **fine** like this, you can use words such as 'very' or 'extremely' in front of it.

He's interested and he'd do a very fine job.
The yellow building appears to be unusually fine by Moscow standards.

You cannot use **fine** as an adverb with this meaning, but you can use the adverb **finely** in front of a past participle.

...finely written novels.

used to mean 'satisfactory' You can also use **fine** to say that something is satisfactory or acceptable.

'Do you want it stronger than that?'—'No, that's fine.'

If you say that you are **fine**, you mean that your health is satisfactory.

'How are you?'—'Fine, thanks.'

When you use **fine** to mean 'satisfactory', you do not use 'very' in front of it, but you can use 'just'.

Everything is just fine.
'Is she settling down nicely in England?'—'Oh, she's just fine.'

In conversation, you can use **fine** as an adverb to mean 'satisfactorily' or 'well'.

We got on fine.
I was doing fine.

You do not use **finely** in sentences like these. You do not say, for example, 'We got on finely'.

<table>
<tr><td>used to mean
'small' or
'narrow'</td><td>You can also use **fine** to say that something is very narrow, or consists of very small or narrow parts.</td></tr>
</table>

...fine hair.
...handfuls of fine sand.

When you use **fine** like this, you can use words such as 'very' in front of it.

These pins are very fine and won't split the wood.

You can use **finely** as an adverb with this meaning.

...finely chopped meat.

finish

When you **finish** what you are doing, you reach the end of it.

Aren't you ever going to finish the ironing?
When he had finished, he closed the file.

You can say that someone **finishes doing** something.

Jonathan finished studying at the West Surrey college three years ago.
I've finished reading your book.

You do not say that someone 'finishes to do' something.

first - firstly

The **first** thing, event, or person of a particular kind is the one that comes before all the others.

The President went on the air to make his first public statement about Watergate.
...the first man in space.

If you want to emphasize that a thing, event, or person is the first one of their kind, you can put 'very' in front of **first**.

The very first thing that happened was that I got ravenously hungry.

'first' used as
an adverb

If an event happens before other events, you say that it happens **first**.

Ralph spoke first.
When people get their newspaper, which page do they read first?

You do not say that something happens 'firstly'.

used as
sentence
adverbs

You can use **first** or **firstly** to introduce the first point in a discussion, the first of a series of questions or instructions, or the first item in a list.

Four tendencies began to converge. First, there was a growing awareness of the true dimensions of the threat.
There are two reasons. Firstly I have no evidence that the original document has been destroyed.

If you want to emphasize that an item is the first one you are going to mention, you can say **first of all**.

There are, first of all, those who have been brought up with little confidence in their own judgement.
First of all dig a little hole.

Note that you do not say 'firstly of all'.

'at first'

When you are contrasting feelings or actions at the beginning of an event with ones that came later, you say **at first**.

At first I was reluctant.
At first I thought that the shop was empty, then from behind one of the counters a man appeared.

Note that you do not use 'firstly' in sentences like these.

first floor

See entry at **ground floor**.

first name

See entry at **Christian name - first name**.

fish

Fish is used as a count noun or an uncount noun.

used as a count noun
A **fish** is a creature that lives in water and has a tail and fins.

How fast is the fish swimming?

In modern English, the plural of 'fish' is **fish**, not 'fishes'.

My sister was singing happily because we'd caught so many fish.

used as an uncount noun
Fish is the flesh of a fish which you eat as food.

Fresh fish is expensive.

fit

clothes
If clothes **fit** you, they are the right size, neither too big nor too small.

...a dress of purple silk that fits her snugly.
He was wearing pyjamas which did not fit him.

When **fit** has this meaning, its usual past tense is **fitted**. However, many American speakers use **fit** as the past tense.

The boots fitted Rudolph perfectly.
The pants fit him well and looked like men's slacks.

'suit'
If clothes make you look attractive, you do not say that they 'fit' you. You say that they **suit** you.

I love you in that dress, it really suits you.

another meaning of 'fit'
If you **fit** something into, onto, or next to something else, you put it into the right hole or space, where it belongs. When **fit** has this meaning, its past tense is always **fitted**.

Philip fitted his key into the lock.
The upper strut was fitted into place.

Fixed pairs

The following lists show pairs of words joined by 'and' or 'or' which always or nearly always occur in the same order. For example, you always say **bread and butter**. You do not say 'butter and bread'.

Nouns:

bits and pieces	friend or foe	nearest and dearest
board and lodging	hands and knees	north and south
body and soul	health and safety	nuts and bolts
bread and butter	heart and soul	pen and paper
cup and saucer	heaven and earth	pros and cons
fish and chips	kith and kin	salt and pepper
flesh and blood	knife and fork	sex and violence
flotsam and jetsam	land and sea	ups and downs
food and water	law and order	women and children

Together, he and I shovelled all the <u>bits and pieces</u> back in the tin box.
Tim crawled on <u>hands and knees</u> out of the water.
The police were at last able to maintain some degree of <u>law and order</u> in the streets.

Adjectives:

alive and well	good or bad	right or wrong
black and white	hot and bothered	safe and sound
born and bred	hot and cold	sick and tired
drunk and disorderly	ready and waiting	

It's nice to know he is <u>alive and well.</u>
...to discuss whether the expansion was <u>right or wrong.</u>
I'm <u>sick and tired</u> of being pushed around.

Adverbs:

back and forth	hither and thither	rightly or wrongly
backwards and forwards	in and out	to and fro
far and wide	loud and clear	up and down
first and foremost	out and about	well and truly
here and now	really and truly	

The plough is drawn <u>backwards and forwards</u> across the field.
His weekly reviews in the Dallas Times Herald have spread his reputation <u>far and wide</u>.
They began jumping <u>up and down.</u>

Verbs:

come and go	huff and puff	wax and wane
ebb and flow	rant and rave	weep and wail
fetch and carry	twist and turn	wine and dine

People are ceaselessly <u>coming and going</u>.
Fish react to the state of the tide as it <u>ebbs and flows</u>.
Doreen was <u>weeping and wailing</u>. 'I've never been in trouble before!'

flammable - inflammable

Both **flammable** and **inflammable** are used to describe materials or chemicals that burn easily.

A window had been smashed and <u>flammable</u> liquid poured in.
...commercial centres, holding large stocks of <u>inflammable</u> materials.

WARNING   **Inflammable** is not the opposite of **flammable**.

flat - apartment

In British English, a **flat** is a set of rooms for living in, usually on one floor of a large building. You can rent a flat or you can own it yourself.

They rented a furnished <u>flat</u> in Rummidge.

In American English, a set of rooms like this is usually called an **apartment**. When it is in a modern building, or when it is owned by the person or people who live there, it is sometimes called a **condominium** or, in conversation, a **condo**.

They pay 2,000 thousand dollars a month for their three-bedroomed apartment.
He urged me to buy a condominium.

In British English, a large building containing flats is called a **block of flats.** In American English, it is called an **apartment house,** an **apartment building,** or an **apartment block.**

The building was pulled down to make way for a block of flats.
The next night police rushed to an apartment house on Charlesgate East.
Several apartment buildings were destroyed.
Stuart began to count the apartment blocks.

flat - flatly

Flat is usually used as a noun or an adjective, but it is sometimes used as an adverb.

'flat' used as a noun

In British English, a **flat** is a set of rooms for living in, usually on one floor of a large building.

...a ground floor flat.

See entry at **flat - apartment.**

'flat' used as an adjective or adverb

Something that is **flat** is not sloping, curved, or pointed.

Every flat surface in our house is covered with junk.
Use a saucepan with a flat base.

If something lies or rests **flat** against a surface, all of it is touching the surface.

He was lying flat on his back.
She let the blade of her oar rest flat upon the water.

Note that you do not say that something lies or rests 'flatly' against a surface.

A **flat** refusal, denial, or rejection is definite and firm, and not likely to be changed.

He has issued a flat denial of these allegations.

'flatly'

The adverb corresponding to this meaning of 'flat' is **flatly,** not 'flat'.

She has flatly refused to go.
The Norwegians and Danes flatly rejected the evidence.

Flatly goes in front of verbs like 'refuse' and 'deny', but you put it after verbs like 'say' and 'state'.

He flatly refused to accept it.
Many scientists flatly denied the possibility.

He declared flatly that he could not leave his country.
He said flatly that he would accept no cub that had been more than twelve hours captive.

flee

See entry at **fly - flee.**

floor

The **floor** of a room is the flat part you walk on.

The book fell to the floor.

A **floor** of a building is all the rooms on a particular level.

...the stairs leading to the ground floor.

18 prisoners seized control of the top floor.

You say that something is **on** a particular floor.

My office is on the second floor.

You do not say that something is 'in' a particular floor.

See also entry at **ground floor.**

'ground'   You do not normally refer to the surface of the earth as the 'floor'. You call it the **ground.**

He set down his bundle carefully on the ground.
The ground all round was very wet and marshy.

However, the surface of the earth in a forest is sometimes referred to as the **forest floor,** and the land under the sea is sometimes called the **sea floor** or the **ocean floor.**

The forest floor is not rich in vegetation.
Some species take rests at night and slumber on the sea floor.

fly - flee

'fly'   **Fly** is usually used as an intransitive verb. Its other forms are **flies, flying, flew, flown.**

When a bird or insect **flies,** it moves through the air.

My canary flew away.

If you **fly** somewhere, you travel there in a plane.

You can fly from Cardiff to Ostend.

Fly is sometimes used to say that someone leaves a place in a hurry.

I'm sorry, I must fly.
By the time they returned, their prisoner had flown.

'flee'   **Flee** is used as a transitive or intransitive verb. Its other forms are **flees, fleeing, fled.**

If you **flee** someone or something or **flee from** them, you get away from them because you think they will harm you.

He had fled his executioners and crossed the ocean into a strange land.
The population prepared to flee the heat for the relative cool of the rivers.
When he reached it, the gazelle fled from him.

If you **flee** a place or **flee from** it, you get away from it quickly, because you think you are in danger there.

Along with thousands of others, he fled the country.
We fled from the hotel that night.
Most of the residents have fled.

Flee is normally used only in writing. In conversation, you usually use other expressions which have the same meaning.

Last Thanksgiving Day I ran away from a mugger in Chicago.
I wanted to get away from the fighting.
You must get out of this area fast!

folk - folks

Folk and **folks** are sometimes used to refer to particular groups of people. Both these words are plural nouns. You always use a plural form of a verb with them.

'folk' **Folk** is sometimes used with a modifier to refer to all the people who have a particular characteristic.

Country folk are a suspicious lot.
She was like all the old folk, she did everything in strict rotation.

However, this is not a common use. You usually say **country people** or **old people,** rather than 'country folk' or 'old folk'.

'folks' In American English, your **folks** are your close family, especially your mother and father.

I don't even have time to write letters to my folks.
Vera's visiting her folks up in Paducah.

Some people use **folks** when addressing a group of people in an informal way. This use is more common in American English than in British English.

That's all for tonight, folks.
They saw me drive out of town taking you folks up to McCaslin.

following

Following is most commonly used in expressions like 'the following day' and 'the following week'. For an explanation of this use, see entry at **next.**

used as a preposition **Following** can also be used as a preposition. It is usually used to indicate that one event happens after another and to some extent as a result of it.

Following that outburst, the general was banished.
Durga Lal died on February 1, following a heart attack.

Sometimes **following** is used simply to say that one event happens after another.

Following a remembrance service for Cunard staff who died in two world wars, a bronze bust of Samuel Cunard will be unveiled.
India were all out for 482 following lunch on the third day.

This use is fairly common, but many people think that it is incorrect. In sentences like these, it is better to use **after,** rather than 'following'.

The declaration criticizes the under-funding of community care after the closure of mental hospitals.
He flew into a rage when he returned to his hotel after Algeria's 1-0 defeat by Egypt.

fond

See entry at **like - dislike.**

foot

part of the body Your **foot** is the part of your body at the end of your leg. Your foot includes your toes.

He kept on running despite the pain in his foot.

When you use **foot** with this meaning, its plural is **feet.**

She's got very small feet.

If someone goes somewhere **on foot,** they walk, rather than using some form of transport.

The city should be explored on foot.

You have to get off the train at the frontier and cross on foot.

Note that you do not say that someone goes somewhere 'by foot'.

measurements A **foot** is also a unit for measuring length, equal to 12 inches or 30.48 centimetres. When **foot** has this meaning, its usual plural is **feet**.

We were only a few feet away from the edge of the cliff.
The planes flew at 65,000 feet.

However, you can use **foot** as the plural in front of words like 'high', 'tall', and 'long'.

She's five foot eight inches tall.

Note that you always use **foot** as the plural in front of another noun. For example, if a gap is twenty feet wide, you refer to it as a 'twenty **foot** gap'. You do not refer to it as a 'twenty feet gap'.

...a forty foot wall.

football

In Britain, **football** is a game played between two teams who kick a round ball around a field in an attempt to score goals. In America, this game is called **soccer**.

In America, **football** is a game played between two teams who throw or run with an oval ball in an attempt to score points. In Britain, this game is called **American football**.

In Britain, two teams play a football **match**. In America, they play a football **game**.

They had sustained injuries in the League match with Millwall on Saturday.
Kitty could hear cheering coming from a football game on the athletic field.

footprint

See entry at **pace**.

footstep

See entry at **pace**.

for

If something is **for** someone, they are intended to have it or benefit from it.

He left a note for her on the table.
She held out the flowers and said, 'They're for you.'
I am doing everything I can for you.

You use **for** in front of a noun group or '-ing' form when you are mentioning the use to which an object is put.

I had two knives with me, one for leather work and one for skinning animals.
The mug had been used for mixing flour and water.

You use **for** in front of a noun group when you are saying why someone does something.

We stopped for lunch by the roadside.
I walked two miles for a couple of pails of water.

You do not use **for** with an '-ing' form when you are saying why someone does something. You do not say, for example, 'He went to the city for finding work'. You say 'He went to the city **to find** work' or 'He went to the city **in order to find** work'.

People would stroll down the path to admire the garden.
He had to hurry in order to reach the next place on his schedule.

duration   You use **for** to say how long something lasts or continues.

I'm staying with Bob DeWeese for a few days.
The five nations agreed not to build any new battleships for a ten-year period.

You also use **for** to say how long something has been the case.

I have known you for a long time.
He has been missing for three weeks.
…artists who have been famous for years.
He hadn't had a proper night's sleep for a month.

WARNING   When you use **for** to say how long something has been the case, you must use a perfect tense. You cannot say, for example, 'I am living here for five years'. You must say 'I **have lived** here for five years'.

'since'   Do not confuse **for** with **since**. You use **since** to say that something has been the case from a particular time in the past until now.

It's been on my desk since 1959.
We had been travelling since dawn.
I had known her since she was twelve.

See entry at **since**.

used to mean 'because'   In stories, **for** is sometimes used to mean 'because'.

This is where he spent a good deal of his free time, for he had nowhere else to go.

See entry at **because**.

forceful

The following words can all be used to describe a person who speaks and acts in a strong, determined, and confident way:

aggressive	forceful	pushy	tyrannical
assertive	overbearing	self-confident	
domineering	positive	strong-willed	

Assertive, forceful, positive, self-confident, and **strong-willed** are complimentary words.

I would like to see sons who are gentle and tender, daughters who can be strong and assertive.
Off-stage she is direct, honest, forceful.
I tried to meet his eyes with self-confident defiance.

Aggressive, domineering, overbearing, pushy, and **tyrannical** are used to show disapproval of someone's behaviour. **Pushy** is used mainly in conversation.

Many of her women friends also had domineering husbands.
We worry about being pushy parents.

forename

See entry at **Christian name - first name**.

forever

Something that will last or continue **forever** will always last or continue.

She would remember his name forever.
They thought that their empire would last forever.

Something that has gone **forever** has gone and will never reappear.

This innocence is lost forever.
They will vanish forever into the grey twilight.

For the above two meanings, you can use the alternative spelling **for ever**.

My fate had been sealed for ever.
The white man's rule will be ended for ever.

Other words and expressions can be used to say how long something lasts. For a graded list, see section on **duration** in entry at **Adverbials**.

If you say that someone **is forever doing** something, you mean that they do it very often.

Babbage was forever spotting errors in their calculations.

For this meaning, the only acceptable spelling is **forever**.

forget

If you **forget** something, you stop thinking about it. The past tense of this verb is **forgot**, not 'forgetted'. The past participle is **forgotten**.

Tim forgot his troubles.
Ash, having forgotten his fear, had become bored and restless.

If you **have forgotten** something that you knew, you can no longer remember it.

I have forgotten where it is.
...a Grand Duke whose name I have forgotten.

If you **forget** something such as a key or an umbrella, you do not remember to take it with you when you go somewhere.

Sorry to disturb you — I forgot my key.

'forget to'   If you **forget to do** something which you had intended to do, you do not do it because you do not remember it at the right time.

I had forgotten to screw in the winding handle.
Don't forget to send your entries by Wednesday to this address.

Note that you do not say that someone 'forgets doing' something.

form

See entry at **class**.

former - late

'former'   You use **former** in front of a noun to indicate that the person you are talking about is no longer the thing referred to by the noun. For example, the **former chairman** of a company used to be the chairman, but is not the chairman now.

...former President Gerald Ford.
...William Nickerson, a former Treasury official.

'late' You use **late** in front of a name or noun to indicate that the person you are talking about has recently died.

...the late Cyril Connolly.
I'd like to talk to you about your late husband.

fortnight

In British English, two weeks is often called a **fortnight**.

I went to Rothesay for a fortnight.
He borrowed it a fortnight ago.

American speakers do not usually use this word.

fortune

Good fortune is good luck.

He has since had the good fortune to be promoted.
He could hardly believe his good fortune.

You do not say that something good that happens is 'a good fortune'. You do not say, for example, 'It's a good fortune I remembered to bring my umbrella'. You say 'It's **lucky** I remembered to bring my umbrella' or 'It's **a good job** I remembered to bring my umbrella'.

It's lucky that I'm going abroad.
It's a good job you were there.

forward - forwards

If you move or look **forward** or **forwards**, you move or look in a direction that is in front of you.

Salesmen rushed forward to serve her.
John peered forward through the twilight.
Ralph walked forwards a couple of steps.

Forwards is only used as an adverb.

'look forward to' If you **are looking forward to** something that is going to happen, you want it to happen because you think you will enjoy it.

He's looking forward to going home.

Note that you do not say that someone is 'looking forwards to' something.

For more information about this use, see entry at **look forward to**.

'forward' used as an adjective **Forward** is also used as an adjective. A **forward** movement is one in which someone or something moves forwards.

...the impetus of his forward movement.
The mercury would be slammed back in its cavity by the forward rush of the bullet.

When **forward** has this meaning, it can only be used in front of a noun.

'forward' used as a verb **Forward** is also used as a verb. If you **forward** a letter to someone, you send it on to them when they have moved to a different address.

Would you mind forwarding my mail to this address?

found

Found is the past tense and past participle of 'find'.

I found a five-pound note in the gutter.
His body has not been found.

See entry at **find**.

Found is also a verb. If someone **founds** a town or an organization, they cause it to be built or to exist. The past tense and past participle of 'found' is **founded**.

Tyndall founded his own publishing company.

free - freely

no controls
You use **free** as an adjective to describe activities which are not controlled or limited.

Within the EC there is free movement of labour.
...a free press.

You do not use **free** as an adverb with this meaning. Instead you use **freely**.

We are all comrades here and I may talk freely.

no payment
If something is **free,** you can have it or use it without paying for it.

The coffee was free.
...free school meals.

The adverb you use with this meaning is **free**, not 'freely'. For example, you say 'Pensioners can travel **free** on the buses'. You do not say 'Pensioners can travel freely on the buses'.

Children can get into the museum free.

releasing
If something is cut or pulled **free**, it is cut or pulled so that it is no longer attached to something or no longer trapped.

She tugged to get it free.
I shook my jacket free and hurried off.

You do not say that something is cut or pulled 'freely'.

frequently

See section on **frequency** in entry at **Adverbials**.

friend

Your **friends** are people you know well and like spending time with. You can refer to a friend who you know very well as a 'good friend', a 'great friend', or a 'close friend'.

He's a good friend of mine.
She later married Shaw's great friend Harley Granville-Barker.
A close friend told me about it.

If someone has been your friend for a long time, you can refer to them as an **old friend**.

I was brought up by an old friend of mother's called Lucy Nye.

'be friends with'
If someone is your friend, you can say that you are **friends with** them.

Dolley continued to be friends with Theodosia.
You used to be great friends with him, didn't you?
I also became friends with Melanie.

friendly

A **friendly** person is kind and pleasant.

Malawians seemed to be the friendliest people in the world.

If you are **friendly to** someone or **friendly towards** someone, you are kind and pleasant to them.

The women had been friendly to Lyn.
I have noticed that your father is not as friendly towards me as he used to be.

If you are **friendly with** someone, you like each other and enjoy spending time together.

I became friendly with a young engineer.

Friendly is never used as an adverb. You do not say, for example, 'He behaved friendly'. You say 'He behaved **in a friendly way**'.

We talk to them in a friendly way.
She looked up at Bal, smiling at him in such a friendly way.

fries

See entry at **chips.**

frighten - frightened

If something **frightens** you, it makes you feel afraid.

Rats and mice don't frighten me.

Frighten is almost always used as a transitive verb. You never say that someone 'frightens'. If you want to say that someone is afraid because of something that has happened or that might happen, you say that they **are frightened.**

I was even more determined not to show I was frightened.
He told the audience not to be frightened.

For more information about **frightened**, see entry at **afraid - frightened.**

'frightening'   Do not confuse **frightened** with **frightening**. Something that is **frightening** causes you to feel fear.

...the most frightening sight he had ever seen.
It is frightening to think what damage could be done.

from

source or origin   You use **from** to say what the source, origin, or starting point of something is.

...wisps of smoke from a small fire.
Get the leaflet from a post office.
The shafts were cut from heavy planks of wood.

If you **come from** a particular place, you were born there, or it is your home.

I come from Scotland.

See entry at **come from.**

time   If something happens **from** a particular time, it begins to happen at that time.

From November 1980, the amount of money you receive may be less.
We had no rain from March to October.

You do not use **from** to say that something began to be the case at a particular time in the past and is still the case now. You do not say, for example, 'I have lived here from 1984'. You say 'I have lived here **since** 1984'.

We've been fighting for this improvement since 1963.

See entry at **since**.

WARNING You do not use **from** to say who wrote a book, play, or piece of music. You do not say, for example, 'Have you seen any plays from Ibsen?' You say 'Have you seen any plays **by** Ibsen?'

...three books by a great Australian writer.
...a collection of pieces by Mozart.

front

The **front** of a building is the part that faces the street or that has the building's main entrance.

'in front of' If you are between the front of a building and the street, you say that you are **in front of** the building.

A crowd had assembled in front of the courthouse.
A soldier was taking snapshots of his friends in front of the National Assembly.

Note that you do not say that you are 'in the front of' a building.

'opposite' If there is a street between you and the front of a building, you do not say that you are 'in front of' the building. You say that you are **opposite** it.

The hotel is opposite a railway station.
Opposite is St Paul's Church.
There was a banner on the building opposite.

frontier

See entry at **border**.

fruit

Fruit is usually used as an uncount noun. Oranges, bananas, grapes, and apples are all **fruit**.

I have eaten fruit all my life.
...fruit imported from Australia.

You can refer to an individual orange, banana, etc as a **fruit,** but this use is not common.

Each fruit contains many juicy seeds.

You do not use a plural form of **fruit** to refer to several oranges, bananas, etc. Instead you use **fruit** as an uncount noun. For example, you say 'I'm going to the market to buy some **fruit**'. You do not say 'I'm going to the market to buy some fruits'.

...a table with some fruit on it.
They gave me fruit and cake and wine.

full

If something is **full of** things or people, it contains a very large number of them.

...a long garden full of pear and apple trees.
His office was full of people.

You do not use any preposition except 'of' after **full** in sentences like these.

full stop - period

In British English, the punctuation mark which you use at the end of a sentence (.) is called a **full stop**. In American English, it is called a **period**. See entry at **Punctuation**.

fun - funny

'fun'   If something is **fun**, it is pleasant, enjoyable, and not serious.

It's fun working for him.

If you have **fun**, you enjoy yourself.

We had great fun sleeping rough on the beaches.
She wanted a bit more fun out of life.

Fun is an uncount noun. You do not say that someone 'has funs' or 'has a great fun'.

'funny'   You say that something is **funny** when it is strange, surprising, or puzzling.

The funny thing is, we went to Arthur's house just yesterday.
'I always thought of him as very ordinary.'—'That's funny. So did I.'
Have you noticed anything funny about this plane?

Several other words can be used to mean 'strange' or 'surprising'. For more information, see entry at **unusual**.

You also say that something is **funny** when it is amusing and makes you smile or laugh.

He told funny stories.
It did look funny upside down.

furniture

Furniture consists of the large moveable objects in a room, such as tables and chairs.

She arranged the furniture.
It's quite trendy to have pine furniture.

Furniture is an uncount noun. You do not talk about 'furnitures'.

further

See entry at **farther - further**.

GRAMMAR   # The Future

For the formation of future tenses, see entry at **Tenses**.

talking about   You can talk about future events in a variety of ways. You use 'will' or
the future   'shall' when making predictions about the future.

The weather tomorrow will be warm and sunny.
I'm sure you will enjoy your visit to the zoo.

You can also use the future continuous tense when you are referring to something that will happen in the normal course of events.

You'll be starting school soon, I suppose.

Once the war is over, they'll be cutting down on staff.

If you are certain that an event will happen, you usually use 'be bound to' in conversation.

Marion's bound to be back soon.
The parade's bound to be cancelled now.

'Be sure to' and 'be certain to' are also sometimes used.

She's sure to find out sooner or later.
He's certain to be elected.

You use 'be going to' when referring to an event that you think will happen fairly soon.

It's going to rain.
I'm going to be late.

You use 'be about to' when referring to an event that you think will happen very soon.

Another 385 people are about to lose their jobs.
She seemed to sense that something terrible was about to happen.
I was just about to serve dinner when there was a knock on the door.

You can also refer to events in the very near future using 'be on the point of'. You use an '-ing' form after it.

She was on the point of bursting into tears.
You may remember that I was on the point of asking you something else when we were interrupted by Doctor Smithers.

intentions and plans

When you are talking about your own intentions, you use 'will' or 'be going to'. When you are talking about someone else's intentions, you use 'be going to'.

I'll ring you tonight.
I'm going to stay at home.

They're going to have a party.

WARNING

People tend to avoid using 'be going to' with the verb 'go'. For example, they would probably say 'I'm going away next week' rather than 'I'm going to go away next week'.

For more information on how to express intentions, see entry at **Intentions.**

You can also talk about people's plans or arrangements for the future using the present continuous tense.

I'm meeting Bill next week.
They're getting married in June.

The future continuous tense is also sometimes used.

I'll be seeing them when I've finished with you.

'Be due to' is used in writing and more formal speech to indicate that an event is intended to happen at a particular time in the future.

He is due to start as a courier shortly.
The centre's due to be completed in 1996.

The simple present tense is used to talk about an event which is planned to happen soon, or which happens regularly, in accordance with a timetable or schedule.

My flight leaves in half an hour.
Our next lesson is on Thursday.

The US Secretary of State flies to Moscow today for a final round of talks.

In writing and broadcasting, 'to'-infinitive clauses are used after 'be' to indicate that something is planned to happen.

A national centre to promote the efficient use of energy is to be set up in Milton Keynes.
The Prime Minister is to visit Hungary and Czechoslovakia in the autumn.

using the future perfect

When you want to talk about something that will happen before a particular time in the future, you use the future perfect tense.

By the time we phone he'll already have started.
By 1992, he will have worked for twelve years.

present tenses in subordinate clauses

In some subordinate clauses, you use a present tense when referring to a future event. For example, in conditional clauses and time clauses, you normally use the simple present tense or present perfect tense when talking about the future.

If he comes, I'll let you know.
Please start when you are ready.
We won't start until everyone arrives.
I'll let you know when I have arranged everything.

You also use a present tense in reason clauses introduced by 'in case'.

It would be better if you could arrive back here a day early, just in case there are some last minute details to talk over.

For further information on tenses used in subordinate clauses, see entries at **if** and **Subordinate clauses.**

In a defining relative clause, you use the simple present tense, not 'will', when you are clearly referring to the future in the main clause.

Any decision that you make will need her approval.
Give my love to any friends you meet.
The next woman I marry is not going to be so damned smart.

However, you use 'will' in the relative clause when you need to make it clear that you are referring to the future, or when the relative clause refers to an even later time.

Thousands of dollars can be spent on something that will be worn for only a few minutes.
The only people who will be killed are those who have knowledge which is dangerous to our cause.
I send my boys to a good public school so that they will meet people who will be useful to them later on.

You use a present tense in reported questions and similar clauses which refer to a future event when the event will happen at about the same time as the reporting or knowing.

I'll telephone you. If I say it's Hugh, you'll know who it is.

However, if the future event is going to happen after the reporting, you use 'will' in the reported question.

I'll tell you what I will do.

In a 'that'-clause after the verb 'hope', you often use the simple present tense to refer to the future.

I hope you enjoy your holiday.

For information on tenses in other 'that'-clauses, see entry at **Reporting.**

G

gain

If you **gain** something such as an ability or quality, you gradually get more of it.

After a nervous start, the speaker began to gain confidence.
This gives you a chance to gain experience.

'earn' You do not say that someone 'gains' wages or a salary. The word you use is **earn**.

She earns sixty pounds a week.

garbage

See entry at **rubbish**.

gas - petrol

'gas' The air-like substance that burns easily and that is used for cooking and heating is called **gas**.

In American English, the liquid that is used as fuel for motor vehicles is also called **gas,** or sometimes **gasoline.**

I'm sorry I'm late. I had to stop for gas.

'petrol' In British English, this liquid is called **petrol.**

Petrol only costs about 30p per gallon there.

gay

In modern English, if you say that a person is **gay,** you mean that they are homosexual.

I told them I was gay.

A homosexual man can be referred to as a **gay.**

Many gays were worried about the new system.

Gay is sometimes used to describe colours, places, or pieces of music which make people feel cheerful because they are bright or lively. This is a rather old-fashioned use.

Pauline wore a gay yellow scarf.

generally

Generally means 'usually', 'in most cases', or 'on the whole'.

Wool and cotton blankets are generally cheapest.
His account was generally accurate.

'mainly' You do not use **generally** to say that something is true about most of something, or about most of the people or things in a group. The word you use is **mainly.**

The molecules from which the DNA is mainly built are of four kinds.
A queue of people, mainly children and old men, had already formed.

gently

If you do something **gently,** you do it carefully and without using force, in order to avoid hurting someone or damaging something.

I shook her gently and she opened her eyes.

'politely' You do not use **gently** to say that someone behaves with good manners. The word you use is **politely.**

He thanked me politely.

geographical

The physical features of an area are often referred to as its **geographical** features.

Many birds follow major geographical features.
...the Casiquare Link, a geographical phenomenon which joins the Orinoco to the Amazon.

A **geographical** area is one which is determined by its physical features, rather than, for example, by administrative or political boundaries.

The country stretches over three very different geographical areas.
There was gradual change over a broad geographical region.

Geographical and **Geographic** occur in the names of some organizations and publications concerned with the subject of geography.

...the Royal Geographical Society of Oslo.
...the National Geographic Society.
...the latest issue of National Geographic.

If you want to say that something relates to the teaching of geography, you use **geography** in front of another noun. You do not use 'geographical' or 'geographic'.

...a geography book.
...my geography course.

get

Get is a very common verb which has several different meanings. Its past tense is **got,** not 'getted'. In British English and formal American English, its past participle is also **got.** However, many American speakers use **gotten** as the past participle. See entry at **gotten.**

used to mean **Get** is very often used to mean 'become'.
'become'
The sun shone and I got very brown.
I was getting quite hungry.

See entry at **become.**

used to form In conversation, you often use **get** instead of 'be' to form passives.
passives
My husband got fined in Germany for crossing a road.
Every time I send a horse to France it gets beaten.
Our car gets cleaned about once every two months.

Note that you only use **get** like this to refer to an event which is not planned or intended, or which happens later or less often than intended.

You do not use **get** to form passives in formal English.

used to describe movement	You use **get** instead of 'go' when you are describing a movement that involves difficulty.

We got along the street as best we could.
They managed to get through without tipping over.

Get is also used in front of 'in', 'into', 'on', and 'out' to describe acts of entering and leaving vehicles and buildings.

Sometimes I would get into my car and drive into San Diego.
I got out of there as fast as possible.

See entries at **go into** and **go out**.

'get to'	When you **get to** a place, you arrive there.

When we got to Firle Beacon we had a rest.

Get to is also used in front of a verb to say that someone gradually acquires a particular attitude, gradually becomes aware of something, or gradually becomes acquainted with someone or something.

I got to hate surprises.
I got to know Shrewsbury.

See entry at **get to - grow to**.

transitive uses of 'get'	If you **get** something, you obtain or receive it.

He's trying to get a flat.
I got the anorak for Christmas.

If you **get** a meal, you prepare it.

He was in the galley getting supper.

See entry at **cook**.

'have got'	**Got** is also used in the expression **have got**. See entry at **have got**.

get away

See entries at **escape** and **leave**.

get to - grow to

You use **get to** or **grow to** in front of another verb to say that someone gradually acquires a particular attitude. **Grow to** is more formal than **get to**.

I got to like the whole idea.
I grew to dislike working for the cinema.

You also use **get to** to say that someone gradually becomes aware of something, or gradually becomes acquainted with someone or something.

I got to realize it more as I grew older.
I got to know a few people.

In American English, if you **get to** do something, you have the opportunity to do it, and you do it.

I got to do a little work in Cuba.
I never got to ride in one again.

Get to is not usually used like this in British English.

get up

See entry at **rise - raise**.

girl

Girl is used in two different ways.

It is used to refer to a female child.

...a girl of eleven.
The boys and girls cheered.

It is also used to refer to a young woman up to the age of about 30.

We'd been invited to the wedding of a girl we knew.
At the next table was a pretty girl waiting for someone.

'little girl'   You can refer to a girl up to the age of 10 as a **little girl.**

She's a very well behaved little girl.

'young woman'   Many young women object to being referred to as **girls.** Instead they prefer to be referred to as **women.** In formal writing, the expression **young woman** is used, instead of 'girl'.

The Society aims to serve the needs of young women.

give

Give is a very common verb which has several meanings. Its past tense is **gave,** not 'gived'. Its past participle is **given.**

Give usually takes an indirect object. For some meanings of **give,** the indirect object must go in front of the direct object. For other meanings, it can go either in front of the direct object or after it.

physical actions   Give is often used to describe physical actions. When you use **give** like this, you put the indirect object in front of the direct object. For example, you say 'He **gave the ball a kick**'. You do not say 'He gave a kick to the ball'.

He gave the door a push.
Judy gave Bal's hand a squeeze.

expressions and gestures   Give is also used to describe expressions and gestures. When **give** is used like this, the indirect object goes in front of the direct object.

She gave Etta a quick, shrewd glance.
As he passed me, he gave me a wink.

effects   You can also use **give** to describe an effect produced by someone or something. Again, you put the indirect object in front of the direct object.

I thought I'd give you a surprise.
That noise gives me a headache.

things   If you **give** someone something, you offer it to them and they take it. When you use **give** like this, the indirect object can go either in front of the direct object or after it. When you put the direct object first, you put 'to' in front of the indirect object.

She gave Minnie the keys.
He gave the letter to the platoon commander.

However, when the direct object is a pronoun and the indirect object is not a pronoun, you must put the direct object first. You say 'He **gave it to his father**'. You do not say 'He gave his father it'.

He poured some whisky and gave it to Atkinson.

| information | You also say that you **give** someone information, advice, a warning, or an order. When **give** is used like this, the indirect object can go either in front of the direct object or after it. |

Castle gave the porter the message.
Dad gave a final warning to them not to look at the sun.
He gave an order to his subordinates.

given name

See entry at **Christian name - first name**.

glad

If you are **glad** about something, you are pleased about it.

I'm so glad that your niece was able to use the tickets.
Ralph was glad of a chance to change the subject.

For a graded list of words indicating how pleased someone is, see entry at **pleased - disappointed**.

| 'happy' | You do not use **glad** in front of a noun, and you do not use it to describe someone's mental state at a particular time in their life. If you want to say that someone is contented and enjoys life, you say that they are **happy**, not 'glad'. |

She always seemed such a happy woman.

| 'cheerful' | If someone shows that they are happy by smiling and laughing a lot, you say that they are **cheerful**. |

She had remained cheerful and energetic throughout the trip.

For a graded list of words indicating how happy someone is, see entry at **happy - sad**.

glasses

A person's **glasses** are two lenses in a frame which they wear to help them to see better.

He took off his glasses.
...a girl with red hair and glasses.

Glasses is a plural noun. You do not talk about 'a glasses'. Instead you talk about **a pair of glasses**.

Gretchen took a pair of glasses off the desk.

After **glasses** you use a plural form of a verb. After **a pair of glasses** you use a singular form.

My glasses are misted up.
A pair of glasses costs more than a pair of tights.

go

| describing movement | When you are describing movement from one place to another, or movement past or through a place, you usually use the verb **go**. See, however, entry at **come**. |

The past tense of 'go' is **went**. The past participle is **gone**.

I went to Stockholm.

A girl went past, smiling to herself.
Celia had gone to school.

using 'get' If a movement involves difficulty, you often use **get**, rather than 'go'. For example, you say 'We managed to **get** over the wall'. You do not say 'We managed to go over the wall'.

It used to take them three days to get to school.
Nobody can get past.
Frankie and Clive were trying to get through the window.

See entry at **get**.

leaving **Go** is sometimes used to say that someone or something leaves a place.

'I must go,' she said.
Our train went at 2.25.

See entry at **leave**.

'let go' If you **let** a person or animal **go,** you release them.

Let me go!
The Afghans had let their camels go.

See entry at **release - let go**.

'have gone' and If someone is visiting a place or now lives there, you can say that they
'have been' **have gone** there.

He has gone to Argentina.
Someone said she'd gone to Wales.

If someone has visited a place and has now returned, American speakers say that they **have gone** there. British speakers say that they **have been** there.

I've never gone to Italy.
I've been to Santander many times.
Have you ever been to France or Germany?

talking about You can use **go** with an '-ing' form to talk about activities.
activities
They went fishing below the falls.
We went exploring together in the fields.

You can also use **go** with 'for' and a noun group to talk about activities, especially in British English.

He went for a hike.
She said you were going for a swim.

WARNING You do not use **go** with a 'to'-infinitive to talk about activities. You do not say, for example, 'They went to fish below the falls' or 'He went to hike'.

'go and' To **go and** do something means to move from one place to another in order to do it.

I'll go and see him in the morning.
Let's go and have a drink somewhere.
I went and fetched another glass.

'be going to' You use **be going to** to talk about the future. For example, if you say that something **is going to** happen, you mean that it will happen, or that you intend it to happen.

She told him she was going to leave her job.
I'm not going to be made a scapegoat.

See entry at **The Future**.

used to mean 'become'	**Go** is sometimes used to mean 'become'. *The water had gone cold.* *The village thought we had gone crazy.* See entry at **become**.

go away

See entry at **leave**.

go into

When you enter a building or room, you usually say that you **go into** it or **go in**.

One day I went into the church.
She took him into a small room, switching on the light as she went in.

'get into'	However, you say that you **get into** a car or **get in**. *I saw him get into a cab.* *I walked to the van, got in and drove away.* You also say that you **get into** a lift, a small boat, or a small plane.
'get on' and 'board'	When you enter a bus, train, large plane, or ship, you say that you **get on** it or **board** it. *George got on the bus with us.* *Griffiths took a taxi to the Town station and boarded a train there.* *Decker boarded another ship, the Panama.*
'embark'	You can also say that someone **embarks on** a ship. *She had embarked on the S.S. Gordon Castle at Tilbury.*
WARNING	You never say that someone 'goes into' any kind of vehicle.
entering with difficulty	If you enter a building or room with difficulty, you say that you **get into** it or **get in**. *We tried to get into the dormitory unnoticed.* *It cost three pounds to get in.*

good - well

'good'	Something that is **good** is pleasant, acceptable, or satisfactory. The comparative form of 'good' is **better**, not 'gooder'. The superlative form is **best**. *Your French is probably better than mine.* *Some of our best English actors have gone to live in Hollywood.*
'well'	**Good** is never used as an adverb. If you want to say that something is done to a high standard or to a great extent, you use **well**, not 'good'. *She speaks French well.* *You say you don't know this man very well?* See entry at **well**. The comparative form of 'well' is **better**, not 'more well'. The superlative form is **best**. *People are better housed than ever before.* *Whatever works best is what she should adopt.* See entry at **better**.

good-looking

See entry at **beautiful**.

goods

Goods are things that are made to be sold. **Goods** is a plural noun. You do not use 'a' in front of it, and you use the plural form of a verb after it.

...a wide range of electrical goods.
You are responsible for seeing that your goods are insured.

'possessions' You do not refer to the things that someone owns as their 'goods'. The word you use is **possessions**.

He had few possessions.
I kept one room locked, with my most treasured possessions inside.

go on

The phrasal verb **go on** can be followed by either an '-ing' form or a 'to'-infinitive, but with different meanings.

If you **go on doing** something, you continue to do it.

I went on writing.
We went on fighting the Incomes Policy for 18 months after that.

If you **go on to do** something, you do it after doing something else.

She went on to talk about the political consequences.
He later went on to form a successful computer company.

go out

When you leave a building or room, you usually say that you **go out** of it or **go out.**

He threw down his napkin and went out of the room.
I went out into the garden.
He bowed and went out.

'get out' However, you say that you **get out** of a car or **get out.**

We got out of the car.
I got out and examined the right rear wheel.

You also say that you **get out** of a lift, plane, or small boat.

'get off' When you leave a bus or train, you say that you **get off.**

When the train stopped, he got off.
Get off at Mayfield Church.

You can also say that you **get off** a plane.

WARNING You never say that someone 'goes out' of any kind of vehicle.

leaving If you leave a building or room with difficulty, you say that you **get out** of it
with difficulty or **get out.**

I got out of the room somehow and made for the bathroom.

got

Got is the past tense of the verb 'get'. In British English and formal American English, it is also the past participle of 'get'. See entry at **get**.

Got is also used in the expression **have got**. See entry at **have got**.

gotten

In spoken American English, **gotten** is often used as the past participle of 'get'. It is used to mean 'obtained', 'received', 'become', or 'caused to be'.

He could have gotten his boots without anyone seeing him.
He'd gotten some tear gas in his eyes.
His leg may have gotten tangled in a harpoon line.
I had gone to work and gotten quite a lot done.

It is also used in many phrasal verbs and phrases.

No one had gotten around to cleaning up the mess.
He must have gotten up at dawn.
We should have gotten rid of him.
She had gotten married and given birth to a child.

You do not use **have gotten** to mean 'possess'. For example, you do not say 'I have gotten a headache' or 'He has gotten two sisters'.

You also do not use **have gotten** to mean 'must'. For example, 'I had gotten to see the President' does not mean 'It was necessary for me to see the President'. It means 'I had succeeded in seeing the President'. See entry at **get to - grow to.**

In British English and formal American English, the past participle of 'get' is **got**, not 'gotten'.

government

The **government** of a country is the group of people responsible for ruling it. After **government** you can use either a singular or plural form of a verb.

The government has had to cut back on public expenditure.
The government have made up their minds that they are going to win no matter what.

go with

See entry at **accompany.**

graceful - gracious

'graceful' **Graceful** people or things move in an attractive way or have an attractive shape.

...graceful dancers.
...a graceful little building.

'gracious' **Gracious** people are polite and pleasant. **Gracious** is a fairly formal word.

...a gracious lady.
...gracious expressions of thanks.

grade

See entry at **class.**

graduate

A **graduate** is someone who has successfully completed a first degree at a university or college.

In America, a **high school graduate** is someone who has completed a course at a high school. See entry at **high school.**

Someone who already has a first degree and who is studying for a higher degree can be called a **graduate student**, a **postgraduate student**, or a **postgraduate**. In America, **graduate student** is the usual term.

great

See entry at **big - large - great**.

greatly

See section on **degree** in entry at **Adverbials**.

Greetings and goodbyes

This entry deals with ways of greeting someone when you meet them, and with ways of saying goodbye. For information on what to say when meeting someone for the first time, see entry at **Introducing yourself and other people**. For information on beginning and ending a telephone conversation, see entry at **Telephoning**.

greetings

The usual way of greeting someone is to say 'Hello'. You can add 'How are you?' or another comment or question.

Hello there, Richard, how are you today?
Hello, Luce. Had a good day?

Note that the greeting 'How do you do?' is used only by people who are meeting each other for the first time. See entry at **Introducing yourself and other people**.

informal greetings

A more informal way of greeting someone is to say 'Hi' or 'Hiya'.

'Hi,' said Brody. 'Come in.'

'Hi' and 'Hiya' are more common in American English than in British English.

You can use other informal expressions to greet friends when you meet them unexpectedly after not seeing them for a long time.

Well, look who's here!
Well, well, it is nice to see you again.

If you meet someone in a place where you did not expect to see them, you can say 'Fancy seeing you here.'

formal greetings

When you greet someone formally, the greeting you use depends on what time of day it is. You say 'Good morning' until about one o'clock. 'Good afternoon' is normal from about one o'clock until about six o'clock. After six o'clock you say 'Good evening'.

Good morning. I can give you three minutes. I have to go out.
Good evening. I'd like a table for four, please.

These greetings are often used by people who are making formal telephone calls, or introducing a television programme or other event.

'Good afternoon. William Foux and Company.'—'Good afternoon. Could I speak to Mr Duff, please?'
Good evening. I am Brian Smith and this is the second of a series of programmes about the University of Sussex.

You can make these expressions less formal by omitting 'Good'.

Greetings and goodbyes

Morning, Alan.
Afternoon, Jimmy.

WARNING You only say 'Goodnight' when you are leaving someone in the evening or going to bed. You do not use 'Goodnight' to greet someone.

'Good day' is old-fashioned and rather formal in British English, although it is more common in American English and Australian English.

'Welcome' can be used on its own or in the ways shown below to greet someone who has just arrived. It is quite formal.

Welcome to Peking.
Welcome home, Marsha.
Welcome back.

replying to a greeting The usual way of replying to a greeting is to use the same word or expression.

'Hello, Sydney.'—'Hello, Yakov! It's good to see you.'
'Good afternoon, Superintendent. Please sit down.'—'Good afternoon, sir.'

If the other person has also asked you a question, you can just answer the question.

'Hello, Barbara, did you have a good shopping trip?'—'Yes, thanks.'
'Hello. May I help you?'—'Yes, I'd like a table, please.'
'Good morning. And how are you this fine day?'—'Very well, thank you.'

Note that if someone says 'How are you?' to you, you say something brief like 'Fine, thanks', unless they are a close friend and you know they will be interested in details of your life and health. It is polite to add 'How are you?' or 'And you?'

greetings on special days There are particular expressions which you use to give someone your good wishes on special occasions such as Christmas, Easter, or their birthday.

At Christmas, you say 'Happy Christmas' or 'Merry Christmas'. At New Year, you say 'Happy New Year'. At Easter, you say 'Happy Easter'. You reply by repeating the greeting, or saying something like 'And a happy Christmas to you too' or 'And you!'

If it is someone's birthday, you can say 'Happy Birthday' to them, or 'Many happy returns'. When someone says this to you, you reply by saying 'Thank you'.

goodbyes You say 'Goodbye' to someone when you or they are leaving.

'Goodbye, dear,' Miss Saunders said.

At night, you can say 'Goodnight'.

'Well, I must be off.'—'Goodnight, Moses dear.'
'Well, goodnight, Flora.'—'Goodnight, Howard.'

People also say 'Goodnight' to people in the same house before they go to bed.

WARNING In modern English, 'Good morning', 'Good afternoon', and 'Good evening' are not used to say goodbye.

informal goodbyes 'Bye' is commonly used as an informal way of saying goodbye.

See you about seven. Bye.

'Bye-bye' is even more informal. It is used between close relatives and friends, and to children.

Bye-bye, dear; see you tomorrow.

If you expect to meet the other person again soon, you can say things like 'See you', 'See you later', 'See you soon', 'See you around', or 'I'll be seeing you.'

See you later maybe.
Must go in now. See you tomorrow.
See you in the morning, Quent.

Some people say 'So long'.

'Well. So long.' He turned and walked back to the car.

You can say 'Take care', 'Take care of yourself', or 'Look after yourself' when you are saying goodbye to a friend or relative.

'Take care.'—'Bye-bye.'
'Look after yourself, Ginny dear.'—'You, too, Mother.'

Many speakers of American English use the expression 'Have a nice day' to say goodbye to people they do not know as friends. For example, employees in some shops and restaurants say it to customers.

'Have a nice day.'—'Thank you.'

'Cheers' and 'cheerio' are used by speakers of British English.

See you at six, then. Cheers!
I'll give Brigadier Sutherland your regards. Cheerio.

formal goodbyes　When you are saying goodbye to someone you do not know very well, you can use a more formal expression such as 'I look forward to seeing you again soon' or 'It was nice meeting you.'

I look forward to seeing you in Washington. Goodbye.
It was nice meeting you, Dimitri. Hope you have a good trip back.
It was nice seeing you again.

grill

See entry at **cook**.

ground floor

In British English, the floor of a building which is level with the ground is called the **ground floor**. The floor above it is called the **first floor**, the floor above that is the **second floor**, and so on.

In American English, the floor which is level with the ground is called the **first floor**, the floor above it is the **second floor**, and so on.

So, for example, the highest floor of a three-storey building is called the **second floor** in British English and the **third floor** in American English.

Groups of things, animals, and people

There are many words which are used in front of 'of' and a plural noun to refer to a group of things, animals, or people. The commonest ones are given here.

Some words can be used to refer to a wide range of things or people:

assortment	cluster	group	set
batch	collection	host	variety
battery	crop	selection	

Groups of things, animals, and people

She joined a group of gossiping villagers in the street.
She may have a collection of old toys left from the time her children were young.

Some words are usually used to refer to people or animals, rather than things:

army	gathering	party
band	horde	swarm
crowd	knot	throng

A large crowd of students gathered to watch the parade.
The couple obliged a horde of journalists with a press conference.
An army of ants crossed the flagstones in two close columns.

indicating shape   Some words indicate the shape of a group of things or people:

circle	jumble	mountain	row	sprinkling
column	line	pile	scatter	stack
heap	mound	ring	scattering	string

He sat down in the middle of the front row of chairs and waited.
Beside her there was a pile of magazines.
The circle of boys broke into applause.

indicating movement or occurrence   Some words indicate the movement or occurrence of a group of things or people:

hail	rash	spate	tide
barrage	series	stream	trickle
flood	shower	string	volley

Throughout the evening an unbroken stream of people came in.
After a spate of protests the authorities reacted by bringing many of them to trial.

typical groups   The following table shows which word is typically used to refer to a group of animals of a particular kind.

ants	an army of ants
bees	a swarm of bees
birds	a flock/flight of birds
cattle	a herd of cattle
cubs	a litter of cubs
deer	a herd of deer
dolphins	a school of dolphins
elephants	a herd of elephants
fish	a shoal of fish
geese	a gaggle of geese
goats	a herd/flock of goats
hounds	a pack of hounds
insects	a swarm/colony of insects
kittens	a litter of kittens
lions	a pride of lions
monkeys	a troop of monkeys
puppies	a litter of puppies
sheep	a flock of sheep
wolves	a pack of wolves

The following table shows which word is typically used to refer to a group of people or things of a particular kind.

actors	a company/troupe of actors
amateurs	a bunch of amateurs
banknotes	a wad/roll of banknotes
bullets	a hail of bullets
cakes	a batch of cakes
cards	a pack/deck of cards
eggs	a clutch of eggs
experts	a team/panel of experts
faces	a sea of faces
fighter planes	a squadron of fighter planes
flowers	a bunch/bouquet of flowers
grapes	a bunch/cluster of grapes
keys	a bunch of keys
papers	a sheaf/bundle of papers
protests	a spate of protests
reporters	a team/crowd/gaggle of reporters
rumours	a spate of rumours
ships	a fleet of ships
steps	a flight of steps
terrorists	a gang of terrorists
thieves	a gang/band/pack of thieves
tourists	a party of tourists
trees	a clump of trees
volunteers	an army of volunteers

grow

When children or young animals **grow,** they become bigger or taller. The past tense of 'grow' is **grew,** not 'growed'. The past participle is **grown.**

Babies who are small at birth grow faster.
The animal grew to a height of over a metre.
Has he grown any taller?

'grow up' When someone **grows up,** they gradually change from a child into an adult. People often talk about the place where they **grew up** or the period during which they **grew up.**

He grew up in Cambridge.
They grew up in the early days of television.

used to mean **Grow** is also used to mean 'become'.
'become'
He seemed to have grown older.

See entry at **become.**

'grow to' **Grow to** is used to say that someone gradually acquires a particular attitude.

I grew to hate those smiling faces.

See entry at **get to - grow to.**

guardian

A young person's **guardian** is someone who is legally appointed to look after their affairs, usually because their parents are dead.

'guard' You do not use **guardian** to refer to a railway official who travels on a train and makes sure that it arrives and leaves at the correct time. This official is called the **guard** or **conductor** in British English. In American English, he or she is called the **conductor.**

guess

If you **guess** that something is the case, you decide that it is probably the case.

I guessed that he might be ill.
She guessed that she was fifty yards from the shore.

You also use **guess** to say that someone finds the correct answer to a problem or question without knowing that it is correct.

I had guessed the identity of her lover.

'I guess' American speakers sometimes say **I guess** to indicate that they think that something is true or likely.

I guess I got the news a day or so late.
'What's that?'—'Some sort of blackbird, I guess.'

American speakers also sometimes reply to a question in an affirmative way by saying '**I guess so**'. Note that they do not say 'I guess it'.

'You think you can find out something about Larry's partners?'—'I guess so.'
'Does that answer your question?'—'Yeah, I guess so.'

American speakers sometimes show agreement with a negative statement, or reply to a negative question in an affirmative way, by saying '**I guess not**'.

'So no one actually saw this shark.'—'No, I guess not.'

guilty

If you feel unhappy because you think you have done something wrong, you can say that you **feel guilty about doing** it.

They feel guilty about having a new baby.
I feel guilty about using all that water.

You do not use a 'to'-infinitive after 'feel guilty'. You do not say, for example, 'They feel guilty to have a new baby'.

gymnasium

A **gymnasium** is a building or large room used for physical exercise, with equipment such as bars, mats, and ropes in it. In conversation, people often refer to a gymnasium as a **gym**.

WARNING You do not use **gymnasium** to refer to a British or American school for older pupils. In Britain, the general term for a school of this kind is **secondary school**. In America, it is **high school**. See entry at **high school**.

H

habit - custom

'habit'   A **habit** is something that an individual person does often or regularly, usually for no particular reason.

> *He had a nervous habit of biting his nails.*
> *I wish I could get out of this habit.*

'custom'   A **custom** is something done by the people in a society in particular circumstances or at a particular time of the year.

> *It is the custom to take chocolates or fruit when visiting a patient in hospital.*
> *My wife likes all the old English customs.*

hair

Hair is used as a count noun or an uncount noun.

used as a
count noun   Each of the thread-like things growing on your head and body is a **hair**. You can refer to several of these things as **hairs**.

> *...two strands of high-purity glass, each thinner than a human hair.*
> *...the black hairs on the back of his hands.*

used as an
uncount noun   However, you do not refer to all the hairs on your head as your **hairs**. You refer to them as your **hair**.

> *I washed my hands and combed my hair.*
> *...a young woman with long blonde hair.*

half - half of

used in front of
noun groups   **Half** or **half of** an amount or object is one of the two equal parts that together make up the whole amount or object.

You use **half** or **half of** in front of a noun group beginning with a determiner. **Half** is more common.

> *He had finished about half his drink.*
> *He drank half of his beer.*

> *She'd known me half her life.*
> *For half of her adult life she has been pregnant.*

Note that in standard English you do not say 'the half of'.

In front of measurement words like 'metre', 'kilogram', or 'hour', you always use **half**, not 'half of'.

> *They were nearly half a mile away.*
> *Boyd Stuart waited in an empty sitting-room for half an hour before the Director came in.*
> *They had been friends for about half a century.*

You use **half of** in front of pronouns. You do not use 'half'.

> *The waitress brought the drink she had ordered, and Ellen drank half of it immediately.*
> *More than half of them have gone back to their home towns.*

Note that you do not use 'they' or 'we' after **half of**. Instead you use **them** or **us**.

Half of them have had no education at all.
If production goes down by half, half of us lose our jobs.

When you use **half** or **half of** in front of a singular noun or pronoun, you use a singular form of a verb after the noun or pronoun.

Half her property belongs to him.
Half of it was exposed above water.

When you use **half** or **half of** in front of a plural noun or pronoun, you use a plural form of a verb after the noun or pronoun.

Half my friends have jobs and wives and children.
Half of them were still married.

used as a pronoun

Half can itself be used as a pronoun.

Roughly half are French and roughly half are from North America.
...some of the money for you, half for me.

used as a noun

You can also use **half** as a noun to talk about a particular part of something.

...the first half of the eighteenth century.
Philip Swallow rented an apartment in the top half of a two-storey house.

hand

Your **hand** is the part of your body at the end of your arm. It includes your fingers and your thumb.

You do not usually refer to a particular person's hand as 'the hand'. You say **his hand** or **her hand**. You refer to your own hand as **my hand**.

The young man held a letter in his hand.
Louise stood shading her eyes with her hand.
I raised my hand.
They keep their hands clean.

However, if you say that someone does something to someone else's hand, you usually use 'the'.

I grabbed Rick by the hand.
Father took his wife by the hand.

handicapped

See entry at **crippled**.

handsome

See entry at **beautiful**.

hang

If you **hang** something somewhere, you place it so that its highest part is supported and the rest is not. When **hang** has this meaning, its past tense and past participle is **hung**.

My sister hung the cups on the dresser hooks.
He had hung the coat where he could see it.

To **hang** a person means to kill them by tying a rope around their neck and taking away the support from under their feet so that they hang in the air. When **hang** has this meaning, its past tense and past participle is **hanged**.

He went off and hanged himself.
Rebecca Smith was hanged in 1849.

Hang has several other meanings and is used in some phrasal verbs. For all these other meanings, the past tense and past participle is **hung**.

Her long hair hung over her face.
The smell of paint hung in the air.
'Good night.' He hung up the phone.

happen

When something **happens,** it takes place without being planned.

Then a strange thing happened.
...a court of inquiry into what happened.

Happen does not have a passive form. You do not say, for example, that something 'was happened'.

'take place',
'occur'
Happen is usually used after vague words like 'something', 'thing', 'what', or 'this'. After words with a more precise meaning, you usually use **take place** or **occur**.

The incident had taken place many years ago.
Mrs Weaver had been in the milking shed when the explosion occurred.

You do not say that a planned event 'happens'. You say that it **takes place**.

The first meeting of the committee took place on 9 January.
The election took place in June.

'happen to'
When something **happens to** someone or something, it takes place and affects them.

I wonder what's happened to Jeremy?
I'm sure something has happened to Molly.
If anything happens to the car, you'll have to pay for it.

Note that in sentences like these you do not use any preposition except 'to' after **happen.**

You use **happen** in front of a 'to'-infinitive to indicate that something happens or is the case by chance. For example, instead of saying 'The two people he wanted to speak to lived in the same street', you can say 'The two people he wanted to speak to **happened to live** in the same street'.

He happened to be at their base when the alert began.
If you happen to see Jane, ask her to phone me.

You often use **happen to be** in sentences beginning with 'there'. For example, instead of saying 'A post office happened to be in the next street', you say '**There happened to be** a post office in the next street'.

There happened to be a policeman on the corner, so I asked him the way.

Note that in sentences like these you must use 'there'. You do not say, for example, 'Happened to be a post office in the next street'.

happy - sad

There are a number of adjectives which are used to indicate how happy or sad someone is. The adjectives in the following list are arranged from 'most happy' to 'least happy':

▶ ecstatic, elated, euphoric

- ▶ joyful, radiant, jubilant
- ▶ happy, cheerful, jolly
- ▶ light-hearted
- ▶ contented, fulfilled
- ▶ dissatisfied, moody, discontented
- ▶ sad, unhappy, depressed, gloomy, glum, dejected, despondent, dispirited
- ▶ miserable, wretched

hard - hardly

'hard' **Hard** can be used as an adjective or an adverb, often with a similar meaning.

They have so much hard work to do.
Many old people have worked hard all their lives.

'hardly' **Hardly** is an adverb. It has a totally different meaning from **hard.** You use **hardly** to say that something is only just true.

I hardly knew him.
You hardly look old enough.

If you use an auxiliary or modal with **hardly,** you put the auxiliary or modal first. You say, for example, 'I **can hardly** see'. You do not say 'I hardly can see'.

Two years before, the wall had hardly existed.
She can hardly wait to begin.
We could hardly move.

WARNING You do not use 'not' with **hardly.** You do not say, for example, 'I did not hardly know him'. You say 'I **hardly** knew him'.

Hardly is sometimes used in longer structures to say that one thing happened immediately after another.

The local police had hardly finished their examination when the CID arrived.

Note that in structures like these you use **when,** not 'than'. You do not say, for example, 'The local police had hardly finished their examination than the CID arrived'.

In stories, **hardly** is sometimes put at the beginning of a sentence, followed by 'had' and the subject.

Hardly had he uttered the words when he began laughing.

'hardly ever' If something **hardly ever** happens, it almost never happens.

I hardly ever spoke to them.
Daisy had women friends whom Tim hardly ever met.

Many other words and expressions can be used to say how frequently something happens. For a graded list, see section on **frequency** in entry at **Adverbials.**

harm

See entry at **damage.**

harmful

If something is **harmful to** someone or **harmful for** them, it has a bad effect on them.

Too much salt can be harmful to a young baby.
There are suggestions that this food could be more harmful for you than the food you normally eat.

You can also say that something is **harmful to** a thing.

Excessive amounts may be harmful to the skin.

You do not say that something is 'harmful for' a thing.

hate

See entry at **like - dislike**.

have

Have is one of the most common verbs in English. It is used in many different ways. Its other forms are **has, having, had.**

used as an auxiliary

Have is often used as an auxiliary.

They have just bought a new car.
She has never been to Rome.
Having been warned beforehand, I knew how to react.

See entries at **Auxiliaries** and **Tenses**.

'Have', 'has', and 'had' are not usually pronounced in full when they come after a pronoun or noun. When you write down what someone says, you usually represent 'have', 'has', and 'had' as **'ve, 's**, and **'d** after a pronoun. You can also represent 'has' as **'s** after a noun.

I've changed my mind.
She's become a very interesting young woman.
I do wish you'd met Guy.
Ralph's told you often enough.

See entry at **Contractions**.

'have to'

Have to is often used to say that someone must do something.

I have to speak to your father.
He had to sit down because he felt dizzy.

See entry at **must**.

actions and activities

Have is often used in front of a noun group to say that someone performs an action or takes part in an activity.

Did you have a look at the shop when you were there?
I'm going to have a bath.

See entry at **have - take**.

causing something to be done

Have can also be used to say that someone arranges for something to be done. When **have** is used like this, it is followed by a noun group and a past participle.

We've just had the house decorated.
Will the shop you're buying the machine from have it installed for you?

You can also use **have** to say that someone causes another person to do something or to be in a particular state. When **have** is used like this, it is followed by a noun group and either an '-ing' form or a past participle.

Alan had me looking for that book all day.
He had me utterly confused.

possession   **Have** is often used to indicate possession.

He had a small hotel.
What is the point in having a mink coat?

In spoken English, **have got** is usually used instead of 'have' to indicate possession.

She's got two sisters.
Have you got any brochures on Holland, please?

See entry at **have got.**

WARNING   You do not usually use a continuous tense of **have.** You either use a simple tense or you use **have got.** Note especially that you do not use a continuous tense in any of the following ways:

You do not use a continuous tense when you are talking about ownership. For example, you do not say 'I am having a collection of old coins'. You say 'I **have** a collection of old coins' or 'I**'ve got** a collection of old coins'. Similarly, you do not use a continuous tense when you are talking about relationships. You do not say 'I am having three sisters' or 'I am having a lot of friends'.

We haven't got a car.
They have one daughter.
I've got loads of friends.

You do not use a continuous tense to say that someone or something has a particular feature. For example, you do not say 'He is having a beard'.

He has nice eyes.
He had beautiful manners.
...machines which have dangerous moving parts.
The door's got a lock on it.

You do not use a continuous tense to say that someone has an illness or disease. For example, you do not say 'She is having a bad cold'.

He had a headache.
Sam's got measles.

You do not use a continuous tense to say how much time someone has in which to do something. For example, you do not say 'He is having plenty of time to get to the airport'.

I haven't got time to go to the library.
He had only a short time to live.
I hope I'll have time to finish it.

using a   Here are some ways in which you do use a continuous tense of **have:**
continuous
tense   You use a continuous tense to say that an activity is taking place. For example, you say 'He **is having** a bath at the moment'. You do not say 'He has a bath at the moment'.

The children are having a party.
I was having a chat with an old friend.

You use a continuous tense to say that an activity will take place at a particular time in the future. For example, you can say 'I**'m having** lunch with Barbara tomorrow'.

We're having a party tonight.
She's having a baby next month.

You also use a continuous tense to talk about continuous or repeated actions, events, or experiences. For example, you can say 'I **am having** driving lessons'.

I'm having an affair with Bernard.
I was already having problems.
Neither of us was having any luck.
You're having a very busy time.

have - take

Have and **take** are both commonly used with nouns as their objects to indicate that someone performs an action or takes part in an activity. With some nouns, you can use either **have** or **take** with the same meaning. For example, you can say '**Have** a look at this' or '**Take** a look at this'. Similarly, you can say 'We **have** our holidays in August' or 'We **take** our holidays in August'.

There is often a difference between British and American usage. For example, British speakers usually say 'He **had** a bath', while American speakers say 'He **took** a bath'.

I'm going to have a bath.
I took a bath, my second that day.

When talking about activities such as walking and swimming, American speakers often use **take.** For example, they say 'He **took** a walk' or 'She **took** a swim'. British speakers sometimes use **have,** but it is much more common in British English to say 'He **went for** a walk' or 'She **went for** a swim'.

Brody decided to take a walk.
I went down to the ocean and took a swim.

After dinner we went for a walk.
She's going for a swim.

meals   In modern English, you use **have** to say that someone eats a meal.

He has his meals at home.
We might have dinner together.

In the past, **take** was sometimes used instead of 'have', but this use now sounds very formal.

I always took my meals at White's.

For more information about verbs used in connection with meals, see entry at **Meals.**

have got

Have got is often used in spoken English with the same meaning as 'have'.

I have got the car.
You have got a problem.

'Have got', 'has got', and 'had got' are not usually pronounced in full. When you write down what someone says, you usually write '**ve got,** '**s got,** or '**d got.**

I've got her address.
He's got a beard now.
They'd got this house just north of the Euston Road.

Have got is not used in formal written English, and is less common in American English than British English.

have got

You cannot use **have got** for all meanings of 'have'. You use it when you are talking about a situation or state, but not when you are talking about an event or action. For example, you say 'I've got a new car', but not 'I've got a bath every morning'.

possession **Have got** is most commonly used to talk about possession, relationships, and qualities or features.

> *I've got a rather curious table.*
> *She's got two sisters.*
> *He's got a lovely smile.*
> *It's a nice town. It's got very nice shops.*

illness You often use **have got** to talk about illnesses.

> *Sam's got measles.*
> *I've got an awful headache.*

availability You also use **have got** to talk about the availability of something.

> *Come in and have a chat when you've got time.*
> *I think we've got an enormous amount to offer.*

future events You can use **have got** with a noun group to mention a future event that you will be involved in.

> *I've got a date.*
> *I've got an appointment with two Americans.*

You can use **have got** with a noun group and an '-ing' form to mention an event that you have arranged or that will affect you.

> *I've got two directors flying out first class.*
> *I've got some more people coming.*

You use **have got** with a noun group and a 'to'-infinitive to say that there is some work that you must do.

> *I've got some work to do.*
> *She's got the house to clean.*

negatives In negative sentences, 'not' goes between 'have' and 'got', and is almost always shortened to 'n't'.

> *He hasn't got a moustache.*
> *I haven't got any graph paper.*

American speakers do not usually use this form. Instead they use the auxiliary 'do', followed by 'not' and 'have'. 'Not' is usually shortened to 'n't'.

> *We don't have a phone.*
> *I'm bored. I don't have anything to do.*

questions In questions, you put the subject between 'have' and 'got'.

> *Have you got enough dusters?*
> *I need a drink. What have you got?*

American speakers do not usually use this form. Instead they use the auxiliary 'do', followed by the subject and 'have'. Some British speakers also use 'do' and 'have'.

> *Do you have her address?*
> *What kind of animals do you have?*

past tense The past tense form of **have got** is quite common in spoken British English.

> *He'd got this interview at Oxford.*
> *I didn't tell them I'd got some other pearls.*

future tense	The future tense of **have got** is hardly ever used. Instead you use the future tense of **have**.

I'm hoping he'll have more positive opinions at some point.
We'll have all morning to get them.

infinitives and participles	Similarly, if you use an infinitive or a participle, you use **have** rather than 'have got'.

People with dishwashers always seem to have tidy kitchens.
I'd like to have a room like yours.
He dreamed of having a car.

have got to

See entry at **must**.

have to

See entry at **must**.

he

He is used as the subject of a verb. You use **he** to refer to a man, boy, or male animal that has already been mentioned, or whose identity is known.

He had a nervous habit of biting his nails.
Bill had flown back from New York and he and his wife took me out to dinner.

When the subject of a sentence is followed by a relative clause, you do not use **he** in front of the main verb. For example, you do not say 'The man who is going to buy my car, he lives in Norwich'. You say 'The man who is going to buy my car lives in Norwich'.

The man who came into the room was small and slender.
Professor Marvin, who was always early, was there already.

he - they

'he'	**He, him, his,** and **himself** are sometimes used to refer back to an indefinite pronoun or to a word such as 'person', 'child', or 'student'.

If anybody complained about this, he was told that things would soon get back to normal.
It won't hurt a child to have his meals at a different time.

Many people object to this use because it suggests that the person referred to is male.

'he or she'	You can sometimes use **he or she, him or her, his or her,** or **himself or herself.**

Teach a child to dial 999 and read out the telephone number from which he or she is speaking.
The important thing is that the student should feel that that bit of writing belongs to him or her.
Nothing excuses the child from his or her own responsibilities.
There were several cases where one of them shot the other and then shot himself or herself.

Many people avoid these expressions because they think they sound clumsy and unnatural, especially when more than one of them is used in the same sentence.

'they'   In conversation, most speakers use **they**, **them**, and **their**.

Nearly everybody thinks they're middle class.
If I think someone may attempt to take an overdose, I will spend hours talking to them.
Don't hope to change anyone or their attitudes.

This use used to be considered incorrect, but it is becoming more common in writing as well as in speech. In this book, we usually use **they**, **them**, and **their**.

It is often possible to avoid all the above uses. You can sometimes do this by using plurals. For example, instead of saying 'Every student has his own room', you can say '**All** the students have **their** own rooms'. Instead of saying 'Anyone who goes inside must take off his shoes', you can say '**People** who go inside must take off **their** shoes'.

headache

If you have a **headache**, you have a pain in your head.

I told Derek I had a headache.

Headache is a count noun. You do not say that someone 'has headache'.

headline

See entry at **title**.

headmaster - principal

In Britain, the teacher in charge of a school is called the **headmaster** or **headmistress**. In America, these terms refer only to teachers in charge of private schools. The teacher in charge of any other kind of school is called the **principal**.

In both Britain and America, the person in charge of a college is often called the **principal**.

hear

If you **can hear** a sound, you are aware of it because it has reached your ears.

I can hear a car.

Note that you usually use **can** in sentences like these. You say, for example, 'I **can hear** a radio'. You do not say 'I hear a radio'. You also do not use a continuous tense. You do not say 'I am hearing a radio'.

The past tense and past participle of 'hear' is **heard** /hɜːd/. If you want to say that someone was aware of something in the past, you use **heard** or **could hear**.

From the far side of the village he heard the wailing of sirens.
Below me I could hear the roar of a waterfall.

However, if you want to say that someone suddenly became aware of something, you must use **heard**.

I heard a shout.

You can use an '-ing' form after **heard** or **could hear** to indicate that someone was aware of something that was continuing to take place.

He heard Alan shouting and laughing.

We could hear birds singing.

You can use an infinitive without 'to' after **heard** to indicate that someone was aware of a complete event or action.

I heard him dash into the bathroom.
I heard Amy O'Shea cry out in fright.

You do not use a 'to'-infinitive with an active form of **hear.** You do not say, for example, 'I heard him to open the door'.

passive use You can use a passive form of **hear,** followed by either a 'to'-infinitive or an '-ing' form.

You use a 'to'-infinitive after a passive form when you are talking about a complete event or action.

He was heard to say 'We're not going to have any more of this.'

You use an '-ing' form when you are talking about an event or action that was continuing to take place.

Her companions could be heard playing games.

See also entry at **listen to.**

help

If you **help** someone, you make something easier for them. When **help** has this meaning, it can be followed by an infinitive, with or without 'to'. For example, you can say 'I **helped him to move** the desk' or 'I **helped him move** the desk'. There is no difference in meaning.

We must try to help students to have confidence in their ability.
Something went wrong with his machine so I helped him fix it.

You can also use **help** as an intransitive verb, followed by an infinitive with or without 'to'. If someone **helps do** something or **helps to do** it, they help other people to do it.

They issued the organization's first pamphlets and helped arrange its first conference.
Dora helped to carry the wounded off the battlefield.

If something **helps do** something or **helps to do** it, it makes it easier for that thing to be done.

The money helped keep me off the streets for a while.
The performance of these actions helped to ease the tension.

You do not use an '-ing' form after **help.** You do not say, for example, 'I helped moving the desk' or 'I helped him moving the desk'.

'cannot help' If you **cannot help** doing something, you are unable to prevent yourself from doing it.

I couldn't help teasing him a little.

You do not use a 'to'-infinitive after **cannot help.** You do not say, for example, 'I couldn't help to tease him a little'.

hen

See entry at **chicken - hen - chick.**

her

Her is used as the object of a verb or preposition. You use **her** to refer to a woman, girl, or female animal that has already been mentioned, or whose identity is known.

They gave her the job.
I knew your mother. I was at school with her.

You do not use **her** as the indirect object of a sentence when you are referring to the same person as the subject. Instead you use **herself.**

Rose bought herself a piece of cheese for lunch.

here

Here refers to the place where you are.

I'm glad you'll still be here next year.
We're allowed to come here at any time.

You never use 'to' in front of **here.** You do not say, for example, 'We're allowed to come to here at any time'.

'here is' and
'here are'
You can use **here is** or **here are** at the beginning of a sentence when you want to draw attention to something or to introduce something. In standard English, you use **here is** in front of a singular noun group and **here are** in front of a plural noun group.

Here is a situation in which our decisions clearly count.
Here are the addresses to which you should apply.

here - hear

These words are both pronounced /hɪə/.

'here'
You use **here** to refer to the place where you are.

Come here.
She left here at eight o'clock.

See entry at **here.**

'hear'
When you **hear** a sound, you are aware of it through your ears.

Did you hear anything unusual?

See entry at **hear.**

high - tall

'high'
You use **high** to describe things which measure a larger distance than usual from the bottom to the top. For example, you talk about a 'high hill' or a 'high fence'.

...the high mountains of northern Japan.
...the high walls of the prison.

'tall'
You use **tall** to describe things which are higher than usual, but which are also much higher than they are wide. So, for example, you talk about a 'tall tree' or a 'tall chimney'.

...tall poles.
...a tall heron standing on one leg.

You always use **tall** when you are talking about people.

...a tall handsome man.

High also means 'a long way above the ground'. For example, you talk about a 'high window' or a 'high shelf'.

...a large room with a <u>high</u> ceiling.

high school

In America, a **high school** is a school for older pupils up to the age of 18. In Britain, the general term for a school of this kind is **secondary school.**

hill - mountain

Hill and **mountain** are both used to refer to areas of land which are much higher than the land surrounding them. Mountains are generally higher than hills. In Britain, the smallest mountains are about 1000 feet (300 metres) higher than the land surrounding them. Mountains usually have steeper sides than hills. The highest parts of a mountain often consist of rock.

him

Him is used as the object of a verb or preposition. You use **him** to refer to a man, boy, or male animal that has already been mentioned, or whose identity is known.

He asked if you'd ring <u>him</u> when you got in.
There's no need for <u>him</u> to worry.

WARNING   You do not use **him** as the indirect object of a sentence when you are referring to the same person as the subject. Instead you use **himself.**

He poured <u>himself</u> a whisky.

hire - rent - let

'hire' and 'rent'   If you pay a sum of money in order to use something for a short period of time, you can say that you **hire** it or **rent** it. **Hire** is more common in British English and **rent** is more common in American English.

We <u>hired</u> a car from a local car agency and drove across the island.
He <u>rented</u> a car for the weekend.

If you make a series of payments in order to use something for a long period, you say that you **rent** it. You do not usually say that you 'hire' it.

A month's deposit may be required before you can <u>rent</u> the house.

'hire out'   If you hire something from someone, you can say that they **hire** it **out** to you.

Holborn library <u>hires out</u> reproductions and original pictures.

'rent out'   If you rent something from someone, you can say that they **rent** it **out** to you.

They had to <u>rent out</u> the upstairs room.

'let' and 'let out'   If you rent a building or piece of land from someone, you can say that they **let** it to you or **let** it **out** to you. The past tense and past participle of 'let' is **let,** not 'letted'.

The cottage <u>was let</u> to an actress from London.
My father owned two houses which he <u>let out</u> as rooms to his friends.

historic - historical

'historic' You use **historic** to say that something was important in history, or that it will be regarded as important in the future.

...their *historic* struggle for emancipation.
...a *historic* decision.

'historical' You use **historical** to say that someone or something really existed or happened in the past, rather than being invented by a writer.

...a *historical* detective.

Historical novels, plays, and films deal with real or imaginary events in the past.

...*Richard of Bordeaux, a historical play by Gordon Daviot.*

Historical occurs in the names of some organizations concerned with the subject of history.

...*the German Historical Institute.*

However, if you want to say that something relates to the teaching of history, you use **history** in front of another noun. You do not use 'historic' or 'historical'.

...a *history* book.
...a *history* lesson.

hit

To **hit** someone or something means to touch them quickly with a lot of force. The past tense and past participle of 'hit' is **hit,** not 'hitted'.

He hit the burglar with a candlestick.
The truck had hit a wall.

hold

When you **hold** something, you carry or support it using your hands or arms. The past tense and past participle of 'hold' is **held,** not 'holded'.

I held the picture up to the light.
A baby should be held for feedings and comforting, and at other times.

used to mean **Hold** is sometimes used with the meaning 'have' or 'possess'. It is used,
'have' for example, with words like 'licence' and 'passport'.

You need to hold a work permit.

It is also used with words like 'opinion'.

I don't hold the right opinions.
This soon dispelled any foolish notions they might hold about Baldwin's ability.

Both of these uses are rather formal, and in conversation you normally use **have,** not 'hold'.

He doesn't need to have a licence.
I have very strong opinions about electoral reform.

holiday - vacation

'holiday' In British English, you refer to a period of time which you are allowed to spend away from work or school as the **holiday** or the **holidays.**

The school had undergone repairs during the holiday.
One day after the Christmas holidays I rang her up.

You refer to a period of time spent away from home enjoying yourself as a **holiday.**

He thought that Vita needed a holiday.
I went to Marrakesh for a holiday.

When you spend a long period of time like this each year, you refer to it as your **holidays.**

Where are you going for your holidays?

Note that you usually use a determiner or a possessive in front of **holiday** or **holidays.** You do not say, for example, 'I went to Marrakesh for holidays'.

If you are **on holiday,** you are spending a period of time away from work or school, or you are spending some time away from home enjoying yourself.

Remember to turn off the gas when you go on holiday.

In American English, a **holiday** is a single day when people do not work, often to commemorate an important event.

In British English, a day like this is called a **bank holiday.**

'vacation' The usual American word for a longer period of time spent away from work or school, or for a period of time spent away from home enjoying yourself, is **vacation.**

Harold used to take a vacation at that time.

At a British university or college, the **vacation** is one of the periods of several weeks when the university or college is officially closed for teaching.

I've a lot of reading to do over the vacation.

'vac' In conversation, British students often refer to one of these periods as the **vac.**

home

Your **home** is the place where you live and feel that you belong. **Home** is most commonly used to refer to a person's house, but it can also be used to refer to a town, a region, or a country.

The old man wants to die in his own home.
Jack dreamed of home from his prisoner-of-war camp.

You do not refer to a particular person's home as 'the home'. You say **his home, her home,** or just **home.**

He had been knifed and robbed near his home.
She was visiting her home in Germany.
Their children have left home.

WARNING You never use 'to' immediately in front of **home.** You do not say, for example, 'We went to home'. You say 'We went **home**'.

Come home with me.

The policeman escorted her home.

If you remain in your house rather than going out somewhere, British speakers say that you **stay at home.** American speakers say that you **stay home.**

Oh, we'll just have to stay at home for the weekend.
What was Cindy supposed to do? Stay home all day and dust the house?

'the home' and 'a home'

You use **the home** or **a home** when you are talking about homes in general.

Their view of women is that their place is in the home.
A home should be as clean as you can get it.

You also use **a home** when you are describing a situation in which someone does not have a place of their own where they can live.

I want a home and children.
I had never had a home of my own.

You use 'a' with an adjective to talk about a particular kind of home. For example, you can say 'She has **a pleasant home**'.

...a happy home.
He has a nice home in Bradford.

homely

In American English, if you say that a person is **homely,** you mean that they are not attractive to look at.

...a sturdy, healthy, but decidely homely child.
A broad grin spread across his homely features.

You cannot use **homely** in this way in British English. If you want to say that someone is not attractive to look at, you say that they are **plain.**

...a plain plump girl with pigtails.

In British English, if you say that someone is **homely,** you mean that they behave kindly and in a simple, unsophisticated way.

He greeted us in his usual homely manner.

homework - housework

'homework'

In British English, **homework** is work that pupils are given to do at home. You say that pupils **do** homework. You do not say that they 'make' homework.

He never did any homework.

'housework'

Housework is work such as cleaning or washing that is done in a house.

She relied on him to do most of the housework.

WARNING

Both **homework** and **housework** are uncount nouns. You do not talk about 'a homework' or 'houseworks'.

hood

See entry at **bonnet - hood.**

hope

Hope is used as a verb or a noun.

used as a verb	If you **hope** that something is true or will happen, you want it to be true or to happen.

She hoped she wasn't going to cry.
I sat down, hoping to remain unnoticed.

'I hope'	You often use **I hope** to express a wish that someone will have a pleasant time. After 'hope' you can use either the future tense or the simple present tense. For example, you can say '**I hope you'll enjoy** the film' or '**I hope you enjoy** the film'.

I hope you'll enjoy your stay in Roehampton.
I hope you get well very soon.

Note that if you say to someone that you **hope they are going to do** something, you are usually asking or reminding them to do something that they may not want to do.

I hope you're going to show me what you're working on.
Next time I come I hope you're going to be a lot more entertaining.

'I hope so'	If someone says that something is the case, or asks you whether something is the case, you can express your wish that it is the case by saying '**I hope so**'.

'I will see you in the church.'—'I hope so.'
'You'll be home at six?'—'I hope so.'

Note that you do not say 'I hope it'.

'I hope not'	Similarly, you can express your wish that something is not the case by saying '**I hope not**'.

'You haven't lost the ticket, have you?'—'I hope not.'

Note that you do not say 'I don't hope so'.

'hope' used as a noun	**Hope** is a feeling of confidence that what you want to happen might happen.

The government ignored the problem in the hope that it would go away.
She never completely gave up hope.

If you think that it is impossible that something will happen, you can say that there is **no hope of** it happening.

There seemed to be no hope of winning.
The infantry had no hope of keeping up with the tanks.

Note that you do not use any preposition except 'of' after **no hope**.

hopefully

used after a verb	If you do something **hopefully**, you do it hoping that a particular thing will happen.

She continued to gaze hopefully in their direction.
'You could find out things,' said Mrs Oliver hopefully, 'and then tell me.'

This use of **hopefully** occurs mainly in books, rather than in conversation.

used as a sentence adverb	**Hopefully** is much more commonly used as a sentence adverb. You add **hopefully** to a statement to indicate that you hope that what you are saying is true or will be true.

Hopefully, future fossil-hunters will unearth some evidence to resolve this question.
We can still try to push things forward, which hopefully would lead to a solution.

This use of **hopefully** is fairly new in British English, and some people object to it. However, it is now very common in conversation and writing. No other English adverb can be used with the same meaning.

horrible - horrid - horrific - horrifying - horrendous

All of these words except **horrid** can be used to describe a very unpleasant and shocking event, experience, or story.

...an imaginary torture, perhaps, but all the more horrible.
It was one of the most horrific experiences of my life.
...horrifying stories.
...the horrendous murder of a prostitute.

In conversation, people use **horrible** and **horrid** to show their dislike for someone or something. These words can be used to describe almost anything which is unpleasant, ugly, disgusting, or depressing.

The hotel was horrible.
His suit was a horrible colour.
We had to live in a horrid little flat.

Horrible is also used in front of a noun to emphasize how bad something is. For example, you can say 'I've made a **horrible** mistake'.

Everything's in a horrible muddle.

Horrendous is usually used to describe something which is extremely difficult to deal with.

...horrendous problems.
The cost can be horrendous.

hospital

A **hospital** is a place where sick people are looked after by doctors and nurses.

In British English, if you want to say that someone is in a hospital without mentioning which hospital they are in, you say they are **in hospital**.

I used to visit him in hospital.
The mother broke down completely and had to go into hospital.

American speakers do not say 'in hospital'. They say **in the hospital**.

She will be better off in the hospital.
She broke a bone in her back and spent some time in the hospital.

In both British and American English, if you want to say that something happened in a particular hospital, you usually say **at the hospital**.

I was working at the hospital.

house

Your **house** is the building where you live and which you own or rent.

You do not usually say 'I am going to my house' or 'She was in her house'. You say 'I am going **home**' or 'She was at **home**'.

Brody arrived home a little before five.
I'll finish the script at home.

See entry at **home**.

housework

See entry at **homework - housework**.

how

ways of
doing things

You use **how** in questions and explanations when you are talking about the way something is done.

How do you get rid of a nasty smell?
Tell me how to get there.
This is how I make a vegetable curry.

WARNING

You do not use **how** to mean 'in the way that'. For example, you do not say 'He walks to work every day, how his father did'. Instead you use **like, as,** or **the way.** See entry at **like - as - the way.**

asking about
someone's
health

You use **how** with 'be' to ask about someone's health.

How are you?
How is she? All right?
How is your son this morning?

WARNING

You do not use **how** to ask what kind of person someone is. For example, if you are asking someone for a description of their boss, you do not say 'How is your boss?' You say '**What** is your boss **like?**'

What's his mother like?

asking about
impressions

You use **how** with 'be' to ask about someone's impressions of something.

How was your trip?
How was the smoked trout?

WARNING

You do not use **how** to ask for a description of a thing or place. For example, if you say 'How is Birmingham?', you are not asking someone what kind of place Birmingham is; you are asking them if they are enjoying living or working there. If you want them to give you a description of Birmingham, you say '**What** is Birmingham **like?**'

What is Fiji like?

You do not say 'How do you think of Birmingham?' You say '**What do you think of** Birmingham?'

What do you think of the photo on the front of The Student?
What did you think of Holland?

commenting on
a quality

In the past, people used to use **how** in front of adjectives to remark about the extent to which someone or something had a quality. For example, they said things like 'How clever he is!' Note the word order here: they did not say 'How he is clever!'

Sentences like these are not usually used in modern English. Instead of 'How clever he is!', people usually say 'He's so clever', 'Isn't he clever?', or 'What a clever man!'

They're so childish.
Aren't they amazing?
What a beautiful girl!

People often use **how** with an adjective and nothing else, when they are commenting on what someone has just said.

'She has a flat there as well.'—'How nice!'
'To my surprise, I found her waiting for me at the station.'—'How kind!'
'I never got as far as reading it.'—'How extraordinary!'

For other ways of commenting on what someone has just said, see entry at **Reactions.**

however

You use **however** when you are adding a comment which contrasts with what has just been said.

The more I talked, the more silent Eliot became. However, I left thinking that I had created quite an impression.
Losing at games doesn't matter to some women. Most men, however, can't stand it.

You also use **however** to say that it makes no difference how something is done.

You can do it however you want.
However we add that up, it does not make a dozen.

'how ever' Sometimes people use **ever** after 'how' at the beginning of a question. They do this to express surprise at something that has happened. For example, instead of saying 'How did you get here?', they say '**How ever** did you get here?'

How ever did you find me?

How ever is always written as two separate words. You do not write, for example, 'However did you find me?'

how much

You use **how much** when you are asking about the price of something. For example, you say '**How much** is that T-shirt?'

I like that dress – how much is it?

Note that you do not say 'How much is the price of that T-shirt?'

You only use **how much** with 'be' when you are asking about the price of something. You do not use it to ask about other amounts of money. You do not say, for example, 'How much is his income?' You say '**What is his income?**', '**What does he earn?**', or '**How much does he earn?**'

Similarly, you do not say 'How much is the temperature outside?' or 'How much is the population of Tokyo?' You say '**What** is the temperature outside?' or '**What** is the population of Tokyo?'

What is the current in the resistor?
What is the lowest temperature it's possible to reach?

huge

See entry at **small - large**.

human - humane

'human' **Human** /hjuːmən/ means 'relating to people'.

...the human body.
...human relationships.

'humane' **Humane** /hjuːmeɪn/ means 'showing kindness and sympathy, especially in preventing or reducing suffering'.

...a humane plea for mercy and compassion.
...the most humane method of killing badgers.

hundred

A hundred or **one hundred** is the number 100.

You can say that there are **a hundred** things or **one hundred** things.

She must have had a hundred cats at least.
The group claimed the support of over one hundred MPs.

Note that you do not say that there are 'hundred' things.

You do not add '-s' to the word **hundred** when you put another number in front of it.

There are more than two hundred languages spoken in Nigeria.

British and American speakers have different ways of expressing some numbers greater than 100. For example, 370 is expressed as **three hundred and seventy** in British English and as **three hundred seventy** in American English.

...nine hundred and eighty-three votes.
...a hundred fifty pounds.

hunting - shooting

In American English, **hunting** is the killing of wild animals or birds as a sport or for food, using guns. In British English, **hunting** usually refers to the chasing and killing of foxes by dogs, followed by people on horseback. The killing of animals and birds with guns is referred to in British English as **shooting**.

hurt

Hurt can be used as a verb or an adjective.

used as a verb

If you **hurt** yourself or **hurt** a part of your body, you accidentally injure yourself. The past tense and past participle of 'hurt' is **hurt,** not 'hurted'.

...a young boy who had fallen down and hurt himself.
How did you hurt your finger?

If a part of your body **hurts,** you feel pain there.

My leg was beginning to hurt.

In American English, you can also say that a person **hurts.**

When that anesthetic wears off, you're going to hurt a bit.

Some British speakers also use **hurt** like this, but this use is not generally accepted in British English.

used as an adjective

You can use **hurt** as an adjective to describe an injured person.

Nobody in the bunker seemed to be hurt.
He was more shaken than hurt.

If someone has a bad injury, you do not say that they are 'very hurt'. You say that they are **badly hurt** or **seriously hurt.**

The soldier was badly hurt.
The injured, two of them seriously hurt, were taken to Peterborough District Hospital.

You do not usually use **hurt** in front of a noun. You do not, for example, talk about 'a hurt soldier'. You say 'an **injured** soldier'. See entry at **injure.**

hyphen

See entries at **Punctuation** and **Spelling.**

I

I

A speaker or writer uses I to refer to himself or herself. I is used as the subject of a verb. It is always written as a capital letter.

I shall be leaving soon.
I like your dress.

You can also use I as part of the subject of a verb. For example, you can say '**My friend and I** are going to Sicily'. Note that you mention the other person first. You do not say 'I and my friend are going to Sicily'.

My mother and I stood beside the road and waited.
My colleagues and I have created a new programme of higher education.

You do not use I after 'is'. See entry at **me**.

'-ic' and '-ical' words

Many adjectives end in '-ic' or '-ical'.

adjectives related to '-ic' nouns

Sometimes an adjective ending in '-ical' is related to a noun ending in '-ic'.

She loved music and played the piano well.
The majority of the finance for musical performances comes from the audiences.

Pareto was a cynic, disillusioned by the society of his day.
...a cynical contempt for truth and decency.

The owner of the hotel is a sports fanatic.
...a fanatical supporter of the government.

The words in the following two lists are nouns ending in '-ic' which have related adjectives ending in '-ical'.

These nouns refer to things:

arithmetic	logic	music
comic	magic	tactic

These nouns refer to people:

comic	cynic	mystic
critic	fanatic	sceptic

Note that 'comic' can refer to a thing (a cartoon magazine) or a person (a comedian).

'Comic', 'fanatic', 'magic', and 'mystic' can themselves be used as adjectives.

Many other nouns end in '-ic', for example 'fabric', 'panic', and 'relic', but they do not have related adjectives ending in '-ical'.

adjectives related to '-ics' nouns

Many nouns end in '-ics'. Sometimes the adjective related to them ends in '-ic' and sometimes it ends in '-ical'.

The following nouns have related adjectives ending in '-ic':

acoustics	athletics	graphics	linguistics
acrobatics	basics	gymnastics	obstetrics
aerobatics	economics	heroics	specifics
aerobics	electronics	histrionics	thermodynamics
aerodynamics	genetics	italics	

...the amazing developments in genetics that have taken place recently.
...the rapid progress being made in the field of genetic research.

...a paper on linguistics and literary criticism.
...students with linguistic ability.

The following nouns have related adjectives ending in '-ical':

aeronautics	ethics	mathematics	statistics
classics	hysterics	physics	tropics

...the doctor's code of ethics.
...the kinds of ethical and moral problems that will arise.

She was having a fit of hysterics.
It's nothing to get hysterical about, darling.

Note that 'logistics' has two related adjectives: 'logistic' and 'logistical'.

'-ic' and '-ical' adjectives

A number of adjectives have forms ending in '-ic' and '-ical', with no great difference in meaning.

There was some scattered ironic applause from the crowd.
He smiled a friendly, slightly ironical smile.

The whole business becomes problematic, tinged with anxiety.
The relationship between private business and government remains unsolved and problematical.

The following pairs of adjectives have similar meanings:

cyclic - cyclical	ironic - ironical
egoistic - egoistical	logistic - logistical
egotistic - egotistical	mystic - mystical
fanatic - fanatical	problematic - problematical
geographic - geographical	rhythmic - rhythmical
geometric - geometrical	syntactic - syntactical

Sometimes there is a difference in meaning or use between pairs of adjectives ending in '-ic' and '-ical'. See entries at **classic - classical**, **comic - comical**, **electric - electrical**, **historic - historical**, and **magic - magical**. See also entry at **economics** for the difference between 'economic' and 'economical'.

other '-ic' adjectives

Some adjectives not mentioned above consist of a noun with '-ic' on the end. The adjective indicates that something is connected with the thing referred to by the noun. For example, if a drink is 'alcoholic', it contains alcohol, something that is 'magnetic' is like a magnet and causes metal objects to stick to it.

Daniel laughed with idiotic pleasure.
He took a carving knife from a magnetic board on the wall.

I was getting more and more journalistic work.
...distributing photographic products to retailers.

Sometimes it may not be very clear what noun an '-ic' adjective is related to. For example, 'ironic' is related to 'irony', not to 'iron'; 'organic' means 'relating to organisms' (living things), not 'relating to an organ'; and 'manic' means 'very energetic or excited', not 'relating to a man'.

identical

If two or more things are **identical,** they are exactly the same in every detail.

...twenty or thirty suitcases with identical blue labels.

You can say that one thing is **identical with** another thing or **identical to** it. There is no difference in meaning.

Chemically, it is almost identical to limestone.
India's internal structure can never be identical with Europe's.

i.e.

See entry at **namely - i.e.**

if

possible
situations

You use **if** to introduce a conditional clause in which you mention a possible situation.

If a tap is dripping, it needs a new washer.
If you can thread a needle, you can mend a fuse.

You can use **if** to mention a situation that might exist in the future. In the conditional clause, you use the simple present tense. You do not use the future tense.

If all goes well, Voyager II will head on to Uranus.
If nuclear weapons are employed in a world war, the world will be destroyed.

You sometimes use **if** in a conditional clause to suggest that someone does something. You usually use the simple present tense in the conditional clause.

If you look in the middle of the picture, you'll see Mrs Galsworthy.

You can use **if** to mention a situation that sometimes existed in the past.

They sat on the grass if it was fine.
If it was raining, we usually stayed indoors.

You can also use **if** to mention something that might have happened in the past, but did not in fact happen. In the conditional clause, you use the past perfect tense. You do not use the simple past tense.

If he had realized that, he would have run away.
If she had not married, she would probably have become something special in her field.

unlikely
situations

You also use **if** in conditional clauses to mention situations that do not exist, or events that are unlikely to happen. In the conditional clause, you use the simple past tense. You do not use a present tense.

The older men would find it difficult to get a job if they left the farm.
If I frightened them, they might take off and I would never see them again.

When the subject of the conditional clause is 'I', 'he', 'she', 'it', 'there', or a singular noun, it is generally considered correct to use **were** in the clause instead of 'was'.

If I were in his circumstances, I would do the same thing.
As regards absolute proof, there is none. If there were, it would be a bad sign.
If education were even better organized, there would be no complaint about the content or level of work required.

However, in conversation people usually use **was** (except in the expression 'If I were you').

If I was an architect, I'd re-design this house.
If it was up there, it would be easier to find.
This would still be true if Britain was out of the Community.

You can use **was** or **were** in conversation, but you should use **were** in formal writing.

in reported questions **If** is also used in reported questions.

I asked her if I could help her.
He inquired if her hair had always been that colour.
I wonder if you'd give the children a bath.

See entry at **Reporting**.

ill - sick

Ill and **sick** are both used to say that someone has a disease or some other problem with their health.

Davis is ill.
Your uncle is very sick.
...a sick child.

Most British speakers do not use **ill** in front of a noun unless they are also using an adverb. For example, they do not talk about 'an ill woman', but they might talk about 'a seriously ill woman'.

...a terminally ill patient.

American and Scottish speakers sometimes use **ill** in front of a noun without using an adverb.

We had to get medical help for our ill sisters.

WARNING You do not say that someone becomes 'iller' or 'more ill'. You say that they become **worse**.

Each day Kunta felt a little worse.

'be sick' To **be sick** means to bring up food from your stomach. See entry at **sick**.

WARNING You do not use **ill** or **sick** to say that someone has received an injury. You say that they are **injured** or **hurt**. See entries at **injure** and **hurt**.

illness - disease

'illness' If you have an **illness,** there is something wrong with your health, so that you cannot work or live normally. An illness can affect several parts of your body. It can last for a long time or a short time, and its effects can be serious or not serious.

Most members believed that Stephen's illness was due to overwork.

You can use adjectives like 'long', 'short', 'serious', and 'mild' in front of **illness.**

He died at the age of 66 after a long illness.
He was still not properly on his feet after a serious illness.

'disease' A **disease** is a particular kind of illness caused by bacteria or an infection. Diseases can often be passed from one person to another.

I have a rare eye disease.
Whooping cough is a dangerous disease for babies.

Animals and plants can also have diseases.

...cattle disease.
...Dutch Elm disease.

illusion - delusion

You can use either of these words to say that someone has a wrong belief.

You have the illusion that you're doing something.
One patient had the delusion that he was Trotsky.

You say that someone is **under** an illusion or delusion.

We were under the happy illusion that we should be able to find a charming country cottage for about £1 a week.
I still laboured under the nice middle-class delusion that everyone was a good guy at heart.

You can also say that someone **suffers from** an illusion or delusion.

A man who has had a leg amputated often suffers from the delusion that the leg is still there.

If you have an **illusion of** something, you believe that it exists when in fact it does not.

We have an illusion of freedom.
In return they are allowed the illusion of a guiltless life.

another meaning of 'illusion' An **illusion** is also something that looks or sounds like one thing, but is either something else or is not there at all.

The thing, being related to his eye-movements, must be some optical illusion.
I fancy I can hear her voice, but that must be an illusion.

You do not use **delusion** with this meaning.

imaginary - imaginative

'imaginary' Something that is **imaginary** exists only in someone's imagination, and not in real life.

Many children develop fears of imaginary dangers.
...pictures of completely imaginary plants.

'imaginative' **Imaginative** people are good at forming ideas of new and exciting things.

...an imaginative schoolteacher.

You can also describe someone's ideas as **imaginative**.

...an imaginative scheme.

imagine

If you **imagine** a situation, you think about it and your mind forms a picture or idea of it.

It's hard to imagine a greater biological threat.
Try to imagine you're sitting on a cloud.

You can use an '-ing' form after **imagine.**

She could not imagine living with Daniel.
It is hard to imagine anyone starting a war.

You do not use a 'to'-infinitive after **imagine.** You do not say, for example, 'She could not imagine to live with Daniel'.

If you say that you **imagine** something is true, you mean that you think it is probably true.

I imagine there would be difficulties if you were expected to make a profit.
I imagine that sooner or later he'll ask you to join him there.

If someone asks you if something is true, you can say '**I imagine so**' or '**I should imagine so**' to indicate that you think it is probably true.

'Can he bite through that?'—'I imagine so.'
'Does she know what kind of tablets she's taken today?'—'I should imagine so.'

Note that you do not say 'I imagine it'.

Instead of saying that you 'imagine something is not' true, you usually say that you **don't imagine it is** true.

I don't imagine the New York Times has much interest in reporting a picnic.

immediately

used as an adverb

Immediately is usually used as an adverb. If something happens **immediately**, it happens without delay.

I have to go down to Brighton immediately. It's very urgent.
She finished her cigarette, then lit another one immediately.

If something happens **immediately after** something else, it happens as soon as the other thing is finished.

He had to see a client immediately after lunch.
They must have contacted him immediately after my meeting with them last Tuesday.

If something is **immediately above** something else, it is above it and very close to it. You can use **immediately** in a similar way with other prepositions such as 'under', 'opposite', and 'behind'.

...a window on the second floor immediately above the entrance.
The first layer of fat is immediately under the skin.
This man had seated himself immediately behind me.

used as a conjunction

In British English (but not American English), **immediately** is also used as a conjunction. You use **immediately** to say that something happens or is done as soon as something else has happened.

Immediately I finish the show I get changed and go home.
Contact can be made immediately the door is opened.

In sentences like these, you do not use a future tense after **immediately.**

You do not say, for example, 'I will do it immediately I will arrive'. You say 'I will do it immediately I **arrive**'.

immigrant

See entry at **emigration - immigration - migration**.

immigration

See entry at **emigration - immigration - migration**.

GRAMMAR **Imperatives**

You use an **imperative** clause when you are telling someone to do something or not to do something. An imperative clause usually has no subject.

form The imperative form of a verb is the same as its base form.

Come here.
Take two tablets every four hours.
Be sensible.
Enjoy yourself.

For a **negative imperative,** you use 'don't' and the base form of the verb. In formal English, you use 'do not' and the base form.

Don't touch that wire!
Don't be afraid of them.
Do not forget to leave the key on the desk.

emphasis and
politeness
An imperative form usually comes at the beginning of a sentence. However, you can put 'always' or 'never' first for emphasis.

Always check that you have enough money first.
Never believe what he tells you.

You can also use 'do' to add emphasis.

Do be careful!

You can add 'please' to the beginning or end of the clause in order to be more polite.

Please don't do that.
Follow me, please.

Question tags are sometimes added after imperative clauses to make them sound more like requests, or to express impatience or anger.

Post that letter for me, will you?
Hurry up, can't you?

See entry at **Requests, orders, and instructions**.

The subject 'you' is sometimes used when people want to indicate which person they are talking to, or want to add emphasis or express anger.

You get in the car this minute!

WARNING An imperative can often sound rude or abrupt. See entries at **Advising someone, Invitations, Requests, orders, and instructions, Suggestions,** and **Warning someone** for detailed information on alternatives to imperatives.

conditional use	Sometimes, when an imperative is followed by 'and' or 'or', it has a meaning similar to a conditional clause beginning 'If you...'. For example, 'Take that piece away, and the whole lot falls down' means 'If you take that piece away, the whole lot falls down'. 'Go away or I'll call the police' means 'If you don't go away, I'll call the police'.

Ask any policeman and he'll tell you he doesn't want a gun.
Say that again, and I'll hit you.
Hurry up, or you'll be late for school.

imply - infer

'imply'	If you **imply** that something is the case, you suggest that it is the case without actually saying so.

Somehow he implied that he was the one who had done all the work.
His tone implied that he hoped that something would happen soon.

'infer'	If you **infer** that something is the case, you decide that it is the case on the basis of the information that you have.

From this we inferred that they were equipped with nuclear weapons.
Darwin saw in the fossil record glimpses of past eras which, he inferred, were linked by steady and continuous change.

important

Important is an adjective. Something that is **important** is very significant, valuable, or necessary.

This is the most important part of the job.
It is important to get on with your employer and his wife.

WARNING	You do not use **important** to say that an amount or quantity is very large. You do not talk, for example, about 'an important sum of money'. Instead you use a word such as **considerable** or **substantial.**

He claimed he had been paid a substantial sum for working for MI5.
A considerable amount of rain had fallen.

in

used to say where something is	You use **in** as a preposition to say where someone or something is, or where something happens.

Colin was in the bath.
I wanted to play in the garden.
How much is the hat in the window?
In Hamburg the girls split up.

In is sometimes used with superlatives. For example, you can say that a particular building is 'the tallest building in Tokyo'.

Hakodate is the oldest port in Hokkaido.
...the biggest lizards in the world.

used to say where something goes	You use **in** as an adverb to say that someone goes into a place, or that something is put into a container.

There was a knock at Howard's door. 'Come in,' he shouted.
She opened her bag and put her diary in.

In is sometimes used as a preposition to mean 'into'.

She threw both letters in the bin.

See entry at **into**.

used with
expressions
of time

In is often used with expressions of time.

You use **in** to say how long something takes.

He learned to drive in six months.
He was dead in a few seconds.

You also use **in** to say how long it will be before something happens in the future.

In another few minutes it will be dark.

You use **in** to say that something happens during a particular year, month, or season.

In 1872, Chicago was burned to the ground.
In April we prepared to make our first trip to Europe.
It'll be warmer in the spring.

You use **in** with 'the' to say that something happens regularly each morning, afternoon, or evening.

I read all the papers in the morning.
You could sit there in the evening and listen to the radio.

See entries at **morning**, **afternoon**, and **evening**.

However, you do not use **in** to say that something happens regularly each night. Instead you use **at** without 'the'.

There were no lights in the street at night.

See entry at **night**.

WARNING

You do not say that something happens 'in' a particular day or date. You say that it happens **on** that day or date.

On Tuesday they went shopping again.
Caro was born on April 10th.

American speakers sometimes omit the **on**.

I've got a party Wednesday.
Friday we had promised that we would have dinner at his house.

You do not say that something lasts or continues 'in' a period of time. You say that it lasts or continues **for** that time.

I have known you for a long time.
I had been with my company for ten years.

See entry at **for**.

used to mean
'wearing'

In is sometimes used to mention what someone is wearing.

The bar was full of men in cloth caps.

See entry at **wear**.

WARNING

You do not use **in** when you are talking about someone's ability to speak a foreign language. You do not say, for example, 'She speaks in Russian'. You say 'She speaks Russian'. See entry at **speak - talk**.

incapable

If someone is **incapable of doing** something, they are unable to do it.

He was incapable of enjoying himself.
She is totally incapable of caring for her baby.

You do not say that someone is 'incapable to do' something.

in case

See entry at **case**.

include

If one thing **includes** another, it has that thing as one of its parts.

He is a former president of the Campania region, which includes Naples.
Their navy includes a large number of destroyers.

You do not use **include** when mentioning all the parts of something. Instead, you use a word such as **comprise**. See entry at **comprise**.

indeed

When you are using 'very' with an adjective or adverb, you can put **indeed** after the adjective or adverb, for extra emphasis.

I think it's very good indeed.
She had got very angry indeed.
They can run very fast indeed.

You do not use **indeed** after an adjective or adverb unless you have put 'very' in front of it. You do not say, for example, 'I think it's good indeed'.

used after
a noun

If you use 'very' with an adjective in front of a noun, you can put **indeed** after the noun.

That's a very good answer indeed.
It is a very rare bird indeed.

Note that you do not say 'That's a good answer indeed' or 'It is a rare bird indeed'.

People often say '**Thank you very much indeed**'.

'I will confirm that by phone or by telex.'—'Thank you very much indeed.'
Thank you very much indeed for having us here.

You do not say 'Thank you indeed'.

indicate - show

Indicate has the general meaning 'show', and you can sometimes use **indicate** and **show** in a similar way, for example when you are talking about evidence or the results of research.

Evidence indicates that the experiments were unsuccessful.
Evidence shows that chronic illness predisposes the sufferer to commit suicide.

However, **indicate** and **show** are not always used in the same way when they have a person as their subject.

If someone **indicates** an object, they show someone else where it is, usually by pointing or nodding towards it. **Indicate** is only used like this in stories.

'The car's just down there,' she said, indicating it with a nod of her head.
She sat down in the armchair that Mrs Jones indicated.

When **indicate** has this meaning, it is sometimes used with an indirect object, although this use is not common. The indirect object always has 'to' in front of it.

Without speaking, he indicated to him the inside of the hut.

If you **show** an object to someone, you hold it up or give or take it to them, so that they can see it and examine it. When **show** has this meaning, it always takes an indirect object. When the indirect object comes after the direct object, you put 'to' in front of the indirect object.

I showed William what I had written.
Fetch that drawing you did and show it to the doctor.

indoors - indoor

'indoors' **Indoors** is an adverb. If you go **indoors,** you go into a building.

Let's go indoors.

If something happens **indoors,** it happens inside a building.

I spent all the evenings indoors.

'indoor' **Indoor** is an adjective used in front of a noun. You use it to describe objects or activities that exist or take place inside a building.

...indoor swimming pools.
...indoor games.

industrious

An **industrious** person works very hard.

Rosa was an industrious student.
The people were industrious and very thrifty.

'industrial' You do not use **industrious** to refer to the work and processes involved in making things in factories. The word you use is **industrial.**

They have increased their industrial production in recent years.
...the future of industrial relations in Britain.

infamous

See entry at **famous.**

infer

See entry at **imply - infer.**

inferior

If one thing is **inferior to** another, it is of poorer quality than the other thing.

His photographs were inferior to those taken by Ernie.
Their air combat skills were inferior to those of our pilots.

Note that you do not use any preposition except 'to' after **inferior.**

GRAMMAR # Infinitives

There are two kinds of infinitive. One kind is called the **'to'-infinitive.** It consists of 'to' and the base form of a verb. The uses of this kind of infinitive are explained in the entry at **'To'-infinitive clauses.**

I wanted to escape from here.

I asked Don Card to go with me.

The other kind of infinitive is sometimes called the **infinitive without 'to'** or the **bare infinitive.** It is the same as the base form of a verb. Its uses are explained in this entry.

They helped me get settled here.

used after other verbs You use an infinitive to refer to a completed action that someone sees, hears, or notices.

She heard him fall down the stairs.
The kids at the Youth Club just don't want to listen to anybody speak.

An infinitive is used in this way after the object of the following verbs:

feel	listen to	observe	watch
hear	notice	see	

These verbs can also have an '-ing' form after their object. See entry at **'-ing' forms.**

'let' and 'make' You use an infinitive after the object of 'let', and after the object of 'make' when it means 'cause or force someone to do something'.

Don't let Tim go by himself!
They made me write all the details down again.

'know' An infinitive can be used after the object of 'know' in negative, simple past clauses or in perfect clauses.

I never knew him smoke before breakfast.
Have you ever known him buy a round?

'help' You can also use an infinitive with 'help'. You can leave out the object if you do not think it is necessary to mention the person who is being helped.

John helped the old lady carry the bags upstairs.
We got up and helped clear up the debris of the party.

'Help' can also be used with a 'to'-infinitive. See entry at **help.**

WARNING When you are using the verbs mentioned above in passive clauses, you do not use an infinitive without 'to' after them. You use a 'to'-infinitive instead.

...magazines which nobody was ever seen to buy.
I resent being made to feel guilty.
...if people are helped to liberate themselves.

used after modals You use an infinitive after all modals except 'ought'.

I must go.
Can you see him?

See entry at **Modals.**

You use an infinitive after the expressions 'had better' and 'would rather'.

I had better go.
Would you rather do it yourself?

You sometimes use an infinitive after 'dare' and 'need'.

I daren't leave before six.
Need you pay him right now?

See entries at **dare** and **need.**

other uses
You can use an infinitive after 'Why' to indicate that you think that an action is foolish or pointless.

Why wait until then?

You can use an infinitive after 'Why not' to suggest what someone should do.

Why not come with us?

You can use an infinitive after 'be' when you are explaining what someone or something does or should do. The subject must be a clause beginning with 'all' or 'what'.

All he did was open the door.
What it does is cool the engine.

WARNING
You cannot use infinitives after prepositions. You can, however, use an '-ing' form. See entry at **'-ing' forms.**

inflammable

See entry at **flammable - inflammable.**

inflate

If you **inflate** something such as a tyre, balloon, or airbed, you fill it full of air or gas.

...a rubber dinghy that took half an hour to inflate.

'blow up'
Inflate is a formal or technical word. In conversation, you usually say that you **blow up** a tyre, balloon, or airbed.

She blew up the airbed.
She would buy her son a dinghy and a pump to blow it up.

influence

used as a noun
You use **influence** as a noun to refer to the power that someone or something has to affect people's behaviour or decisions.

His wife had a lot of influence.
His teachings still exert a strong influence.

If you want to mention the person or thing affected, you use 'on'.

He was a bad influence on the children.
We shall be looking at the influence of religion on society.

WARNING
You do not use **influence** to refer to a change or event that is the result of something. The word you use is **effect.**

The towers have a great effect on the sound of the bells.
The intense heat had no effect on the spacecraft.

See entry at **affect - effect.**

used as a verb
You can also use **influence** as a verb. You say that one person or thing **influences** another.

I didn't want him to influence me in my choice.
There was little opportunity to influence foreign policy.

Note that when you use **influence** as a verb, you do not use 'on' after it.

inform

If you **inform** someone **of** something, you tell them about it.

He intended to inform her of his objections.

Inform is often followed by a 'that'-clause.

I informed her that I was unwell.
She informed me that she had not changed her plans.

You do not usually omit 'that' after **inform**. You do not say, for example, 'I informed her I was unwell'.

'tell'   **Inform** is a fairly formal word. In conversation, you usually use **tell**. See entry at **tell**.

information

Information consists of facts that you obtain or receive.

It is mainly used to obtain information required by government departments.
Whenever he wanted information, he could get it immediately.

Information is an uncount noun. You do not use 'an' in front of it, and you do not talk about 'informations'. However, you can talk about a **piece of information**.

I kept wondering what use I could make of this piece of information.

You say that you **give** people information.

He thought I'd given them the information.

You do not say that you 'tell' people information.

You refer to information **about** something or **on** something.

I'd like some information about trains, please.
I'm afraid that I have no information on that.

'news'   You do not use **information** to refer to descriptions of recent events in newspapers or on television or radio. The word you use is **news**.

He's recently been in the news.
It was on the news at 8.30.

See entry at **news**.

in front of

See entry at **front**.

GRAMMAR   ## '-ing' adjectives

A large number of adjectives end in '-ing'.

related to
transitive verbs   Many '-ing' adjectives have the same form as the present participle of a transitive verb, and are similar in meaning. For example, 'an astonishing fact' is a fact that astonishes you.

...her annoying habit of repeating what I had just said.
...a brilliantly amusing novel.

Note that '-ing' adjectives of this kind often describe the person or thing causing a feeling, as in 'a boring lecture', whereas '-ed' adjectives describe the person or thing affected by a feeling, as in 'a bored student'. See entry at **'-ed' adjectives.**

When a transitive verb does not refer to causing a feeling, you can often put the object of the verb in front of the '-ing' form to form a compound adjective.

The news was listened to by at least half the German-speaking population.
Each colony would be completely self-governing.

related to intransitive verbs

Some '-ing' adjectives are related to intransitive verbs. They describe processes, changes, or states. For example, if there is a 'decreasing' number of things, the number of things is getting smaller; an 'existing' law is one which already exists. When an '-ing' word of this kind is used after 'be', it forms part of a continuous tense.

The crying made her look so old and vulnerable, like a miserable, sick, ageing monkey.
Much of the world's tanker fleet is ageing.

...an increasing amount of leisure time.
Efficiency and productivity are increasing.

Here is a list of common '-ing' adjectives related to intransitive verbs:

ageing	decreasing	existing	recurring	rising
bleeding	diminishing	increasing	reigning	
booming	dwindling	living	remaining	
bursting	dying	prevailing	resounding	

related to verbs but different in meaning

A few '-ing' adjectives are related to verbs in form, but have a different meaning from the usual or commonest meaning of the verb. For example, the verb 'dash' usually means 'move quickly', but someone or something that is 'dashing' is stylish and attractive.

She kept dashing out of the kitchen to give him a kiss.
I used to be told I looked quite dashing.

The following adjectives have a different meaning from the verb they appear to be related to:

becoming	engaging	promising
dashing	fetching	retiring
disarming	halting	trying

not related to verbs

A few '-ing' adjectives are not related to verbs at all. For example, there are no verbs 'to appetize', 'to bald', or 'to scathe'. The following '-ing' adjectives are not related to verbs:

appetizing	enterprising	neighbouring
balding	excruciating	scathing
cunning	impending	unwitting

...the appetizing aromas of the dishes I produced for myself.
Pitman glanced at the fat, balding man sitting beside him.
He launched into a scathing attack on Gates.

used for emphasis in informal speech

A small group of '-ing' adjectives are used in informal speech for emphasis:

blinking	blooming	flipping	stinking
blithering	flaming	raving	thundering

These adjectives are always used in front of a noun, never after a link verb.

If you plan to join the others, you might tell your <u>blinking</u> brother.

Several of these adjectives are usually used with a particular noun, as shown in the examples below.

He's in America, according to that <u>blithering idiot</u> Pete.
I knew that I was carrying on a dialogue with a <u>raving lunatic.</u>
Nobody must get in here and make a <u>thundering nuisance</u> of themselves.

GRAMMAR   **'-ing' forms**

'-ing' forms are also called **present participles.** Most '-ing' forms are formed by adding '-ing' to the base form of a verb, for example 'asking', 'eating', and 'passing'. Sometimes there is a change in spelling, as in 'dying', 'making', and 'putting'. For a table showing these changes, see entry at **Verbs.**

For information about '-ing' forms used as adjectives, see entry at **'-ing' adjectives.**

For the use of '-ing' forms in sentences such as 'It was difficult saying goodbye', see entry at **it.**

continuous tenses
One common use of '-ing' forms is as part of continuous tenses of verbs.

He <u>was sleeping</u> in the other room.
Cathy <u>has been looking</u> at the results.

See entries at **Tenses** and **Continuous tenses.**

after verbs
When you are talking about someone's behaviour in relation to an action, or their attitude towards doing it, you often use a verb followed by a clause beginning with an '-ing' form (an **'-ing' clause.**)

He wisely <u>avoided mentioning the incident to his boss.</u>
They <u>enjoy working together.</u>
You must <u>keep trying.</u>

The following verbs can be followed by an '-ing' clause:

admit	deny	fancy	miss	risk
adore	describe	finish	postpone	stop
avoid	detest	imagine	practise	suggest
commence	dislike	involve	recall	
consider	dread	keep	resent	
delay	enjoy	mind	resist	

'Need', 'require', and 'want' can be followed by an '-ing' form which has a passive meaning. For example, if you say that something 'needs doing', you mean that it needs to be done.

It <u>needs dusting.</u>
The beans <u>want picking.</u>

'Deserve' and 'merit' are also sometimes used in this way.

'-ing' forms

<table>
<tr><td>choice of
'-ing' form and
'to'-infinitive</td><td>After some verbs, you can use an '-ing' clause or a 'to'-infinitive clause without greatly changing the meaning.</td></tr>
</table>

choice of '-ing' form and 'to'-infinitive

After some verbs, you can use an '-ing' clause or a 'to'-infinitive clause without greatly changing the meaning.

It started raining soon after we set off.
Then it started to rain.

Here are some common verbs which can be followed by an '-ing' clause or a 'to'-infinitive clause:

begin	continue	intend	prefer
bother	deserve	like	start
cease	hate	love	

After the verbs 'go on', 'regret', 'remember', and 'try', an '-ing' form has a different meaning from a 'to'-infinitive. See entries at **go on, regret - be sorry, remember,** and **try - attempt**.

after the object of a verb

Some verbs, particularly verbs of perception, are used with an object and an '-ing' clause. The '-ing' clause indicates what the person or thing referred to by the object is doing.

I saw him looking at me.

The following verbs are commonly used with an object and an '-ing' clause:

catch	imagine	notice	save	stop
feel	keep	observe	see	watch
find	leave	picture	send	
hear	listen to	prevent	spot	

Some of these verbs can also be used with an object and an infinitive without 'to'. See entry at **Infinitives**.

'-ing' forms after conjunctions

You can use '-ing' forms after some subordinating conjunctions, with no subject or auxiliary. Note that you can only do this when the subject would be the same as the one in the main clause, or when it is not specific.

I deliberately didn't read the book before going to see the film.
When buying a new car, it is best to seek expert advice.

See entry at **Subordinate clauses**.

separate '-ing' clauses

When you are describing two actions done by the same person at about the same time, you can use an '-ing' clause in front of the main clause. You can also put the '-ing' clause after the main clause, if it is clear who the subject is.

Walking down Newbury Street, they spotted the same man again.
He looked at me, suddenly realising that he was talking to a stranger.

If you want to indicate that someone did one thing immediately after another, you can mention the first thing they did in an '-ing' clause in front of the main clause.

Leaping out of bed, he dressed so quickly that he put his boots on the wrong feet.

WARNING

You should not use an '-ing' clause in front of a main clause when the subject of the '-ing' clause is not the same as the subject of the main clause. If you say 'Driving home later that night, the streets were deserted', you are suggesting that the streets were driving.

However, if the verb in the main clause is transitive and active, you can use an '-ing' clause which relates to the object after the main clause. For example, you could say 'They spotted the same man again, walking down

Newbury Street', meaning that the man was walking down Newbury Street. You should try to avoid making your sentence ambiguous.

active meaning   When an '-ing' form is used to begin a clause, it has an active meaning.

'You could play me a tune,' said Simon, <u>sitting</u> down.
<u>Glancing</u> at my clock, I saw that it was midnight.

Combinations beginning with 'having' are sometimes used, especially in writing. For example, instead of writing 'John, who had already eaten, left early', you could write 'John, having already eaten, left early'.

Ash, <u>having forgotten</u> his fear, had become bored and restless.
<u>Having beaten</u> Rangers the previous week, Aberdeen were entitled to be confident about their ability to cope with Celtic.

passive meaning   '-ing' clauses beginning with 'having been' and a past participle have a passive meaning.

<u>Having been declared</u> insane, he was confined for four months in a prison hospital.

subject and '-ing' form   In writing, you can use a clause containing a subject and an '-ing' form when you want to mention a fact or situation that is relevant to the fact stated in the main clause, or is the reason for it.

Bats are surprisingly long-lived creatures, <u>some having a life-expectancy of around twenty years.</u>
<u>Her eyes glistening with tears,</u> she stood up and asked the Council: 'What am I to do?'
<u>Ashton being dead,</u> the whole affair must now be laid before Colonel Browne.
<u>The subject having been opened,</u> he had to go on with it.

You do this when the subject of the '-ing' clause is closely connected with the subject of the main clause, or when the '-ing' form is 'being' or 'having'.

'With' is sometimes added at the beginning of clauses of this type.

The old man stood up <u>with tears running down his face.</u>

'With' is always used when the two subjects are not closely connected and the '-ing' form is not 'being' or 'having'.

<u>With the conditions increasing from breezy to windy,</u> she had plenty of chances to show off her control.
Our correspondent said it resembled a frontline city, <u>with helicopters patrolling overhead.</u>

after a noun   You can use an '-ing' clause after a noun, 'those', or an indefinite pronoun to identify or describe someone by saying what they do or are doing.

She is now a British citizen <u>working for the Medical Research Council.</u>
Many of those <u>crossing the river</u> had brought books.
Anyone <u>following this advice</u> could find himself in trouble.

The '-ing' clause has a similar function to a relative clause.

used like nouns   You can use '-ing' forms like nouns. When used like this, they are sometimes called **gerunds** or **verbal nouns.** They can be the subject, object, or complement of a clause.

Does slow <u>talking</u> point to slow mental development?
...policemen who regarded unnecessary <u>walking</u> as inherently suspicious.
His hobby was <u>collecting</u> old coins.

They can be used after prepositions, including 'to'.

They get a considerable thrill <u>from taking</u> it home and <u>showing</u> it to their parents.
Local corner shops object <u>to seeing</u> their more expensive personal service undermined <u>by</u> cut-price supermarket-style <u>selling</u>.

When you are not using a determiner in front of an '-ing' form, the '-ing' form can have a direct object. When you are using a determiner, you use 'of' to introduce the object.

I somehow didn't get round to <u>taking the examination</u>.
India now retain only a remote chance of <u>winning the trophy</u>.

What you've just heard was an interview recorded during <u>the making of Karel Reisz's film</u>.
...charges relating to <u>the illegal taking of wild birds' eggs</u>.

The object of the verb is put in front of the '-ing' form to form a compound noun if you are referring to a common type of activity, such as a type of job or hobby.

He regarded <u>film-making</u> as the most glamorous job on earth.
As a child, his interests were drawing and <u>stamp collecting</u>.

Note that you use a singular form for the object. For example, you refer to 'stamp collecting', not 'stamps collecting'.

You can use an '-ing' form with a possessive. This is rather formal.

<u>Your being</u> in the English department means that you must have chosen English as your main subject.
'I think <u>my mother's being</u> American had considerable advantage,' says Lady Astor's son.

You can use an '-ing' form in a similar way with a pronoun or noun. This is less formal.

What do you reckon on the prospects of <u>him being</u> re-elected?

A few nouns ending in '-ing', particularly ones referring to leisure activities, are not related to verbs but are formed from other nouns, or are much commoner than the related verbs.

ballooning	hang-gliding	power-boating	skydiving
caravanning	pot-holing	skateboarding	tobogganing

Camping and <u>caravanning</u> are increasingly cost-attractive.
<u>Skateboarding</u> has come back with a vengeance.

other uses A few '-ing' forms are used as subordinating conjunctions:

assuming	presuming	supposing
considering	providing	

The payments would gradually increase to £1,298, <u>assuming</u> interest rates stayed the same.
<u>Supposing</u> you heard that I'd died in the night, what would you feel?

A few '-ing' forms are used as prepositions or in compound prepositions:

according to	considering	excluding	owing to
barring	depending on	following	regarding
concerning	excepting	including	

The property tax would be set <u>according to</u> the capital value of the home.

There seems no reason why, barring accidents, Carson should not surpass the late Doug Smith's total.
We had already closed the party down shortly after midnight, following complaints from residents.

injure

To **injure** someone means to damage a part of their body.

The earthquake killed 24,000 people and injured 77,000.

If you accidentally damage a part of your body, you can say that you **injure** yourself or **injure** that part of your body.

He's going to injure himself if he isn't careful.
Peter recently injured his right hand in a training accident.

WARNING   **Injure** cannot be used as an intransitive verb. You do not say, for example, 'He injured in a car accident'. You say 'He **was injured** in a car accident'.

A 74-year-old man was killed and five other people were injured when three cars crashed on the A21 near Tonbridge.

A number of other verbs are used to refer to damage done to a person's body. For more information, see entry at **damage**.

'injured' used as   **Injured** is often used as an adjective.
an adjective

Thousands of injured people still lay among the ruins.
East Grinstead won 3-1 without van Asselt, who was injured.

Adverbs such as 'badly', 'seriously', and 'critically' are often used in front of **injured**.

She was not badly injured.
A man lay critically injured for eight hours after his car skidded off a road and smashed into trees.

See also entry at **hurt**.

inquire - enquire

If you **inquire** or **enquire** about something, you ask for information about it. There is no difference in meaning between these words. **Inquire** is more common, especially in American English.

We inquired about the precise circumstances surrounding the arrest.
I enquired about the scenery and Beaumont told me it was being built in a carpenter's shop in Waterloo.

You can use **inquire** or **enquire** with a 'wh'-clause.

She inquired how Ibrahim was getting on.
I enquired what the matter was.

In writing, **inquire** and **enquire** are sometimes used in quote structures.

'Anything you need?' inquired the girl.
'Who compiles these reports?' Philip enquired.

WARNING   You do not use these verbs with a direct object. You do not say, for example, 'He inquired her if she was well'.

'ask'   **Inquire** and **enquire** are fairly formal words. In conversation, people usually use **ask**. **Ask** can be used with or without a direct object.

She asked about his work.
I asked him what he wanted.

insane

See entry at **mad**.

insensible

If you are **insensible to** a physical sensation, you are unable to feel it. **Insensible** is a formal word.

We believe that all animals should be rendered insensible to pain before slaughter.

Insensible is not the opposite of 'sensible'. If someone behaves in a way that is not sensible, you do not say that they are 'insensible'. You say, for example, that they or their actions are **silly** or **foolish.**

You're a silly little boy.
It would be foolish to tell such things to a total stranger.

inside

used as a preposition

When someone or something is in a building or vehicle, you can say that they are **inside** it.

The policemen inside the building opened fire on the crowd.
Two minutes later we were safely inside the taxi.

You do not say that someone is 'inside of' a building or vehicle.

used as an adverb

Inside can also be used as an adverb.

My main concern was to get the man away from the house because my wife and children were inside.
'I have been expecting you,' she said, inviting him inside.

insist

If someone **insists on doing** something, they say very firmly that they will do it, and they do it.

Mr Corleone is a man who insists on hearing bad news at once.
He insisted on paying for the meal.

Note that you do not say that someone 'insists to do' something.

in spite of - despite

'in spite of'

You use **in spite of** when you are mentioning circumstances which surprisingly do not prevent something from happening or being true. Note that the spelling is **in spite of**, not 'inspite of'.

The morning air was still clear and fresh, in spite of all the traffic and the crowd.
In spite of poor health, my father was always cheerful.

WARNING

You do not use **in spite of** to say that something will not be affected by any circumstances. You do not say, for example, 'Everyone can take part, in spite of their ability'. You say 'Everyone can take part **regardless of** their ability' or 'Everyone can take part **whatever** their ability'.

If they are determined to strike, they will do so regardless of what the law says.
A winning team will always attract support, whatever the facilities provided.

You also do not use **in spite of** as a conjunction. You do not say, for example, 'In spite of we protested, they took him away'. You say '**Although** we protested, they took him away'.

Although he was late, he stopped to buy a sandwich.
Gretchen kept her coat on, although it was warm in the room.

'despite' **Despite** means the same as **in spite of.** You do not use 'of' after **despite.**

Despite the differences in their ages they were close friends.
The cost of public services has risen steeply despite a general decline in their quality.

instead - instead of

'instead' **Instead** is an adverb. You use it when you are saying that someone does something rather than doing something else that you have just mentioned.

Judy did not answer. Instead she looked out of the taxi window.
Robert had a great desire to turn away, but instead he led her towards the house.

'instead of' **Instead of** is a preposition. You use it to introduce something which is not done, not used, or not true when you are contrasting it with something which is done, is used, or is true.

I'm tired of sleeping in the mud instead of a nice warm bed.
If you want to have your meal at seven o'clock instead of five o'clock, you can.

You can say that someone does something **instead of doing** something else.

You could always write this instead of using your word processor.
I went up the tributary instead of sticking to the river.

You do not say that someone does something 'instead to do' something else.

instruct

If you **instruct** someone to do something, you tell them to do it. When **instruct** has this meaning, it is followed by an object and a 'to'-infinitive.

The judge instructed them to keep silent.
General Geldenhuys has instructed me to take a full statement from you.

You do not use **instruct** like this without an object. You do not say, for example, 'He instructed to take the prisoners away'. Instead you can say 'He **gave instructions for** the prisoners **to be taken away**' or 'He **gave instructions that** the prisoners **should be taken away**'.

She gave instructions for Lady Illingworth to be cremated.
You had given instructions that physical force should if necessary be used.

another **Instruct** has another meaning. To **instruct** people in a subject or skill
meaning means to teach it to them.

Reg Renn instructs the trainees at the college's motor vehicle unit.

insure

See entry at **assure - ensure - insure.**

intelligent - intellectual

'intelligent' Someone who is **intelligent** can learn new things quickly and understand things which are not simple.

Jo is an intelligent student.
Four of them were highly intelligent women.

'intellectual' Someone who is **intellectual** is interested in ideas or theories, rather than in practical matters.

Who's your intellectual friend?
Dürer was immersed in the intellectual life of his time.

intense - intensive

'intense' **Intense** means 'very great or strong'.

...intense heat.
I could not help feeling intense discomfort.

'intensive' **Intensive** activities involve using a lot of energy or effort in order to achieve something in a short time.

Intensive training courses are provided by the local authority.
...my last intensive preparations for my Ph.D.

intention

When someone intends to do something, you can talk about their **intention to do** it or their **intention of doing** it.

My opponent has declared his intention to petition the Election Court.
They announced their intention of cutting down all the trees.

You can say that **it is someone's intention to do** something.

It had been her intention to walk around Ougadougou.
It is still my intention to resign.

You do not say that 'it is someone's intention of doing' something.

'with the intention' When someone does something because they intend to do something else, you can say that they do the first thing **with the intention of doing** the second thing.

The troops had come with the intention of firing on the crowd.

You do not say that someone does something 'with the intention to do' something else.

'no intention' You can say that someone **has no intention of doing** something.

She had no intention of spending the rest of her life working as a waitress.

You do not say that someone 'has no intention to do' something.

Intentions

When you want to express an intention, especially one relating to an immediate action, you can say 'I'm going to...'.

I'm going to call my father.
I'm going to have a bath.

I'm going to kill you, Max.

You can also say 'I think I'll...'.

I think I'll do some more typing.
I think I'll go to sleep now.

You can use the present continuous tense when you regard your intention as a fixed plan or have already made the necessary arrangements.

I'm taking it back to the library soon.
I'm going away.

The future continuous tense is also sometimes used.

I'll be waiting.

You can also express an intention by saying 'I've decided to...'.

I've decided to clear this place out.
I've decided to go there.

To express a negative intention, you say 'I'm not going to...' or 'I've decided not to...'.

I'm not going to make it easy for them.
I've decided not to take it.

vague intentions   If your intention is not a firm one, you can say 'I'm thinking of...'.

I'm thinking of going to the theatre next week.
I'm thinking of giving it up altogether.
I'm thinking of writing a play.

You can also say 'I might...' or 'I may...'.

I might do that or I might go to Ireland.
I might stay a day or two.
I may come back to Britain, I'm not sure.

If you feel that your intention might surprise the person you are talking to, or are not sure that they will approve of it, you say 'I thought I might...'.

I thought I might buy a house next year.
I thought I might get him over to dinner one evening.

To express a vague negative intention, you can say 'I might not...'.

I might not go.

firm intentions   You use 'I'll' to express a firm intention, especially when making arrangements or reassuring someone.

I'll buy one as soon as I can.
I'll do it this afternoon and ring you back.
I'll explain its function in a minute.

To express a firm negative intention, you can say 'I won't...'.

I won't go.
I won't give you any trouble.
I won't let my family suffer.

expressing   A more formal way of expressing an intention is to say 'I intend to...'.
intentions
formally   *I intend to carry on with it.*
I intend to go into this in rather more detail this term.
I intend to be conciliatory.

'I intend' is also occasionally followed by an '-ing' form.

I intend retiring to Florence.

The emphatic expression 'I have every intention of...' is also sometimes used.

I have every intention of buying it.

Even more formal expressions are 'My intention is to...' and 'It is my intention to...'.

My intention is to provide a reconstruction of this largely discredited ideology.
It is still my intention to resign if they wilfully fail to print the story.

To express a negative intention formally, you can say 'I don't intend to...'.

I don't intend to investigate that at this time.
I don't intend to stay too long.

You can also say 'I have no intention of...'. This is more emphatic.

I have no intention of making a run for it.
I have no intention of retiring.
I've no intention of marrying again.

involuntary actions   Note that 'be going to', 'might', 'may', and 'will' are also used to make statements about involuntary future actions.

If you keep chattering I'm going to make a mistake.
I might not be able to find it.
I may have to stay there awhile.
If I don't have lunch, I'll faint.

interested - interesting

'interested'   If you want to know more about something or someone, you can say that you are **interested in** them.

I'm very interested in birds.
Ellen seemed genuinely interested in him and his work.

Note that you do not use any preposition except 'in' after **interested.**

For information about other words which can be used to say that you want to know more about a person, see entry at **curious.**

If you want to do something, you can say that you are **interested in doing** it.

I was interested in seeing different kinds of theatre.
I'm only interested in finding out what the facts are.

You do not say that you are 'interested to do' something.

'interesting'   Do not confuse **interested** with **interesting.** You say that someone or something is **interesting** when they have qualities or features which make you want to know more about them.

I've met some very interesting people.
...some interesting old coins.

WARNING   You do not use **interesting** to describe things which result in your receiving a lot of money. For example, if you earn a large salary, you do not say that your job is 'interesting'. You say that it is **well-paid.**

They go on to get university degrees and well-paid careers in business.
Sylvia found herself a series of quite well-paid secretarial jobs.

interior

The **interior** of a building or vehicle is the inside part of it.

...the fire that destroyed the interior of the Savoy Theatre.
The car's interior was becoming stuffy.

Interior is often used as an adjective in front of a noun to refer to an inside part of a building or vehicle.

The interior walls were coated with green mould.
I put the interior light on and looked at her.

'internal'   You do not usually use **interior** to refer to the inside parts of other things. Instead you use **internal**.

All the internal organs are in groups of five.

into

The preposition **into** is usually used in connection with movement of some kind. You use **into** to say where someone or something goes, or where something is put.

I went into the church.
He shook a little dust into the basin.

However, in front of 'here' and 'there', you use **in**, not 'into'.

Come in here.
She went in there and stood at the foot of his bed.

After verbs meaning 'put', 'throw', 'drop', or 'fall', you can use **into** or **in** with the same meaning.

William put the letter into his pocket.
He locked the bag and put the key in his pocket.

He crumpled the envelope up and threw it into his wastebasket.
She threw both letters in the bin.

He fell into an ornamental pond.
The dog slipped and fell in the water.

intolerable - intolerant

'intolerable'   If a situation is **intolerable**, it is so bad that you cannot bear it.

They find this situation intolerable.
...the things that made his life intolerable.

'intolerant'   Someone who is **intolerant** tries to prevent people from behaving in ways that they do not approve of, or from expressing opinions that they do not agree with.

She is intolerant by nature.
...intolerant regimes.

Introducing yourself and other people

introducing   When you meet someone for the first time, and they do not already know
yourself   who you are, you can introduce yourself by saying who you are. You may need to say 'Hello' or make a remark first.

'I'm Helmut,' said the boy. 'I'm Edmond Dorf,' I said.
Come with me, sir. I'm the captain.

Introducing yourself and other people

'I don't think we've met, have we? Are you visiting here?'—'Yes. I'm Philip Swallow.'
I had better introduce myself. I am Colonel Marc Rodin.
May I introduce myself? The Reverend John Hunt.
You must be the Kirks. My name's Macintosh.

In formal situations, people sometimes say 'How do you do?' when introducing themselves.

I'm Nigel Jessop. How do you do?

introducing other people

If you are introducing people who have not met each other before, you say 'This is...'. You introduce each person, unless you have already told one of them who they are going to meet.

'This is Bernadette, Mr Zapp,' said O'Shea.

You use an appropriate form of each person's name, depending on how formal the occasion is. See entry at **Names and titles.**

Note that 'these' is rarely used, although you might say, for example, 'These are my children'. When you are introducing a couple, you can use 'this' once instead of repeating it.

This is Mr Dixon and Miss Peel.

You can just say the name of the person or people you are introducing, indicating with your hand which one you mean.

more formal introductions

If you need to be more formal, you first say something like 'May I introduce my brother', 'Let me introduce you to my brother', or 'I'd like to introduce my brother'.

By the way, may I introduce my wife? Karin – Mrs Stannard, an old friend.
Let me introduce everybody to everybody. My brother, Rudolph; my sister, Gretchen; my wife, Teresa; my manager, Mr Schultz.
Bill, I'd like to introduce Charlie Citrine.

You can also say 'I'd like you to meet...'.

Officer O'Malley, I'd like you to meet Ted Peachum.

more casual introductions

A more casual way of introducing someone is to say something like 'You haven't met John Smith, have you?', 'You don't know John, do you?', or 'I don't think you know John, do you?'

'I don't think you know Colonel Daintry.'—'No. I don't think we've met. How do you do?'

If you are not quite sure whether an introduction is necessary, you can say something like 'Have you met...?' or 'Do you two know each other?'

'Do you know my husband, Ken?'—'Hello. I don't think I do.'

If you are fairly sure that the people have met each other before, you say something like 'You know John, don't you?' or 'You've met John, haven't you?'

Hello, come in. You've met Paul.

responding to an introduction

When you have been introduced to someone, you both say 'Hello'. If you are both young and in an informal situation, you can say 'Hi'. If you are in a formal situation, you can say 'How do you do?'

'Francis, this is Father Sebastian.'—'Hello, Francis,' Father Sebastian said, offering his hand.
How do you do? Elizabeth has spoken such a lot about you.

People sometimes say 'Pleased to meet you' or 'Nice to meet you', especially in more formal situations.

Pleased to meet you, Doctor Floyd.
It's so nice to meet you, Edna. Ginny's told us so much about you.

invaluable

If you say that someone or something is **invaluable,** you mean that they are extremely useful.

He was an invaluable source of information.
This experience proved invaluable later on.

Invaluable is not the opposite of 'valuable'. If you want to say that an object has no value at all, you can say that it is **worthless** or **not worth anything.**

The goods are often worthless by the time they arrive.
I started collecting his pictures when they weren't worth anything.

invent

If someone **invents** something new, they are the first person to think of it or make it.

Walter Hunt and Elias Howe invented the sewing machine.

'discover' You do not use **invent** to say that someone finds out about something which exists but which was not previously known. The word you use is **discover.**

Herschel discovered a new planet.
We discovered a way to get rid of it.

GRAMMAR # Inversion

Inversion means changing the normal word order in a sentence by putting part or all of the verb group in front of the subject. Usually an auxiliary is put in front of the subject, and the rest of the verb group is put after the subject. If no other auxiliary is used, a form of 'do' is used, unless the verb is 'be'.

in questions Inversion is normal in questions.

Are you ready?
Can John swim?
Did he go to the fair?
Why did you fire him?
How many are there?

You do not need to use inversion when you are expecting someone to confirm what you are saying, or when you want to express a reaction such as surprise, interest, doubt, or anger about what has just been said.

You've been having trouble?
She's not going to do it?
'She's gone home.'—'She's gone back to Montrose?'

WARNING You must use inversion in a question that begins with a 'wh'-word, unless the 'wh'-word is the subject. For example, you must say 'What did she think?', not 'What she thought?'

Inversion is not used in reported questions. You do not say, for example,

'She asked what was I doing'. You say 'She asked what I was doing'. See entry at **Reporting**.

after place adverbials

Inversion occurs in descriptions of a place or scene when an adverbial of place is put at the beginning of a clause. This type of structure is found mainly in writing.

On the ceiling hung dustpans and brushes.
Beyond them lay the fields.
Behind the desk was a middle-aged woman.

Note that in this kind of inversion the main verb is put in front of the subject.

Inversion is used in speech after 'here' and 'there' when you are drawing attention to something.

Here's the money, go and buy yourself a watch.
Here's my card!
Here comes the cloud of smoke.
There's another one!

WARNING

You do not use inversion when the subject is a personal pronoun.

Here he comes.
There she is.

after negative adverbials

Inversion occurs when broad negative adverbs or other negative adverbials are put at the beginning of a clause for emphasis. This structure is used in formal speech and writing.

Never have I experienced such agony.
Seldom have enterprise and personal responsibility been more needed.
Rarely has so much time been wasted by so many people.
The police said the man was extremely dangerous and that on no account should he be approached.

Note that inversion also occurs in formal speech and writing after adverbials preceded by 'only'.

Only then would I ponder the contradictions inherent in my own personality.

See entry at **only**.

after 'neither' and 'nor'

You use inversion after 'neither' and 'nor' when you are saying that the previous negative statement also applies to another person or group.

'I can't remember.'—'Neither can I.'
Research assistants don't know how to do it, and nor do qualified tutors.

after 'so'

You use inversion after 'so' when you are saying that the previous positive statement also applies to another person or group.

'I've been through the Ford works at Dagenham.'—'So have I.'
'I hate KB.'—'So do I. A most unsociable place, isn't it?'
'Skating's just a matter of practice.'—'Yes, well, so is skiing.'
Bioff went to jail. So did the national president.

Note that when 'so' is used to express surprise or to emphasize that someone should do something, inversion does not occur.

'It's on the table behind you.'—'So it is!'
'I feel very guilty about it.'—'So you should.'

| other uses | Inversion occurs in conditional clauses that are not introduced by a conjunction. This structure is formal. |

Had the two tied, victory would have gone to Todd.

Inversion can occur in comparisons after 'as'.

The piece was well and confidently played, as was Peter Maxwell Davies' 'Revelation and Fall'.
Their father, George Churchill, also made jewellery, as did their grandfather.

Inversion is often used after a quote. See entry at **Reporting**.

inverted commas

See section on **direct speech** in entry at **Punctuation.**

Invitations

There are several ways of inviting someone to do something or to come to a place.

| polite invitations | The usual polite way to invite someone to do something is to say 'Would you like to...?' |

Would you like to come up here on Sunday?
Well, would you like to comment on that, Tessa?
Would you like to look at it, Ian?

Another polite form of invitation is 'please' with an imperative. This form of invitation is used mainly by people who are in charge of a situation.

Please help yourselves to another drink.
Sit down, please.

| informal invitations | In informal situations, you can use an imperative form without 'please'. However, you should only do this if it is clear that you are giving an invitation rather than an order. |

Come and have a drink, Max.
Look, come to a party at my home tonight.
Sit down, sit down. I'll order tea.
Stay as long as you like.

| persuasive invitations | You can make your invitation more persuasive or firm by putting 'do' in front of the imperative. You do this especially when the other person seems reluctant to do what you are inviting them to do. |

Do sit down.
What you said just now about Seaford sounds most intriguing. Do tell me more.

You can also say 'Wouldn't you like to...?' when you want to be persuasive.

Wouldn't you like to come with me?

When you want to be very polite and persuasive, you can say 'Won't you...?'

Won't you take off your coat?
Won't you sit down, Sir Clarence, and have a bite to eat?

Invitations

very emphatic invitations

If you know the person you are inviting well, and you want to make your invitation very emphatic, you can say 'You must...'. You use this form of invitation when inviting someone to do something in the future, rather than immediately.

You must come and stay.
You must come to Rome!

casual invitations

A casual, non-emphatic way of inviting someone to do something is to say 'You can...' or 'You could...'. You can add 'if you like'.

Well, when I get my flat, you can come and stay with me.
You can tell me about your people, if you like.

'You're welcome to...' is another way of starting a casual invitation, but is more friendly.

You're welcome to live with us for as long as you like.
The cottage is about fifty miles away. But you're very welcome to use it.

Another way of making an invitation seem casual is to say 'I was wondering if...'.

I was wondering if you'd care to come over next weekend.
I was wondering if you're free for lunch.

indirect invitations

An invitation can be indirect. For example, you can invite someone to do something in the future by saying 'I hope you'll...'. You use this form of invitation especially when you are not confident that the other person will accept your invitation.

I hope you'll be able to stay the night. We'll gladly put you up.
I hope, Kathy, you'll come and see me again.

You can also invite someone indirectly using 'How would you like to...?' or 'Why don't you...?'

How would you like to come and work for me?
Why don't you come to the States with us in November?

You can also use a question beginning with 'How about' followed by an '-ing' form or a noun.

Now, how about coming to stay with me, at my house?
How about a spot of lunch with me, Mrs Sharpe?

You can also use a statement that begins with 'You'll' and ends with the tag 'won't you?' This implies that you are expecting the other person to accept.

You'll bring Angela up for the wedding, won't you?

inviting someone to ask you for something

You can invite someone else to ask you for something by saying 'Don't hesitate to...'. This form of invitation is polite and emphatic, and is usually used between people who do not know each other well.

Should you have any further problems, please do not hesitate to telephone.
When you want more, don't hesitate to ask me.

responding to an invitation

If you want to accept an invitation, you say 'Thank you' or, more informally, 'Thanks'. You can also say something like 'Yes, I'd love to' or 'I'd like that very much'.

'We have quite a good stream on the property. If you'd like to give it a try, just come any time.'—'Thank you. I'll come round sometime.'
'You could come and tutor me in physics and maths.'—'Yes, I'd love to.'
'Won't you join me and the girls for lunch, Mr Jordache?'—'Thanks, Larsen. I'd like that very much.'

If you want to decline an invitation to visit someone or go somewhere with them, you can say something like 'I'm sorry, I can't', 'I'm afraid I'm busy then', or 'I'd like to, but...'.

'I'm phoning in the hope of persuading you to spend the day with me.'—'Oh, I'm sorry, I can't.'
'I would like it very much if you could come on Sunday.'—'I'm afraid I'm busy.'
'Why don't you come? We're having a party.'—'It sounds like fun. But I'm afraid I'm tied up at the moment.'
'Would you like to stay for dinner?'—'I'd like to, but I can't.'

You can also decline an invitation by saying 'No, thanks', 'Thanks, but...', or 'I'm all right, thanks'.

'Come home with me.'—'No thanks. I don't want to intrude on your family.'
'Won't you take off your coat?'—'Thanks, but I can't stop.'
'Eat with us.'—'Thanks, but I've eaten.'
'Would you like to lie down?'—'No, I'm all right.'

invite

If you **invite** someone to a party or a meal, you ask them to come to it.

The Hogans invited me to a cocktail party.
He invited Alexander to dinner.

Note that you must use 'to' in sentences like these. You do not say 'I invited her my party'.

When you ask someone to do something which you think they will enjoy, you can say that you **invite** them **to do** it.

He invited Axel to come with him.
Dr Kiryushin invited Medvedev and his son to visit him.

You do not say that you invite someone 'for doing' something.

involved

used after a link verb
The adjective **involved** is usually used after a link verb such as 'be' or 'get'.

If you are **involved in** an activity, you are taking part in it.

Should religious leaders get involved in politics?
In all, 6000 companies are involved in producing the parts that are needed for these aircraft.

used after a noun
Involved can also be used immediately after a noun. The people **involved** in something are the people affected by it or taking part in it.

We never managed to get anything done, simply because of the large number of people involved.
He felt justified in protecting the children involved by separating them from their mother.

You also use **involved** immediately after a noun when you are mentioning an important aspect of something that is being discussed.

There is quite a lot of work involved.
She had no real understanding of the problems involved.

another meaning

Involved has another meaning. If you say that a process or situation is involved, you mean that it is very complicated. When involved has this meaning, it can only go after a verb or in front of a noun.

The problem's a little bit more <u>involved</u> than I suggested.
We had long, <u>involved</u> discussions.

GRAMMAR **Irregular verbs**

An **irregular verb** has a past form or a past participle which is not formed by adding '-ed'.

A few irregular verbs have regular past forms, but two past participle forms, one of which is irregular. The commoner one is given first.

base form	past form	past participle
mow	mowed	mowed, mown
prove	proved	proved, proven
sew	sewed	sewn, sewed
show	showed	shown, showed
sow	sowed	sown, sowed
swell	swelled	swollen, swelled

Some irregular verbs have two past forms and two past participle forms. If there is a regular form, it is given first in the following table, unless it is much less common than the irregular one.

base form	past form	past participle
bid	bid, bade	bid, bidden
burn	burned, burnt	burned, burnt
bust	busted, bust	busted, bust
dream	dreamed, dreamt	dreamed, dreamt
dwell	dwelled, dwelt	dwelled, dwelt
hang	hanged, hung	hanged, hung
kneel	kneeled, knelt	kneeled, knelt
lean	leaned, leant	leaned, leant
leap	leaped, leapt	leaped, leapt
lie	lied, lay	lied, lain
light	lit, lighted	lit, lighted
smell	smelled, smelt	smelled, smelt
speed	sped, speeded	sped, speeded
spell	spelled, spelt	spelled, spelt
spill	spilled, spilt	spilled, spilt
spoil	spoiled, spoilt	spoiled, spoilt
weave	wove, weaved	woven, weaved
wet	wetted, wet	wetted, wet
wind	wound, winded	wound, winded

With a few verbs, different forms are used for different meanings. For example, the past form and the past participle of the verb 'hang' is 'hung' for most of its meanings. However, 'hanged' is used when it means 'executed by hanging'. See entries at **bid, hang, lay - lie, speed, weave,** and **wind**.

The following table shows verbs which have irregular past forms and past participles.

base form	past form	past participle	base form	past form	past participle
arise	arose	arisen	hold	held	held
awake	awoke	awoken	hurt	hurt	hurt
bear	bore	borne	keep	kept	kept
beat	beat	beaten	know	knew	known
become	became	become	lay	laid	laid
begin	began	begun	lead	led	led
bend	bent	bent	leave	left	left
bet	bet	bet	lend	lent	lent
bind	bound	bound	let	let	let
bite	bit	bitten	lose	lost	lost
bleed	bled	bled	make	made	made
blow	blew	blown	mean	meant	meant
break	broke	broken	meet	met	met
breed	bred	bred	pay	paid	paid
bring	brought	brought	put	put	put
build	built	built	quit	quit	quit
burst	burst	burst	read	read	read
buy	bought	bought	rend	rent	rent
cast	cast	cast	ride	rode	ridden
catch	caught	caught	ring	rang	rung
choose	chose	chosen	rise	rose	risen
cling	clung	clung	run	ran	run
come	came	come	saw	sawed	sawn
cost	cost	cost	say	said	said
creep	crept	crept	see	saw	seen
cut	cut	cut	seek	sought	sought
deal	dealt	dealt	sell	sold	sold
dig	dug	dug	send	sent	sent
draw	drew	drawn	set	set	set
drink	drank	drunk	shake	shook	shaken
drive	drove	driven	shed	shed	shed
eat	ate	eaten	shine	shone	shone
fall	fell	fallen	shoe	shod	shod
feed	fed	fed	shoot	shot	shot
feel	felt	felt	shrink	shrank	shrunk
fight	fought	fought	shut	shut	shut
find	found	found	sing	sang	sung
flee	fled	fled	sink	sank	sunk
fling	flung	flung	sit	sat	sat
fly	flew	flown	slay	slew	slain
forbear	forbore	forborne	sleep	slept	slept
forbid	forbade	forbidden	slide	slid	slid
forget	forgot	forgotten	sling	slung	slung
forgive	forgave	forgiven	slink	slunk	slunk
forsake	forsook	forsaken	speak	spoke	spoken
forswear	forswore	forsworn	spend	spent	spent
freeze	froze	frozen	spin	spun	spun
get	got	got	spread	spread	spread
give	gave	given	spring	sprang	sprung
go	went	gone	stand	stood	stood
grind	ground	ground	steal	stole	stolen
grow	grew	grown	stick	stuck	stuck
hear	heard	heard	sting	stung	stung
hide	hid	hidden	stink	stank	stunk
hit	hit	hit	strew	strewed	strewn

base form	past form	past participle	base form	past form	past participle
stride	strode	stridden	think	thought	thought
strike	struck	struck	throw	threw	thrown
string	strung	strung	thrust	thrust	thrust
strive	strove	striven	tread	trod	trodden
swear	swore	sworn	understand	understood	understood
sweep	swept	swept	wake	woke	woken
swim	swam	swum	wear	wore	worn
swing	swung	swung	weep	wept	wept
take	took	taken	win	won	won
teach	taught	taught	wring	wrung	wrung
tear	tore	torn	write	wrote	written
tell	told	told			

Note that 'gotten' is often used instead of 'got' as the past participle of 'get' in spoken American English. See entry at **gotten**.

irritated

See entry at **nervous**.

issue

If something **is issued to** you, it is officially given to you.

Radios were issued to the troops.
The boots issued to them had fallen to bits.

In British English, you can also say that someone **is issued with** something.

She was issued with travel documents.
Some of the soldiers fighting in Turkey were issued with caviar as part of their rations.

American speakers do not say that someone 'is issued with' something.

it

used to refer to things

You use **it** to refer to an object, animal, or other thing that has just been mentioned.

...a tray with glasses on it.
The horse must have been thirsty, because it went straight to the fountain and drank.
The strike went on for a year before it was settled.

WARNING

When the subject of a sentence is followed by a relative clause, you do not use **it** in front of the main verb. You do not say, for example, 'The town where I work, it is near London'. You say 'The town where I work **is** near London'.

The bitter fighting which has split the Party in recent years has finally reached the General Council.
The interest which inspired these investigations came from Tarski's paper 'On the Concept of Logical Consequence'.
The cave, which Ralph Solecki has been excavating, has yielded a rich selection of Neanderthal remains.

used to refer to situations	You can also use **it** to refer to a situation, fact, or experience. *I like it here.* *She was frightened, but tried not to show it.*
WARNING	You often refer to something such as an experience or wish using an '-ing' form or 'to'-infinitive after a verb such as 'like'. When you do this, you do not use **it** in front of the '-ing' form or infinitive.

For example, you do not say 'I like it, walking in the park'. You say 'I like walking in the park'. Similarly, you do not say 'I prefer it, to make my own bread'. You say 'I prefer to make my own bread'.

I like being in your house.
I enjoy bathing in the sea.
I want to be an actress.

used with link verbs

It is often used as the subject of a link verb such as 'be'. Usually **it** refers to something that has just been mentioned.

I like your Hungarian accent. I think it's quite attractive.
So you don't like them? It's a pity.

You can also use **it** as the subject of 'be' to say what the time, day, or date is.

It's seven o'clock.
It's Sunday morning.

You can also use **it** as the subject of a link verb to describe the weather or the light.

It was terribly cold.
It was a windy afternoon.
It's getting dark.

used to describe an experience

You can use **it** with a link verb and an adjective to describe an experience. After the adjective, you use an '-ing' form or a 'to'-infinitive. For example, instead of saying 'Walking by the lake was nice', people usually say '**It was** nice walking by the lake'.

It's nice hearing your voice again.
It was sad to see her the victim of continual pain.

You can use **it** with a link verb and an adjective to describe the experience of being in a particular place. After the adjective, you use an adverbial such as 'here' or 'on the beach'.

It is very quiet and pleasant here.
It was warm in the restaurant.
It was cosy in the car.

used to comment on a situation

You can use **it** with an adjective or noun group to comment on a whole situation. After the adjective or noun group, you use a 'that'-clause.

It is lucky that I am going abroad.
It's strange you should come today.
It's a pity you didn't stay.
It's a wonder he hasn't been in jail before this.

After an adjective, you can sometimes use a 'wh'-clause instead of a 'that'-clause.

It's funny how people change.
Get a carpet cleaner to do your carpets. It's amazing what they can do.

WARNING

You do not use **it** with a link verb and a noun group to say that something exists or is present. You do not say, for example, 'It's a lot of traffic on this road tonight'. You say '**There's** a lot of traffic on this road tonight'.

There's a lecturer in the Law Faculty called Hodgson.
There was no room in the cottage.
There will be no one to help you.

See entry at **there.**

its - it's

'its' **Its** is a possessive determiner. You use **its** to indicate that something belongs or relates to a thing, place, animal, or child.

He discovered the river had lost its beauty.
The pig managed to keep its balance.
She hoisted the child on her shoulder and started patting its back.

'it's' **It's** is a shortened form of 'it is' or 'it has'.

It's just like the ticking of a clock.
It's been very nice talking to you.

J

jam

See entry at **marmalade.**

jewellery - jeweller's

'jewellery' **Jewellery** consists of valuable ornaments that people wear, such as rings, bracelets, and necklaces.

She was wearing a lot of jewellery.
Some of her jewellery was missing.

Jewellery is an uncount noun. You do not talk about 'jewelleries'.

'jeweller's' A shop where you buy jewellery is called a **jeweller's** or a **jeweller**. You do not call it a 'jewellery'.

...a large modern jeweller's.

Jewellery and **jeweller** are usually spelled **jewelry** and **jeweler** in American English.

job

See entry at **work.**

joke

A **joke** is something which you say or do in order to make people laugh. There are three kinds of joke.

When someone **makes** or **cracks** a joke, they make a witty remark.

Sometimes he made a joke about people going by.

He even <u>cracked</u> the odd joke about my drinking too much.

A **joke** is also something clever or funny which you have heard, read, or invented at an earlier time and which you repeat to amuse people. When **joke** has this meaning, you say that someone **tells** a joke.

Tell Uncle Henry the joke you <u>told</u> us.
He has a way of screwing up his face when he is <u>telling</u> a joke.

A **joke** is also something that is done to make someone appear foolish. When **joke** has this meaning, you say that someone **plays** a joke **on** someone else.

They're <u>playing</u> a joke <u>on</u> you.

WARNING   You never say that someone 'says' or 'does' a joke.

jolly

See entry at **happy - sad.**

journal

A **journal** is a magazine for people with a particular interest. Many magazines have 'Journal' as part of their name.

...the British Medical <u>Journal</u>.

Journal is also an old-fashioned or literary word for a diary.

He had been keeping a <u>journal</u> of his travels.

WARNING   You do not refer to a newspaper as a 'journal'.

journey

When you **make** a **journey,** you travel from one place to another.

He <u>made</u> the <u>journey</u> to Mardan.
He <u>had made</u> a tortuous <u>journey</u> across the Pacific.

You can also say that someone **goes on** a **journey.**

He <u>went on</u> a <u>journey</u> to London.

You do not say that someone 'does' a journey.

'trip'   When someone makes a journey to a place and back again, you can refer to it as a **trip.**

...a return <u>trip</u> from Los Angeles to New York.

'voyage'   A **voyage** is a long journey in a ship or spacecraft.

The ship's <u>voyage</u> is over.
...the <u>voyage</u> to the moon in 1972.

just

You use **just** to say that something happened a very short time ago. British speakers usually use the present perfect tense with **just.** For example, they say 'I've **just** arrived'.

I've <u>just</u> sold my car.
I've <u>just</u> finished going through Section 6.

American speakers usually use the simple past tense. Instead of saying 'I've just arrived', they say 'I **just** arrived'.

He just died.
I just broke the pink bowl.

Some British speakers also use the simple past tense, but in Britain this use is usually regarded as incorrect.

WARNING

You do not use **just** with adverbs such as 'partly' to give the meaning 'not completely'. You do not say, for example, 'The job is just partly done'. You say 'The job is **only partly** done'.

This is only partly true.
He was only partially successful.
Dazed and only half awake, he was still in his underwear.

just now

See entry at **now**.

K

keep

used as a transitive verb

To **keep** someone or something in a particular state or place means to cause them to remain in that state or place. The past tense and past participle of 'keep' is **kept,** not 'keeped'.

She kept her arm around her husband as she spoke.
They had been kept awake by nightingales.

used as an intransitive verb

To **keep** in a particular state means to remain in that state.

They've got to hunt for food to keep alive.

If a sign says '**Keep Out**', it is warning you not to go somewhere.

used with an '-ing' form

Keep can be used in two different ways with an '-ing' form.

You can use it to say that something is repeated many times.

The phone keeps ringing.
My mother keeps asking questions.

You can also use it to say that something continues to happen and does not stop.

A van began hooting to get by. Bessie kept running.
The bonfire is still burning. I think it'll keep going all night.

For emphasis, you can use **keep on** instead of 'keep'.

The tank kept on going.

WARNING

You never say that someone or something 'keeps to do' something.

kerb

See entry at **curb - kerb**.

kind

Kind is used as a noun or an adjective.

used as a noun You use it as a noun to talk about a class of people or things. **Kind** is a count noun. After words like 'all' and 'many', you use **kinds**, not 'kind'.

It will give you an opportunity to meet all kinds of people.
Soil derives from many kinds of rock.
The trees were filled with birds of all kinds.

After **kinds of** you can use either the plural or singular form of a noun. For example, you can say 'I like most kinds of **cars**' or 'I like most kinds of **car**'. The singular form is more formal.

…trying to communicate with different kinds of people.
People have been working hard to produce the kinds of courses that we need.

I've seen this in several kinds of profession.
There will be two kinds of certificate.

After **kind of** you use the singular form of a noun.

He gave me the fleshy leaf of a kind of cactus.
She makes the same kind of point in another essay.

In conversation, 'these' and 'those' are often used with **kind**. For example, people say 'I don't like these kind of films' or 'I don't like those kind of films'. This use is generally thought to be incorrect, and it is best to avoid it. Instead you should say 'I don't like **this kind of film**' or 'I don't like **that kind of film**'.

There are problems with this kind of explanation.
We're always equipped to handle that kind of question.

You can also say 'I don't like films **of this kind**'.

This appears to be the natural way of interpreting data of this kind.

In conversation, people often say **like this, like that,** or **like these.**

I hope we see many more enterprises like this.
I'd read a few books like that.
I'm sure they don't have chairs like these.

Some people use **kind of** when they are describing something in a vague or uncertain way. For more information about this use, see entry at **sort of - kind of.**

used as an adjective When **kind** is used as an adjective, it has a totally different meaning. You use it to describe gentle, caring behaviour.

Gertrude had been immensely kind.
His voice was very kind.

You also use it to describe people who always behave in this way.

He was a thoroughly kind and generous man.
I find them all very pleasant and extremely kind and helpful.

You say that someone is **kind to** someone else.

She's been very kind to you.
He was so kind to young people.

Note that when **kind** has this meaning, you do not use any preposition except 'to' after it.

kindly

Kindly is used as an adverb or an adjective.

used as an adverb	If you do something **kindly,** you do it in a kind way.

Priscilla played with Edal <u>kindly</u> and patiently.
She smiled very <u>kindly</u>.

You can use **kindly** to show that you are grateful to someone.

They <u>kindly</u> contributed to our funds.
Manfred and Mrs Mount are very <u>kindly</u> taking me back.

Some people use **kindly** when they are asking someone to do something in an annoyed way. This is a rather old-fashioned use.

<u>Kindly</u> stand back a minute, please.

'take kindly'   If you do not **take kindly to** something, you are very unwilling to accept it.

He doesn't <u>take too kindly to</u> discipline.
They have been left with nothing but their expectations and are unlikely to <u>take kindly to</u> disappointment.

used as an adjective   **Kindly** is sometimes used as an adjective with the same meaning as 'kind'. This is a rather old-fashioned use.

They are <u>kindly</u> people.
He had been given shelter by a <u>kindly</u> villager.

know

awareness of facts   If you **know** that something is the case, you are aware that it is the case. The past tense of 'know' is **knew**, not 'knowed'. The past participle is **known.**

I <u>knew</u> that she had recently graduated from law school.
I <u>should have known</u> that the Times can never be wrong.

WARNING   You never use a continuous tense with **know.** You do not say, for example, 'I am knowing that this is true'. You say 'I **know** that this is true'.

'I know'   In British English, if someone tells you a fact that you already know, you do not say 'I know it'. You say '**I know**'.

'The stuff's very good.'—'I <u>know</u>.'
'That's not their fault, Peter.'—'Yes, I <u>know</u>.'

Some American speakers say '**I know it**'.

'For God's sake, man, this town is dying!'—'I <u>know it</u>, Larry.'

'want to know'   You use **want to know** in front of a 'wh'-clause to say that someone requires some information.

Mrs Fleming <u>wants to know</u> what you feel about it.
Celia <u>wants to know</u> what really happened.

'let...know'   If you say that you will **let** someone **know** something, you mean that you will give them some information when you receive it, or if you receive it.

I'll find out about the car and <u>let</u> you <u>know</u> what's happened.
You will <u>let</u> me <u>know</u> if she turns up again, won't you?

acquaintance and familiarity   If you **know** a person, place, or thing, you are acquainted with them or are familiar with them.

Do you <u>know</u> David?
He <u>knew</u> London well.
Do you <u>know</u> the poem 'Kubla Khan'?

'get to know'   If you want to say that someone gradually becomes acquainted with a person or gradually becomes familiar with a place, you say that they **get to know** the person or place.

I got to know some of the staff quite well.
I really wanted to get to know America.

WARNING   You do not use **know** without 'get to' to mean 'become acquainted with'.

'know how to'   If you **know how to** do something, you have the necessary knowledge to do it.

No one knew how to repair it.
Do you know how to drive?

You do not say that someone 'knows to' do something.

knowledge

Knowledge is information and understanding about a subject, which people have in their minds.

...advances in scientific knowledge.
All knowledge comes to us through our senses.

Knowledge is an uncount noun. You do not talk about 'knowledges' or 'a knowledge'.

You talk about someone's **knowledge of** a subject.

Her knowledge of French and Italian was good.
My knowledge of the play was a great help.

Note that you do not use any preposition except 'of' after **knowledge**.

L

lack

Lack is used as a noun or a verb.

used as a noun   If there is a **lack of** something, there is not enough of it, or it does not exist at all.

I hated the lack of privacy in the dormitory.

used as a verb   If someone or something **lacks** a quality, they do not have it.

...the child who lacks self-confidence.
Their work is repetitive and lacks variety.

Note that you do not say that someone or something 'lacks of' a quality.

lady

See entry at **woman - lady**.

lake - pool - pond

These words all refer to areas of water surrounded by land.

'lake' A **lake** is a large area of fresh water, on which ships or boats can sail.

'pool' A **pool** is a small area of still or slow-moving water. You can see pools of salt water close to the sea on some coasts. Rivers often pass through pools.

'pond' A **pond** is a very small area of fresh water. Ponds are usually created artificially. Many English villages have ponds with ducks on them, and people sometimes have small ponds in their gardens with fish in them.

landscape

See entry at **scene - sight**.

lane

A **lane** is a narrow road which can be used by vehicles, especially in the country.

'path' You do not use **lane** to refer to a strip of ground which people walk along and which vehicles cannot use. The word you use is **path** or **footpath**.

large

See entries at **big - large - great** and **small - large**.

last - lastly

Last is used as an adjective or an adverb.

'last' used as
an adjective

The **last** thing, event, or person of a particular kind is the one that comes after all the others.

He missed the last bus.
They met for the last time just before the war.
He was the last man out of Esseph at the time of its earthquake.

If you want to emphasize that someone or something is the last one of their kind, you can put 'very' in front of **last**.

Those were his very last words.
Gillian and I would stand outside our doors until the very last minute.

Latest is sometimes used in a similar way. See entry at **latest - last**.

'last' used as
an adverb

If something **last** happened on a particular occasion, it has not happened since then.

They last saw their homeland nine years ago.
It's a long time since we met last.

If an event is the final one in a series of similar events, you can say that it happens **last**. You put **last** at the end of a clause.

He added the milk last.
Mr Ross was meant to have gone first, but in fact went last.

'lastly' You can also use **lastly** to say that an event is the final one in a series. You put **lastly** at the beginning of a clause.

Lastly he jabbed the knife hard into the trunk of the tree.

However, **last** and **lastly** are not always used in the same way. You usually use **last** to say that an event is the final one in a series of similar events. You use **lastly** when you are talking about events which are not similar.

For example, if you say 'George rang his aunt **last**', you usually mean that

George had rung several people and that his aunt was the last person he rang. If you say 'Lastly George rang his aunt', you mean that George had done several things and that the last thing he did was to ring his aunt.

Lastly has a much more common use. You use it to introduce a final point in a discussion, ask a final question, give a final instruction, or mention a final item in a list.

And lastly, we need to examine the extent to which the relative value of benefits has changed.
Lastly I would like to ask about your future plans.

'at last'

At last and at long last are used to indicate that something that you have been waiting for or expecting for a long time has happened. These expressions usually go at the beginning or end of a clause.

I'm free at last.
At long last I've found a girl who really loves me.

'last' with time expressions

You use last in front of a word such as 'week' or 'month' to say when something happened. For example, if it is August and something happened in July, you say that it happened last month.

He opened up another shop last month.
The group held its first meeting last week.

Note that you do not say that something happened 'the last month' or 'the last week'.

Last can be used in a similar way in front of the names of festivals, seasons, months, or days of the week.

Last Christmas he insisted on dressing up as Santa Claus.
She died last autumn.
Police seized other documents at his home last March.
We saw a rare sight last Saturday.

However, you do not use last like this in front of 'decade' or 'century'. You do not say, for example, that something happened 'last decade'. You say that it happened in the last decade or during the last decade.

This was well known during the last century.

You also do not say 'last morning' or 'last afternoon'. You say yesterday morning or yesterday afternoon.

It's not so warm this morning as it was yesterday morning.
Yesterday afternoon we drove down the road from Wells Summit.

You do not say 'last evening'. You say yesterday evening or last night.

The students voted to endorse the 'sit-in' already initiated by 150 left-wing extremists yesterday evening.
I've been thinking about what we said last night.

'previous' and 'before'

When you are describing something that happened in the past and you want to refer to an earlier period of time, you use previous or before instead of 'last'. For example, if you are talking about events that happened in 1983 and you want to mention something that happened in 1982, you say that it happened the previous year or the year before.

We had had a row the previous night.
His village had been destroyed the previous summer.
The two had met in Bonn the weekend before.
The quarrel of the night before seemed forgotten.

'before last' You use **before last** to refer to the period of time immediately before the most recent one of its kind. For example, **the year before last** means 'the year before last year'.

Eileen was visiting friends made on a camping holiday <u>the year before last</u>.
'When did he arrive?'—'The afternoon before last.'

'the last' You can also use **last** to refer to any period of time measured back from the present. For example, if it is July 16th and you want to refer to the period from July 2nd to the present, you refer to it as **the last fortnight**. Note that you must use 'the'. If you want to say that something happened during this period, you say that it happened **in the last fortnight** or **during the last fortnight**.

How many passports issued <u>in the last hundred days</u> remain to be checked?
All this has happened <u>during the last few years</u>.

Note the order of words in these examples. You do not say 'the hundred last days' or 'the few last years'.

late - lately

'late' **Late** is used as an adjective or an adverb.

If you are **late** for something, you arrive after the time that was arranged.

I was ten minutes <u>late</u> for my appointment.

You can also say that someone arrives **late**.

Etta arrived <u>late</u>.

You do not say that someone arrives 'lately'.

For another meaning of **late**, see entry at **former - late**.

'lately' You use **lately** to say that something has been happening since a short time ago.

As you know, I've <u>lately</u> been dabbling in psychology.

For more information about this use, see entry at **recently - newly - lately**.

latest - last

You use **latest** or **last** to talk about one of a series of events which is continuing to happen, or one of a series of things which someone is continuing to have or produce.

events If one of a series of events is happening now or has just happened, you refer to it as the **latest** one.

The <u>latest</u> closure marks yet another chapter in the history of Gebeit.

You refer to the event before the latest one as the **last** one. If no event of the kind you are talking about has happened recently, you refer to the most recent one as the **last** one.

...the weeds that had grown since the <u>last</u> harvest.

things you have or produce If someone keeps having or producing a series of things, you refer to the one they have now or the one they have produced most recently as their **latest** one.

...her <u>latest</u> boyfriend.
...his <u>latest</u> novel, 'The Comfort of Strangers'.

You refer to the one before their latest one as their **last** one. If they have not had or produced one recently, you refer to their most recent one as their **last** one.

Loach has not been idle since Family Life, his last film for the cinema.

You can talk about more than one thing in this way by putting **last** in front of a number. For example, you can talk about 'his **last three** books'.

Her last two pictures have been disasters.

lawful

See entry at **legal - lawful - legitimate**.

lawyer

Lawyer is a general term for a person who is qualified to advise people about the law and represent them in court.

'barrister' In Britain, a **barrister** is a lawyer who speaks in the higher courts of law on behalf of either the prosecution or the defence.

'advocate' In Scotland, a barrister is usually called an **advocate**.

'solicitor' In Britain, a **solicitor** is a lawyer who gives legal advice to clients, prepares legal documents and cases, and in certain limited circumstances may represent a client in court.

'attorney' In America, an **attorney** is a lawyer who acts for someone in a legal matter and is qualified to represent them in court.

lay - lie

'lay' **Lay** is a transitive verb, and it is also a past tense of another verb, **lie**.

To **lay** something somewhere means to put it there carefully.

Take the top sheet and lay it in the centre of the bed.

The other forms of 'lay' are **lays, laying, laid**.

He lays the negatives in the frame.
'I couldn't get a taxi,' she said, laying her hand on Nick's sleeve.
She laid the cigarette in the ash-tray.

'lie' used as a verb **Lie** is used as an intransitive verb with two different meanings.

To **lie** somewhere means to be there in a horizontal position, or to get into that position.

She would lie on the floor in her overalls.

When **lie** is used like this, its other forms are **lies, lying, lay, lain**. The past participle **lain** is rarely used.

A dress lies on the floor.
The baby was lying on the table.
I lay in bed in the dormitory.

To **lie** means to say or write something which you know is untrue. When **lie** is used like this, its other forms are **lies, lying, lied**.

Why should he lie to me?
Rudolph was sure that Thomas was lying.
He had lied about never going back.

Lie is also used as a noun. A **lie** is something that someone says or writes which they know is untrue.

He knew that all these statements were lies.

You say that someone **tells** a lie.

I have never told a lie to my pupils.

You do not say that someone 'says' a lie.

lead

Lead is used with various related meanings as a verb, singular noun, or count noun, and with a totally different meaning and pronunciation as an uncount noun.

used as a verb If you **lead** /liːd/ someone somewhere, you show them the way by going in front of them, or by walking beside them holding their hand or arm. The past tense and past participle of 'lead' is **led** /led/, not 'leaded'.

My mother took me by the hand and led me downstairs.

'drive' and 'take' You do not say that you 'lead' someone somewhere in a car. You say that you **drive** or **take** them there.

Ginny drove Mrs Yancy to the airport.
It's his turn to take the children to school.

used as a singular noun The person who has the **lead** in a race or competition is the one who is winning.

This win gave him the overall lead.

You often say that someone is **in the lead**.

Hammond was well in the lead for the first 40 minutes.

used as a count noun A dog's **lead** is a chain or long piece of leather or plastic which is attached to the dog's collar so that you can control the dog.

Always keep your dog on a lead in the street.

used as an uncount noun **Lead** /led/ is a soft, grey, heavy metal.

...the lead spire of the church.

learn

knowledge and skills When you **learn** something, you obtain knowledge or a skill as a result of studying or training. The past tense and past participle of 'learn' can be either **learned** or **learnt**.

She soon learned to paint anything she chose.
He had never learnt to read and write.

'teach' You do not say that you 'learn' someone something or 'learn' them how to do something. The word you use is **teach**.

Mother taught me how to read.

See entry at **teach**.

learning from experience You can use **learn** to say that someone becomes wiser or better able to do something as the result of an experience.

Industry and commerce have learned a lot in the last few years.

You say that someone **learns** something **from** an experience.

They had learned nothing from their early victories.

You do not use any preposition except 'from' in a sentence like this.

information	**Learn** can also be used to say that someone receives some information. After **learn,** you use 'of' and a noun group, or you use a 'that'-clause.

He had learned of his father's death in Australia.
He had learned that the plot had been exposed.

leave

movement from a place	You use **leave** to say that someone moves away from a place in order to go somewhere else. The past tense and past participle of 'leave' is **left,** not 'leaved'.

They left the house to go for a walk after tea.
I'd left Pretoria in a hurry.

Note that you do not say that someone 'leaves from' a place.

'get away from' and 'depart from'	You can also say that someone **gets away from** or **departs from** a place. **Get away from** usually indicates that someone is eager or anxious to leave a place. **Depart** is a formal word.

You've got to get away from home.
When you depart from the airport, you will be driven to Paris.

intransitive uses	You can use **leave** as an intransitive verb.

He stood up to leave.

You can also say that someone **goes, gets away, goes away,** or **departs.**

'I must go,' she said.
She wanted to get away.
I like parents to come into school but I do not like them to go away with a misunderstanding.
They watched the visitor depart as quietly as he had come.

Get away and **go away** are often used to say that someone leaves a place and spends a period of time somewhere else, especially as a holiday.

It's nice to get away in the autumn.
What did you do over the summer? Did you go away?

transport	You can say that a train, ship, or other means of transport **leaves, goes,** or **departs** at a particular time or from a place.

My train leaves Euston at 11.30.
Our train went at 2.25.
Ships carrying toys and books were preparing to depart from Dover.

Note that you do not say that a train or ship 'goes away'.

movement to a place	When a person or vehicle moves away from a place in order to go to another place, you can say that they **leave for** or **depart for** the second place.

She left for Geneva on May 5th.
He would breakfast with his staff and then depart for Germany.

Note that you do not use any preposition except 'for' in sentences like these.

movement from a person	You can say that someone **leaves** or **gets away from** a person or group of people. You use **get away from** to indicate that someone is eager or anxious to move away from the person or group.

I left Conrad and joined the Count at his table.
I wish you could get away from all those people.

Note that you do not say that someone 'departs from' a person or group of people.

If someone tells you to **go away,** they are telling you firmly that they do not want to speak to you or to spend any more time in your company.

There was a knock at the door. 'Go away!' Stroganov called.
Go away now and leave me alone.

left hand - left-handed

'left hand' The **left hand** part of something is the part which is towards your left.

We were on the left hand side of the road.

'left-handed' **Left-handed** people use their left hand rather than their right hand for activities such as writing.

legal - lawful - legitimate

'legal' and **Legal** and **lawful** both mean 'allowed by law'. **Lawful** is a formal word.
'lawful'
Talks have begun for legal retirement at 60.
Capital punishment is legal in many countries.
...lawful publications.
All his activities had been perfectly lawful.

'legitimate' **Legitimate** means 'correct or acceptable according to a law or rule'.

...a legitimate business transaction.

Legitimate can also mean 'justifiable under the circumstances'.

Religious leaders have a legitimate reason to be concerned.

If someone is **legitimate,** their parents were married at the time they were born.

...evidence that he was his father's legitimate son.

another **Legal** also means 'relating to the law'. You cannot use **lawful** or **legitimate**
meaning of with this meaning.
'legal'
...the British legal system.
...legal language.

'law' in front of You use **law,** not 'legal', in front of a noun when you are talking about
nouns someone or something connected with the study of law.

...a law student.
He had only just received his law degree.

Law also appears in the names of some places and institutions connected with the law.

...the Law Courts.
...the Law Society.

legible

See entry at **readable.**

lend

See entry at **borrow - lend.**

less

used in front of nouns

You use **less** in front of an uncount noun to say that one quantity is not as big as another, or that a quantity is not as big as it was before.

A shower uses less water than a bath.
His work gets less attention than it deserves.
In Catherine's case it has led to divorce and much less time for her child.

Less is sometimes used in front of plural nouns.

This proposal will mean less jobs and a dwindling rail network.
Less people are going to university than usual.

Some people object to this use. They say that you should use **fewer** in front of plural nouns, not 'less'.

There are fewer trees here.
The new technology allows products to be made with fewer components than before.

However, **fewer** sounds formal when used in conversation. As an alternative to 'less' or 'fewer', you can use **not as many** or **not so many** in front of plural nouns. These expressions are acceptable in both conversation and writing.

There are not as many cottages as there were.
There aren't so many trees there.

Note that after 'not as many' and 'not so many' you use **as**, not 'than'.

'less than' and 'fewer than'

You use **less than** in front of a noun group to say that an amount or measurement is below a particular point or level.

Half of all working women earned less than twenty pounds a week.
I travelled less than 3000 miles.

Less than is sometimes used in front of a noun group referring to a number of people or things.

The whole of Switzerland has less than six million inhabitants.
The country's standing army consisted of less than a hundred soldiers.

Some people object to this use. They say that you should use **fewer than**, not 'less than', in front of a noun group referring to people or things.

He had never been in a class with fewer than forty children.
In 1900 there were fewer than one thousand university teachers.

You can use **less than** in conversation, but you should use **fewer than** in formal writing.

However, **fewer than** can only be used when the following noun group refers to a number of people or things. You do not use **fewer than** when the noun group refers to an amount or measurement.

'no less than'

You use **no less than** or **no fewer than** in front of a number to show that you think that it is surprisingly large.

By 1880, there were no less than fifty-six coal mines.
No fewer than five cameramen lost their lives.

In formal writing, you should use **no fewer than**, rather than 'no less than'.

'less' used in front of adjectives

Less can be used in front of an adjective to say that someone or something has a smaller amount of a quality than they had before, or a smaller amount than someone or something else has.

From this time on, I felt less guilty.
Most of the other plays were less successful.

You do not use **less** in front of the comparative form of an adjective. You do not say, for example, 'It is less colder than it was yesterday'. You say 'It is **less cold** than it was yesterday'.

'not as ... as' In conversation, people do not usually use **less** in front of adjectives. They do not say, for example, 'It is less cold than it was yesterday'. They say 'It is **not as cold as** it was yesterday'.

No 14 Sumatra Road was not as pretty as Walnut Cottage.

Not so is also sometimes used, but this is less common.

The young otter is not so handsome as the old one.

Note that after 'not as' and 'not so', you use **as,** not 'than'.

let

Let is used to say that someone allows someone else to do something. After the object, you use an infinitive without 'to'.

The farmer lets me live in a caravan behind his barn.
She never lets her leave home.
They sit back and let everyone else do the work.

You do not use a 'to'-infinitive or an '-ing' form after **let.** You do not say, for example, 'He lets me to use his telephone' or 'He lets me using his telephone'.

The past tense and past participle of 'let' is **let,** not 'letted'.

He let Jack lead the way.
She had let him go off with her papers.

There is no passive form of **let.** You do not say, for example, 'He was let go' or 'He was let to go'. If you want to use a passive form, you use a different verb, such as **allow** or **permit.**

Perhaps when he grew up he would be allowed to do as he pleased.
She was the only prisoner permitted to enter my cell.

'let ... know' If you **let** someone **know** something, you tell them about it.

I'll find out about the car and let you know what happened.
It doesn't matter so long as she lets her doctor know.

'let me' People often use **let me** when they are offering to do something for someone.

Let me show you.
Let me help you off with your coat.

For other ways of making an offer, see entry at **Offers.**

another meaning **Let** has another meaning. If you **let** your house or land to someone, you allow them to use it in exchange for regular payments. See entry at **hire - rent - let.**

let go

See entry at **release - let go.**

let's - let us

making a suggestion You use **let's** when you are suggesting that you and someone else should do something. **Let's** is short for 'let us'. It is followed by an infinitive without 'to'.

Let's go outside.
Let's creep forward on hands and knees.

The full form **let us** is used with this meaning only in formal English.

Let us postpone the matter.

If you are suggesting that you and someone else should not do something, you say **let's not.**

Let's not talk about that.
Let's not waste time.

Some British speakers say **don't let's.**

Don't let's tell anyone.

For other ways of making suggestions, see entry at **Suggestions.**

making a request You can use **let us** when you are making a request on behalf of yourself and someone else. In sentences like these, you do not shorten **let us** to 'let's'.

Let us know what progress has been made.
Give us food! Don't let us die.

Letter writing

When you are writing a letter, the language you use and the layout of the letter will depend on how formal the letter is.

formal letters If you are writing a formal letter, such as a business letter or an application for a job, you use formal language, as in the example below.

80 Green Road
Moseley
Birmingham
B13 9PL

29/4/92

The Personnel Manager
Cratex Ltd.
21 Fireside Road
Birmingham
B15 2RX

Dear Sir

I am writing in response to the advertisement your company placed in the Times dated 28/4/92. Could you please send me an application form and details about the job. I have recently graduated from Southampton University in Mechanical Engineering. I look forward to hearing from you soon.

Yours faithfully

J. Laker.

James Laker

Letter writing

address and date You put your address in the top right-hand corner. You can put a comma at the end of each line, and a full stop at the end of the last one, but this is not necessary. You do not put your name above the address.

You put the date under your address. If you are using headed notepaper, you put the date above the address of the person you are writing to or at the right-hand side of the page. You can write the date in several different ways, for example '29.4.92', '29/4/92', '29 April 1992', or 'April 29th, 1992'. Note that in American English the month is put in front of the day, for example '4/29/92'.

You put the name or job title and the address of the person you are writing to on the left-hand side of the page, usually starting on the line below the date.

beginning a formal letter You begin a formal letter with the person's title and surname, for example 'Dear Mr Jenkins', 'Dear Mrs Carstairs', or 'Dear Miss Stephenson'. See entry at **Names and titles** for information on titles.

If you do not know whether the woman you are writing to is married or not, you can use the title 'Ms'. Some younger women prefer 'Ms' to 'Mrs' and 'Miss', especially if they have married but not changed their surname. However, some older women do not like this title.

In less formal letters, people sometimes use the person's first name and surname after 'Dear', for example 'Dear Fiona Smart'.

If you are writing a very formal letter, or do not know the person's name, you use 'Dear Sir' or 'Dear Madam'. If you are not sure whether the person you are writing to is a man or a woman, it is safest to write 'Dear Sir or Madam'. When writing to a company, 'Dear Sirs' is used in British English and 'Gentlemen' in American English.

People writing in the American style put a colon after the 'Dear...' expression, for example 'Dear Mr. Jones:'. If you are writing in the British style, you can either use a comma or have no punctuation.

ending a formal letter If you begin the letter using the person's title and surname (for example 'Dear Mrs Carstairs'), you finish with 'Yours sincerely'. If you want to be less formal, you can finish with 'Yours'. If you begin your letter with 'Dear Sir', 'Dear Madam', or 'Dear Sirs', you finish with 'Yours faithfully'.

In American English, the usual way of finishing a letter is with the expression 'Sincerely yours' or, more formally, 'Very truly yours'.

You write your signature underneath the expression you finish with. You can type your name (or write it in capitals) underneath your signature. If you are writing a business letter, you can also put your job title.

informal letters If you are writing a letter to a friend or relative, you use informal language, as in the example opposite. Informal letters are usually handwritten, although some people type them.

address and date You put your address and the date, or just the date, in the top right-hand corner. You do not put the address of the person you are writing to at the top of the letter.

beginning an informal letter You normally begin an informal letter to a friend using 'Dear' and the person's first name, for example 'Dear Louise'. When people are writing to a relative, they use the person's 'relative' title, for example 'Dear Mum', 'Dear Grandpa', or 'Dear Grandma'. If you are very fond of the friend or relative you are writing to, you can begin your letter with something like 'My dearest Sara' or 'Darling Alison'.

In a handwritten letter, people usually begin the first sentence under the

> 63 Pottery Road
> Birmingham
> B13 8AS
>
> 18/4/92
>
> Dear Mario,
>
>   How are you? Thanks for the letter telling me that you'll be coming over to England this summer. It'll be good to see you again. You must come and stay with me in Birmingham.
>
>   I'll be on holiday when you're here as the University will be closed, so we can have some days out together. Write or phone me to tell me when you want to come and stay.
>
>   All the best,
>
>   Dave

end of the person's name, and start each paragraph a little way in from the left-hand side of the page.

ending an informal letter

The expression you use to end an informal letter with depends on whether you are a man or a woman. 'Love' is used by women in most informal letters, but by men only when writing to close female friends or relatives. 'Yours', 'Best wishes', and 'All the best' are used by men in most informal letters, and by women who are writing to someone they are not particularly fond of. 'Lots of love' is used by men and women when writing to someone they are very fond of, but is not often used by men writing to men.

The expression at the end of an informal letter is usually written towards the right of the page, with the signature a little further to the right.

addressing an envelope

The example at the top of the next page shows how to write the name and address on an envelope. Some people put a comma at the end of each line, and a full stop after the county or country.

You usually use the title, initial or initials, and surname of the person you are writing to. When writing to a married couple, you usually use only the husband's initials, for example 'Mr and Mrs G T Black'.

When writing to a married woman, people used to use her husband's initials. However, people nowadays tend to use the woman's own initials, unless they are sending a very formal letter or writing to someone who prefers the old style of address.

You can also use the person's title, first name, and surname: 'Miss Sarah Wilkins'. When the letter is informal, you can just use their first name and surname, or their initial (or initials) and surname: 'Sarah Wilkins' or 'S Wilkins'.

```
Miss S Wilkins
13 Magpie Close
Guildford
Surrey
GL4 2PX
```

If you are writing to someone who is temporarily staying with someone else or staying in a particular place, you put their name first and then, on the line below, put 'c/o' in front of the name of the other person or the place, as in the example below. 'c/o' stands for 'care of'.

```
Mr JL Martin
c/o Mrs P Roberts
28 Fish Street
Cambridge
CB2 8AS
```

When sending a letter to a place in Britain or the USA, you should put the postcode or zip code (the set of letters and numbers at the end of the address) on a separate line.

lettuce

See entry at **salad - lettuce**.

level

A **level** is a point on a scale, for example a scale of amount or importance.

The noise levels were too high.
We now have a high level of unemployment.
These decisions are made well below the level of top management.

You say that something is **at** a particular level.

Mammals maintain their body temperature at a constant level.
Women must have a voice at all levels in the union.

You do not use any preposition except 'at' in sentences like these.

library

A **library** is a building where books are kept which people can look at or borrow.

A **library** is also a private collection of books, or a room in a large house where books are kept.

'bookshop' You do not refer to a shop where you can buy books as a 'library'. In Britain, a shop like this is called a **bookshop.** In America, it is called a **bookstore.**

licence - license

'licence' In British English, a **licence** is an official document which gives you permission to do, use, or own something.

He was given a marriage licence.
Keep your driving licence on you.

'license' used as a noun In American English, this word is usually spelled **license.**

They had never intended to give Ivor a hunting license.

'license' used as a verb In both British and American English, if you **are licensed** to do something, you have official permission to do it.

These men are licensed to carry firearms.

lie

See entry at **lay - lie.**

lift

If you give someone a **lift,** you drive them in your car from one place to another.

She offered me a lift home.

In British English, a **lift** is also a device that moves up and down inside a tall building and carries people from one floor to another.

I took the lift to the eighth floor.

'elevator' In American English, a device like this is called an **elevator.**

light

If you **light** something such as a cigarette or candle, you make it start burning. The past tense and past participle of 'light' is either **lit** or **lighted.** **Lit** is more common.

He lit a cigarette.
I lighted a candle.

You can say that a street, building, or room **is lit** or **is lighted** by a particular kind of light, for example electricity.

...a room lit by candles.
The room was lighted by a very small, dim bulb.

For both meanings of 'light', you use **lighted,** not 'lit', in front of a noun.

Mitchell took the lighted cigarette from his lips.
I noticed a lighted window across the street.

However, after an adverb you use **lit**.

...a freshly lit cigarette.
...the dimly lit department store.

like

Like is used with one meaning as a preposition or conjunction, and with another meaning as a verb.

used as a preposition

If one person or thing is **like** another, they have similar characteristics or behave in a similar way.

He looked like Clark Gable.
The lake was like a bright blue mirror.

If you ask someone what something is **like**, you are asking them to describe it.

What was Essex like?
What did they taste like?

used as a conjunction

In conversation, you can say that something is **like** you remembered it or **like** you imagined it.

Is it like you remembered it?

In writing, it is better to say that something is **how** you remembered or imagined it.

You can use **like** with 'do' when you are comparing someone's behaviour or appearance to another person's. For example, you can say 'She swims in the lake every day, **like** her mother **did**'. For more information about this use, see entry at **like - as - the way**.

Some speakers use **like** with other verbs to describe how someone or something looks, or how someone behaves.

He did it like he was used to it.

This use is generally regarded as incorrect. Instead of 'like', it is better to use **as if** or **as though**. See entry at **as if**.

used as a verb

If you **like** someone or something, you find them pleasant or attractive.

She's a nice girl, I like her.
Very few of the women liked Saigon.

For a graded list of verbs and expressions used to express liking or dislike, see entry at **like - dislike**.

WARNING

You do not use a continuous tense of **like**. You do not say, for example, 'I am liking peanuts'. You say 'I **like** peanuts'.

You can use **like** in front of an '-ing' form to say that you enjoy an activity.

I like reading.

You can add 'very much' to emphasize how much you like someone or something, or how much you enjoy an activity.

I like him very much.
I like driving very much.

WARNING

Note that you put 'very much' after the object, not after **like**. You do not say, for example, 'I like very much driving'.

If someone asks you if you like something, you can say 'Yes, I **do**.' You do not say 'Yes, I like.'

'Do you like walking?'—'Yes I do, I love it.'

WARNING

You do not use **like** immediately in front of a clause beginning with 'when' or 'if'. For example, you do not say 'I like when I can go home early'. You say 'I **like it** when I can go home early'.

They don't like it when you're nice.
He felt his father would like it if he took some.

'would like'

You say **'Would you like...?'** when you are offering something to someone.

Would you like some coffee?

Note that you do not say 'Do you like some coffee?'

You say **'Would you like...'** followed by a 'to'-infinitive when you are inviting someone to do something.

Would you like to meet him?

Note that you do not use an '-ing' form after **'Would you like...'**. You do not say, for example, 'Would you like meeting him?'

For more information about making invitations, see entry at **Invitations**.

You can say **'I'd like...'** when asking for something in a shop or café.

I'd like some apples, please.

For more information about asking for something, see section on **asking as a customer** in entry at **Requests, orders, and instructions**.

You say **'I'd like you to...'** when you are telling someone to do something in a fairly polite way.

I'd like you to tell them where I am.

For more information about ways of telling people to do something, see section on **orders and instructions** in entry at **Requests, orders, and instructions**.

like - as - the way

used as conjunctions

You can use **like, as,** or **the way** as conjunctions when you are comparing one person's behaviour or appearance to another's. In the clause which follows the conjunction, the verb is usually 'do'.

For example, you can say 'He walked to work every day, **like** his father had done', 'He walked to work every day, **as** his father had done', or 'He walked to work every day, **the way** his father had done'.

How can you live like she does?
They were people who spoke and thought as he did.
Start lending things, the way people did in the war.

Learners used to be taught that only **as** was correct in sentences like these, but this use now sounds rather formal or literary. In conversation, people usually use **like** or **the way**.

used as prepositions

Like and **as** can be used as prepositions, but their meaning is not usually the same. For example, if you do something **like** a particular kind of person, you do it the way that kind of person would do it, although you are not that kind of person.

We worked like slaves.

If you do something **as** a particular kind of person, you are that kind of person.

Over the summer she worked as a waitress.
I can only speak as a married man without children.

like - dislike

The verbs and expressions in the following list are all used to indicate how much someone likes or dislikes something. They are arranged from 'like most' to 'dislike most':

► adore
► love, be crazy about, be mad about, be a great fan of
► like, be fond of, be keen on
► don't mind
► dislike
► hate
► can't stand, can't bear, detest, loathe

likely

used as an adjective

Likely is usually used as an adjective. You say, for example, that something is **likely to** happen.

These services are likely to be available to us all before long.

You can also say that **it is likely that** something will happen.

It is likely that there will be a major use of coal to make oil.

used as an adverb

In conversation, **likely** is sometimes used as an adverb with 'most', 'more than', or 'very' in front of it, or as part of the phrase 'more likely than not'. You do not use it as an adverb on its own.

One pupil will have been taught, most likely, by five people.
More than likely they have only so many rooms on allocation.
More likely than not he will realize he is beaten.

linguistic - linguistics

'linguistic'

Linguistic is an adjective. It means 'related to language'.

…linguistic development between the ages of nought and four.

'linguistics'

Linguistics is a noun. It refers to the study of the ways in which language works.

Are you still doing research into linguistics?

You use **linguistics,** not 'linguistic', in front of another noun when you are talking about something that relates to linguistics.

I'm in the middle of writing a linguistics essay.
I read quite a few linguistics books.

GRAMMAR # Linking adverbials

Linking adverbials are words and phrases which indicate a connection between one clause or sentence and another. They are usually put at the beginning of the clause, or after the subject or the first auxiliary.

It will never be possible to release these criminals. Moreover, as the years go by, there are bound to be other similar cases.
The effect on wild flowers, however, has been enormous.
He has seen it all before and has consequently developed a feeling for what will happen next.

| adding information | Some linking adverbials are used to indicate that you are adding an extra point or piece of information. |

also	at the same time	furthermore	on top of that
as well	besides	moreover	too

His first book was published in 1932, and it was followed by a series of novels. He also wrote a book on British pubs.
This limits both their reliability and their scope. The smaller nations, moreover, cannot afford them.

See also entry at **also - too - as well**.

| giving a parallel | Other linking adverbials are used to indicate that you are giving another example of the same point, or are using the same argument in two different cases. |

again	equally	likewise
by the same token	in the same way	similarly

Retaining nuclear weapons may be significantly different from acquiring them, and, by the same token, relinquishing them may be different from refraining from acquiring them.
I still remember clearly the time and place where I first saw a morning glory in full bloom. Similarly, I remember the first occasion when I saw a peacock spread its tail.

| contrasting | Another group of linking adverbials are used to indicate that you are making a contrast or giving an alternative. |

all the same	even so	nonetheless	still
alternatively	however	on the contrary	then again
by contrast	instead	on the other hand	though
conversely	nevertheless	rather	

They were too good to allow us to score, but all the same they didn't play that well.
I would not have been surprised if he had smashed the bottle in my face. Instead, he sank back in his chair, gasping for breath.
He always had good manners. He was very quiet, though.

See entry at **although - though** for information on the position of 'though'.

| indicating a result | Some linking adverbials are used to indicate that the situation you are about to mention exists because of the fact you have just mentioned. |

accordingly	consequently	so	therefore
as a result	hence	thereby	thus

Sales are still running at a lower rate than a year ago. Consequently stocks, with their attendant cost, have grown.
The terrain was more thickly wooded here, and thus more favourable to the defenders.

'So' is always put at the beginning of the clause.

His father had been a Member of Parliament and Chairman of the Isle of Wight County Council. So, as with so many of his famous family, Sir Charles Baring's own life was dominated by public service.

indicating	Adverbials of time are often used to link two sentences by indicating that		
sequence	one event took place after another.		

afterwards	finally	next	suddenly
at last	immediately	presently	then
at once	instantly	since	within minutes
before long	last	soon	within the hour
eventually	later	soon after	
ever since	later on	subsequently	

Philip had a shrimp salad sandwich with Sy Gootblatt in the Silver Steer restaurant on campus. <u>Afterwards,</u> Sy went back to his office.

See entries at **after - afterwards, finally, last - lastly, presently,** and **soon.**

Some adverbials of time are used to indicate that one event took place or will take place before another.

beforehand	first	meanwhile
earlier	in the meantime	previously

Then he went out to Long Beach to thank his benefactor. Arrangements had been made <u>beforehand,</u> of course.
Ask the doctor to come as soon as possible. <u>Meanwhile,</u> give first-aid treatment.

See also entry at **first - firstly.**

A few adverbials are used to indicate that an event took place at the same time as another event.

at the same time	simultaneously
meanwhile	throughout

Barrie and John very unselfishly offered to go back down. <u>Meanwhile,</u> the Italians were just coming into sight.

listen to

If you **listen to** a sound or **listen to** a person who is talking, you pay attention to the sound or to what the person is saying.

I do my ironing while <u>listening to</u> the radio.
<u>Listen</u> carefully <u>to</u> what he says.
They wouldn't <u>listen to</u> me.

WARNING

Listen is not a transitive verb. You do not say that someone 'listens' a sound or 'listens' a person.

If you have been to a musical performance, you do not usually say that you 'listened to' the music or 'listened to' the performer. You say that you **heard** them.

That was the first time I ever <u>heard</u> Jimi Hendrix.

See also entry at **hear.**

literal - literary - literate

'literal'

The **literal** meaning of a word is its most basic meaning.

She was older than I was, and not only in the <u>literal</u> sense.
Tristan's first words were Tykki Dyw, Cornish for butterfly. Its <u>literal</u> meaning is 'beautiful little thing of God'.

'literary' **Literary** words and expressions are used to create a special effect in poems or novels, and are not usually used in ordinary speech or writing.

'Awaken' and 'waken' are old-fashioned or literary words.

Literary also means 'connected with literature'.

...literary critics.
...literary magazines.

'literate' A **literate** person is able to read and write.

Only half the children are literate.

little - a little

'little' used as an adjective **Little** is usually used as an adjective. You use it to talk about the size of something.

...a little table with a glass top.

See entry at **small - little.**

'a little' used as an adverb **A little** is usually used as an adverb. You use it after a verb, or in front of an adjective or another adverb. It means 'to a small extent or degree'.

The economy is expected to slow down a little.
Trading is thought to have been a little disappointing.
The local football team is doing a little better.
The celebrations began a little earlier than expected.

Note that you do not use **a little** in front of an adjective when the adjective comes in front of a noun.

Several other words and expressions can be used to express degree. For a graded list, see section on **degree** in entry at **Adverbials**. See also section on **submodifiers** in entry at **Adverbs**.

used in front of nouns **Little** and **a little** are also used in front of nouns to talk about quantities. When they are used like this, they do not have the same meaning.

You use **a little** simply to indicate that you are talking about a small quantity or amount of something. When you use **little** without 'a', you are emphasizing that there is only a small quantity or amount of something.

So, for example, if you say 'I have **a little** money', you are simply saying that you have some money. However, if you say 'I have **little** money', you mean that you do not have enough money.

I had made a little progress.
It is clear that little progress was made.

He started a new business with a little help from his friends.
Having an independent allowance will be little help.

used as pronouns **Little** and **a little** can be used in similar ways as pronouns.

Beat in the eggs, a little at a time.
Little has changed.

'not much' In conversation, people do not usually use **little** without 'a'. Instead they use **not much**. For example, instead of saying 'I have little money', they say 'I **haven't got much** money' or 'I **don't have much** money'.

I haven't got much appetite.
You haven't got much to say to me, have you?
We probably don't have much time.
You don't have much contact with other people.

You do not use **little** or **a little** when you are talking about a small number of people or things. You do not say, for example, 'She has a little hens'. You say 'She has **a few** hens'. Similarly, you do not say 'Little people attended his lectures'. You say '**Few** people attended his lectures', or '**Not many** people attended his lectures'. See entry at **few - a few.**

live

If you **live** in a particular place, it is your home.

I have some friends who live in Wandsworth.
I live in a flat just down the road from you.

When you are simply saying that a place is someone's home, you do not use a continuous tense. You only use a continuous tense when you are saying that someone has just moved to a place, or that it is their home for a temporary period.

Her husband had been released from prison and was now living at the house.
Remember that you are living in someone else's home.
We have to leave Ziatur, the town where we have been living.

If you want to say how long you have been living in a place, you use **for** or **since.** You say, for example, 'I have been living here **for** four years', 'I have been living here **since** 1988', or 'I have lived here **since** 1988'. You do not say 'I am living here for four years' or 'I am living here since 1988'.

He has been living in France now for almost two years.
His wife and their youngest child have been living since May 29 on Cistern Key, a tiny island about 40 miles south of Nassau.
She has lived there since she was six.

See entries at **for** and **since.**

'leave'   Do not confuse **live** /lɪv/ with **leave** /liːv/. If you **leave** a place, you go away from it.

We will leave the town by the old road.

See entry at **leave.**

locality - location

'locality'   You can refer to a part of a city or the countryside as a **locality.**

...people living in the same locality.
Young people should be encouraged to have a pride in their locality.

'location'   The **location** of something is the place where it is.

...the size and location of your office.
The location of the new institution has not yet been decided.

lonely - lonesome

'lonely'   In British English, someone who is **lonely** is unhappy because they are alone.

Since he left India he had been lonely and homesick.

'lonesome'   American speakers usually say **lonesome,** not 'lonely'.

I bet you told her how lonesome you were.

long

used to talk about length	You use **long** when you are talking about the length of something.

...an area up to 3000 feet long and 900 feet wide.
How long is that side of the triangle?

talking about distance	You use **a long way** to talk about the distance from one place to another. You say, for example, 'It's **a long way** from here to Birmingham'.

I'm a long way from London.

You do not say 'It's long from here to Birmingham' or 'I'm long from London'.

In negative sentences, you use **far**. You say, for example, 'It's **not far** from here to Birmingham'.

They had rented a villa not far from the Hotel Miranda.

You also use **far** in questions. You say, for example, 'How **far** is it from here to Birmingham?'

How far is Amity from here?

You do not use **long** in negative sentences and questions like these.

When you are talking about the extent of a journey, you use **as far as**, not 'as long as'. You say, for example, 'We walked **as far as** the church'.

Vita and Rosamund went with Harold as far as Bologna.

used to talk about time	In a negative sentence or a question, you can use **long** as an adverb to mean 'a long time'.

Wilkins hasn't been with us long.
Are you staying long?

You can also use **long** to mean 'a long time' after 'too' or in front of 'enough'.

He's been here too long.
You've been here long enough to know what we're like.

However, you do not use **long** with this meaning in any other kind of positive sentence. Instead you use **a long time**.

We may be here a long time.
It may seem a long time to wait.

The comparative and superlative forms **longer** and **longest** can be used with this meaning in any kind of positive sentence.

Uncertainty has persisted longer than expected.
Korda's performance will linger longest in the memory.

Several other words and expressions can be used to say how long something lasts. For a graded list, see section on **duration** in entry at **Adverbials**.

'no longer'	When something that happened in the past does not happen now, you can say that it **no longer** happens or that it does not happen **any longer**.

We no longer feed our infants in this way.
She could not doubt it any longer.

For more information, see section on **any longer** in entry at **any more**.

look

If someone directs their eyes towards something, you say that they **look at** it.

Lang looked at his watch.
She looked at the people around her.

When **look** has this meaning, it must be followed by 'at'. You do not say, for example, 'Lang looked his watch'.

Do not confuse **look** with **see** or **watch**. For an explanation of the differences, see entry at **see - look at - watch**.

If you want to say that someone shows a particular feeling when they look at someone or something, you indicate this using an adverb, not an adjective. For example, you say 'She looked **sadly** at her husband'. You do not say 'She looked sad at her husband'.

Jack looked uncertainly at Ralph.
Wilson looked glumly at Pearson.

'look and see' If you intend to use your eyes to find out if something is the case, you say that you will **see** or **look and see** if it is the case.

Have a look at your wife's face to see if she's blushing.
Now let's look and see whether that's true or not.

You do not say that you will 'look' if something is the case.

You can use **see** to say that you will find out about something, even if you are not talking about using your eyes. For example, you can say 'I'll **see** if George is in his office', and then find out whether George is in his office by making a phone call there.

I'll just see if he's at home.
I'll see if I can borrow a car for the weekend.

used to mean 'seem' **Look** can also be used to mean 'seem' or 'appear'. When you use **look** like this, you use an adjective after it, not an adverb. For example, you say 'She looked **sad**'. You do not say 'She looked sadly'.

You look very pale.
The place looked a bit bare.

You only use **look** to mean 'seem' when talking about the appearance of something.

look after - look for

'look after' If you **look after** someone or something, you take care of them.

She will look after the children during their holidays.
It doesn't worry me who owns the club so long as it is looked after.

'look for' If you **look for** someone or something, you try to find them.

Were you looking for me, Miss Nicandra?
He looked for his shoes under the bed.

look forward to

If you **are looking forward to** something that you are going to experience, you are pleased or excited about it.

They're so much looking forward to the opportunity to watch our programmes.
Is there any particular thing you are looking forward to next year?

WARNING	You do not use this expression without 'to'. You do not say, for example, 'I am looking forward the party'. You also do not say that someone 'is looking forwards to' something.
used with an '-ing' form	You can use an '-ing' form after **look forward to**.

He's looking forward to going home.
I look forward to seeing you in Washington.

You do not use an infinitive after **look forward to**. You do not say, for example, 'He's looking forward to go home'.

loose - lose

'loose'
Loose /luːs/ is an adjective. It means 'not firmly fixed', or 'not tight'.

The doorknob is loose.
Mary wore loose clothes.

'lose'
Lose /luːz/ is a verb. If you **lose** something, you no longer have it, or you cannot find it.

I do not want to lose my job.
The woods are so thick you could lose a cat in them.

The other forms of **lose** are **loses, losing, lost**.

They were willing to risk losing their jobs.
He had lost his passport somewhere.

lorry - truck

'lorry'
In British English, a **lorry** is a large motor vehicle used for transporting goods by road.

'truck'
In American English, a vehicle like this is called a **truck**. In British English, small open lorries are sometimes called **trucks**.

In British English, open vehicles used for transporting goods by rail are sometimes called **trucks**. See entry at **carriage**.

lose

See entry at **loose - lose**.

lot

'a lot of' and 'lots of'
You use **a lot of** or **lots of** in front of a noun when you are talking about a large number of people or things, or a large quantity or amount of something. For example, you can talk about 'a lot of money' or 'lots of money'. **Lots of** is only used in conversation.

A lot of people thought it was funny.
We have quite a lot of newspapers.
There's a lot of research to be done.
You've got lots of time.

When you use **a lot of** or **lots of** in front of a plural count noun, you use a plural form of a verb with it.

A lot of people come to our classes.
Lots of people think that the rust on a nail brings the danger of tetanus.

When you use **a lot of** or **lots of** in front of an uncount noun, you use a singular form of a verb with it.

A lot of money is spent on things that are eaten or drunk between meals.
There is lots of money to be made in advertising.

'a lot' and 'lots'   You use **a lot** to refer to a large quantity or amount of something.

I'd learnt a lot.
I feel that we have a lot to offer.

You use **a lot** as an adverb to mean 'to a great extent' or 'often'.

You like Ralph a lot, don't you?
They talk a lot about equality.

Many other words and expressions can be used to say that something is the case to a smaller or greater extent. For a graded list, see section on **degree** in entry at **Adverbials.**

You also use **a lot** in front of comparatives. For example, if you want to emphasize the difference in age between two things, you can say that one thing is **a lot older** than the other.

The weather's a lot warmer there.
I've known people who were in a lot more serious trouble than you.

You also use **a lot** or **lots** with 'more' to emphasize the difference between two quantities or amounts. **Lots** is only used in conversation.

He had gained a lot more sleep than the others.
She meets lots more people than I do.

Far is used in a similar way.

He had to process far more information than before.
Professional training was provided in far more forms than in Europe.

loudly

See entry at **aloud - loudly.**

love

The verb **love** is usually used to express a strong feeling of affection for a person or place.

She loved her husband deeply.
He had loved his aunt very much.
He loved his country above all else.

If you want to say that something gives you pleasure, or that you enjoy a person's company, you usually say **like,** not 'love'.

I like reading.
We liked him very much.

In conversation, people sometimes use **love** to emphasize that they like a thing or activity very much.

I love your new hairdo.
I love reading his plays.

For a list of words and expressions used to express liking, see entry at **like - dislike.**

low - lowly

'low'   **Low** is used as an adjective or an adverb.

Something that is **low** measures a short distance from the bottom to the top.

...a low brick wall.
...low hills.

You also say that something is **low** when it is very close to the ground.

She made a low curtsey.
...a chain hanging in a low loop across the inner arch.

You can use **low** as an adverb to say that something moves close to the ground. For example, you can say 'He bowed **low**'.

I asked him to fly low over the beach.

Note that you do not say 'He bowed lowly' or 'I asked him to fly lowly over the beach'.

Low also means 'small in amount, value, or degree'.

...workers on low incomes.
...low expectations.

Low is not used as an adverb with this meaning, except in front of 'paid'.

As with most low paid women's work, it's dull, repetitive and labour intensive.

Like the adjective, the adverb **low** has the comparative and superlative forms **lower, lowest.**

In a series of quick, jerky movements he bent lower and lower.
...the lowest paid workers in the country.

'lowly'   **Lowly** is an adjective. It is a literary word meaning 'low in rank, status, or importance'.

...a lowly employee.
...his lowly social origins.

The comparative and superlative forms of 'lowly' are **lowlier** and **lowliest.**

luck

Luck is success that comes to you by accident rather than by your own efforts.

I had some wonderful luck.
All he did was shake hands and wish me luck.

Luck is an uncount noun. You do not talk about 'lucks' or 'a luck'.

lucky

You say that someone is **lucky** when something nice happens to them, or when they always seem to have good luck.

You're a lucky girl.
He was the luckiest man in the world.

'happy'   You do not use **lucky** to say that someone has feelings of pleasure and contentment. The word you use is **happy.**

Sarah's such a happy person.
Barbara felt tremendously happy.

luggage - baggage

In British English, both these words refer to the bags and suitcases that you take with you when you travel, together with their contents. **Luggage** is more common than **baggage.**

In American English, **luggage** refers to empty bags and suitcases. **Baggage** refers to bags and suitcases with their contents.

Both these words are uncount nouns. You do not talk about 'luggages' or 'a baggage'.

lunch

See entry at **dinner**.

luxury - luxurious

'luxury'   **Luxury** is great comfort among beautiful and expensive surroundings.

We lived in great luxury.
...a life of luxury.

Luxury is often used as an adjective in front of a noun. You use it to talk about a class of comfortable, expensive things, or to identify something as belonging to such a class.

The Government eliminated rent controls on luxury apartments.
...a luxury car for the President.

Note that although you can talk about 'luxury goods', you do not talk about 'luxury things'. Instead you say **luxuries.**

We are not able to afford luxuries.

'luxurious'   You use **luxurious** to describe something as being comfortable and expensive, without identifying it as belonging to a particular class. You can use words like 'very' and 'more' in front of **luxurious.**

He let himself fall into the most luxurious of the armchairs.

GRAMMAR   **'-ly' words**

adverbs related   Most **'-ly' words** are adverbs of manner, aspect, opinion, degree, or extent.
to adjectives   They are formed from adjectives and have a similar meaning to the adjective.

They were hoping to bring a quick end to the civil war.
...tasks that I would ordinarily have expected to finish quickly and easily.

She succeeded in retaining her political independence.
...where societies remained politically independent of their neighbours.

This is hardly surprising.
Surprisingly, I was not dismissed.

It is very easy to do severe damage to your eyes.
The roots are severely damaged.

Usually you just add '-ly' to the end of an adjective when forming an adverb.

bad — badly
beautiful — beautifully
quiet — quietly
safe — safely

Sometimes a spelling change has to be made, depending on the ending of the adjective.

	adjective	adverb
'-le' changes to '-ly'	gentle	gently
'-y' changes to '-ily'	easy	easily
'-ic' changes to '-ically'	automatic	automatically
'-ue' changes to '-uly'	true	truly
'-ll' changes to '-lly'	full	fully

Note that:

● the adverb related to 'whole' is spelled 'wholly'

● one-syllable adjectives ending in '-y' usually have '-ly' added in the normal way: 'wryly', 'shyly'

● the adverb related to 'dry' can be spelled 'drily' or 'dryly'

● the adverb formed from 'public' is 'publicly'

For more information about '-ly' adverbs of manner, aspect, opinion, degree, and extent, see entry at **Adverbials.**

adverbs related to nouns   The adverbs in the following examples are formed from nouns, not from adjectives.

The other change, <u>namely</u> the increase in electronic equipment, has slowed down.
Here the problem is <u>partly</u> economic.
I am <u>purposely</u> picking out examples of children with mixed rates of development.

adverbs not related to adjectives or nouns   A few '-ly' adverbs are not directly related to any adjective or noun.

accordingly	manfully	presumably
exceedingly	mostly	

This way you have a clear picture of how much you have to repay and can plan <u>accordingly</u>.
I could just see Simon <u>manfully</u> wielding a shovel.

'-ly' adjectives   Some '-ly' words are adjectives, not adverbs.

Current solar cells are too <u>costly</u> for commercial use.
...an <u>elderly</u> man with bushy eyebrows.
My husband said how <u>lonely</u> he had been while I was away.
I mustn't ask <u>silly</u> questions any more.

WARNING   You cannot form adverbs from these adjectives. However, you can use them in prepositional phrases with nouns such as 'way', 'manner', or 'fashion'. For example, you can say 'He smiled in a friendly way'.

Note that 'kindly' is used as an adjective and an adverb. See entry at **kindly.**

adjectives related to nouns   Many adjectives ending in '-ly' are formed from nouns referring to people, and indicate a quality that those people typically have or should have.

brotherly	friendly	miserly	saintly	soldierly
cowardly	gentlemanly	motherly	scholarly	womanly
fatherly	manly	neighbourly	sisterly	

Tell them how <u>cowardly</u> you were as a boy at school.
He assumed an expression of <u>saintly</u> resignation.
She treated him in a cordial, <u>sisterly</u> way.

adjectives and adverbs	Some '-ly' words are both adjectives and adverbs. They are related to nouns and describe things that happen at regular intervals.

daily	hourly	quarterly	yearly
fortnightly	monthly	weekly	

...daily or weekly visits to a children's clinic.
Maids were usually paid monthly.

M

machine

A **machine** is a piece of equipment which uses electricity or some other form of power to perform a particular task.

...a washing machine.
...a machine which could perform calculations.

'motor'
When a machine operates by electricity, you refer to the part of the machine that converts power into movement as the **motor**.

'engine'
You do not use **machine** to refer to the part of a vehicle that provides the power that makes the vehicle move. This part of a car, bus, lorry, or plane is usually called the **engine**.

He couldn't get his engine started.
The starboard engines were already running.

You talk about the **engine** of a ship, but the **motor** of a small boat.

Black smoke belched from the engine into the cabin.
We patched leaks, overhauled the motor, and refitted her.

machinery

You can refer to machines in general as **machinery**.

Machinery is being introduced to save labour.
...a manufacturer of farm machinery.

Machinery is an uncount noun. You do not talk about 'machineries' or 'a machinery'. However, you can talk about a **piece of machinery**.

He was called out to do some work on a piece of machinery that had broken down.

mad

In the past, when someone had a mental illness which made them behave in strange ways, people used to say that they were **mad** or **insane**. Nowadays these words are not usually used about living people, as they are thought to be offensive. People usually say that someone is **mentally ill**.

They were found to be <u>mentally ill</u>.
...the treatment of <u>mentally ill</u> patients.

A number of other words are used to talk about people who have a mental illness. These words are discussed in the entry at **madness**.

other meanings of 'mad'

It is fairly common to describe a foolish action or proposal as **mad** or **insane**.

Anyone could see it was a <u>mad</u> idea.
...the Community's <u>insane</u> agricultural policy.

In conversation, **mad** is sometimes used to mean 'angry'. If you are **mad at** someone, you are angry with them.

Jeannie gets <u>mad</u> when you talk like that.
I guess that they're <u>mad at</u> me for getting them up so early.

'mad about'

If you are **mad about** something that has happened, you are angry about it.

She was <u>mad about</u> missing a projected holiday in Juan-les-Pins.

If you are **mad about** something such as an activity, you like or enjoy it very much.

How is Rosalind? Still <u>mad about</u> ponies?
She loved dancing and was <u>mad about</u> the cinema.

You do not use **mad** in any of these ways in formal writing.

made

Made is the past tense and past participle of the verb **make**. See entry at **make**.

'made from' and 'made of'

If one thing has been produced from another in such a way that the original thing is completely changed, you can say that the first thing is **made from**, **made out of**, or **made of** the second thing.

Our rope was <u>made from</u> ordinary hemp.
...artificial meat <u>made out of</u> soya-bean protein.
...cloth <u>made of</u> goats' hair.

If you want to indicate that one thing has been produced from another in an unusual or surprising way, you usually use **made out of**.

...a loincloth <u>made out of</u> a kitchen towel.

If you are mentioning the parts or materials from which something is constructed, you use **made of** or **made out of**. You do not use 'made from'.

My cabin was <u>made of</u> logs.

madness

You should be careful which words you use to refer to someone who has an abnormal mental condition. The adjectives **mad, insane, crazy, demented,** and **deranged,** and the nouns **lunatic, maniac,** and **madman** are usually avoided nowadays in serious speech and writing because they are thought to be offensive.

Instead, you can say that someone is **mentally ill**. If their condition is less severe, you can say that they are **mentally disturbed** or **unbalanced**, or that they have **psychological problems**.

At least ninety percent of the men and women who kill themselves are <u>mentally ill</u>.

...an institution for <u>mentally disturbed</u> children.
...the area of the jail reserved for women <u>with psychological problems.</u>

magazine

A **magazine** is a weekly or monthly publication containing articles, photographs, and advertisements.

'shop'   You do not use **magazine** to refer to a building or part of a building where things are sold. The word you use is **shop.**

magic - magical

'magic' used as a noun   **Magic** is a special power that occurs in children's stories and that some people believe exists. It can make apparently impossible things happen.

Janoo-Bai was suspected of practising <u>magic.</u>

'magic' used as an adjective   You use **magic** in front of a noun to indicate that an object or utterance does things or appears to do things by magic.

...<u>magic</u> mushrooms.
...the <u>magic</u> password.

'magical'   **Magical** can be used with a similar meaning.

...<u>magical</u> garments.
...a <u>magical</u> food.

You also use **magical** to say that something involves magic or is produced by magic.

...<u>magical</u> processes.
Explanations are found for what seemed <u>magical.</u>

another meaning   **Magic** and **magical** can also be used to say that something is wonderful and exciting.

...a truly <u>magic</u> moment.
The journey had lost its <u>magical</u> quality.

mail

See entry at **post - mail.**

majority

If something is true of **the majority** of the people or things in a group, it is true of more than half of them.

The <u>majority</u> of young mothers are totally dependent on their husbands' salaries.
This is true in the <u>majority</u> of cases.

When **the majority** is not followed by 'of', you can use either a singular or plural form of a verb after it.

This tax will soon be abolished as far as the majority <u>is</u> concerned.
The majority <u>feel</u> threatened by change.

However, when you use **the majority of** followed by a plural noun or pronoun, you must use a plural form of a verb after it.

The majority of birds <u>have</u> much to gain from remaining inconspicuous.

'most of'   You do not use **the majority** when you are talking about an amount of something or part of something. You do not say, for example, 'The majority of the forest has been cut down'. You say '**Most of** the forest has been cut down'.

<u>Most of</u> the wood was rotten.

Mrs Leonard did <u>most of</u> the work.

See entry at **most**.

make

Make is a very common verb which is used in many different ways. The past tense and past participle of 'make' is **made.**

performing an action

Make is most commonly used to say that someone performs an action. For example, if someone suggests something, you can say that they **make** a suggestion. If someone promises something, you can say that they **make** a promise.

I think that I <u>made</u> the wrong decision.
He <u>made</u> the shortest speech I have ever heard.
In <u>1978</u> he <u>made</u> his first visit to Australia.

Here is a list of common nouns that you can use with **make** in this way:

arrangement	enquiry	point	speech	visit
choice	journey	promise	suggestion	
comment	noise	remark	tour	
decision	plan	sound	trip	

You do not use **make** when you are talking generally about action, rather than mentioning a particular action. Instead you use **do.** For example, if someone is unsure what action to take, you do not say they do not know what to 'make'. You say that they do not know what to **do.**

What have you <u>done</u>?
You've <u>done</u> a lot to help us.
We'll see what can be <u>done</u>.

making an object or substance

If you **make** an object or substance, you construct or produce it.

Sheila <u>makes</u> all her own clothes.
You can <u>make</u> petroleum out of coal.

You can also say that someone **makes** a meal or a drink.

I <u>made</u> his breakfast.

See entry at **cook**.

When **make** is used to talk about constructing or producing something, it can have an indirect object. You say that you **make** someone something, or **make** something **for** them.

I have <u>made</u> you a drink.
We <u>made</u> collars for the horses.
I shall have a copy <u>made for</u> you.

making someone do something

If someone forces you to do something, you can say that they **make you do** it.

You've got to <u>make him listen</u>.
He meant to <u>make them sit still</u>.

Note that in active sentences like these, you do not use a 'to'-infinitive after **make**. You do not say, for example, 'You've got to make them to listen'.

However, in passive sentences you must use a 'to'-infinitive.

He is <u>made to pay back</u> the debt.
One old woman <u>was made to wait</u> more than an hour.

| used to mean 'be' | **Make** is sometimes used instead of 'be' to say how successful someone is in a particular job or role. For example, instead of saying 'He will be a good prime minister', you can say 'He will **make** a good prime minister'. |

You really mean it when you say he'll make a good president?
They make a good team.

| used as a noun | **Make** is sometimes used as a noun. The **make** of something such as a car or radio is the name of the company that made it. |

My own boots were a different make.

Make is usually followed by 'of' and another noun. After **makes of** you use either the plural or singular form of a noun. For example, you can say 'We sell all makes of **cars**' or 'We sell all makes of **car**'. The singular form is more formal.

There are now over a hundred makes of micro-computers for sale.
...tests on well-known makes of car.

After **make of** you use the singular form of a noun.

She can spot the make of typewriter a secretary is using.

make up

See entry at **comprise**.

male - masculine

| 'male' | **Male** means 'relating to the sex that cannot have babies'. You can use **male** as an adjective to talk about either people or animals. |

...male nurses.
...a young male chimpanzee.

You can use **male** as a noun to talk about an animal.

The males establish a breeding territory.

You do not usually use **male** as a noun to talk about men or boys.

| 'masculine' | **Masculine** means 'typical of men, rather than women'. |

...masculine pride.
...a masculine cough.

You do not use **masculine** to talk about animals.

Male and female

| pronouns and determiners | The fact that you are referring to a male person or a female person makes a difference grammatically only when you are using personal pronouns, reflexive pronouns, possessive pronouns, or possessive determiners. |

She sat twisting her hands together.
When he had finished he washed his hands and face.
She managed to free herself.

See entries at **Possessive determiners** and **Pronouns**.

If you are referring to more than one person, there is only one pronoun or determiner of each type to use. For example, the subject pronoun you use to refer to a group of men, a group of women, a group of men and women, or one man and one woman together is 'they'.

Boys are taught that they mustn't show their feelings.
People were looking to me as though they thought I might know the secret.
They had been married for forty-seven years.

'she' and 'her' for things

Although 'it' and 'its' are generally used when referring to a thing, 'she' and 'her' are sometimes used when referring to countries, ships, and cars.

Mr Gerasimov has a high regard for Britain and her role in Europe.
When the repairs had been done she was a fine and beautiful ship.

modifiers

If you need to indicate someone's sex when using a noun to refer to them, you can use 'woman', 'female', or 'male' in front of the noun. You do not use 'man' in front of a noun.

We went to the home of a woman factory worker named Liang.
A female employee was dismissed because her husband was working for a rival firm.
He asked some other male relatives for help.

Note that 'women', not 'woman', is used in front of a plural noun.

I did a survey on women lawyers.

nouns referring to males or females

English nouns are not generally masculine, feminine, or neuter. Some nouns, however, are used to refer only to males and others only to females.

He announced that he was a policeman.
The bride was very young.

Words that refer only to women often end in '-ess', for example 'actress', 'waitress', and 'hostess'. Another ending is '-woman', as in 'policewoman'.

She told me she intended to be an actress.
...Margaret Downes, who is this year's chairwoman of the examination committee.

Fewer words ending in '-ess' are used in modern English than were used in the past. For example, people nowadays refer to a woman who writes books as an 'author', not an 'authoress'.

male relatives

The following words are used to refer to male relatives:

brother	godfather	husband	stepbrother
brother-in-law	godson	nephew	stepfather
father	grandfather	son	stepson
father-in-law	grandson	son-in-law	uncle

female relatives

The following words are used to refer to female relatives:

aunt	godmother	mother-in-law	stepdaughter
daughter	grandmother	niece	stepsister
daughter-in-law	granddaughter	sister	stepmother
goddaughter	mother	sister-in-law	wife

men with a particular job or rank

The following words are used to refer to men who have a particular occupation or rank:

barber	craftsman	lord	salesman
barman	duke	mailman	schoolmaster
baron	emperor	marquis	seaman
baronet	fisherman	master	serviceman
businessman	footman	monk	sportsman
butler	gunman	orderly	squire
churchman	hangman	playboy	steward
clergyman	headmaster	policeman	stunt man
commissionaire	host	postman	valet
con-man	king	postmaster	waiter
count	knight	prince	workman

women with a particular job or rank

The following words are used to refer to women who have a particular occupation or rank:

actress	duchess	mistress	spokeswoman
air hostess	empress	nun	sportswoman
ballerina	governess	policewoman	stewardess
barmaid	headmistress	postmistress	stunt woman
baroness	hostess	priestess	usherette
chairwoman	housewife	princess	waitress
chambermaid	maid	proprietress	
comedienne	manageress	queen	
countess	matron	schoolmistress	

other male people

These words are also used to refer only to men or boys:

bachelor	bridegroom	fiancé	lad	suitor
boy	buddy	gentleman	man	widower
boyfriend	chap	guy	schoolboy	

Note that you do not usually refer to a man or boy as a 'male'.

other female people

These words are also used to refer only to women or girls:

blonde	fiancée	lady	widow
bride	girl	lass	woman
bridesmaid	girlfriend	mistress	
brunette	goddess	schoolgirl	
countrywoman	heiress	spinster	

Note that you should not refer to a woman as a 'female', as some people find this offensive.

'-man' and '-person'

Words ending in '-man' are used either to refer only to men or to refer to both men and women. For example, a 'workman' is a man, but a 'spokesman' can be a man or a woman. The words ending in '-man' in the lists of male words above are generally used to refer only to men.

When women begin to do a job that used to be done only by men, the word ending in '-man' is sometimes still used. Sometimes a new word is invented to refer to women doing the job, for example 'policewoman'. However, it is becoming more common to use terms which do not indicate the sex of the person who has a particular job. For example, 'police officer' is used instead of 'policeman' or 'policewoman', and 'head teacher' is used instead of 'headmaster' or 'headmistress'. Words ending in '-person' are also sometimes used. See entries at **chairman** and **spokesman**.

nationality words A few nouns which refer to a person of a particular nationality are used only for a man or only for a woman, for example 'Englishman' and 'Englishwoman'. See entry at **Nationality words**.

nouns referring to animals Most names of animals are used to refer to both male and female animals, such as 'cat', 'elephant', and 'sheep'.

In some cases there are different words that refer specifically to male animals or female animals. For example, a 'ram' is a male sheep and a 'ewe' is a female sheep. However, most of these words are rarely used, or are used mainly by people who have a special interest in animals, such as farmers or vets. The ones most commonly used are 'bull' (for a male cow) and 'hen' (for a female chicken).

man

A **man** is an adult male human being. The plural of 'man' is **men**, not 'mans'.

Larry was a handsome man in his early fifties.
He was visited by two men in the morning.

Man is sometimes used to refer to human beings in general. For example, instead of saying 'Human beings are destroying the environment', you can say '**Man** is destroying the environment'. Note that when **man** has this meaning, you do not use 'the' in front of it.

Man is a rational animal.
...the most dangerous substance known to man.

Men is sometimes used to refer to all human beings, considered as individuals.

All men are born equal.
Darwin concluded that men were descended from apes.

'mankind' **Mankind** is used to refer to all human beings, considered as a group.

You have performed a valuable service to mankind.

Some people object to the use of **man, men,** and **mankind** to refer to human beings of both sexes, because they think it suggests that men are more important than women.

another meaning of 'man' In conversation, a woman's boyfriend or the man she is married to can be referred to humorously as her **man**.

The two women have abandoned their men and are going to spend an evening in town.

'husband' However, you do not usually refer to the man a woman is married to as her 'man'. You refer to him as her **husband**.

manage

If you **manage to do** something, you succeed in doing it.

Manuelito managed to avoid capture.
Did you manage to get anything to eat?

Note that you use a 'to'-infinitive, not an '-ing' form, after **manage**.

'arrange'
You do not use a 'that'-clause after **manage**. You do not say, for example, that you 'manage that something is done'. You say that you **arrange for it to be done.**

He had arranged for roadblocks to be erected.

You also do not say that you 'manage that someone does something'. You say that you **arrange for them to do it.**

I had arranged for a photographer to take pictures of the body.

manifestation

A **manifestation** of something is a sign that it is happening or that it exists.

...the first manifestations of the Computer Revolution.

'demonstration'
You do not use **manifestation** to refer to a public meeting or march held to show opposition to something or support for something. The word you use is **demonstration.**

The opposition staged a huge demonstration.
There were a series of demonstrations against the visit.

See entry at **demonstration.**

mankind

See entry at **man.**

manufacture

Manufacture refers to the making of a product using machinery. **Manufacture** is an uncount noun.

...the manufacture of nuclear weapons.

'factory'
You do not use **manufacture** to refer to a building where machines are used to make things. A building like this is usually called a **factory.** See entry at **factory.**

many

You use **many** immediately in front of the plural form of a noun to talk about a large number of people or things.

Many girls report that the experience is unpleasant.
Capital punishment is legal in many countries.

'many of'
When you want to talk about a large number of the people or things belonging to a particular group, you use **many of** in front of a plural pronoun, or in front of a plural noun group beginning with 'the', 'these', 'those', or a possessive.

Many of them are being forced to give up.
Many of the inhabitants had fair skins.
To the outside world many of these displays would be meaningless.
Many of his books are still available.
This enables scientists to confirm many of Einstein's ideas about relativity.

'many' used as a pronoun
Many is sometimes used as a pronoun to refer to a large group of people or things. This is a fairly formal use.

Many were still lying where they had been injured.

WARNING
You do not use **many** or **many of** to talk about a large quantity or amount of something. Instead you use **much** or **much of.** See entry at **much.**

'many more' You can use **many** with 'more' to emphasize the difference in size between two groups of people or things.

I know many more country people than I do town people.
Why does man seem to have many more diseases than animals have?

mark

A **mark** is a small stain or damaged area on a surface.

...grease marks.
There seems to be a dirty mark on it.

A **mark** is also a number or letter which indicates your score in a test or examination.

You need 120 marks out of 200 to pass.

Mark sometimes appears in the name of a vehicle or machine, followed by a number.

...the Harvard Mark 1.

'make' However, you do not refer to a type of product as a 'mark'. If you want to indicate which company makes a product, you use the noun **make**.

She couldn't tell what make of car he was driving.

See entry at **make**.

marmalade

Marmalade is a sweet food made from oranges, lemons, limes, or grapefruit. In Britain, people spread it on bread or toast and eat it as part of their breakfast.

'jam' and 'jelly' Note that in English **marmalade** refers only to a food made from oranges, lemons, limes, or grapefruit. You do not use it to refer to a similar food made from some other fruit, for example blackberries, strawberries, or apricots. A food like this is called **jam** in British English, and **jam** or **jelly** in American English.

marriage

Marriage refers to the state of being married, or to the relationship between a husband and wife.

I never wanted marriage.
It has been a happy marriage.

You can also use **marriage** to refer to the act of getting married.

Victoria's marriage to her cousin was not welcomed by her family.

'wedding' However, you do not usually use **marriage** to refer to the ceremony in which two people get married. The word you use is **wedding**.

He had been invited to the wedding.

married - marry

'married to' If you are **married to** someone, they are your husband or wife.

Her daughter was married to a Frenchman.

'marry' When you **marry** someone, you become their husband or wife during a special ceremony.

I wanted to marry him.

Note that you do not say that someone 'marries to' someone else.

'get married'   You do not usually use **marry** without an object. You do not say, for example, that a person 'marries' or that two people 'marry'. You say that they **get married**.

I'm getting married next month.
When they got married, he wanted a big ceremony.

In stories, **marry** is sometimes used without an object. This is an old-fashioned use.

Your sister and I have every right to marry if we wish to.

marsh - bog - swamp

These three words all refer to areas of very wet land.

'marsh'   A **marsh** is any area of low land that is wet and muddy because water cannot drain away from it properly.

'bog'   A **bog** is an area of very soft, wet land which is dangerous to cross. Bogs consist of decaying plant material.

'swamp'   A **swamp** is a wild area of very wet land with flowers and sometimes trees growing in it.

masculine

See entry at **male - masculine**.

match

If one thing has the same colour or design as another thing, you say that the first thing **matches** the other thing.

The lampshades matched the curtains.
The lilac of the beads round her neck did not quite match the dress.

You do not say that one thing 'matches to' another thing.

mathematics

Mathematics is the study of numbers, quantities, and shapes. When mathematics is taught as a subject at school, it is usually called **maths** in British English, and **math** in American English.

I enjoyed maths and that was my best subject.
...methods for teaching English or Math.

When you are talking about mathematics as a science, rather than as a subject taught at school, you call it **mathematics,** not 'maths' or 'math'.

...the laws of mathematics.

All these words are uncount nouns and are used with a singular form of a verb. So, for example, you say 'Maths **is** my favourite subject'. You do not say 'Maths are my favourite subject'.

matter

talking about   The **matter** is used after 'what', 'something', 'anything', or 'nothing' to talk
a problem   about a problem or difficulty. You use **the matter** as if it was an adjective like 'wrong'. For example, instead of saying 'Is something wrong?' you can say 'Is something **the matter**?'

What's the matter?

There's something the matter with your eyes.
Is anything the matter?
They told me there was nothing the matter.

You do not use **the matter** with this meaning in other types of sentence. You do not say, for example, 'The matter is that we don't know where she is'. Instead you say **the problem** or **the trouble**.

The problem is that she can't cook.
The trouble is wars are not the product of rational thought, they're the product of emotions.

'It doesn't matter' When someone apologizes to you, you can say '**It doesn't matter.**' You do not say 'No matter'.

'I've only got dried milk.'—'It doesn't matter.'

For other ways of replying to an apology, see entry at **Apologizing**.

'no matter' You use **no matter** in expressions such as 'no matter what' and 'no matter how' to indicate that something happens or is true in all circumstances.

They smiled almost continuously, no matter what was said.
I told him to report to me after the job was completed, no matter how late it was.

You do not use **no matter** to mention something which makes your main statement seem surprising. You do not say, for example, 'No matter the rain, we carried on with the game'. You say '**In spite of** the rain, we carried on with the game'.

In spite of poor health, my father was always cheerful.
The morning air was still clear and fresh in spite of all the traffic.

used as a count noun A **matter** is a situation that someone has to deal with.

It was a purely personal matter.
She's very honest in money matters.
This is a matter for the police.

You can use the plural form **matters** to refer to a situation that has just been discussed.

There is only one applicant, which simplifies matters.
The murder of Jean-Marie will not help matters.

When **matters** has this meaning, you do not put 'the' in front of it.

may

See entry at **might - may**.

maybe - perhaps

You use **maybe** or **perhaps** to indicate that something is possible, although you are not certain about it. There is no difference in meaning between these words.

Maybe he was wrong.
Perhaps Andrew is right after all.

Maybe is normally used only at the beginning of a clause.

Maybe he'll be prime minister one day.
If you begin, maybe other customers will come.

Perhaps can be used in other positions in a clause.

If you live in the country, you can, perhaps, profit by buying and freezing local produce.
The Allies had better luck, perhaps, than they deserved.
It was perhaps Ellen's unconventional approach to life that made her such a great actress.

Many other words can be used to indicate how certain you are about something. For a graded list, see section on **probability** in entry at **Adverbials.**

WARNING

Do not confuse **maybe** /meɪbiː/ with **may be** /meɪbiː/. **May be** is used in sentences such as 'He may be the best person for the job'. See entry at **might - may.**

me

Me is used as the object of a verb or preposition. You use **me** to refer to yourself.

He told me about it.
He looked at me reproachfully.

WARNING

In standard English, you do not use **me** as the indirect object of a sentence when 'I' is the subject. You do not say, for example, 'I got me a drink'. You say 'I got **myself** a drink'.

I poured myself a small drink.
I had set myself a time limit of two years.

In standard English, you do not use **me** as part of the subject of a sentence. You do not say, for example, 'Me and my friend are leaving'. You say '**My friend and I** are leaving'.

My sister and I were a bit worried.
Father and I both saw him.

'it's me'

If you are asked 'Who is it?', you can say 'It's **me**', or just '**Me**'.

'Who is it?'—'It's me, Frank Rogers.'

It used to be considered correct to say 'It is I', but no one says this now.

In conversation, if you want to emphasize that something applies to you rather than to anyone else, you can say '**it's me...**' followed by a relative clause. For example, instead of saying 'She wants me', you can say '**It's me** she wants'. Note that you do not say 'It's I she wants'.

As long as it's me who's doing it, then it's all right.

In sentences like this, you can say '**I'm the one...**' instead of 'it's me...'.

I'm always the one who's got to do the talking.
I'm the one who gets sued if things don't go the way they should go.

If someone asks who did something, you can say '**Me**' or '**I did**'. You do not say 'I'.

'I'm all for decent reserve.'—'Who mentioned "decent"?'—'I did.'

Meals

The meanings of words referring to meals, and the ways that these words are used, are explained below. Some words for meals are used by different people to refer to different meals.

'breakfast'   **Breakfast** is the first meal of the day. You eat it in the morning, just after you get up.

'dinner'   In Britain, people usually call their main meal of the day **dinner.** Some people have this meal in the middle of the day, and others have it in the evening.

However, some people call their main meal **tea** or **supper,** if they eat it in the evening.

'lunch'   People who call their evening meal 'dinner' usually refer to a meal eaten in the middle of the day as **lunch.**

'luncheon'   **Luncheon** is a formal and rather old-fashioned word for 'lunch'.

'tea'   **Tea** can be a light meal eaten in the afternoon, usually consisting of sandwiches and cakes, with tea to drink. This meaning of 'tea' is used mainly in Britain, by middle-class people. The expression **afternoon tea** is often used in hotels and restaurants.

Tea can also be a main meal that is eaten in the early evening. This meaning of 'tea' is often used by working-class people in Britain. It is also more common in northern parts of Britain, and in Australia and New Zealand. The expression **high tea** is also used in Britain.

'supper'   Some people call a large meal they eat in the early part of the evening **supper.** Other people use **supper** to refer to a small meal eaten just before going to bed at night.

more formal terms   You can refer to a meal that you eat in the middle of the day as a **midday meal.** Similarly, you can refer to a meal that you eat in the evening as an **evening meal.** However, these terms are not normally used in conversation to refer to meals eaten at home, only to meals provided for you, for example at school or in lodgings.

'at' and 'over'   You indicate that someone does something while they are having a meal using the preposition **at.**

He had told her at lunch that he couldn't take her to the game tomorrow.
Mrs Zapp was seated next to me at dinner.

However, you usually use **over** when talking about an event that takes some time, especially when saying that people discuss something while having a meal.

It's often easier to discuss difficult ideas over lunch.
He said he wanted to reread it over lunch.

'for' and 'to'   When you talk about what a meal consists of, you say what you have **for** breakfast, lunch, and so on.

They had hard-boiled eggs for breakfast.
What's for dinner?

When you invite someone to have a meal with you, for example at your house, you say that you ask them **for** the meal or **to** the meal.

Why don't you join me and the girls for lunch, Mr Jordache?
Stanley Openshaw invited him to lunch once.

'have'   You often use 'have' to say that someone eats a meal. You can say, for example, that someone **has breakfast** or **has their breakfast.**

When we've had breakfast, you can phone for a taxi.
That Tuesday, Lo had her dinner in her room.

Note that you do not say that someone 'has a breakfast' or 'has the breakfast'.

'make'   When someone prepares a meal, you can say, for example, that they **make breakfast, make the breakfast,** or **make their breakfast.**

I'll go and make dinner.
He makes the breakfast every morning.
She had been making her lunch when he arrived.

Note that you do not say that someone 'makes a breakfast'.

'a' with meals   Words referring to meals can be used either as uncount nouns or as count nouns. However, these words are not generally used with 'a'. For example, you do not say 'I had a lunch with Deborah' or 'I had a dinner early'. You say 'I had **lunch** with Deborah' or 'I had **dinner** early'. You can, however, use 'a' when you are describing a meal.

They had a quiet dinner together.
He was a big man and needed a big breakfast.

meal times   When you want to refer to the period of the day when a particular meal is eaten, you can use a compound noun consisting of a word referring to a meal and the word 'time'. The compound noun can be hyphenated or written as two separate words.

I shall be back by dinner-time.
It was almost lunch time.

The forms 'dinnertime', 'lunchtime', 'suppertime', and 'teatime' are also used. 'Breakfast time' is never written as one word.

He had a great deal to do before lunchtime.

---

mean

'mean' used   **Mean** is usually used as a verb. Its past tense and past participle is **meant**
as a verb   /ment/, not 'meaned'.

You use **mean** when you are talking about the meaning of a word or expression. For example, you might say 'What does "promissory" **mean**?'

What does 'imperialism' mean?
'Pandemonium' means 'the place of all devils'.

Note that you must use the auxiliary 'does' in questions like these. You do not say, for example, 'What means "promissory"?'

You can use **mean** with an '-ing' form to say what an attitude or type of behaviour implies or involves.

Being aware means being free from prejudice.
Some people will buy them even if it means defying the law.

What someone **means** is what they are referring to or are intending to say.

I know the guy you mean.
I thought you meant you wanted to take your own car.

WARNING   You do not use **mean** when you are talking about people's opinions or beliefs. You do not say, for example, 'Most of the directors mean he should resign'. You say 'Most of the directors **think** he should resign'. Similarly, you do not say 'His subjects mean that he is descended from God'. You say 'His subjects **believe** that he is descended from God'.

I think a woman has as much right to work as a man.
Most scientists believe the atmosphere of Jupiter is too unstable for life.

'means' used
as a noun

A **means** of doing something is a method or thing that makes it possible.

Scientists are working to devise a means of storing this type of power.
The essential means of transport for the islanders remains the donkey.

The plural of 'means' is also **means.**

An attempt was made to sabotage the ceremony by violent means.

'by means of'

If you do something **by means of** a particular method or object, you do it using that method or object.

The rig is anchored in place by means of steel cables.

'by all means'

You can say **'by all means'** to indicate that you are very willing to allow something to be done.

If you feel you need to ask any questions, by all means do so.
'Would it be all right if I left a bit early?'—'Yes, yes, by all means.'

WARNING

You do not use **by all means** to mean 'using whatever methods are necessary'. You do not say, for example, 'He was determined to become leader by all means'. You say 'He was determined to become leader **by whatever means'.**

Should not its alleviation by whatever means be the prime consideration?

'mean' used as
an adjective

Someone who is **mean** is unwilling to spend much money or to use much of something. You describe someone as **mean** when you disapprove of their behaviour.

Become a regular customer and don't be mean with the tips.

similar
adjectives

The following adjectives can also be used to describe someone who does not spend much money:

economical	parsimonious	thrifty
frugal	penny-pinching	tight
miserly	stingy	tight-fisted

Economical and **frugal** are neutral words.

Spaghetti, ravioli, and noodles have for years been the staple dishes of economical Italian countryfolk.
Make some stringent economies, be as frugal as a monk.

Thrifty is a complimentary word.

The people were industrious and very thrifty.

Miserly, parsimonious, penny-pinching, stingy, tight, and **tight-fisted** are used to show disapproval. **Parsimonious** is a formal word.

He was commercially stingy, absorbed with the cost of glue, paper clips and string.
At home he was churlish, parsimonious, and unloving to his daughters.

Penny-pinching is used mainly by journalists and public speakers.

He said the Government's penny-pinching policies were causing loss of life.

meaning

The **meaning** of a word, expression, or gesture is the thing or idea that it refers to or represents.

The word 'guide' is used with various meanings.
This gesture has the same meaning throughout Italy.

The **meaning** of what someone says is what they intend to express.

The meaning of the remark was clear.

'intention' You do not use **meaning** to refer to what someone intends to do. You do not say, for example, 'His meaning was to reach the border before nightfall'. You say 'His **intention** was to reach the border before nightfall'.

Their intention was to make the trip inconspicuous.

'opinion' You also do not use **meaning** to refer to what someone thinks about a particular matter. You do not say, for example, 'I think he should resign. What's your meaning?' You say 'I think he should resign. What's your **opinion**?'

My opinion is that a farm-worker is as important as a skilled man in any other industry.
If you want my honest opinion, I don't think it will work.

measurement

A **measurement** is a result obtained by measuring something.

Check the measurements carefully.
Every measurement was exact.

'measure' You do not use **measurement** to refer to an action taken by a government. The word you use is **measure**.

Measures had been taken to limit the economic decline.
Day nurseries were started as a war-time measure to allow mothers to work.

Measurements

You can refer to a size, area, volume, weight, distance, speed, or temperature by using a number or general determiner in front of a **measurement noun**.

They grow to twenty feet.
At this point, the city covered approximately 6 hectares.
...blocks of stone weighing up to a hundred tons.
They may travel as far as 70 kilometres in their search for fruit.
Reduce the temperature by a few degrees.

metric and imperial measurements In Britain, two systems of measurement are used – the **metric system** and the **imperial system**. The metric system is now commonly used for most purposes, but the imperial system is still used for people's heights and weights, drinks in pubs, distances on road signs, and sports such as cricket, football, and horseracing.

Each system has its own measurement nouns, as shown in the table opposite. Their abbreviations are shown in brackets.

	metric units		imperial units	
size/distance	millimetre	(mm)	inch	(in or ")
	centimetre	(cm)	foot	(ft or ')
	metre	(m)	yard	(yd)
	kilometre	(km)	mile	(m)
area	hectare	(ha)	acre	(a)
volume	millilitre	(ml)	fluid ounce	(fl oz)
	centilitre	(cl)	pint	(pt)
	litre	(l)	quart	(q)
			gallon	(gal)
weight	milligram	(mg)	ounce	(oz)
	gram	(g)	pound	(lb)
	kilogram	(kg)	stone	(st)
	tonne	(t)	hundredweight	(cwt)
			ton	(t)

If you are using metric units, you use decimal numbers. For example, you say that something is '1.68 metres long' or weighs '4.8 kilograms'. With imperial units, fractions are often used instead, for example 'six and three-quarter inches' or 'one and a half tons of wheat'.

'Kilo' is sometimes used instead of 'kilogram', and 'metric ton' instead of 'tonne'.

In America, the metric system is not commonly used, except for military, medical, and scientific purposes. The spellings 'meter' and 'liter' are used instead of 'metre' and 'litre'. The terms 'stone' and 'hundredweight' are very rarely used. Note that U.S. pints, quarts, and gallons are different from British ones.

size When you want to state the size of something, you usually use a number, a measurement noun, and an adjective. The verb you use is 'be'.

The water was fifteen feet deep.
The altar is to be 90 centimetres high.
One of the layers is six metres thick.
He was about six feet tall.

As well as the plural form 'feet', the singular form 'foot' can be used with numbers.

The spears were about six foot long.

If you are expressing size using feet and inches, you do not have to say 'inches'. For example, you can say that something is 'two foot six long'.

However, you do not say 'two feet six' or 'two foot six inches'.

He's Italian, and immensely tall, six feet six inches.

The following adjectives can be used after measurement nouns indicating size:

deep	long	thick
high	tall	wide

Note that you do not use adjectives such as 'narrow', 'shallow', 'low', or 'thin'.

When mentioning someone's height, you can use the adjective 'tall' or leave it out.

Measurements

She was six feet tall.
He was six foot six.

Note that you do not use the adjective 'high' for people.

When describing how wide something is, you can use 'across' instead of 'wide'.

…a squid that was 21 metres long with eyes 40 centimetres across.

Instead of using an adjective when stating size, you can use one of the following prepositional phrases after the measurement noun.

in depth	in length	in width
in height	in thickness	

They are thirty centimetres in length.
He was five feet seven inches in height.

When asking a question about the size of something, you use 'how' and the adjectives listed earlier. You can also use the less specific adjective 'big'.

How tall is he?
How big is it going to be?

size of circular objects and areas If you are talking about the size of a circular object or area, you can give its circumference (edge measurement) or diameter (width) using 'in circumference' or 'in diameter'.

Some of its artificial lakes are ten or twenty kilometres in circumference.
They are about nine inches in diameter.

You can also say that something has a 'radius' (half the diameter) of a particular length. However, you do not say 'in radius'.

It had a radius of fifteen kilometres.

size by dimensions If you want to describe the size of an object or area fully, you can give its **dimensions**; that is, you can give the measurements for its length and width, or length, width, and depth. When you give the dimensions of an object or area, you separate the figures using 'and', 'by', or the multiplication sign 'x'. You use the verb 'be' or 'measure'.

Each frame was four metres tall and sixty-six centimetres wide.
The island measures about 25 miles by 12 miles.
It was an oblong box about fifteen by thirty centimetres.
The box measures approximately 26 inches wide x 25 inches deep x 16 inches high.

As shown above, you can use adjectives such as 'long' and 'wide' or leave them out.

You can add 'in size' after the dimensions if you want to be precise.

…two sections, each 2 x 2 x 1 metres in size.

area Area is often expressed by using 'square' in front of units of length. For example, a 'square metre' has the same area as a square whose sides are one metre long.

He had cleared away about three square inches.
They are said to be as little as 300 sq cm.
…a couple of square yards.

You can add 'in area' if you want to be precise.

These hot spots are often hundreds of square miles in area.

If you are talking about a square object or area, you can give the length of each side followed by the word 'square'.

Each family has only one room eight or ten feet square.
...an area that is 25 km square.

Do not confuse the two uses of 'square'. A room five metres square has an area of twenty-five square metres.

When talking about large areas of land, the words 'hectare' and 'acre' are often used.

In 1975 there were 1,240 million hectares under cultivation.
His land covers twenty acres.

volume The volume of an object is the amount of space it occupies or contains.

Volume is usually expressed by using 'cubic' in front of units of length. For example, you can say '10 cubic centimetres' or '200 cubic feet'.

Its brain was close to 500 cubic centimetres (49 cubic inches).

Units of volume such as 'litre' and 'gallon' are used to refer to quantities of liquids and gases.

Wine production is expected to reach 4.1 billion gallons this year.
The amount of air being expelled is about 1,000 to 1,500 mls.

Note that, in Britain, 'a pint' by itself often refers to a pint of beer.

A lorry driver came into the pub for a pint.

distance You can indicate the distance from one thing to another by using a number and measurement noun in front of 'from', 'away from', or 'away'.

...when the fish are 60 yds from the beach.
These offices were approximately nine kilometres away from the centre.
She sat down about a hundred metres away.

Distance can also be indicated by stating the time taken to travel it.

It is half an hour from the Pinewood Studios and forty-five minutes from London.
They lived only two or three days away from Juffure.

The method of travelling can be stated to be more precise.

It is less than an hour's drive from here.
It's about five minutes' walk from the bus stop.

If you want to know the distance to a place, you use 'how far', usually with 'from', or with impersonal 'it' and 'to'.

How far is Chester from here?
How far is it to Charles City?
'How far is it?'—'A hundred and fifty kilometres from here.'

Note that 'far' is not used when stating distances. See entry at **far**.

distance and position To indicate both the distance and the position of something in relation to another place or object, the distance can be stated in front of the following prepositions:

above	below	inside	outside	underneath
across	beneath	into	over	up
along	beyond	off	past	
behind	down	out of	under	

He guessed that he was about ten miles above the surface.

Measurements

Maurice was only a few yards behind him.
At a cafe a hundred metres down the street he again used the phone.

All the words in the list above, except 'across', 'into', 'over', and 'past', can be used as adverbs after the distance. The adverbs 'apart', 'in', 'inland', 'offshore', 'on', and 'out' can also be used.

These two fossils had been lying about 50 feet apart in the sand.
We were now forty miles inland.
A few metres further on were other unmistakable traces of disaster.

The distance can also be stated in front of phrases such as 'north of', 'to the east of', and 'to the left'.

He was some miles north of Ayr.
The low crest 1,000 metres away to the east was dimly visible.
The maker's name was engraved a millimetre to the right of the '2'.
It had exploded 100 yards to their right.

weight When you want to state how much an object or animal weighs, you use the verb 'weigh'.

The statue weighs fifty or more kilos.
The calf weighs 50 lbs.

When you want to state how much a person weighs, you can use 'weigh' or 'be'. In Britain, you usually use the singular form 'stone'.

He weighs about nine and a half stone.
You're about ten and a half stone.

If you express weight using stones and pounds, you can leave out the word 'pounds'. For example, you can say that someone weighs 'twelve stone four'. Note that you do not usually say 'twelve stones four' or 'twelve stone four pounds'.

You do not say 'two pounds heavy', but you can say 'two pounds in weight'.

I put on nearly a stone in weight.

In America, all weights are normally expressed in 'pounds' or 'tons'. 'Stone' and 'hundredweight' are very rarely used.

Philip Swallow weighs about 140 pounds.

Americans often omit the words 'hundred' and 'pounds' when talking about a person's weight.

I bet he weighs one seventy, at least.

When asking about the weight of something or someone, you can use 'how much' and 'weigh'.

How much does the whole thing weigh?

You can also use 'how heavy'.

How heavy are they?

temperature You express temperature using either degrees centigrade (often written °C), or degrees Fahrenheit (often written °F). In everyday language the metric term 'centigrade' is used, whereas in scientific language 'Celsius' is used to refer to the same scale of measurement.

The temperature was still 23 degrees centigrade.
...about 30 degrees Celsius.
It was 9°C, and felt much colder.
The temperature was probably 50°F.

If the scale is known, 'degrees' can be used by itself.

It's 72 degrees down here and we've had a dry week.

In cold weather, temperatures are often stated as 'degrees below freezing' or 'degrees below zero'.

...when the temperature is fifteen degrees below freezing.
It's amazingly cold: must be twenty degrees below zero.

speed, rates, and ratios
You talk about the speed of something by saying how far it travels in a particular unit of time. To do this, you use a noun such as 'kilometre' or 'mile', followed by 'per', 'a', or 'an', and a noun referring to a length of time.

Wind speeds at the airport were 160 kilometres per hour.
Warships move at about 500 miles per day.

When writing about speeds, rates, or pressures, you can use the symbol '/' instead of 'per' between abbreviations for the units of measurement.

...a velocity of 160 km/sec.

'Per', 'a', and 'an' are also used when talking about other rates and ratios.

...a heart rate of 70 beats per minute.
He earns two rupees a day collecting rags and scrap paper.
In Java a quarter of the annual rainfall comes in showers of sixty millimetres an hour.

'Per' can also be used in front of a word that does not refer to a length of time or a unit of measurement.

In Indonesia there are 18,100 people per doctor.
I think we have more paper per employee in this department than in any other.

Note that 'per head' or 'a head' are often used instead of 'per person' or 'a person'.

The average cereal consumption per head per year in the U.S.A. is 900 kg.

You can also use 'to the' when you are talking about rates and ratios.

The exchange rate would soon be $2 to the pound.
Those German Fords got forty-three miles to the gallon.
...about 2 cwt (101 kg) to the acre.

measurements used as modifiers and qualifiers
Expressions indicating size, area, volume, distance, and weight can be used as modifiers in front of a noun.

...a 5 foot 9 inch bed.
...70 foot high mounds of dust.
15 cm x 10 cm posts would be ideal.
...a 2-litre engine.
The 4,700 pound bomb was dropped on a single target.

Note that you can use adjectives like 'long' and 'high', but you do not have to.

If the expression consists simply of a number and a measurement noun, it is often hyphenated.

...a five-pound bag of lentils.
We finished our 500-mile journey at 4.30 p.m. on the 25th September.
...a ten-acre farm near Warwick.

WARNING
The measurement noun is singular, not plural, even though it comes after a number. For example, you do not say 'a ten-miles walk'. You say 'a ten-mile walk'.

However, the plural form is used in athletics, because the measurement is really the name of a race. For example, 'the 100 metres record' means 'the record for the 100 metres (race)'.

...winning the 100 metres breaststroke.

You can use measurement expressions, usually ending in an adjective or 'in' phrase, after a noun.

There were seven main bedrooms, four bathrooms and a sitting-room fifty feet long.
...long thin strips 6mm (quarter inch) wide.
...a giant planet over 30,000 miles in diameter.

You can also indicate the area or weight of something using '-ing' forms such as 'covering', 'measuring', or 'weighing'.

...a largish park covering 40,000 square feet.
...a square area measuring 900 metres on each side.
...an iron bar weighing fifteen pounds.

You can also indicate the area or volume of something using a phrase beginning with 'of'.

...industrial units of less than 15,000 sq ft.
At the beginning of the century Britain ruled an empire of 13 million square miles and 360 million people.
...vessels of 100 litres.

size of something abstract

If you want to indicate how great something abstract such as an area, speed, or increase is, you use 'of'.

There were fires burning over a total area of about 600 square miles.
...speeds of nearly 100 mph.
...an average annual temperature of 20°.
...an increase of 10 per cent.

You can also sometimes use a modifier, for example when talking about percentages or salaries.

...a 71 per cent increase in earnings.
...his £25,000-a-year salary.

measurement nouns before 'of'

Measurement nouns are often used in front of 'of' to refer to an amount of something which is a particular length, area, volume, or weight.

...20 yds of nylon.
Americans consume about 1.1 billion pounds of turkey and 81 million gallons of hard liquor at this time.

In addition to units of measurement, people often use 'a half' by itself when referring to half a pint of a drink in a pub, and 'a quarter' when referring to a quarter of a pound of something such as vegetables.

I'll have a half of lager.
A quarter of mushrooms, please.

For information on other ways of referring to amounts, see entries at **Quantity** and **Pieces and amounts**.

media

Media is a noun, and it is also a plural form of another noun, 'medium'.

'the media'   You can refer to television, radio, and newspapers as **the media.**

I don't think he will want to say anything to the media.

It is usually regarded as correct to use a plural form of a verb with **the media,** but some people use a singular form.

The media have generally refrained from comment.
The media is full of pictures of tearful, anxious families.

You can use a singular or plural form in conversation, but you should use a plural form in formal writing.

'medium'   A **medium** is a way of expressing your ideas or communicating with people. The plural of 'medium' is either **mediums** or **media.**

He would prefer to be remembered for his talents in other mediums besides photography.
They are encouraged to explore different methods of study and of presentation, including media other than the written word.

meet

Meet is usually used as a verb. Its past tense and past participle is **met,** not 'meeted'.

When you **meet** someone, you happen to be in the same place and you start talking to each other.

I met a Swedish girl on the train.
I have met you here before.

When this meeting is intentional, you can say that you **meet** or **meet with** the other person. **Meet with** is especially common in American English.

I went with Mrs Mellish to meet some of the teachers.
We can meet with the professor Monday night.

memoirs

When someone writes their **memoirs,** they write a book about people and events that they remember.

He was busy writing his memoirs.
They're making a movie of his war memoirs.

'memories'   You do not use **memoirs** to refer to things that you remember about the past. The word you use is **memories.**

My memories of a London childhood are happy ones.
One of my earliest memories is of a total eclipse of the sun.

memory

Your **memory** is your ability to remember things.

You've got such a wonderful memory.
A few things stand out in my memory.

A **memory** is something that you remember.

...a memory of an old friend.
She had no memory of what had happened.

'souvenir'   You do not use **memory** to refer to an object which you buy or keep to remind you of a holiday, place, or event. An object like this is called a **souvenir** /suːˈvənɪə/.

He kept the spoon as a souvenir of his journey.

merry-go-round

See entry at **roundabout**.

metre - meter

'metre' In British English, a **metre** is a unit of length equal to 39.37 inches.

The blue whale grows to over 30 metres long.

'meter' In American English, this word is spelled **meter**.

I stopped about fifty meters down the road.

In both British and American English, some kinds of measuring devices are also called **meters**.

...a parking meter.
He'd come to read the gas meter.

middle - centre

'middle' The **middle** of a two-dimensional shape or area is the part that is furthest from its sides, edges, or boundaries.

In the middle of the lawn was a great cedar tree.
Foster was standing in the middle of the room.

'centre' **Centre** is used in a similar way, but it usually refers to a more precise point or position. For example, in mathematics you talk about the **centre** of a circle, not the 'middle'.

...the centre of the cyclone.

'center' In American English, this word is spelled **center**.

At the center of the monument was a photograph.

other meanings The **middle** of a road or river is the part that is furthest from its sides or
of 'middle' banks.

...white lines painted along the middle of the highway.
We managed to pull on to a sandbank in the middle of the river.

You do not talk about the 'centre' of a road or river.

The **middle** of an event or period of time is a period which is halfway between its beginning and its end.

We landed at Canton in the middle of a torrential storm.
...the middle of December.

You do not talk about the 'centre' of an event or period of time.

Middle Ages - middle age

'Middle Ages' In European history, **the Middle Ages** were the period between approximately 1000 AD and 1400 AD.

This practice was common throughout the Middle Ages.

'middle age' **Middle age** is the period in a person's life when they are no longer young but are not yet old.

...the discontents of middle age.
...a man in late middle age.

'middle-aged' When someone has reached this period of their life, you can say that they are **middle-aged**.

The boss was a middle-aged woman.

might - may

Might and **may** are used mainly to talk about possibility. They can also be used to make a request, to ask permission, or to make a suggestion. When **might** and **may** can be used with the same meaning, **may** is more formal than **might**.

Might and **may** are called **modals**. See entry at **Modals**.

In conversation, the negative form **mightn't** is often used. The form **mayn't** is much less common. People usually use the full form **may not**.

He mightn't have time for such things.
It may not be quite so depressing as you think.

possibility:
the present and
the future

You can use **might** or **may** to say that it is possible that something is true or that something will happen in the future.

His route from the bus stop might be the same as yours.
This may be why women enjoy going back to work.

They might be able to remember what he said.
Clerical work may be available for two students who want to learn about publishing.

You can use **could** in a similar way, but only in positive sentences.

Don't eat it. It could be a toadstool.

See entry at **can - could - be able to**.

You can use **might well** or **may well** to indicate that it is fairly likely that something is the case.

You might well be right.
I think that may well have been the intention.

You use **might not** or **may not** to say that it is possible that something is not the case.

He might not be in England at all.
That mightn't be true.
That may not sound very imposing.

WARNING

You do not use **might not** or **may not** to say that it is impossible that something is the case. Instead you use **could not, cannot,** or **can't**.

...knowledge which could not have been gained in any other way.
Kissinger cannot know what the situation is in the country.
You can't talk to the dead.

You never use **may** when you are asking if something is possible. You do not say, for example, 'May he be right?' You say '**Might** he be right?' or, more usually, '**Could** he be right?'

Might it be even earlier?
Could this be true?
Could he remember having seen the picture before?

Similarly, you do not say 'What may happen?' You usually say 'What **is likely to** happen?'

What are likely to be the ecological effects of intensive agricultural production?

possibility:
the past

You use **might** or **may** with 'have' to say that it is possible that something happened in the past, but you do not know whether it happened or not.

Grandpapa might have secretly married Pepita.
I may have seemed to be overreacting.

Could have can be used in a similar way.

It is just possible that such a small creature could have preyed on dinosaur eggs.

However, if something did not happen and you want to say that there was a possibility of it happening, you can only use **might have** or **could have**. You do not use 'may have'. For example, you say 'If he hadn't hurt his ankle, he **might have** won the race'. You do not say 'If he hadn't hurt his ankle, he may have won the race'.

A lot of men died who might have been saved.

You use **might not** or **may not** with 'have' to say that it is possible that something did not happen or was not the case.

They might not have considered me as their friend.
My father mightn't have been to blame.
The parents may not have been ready for this pregnancy.

WARNING

You do not use **might not** or **may not** with 'have' to say that it is impossible that something happened or was the case. Instead you use **could not have** or **cannot have**.

The measurement couldn't have been wrong.
The girls cannot have been seriously affected by the system.

requests and permission

May and **might** are sometimes used when someone is making a request, or asking or giving permission. These are formal uses.

May I look round?
Might we leave our bags here for a moment?
You may speak.

For more information, see entries at **Requests, orders, and instructions** and **Permission.**

suggestions

Might is often used in polite suggestions.

You might like to comment on his latest proposal.
I think it might be a good idea to stop the recording now.

For more information about ways of making a suggestion, see entry at **Suggestions.**

migrate - migration - migrant

See entry at **emigration - immigration - migration.**

mill

See entry at **factory.**

million

A million or **one million** is the number 1,000,000.

You do not add '-s' to the word **million** when you put another number in front of it. You do not say, for example, 'five millions people'. You say 'five **million** people'.

...130 million litres.

mind

Mind is used as a noun or a verb.

used as a noun

Your **mind** is your ability to think.

...the evolution of the human mind.

'make up one's mind'	When someone decides to do something, you can say that they **make up their mind** to do it.

Egged on by Iago, Othello makes up his mind to kill Desdemona.
She made up her mind to write to Teddy Boylan.

Note that you use a 'to'-infinitive, not an '-ing' form, after this expression.

used as a verb	If you have no objection to doing something, you can say that you **don't mind doing** it.

I don't mind walking.

You do not say that you 'do not mind to do' something.

You can indicate that you do not object to a situation or proposal by saying **'I don't mind'**.

'Do you want me to go and do it?'—'I don't mind, if you want to.'
If the public thinks of me as Alf, I don't mind.
It was raining, but he didn't mind.

Note that you do not use 'it' after **mind** in sentences like these.

minority

If something is true of **a minority** of the people or things in a group, it is true of less than half of the whole group.

These values are accepted by only a minority of the population.

You can talk about **a small minority** (for example 8%) or **a large minority** (for example 40%).

Only a small minority of children get a chance to benefit from the system.
The incomes of a large minority of tenants are inadequate to enable them to pay their rents.

When **a minority** is not followed by 'of', you can use either a plural or singular form of a verb after it. The plural form is more common.

Only a minority were active in pursuing their beliefs.

When you use **a minority of** followed by a plural noun, you must use a plural form of a verb after it.

Only a minority of people ever become actively engaged on any issue.

miserable

See entry at **happy - sad**.

mistake

A **mistake** is something incorrect or unfortunate that someone does, such as spelling a word wrongly. You say that someone **makes** a mistake.

He had made a terrible mistake.
We made the mistake of leaving our bedroom window open.

You do not say that someone 'does' a mistake.

'fault'	You do not use **mistake** to refer to something wrong in a machine or structure. The word you use is **fault**.

There's usually a fault in one of the appliances.
The machine has developed a fault.

'in mistake for'	If someone has taken something when they intended to take something else, you say that they took the first thing **in mistake for** the second thing.

I had taken Ewen Waite's gun in mistake for my own.

You can use **in mistake for** in a similar way with several other verbs.

The root of aconite has frequently been eaten in mistake for that of horseradish.

'by mistake'	However, you do not say that someone does something 'in mistake'. You say that they do it **by mistake.**

I once burst into his bedroom by mistake.
Griffiths thought he had been sent there by mistake.

misused

See entry at **disused - unused - misused.**

GRAMMAR # Modals

Modals are a type of auxiliary verb. They are used, for example, to indicate the possibility or necessity of an event, and to make requests, offers, and suggestions. They can also be used to make what you are saying more tactful or polite.

The following words are modals:

can	might	shall	would
could	must	should	
may	ought	will	

A modal is always the first word in a verb group. All modals except 'ought' are followed by the base form of a verb (the infinitive without 'to'), unless the verb has already been mentioned (see entry at **Ellipsis**).

I must leave fairly soon.
Things might have been so different.
People may be watching.

'Ought' is followed by a 'to'-infinitive.

She ought to go straight back to England.
Sam ought to have realized how dangerous it was.

Modals have only one form. There is no '-s' form for the third person singular of the present tense, and there are no '-ing' or '-ed' forms.

There's nothing I can do about it.
I'm sure he can do it.

short forms	'Shall', 'will', and 'would' are not usually pronounced in full. When you write down what someone says, or write in a conversational style, you usually represent 'shall' and 'will' using 'll, and 'would' using 'd, after pronouns. See entry at **Contractions.**

I'll see you tomorrow.
Posy said she'd love to stay.

You can also represent 'will' as 'll after a noun.

My car'll be outside.

'Shall', 'will', and 'would' are never shortened if they come at the end of a sentence.

Paul said he would come, and I hope he <u>will</u>.

Remember that 'd is also the short form of the auxiliary 'had'.

<u>I'd</u> heard it many times.

The auxiliary 'have' is not usually pronounced in full after 'could', 'might', 'must', 'should', and 'would'. The contractions 'could've', 'might've', 'must've', 'should've', and 'would've' are occasionally used in writing when reporting a conversation.

I <u>must've</u> fallen asleep.
You <u>should've</u> come to see us.

'Not' is not usually pronounced in full after a modal. You usually represent what someone says using 'nt after the modal. See entry at **Contractions.**

For more information about the uses of modals, see the individual entries for each word. See also entries at **Advising someone, Invitations, Offers, Opinions, Permission,** and **Suggestions.** For information on the use of 'will' to talk about the future and 'would' to talk about the past, see entries at **The Future** and **The Past.**

modern

See entry at **new.**

Modifiers

A **modifier** is a word or group of words which comes in front of a noun and adds information about the thing which the noun refers to. Modifiers can be:

● **adjectives**

This is the <u>main</u> bedroom.
After the crossroads look out for the <u>large white</u> building.
A <u>harder</u> mattress often helps with back injuries.

See entry at **Adjectives.**

● **nouns**

...the <u>music</u> industry.
...<u>tennis</u> lessons.

See entries at **Noun modifiers** and **Possession and other relationships.**

● **place names**

...a <u>London</u> hotel.
...<u>Arctic</u> explorers.

See entry at **Places.**

● **place and direction adverbs**

...the <u>downstairs</u> television room.
The <u>overhead</u> light went on.

See entry at **Places.**

● **times**

Castle was usually able to catch the six thirty-five train from Euston.
Every morning he would set off right after the eight o'clock news.

See entry at **Time**.

moment

A **moment** is a very short period of time.

She hesitated for only a moment.
A few moments later he heard footsteps.

'the moment'   **The moment** is often used as a conjunction to say that something happens
or is done at the same time as something else, or immediately after it.

The moment I saw this, it appealed to me.

When you use **the moment** like this to talk about the future, you use the
simple present tense after it. You do not use a future tense.

The moment he shows up I want to see him.

momentarily

Something that happens **momentarily** happens for only a short time.

She shivered momentarily.
I had momentarily forgotten.

In American English, **momentarily** is also used to mean 'very soon indeed',
especially in announcements about the arrival or departure of planes.
Momentarily is not used like this in British English.

We will arrive momentarily in Paris.

momentary - momentous

'momentary'   Something that is **momentary** lasts for only a short time.

There was a momentary pause.

'momentous'   A **momentous** event or decision is very important, because of the effects it
will have.

It was here that the momentous discovery was made.
He would be forced to make a momentous decision by the end of the day.

money

Money is the coins or bank notes that you use to buy things. **Money** is an
uncount noun. You do not talk about 'moneys' or 'a money'.

I spent all my money on sweets.
I had very little money left.

After **money** you use a singular form of a verb.

My money has been returned to me.
Money isn't everything.

Money

British currency consists of **pounds** and **pence**. There are a hundred pence
in a pound.

| writing amounts of money | When you write amounts of money in figures, the pound symbol £ is shown in front of the figures. For example, 'two hundred pounds' is written as '£200'. |

'Million' is sometimes abbreviated to 'm', and 'billion' to 'bn'. 'k' and 'K' are sometimes used as abbreviations for 'thousand' when people's salaries are being mentioned.

About £20m was invested in the effort.
...generating revenues of £6bn.
...Market Manager, £30K + bonus + car.

If an amount of money consists only of pence, you put the letter 'p' after the figures. For example, 'fifty pence' is written as '50p'.

If an amount of money consists of both pounds and pence, you write the pound symbol and separate the pounds and the pence with a full stop. You do not write 'p' after the pence. For example, 'two pounds fifty pence' is written as '£2.50'.

| saying amounts of money | When saying aloud an amount of money that consists only of pence, you say the word 'pence' or the letter 'p' (pronounced like 'pea') after the number. |

When saying aloud an amount of money that consists of pounds and pence, you do not usually say the word 'pence'. For example, you say 'two pounds fifty'.

WARNING

In conversation, people sometimes say 'pound' not 'pounds'. For example, 'I get ten pound a week'. However, many people regard this as incorrect, so you should say 'pounds'.

The words 'pounds' and 'pence' are often left out when it is clear which you are referring to.

At the moment they're paying 75p for their meal, and it costs us ninety-eight.
'I've come to pay an account.'—'All right then, fine, that's four seventy-eight sixty then, please.'

In very informal speech, 'quid' is often used instead of 'pound' or 'pounds'.

'How much did you have to pay?'—'Eight quid.'

| asking and stating the cost of something | When you ask or state the cost of something, you use the verb 'be'. You begin a question about cost with 'How much...'. |

How much is that?
How much is it to park?
The cheapest is about eight pounds.

You can also use the verb 'cost'. This is slightly more formal.

How much will it cost?
They cost several hundred pounds.

You can mention the person buying something by adding a pronoun or other noun group after 'cost'.

It would cost me around six hundred.

| notes and coins | You use 'notes' to refer to paper money. In British currency, there are notes worth five, ten, twenty, and fifty pounds. |

You didn't have a five-pound note, did you?
Several paid on the spot in notes.

Note that you do not say 'a five-pounds note'.

You use 'coins' to refer to metal money. In British currency, there are coins worth one, two, five, ten, twenty, and fifty pence, and one pound.

You should make sure that you have a ready supply of coins for telephoning.

If you want to refer to a coin that is worth a particular amount, you usually use the word 'piece'.

That fifty pence piece has been there all day.
The machine wouldn't take 10p pieces.

You can refer to coins that you have with you as 'change'.

He rattled the loose change in his pocket.

expressing a rate
When you want to express the rate at which money is spent or received, you use 'a' or 'per' after the amount. 'Per' is more formal.

He gets £35 a week.
Farmers spend more than half a billion pounds per year on pesticides.

'Per annum' is sometimes used instead of 'per year'.

...staff earning less than £7,500 per annum.

expressing quantity by cost
You can talk about a quantity of something by saying how much it costs using 'worth of'.

You've got to buy thousands of pounds worth of stamps before you get a decent one.
He owns some 20 million pounds worth of property in Mayfair.

American currency
American currency consists of **dollars** and **cents**. There are a hundred cents in a dollar.

Americans use the word 'bill' to refer to paper money. There are bills worth one, two, five, ten, twenty, fifty, and a hundred dollars.

Ellen put a five-dollar bill and three ones on the counter.

There are coins worth one, five, ten, and twenty-five cents. These are often referred to by the special words 'penny', 'nickel', 'dime', and 'quarter'.

I had just that - a dollar bill, a quarter, two dimes and a nickel, and three pennies.

In very informal speech, 'buck' is often used instead of 'dollar'.

I got 500 bucks for it.

When writing amounts of money, you use the dollar symbol $, or 'c' for cents. For example, 'two hundred dollars' is written as '$200', 'fifty cents' is written as '50c', and 'two dollars fifty cents' is written as '$2.50'.

Note that when saying aloud amounts of money, you always say the word 'cents'. You never say 'c'.

other currencies
Many countries use the same units for their currencies. If you need to indicate which country's currency you are talking about, you use a nationality adjective.

...a contract worth 200 million Canadian dollars.
It cost me about thirteen hundred Swiss francs.

Note that some currencies have some units in common, but also have some different units. For example, Britain uses 'pounds' and 'pence', but Egypt uses 'pounds' and 'piastres'.

Currencies have different values, so when you change money from one currency to another, you need to know the **exchange rate.** When talking about exchange rates, you say how many units of one currency there are 'to the' other unit of currency.

The rate of exchange while I was there was 11.20 francs to the pound.

moral - morality - morale

'moral'
Moral /mɒrəl/ is used as an adjective, a count noun, or a plural noun.

When you use it as an adjective, it means 'relating to right and wrong behaviour'.

I have noticed a fall in moral standards.
It is our moral duty to stay.

The **moral** of a story is what it teaches you about how you should or should not behave.

The moral is clear: you must never marry for money.

Morals are principles of behaviour.

There can be no doubt about the excellence of his morals.
We agreed that business morals nowadays were very low.

'morality'
Morality /mərælətɪ/ is the idea that some forms of behaviour are right and others are wrong.

Punishment always involves the idea of morality.
Sexual morality was enforced by the fear of illegitimacy.

'morale'
Your **morale** /mɒrɑːl/ is the amount of confidence you have when you are in a difficult or dangerous situation.

The morale of the men was good.

more

talking about a greater number or amount
You use **more** or **more of** to indicate that you are talking about a greater number of people or things, or a greater amount of something.

You use **more** in front of a noun which does not have a determiner or possessive noun in front of it.

There are more people getting a better education than ever.
Better management may enable one man to milk more cows.
They are offered more food than they need.

You use **more of** in front of a pronoun, or in front of a noun which has a determiner or possessive noun in front of it.

There are more of them seeking jobs than ever.
As my children grew into teenagers, they needed more of my time.
He knew more of Mr Profumo's statement than he had hitherto admitted.

talking about an additional number or amount
You also use **more** or **more of** to talk about an additional number of people or things, or an additional amount of something.

More officers will be brought in.
We need more information.

More of the land is needed to grow crops.
I sipped a little more of Otto's scotch.

used with modifiers

You can use words such as 'some' and 'any' and expressions such as 'a lot' in front of **more** and **more of**.

Bond promised he would buy her some more diamonds.
I don't want to hear any more of this crazy talk.
It will give us a lot more freedom.
People are concerned about crime because there is much more of it.

These words and expressions can be used in front of **more** and **more of** when they are followed by a plural form:

any	many	some	a great many
far	no	a few	a lot
lots	several	a good many	

Note that you do not use 'many', 'several', 'a few', 'a good many', or 'a great many' in front of **more** or **more of** when they are followed by an uncount noun or a singular pronoun.

These words and expressions can be used in front of **more** and **more of** when they are followed by an uncount noun or a singular pronoun:

any	much	some	a great deal
far	no	a bit	a little
lots	rather	a good deal	a lot

'more than'

If you want to say that the number of people or things in a group is greater than a particular number, you use **more than** in front of the number.

He saw more than 800 children.
By the age of five, the child had a vocabulary of more than 2,000 words.
He had been awake for more than forty-eight hours.

When you use **more than** in front of a number and a plural noun, you use a plural form of a verb after it.

More than 17,000 children are said to have written to Richard.
More than 100 people were arrested.

used as an adverb

More is used as an adverb to mean 'to a greater extent or degree'.

The books that are true to life will attract them more.
I couldn't have agreed more.

used in comparatives

More is also used in front of adjectives and adverbs to form comparatives.

Your child's health is more important than the doctor's feelings.
Next time, I will choose more carefully.

See entries at **Comparative and superlative adjectives** and **Comparative and superlative adverbs**.

morning

The **morning** is the part of each day which begins when you get up or when it becomes light outside, and which ends at noon or lunchtime.

the present day

You refer to the morning of the present day as **this morning**.

His plane left this morning.
'When did it come?'—'This morning.'

You refer to the morning of the previous day as **yesterday morning**.

Yesterday morning there were more than 1,500 boats waiting in the harbour for the weather to improve.

If you want to say that something will happen during the morning of the next day, you say that it will happen **tomorrow morning** or **in the morning**.

You've got to be in court <u>tomorrow morning</u>.
Phone him <u>in the morning</u>.

single events in the past

If you want to say that something happened during a particular morning in the past, you use **on**.

She left after breakfast <u>on Saturday morning</u>.
<u>On the morning of our departure</u>, an old man came up and spoke to him.

If you have been describing what happened during a particular day, you can then say that something happened **that morning** or **in the morning**.

<u>That morning</u> I flew from East London to Johannesburg.
The tracks told me what had happened <u>in the morning</u>.

If you are talking about a day in the past and you want to mention that something had happened during the morning of the day before, you say that it had happened **the previous morning**.

My head felt clear, as it had been <u>the previous morning</u>.

If you want to say that something happened during the morning of the next day, you say that it happened **the next morning, in the morning, next morning,** or **the following morning**.

<u>The next morning</u> I got up early and ate my breakfast.
<u>In the morning</u> Bernard wanted to go out for fresh milk.
<u>Next morning</u> we drove over to Leysin.
The ship was due to sail <u>the following morning</u>.

In stories, if you want to say that something happened during a morning in the past, without saying which morning, you say that it happened **one morning**.

<u>One morning</u> there was a fire in the prison camp.

You can also say, for example, that something happened **one January morning** or **on a January morning**.

<u>One breezy March morning,</u> Miss Clare was upstairs making her lodger's bed.
<u>One morning in 1936</u> I accompanied Bertha to church.
<u>On a fine May morning</u> Washington reviewed the troops.

talking about the future

If you want to say that something will happen during a particular morning in the future, you use **on**.

They're coming to see me <u>on Friday morning</u>.

If you are already talking about a day in the future, you can say that something will happen **in the morning**.

The teams will arrive at Orpington on Sunday, when the South of England will play Vermont <u>in the morning</u>.

If you are talking about a day in the future and you want to say that something will happen during the morning of the next day, you say that it will happen **the following morning**.

We will arrive in Delhi on Friday evening and set off for Nepal <u>the following morning</u>.

regular events

If something happens or happened regularly every morning, you say that it happens or happened **in the morning** or **in the mornings**.

I read all the papers <u>in the morning</u>.
The museums may open only <u>in the mornings</u>.

I had to get up very early <u>in the morning</u>.

She stayed in bed in the mornings.

If you want to say that something happens or happened once a week during a particular morning, you use **on** followed by the name of a day of the week and **mornings.**

You can deposit and withdraw money on Saturday mornings.
My father mended shoes on Sunday mornings.

exact times   If you have mentioned an exact time and you want to make it clear that you are talking about the period between midnight and noon rather than the period between noon and midnight, you add **in the morning.**

They often hold policy meetings at seven in the morning.
It was five o'clock in the morning.

most

used to mean 'the majority' or 'the largest part'   You use **most** or **most of** to indicate that you are talking about the majority of a group of things or people, or the largest part of something.

You use **most** in front of a plural noun which does not have a determiner or possessive noun in front of it.

Most people don't enjoy their own parties.
In most schools, sports are compulsory.

You use **most of** in front of a pronoun, or in front of a noun which has a determiner or possessive noun in front of it.

Most of us have strong views on politics.
The trees cut out most of the light.
He used to spend most of his time in the library.
Most of the region's timber is imported.

Note that when you use **most** like this, you do not use a determiner in front of it.

You also do not talk about 'the most part' of something. You do not say, for example, 'She had drunk the most part of the wine'. You say 'She had drunk **most of** the wine'.

used to form superlatives   **Most** is used in front of adjectives and adverbs to form superlatives.

The head is the most sensitive part of the body.
It was one of the most important discoveries ever made.
These are the works I respond to most strongly.

See entries at **Comparative and superlative adjectives** and **Comparative and superlative adverbs.**

used to mean 'very'   Some people use **most** in front of adjectives and adverbs to mean 'very'. They do this when they are expressing their opinion of something. They do not use **most** in front of very common words like 'good' or 'big'.

The film is most disturbing.
He always acted most graciously.

'really'   **Most** is more emphatic than **very,** but it sounds rather formal and old-fashioned. In conversation, if you want to use a stronger word than 'very', you usually use **really. Really** can be used with any qualitative adjective.

It was really good, wasn't it, Andy?
These fires produce really obnoxious fumes.
We're doing really well actually.

motor

See entry at **machine.**

mountain

See entry at **hill - mountain**.

movie

See entry at **film**.

much

You use **very much** to say that something is true to a great extent.

I enjoyed it very much.
I doubt it very much.

When **very much** is used with a transitive verb, it usually goes after the object. You do not use it immediately after the verb. You do not say, for example, 'I enjoyed very much the party'. You say 'I enjoyed the party **very much**'.

When **very much** is used with an intransitive verb followed by a 'that'-clause or a 'to'-infinitive, you can put **very much** either in front of the verb or after it. For example, you can say 'She **very much wants** to come' or 'She **wants very much** to come'.

We very much hope he'll continue to be able to represent you.
I hope very much you will be coming on Saturday.

We'd very much like to give you a present.
He would like very much to write to Dennis himself.

WARNING In positive sentences, you do not use **much** without 'very'. You do not say, for example, 'I enjoyed it much' or 'We'd much like to give you a present'.

In negative sentences, you can use **much** without 'very'.

I didn't like him much.
The situation isn't likely to change much.

You can also use **much** in negative sentences and questions to mean 'often'.

She doesn't talk about them much.
Does he come here much?

WARNING You do not use **much** in positive sentences to mean 'often'. You do not say, for example, 'He comes here much'.

Many other words and expressions can be used to indicate degree. For a graded list, see section on **degree** in entry at **Adverbials**.

used with adjectives **Much** and **very much** are used in front of comparatives (see below), but are not usually used in front of other adjectives. However, you can use them in front of '-ed' words.

Education is a much debated subject.
She was very much attached to her husband.

You can use **very much** in front of 'afraid', 'alike', 'alive', and 'awake'.

I am very much afraid that she will end by marrying her cousin.
Dolly and Molly were very much alike.
The animal was not dead but very much alive.
The children were very much awake.

used with comparatives You often use **much** or **very much** in front of comparative adjectives and adverbs. For example, if you want to emphasize the difference in size between two things, you can say that one thing is **much bigger** or **very much bigger** than the other.

She was much older than me.

Now I feel much more confident.
The new machine was very much bigger and very much more complicated.
This could all be done very much more quickly.

Much more and **very much more** can be used in front of a noun to emphasize the difference between two quantities or amounts.

She ought to have been allowed much more time.
Children, whose bones are growing, need much more calcium than adults.
We get very much more value for money.

used with
superlatives

Much is sometimes used in front of superlative adjectives.

I thought he was much the best speaker.
...the Svalbard group of islands, of which Spitzbergen is much the largest.

used with
adverbials and
noun groups

You use **very much** in front of adverbials. You do not use 'very'.

She does things very much her own way.
Battle damage and fatigue left the eventual outcome of the fighting very much in doubt.

Very much is sometimes used in front of noun groups. You use it to emphasize that someone or something has all the qualities you would expect a particular kind of person or thing to have.

He was very much a seaman.
He was very much a man of the people.

'much too'

You use **much too** in front of an adjective to say that something cannot be done or achieved because someone or something has too much of a quality.

I knew where it was, but was much too polite to say.
The rooms were much too cold for comfort.
The price is much too high.

Note that in sentences like these you put **much** in front of 'too', not after it. You do not say, for example, 'The rooms were too much cold for comfort'.

If there is very much more of something than is necessary or desirable, you can say that there is **much too much** of it.

Eating much too much salt can be dangerous during pregnancy.

However, if there is a very much larger number of people or things than is necessary or desirable, you do not usually say that there are 'much too many' of them. You say that there are **far too many** of them.

Every middle-class child gets far too many toys.

used as a
determiner

You use **much** in front of an uncount noun when you are talking about a large quantity or amount of something. **Much** is usually used like this in negative sentences, in questions, or after 'too', 'so', or 'as'.

I don't think there is much danger.
Is this going to make much difference?
It gave the President too much power.
There is so much financial hardship.
It absorbs as much heat as possible.

'much of'

In front of 'it', 'this', or 'that', you use **much of,** not 'much'.

I still remember much of it in some detail.
Much of this could be glossed over.

You also use **much of** in front of a noun group which begins with a determiner or a possessive.

Much of the recent trouble has come from outside.
Caroline devoted much of her life to education.

used as a   You can use **much** as a pronoun to refer to a large quantity or amount of
pronoun   something.

There wasn't much to do.
Much has been gained from our discussions.

Note that you do not usually use **much** as an object pronoun in positive
sentences. Instead you use **a lot.** For example, instead of saying 'He
knows much about butterflies', you say 'He knows **a lot** about butterflies'.

I think he knows a lot about protection.
I suppose they learned a lot by doing it.

See entry at **lot.**

'how much'   You use **how much** when you are asking about the price of something.

I like that dress – how much is it?

See entry at **how much.**

WARNING   You do not use **much** or **much of** to talk about a large number of people or
things. Instead you use **many** or **many of.** See entry at **many.**

music - musical

'music'   **Music** is the sound that people make when they sing or play instruments.
Music is an uncount noun. You use the singular form of a verb after it.

Loewe's music is pure and entrancing.

You do not call a musical composition a 'music'. You call it a **piece of
music.**

*The only pieces of music he knew were the songs in the school's
songbook.*

'musical' used   **Musical** is used as an adjective or a noun. You use it as an adjective to
as an adjective   describe things which are connected with the playing or studying of music.

...musical instruments.
...a musical career.
...one of London's most important musical events.

Someone who is **musical** has a natural ability and interest in music.

He came from a musical family.

However, a student who studies music is called a **music student,** not a
'musical student'. Someone who teaches music is a **music teacher,** not a
'musical teacher'. Here is a list of nouns in front of which you use **music,**
not 'musical':

critic	lesson	shop
department	library	student
festival	room	teacher

'musical' used   A **musical** is a play or film that uses singing and sometimes dancing as
as a noun   part of the story.

She appeared in the musical 'Oklahoma'.

must

Must is usually used to say that something is necessary. It can also be used to say that you believe that something is true. **Must** is called a **modal**. See entry at **Modals**.

The expressions **have to, have got to,** and **need to** can sometimes be used with the same meaning as **must**. **Have got to** is not used in formal English.

The negative form of 'must' is **must not** or **mustn't**. The negative forms of 'have to' and 'have got to' are **don't have to** and **haven't got to**. The negative form of 'need to' is **need not, needn't** or **don't need to**. However, these negative forms do not all have the same meaning. This is explained below under **negative necessity**.

necessity in the present

Must, have to, have got to, and **need to** are all used to say that it is necessary that something is done.

I must leave fairly soon.
It must be protected at all costs.
You have to find some compromise.
We've got to get up early tomorrow.
A number of points need to be made about this.

After **must** you use an infinitive without 'to'. You do not use a 'to'-infinitive.

If you want to say that someone is required to do something regularly, for example because it is part of their job, you use **have to**. You do not use 'must'.

She has to do the housework while her brother reads.
He has no secretarial help and has to do everything for himself.

If you want to say that someone is required to do something on a particular occasion, you use **have got to**.

I've got to report to the office.
We've got to get in touch with the builders.

In formal English, **must** is used to say that someone is required to do something by a rule or law.

People who qualify must apply within six months.

necessity in the past

If you want to say that something was necessary in the past, you use **had to**. You do not use 'must'.

She had to go to work immediately.
We had to keep still for about four minutes.

necessity in the future

If you want to say that something will be necessary in the future, you use **will have to**.

He'll have to go to the casualty department.

negative necessity

You use **must not** or **mustn't** to say that it is important that something is not done.

You must not accept it.
We mustn't forget the paraffin.

If you want to say that it is not necessary that something **is** done, you use **don't have to, haven't got to, needn't,** or **don't need to**.

I don't have to do it any longer.
It's all right if you haven't got to work.
You needn't put the units in every time.
You don't need to go into all the details.

You do not use **must not, mustn't,** or **have not to** to say that it is not necessary that something is done.

If you are talking about the past and you want to say that it was not necessary for something to be done on a particular occasion, you use **didn't have to** or **didn't need to.**

Fortunately, she didn't have to choose.
I didn't need to say anything at all.

strong belief You use **must** to say that you strongly believe that something is the case, because of particular facts or circumstances.

There must be some mistake.
Oh, you must be Sylvia's husband.

Have to and **have got to** can also be used in this way, but not when the subject is 'you'.

It has to be the explanation.
Money has got to be the reason.

You can use **must** with 'be' and an '-ing' form to say that you believe something is happening.

She must be exaggerating.
You must be getting old.

You do not use **must** with an infinitive to say that you believe something is happening. You do not say, for example, 'He isn't in his office. He must work at home'. You say 'He isn't in his office. He **must be working** at home'.

If you want to say that you believe something is not the case, you use **cannot** or **can't.** You do not use 'must' or 'have to' with 'not'.

The two messages cannot both be true.
You can't have forgotten me.

See entry at **can - could - be able to.**

mutual

You describe a feeling as **mutual** when two people or groups feel it about each other.

I didn't like him and I was sure the feeling was mutual.
There had been a great measure of mutual respect.

You describe behaviour as **mutual** when two people or groups behave in the same way towards each other.

Single parents can join self-help groups for social life and mutual help.
They are in danger of mutual destruction.

Mutual is also used to indicate that two people have the same feeling about something, are interested in the same thing, or know the same person.

...their mutual indifference to children.
We discovered we had mutual interests in cricket and music.
They had no mutual acquaintances.

This last use is very common in written and spoken English, but some people consider it to be incorrect. You can avoid it by using other expressions. For example, instead of saying 'We discovered we had mutual friends' you can say 'We discovered we had **some of the same** friends'. Instead of talking about 'our mutual love of music' you can say 'the love **we both had** for music'.

N

name

If you **name** someone or something, you give them a name.

She wanted to name the baby Colleen.
He named his horse Circuit.

'name after' In British English, if you intentionally give someone or something the same name as a particular person or thing, you say that you **name** them **after** that person or thing.

She was named after her mother.
William Floyd later achieved immortality by having a motorway named after him.

'name for' American speakers usually say that you **name** someone or something **for** a person or thing.

They had a son, James, named for me.
They also named a locomotive for him.

named

See entry at **called - named**.

namely - i.e.

Namely and **i.e.** are both used to give more information about something that you have just mentioned.

'namely' You use **namely** to say exactly what you mean when you have just referred to something in a general or indirect way.

I shall now turn to the fourth factor, namely markets.
This virus was shown to be responsible for causing a very common illness, namely glandular fever.

'i.e.' You use **i.e.** when you are giving an explanation of a word or expression that you have just used.

You must be an amateur, i.e. someone who has never competed for prize money in athletics.
A good pass in French (i.e. at least grade B) is desirable.

Names and titles

This entry gives basic information about names and titles, and explains how you use them when talking or writing about people.

You also use a person's name or title when you talk or write to them. For information on using names and titles when talking to someone, see entry at **Addressing someone.** For information on using names and titles when writing to someone, see entry at **Letter writing.**

kinds of names People in English-speaking countries have a **first name,** which is chosen by their parents, and a **surname,** which is the last name of their parents or one of their parents.

Many people also have a **middle name,** which is also chosen by their parents. This name is not generally used in full, but the initial is sometimes given, especially in the United States.

...the assassination of John F Kennedy.

Christians use the term **Christian name** to refer to the names they choose for their children. On official forms, the term **first name** or **forename** is used.

In the past, married women always used their husband's surname. Nowadays, some women continue to use their own surname after getting married.

short forms People often use an informal and usually shorter form of someone's first name, especially in conversation. Many names have traditional short forms. For example, if someone's first name is 'James', people may call him 'Jim' or 'Jimmy'.

nicknames Sometimes a person's friends invent a name for him or her, for example a name that describes them in some way, such as 'Lofty' (meaning 'tall'). This kind of name is called a **nickname.**

spelling People's names begin with a capital letter.

...John Bacon.
...Jenny.
...Smith.

In names beginning with Mac, Mc, or O', the next letter is often a capital.

Elliott is the first athlete to be coached by McDonald.
...the author of the article, Mr Manus O'Riordan.

In Britain, some people's surnames consist of two names joined by a hyphen or written separately.

...John Heath-Stubbs.
...Sir Patrick McNair-Wilson.
...Ralph Vaughan Williams.

initials Someone's **initials** are the capital letters that begin their first name, middle name, and surname, or just their first name and middle name. For example, if someone's full name is 'Elizabeth Margaret White', you can say that her initials are 'EMW', or that her surname is 'White' and her initials are 'EM'. Sometimes a dot is put after each initial: E.M.W.

referring to someone When you refer to someone, you use their first name if the person you are talking to knows who you mean.

John and I have discussed the situation.
Have you seen Sarah?

If you need to make it clear who you are referring to, or do not know them well, you usually use both their first name and their surname.

If Matthew Davis is unsatisfactory, I shall try Sam Billings.

You use their **title** and their surname if you do not know them as a friend and want to be polite. People also sometimes refer to people much older than themselves in this more polite way.

Mr Nichols can see you now.
We'd better not let Mrs Townsend know.

Information on **titles** is given later in this entry.

You do not generally use someone's title and full name in conversation. However, people are sometimes referred to in this way in broadcasting and formal writing.

An even more ambitious reading machine has been developed by Professor Jonathan Allen at the Massachusetts Institute of Technology.

In general, you only use someone's initials and surname in writing, not in conversation. However, some well-known people (especially writers) are known by their initials rather than their first name, for example 'T.S. Eliot' and 'J.G. Ballard'.

You refer to famous writers, composers, and artists using just their surname.

...the works of Shakespeare.

Other famous people are also sometimes referred to in this way. In Britain, men are more often referred to by their surnames than women.

referring to relatives
Nouns such as 'father', 'mum', 'grandpa', and 'granny', which refer to your parents or grandparents, are also used as names.

Mum will be pleased.
You can stay with Grandma and Grandpa.

referring to a family
You can refer to a family or a married couple with the same surname by using 'the' and the plural form of that name.

...some friends of hers called the Hochstadts.

using a determiner with names
When you use a person's name, you usually use it without a determiner. However, in formal or business situations, you can put 'a' in front of someone's name when you do not know them or have not heard of them before.

You don't know a Mrs Burton-Cox, do you?
Just over two years ago, a Mr Peter Walker agreed to buy a house from a Mrs Dorothy Boyle.

You can use a famous person's name with 'another' in front of it to mean someone like that person.

He dreamed of becoming another Joseph Conrad.
What we need is another Churchill.

You can check that someone actually means a well-known person, or simply express surprise, using 'the' /ðiː/ emphatically.

You actually met the George Harrison?

titles
A person's **title** shows their social status or job.

You use a person's title and surname, or their title, first name, and surname, as explained above. The titles that are most commonly used are 'Mr' for a man, 'Mrs' for a married woman, and 'Miss' for an unmarried woman. Married women who have not taken their husband's surname are also sometimes called 'Miss'. Some younger women prefer 'Ms' to 'Mrs' or 'Miss', especially if they have married but not changed their surname.

The following titles are also used in front of someone's surname, or first name and surname:

Ambassador	Canon	Governor	President
Archbishop	Cardinal	Inspector	Professor
Archdeacon	Constable	Judge	Rabbi
Baron	Councillor	Justice	Superintendent
Baroness	Doctor	Nurse	Viscount
Bishop	Father	Police Constable	Viscountess

Inspector Flint thinks I murdered her.
...representatives of President Anatolijs Gorbunovs of Latvia.

Titles indicating rank in the armed forces, such as 'Captain' and 'Sergeant', are also used in front of someone's surname, or first name and surname.

General Haven-Hurst wanted to know what you planned to do.
...his nephew and heir, Colonel Richard Airey.

The following titles are used in front of someone's first name alone:

Emperor	King	Prince	Queen
Empress	Pope	Princess	Saint

...Queen Elizabeth II.
...Saint Francis.

'Emperor' and 'Empress' usually have 'the' in front of them.

...the Emperor Theodore.

You can use the title 'Sir' or 'Dame' in front of a person's first name and surname or, when it is clear who you mean, in front of their first name alone.

...his successor, Sir Peter Middleton.
Sir Geoffrey was not consulted over these changes.

You can use 'Lord' and 'Lady' in the same way when you are referring to someone who inherited their title and has high rank.

...the Queen's niece, Lady Sarah Armstrong-Jones.
...Lady Diana's wedding dress.

When you are using 'Lord' or 'Lady' to refer to someone who was given their title, you use it in front of the person's surname.

Lord Mackay has written to Judge Pickles seeking an explanation.

When you are using 'Lady' to refer to the wife of a knight, you use it in front of the person's surname.

Vita hated being Lady Nicolson.
...Sir John and Lady Mills.

'Earl' and 'Countess' are used in front of a person's surname.

...Earl Mountbatten of Burma.

Titles are occasionally combined. For example, armed forces titles and 'Professor' can be used in front of 'Sir'. 'Justice' is preceded by 'Mr', 'Mrs', or 'Lord'.

...General Sir Ian Hamilton.
...Mr Justice Melford Stevenson.

You can use 'the' in front of a job title with no name after it, if it is clear who you mean.

...the Queen.
...the Prime Minister.

titles of relatives   The only words which are generally used in modern English in front of names when referring to relatives are 'Uncle', 'Aunt', 'Auntie', 'Great Uncle', and 'Great Aunt'. You use them in front of the person's first name.

...Aunt Jane.

'Father' is used as the title of a priest, 'Brother' as the title of a monk, and

'Mother' or 'Sister' as the title of a nun, but these words are not used in front of the names of relatives.

titles before 'of' A title can sometimes be followed by 'of' to show what place, organization, or part of an organization the person with the title has authority over.

...the President of the United States.
...the Prince of Wales.
...the Bishop of Birmingham.

The following titles can be used after 'the' and in front of 'of':

Archbishop	Duke	Marchioness	Prince
Bishop	Earl	Marquis	Princess
Chief Constable	Emperor	Mayor	Queen
Countess	Empress	Mayoress	
Dean	Governor	President	
Duchess	King	Prime Minister	

plurals of titles You can use plurals of titles. However, they are rather formal, especially when used in front of a name rather than in front of 'of'.

...the Presidents of Colombia, Venezuela and Panama.
...Presidents Carter and Thompson.

WARNING There is no plural of 'Ms'. People hardly ever use the plural of 'Mrs'. 'Messrs', the plural of 'Mr', and 'Misses', the plural of 'Miss', are used only in very formal English or in humorous writing and speech. 'Misses' is usually preceded by 'the'.

...your solicitors, Messrs Levy and McRae.
The Misses Seeley had signed the petition.

very formal titles When you refer formally to someone important such as a king or queen, an ambassador, or a judge, you use a title consisting of a possessive determiner in front of a noun. For example, if you want to refer to the Queen, you can say 'Her Majesty the Queen' or 'Her Majesty'. The possessive determiner is usually spelled with a capital letter.

Her Majesty must do an enormous amount of travelling each year.
...Her Royal Highness, Princess Alexandra.
His Excellency is occupied.

nation

You use **nation** to refer to a country, together with its social and political structures.

He said that Britain was no longer a militarily powerful nation.

You can also use **nation** to refer to the inhabitants of a country.

He appealed to the nation for self-restraint.

However, you do not use **nation** simply to refer to a place. You do not say, for example, 'What nation do you come from?' When you are referring to a place, you use **country**, not 'nation'.

There are over a hundred edible species growing in this country.
Mexico is a large and diverse country.

national - nationalist

'national'   **National** is used to describe something that belongs to or is typical of a particular country or nation.

...*the national economy.*
...*changes in the national diet.*

'nationalist'   **Nationalist** is usually used as a noun. A **nationalist** is someone who tries to obtain political independence for his or her country.

...*a great Indonesian nationalist.*

You can also use **nationalist** as an adjective to describe people, movements, or ideas.

Nationalist leaders demanded the extension of democratic rights.
...*the nationalist movements of French West Africa.*

'nationalistic'   If someone is very proud of their country and thinks it is better than other countries, you can say that they or their views are **nationalistic**. This word is always used to indicate disapproval of someone's views.

...*an attempt to arouse nationalistic passions against the foreigner.*

'patriotic'   Normally, if someone is proud of their country, you say that they or their feelings are **patriotic**. This word is usually used to indicate approval of someone's feelings.

...*an earnest wish to enlist the patriotic spirit of the nation.*
I believe that this is the only way that an ordinary person can inspire others to be patriotic.

nationality

You use **nationality** to say what country someone legally belongs to. For example, you say that someone 'has Belgian **nationality**'.

He's got British nationality.
They have the right to claim Hungarian nationality.

You do not use **nationality** to talk about things. You do not say, for example, that something 'has Swedish nationality'. You say that it **comes from** Sweden or **was made in** Sweden.

Most of the bauxite comes from Jamaica.
They use parts made in Britain to assemble their tractors.

Nationality words

When talking about people and things from a particular country, you use one of three types of words:

- an adjective indicating the country, such as 'French' in 'French wine'

- a noun referring to a person from the country, such as 'Frenchman'

421

● a noun preceded by 'the' which refers to all the people of the country, such as 'the French'

In many cases, the word for a person who comes from a particular country is the same as the adjective, and the word for all the people of the country is the plural form of this. Here are some examples:

country	adjective	person	people
America	American	an American	the Americans
Australia	Australian	an Australian	the Australians
Belgium	Belgian	a Belgian	the Belgians
Canada	Canadian	a Canadian	the Canadians
Chile	Chilean	a Chilean	the Chileans
Germany	German	a German	the Germans
Greece	Greek	a Greek	the Greeks
India	Indian	an Indian	the Indians
Italy	Italian	an Italian	the Italians
Mexico	Mexican	a Mexican	the Mexicans
Norway	Norwegian	a Norwegian	the Norwegians
Pakistan	Pakistani	a Pakistani	the Pakistanis

All nationality adjectives that end in '-an' follow this pattern.

All nationality adjectives that end in '-ese' also follow this pattern. However, the plural form of these words is the same as the singular form. For example:

country	adjective	person	people
China	Chinese	a Chinese	the Chinese
Portugal	Portuguese	a Portuguese	the Portuguese
Vietnam	Vietnamese	a Vietnamese	the Vietnamese

A form ending in '-ese' is in fact not commonly used to refer to one person. For example, people tend to say 'a Portuguese man' or 'a Portuguese woman' rather than 'a Portuguese'.

Note that 'Swiss' also follows this pattern.

There is a group of nationality words where the word for all the people of a country is the plural of the word for a person from that country, but the adjective is different. Here are some examples:

country	adjective	person	people
Czechoslovakia	Czechoslovakian	a Czech	the Czechs
Denmark	Danish	a Dane	the Danes
Finland	Finnish	a Finn	the Finns
Iceland	Icelandic	an Icelander	the Icelanders
New Zealand	New Zealand	New Zealander	the New Zealanders
Poland	Polish	a Pole	the Poles
Sweden	Swedish	a Swede	the Swedes
Turkey	Turkish	a Turk	the Turks

Another group of nationality words have a special word for the person who comes from the country, but the adjective and the word for the people are the same. Here are some examples:

country	adjective	person	people
Britain	British	a Briton	the British
England	English	an Englishman an Englishwoman	the English
France	French	a Frenchman a Frenchwoman	the French
Holland	Dutch	a Dutchman a Dutchwoman	the Dutch
Ireland	Irish	an Irishman an Irishwoman	the Irish
Spain	Spanish	a Spaniard	the Spanish
Wales	Welsh	a Welshman a Welshwoman	the Welsh

'Briton' is used only in writing, and is not common.

The adjective relating to 'Scotland' is usually 'Scottish'. 'Scotch' is old-fashioned. A person from Scotland is 'a Scot', 'a Scotsman', or 'a Scotswoman'. You usually refer to all the people in Scotland as 'the Scots'.

referring to a person
Instead of using a nationality noun to refer to a person from a particular country, you can use a nationality adjective followed by a noun such as 'man', 'gentleman', 'woman', or 'lady'.

...an Indian gentleman.
...a French lady.

If someone uses a nationality noun in the singular, they are more likely to be referring to a man of a particular nationality than a woman. When people want to refer to a woman of a particular nationality, they tend to use a nationality adjective followed by a noun such as 'woman' or 'girl'.

He had married a Spanish girl.
An American woman in her sixties told me that this was her first trip abroad.

People usually use nationality adjectives rather than nouns after 'be'. For example, you would say 'He's Polish' rather than 'He's a Pole'.

Plural nationality nouns ending in '-men' sometimes refer to both men and women. Similarly, singular nouns ending in '-man' are sometimes used to refer in a general way to a person of a particular nationality.

...advice that has strongly antagonized many ordinary Frenchmen.
...if you're a Frenchman or a German.

referring to the people
When you are saying something about a nation, you use a plural form of the verb, even when the nationality word you are using does not end in '-s'.

The British are worried about the prospect of cheap imports.

You can use plural nouns ending in '-s' on their own to refer to the people of a particular country.

There is no way in which Italians, for example, can be prevented from entering Germany or France to seek jobs.

You can use a general determiner, a number, or an adjective in front of a plural noun to refer to some of the people of a particular country.

Many Americans assume that the British are stiff and formal.
There were four Germans with Dougal.
Increasing numbers of young Swedes choose to live together rather than to marry.

WARNING
You cannot use nationality words which do not end in '-s' like this. For example, you cannot say 'many French', 'four French', or 'young French'.

You can also use the name of a country to mean the people who belong to it or who are representing it officially. You use a singular form of a verb with it.

…the fact that Britain has been excluded from these talks.

country as modifier
If there is no adjective that indicates what country someone or something belongs to, you can use the name of the country as a modifier.

…the New Zealand government.

combining nationality adjectives
You can usually combine nationality adjectives by putting a hyphen between them when you want to indicate that something involves two countries.

…joint German-American tactical exercises.
…the Italian-Swiss border.

There are a few special adjectives which are only used in this sort of combination, in front of the hyphen.

Anglo- (England or Britain)
Euro- (Europe)
Franco- (France)
Indo- (India)
Italo- (Italy)
Russo- (Russia)
Sino- (China)

…Anglo-American trade relations.

language
Many nationality adjectives can be used to refer to the language that is spoken in a particular country or that was originally spoken in a particular country.

She speaks French so well.
There's something written here in Greek.

cities, regions, and states
There are a number of nouns which are used to refer to a person from a particular city, region, or state.

…a 23-year-old New Yorker.
Perhaps Londoners have simply got used to it.
Captain Cook was a hard-headed Yorkshireman.
Their children are now indistinguishable from other Californians.

Similarly, there are a number of adjectives which show that a person or thing comes from or exists in a particular city or state.

…a Glaswegian accent.
…a Californian beach.

nationalized - naturalized

'nationalized'
A nationalized industry has been brought under the control of the state.

Nationalized industries are continually at risk from political interference.

'naturalized'
If you become a naturalized citizen of a country, you legally become a citizen of that country, although you were not born there.

Mr Georgiadis is a naturalized British citizen of Greek origin.
Melville became a naturalized Frenchman last month.

nature

Nature is used to talk about all living things and natural processes.

Nature provides most animals with weapons of defence.
It is obvious from observing nature that growing a single crop is not in the natural order of things.

When **nature** has this meaning, you do not use 'the' in front of it.

'the country' You do not use **nature** to refer to land which is situated away from towns and cities. You refer to this land as **the country** or **the countryside.**

We live in the country.
We longed for the English countryside.

near - close

If something is **near, near to,** or **close to** a place or thing, it is a short distance from it. When **close** has this meaning, it is pronounced /kləʊs/.

I live now in Reinfeld, which is near Lübeck.
I stood very near to them.
They owned a sheep station close to the sea.

'nearby' When **near** and **close** have this meaning, you do not use them immediately in front of a noun. Instead you use **nearby.**

He was taken to a nearby building to recuperate.
He took the bag and tossed it into some nearby bushes.

However, the superlative form **nearest** can be used immediately in front of a noun.

They rush, stumbling, for the nearest exit.

other meanings You can use **near** immediately in front of a noun to say that something is almost a particular thing.

...a state of near chaos.
The right and left arms of the sea wall formed a near circle.

You can also use **near** immediately in front of an adjective and a noun to say that something almost has the quality described by the adjective.

...a near fatal accident.
The Government faces a near impossible dilemma.

You can use **near, near to,** or **close to** immediately in front of a noun to say that someone or something is almost in a particular state.

Her father was angry, her mother near tears.
...her anxiety on finding him again near to death.
She was close to tears.

You can refer to someone you know well as a '**close** friend'.

His father was a close friend of Peter Thorneycroft.

You do not refer to someone as a 'near' friend.

You can refer to someone who is directly related to you as a '**close** relative'.

She had no very close relatives.

You can also refer to someone as a '**near** relative', but this is less common.

WARNING Do not confuse the adjective **close** with the verb **close** /kləʊz/. If you **close** something, you move it so that it fills a hole or gap. See entry at **close - closed - shut.**

nearly

See entry at **almost - nearly.**

necessary

If **it is necessary to do** a particular thing, that thing must be done.

It is necessary to act fast.
It is necessary to examine this claim before we proceed any further.

used with 'for'   You can say that it is necessary **for someone** to do something.

It was necessary for me to keep active and not think about Sally.
In the early years, it is necessary for governments to directly subsidize rents.

Note that if you use **necessary** in sentences like these, the subject must be 'it'. You do not say, for example, 'She was necessary to make several calls'. You say '**It was necessary for her** to make several calls'.

However, in conversation people would normally say '**She had to** make several calls'. For more information on this use of **have to,** see entry at **must.**

If one thing is **necessary for** another, the second thing can only happen or exist if the first one happens or exists.

These weapons are necessary for the defence of our country and our free way of life.

used with 'to'   If something is **necessary to** someone, they must have it.

Solitude, no doubt, is necessary to the poet and the philosopher.

need

Need is used as a verb or a noun.

The verb has the negative forms **need not** and **do not need.** The contracted forms **needn't** and **don't need** are also used. However, you cannot use all these forms for all meanings of **need.** This is explained below.

used as a
transitive verb   If you **need** something, it is necessary for you to have it.

These animals need food throughout the winter.
I don't need any help, thank you.

For this meaning of **need,** the negative form is **do not need.**

You do not need a boat to benefit from the riches of the sea.
I didn't need any further encouragement.

WARNING   You do not use a continuous form of **need.** You do not say, for example, 'We are needing some milk'. You say 'We **need** some milk'.

used as an
intransitive verb
or modal   If you **need to do** something, it is necessary for you to do it.

To pass examinations you need to work effectively.
For an answer to these problems we need to look elsewhere.

Note that you must use 'to' in sentences like these. You do not say, for example, 'To pass examinations you need work effectively'.

However, in negative statements and questions, you can use either **need to** or **need.** You can say, for example, 'He **doesn't need to** go' or 'He **needn't** go'. Note that you do not say 'He doesn't need go' or 'He needn't to go'.

You don't need to shout.
You needn't talk about it unless you feel like it.

'Congratulations, Mrs Taylor.'—'What on?'—'Do I need to say?'
Need I remind you that you owe the company twelve-and-a-half thousand pounds?

'must not'   Note that if you say that someone **doesn't need to** do something or **need not** do something, you are saying that it is not necessary for them to do it. If you want to say that it is necessary for someone **not** to do something, you do not use **need**. Instead you use **must not** or **mustn't**.

You must not accept it.
We mustn't forget the paraffin.

See entry at **must**.

talking about   If you are talking about the past and you want to say that it was not
the past   necessary for someone to do something on a particular occasion, you say that they **didn't need to** do it or they **didn't have to** do it. You do not say that they 'needn't' do it.

I didn't need to say anything at all.
Fortunately, she didn't have to choose.

However, in a reporting clause you can use **needn't**.

They knew they needn't bother about me.

If someone has done something and you want to say that it was not necessary, you can say that they **needn't have** done it.

I was wondering whether you were getting properly fed and looked after, but I needn't have worried, need I?

'need' with   You can use **need** with an '-ing' form to say that something ought to have
'-ing' forms   something done to it. For example, you usually say 'The cooker **needs cleaning**', rather than 'The cooker needs to be cleaned'.

The scheme needs improving.
...things that needed doing.

used as a noun   When someone needs something, you can talk about their **need for** it or their **need of** it. **Need for** is more common.

...the centre's need for fresh supplies.
...his need for forgiveness.
It was a matter of recognizing my need of others.

You can also say that someone is **in need of** something. You do not say that someone is 'in need for' something.

He felt in need of a rest.
The blackboards are in need of repair.

'no need'   If you want to say that it is unnecessary to do something, you can say **there is no need to** do it.

There is no need to worry.
There was no need to search any more, because they had found the truth.

You do not say 'it is no need to' do something.

negligent - negligible

'negligent'   If someone has been **negligent,** they have not performed their duties carefully enough.

He said the organisers of the march had been negligent and irresponsible.

'negligible' If something is **negligible,** it is so small or unimportant that it is not worth considering.

The damage appears to have had a negligible effect on the yacht's speed.
They can make extra copies of videotapes at a negligible cost.

neither

You use **neither** or **neither of** to make a negative statement about two people or things. You use **neither** in front of the singular form of a count noun. You use **neither of** in front of a plural pronoun or a plural noun group beginning with 'the', 'these', 'those', or a possessive.

So, for example, you can say '**Neither child** was hurt' or '**Neither of the children** was hurt'. There is no difference in meaning.

Neither man spoke or moved.
Neither of them spoke for several moments.

WARNING You do not use **neither** without 'of' in front of a plural form. You do not say, for example, 'Neither the children was hurt'. You also do not use 'not' after **neither.** You do not say, for example, 'Neither of the children wasn't hurt'.

People sometimes use a plural form of a verb after **neither of** and a noun group. For example, they say 'Neither of the children **were** hurt'.

Neither of them are particularly obvious.
...in those moments when neither of you are speaking.

This use is acceptable in conversation, but in formal writing you should always use a singular form of a verb after **neither of.**

used as a **Neither** can be used on its own as a pronoun. This is a fairly formal use.
pronoun
Neither was suffering pain.
She chose first one, then another, but neither was to her satisfaction.

adding a clause When a negative statement has been made, you can use **neither** to indicate that this statement also applies to another person or thing. You put **neither** at the beginning of the clause, followed by an auxiliary, a modal, or 'be', then the subject.

'I didn't invite them.'—'Neither did I.'
I was not what I pretended and neither were they.

neither ... nor

In writing and formal speech, **neither** and **nor** are used to link two words or expressions of the same type in order to make a negative statement about two people, things, qualities, or actions. You put **neither** in front of the first word or expression and **nor** in front of the second one.

For example, instead of saying 'The President did not come and the Vice-President did not come' you can say '**Neither** the President **nor** the Vice-President came'.

Neither he nor Melanie owe me any explanation.
He neither drinks nor smokes.

WARNING You do not use 'or' after **neither.** You do not say, for example, 'He neither drinks or smokes'.

You always put **neither** immediately in front of the first of the words or expressions linked by 'nor'. You do not put it any earlier in the sentence. You do not say, for example, 'She neither ate meat nor fish'. You say 'She ate **neither meat nor fish**'.

In conversation, people do not usually use **neither** and **nor.** Instead of saying 'Neither the President nor the Vice-President came', you would normally say 'The President didn't come and **neither did** the Vice-President'.

Margaret didn't talk about her mother and neither did Rosa.
I won't give in to their threats, and neither will my colleagues.

Instead of saying 'She ate neither meat nor fish', you would normally say 'She **didn't** eat meat **or** fish'. Instead of saying 'She neither smokes nor drinks', you would say 'She **doesn't** smoke **or** drink'.

Karin's from abroad and hasn't any relatives or friends here.
You can't run or climb in shoes like that.

nervous

If you are **nervous,** you are rather frightened about something that you are going to do or experience.

…the child who is nervous about starting school.

'anxious'　If you are worried about something that might happen to someone else, you do not say that you are 'nervous'. You say that you are **anxious.**

It's time to be going home – your mother will be anxious.
I had to deal with calls from anxious relatives.

See entry at **anxious.**

'irritated'　If something annoys you because you cannot stop it continuing, you do not say that it makes you 'nervous'. You say that you are **irritated** by it.

I was irritated by her solicitous attitude.

never

You use **never** to say that something did not, does not, or will not happen at any time.

She never asked him to lend her any money.
I will never give up.

WARNING　You do not use 'do' in front of **never.** You do not say, for example, 'He does never write to me'. You say 'He **never writes** to me'.

He never complains.
He never speaks to you, does he?

However, for emphasis, people sometimes use 'do' after **never.** They say, for example, 'He **never does write** to me'.

I never do see her now.
I never did want a council house.

WARNING　You do not usually use another negative word with **never.** You do not say, for example, 'I haven't never been there' or 'They never said nothing'. You say 'I have **never** been there' or 'They **never** said **anything**'.

It was an experience I will never forget.
I've never seen anything like it.

Similarly, you do not use **never** if the subject of a clause is a negative word such as 'nothing' or 'no one'. Instead you use **ever.** You say, for example, 'Nothing will **ever** happen'. You do not say 'Nothing will never happen'.

Nothing ever changes.

No one will ever know.
Nobody ever mentioned this to me.

position in clause

If you are not using an auxiliary or modal, you put **never** in front of the verb, unless the verb is 'be'.

He never allowed himself to lose control.
They never take risks.

If the verb is 'be', you usually put **never** after it.

The road alongside the river was never quiet.

If you are using an auxiliary or modal, you put **never** after it.

I have never known a year quite like this.
My husband says he will never retire.
He could never overtake his opponent.

However, if you are using 'do' for emphasis, you put **never** in front of it (see above).

If you are using more than one auxiliary or modal, you put **never** after the first one.

He was one of the few people there who had never been arrested.
The answers to such questions would never be known with certainty.

If you are using an auxiliary on its own, you put **never** in front of it.

I do not want to marry you. I never did. I never will.

In stories, **never** is sometimes put first for emphasis, followed by an auxiliary and the subject of the clause.

Never had Dixon been so glad to see Margaret.
Never had two hours gone so slowly.

'never' with an imperative

You can use **never** with an imperative instead of 'do not'. You do this when you want to emphasize that something should not be done at any time.

Never let them sit on your lap.
Never use a natural fibre such as string to hang pictures.

new

You use **new** to describe things which were created, made, built, or begun a short time ago.

There was a new book by R.D. Laing lying on the table.
...new methods of medical care.
...smart new houses.

You also use **new** to describe something which has replaced something else.

They would have to decorate and get new furniture.
He loved his new job.

There are several other words which have a similar meaning to **new**:

'recent'

Recent is used to describe events and periods of time that occurred a short time ago.

...the recent kidnapping of a British judge.
The energy conservation budget has been substantially reduced in recent years.

You do not usually use **recent** to describe objects, but you can use it to describe things such as newspaper articles and photographs.

...a recent report from the Food and Agriculture Organization.
You will need to take with you your passport and two recent black and white photographs.

You can also use **recent** to describe governments and people with particular jobs.

No recent government has shown much enthusiasm for building up a more robust wood-processing industry.
Many recent composers have been less imaginative.

'modern' and 'present-day'
You use **modern** or **present-day** to describe things that exist now, when you want to emphasize that they are different from earlier things of the same kind.

...modern power stations.
...the stresses of modern life.
By present-day standards, its technology was, of course, cumbersome and limited.

'contemporary'
Contemporary has the same meaning as **modern** and **present-day,** but it is usually used only to describe abstract things or things relating to the arts.

What is women's situation in contemporary society?
Contemporary music is played there now.

You also use **contemporary** to indicate that something existed in the past at the same time as something else that you have been talking about.

Contemporary records of the case do not, however, mention these two items.

'current'
Current is used to describe things that exist now, but that might end or change soon.

...the root causes of our current crisis.
...Kitty King, Boyd Stuart's current girlfriend.

newly

See entry at **recently - newly - lately.**

news

News is information that you give to someone about a recent event or a recently changed situation.

I've got some good news for you.
Thousands of people gathered outside the Mandelas' house on hearing news of his release.

You also use **news** to refer to descriptions of recent events on television or radio or in a newspaper.

They continued to broadcast up-to-date news and pictures of these events.

News looks like a plural noun but is in fact an uncount noun. You use a singular form of a verb after it.

The news is likely to be received with apprehension.
I was still lying helpless in bed when the news was brought to me.

You talk about **this news,** not 'these news'.

I had been waiting at Camp 3 for this news.

You do not talk about 'a news'. You refer to a piece of information as **some news, a bit of news,** or **a piece of news.**

I've got some good news for you.
I've had a bit of bad news.
A respectful silence greeted this piece of news.

You refer to a description of an event on television or in a newspaper as **a news item** or **an item of news.**

...a small news item in The Times last Friday.
An item of news in the Sunday paper caught my attention.

next

Next is usually used to say when something will happen. It can also be used to talk about the physical position of something, or the position that something has in a list or series.

talking about the future You use **next** in front of words such as 'week', 'month', or 'year' to say when something will happen. For example, if it is Wednesday and something is going to happen on Monday, you can say that it will happen **next week.**

I'm getting married next month.
I don't know where I will be next year.

Note that you do not use 'the' or a preposition in front of **next.** You do not say, for example, that something will happen 'the next week' or 'in the next week'.

You can also use **next** without 'the' or a preposition in front of 'weekend' or in front of the name of a season, month, or day of the week.

Next weekend there is a by-election in Marseilles.
You must come and see us next autumn.
He said he would be seventy-five next April.
Let's have lunch together next Wednesday.

However, you do not use **next** like this in front of 'decade' or 'century'. You do not say, for example, that something will happen 'next decade'. You say that it will happen **in the next decade** or **during the next decade.**

The population aged between 5 and 14 in the developing countries will increase in the next decade from 550 million to 725 million.
Academics from the United States will address a conference on higher education during the next decade.

You do not say that something will happen 'next day'. You say that it will happen **tomorrow.** Similarly, you do not say that something will happen 'next morning', 'next afternoon', 'next evening', or 'next night'. You say that it will happen **tomorrow morning, tomorrow afternoon, tomorrow evening,** or **tomorrow night.**

Can we meet tomorrow at five?
I'm going down there tomorrow morning.
We're all having dinner together tomorrow night.

WARNING You do not usually use **next** to refer to a day in the same week. For example, if it is Monday and you intend to ring someone in four days' time, you do not say 'I will ring you next Friday'. You say 'I will ring you **on Friday**'.

He's going off to scout camp on Friday.

If you want to make it completely clear that you are talking about a day in the same week, you use **this.**

The film opens this Thursday at various ABC Cinemas in London.

Similarly, you can say that something will happen **this weekend.**

I might be able to go skiing this weekend.

You use **the next** to refer to any period of time measured forward from the present. For example, if it is July 2nd and you want to say that something will happen between now and July 23rd, you say that it will happen **in the next three weeks** or **during the next three weeks**.

Mr John MacGregor will make the announcement in the next two weeks.
More than 2,000 of the country's 8,000 state-owned companies are expected to go out of business during the next six months.

talking about the past

When you are talking about the past and you want to say that something happened on the day after events that you have been describing, you say that it happened **the next day** or **the following day**.

I telephoned the next day and protested to the receptionist.
The following day I went to speak at a conference in Scotland.

In stories, **next day** is sometimes used, especially at the beginning of a clause.

Next day we all got up rather early.

Next, the next, and **the following** can also be used in front of 'morning'.

Next morning he began to work but felt uninspired.
The next morning, as I left for the office, a letter arrived for me.
The following morning he checked out of the hotel and took the express to Paris.

However, in front of 'afternoon', 'evening', or the name of a day of the week you normally only use **the following**.

I arrived at the village the following afternoon.
He was due to start the following Friday.

talking about physical position

You use **next to** to say that someone or something is by the side of a person or object.

She went and sat next to him.
There was a bowl of goldfish next to the bed.

If you talk about **the next room,** you are referring to a room that is separated by a wall from the one you are in.

I can hear my husband in the next room, typing away.

Similarly, if you are in a theatre or a bus, **the next seat** is a seat which is by the side of the one you are sitting in.

He became aware that the girl in the next seat was studying him with interest.

You can use **next** like this with a few other nouns, for example 'desk', 'bed', or 'compartment'.

WARNING

However, you do not use **next** simply to say that a particular thing is closer than anything else of its kind. You do not say, for example, 'They took him to the next hospital'. You say 'They took him to **the nearest hospital**'.

The nearest town is Brompton.
The nearest beach is 15 minutes' walk away.

talking about a list or series

The **next** one in a list or series is the one that comes immediately after the one you have been talking about.

And this leads directly into our next item, which comes from Kano in northern Nigeria.

The **next** thing **but one** in a list or series is the one that comes after the next one.

The next section but one depicts the violence which has become common in the city.

nice

Nice is a very common adjective. You use it to show that you like someone or something, or that something gives you pleasure.

He has nice eyes.
It's a very nice town.
I got a nice hat and a green dress.

Some people object to the use of **nice** because they say it does not have a clear meaning. This is only partly true.

talking about people When you use **nice** to talk about people or their behaviour, its meaning is clear. If you say that someone is 'a **nice** man' or 'a **nice** woman', you mean that they are kind and thoughtful.

They seemed very nice men.
We've got very nice neighbours.

You can say that it is **nice of** someone to do something. This is a way of showing gratitude when someone has behaved in a kind and thoughtful way.

It's nice of you to say that.
How nice of you to come.

If someone is **being nice to** someone else, they are behaving in a pleasant and friendly way towards them, even though they may not like them.

Promise you'll be nice to her when she comes back.

talking about enjoyment You can use **nice** with some nouns to talk about spending time in a pleasant way. This is a very common use. For example, if you say 'Have a **nice** evening', you are saying to someone that you hope they will spend the evening in a pleasant way. Similarly, if you say 'Did you have a **nice** holiday?', you are asking someone if they enjoyed their recent holiday.

They were having a nice time.
'Have a nice weekend.'—'You too.'

talking about things and places In conversation, you can use **nice** to say that you like a thing or place. However, in formal writing it is better to find another adjective which expresses your meaning more exactly.

...a delightful room.
...a bottle of nail polish in an attractive shade.
It is one of the pleasantest places I know.

'nice' with other adjectives In conversation, **nice** is often used with other adjectives. For example, you can say that a room is **nice and warm** or describe it as a **nice, warm** room. When you use **nice** like this, you are saying that the room is nice because it is warm.

The room is nice and clean.
It's nice and peaceful here.
I want a nice, warm, comfortable bed.

night

Night is the period during each twenty-four hours when it is dark. If something happens regularly during this period, you say that it happens **at night**.

It hunts at night for insects, small reptiles and even baby birds.

I used to lie awake at night watching the rain seep through the ceiling.

A **night** is one of these periods of darkness. You usually refer to a particular period as **the night.**

He was at the hotel and intended to spend the night there.
Is that what you've come out here in the middle of the night to tell me?

the previous night If you want to say that something happened during the night before the present day, you say that it happened **in the night, during the night,** or **last night.**

I didn't hear Sheila in the night.
I had the strangest dream last night.

You can also say that a situation existed **last night.**

I didn't manage to sleep much last night.

Note that **last night** is also used to say that something happened during the previous evening.

I met your husband last night.

If you are talking about a day in the past and you want to say that something happened the night before that day, you say that it happened **in the night, during the night,** or **the previous night.**

He had died in the night.
There had been reports that a motorized division had crossed the border during the night.
...the hill they had climbed the previous night.

exact times If you have mentioned an exact time and you want to make it clear that you are talking about the early part of the night rather than the morning, you add **at night.**

This took place at eleven o'clock at night on our second day of travel.

However, if you are talking about a time after midnight and you want to make it clear that you are talking about the night and not the afternoon, you say **in the morning.**

It was five o'clock in the morning.

no

used as a reply **No** is used as a negative reply.

'Is he down there already?'—'No, he's not there.'
'Did you come alone?'—'No. John's here with me.'

Note that **no** is used as a negative reply to negative questions. For example, if you are Spanish and someone says to you 'You aren't Italian, are you?', you say **'No'.** You do not say 'Yes'.

'You don't smoke, do you?'—'No.'
'It won't take you more than ten minutes, will it?'—'No.'

used as a determiner **No** is used in front of nouns as a negative determiner. It means 'not any'. For example, instead of saying 'She doesn't have any friends', you can say 'She has **no friends'.**

I have no complaints.
My children are hungry. We have no food.

used with comparatives **No** is used in front of comparative adjectives instead of 'not'. For example, instead of saying 'She isn't taller than her sister', you say 'She is **no taller** than her sister'.

The woman was no older than Kate.
...shells no bigger than a little fingernail.

However, you do not use **no** and a comparative in front of a noun. You do not talk, for example, about 'a no older woman' or 'a no bigger shell'.

used with 'different' **No** is used in front of 'different' instead of 'not'.

The tasks which confront him are no different from those which faced his predecessor.

used to forbid things **No** is often used on notices to tell you that something is not allowed. **No** is followed by an '-ing' form or a noun.

No smoking.
No entry.
No dogs.
No wheeled vehicles beyond this point.

nobody

See entry at **no-one**.

noise

See entry at **sound - noise**.

no longer

See entry at **any more**.

none

'none of' You use **none of** in front of a plural noun group to make a negative statement about every thing or person in a particular group.

None of these suggestions is very helpful.
None of his rivals could mount a challenge.

You use **none of** in front of a noun group containing an uncount noun to make a negative statement about every part of something.

None of the mail would be sent out after D-day.

You can use **none of** in front of a singular or plural pronoun.

None of this seems to have made any impression on him.
We had none of these at home.

You do not use 'we' or 'they' after **none of**. Instead you use **us** or **them**.

None of us had been responsible for the reports.
None of them had learned anything about the teaching of reading.

When you use **none of** in front of a plural noun or pronoun, you can use either a plural or singular form of a verb after it. The singular form is more formal.

None of his books have been published in England.
None of their matches has been staged at Old Trafford.

None of them are real.
None of them is impressed.

When you use **none of** in front of an uncount noun or a singular pronoun, you use a singular form of a verb after it.

None of the wheat was ruined.
Yet none of this has seriously affected shares.

used as a pronoun	**None** can be used on its own as a pronoun.

There were none left.
He asked for some documentary proof. I told him that I had none.

You do not usually use any other negative word after **none of** or **none**. You do not say, for example, 'None of them weren't ready'. You say 'None of them **were** ready'.

Similarly, you do not use **none of** or **none** as the object of a sentence which already has a negative word in it. You do not say, for example, 'I didn't want none of them'. You say 'I didn't want **any** of them'.

You only use **none of** or **none** to talk about a group of three or more things or people. If you want to talk about two things or people, you use **neither of** or **neither**. See entry at **neither**.

no-one

No-one or **nobody** means 'not a single person', or 'not a single member of a particular group'. There is no difference in meaning between **no-one** and **nobody**.

No-one can also be written **no one**. **Nobody** is always written as one word.

You use a singular form of a verb with **no-one** or **nobody**.

A drum of chemicals exploded but no-one was killed.
Nobody knows where he is.

You do not usually use any other negative word after **no-one** or **nobody**. You do not say, for example, 'No-one didn't come'. You say 'No-one **came**'.

Similarly, you do not use **no-one** or **nobody** as the object of a sentence which already has a negative word in it. You do not say, for example, 'We didn't see no-one'. You say 'We didn't see **anyone**' or 'We didn't see **anybody**'.

You mustn't tell anyone.
He didn't trust anybody.

You do not use 'of' after **no-one** or **nobody**. You do not say, for example, 'No-one of the children could speak French'. You say '**None** of the children could speak French'.

None of the women I spoke with regretted making this change.
It was something none of us could possibly have guessed.

See entry at **none**.

nor

'neither...nor'	You can use **nor** with 'neither' to make a negative statement about two people or things.

Neither Margaret nor John was there.
He spoke neither English nor French.

For a full explanation, see entry at **neither ... nor**.

used to link clauses	**Nor** is also used to link negative clauses. You put **nor** at the beginning of the second clause, followed by an auxiliary, a modal, or 'be', followed by the subject and the main verb, if there is one.

The officer didn't believe me, nor did the girls when they came back.
This argument fails to explain how the present developed countries were

able to progress, _nor does it explain_ the recent success of some of the developing countries.

You can put 'and' or 'but' in front of **nor.**

I would have nothing to do with it, and nor would most of us.
Institutions of learning are not taxed; but nor, in many cases, are they much respected.

You do not normally begin a sentence with **nor,** but you can sometimes do so when you want to make the sentence seem more dramatic or forceful.

Despite these strong calls, there has been little official action. Nor has the government shown interest in assessing energy conservation's cost-effectiveness.
I do not want these letters. Nor do I even want any copies.

'nor' in replies   You can reply to a negative statement using **nor.** You do this to indicate that what has just been said also applies to another person or thing.

'I don't like him.'—'Nor do I.'
'I can't stand much more of this.'—'Nor can I.'

normally

See section on **frequency** in entry at **Adverbials.**

north

The **north** is the direction which is on your left when you are looking towards the direction where the sun rises.

The land to the north and east was low-lying.
There is a possibility of colder weather and winds from the north.

A **north** wind blows from the north.

The north wind was blowing straight into her face.

The **north** of a place is the part that is towards the north.

Poaching started in the north of the country.
The best asparagus comes from the Calvados region in the north of France.

North occurs in the names of some countries, states, and regions.

They have hopes for business in North Korea.
...the mountains of North Carolina.
...ecological damage in North America.

'northern'   However, you do not usually talk about a 'north' part of a country or region. You talk about a **northern** part.

...Soya, the northern cape of Japan.
...the northern tip of Caithness.

Similarly, you do not talk about 'north Europe' or 'north England'. You say **northern** Europe or **northern** England.

Bowman had flown over northern Canada.

northerly

If something moves in a **northerly** direction, it moves towards the north.

We continued in a northerly direction.

However, a **northerly** wind blows **from** the north.

...a northerly wind blowing off the sea.

The most **northerly** of a group of things is the one that is furthest to the north.

The most northerly of all monkeys is a macaque, living in Japan.
...the Summer solstice, when the sun reaches its most northerly point.

northwards

If you move or look **northwards,** you move or look towards the north.

Morning Rose moved off slowly northwards from the jetty.

Northwards is only used as an adverb.

'northward'   In American English and old-fashioned British English, **northward** is often used instead of 'northwards'.

We struck off northward through the woods.

In both British and American English, **northward** is sometimes used as an adjective in front of a noun.

...the northward offensive of the Northern Army Group.

no sooner

See entry at **soon.**

not

Not is used with verbs to form negative sentences.

position of 'not'   You put **not** after the first auxiliary or modal, if there is one.

They are not seen as major problems.
They might not even notice.
Most people suffering from the disease have not been exposed unduly to radiation.

If there is no other auxiliary, you use 'do' as the auxiliary. After **not** you use the base form of a verb.

The girl did not answer.
He does not speak English very well.

In conversation, when 'not' is used after 'be', 'have', 'do', or a modal, it is not usually pronounced in full. When you write down what someone says, you usually represent 'not' as **n't** and add it to the verb in front of it. In some cases, the verb also changes its form. For an explanation of these changes, see entry at **Contractions.**

Note that with almost all verbs you do not use **not** without an auxiliary. You do not say, for example, 'I not liked it' or 'I liked not it'. You say 'I **didn't like** it'.

There are two exceptions to this. When you use **not** with 'be', you do not use an auxiliary. You simply put **not** after 'be'.

I'm not sure about this.
The program was not a success.

When 'have' is used as a main verb with **not,** it is sometimes used without an auxiliary, but only in the contracted forms 'hasn't', 'haven't', and 'hadn't'.

You haven't any choice.
The sky hadn't a cloud in it.

However, it is more common to use the forms 'doesn't have', 'don't have', and 'didn't have'.

This question doesn't have a proper answer.
We don't have any direct control of the rents.
I didn't have a cheque book.

When you use **not** to make what you are saying negative, you do not usually use another negative word such as 'nothing', 'never', or 'none'. You do not say, for example, 'I don't know nothing about it'. You say 'I don't know **anything** about it'.

'not really' You can make a negative statement more polite or less strong by using 'really' after **not**.

Winning or losing is not really important.
It doesn't really matter.
I don't really want to be part of it.

You can reply to some questions by saying '**Not really**'. See entry at **Replies**.

'not very' When you make a negative statement using **not** and an adjective, you can make the statement less strong by putting 'very' in front of the adjective.

The fees are not very high.
I'm not very interested in the subject.
That's not a very good arrangement.

Although you can say that something is 'not very good', you do not use **not** in front of other words meaning 'very good'. You do not say, for example, that something is 'not excellent' or 'not marvellous'.

used with negative adjectives You can make a positive statement by using **not** in front of an adjective that already has a negative meaning. For example, if you say that something is **not unreasonable,** you mean that it is quite reasonable.

Frost and snow are not uncommon during these months.
It is not unlikely that they could change again.

When you use 'a' and a short adjective in statements like these, you put **not** in front of 'a'. With long adjectives, you can put **not** either in front of 'a' or after it.

It's not a bad idea.
It is not an unpleasant feeling.
This is a not unreasonable interpretation.

used with 'to'-infinitives You can use **not** with a 'to'-infinitive. You put **not** in front of 'to', not after it.

The Prime Minister has asked his ministers not to discuss the issue publicly any more.
I decided not to go in.
Be careful not to overdo it.

'not' in contrasts You can use **not** to link two words or expressions. You do this to point out that something is the case, and to contrast it with what is not the case.

The plaque confirmed that the paintings were a gift, not a bequest.
The world can only be grasped by action, not by contemplation.

You can make a similar contrast by changing the order of the words or expressions. When you do this, you put **not** in front of the first word or expression and **but** in front of the second one.

A passport was now not a right but a privilege.
Industry is owned and controlled not by you, but by your employer.

used with sentence adverbs	You can use **not** with 'surprisingly', 'unexpectedly', or 'unusually' to make a negative comment on a statement. *Not surprisingly, the Council rejected the suggestion.* *Not unexpectedly, the revelation caused enormous interest.* *But, not unusually, Jo surprised me.*
'not all'	**Not** is sometimes used with 'all' and with words beginning with 'every-' to form the subject of a sentence. For example, instead of saying 'Some snakes are not poisonous', you can say '**Not all** snakes are poisonous'. *Not all the houses we get offered have central heating.* *Not everyone agrees with me.*
'not only'	**Not only** is often used with 'but' or 'but also' to link two words or word groups. For an explanation of this use, see entry at **not only**.

notable

See entry at **noticeable - notable**.

nothing

Nothing means 'not a single thing', or 'not a single part of something'.

You use a singular form of a verb with **nothing**.

Nothing is happening.
Nothing has been discussed.

WARNING	You do not usually use any other negative word such as 'not' after **nothing**. You do not say, for example, 'Nothing didn't happen'. You say 'Nothing **happened**'. Similarly, you do not use **nothing** as the object of a sentence which already has a negative word in it. You do not say, for example, 'I couldn't hear nothing'. You say 'I couldn't hear **anything**.' *I did not say anything.* *He never seemed to do anything at all.*
'nothing but'	**Nothing but** is used in front of a noun group or an infinitive without 'to' to mean 'only'. For example, instead of saying 'In the fridge there was only a piece of cheese', you can say 'In the fridge there was **nothing but** a piece of cheese'. *For a few months I thought and talked of nothing but Jeremy.* *He did nothing but complain.*

notice

Notice is used as a noun or a verb.

used as a noun	A **notice** is a sign in a public place which gives information or instructions. *There was a notice on the lift saying it was out of order.*
'note'	You do not use **notice** to refer to a short, informal letter. The word you use is **note**. *I shall have to write a note to Eileen's mother to explain her hurt arm.*
'take notice'	If you **take notice of** someone or something, you pay attention to them. *I'll make her take notice of me.* *Write a letter to your MP. He has to take notice of his post.* When someone does not pay any attention to someone or something, you can say that they **take no notice** of them or **do not take any notice** of them.

Her mother took no notice of her weeping.
They refused to take any notice of one another.

'notice' used as a verb

If someone becomes aware of something, you do not say that they 'take notice of' it. You say that they **notice** it.

I've noticed your hostility towards him.
He noticed two grey trucks parked near his house.

noticeable - notable

'noticeable'

Something that is **noticeable** is large enough or clear enough to be noticed.

The teachers report a noticeable increase in the amount of reading done by the pupils.
I experienced no noticeable ill effects.

'notable'

Something that is **notable** is important or remarkable. **Notable** is a fairly formal word.

His most notable journalistic achievement was to bring out his own paper.
The second notable event was the sudden disappearance of Martha.

not only

used with 'but' or 'but also'

You use **not only** to link two words or word groups referring to things, actions, or situations. You put **not only** in front of the first word or group, and **but** or **but also** in front of the second one. The second thing mentioned is usually more surprising, informative, or important than the first one.

The government radio not only reported the demonstration, but announced it in advance.
Some parents are not only concerned with safety but also sceptical of the educational value of such trips.
We are interested in assessing not only what the children have learnt but how they have learnt it.

used with a pronoun

When you are linking word groups that begin with a verb, you can omit **but** or **but also** and use a personal pronoun instead. For example, instead of saying 'Margaret not only came to the party but brought her aunt as well', you can say 'Margaret not only came to the party, **she** brought her aunt as well'.

Imported taps not only provide more variation, they are often more attractively designed.
Her interest in your work has not only continued, it has increased.

putting 'not only' first

For emphasis, you can put **not only** first, followed by an auxiliary or 'be', then the subject, then the main verb.

Not only did they send home substantial earnings, but they also saved money.
Not only do they rarely go on school outings, they rarely, if ever, leave Brooklyn.

Not only must come first when you are linking two clauses which have different subjects.

Not only were the locals all old, but the women still dressed in long black dresses.
Not only were the instruments unreliable, the crew had not flown together before.

'not just'   **Not just** is sometimes used instead of **not only**.

It is <u>not just</u> the most fashionable but also one of the best restaurants in the West End.
I want to see more and more people <u>not just</u> voting in polling stations, but formulating the policies of the political parties.

Not just is used only in front of adjectives, nouns, phrases, and participles. You do not use it in front of verbs.

notorious

See entry at **famous**.

GRAMMAR # Noun groups

A **noun group**, or **noun phrase**, is a group of words which acts as the subject, complement, or object of a clause, or as the object of a preposition.

He was eating <u>an apple</u>.
He was using <u>blue ink</u>.
<u>Strawberries</u> are very expensive now.
That's <u>a good idea</u>.
She wanted <u>a job</u> in <u>the oil industry</u>.

A noun group can consist of a noun by itself, or it can also contain a determiner, adjective, or other modifier or qualifier.

...picking <u>apples</u> on an autumn afternoon.
Peel, core, and slice <u>the apples</u>.
She noticed the two <u>apple trees</u>, already bearing a crop of <u>small green apples</u>.
<u>The apples hanging above us</u> were tinged with pink.

A noun group can also be a pronoun.

I've got two boys, and <u>they</u> both enjoy playing football.
<u>Someone</u> is coming to mend <u>it</u> tomorrow.

See also entries at **Adjectives, Determiners, Modifiers, Nouns, Pronouns,** and **Qualifiers.**

GRAMMAR # Noun modifiers

A **noun modifier** is a noun that is used in front of another noun to give more specific information about someone or something. It is nearly always singular.

...the <u>car</u> door.
...a <u>football</u> player.
...a <u>surprise</u> announcement.

A few plural nouns remain plural when used as modifiers. See section on **plural nouns** in entry at **Nouns.**

The use of noun modifiers is very common in English. You can use noun modifiers to indicate a wide range of relationships between two nouns. For example, you can indicate:

- what something is made of, as in 'cotton socks'

- what is made in a particular place, as in 'a glass factory'

- what someone does, as in 'a football player'

- where something is, as in 'my bedroom curtains' and 'Brighton Technical College'

- when something happens, as in 'the morning mist' and 'her wartime activities'

- the nature or size of something, as in 'a surprise attack' and 'a pocket chess-set'

See also entry at **Possession and other relationships**.

Noun modifiers can be used together.

...car body repair kits.
...a family dinner party.
...a Careers Information Officer.

Adjectives can be put in front of a noun modifier.

...a long car journey.
...a new scarlet silk handkerchief.
...complex business deals.

---

noun phrases

See entry at **Noun groups**.

GRAMMAR **Nouns**

A **noun** is used to identify a person or thing. Nouns can be classified into six main grammatical types: count nouns, uncount nouns, singular nouns, plural nouns, collective nouns, and proper nouns.

count nouns Nouns referring to things which can be counted are called **count nouns**. They have two forms, singular and plural. The plural form usually ends in 's'. For full information on how to form plurals, see entry at **Plural forms of nouns**.

The singular form of a count noun is always preceded by a determiner such as 'a', 'another', 'every', or 'the'.

They left the house to go for a walk after tea.

When you use a singular form as the subject of a verb, you use a singular verb form.

My son likes playing football.
The address on the letter was wrong.

The plural form of a count noun can be used with or without a determiner. You do not use a determiner if you are referring to a type of thing in general. You use a determiner such as 'the' or 'my' if you are referring to a particular group of things. You use a determiner such as 'many' or 'several' when you are indicating how many things there are.

Does the hotel have large rooms?
The rooms at Watermouth are all like this.

The house had many rooms and a terrace with a view of Etna.

When you use a plural form as the subject of a verb, you use a plural verb form.

These cakes are delicious.

Count nouns can be used after numbers.

...one table.
...two cats.
...three hundred pounds.

uncount nouns   Nouns which refer to things such as substances, qualities, feelings, and types of activity, rather than to individual objects or events, are called **uncount nouns**. These nouns have only one form.

I needed help with my homework.
The children had great fun playing with the puppets.

WARNING   Some nouns which are uncount nouns in English are count nouns or plural nouns in other languages.

advice	furniture	knowledge	money
baggage	homework	luggage	news
equipment	information	machinery	traffic

Uncount nouns are not used with 'a' or 'an'. They are used with 'the' or possessive determiners when they refer to something that is specified or known.

I liked the music, but the words were boring.
Eva clambered over the side of the boat into the water.
She admired his vitality.

When you use an uncount noun as the subject of a verb, you use a singular verb form.

Electricity is dangerous.
Food was expensive in those days.

Uncount nouns are not used after numbers. It is possible to refer to a quantity of something which is expressed by an uncount noun by using a word like 'some', or a phrase like 'a piece of'. See entry at **Quantity**.

I want some privacy.
I pulled the two pieces of paper from my pocket.

WARNING   Some uncount nouns end in '-ics' or '-s' and therefore look like plural count nouns.

Mathematics is too difficult for me.
Measles is in most cases a harmless illness.

These nouns usually refer to:

- subjects of study and activities

acoustics	classics	gymnastics	obstetrics
aerobics	economics	linguistics	physics
aerodynamics	electronics	logistics	politics
aeronautics	ethics	mathematics	statistics
athletics	genetics	mechanics	thermodynamics

- games

billiards	cards	darts	skittles
bowls	checkers	draughts	tiddlywinks

- illnesses

diabetes	mumps	rickets
measles	rabies	shingles

mass nouns A **mass noun** is a noun referring to a substance which is usually used as an uncount noun but which can be used as a count noun to refer to quantities or types of the substance. For example, you can ask for 'three coffees', meaning 'three cups of coffee', or talk about 'different cheeses', meaning 'different types of cheese'.

We asked for two coffees.
...profits from low-alcohol beers.
...the use of small amounts of nitrogen in making certain steels.

singular nouns There are some nouns, and some particular meanings of nouns, which are only used in the singular form. **Singular nouns** are always used with a determiner and take a singular verb.

The sun was shining.
He's always thinking about the past and worrying about the future.
They were beginning to find Griffiths' visits rather a strain.
There was a note of satisfaction in his voice.

plural nouns Some nouns have only a plural form. For example, you can buy 'goods', but not 'a good'. Other nouns have only a plural form when they are used with a particular meaning.

Take care of your clothes.
The weather conditions were the same.

WARNING Plural nouns are not usually used after numbers. For example, you do not say 'two clothes' or 'two goods'.

Some plural nouns refer to single items that have two linked parts: things that people wear or tools that people use. These plural nouns are:

glasses	knickers	pyjamas	tights
jeans	pants	shorts	trousers

binoculars	pliers	scissors	tweezers
pincers	scales	shears	

You use 'some' in front of these words when talking about one item.

I wish I'd brought some scissors.

You can also use 'a pair of' when talking about one item, and 'two pairs of', 'three pairs of', and so on when talking about more than one item.

I was sent out to buy a pair of scissors.
Liza had given me three pairs of jeans.

Many plural nouns lose their '-s' and '-es' endings when they are used in front of other nouns.

...my trouser pocket.
...pyjama trousers.

However, some plural nouns keep the same form when used in front of other nouns.

arms	clothes	jeans
binoculars	glasses	sunglasses

...arms control.
...clothes pegs.

collective nouns Some nouns, called **collective nouns,** refer to a group of people or things.

army	crew	gang	navy	team
audience	enemy	government	press	
committee	family	group	public	
company	flock	herd	staff	

The singular form of these nouns can be used with a singular or plural verb form, depending on whether the group is seen as one thing or as several things.

Our family isn't poor any more.
My family are perfectly normal.

When referring back to a collective noun, you usually use a singular pronoun or determiner if you have used a singular verb. You use a plural pronoun or determiner if you have used a plural verb.

The government has said it would wish to do this only if there was no alternative.
The government have made up their minds that they're going to win.

However, plural pronouns and determiners are sometimes used to refer back to a collective noun even when a singular verb has been used. This is done especially in a separate clause.

The team was not always successful but their rate of success far exceeded expectations.
His family was waiting in the next room, but they had not yet been informed.

Names of organizations and groups such as football teams also behave like collective nouns.

Liverpool is leading 1-0.
Liverpool are attacking again.

WARNING Although you can use a plural verb after the singular form of a collective noun, these singular forms do not behave exactly like plural count nouns. Numbers cannot be used in front of them. For example, you cannot say 'Three crew were killed'. You have to say 'Three of the crew were killed' or 'Three members of the crew were killed'.

Most of the collective nouns listed above have ordinary plural forms, which refer to more than one group. However, 'press' (meaning 'newspapers' or 'journalists') and 'public' (meaning 'the people of a country') do not have plural forms.

proper nouns Names of people, places, organizations, institutions, ships, magazines, books, plays, paintings, and other unique things are **proper nouns** and are spelled with initial capital letters. A proper noun is sometimes used with a determiner but normally has no plural. See entries at **Names and titles** and **Places.**

> ...Mozart.
> ...Romeo and Juliet.
> ...the President of the United States.
> ...the United Nations.
> ...the Seine.

compound nouns **Compound nouns** are made up of two or more words. Some are written as separate words, some are written with hyphens between the words, and some have a hyphen between the first two words.

> His luggage came sliding towards him on the <u>conveyor belt.</u>
> There are many <u>cross-references</u> to help you find what you want.
> It can be cleaned with a spot of <u>washing-up liquid.</u>

Some compound nouns are written in several ways. A Cobuild dictionary will tell you how you should write each compound noun.

For information on compound nouns ending in 'ing', see entry at '**-ing**' **forms.** For information on the plurals of compound nouns, see entry at **Plural forms of nouns.**

abstract and concrete nouns An **abstract noun** is a noun which refers to a quality, idea, or experience rather than something that can be seen or touched.

> ...a boy or girl with <u>intelligence.</u>
> We found Alan weeping with <u>relief</u> and <u>joy.</u>
> I am stimulated by <u>conflict.</u>

Abstract nouns are usually uncountable. However, abstract nouns referring to a particular instance of something are countable.

> Russia had been successful in previous <u>conflicts.</u>

A **concrete noun** is a noun which refers to something that can be seen or touched. Nouns referring to objects, animals, and people are usually countable.

> ...a broad <u>highway</u> with shady <u>trees.</u>

A few nouns that refer to groups of objects, such as 'furniture' and 'equipment', are uncountable. See section above on **uncount nouns.**

Nouns referring to substances are usually uncountable.

> There is not enough <u>water.</u>

However, nouns which are being used to refer to a particular quantity or variety of a substance are countable. See section above on **mass nouns.**

nouns followed by prepositions   Some nouns, especially abstract nouns, are often followed by a prepositional phrase to show what they relate to. There is often little or no choice about which preposition to use after a particular noun.

I demanded access to a telephone.
...his authority over them.
...the solution to our energy problem.

The following nouns usually or often have 'to' after them:

access	antidote	immunity	resistance
addiction	approach	incitement	return
adherence	aversion	introduction	sequel
affront	contribution	preface	solution
allegiance	damage	prelude	susceptibility
allergy	devotion	recourse	threat
allusion	disloyalty	reference	vulnerability
alternative	exception	relevance	witness
answer	fidelity	reply	

The following nouns usually or often have 'for' after them:

admiration	desire	provision	substitute
appetite	disdain	quest	sympathy
aptitude	dislike	recipe	synonym
bid	disregard	regard	taste
craving	disrespect	remedy	thirst
credit	hunger	respect	
cure	love	responsibility	
demand	need	room	

The following nouns usually or often have 'on' or 'upon' after them:

assault	constraint	embargo	restriction
attack	crackdown	hold	stance
ban	curb	insistence	tax
comment	dependence	reflection	
concentration	effect	reliance	

The following nouns usually or often have 'with' after them:

affinity	dealings	familiarity	intersection
collusion	dissatisfaction	identification	sympathy

The following nouns usually or often have 'with' or 'between' after them:

collision	correspondence	link	relationship
connection	encounter	parity	
contrast	intimacy	quarrel	

Many other nouns are usually or often followed by a particular preposition. The following list indicates which preposition follows each noun.

authority over	foray into	reaction against
control over	freedom from	relapse into
departure from	grudge against	safeguard against
escape from	insurance against	
excerpt from	quotation from	

As you can see from the lists given above, it is often the case that words with a similar meaning are typically followed by the same preposition. For example, 'appetite', 'craving', 'desire', 'hunger', and 'thirst' are all followed by 'for'. For full information on prepositions used after nouns, see the Collins Cobuild Guide to Prepositions.

now

Now is usually used to contrast a situation in the present with an earlier situation.

She gradually built up energy and is now back to normal.
He knew now that he could rely completely on Paul Irving.
Now he felt safe.

'right now' and 'just now'

In conversation, you use **right now** or **just now** to say that a situation exists at present, although it may change in the future.

Right now, life doesn't seem worth living.
I'm awfully busy just now.

You also use **right now** to emphasize that something is happening now.

The crisis for forests in many countries is occurring right now.

If you say that something happened **just now,** you mean that it happened a very short time ago.

I telephoned him again just now and he's ready to come down if you want him.
I told you a lie just now.

If something is going to be done **now** or **right now,** it is going to be done immediately, without any delay.

He wants you to come and see him now, in his room.
I guess we'd better do it right now.

You do not use **right now** or **just now** in formal writing.

nowadays

Nowadays means 'at the present time, in contrast with the past'.

Life is so complicated nowadays.
Why don't we ever see Jim nowadays?

Note that **nowadays** is an adverb, not an adjective. You do not use it in front of a noun. You do not talk, for example, about 'nowadays children'. However, you can use **nowadays** immediately after a noun. You can say, for example, 'Children **nowadays** have much more money'.

Kids nowadays are lazy.
People nowadays have much greater expectations about their rights.

nowhere

You use **nowhere** to say that there is no place where something happens or can happen.

There's nowhere for either of us to go.
There was nowhere to hide.

Nowhere is sometimes put first for emphasis, followed by 'be' or an auxiliary and the subject of the clause.

Nowhere are they overwhelmingly numerous.
Nowhere have I seen any serious mention of this.

WARNING
You do not usually use another negative word with **nowhere**. You do not say, for example, 'I couldn't find her nowhere'. You say 'I couldn't find her **anywhere**'.

I changed my mind and decided not to go anywhere.

number

'a number of'
A number of things or people means several things or people. You use a plural form of a verb after **a number of**.

A number of key issues remain unresolved.
An increasing number of women are taking up self-defence.

'the number of'
When you talk about **the number of** people or things of a particular kind, you are talking about an actual number. After **the number of** you use a singular form of a verb.

In the last 30 years, the number of electricity consumers has risen by 50 per cent.

When you use **number** in either of these ways, you can use 'large' or 'small' with it.

His private papers revealed little of interest except a large number of unpaid bills.
The small number of members was made up for by a diversity of styles.

However, you do not use 'big' or 'little' with **number** in sentences like these.

Numbers and fractions

This entry deals with:

- **numbers,** such as 4, 108, and 1,001

- **Roman numerals,** such as IV, XII, and XXXII

- **ordinal numbers,** such as 'seventh', 'twenty-first', and '63rd'

- **fractions, decimals,** and **percentages,** such as $\frac{1}{2}$, 3.142, and 21%

- ways of indicating **approximate numbers**

Numbers and fractions

The following table shows the names of numbers. These numbers are sometimes called **cardinal numbers.** You can see from the numbers in this table how to form all the other numbers.

0	zero, nought, nothing, oh	26	twenty-six
1	one	27	twenty-seven
2	two	28	twenty-eight
3	three	29	twenty-nine
4	four	30	thirty
5	five	40	forty
6	six	50	fifty
7	seven	60	sixty
8	eight	70	seventy
9	nine	80	eighty
10	ten	90	ninety
11	eleven	100	a hundred
12	twelve	101	a hundred and one
13	thirteen	110	a hundred and ten
14	fourteen	120	a hundred and twenty
15	fifteen	200	two hundred
16	sixteen	1000	a thousand
17	seventeen	1001	a thousand and one
18	eighteen	1010	a thousand and ten
19	nineteen	2000	two thousand
20	twenty	10,000	ten thousand
21	twenty-one	100,000	a hundred thousand
22	twenty-two	1,000,000	a million
23	twenty-three	2,000,000	two million
24	twenty-four	1,000,000,000	a billion
25	twenty-five		

In the past, British speakers used 'billion' to mean a million million. However, nowadays they usually use it to mean a thousand million, like American speakers.

WARNING When you use 'hundred', 'thousand', 'million', or 'billion', they remain singular even when the number in front of them is greater than one.

...six hundred miles.
...a thousand billion pounds.

You do not use 'of' after these words when referring to an exact number. For example, you do not say 'five hundred of people'; you say 'five hundred people'.

For information on using these words to refer to less exact numbers, see the section on **approximate numbers** later in this entry.

'Dozen' is used in a similar way to these words. It is used to refer to twelve things. See entry at **dozen.**

expressing numbers Numbers over 100 are generally written in figures. However, if you want to say them aloud, or want to write them in words rather than figures, you put 'and' in front of the number expressed by the last two figures. For example, 203 is said or written as 'two hundred and three' and 2840 is said or written as 'two thousand, eight hundred and forty'.

Four hundred and eighteen men were killed and a hundred and seventeen wounded.

'And' is usually omitted in American English.

...one hundred fifty dollars.

If you want to say or write in words a number between 1000 and 1,000,000, there are various ways of doing it. For example, the number 1872 is usually said or written in words as 'one thousand, eight hundred and seventy-two' when it is being used to refer to a quantity of things. Four-figure numbers ending in 00 can also be said or written as a number of hundreds. For example, 1800 can be said or written as 'eighteen hundred'.

If the number 1872 is being used to identify something, it is said as 'one eight seven two'. You always say each figure separately like this with telephone numbers. If a telephone number contains a double number, you use the word 'double'. For example, 1882 is said as 'one double eight two'.

If you are mentioning the year 1872, you usually say 'eighteen seventy-two'. See entry at **Days and dates.**

When numbers over 9999 are written in figures, a comma is usually put after the fourth figure from the end, the seventh figure from the end, and so on, dividing the figures into groups of three, for example 15,000 or 1,982,000. With numbers between 1000 and 9999, a comma is sometimes put after the first figure, for example 1,526.

position   When you use a determiner and a number in front of a noun, you put the determiner in front of the number.

...*the three young men.*
...*my two daughters.*
All three candidates are coming to Blackpool later this week.

When you put a number and an adjective in front of a noun, you usually put the number in front of the adjective.

...*two small children.*
...*fifteen hundred local residents.*
...*three beautiful young girls.*

However, you can put a few adjectives such as 'following' and 'only' after numbers. See the section on **specifying adjectives** in the entry at **Adjectives.**

agreement   When you use any number except 'one' in front of a noun, you use a plural noun and a plural verb.

...*a hundred years.*
Seven guerrillas were wounded.
There were ten people there, all men.

However, when you are talking about an amount of money, a period of time, or a distance, speed, or weight, you usually use a singular verb.

Three hundred pounds is a lot of money.
Ten years is a long time.
90 miles an hour is much too fast.

numbers
as pronouns   When it is clear what sort of thing you are referring to, you can use a number without a noun following it. Numbers can be used on their own or with a determiner.

They bought eight companies and sold off five.
These two are quite different.
The best thirty have the potential to be successful journalists.
The two in front stared glumly ahead.

You use 'of' to indicate the group that a number of people or things belong to.

I saw four of these programmes.
All four of us wanted to get away from the Earl's Court area.

numbers in compound adjectives

Numbers can be used as part of **compound adjectives.** These adjectives are usually hyphenated.

He took out a five-dollar bill.
I wrote a five-page summary.

Note that the noun remains singular even when the number is two or more and that compound adjectives formed like this cannot be used as complements. For example, you cannot say 'My essay is five-hundred-word'. Instead you would probably say 'My essay is five hundred words long'.

'one'

'One' is used as a number in front of a noun to emphasize that there is only one thing or to show that you are being precise. It is also used when you are talking about a particular member of a group. 'One' is followed by a singular noun and is used with a singular verb.

There was only one gate into the palace.
This treaty was signed one year after the Suez Crisis.
One member declared that he would never vote for such a proposal.

When no emphasis or precision is wanted, you use 'a' instead.

A car came slowly up the road.

'zero'

The number 0 is not used in ordinary English to indicate that the number of things you are talking about is zero. Instead the determiner 'no' or the pronoun 'none' is used, or 'any' is used with a negative.

She had no children.
Sixteen people were injured but luckily none were killed.
There weren't any seats.

See entries at **no** and **none.**

There are several ways of expressing the number 0:

● as 'zero', when expressing some numerical values, for example temperatures, taxes, and interest rates

It was fourteen below zero when they woke up.
...zero tax liability.
...lending capital to their customers at low or zero rates of interest.

● as 'nought', when expressing some numerical values. For example, 0.89 is said as 'nought point eight nine'.

x equals nought.
...linguistic development between the ages of nought and one, one and two etc.

● as 'nothing', when talking informally about calculations

Subtract nothing from that and you get a line on the graph like that.
'What's the difference between this voltage and that voltage?'—'Nothing.'

● like 'oh' or the letter O, when reading out numbers figure by figure. For example, the telephone number 021 4620 is said as 'oh two one, four six two oh'; and the decimal number .089 is said as 'point oh eight nine'.

● as 'nil', in sports scores and informal speech and writing

The England Women's XI beat them by one goal to nil.
It used to be a community of 700 souls. Now the population is precisely nil.

Roman numerals

In a few situations, numbers are expressed in Roman numerals. Roman numerals are in fact letters:

I = 1
V = 5
X = 10
L = 50
C = 100
M = 1000

These letters are used in combination to express all numbers. A smaller Roman numeral is subtracted from a larger one if put in front of it. It is added to a larger numeral if put after it. For example, IV is 4 and VI is 6.

Roman numerals are used after the name of a king or queen when other kings or queens have had the same name.

...Queen Elizabeth II.

This would be said as 'Queen Elizabeth the Second'.

Roman numerals are often used to number chapters and sections of books, plays, or other pieces of writing.

Chapter IV: Summary and Conclusion.
...stalking upstage as the curtain fell on Act I.

Roman numerals are also sometimes used to express dates formally, for example at the end of films and television programmes. For example, '1992' can be written as 'MCMXCII'.

ordinal numbers

If you want to identify or describe something by indicating where it comes in a series or sequence, you use an **ordinal number.**

Quietly they took their seats in the first three rows.
Flora's flat is on the fourth floor of this five-storey block.

The following table shows the ordinal numbers.

1st	first	26th	twenty-sixth
2nd	second	27th	twenty-seventh
3rd	third	28th	twenty-eighth
4th	fourth	29th	twenty-ninth
5th	fifth	30th	thirtieth
6th	sixth	31st	thirty-first
7th	seventh	40th	fortieth
8th	eighth	41st	forty-first
9th	ninth	50th	fiftieth
10th	tenth	51st	fifty-first
11th	eleventh	60th	sixtieth
12th	twelfth	61st	sixty-first
13th	thirteenth	70th	seventieth
14th	fourteenth	71st	seventy-first
15th	fifteenth	80th	eightieth
16th	sixteenth	81st	eighty-first
17th	seventeenth	90th	ninetieth
18th	eighteenth	91st	ninety-first
19th	nineteenth	100th	hundredth
20th	twentieth	101st	hundred and first
21st	twenty-first	200th	two hundredth
22nd	twenty-second	1000th	thousandth
23rd	twenty-third	1,000,000th	millionth
24th	twenty-fourth	1,000,000,000th	billionth
25th	twenty-fifth		

Numbers and fractions

written forms
As shown in the table, ordinals can be written in abbreviated form, especially in dates.

He lost his job on January 7th.
...the 1st Division of the Sovereign's Escort.
Our address is: 5th Floor Waterloo House, Waterloo Street, Leeds.

ordinals as modifiers
Ordinals are used in front of nouns, preceded by a determiner. They are not usually used as complements after link verbs like 'be'.

He took the lift to the sixteenth floor.
...on her twenty-first birthday.

They are used after 'come' or 'finish' when giving the results of a race or competition.

An Italian came second.

Ordinals are included in the small group of adjectives that are put in front of cardinal numbers, not after them.

The first two years have been very successful.
Your second three minutes are up, caller.

ordinals as pronouns
When it is clear what sort of thing you are referring to, you can use an ordinal number without a noun following it. Note that you must use a determiner.

A second pheasant flew up. Then a third and a fourth.
There are two questions to be answered. The first is 'Who should do what?'
The second is 'To whom should he be accountable?'

You use 'of' to indicate the group that the person or thing belongs to.

This is the third of a series of programmes from the University of Sussex.
Tony was the second of four sons.

fractions
When you want to indicate how large a part of something is compared to the whole of it, you use a **fraction**, such as 'a third' or 'two fifths', followed by 'of' and a noun group referring to the whole thing. Most fractions are based on ordinal numbers. The exceptions are the words 'half' (one of two equal parts) and 'quarter' (one of four equal parts).

You can write a fraction in figures. For example, 'a half' can be written as $\frac{1}{2}$, 'a quarter' as $\frac{1}{4}$, 'three-quarters' as $\frac{3}{4}$, and 'two thirds' as $\frac{2}{3}$.

When referring to one part of something, you usually use 'a'. You only use 'one' in formal speech and writing or when you want to emphasize the amount.

This state produces a third of the nation's oil.
You can take out a fifth of your money on demand.
...one quarter of the total population.

You do not usually use 'a' with 'half', except when using it in combination with a whole number. Also, 'half' can be used in front of a noun group without 'of' after it. See entry at **half - half of.**

Plural fractions are often written with a hyphen.

More than two-thirds of the globe's surface is water.
He was not due at the office for another three-quarters of an hour.

You can put an adjective in front of a fraction, after 'the'.

...the southern half of England.
...in the last quarter of 1980.
...the first two-thirds of this century.

...the remaining three-quarters of the population.

When you use 'a half' and 'a quarter' in combination with whole numbers, they come in front of the plural noun you are using.

...one and a half acres of land.
...four and a half centuries.
...five and a quarter days.

However, if you are using 'a' instead of the number 'one', the noun is singular and comes in front of the fraction.

...a mile and a half below the surface.
...a mile and a quarter of motorway.

agreement   When you talk about part of a single thing, you use a singular form of a verb.

Half of our work is to design programmes.
Two fifths of the forest was removed.

However, when you talk about part of a group of things, you use a plural form of the verb.

Two fifths of the dwellings have more than six people per room.
A quarter of the students were seen individually.

fractions   When it is clear who or what you are referring to, you can use fractions
as pronouns   without 'of' and a noun group.

Most were women and about half were young with small children.
One fifth are appointed by the Regional Health Authority.

decimals   **Decimals** are a way of expressing fractions. For example, 0.5 is the same as $\frac{1}{2}$ and 1.4 is the same as $1\frac{2}{5}$.

...an increase of 16.4 per cent.
The library contains over 1.3 million books.

You say the dot as 'point'. For example, 1.4 is said as 'one point four'.

WARNING   You do not use a comma in decimal numbers in English.

Numbers which look like decimal numbers are used when referring to one of a number of sections, tables, or illustrations that are closely connected.

Domestic refuse, for example, can be dried and burnt to provide heat (see section 3.3).
The normal engineering drawing is quite unsuitable (figure 3.4).

percentages   Fractions are often given a special form as a number of hundredths. This type of fraction is called a **percentage.** For example, 'three hundredths', expressed as a percentage, is 'three per cent'. This is often written as 3%.

About 20 per cent of student accountants are women.
...interest at 10% per annum.

approximate   You can refer to a large number imprecisely by using 'several', 'a few', or 'a
numbers   couple of' in front of 'dozen', 'hundred', 'thousand', 'million', or 'billion'.

...several hundred people.
A few thousand cars have gone.
...life a couple of hundred years ago.

You can be even more imprecise, and emphasize how large the number is, by using 'dozens', 'hundreds', 'thousands', 'millions', or 'billions', followed by 'of'.

That's going to take hundreds of years.

We travelled <u>thousands of</u> miles across Europe.

People often use plural forms when they are exaggerating.

I was meeting <u>thousands of</u> people.
Do you have to fill in <u>hundreds of</u> forms before you go?

The following expressions are used to indicate that a number is approximate and that the actual figure could be larger or smaller:

about	odd	roughly
approximately	or so	some
around	or thereabouts	something like

You put 'about', 'approximately', 'around', 'roughly', 'some', and 'something like' in front of a number.

<u>About 85</u> students were there.
It costs <u>roughly £55</u> a year to keep a cat in food.
Harrington has cheated us out of <u>something like thirty thousand</u> quid over the past two years.
I found out where this man lived, and drove <u>some four</u> miles inland to see him.

Note that this use of 'some' is quite formal.

You put 'odd', 'or so', and 'or thereabouts' after a number or the noun that follows a number.

...a <u>hundred odd</u> acres.
The car should be here in <u>ten minutes or so</u>.
Get the temperature to <u>30°C or thereabouts</u>.

minimum numbers The following expressions indicate that a number is a minimum figure and that the actual figure may be larger:

a minimum of	from	more than	over
at least	minimum	or more	plus

You put 'a minimum of', 'from', 'more than', and 'over' in front of a number.

He needed <u>a minimum of 26</u> Democratic votes.
...3 course dinner <u>from £15</u>.
...a school with <u>more than 1300</u> pupils.
The British have been on the island for <u>over a thousand</u> years.

You put 'or more', 'plus', and 'minimum' after a number or after the noun that follows a number.

...a choice of <u>three or more</u> possibilities.
This is the worst disaster I can remember in my <u>25 years plus</u> as a police officer.
They should be getting <u>£38 a week minimum</u>.

'Plus' is sometimes written as the symbol '+', for example in job advertisements.

<u>2+ years'</u> experience of market research required.

You usually put 'at least' in front of a number.

She had <u>at least a dozen</u> brandies.
It was a drop of <u>at least two hundred</u> feet.

However, this expression is sometimes put after a number or noun. This position is more emphatic.

I must have slept <u>twelve hours at least</u>.

maximum numbers

The following expressions indicate that a number is a maximum figure and that the actual figure is or may be smaller:

almost	at the most	nearly	under
a maximum of	fewer than	no more than	up to
at most	less than	or less	
at the maximum	maximum	or under	

You put 'almost', 'a maximum of', 'fewer than', 'less than', 'nearly', 'no more than', 'under', and 'up to' in front of a number.

The company now supplies almost 100 of Paris's restaurants.
...a puppy less than seven weeks old.
We managed to finish the entire job in under three months.

You put 'at the maximum', 'at most', 'at the most', 'maximum', 'or less', and 'or under' after a number or the noun that follows a number.

They might have IQs of 10, or 50 at the maximum.
The area would yield only 200 pounds of rice or less.

indicating a range of numbers

You can indicate a range of numbers using 'between' and 'and', or 'from' and 'to', or just 'to'.

Most of the farms are between four and five hundred years old.
My hospital groups contain from ten to twenty patients.
...peasants owning two to five acres of land.

'Anything' is used in front of 'between' and 'from' to emphasize how great a range is.

An average rate of anything between 25 and 60 per cent is usual.
It is a job that takes anything from two to five weeks.

A hyphen is used between two figures to indicate a range. It is said as 'to'.

Allow to cool for 10-15 minutes.
In 1965-9, people drank a little more, namely 6.0 litres of alcohol.
...the Tate Gallery (open 10 a.m.-6 p.m., Sundays, 2-6).

When mentioning two numbers that follow each other in a range or sequence, you can use the symbol ' / ' (said aloud as 'stroke', 'slash', or 'to').

The top ten per cent of income earners gained 25.8 per cent of all earned income in 1975/6.
Write for details to 41/42 Berners Street, London.

O

obedient

The following words can all be used to describe someone who does what they are told and can be controlled easily:

acquiescent	obedient	submissive	tractable
compliant	servile	subservient	
docile	slavish	tame	

Obedient usually shows approval, especially when you are talking about children or people who are under strict authority.

She was, on the whole, an obedient little girl.
Everyone ought to do military training. It would do them good and make them obedient.
...a continuous supply of cheap and obedient labour.

Acquiescent, compliant, docile, submissive, and **tractable** often show approval but are also sometimes used to indicate mild disapproval.

The soldiers were grateful and docile, and did not pester her.
...men who preferred their women to be submissive.

Acquiescent, compliant, and **tractable** are formal words.

Some children seem to be totally acquiescent, always agreeing with the adult's view.
She was fed up with being eternally compliant.
The inhabitants of these territories were peaceful and tractable.

Subservient and **tame** show mild disapproval.

His gesture of respect seemed old-fashioned and subservient.
I became eager to prove I was no tame victim of my background.

Servile and **slavish** show strong disapproval.

Those who carried on business did so as the servile agents of these men, not as free merchants.
...a slavish conformity to the styles of their classmates.

animals Note that **tame** is more commonly used to describe an animal of a kind that usually lives in the wild which has been born in captivity or has become used to people.

He sometimes let her play with his tame gazelle.

Docile and **obedient** are also used to describe animals. When used like this, they show approval.

Remember that although dormice are in general docile animals, they can give you a very nasty bite.
You cannot begin show jumping until your horse is obedient and supple.

obey

If you **obey** someone who has authority over you, you do what they tell you to do.

She wanted her daughter to obey her.
Why should men serve and obey the monarch?
Alfonsin issued the same order three times, but he was not obeyed.

You can also **obey** an order or instruction.

In all 198 NCOs and men refused to obey orders.
Be careful to obey the manufacturer's washing instructions.

Note that you do not say that someone 'obeys to' a person, order, or instruction.

object

Object is used as a noun or a verb. When it is a noun, it is pronounced /ɒbdʒekt/. When it is a verb, it is pronounced /əbdʒekt/.

used as a noun   You can refer to anything which has a fixed shape and which is not alive as an **object**.

...the shabby, black object he was carrying.
The icon is an object of great beauty.

A person's **object** is their aim or purpose.

The minder's object is to keep the child asleep.
The object, of course, is to persuade people to remain at their jobs.

used as a verb   If you **object to** something that is proposed or being done, you do not approve of it, or you say that you do not approve of it.

He does not object to loans in principle.
People have the opportunity to object to proposed developments in their neighbourhood.

If you **object to doing** something that you have been asked to do, you say that you do not think you should do it.

The women objected to cooking in the midday sun.
This group did not object to returning.

Note that you use an '-ing' form, not an infinitive, after **object to.**

If it is clear what you are referring to, you can use **object** without 'to'.

The men objected and the women supported their protest.
Other authorities will still have the right to object.

If you want to say why someone does not approve of something or does not agree with something, you can use **object** with a 'that'-clause. For example, you can say 'They wanted me to do some extra work, but I **objected that** I had too much to do already'. This is a fairly formal use.

The others quite rightly object that he is holding back the work.
First, it can be objected that poverty particularly affects two groups omitted from the survey.

GRAMMAR   # Objects

direct objects   The **object** of a verb or clause is a noun group which refers to the person or thing that is involved in an action but does not perform the action. The object comes after the verb. It is sometimes called the **direct object**.

He closed the door.
It was dark by the time they reached their house.
Some of the women noticed me.

indirect objects	Some verbs have two objects. For example in the sentence 'I gave John the book', 'the book' is the direct object, and 'John' is the **indirect object.** The indirect object usually refers to the person who benefits from an action or receives something as a result of it.

You can put an indirect object in front of the direct object or in a prepositional phrase after the direct object.

Dad gave me a car.
He handed his room key to the receptionist.

For more information, see section on **ditransitive verbs** in entry at **Verbs.**

prepositional objects	Prepositions also have objects. The noun group after a preposition is sometimes called the **prepositional object.**

I climbed up the tree.
Miss Burns looked calmly at Marianne.
Woodward finished the second page and passed it to the editor.

See entry at **Prepositions.**

---

obligation - duty

If you say that someone has an **obligation to do** something or a **duty to do** something, you mean that they ought to do it, because it is their responsibility. When **obligation** and **duty** are used like this, they have the same meaning.

The Government has an obligation to reverse the decline of this important industry.
Perhaps it was his duty to inform the police of what he had seen.

'duties'	Your **duties** are the things that you do as part of your job.

She has been given a reasonable time to learn her duties.
They also have to carry out many administrative duties.

You do not refer to the things that you do as part of your job as 'obligations'.

oblige

If something **obliges** you to do something, it makes it necessary for you to do it.

Politeness obliged me to go on with the conversation.
Security requirements obliged her to stop.

'feel obliged'	If someone feels that they must do something, for example in order to be polite or because they think it is their duty, you can say that they **feel obliged** to do it.

He looked at me so blankly that I felt obliged to explain.

WARNING	You do not use **oblige** in impersonal structures. You do not say, for example, 'He looked at me so blankly that it obliged me to explain'.

observance

The **observance** of a rule or custom is the practice of obeying it or following it. **Observance** is a fairly formal word.

We are seeking to underpin trade union authority through the observance of agreed procedures.

'observation'   You do not use **observance** to refer to the activity of watching someone or something carefully. The word you use is **observation**.

Stephens had crashed and was taken to hospital for observation.
By far the greatest part of his work is careful observation and precise thinking.

obstinate

See entry at **stubborn**.

obtain

If you **obtain** something that you want or need, you get it.

...my attempt to obtain employment.
He had obtained the papers during occasional visits to Berlin.

'get'   **Obtain** is a formal word. You do not usually use it in conversation. Instead you use **get**.

...one's chances of getting a good job.
He's trying to get a flat.

In writing, **obtain** is often used in the passive.

All the above items can be obtained from Selfridges.
You need to know where this kind of information can be obtained.

You do not usually use **get** in the passive. You do not say, for example, 'Maps can be got from the Tourist Office'. You say 'Maps **can be obtained** from the Tourist Office' or, in conversation, '**You can get** maps from the Tourist Office'.

obvious

If something is **obvious,** you can easily see it or understand it.

It was painfully obvious that I knew very little about it.
For obvious reasons, I preferred my house to his.

You can say that something is **obvious to** someone.

The reasons are obvious to all of us.
It must have been obvious to everyone in Bristol what was happening.

Note that you do not use any preposition except 'to' after **obvious** in sentences like these.

occasion

An **occasion** is a time when a particular event happens or a particular situation arises.

I remember the occasion vividly.
There are occasions when you must refuse.

You often say that something happens **on** a particular occasion.

I think it would be better if I went alone on this occasion.
I met him only on one occasion.

An **occasion** is also an important event, ceremony, or celebration.

It was a fitting conclusion to a memorable occasion.
They have the date fixed for the big occasion.

**'opportunity' and
'chance'**
You do not use **occasion** to refer to a situation in which it is possible for someone to do something. Instead you use **opportunity** or **chance**.

In February 1960 I had the <u>opportunity</u> of hearing a fascinating dissertation by Dr Timothy Leary.
She put the phone down before I had a <u>chance</u> to reply.

See entries at **opportunity** and **chance**.

occasionally

See section on **frequency** in entry at **Adverbials**.

occupation

See entry at **work**.

occur

You can say that an event **occurs**.

...the chances of an accident <u>occurring</u>.
Mrs Weaver had been in the milking shed when the explosion <u>occurred</u>.
Mistakes are bound to <u>occur</u>.

However, you only use **occur** to talk about events which are not planned.

Occur is a fairly formal word. In conversation, you usually say that an event **happens**.

You might have noticed what <u>happened</u> on Tuesday.
A curious thing <u>has happened</u>.

See entry at **happen**.

You do not say that a planned event 'occurs' or 'happens'. You say that it **takes place**.

The first meeting of this committee <u>took place</u> on 9 January.
These lessons <u>took place</u> twice a week.

You do not use 'occur to' to say that someone is affected by an event. You do not say, for example, 'I wonder what's occurred to Jane'. You say 'I wonder what**'s happened to** Jane'.

She no longer cared what <u>happened to</u> her.
It couldn't <u>have happened to</u> a nicer man.

If an idea **occurs to** you, you suddenly think of it.

The idea <u>had never even occurred to</u> him before.
The thought <u>had just occurred to</u> him.

If you want to say what the idea is, you usually use 'it' as the subject of **occur** and mention the idea in a 'that'-clause or a 'to'-infinitive clause.

It occurred to him <u>that he hadn't eaten anything since the night before</u>.
It occurred to him <u>to tell the colonel of the problem</u>.

of

**possession and
other
relationships**
Of is used to indicate possession. It can also be used to indicate other kinds of relationship between people or things.

...the home <u>of a sociology professor</u>.
...the sister <u>of the Duke of Urbino</u>.
At the top <u>of the hill</u> Hilary Jackson paused for breath.

You can use **of** in front of a possessive pronoun such as 'mine', 'his', or 'theirs'. You do this to indicate that someone is one of a group of people or things connected with a particular person. For example, instead of saying 'He is one of my friends', you can say 'He is a friend **of mine**.'

He's a very good friend of mine.
I talked to a colleague of yours recently.

You can use **of** like this in front of other possessives.

…a friend of my mother's.
She was a great friend of Lorna Cook's.

The 's is sometimes omitted, especially in American English.

…a close friend of Mr Reagan.

Of is also sometimes used with a possessive after a noun group beginning with 'this', 'that', 'these', or 'those'.

…this experiment of mine.
Jennifer, you didn't force open that antique desk of mine, did you?
…those brilliant shining eyes of hers.

WARNING

You do not use **of** in front of a personal pronoun such as 'me', 'him', or 'them'. You do not say, for example, 'the sister of me'. Instead you use a **possessive determiner** such as 'my', 'his', or 'their'.

My sister came down the other week.
He had his hands in his pockets.
…the future of our society.

See entry at **Possessive determiners**.

You do not usually use **of** in front of short noun groups. Instead you use 's or the apostrophe '. For example, instead of saying 'the car of my friend', you say '**my friend's** car'.

…Ralph's voice.
…Mr Duffield's sister.
…the President's conduct.
…my colleagues' offices.

See entry at **'s.**

For more information about possession, see entry at **Possession and other relationships**.

descriptions

You can sometimes use **of** and a noun group to describe something, instead of using an adjective and a submodifier. For example, instead of saying that something is 'very interesting', you can say that it is **of great interest**. This is a rather formal use.

It will be of great interest to you.
The result is of little importance.
…a film of considerable character and intelligence.

When you use an adjective to comment on an action, you can put **of** and a pronoun after the adjective. The pronoun refers to the person who has performed the action. For example, you can say 'That was **stupid of you**'.

It was brave of them.
I'm sorry, that was silly of me.

authorship

You do not talk about a book 'of' a particular author, or a piece of music 'of' a particular composer. Instead you use **by**.

…three books by a great Australian writer.
…a collection of pieces by Mozart.

Similarly, you use **by** to indicate who painted a picture.

...the famous painting <u>by</u> Rubens, The Straw Hat.

A picture **of** a particular person shows that person as the subject of the picture.

...Felix Topolski's painting <u>of</u> Tony Benn.

location   You can talk about the capital **of** a country, state, or province.

...Ulan Bator, the capital <u>of</u> Mongolia.

However, you do not talk about a town or village 'of' a particular country or area. Instead you use **in**.

...an old Spanish colonial town <u>in</u> Southern Ecuador.
My favourite town <u>in</u> Shropshire is Ludlow.

You also use **in**, rather than 'of', after superlatives. For example, you talk about 'the tallest building **in** Tokyo'. You do not say 'the tallest building of Tokyo'.

Hakodate is the oldest port <u>in</u> Hokkaido.
...the biggest lizards <u>in</u> the world.

materials   In literary or old-fashioned writing, **of** is sometimes used with a noun group to mention the material from which something has been made.

The walls were <u>of bare plaster</u>.
...houses <u>of brick and stone</u>.

off

You use **off** as a preposition or adverb to say that something is removed from an object or surface.

He took his hand <u>off</u> her arm.
I knocked the clock <u>off</u> the bedside table.
The paint was peeling <u>off</u>.

WARNING   You do not use 'of' after **off**. You do not say, for example, 'I knocked the clock off of the bedside table'.

Off is also used as an adverb to say that someone leaves a place.

The sailors ran <u>off</u>.
He started the motor and drove <u>off</u> immediately.

offer

If you **offer** something to someone, you ask them if they would like to have it or use it.

She took two biscuits when he <u>offered</u> them.
He <u>offered</u> me a cigarette. I shook my head.

'give'   If you put something in someone's hand expecting them to take it, and they do take it, you do not say that you 'offer' it to them. You say that you **give** it to them.

She <u>gave</u> Minnie the keys.
He <u>gave</u> me a small chunk of ironstone.

'offer to'   If you **offer to do** something, you say that you are willing to do it.

He <u>offered to take</u> her home in a taxi.
I <u>offered to answer</u> any questions they might have.

'invite'   If someone asks you to do something that they think you will want to do, you do not say that they 'offer' you to do it. You say that they **invite** you to do it.

I was <u>invited</u> to attend future meetings.
She never once <u>invited</u> him to sit with them.

Offers

offering something to someone

There are several ways of offering something to someone.

A polite way of offering something is to say 'Would you like...?'

Would you like another biscuit or something?
I was just making myself some tea. Would you like some?

When talking to someone you know well, you can use the less polite form 'Do you want...?'

Do you want a biscuit?
Do you want a coffee?

If you know the other person well, and you want to be persuasive, you can use the imperative form 'have'.

Have some more tea.
Have a chocolate biscuit.

You can also use just a noun group, making it sound like a question.

'Tea?'—'Yes, thanks.'
Ginger biscuit?

other ways of offering something

If what you are offering is not immediately available, you can say something like 'Can I get you something?' or 'Let me get you something to eat'.

Can I get you anything?
Sit down and let me get you a cup of tea or a drink or something.

If you want the other person to take what they need, you say 'Help yourself'.

Help yourself to sugar.
'Do you suppose I could have a drink?'—'Of course. You know where everything is. Help yourself.'

A casual, non-emphatic way of offering something is to say 'You can have...' or, if appropriate, 'You can borrow...'.

You can borrow my pen if you like.

Note that a British person might say 'Fancy some coffee?' or 'Fancy a biscuit?' as a way of informally offering something.

offering to help or do something

If you want to offer to help someone or to do something for them, you say 'Shall I...?' You can use this kind of question whether you are offering to do something immediately or at some time in the future.

Shall I fetch another doctor?
'What's the name?'—'Khulaifi. Shall I spell that for you?'
Shall I come tomorrow night?

confident offers

If you are fairly sure that the other person wants to have something done for them at that moment, you can say 'Let me...'.

Let me buy you a drink.
Let me help.
Let me show you the rest of the house.

If you want to make an offer in a firm but friendly way, you say 'I'll...'.

Leave everything, I'll clean up.
Come on out with me. I'll buy you a beer.
I'll give you a lift back.

Offers

less confident or firm offers

If you are not sure whether the other person wants you to do something, you can say 'Do you want me to...?' or, more politely, 'Would you like me to...?' However, this can sound as if you are rather reluctant to do what you are offering to do.

Do you want me to check his records?
Do you want me to go with you?
Would you like me to read to you tonight?

You can also say 'Do you want...?', 'Do you need...?', or, more politely, 'Would you like...?', followed by a noun referring to an action. Although you do not say directly that you are offering to do something, that is what you are implying.

Do you want a lift?
Are you all right, Alan? Need any help?

'Can I...?' is also sometimes used, by people who know each other slightly or have just met.

Can I give you a lift anywhere?

Another way of making an offer when you are not sure that it is necessary is to add 'if you want' or 'if you like' after using 'I'll' or 'I can'.

I'll drive it back if you want.
I can show it to you now if you like.

offers to a customer

Employees of a shop or company sometimes say 'Can I...' or 'May I...' when they are politely offering to help a customer on the phone or in person.

Flight information, can I help you?
What can I do for you?

very formal offers

In a few circumstances, it may be appropriate to make a very formal, polite offer, like the one below, but this style is much too formal for an ordinary, everyday situation.

I should very much appreciate it if you'd allow me to make a contribution towards the airline tickets, by way of a wedding present.

replying to an offer

The usual way of accepting an offer is to say 'Yes, please'. You can also say 'Thank you' or, informally, 'Thanks'.

'Shall I read to you?'—'Yes, please.'
'Have another whiskey.'—'Thank you. I will.'
'Have a cup of coffee.'—'Thank you very much.'
'You can take the jeep.'—'Thanks.'

If you want to show that you are very grateful for an offer, especially an unexpected one, you can say something like 'Oh, thank you, that would be great' or 'That would be lovely'. You can also say 'That's very kind of you', which is more formal.

'Shall I run you a bath?'—'Oh, yes, please! That would be lovely.'
'I'll have a word with him and see if he can help.'—'That's very kind of you.'

The usual way of refusing an offer is to say 'No, thank you' or, informally, 'No, thanks'.

'Would you like some coffee?'—'No, thank you.'
'Do you want a biscuit?'—'No, thanks.'

You can also say things like 'No, I'm fine, thank you', 'I'm all right, thanks', or 'No, it's all right.'

'Is the sun bothering you? Shall I pull the curtain?'—'No, no, I'm fine, thank you.'

'Do you want a lift?'—*'No, it's all right, thanks, I don't mind walking.'*

Note that you do not refuse an offer by just saying 'Thank you'.

If someone says they will do something for you, you can refuse their offer politely by saying 'Please don't bother.'

'I'll get you some sheets.'—*'Please — don't bother.'*

---

officer - official

'officer' An **officer** is a person who has a position of authority in the armed forces.

...a retired army officer.

Officer is also used in the name of some people's jobs.

He was arrested and charged with assaulting a police officer.
Suddenly the press officer came out and announced the result.

'official' An **official** is a person who holds a position of authority in an organization, especially a government department or a trade union.

At present, the development effort is mainly carried on by government officials.
He brought an action against the union officials who had insisted on his dismissal.

'office worker' You do not use **officer** or **official** to refer to someone who works in an office. A person like this is called an **office worker**.

Office workers have been found to make more mistakes when distracted by traffic noise.

often

If something happens **often**, it happens many times.

position in clause If there is no auxiliary, you put **often** in front of the verb, unless the verb is 'be'. If the verb is 'be', you put **often** after it.

We often get very cold winters here.
They often tell you what they want to believe themselves.
They were often hungry.

If there is an auxiliary, you put **often** after it.

She has often spoken of the individual's 'right to choose'.
He had often pointed this out to Lucy.

If there is more than one auxiliary, you put **often** after the first one.

The facts had often been distorted.
It's a word you must often have come across.

If a sentence is fairly short, you can put **often** at the end of it.

He's in London often.
He could see Gertrude often.

In writing, **often** is sometimes put at the beginning of a long sentence.

Often in the evening the little girl would be clutching at my knees while I held the baby up on my shoulder.

WARNING You do not use **often** to talk about something that happens several times within a short period of time. You do not say, for example, 'I often phoned her yesterday'. You say 'I phoned her **several times** yesterday' or 'I **kept phoning** her yesterday'.

That fear was expressed several times last week.
She kept trying to get her husband away to go to lunch.

For a graded list of words used to say how frequently something happens, see section on **frequency** in entry at **Adverbials**.

<table>
<tr><td>other uses of
'often'</td><td>You use **often** with 'how' when you are asking about the number of times that something happens or happened.</td></tr>
</table>

How often do you need to weigh the baby?
How often have you done this programme?

Often can also be used to say that something is done just once by many people, or that something is true about many people.

People often asked me why I didn't ride more during the trip.
Old people often don't like raw cabbage.

old

Old is most commonly used to state the age of a person or thing. For example, you say that someone 'is forty years **old**'.

The Law required witnesses to be at least fourteen years old.
...bone fragments which are three-and-a-half million years old.

You can also describe someone as, for example, 'a **forty-year-old** man'. Note that you do not say 'a forty-years-old man'.

...a sixty-year-old man.
Sue lives with her five-year-old son John in the West Country.

You can also say that someone is 'a man of forty'. However, you do not say 'a man of forty years old'.

Mary is a tall, strong woman of thirty.
A man of 82, who has already graduated there, hopes to achieve a doctorate in philosophy.

For a discussion of the different ways of expressing age, see entry at **Age**.

asking about age	You use **old** after 'how' when you are asking about the age of a person or thing.

'How old's your daughter Dorothy?'—'She's eighteen.'
'How old are you?'—'I'll be eight next year.'
'How old is the Taj Mahal?'—'It was built about 1640, I think.'

'older' and 'oldest'	The usual comparative and superlative forms of 'old' are **older** and **oldest**.

Harriet was ten years older than I was.
It claims to be the oldest insurance company in the world.

However, the forms **elder** and **eldest** are sometimes used. For a full explanation, see entry at **elder**.

another meaning of 'old'	You can also use **old** to describe someone who has lived a very long time.

...a little old lady.
He was emaciated and he looked really old.

'elderly' and 'aged'	This use of **old** can sometimes sound impolite. **Elderly** is a more polite word.

I keep house for my elderly mother.
Like many elderly people, Mrs Carstairs could remember voices better than she did faces.

Old people are often referred to as **the elderly** or **the aged**.

...organizations which help the elderly.
Hospital food seldom caters for the special needs of the aged.

Note that **aged** is pronounced /ˈeɪdʒɪd/ when it is used like this. Its usual pronunciation, for example when talking about 'children aged five', is /eɪdʒd/.

old friends and enemies

An **old** friend or **old** enemy is someone who has been your friend or enemy for a long time. He or she is not necessarily an old person.

Some of the lads had taken the opportunity to visit old friends.
He realized that the leader was an old enemy of his.

'old' used to describe objects

An **old** building or other object was built or made a long time ago.

...a massive old building of crumbling red brick.
...wardrobes full of old clothes.
We got into his battered old car.

'ancient'

You can describe a very old building or object as **ancient**.

...the restoration of their ancient halls and manors.
They discovered an ancient manuscript hidden in a chimney.

Ancient is also used to describe people who lived a very long time ago.

The number zero was unknown to the ancient Greeks and Romans.

'old' used to mean 'former'

Old is sometimes used to mean 'former'.

...his old job at the publishing company.
Miss McDonald, our old maths teacher, was there.

on

used to say where something is

On is usually used as a preposition. You use **on** to say where someone or something is by mentioning the object or surface that is supporting them.

When I came back, she was just sitting on the stairs.
Large, soft cushions lay on the floor.
There was a photograph of a beautiful girl on Daintry's desk.

On is used in some other ways to say where someone or something is. For example, you use it to mention an area of land where someone works or lives, such as a farm, building site, or housing estate.

Not many girls today want to live on a farm.
...a labourer who worked on my father's building site.

You also use **on** to mention an island where something exists or happens.

This plant is now found only on Lundy in the Bristol Channel.
I was born on Honshu, the main island.

Note that you usually use **in** or **at** to say where something is. See entries at **in** and **at**.

used to say where something goes

You can use **on** to say where someone or something falls or is put.

He fell on the floor.
I put a hand on his shoulder.

Onto is used in a similar way. See entry at **onto**.

You use **on** after 'get' to say that someone enters a bus, train, or ship.

George got on the bus with us.

For more information, see entry at **go into**.

used to talk about time	You say that something happens **on** a particular day or date.

She intended to come to see the play on the following Friday.
Caro was born on April 10th.

For more information, see entry at **Days and dates**.

You can sometimes use **on** to say that one thing happens immediately after another. For example, if something happens **on** someone's arrival, it happens immediately after they arrive.

'It's so unfair,' Clarissa said on her return.

the subject of a book	You use **on** to say what the subject of a book is.

...a book on astronomy.
...his book on the First World War.

WARNING	However, you do not use **on** to say what a novel or play deals with. You do not say, for example, 'The Coral Island is on three boys on a desert island'. You say 'The Coral Island is **about** three boys on a desert island'.

...a nail-biting novel about a sinister teenage secret society.
...a Norwegian story about a king who has seven sons.

used as an adverb	**On** is sometimes used as an adverb, usually to indicate that something continues to happen or be done.

His spirit lives on.
She plodded on, silently thinking.
I flew on to California.

once

used to mean 'only one time'	If something happens **once**, it happens only one time.

I've been out with him once, that's all.
I have never forgotten her, though I saw her only once.

When **once** is used with this meaning, it usually goes at the end of a clause.

used to talk about the past	You also use **once** to indicate that something happened at an unspecified time in the past.

I once investigated this story and it seems to be wholly untrue.
Once we were stopped by a woman in a long cotton dress.

When **once** is used with this meaning, it usually goes in front of a verb or at the beginning of a clause.

You also use **once** to say that something was the case in the past, although it is no longer the case.

He had once been a big star but now he was finished.
These carvings were once brightly coloured.
She was in the trade herself once.

When **once** is used with this meaning, it usually goes after 'be' or an auxiliary, or at the end of a clause.

WARNING	You do not use **once** to indicate that something will happen at some time in the future. Instead you use **one day** for events in the distant future, or **sometime** for events in the fairly near future.

One day, you'll be very glad we stopped you.
I'll give you a ring sometime.

'at once'	If you do something **at once**, you do it immediately.

She stopped playing at once.
I knew at once that something was wrong.

one

used in front of a noun	**One** is the number 1. You use **one** in front of a noun to emphasize that you are talking about a single thing or person.

He balanced himself on one foot.
The two friends share one job.

Note that **one** is used like this for emphasis only. Normally, you use **a** or **an** to talk about a single thing or person.

used instead of a noun group
You can use **one** instead of a noun group beginning with 'a' when it is clear what sort of thing you are talking about. For example, instead of saying 'If you want a drink, I'll get you a drink', you say 'If you want a drink, I'll get you **one**'.

Both parents have an equal right to a career if they want one.
Although she wasn't a rich customer, she looked and acted like one.
The cupboards were empty except for one at the top of the bookshelves.

Note that you cannot use a plural form of **one** in this kind of sentence. You do not say, for example, 'If you like grapes, I'll get you ones'. You say 'If you like grapes, I'll get you **some**'.

The shelves contained Daisy's books, mostly novels but some on occult or mystical subjects.
We need more anti-tank helicopters. There are some, but we need more.

used instead of a noun
You can use **one** or **ones** instead of a count noun when the noun comes after an adjective. For example, instead of saying 'I've had this car a long time, and I'm thinking of getting a new car', you say 'I've had this car a long time, and I'm thinking of getting **a new one**'.

I got this trumpet for thirty pounds. It's quite a good one.
This idea has become a very influential one.
...buying old houses and building new ones.
They created a single strong organization instead of two weak ones.

You can also use **one** or **ones** instead of a count noun in front of a relative clause or a prepositional phrase.

...a slightly higher class than the one you were born into.
Could I see that map again — the one with lines across it?
...the students I like most, the ones I really feel a sense of identity with.

You can use **one** instead of a singular count noun when the noun comes immediately after any determiner except 'a'. For example, instead of saying 'I bought these masks when I was in Africa. That mask came from Kenya', you say 'I bought these masks when I was in Africa. **That one** came from Kenya'.

We'll have to have a small fire. This one's too big.
He took the steel tubes and wrapped each one carefully in the sacking.
She had a plateful, then went back for another one.

WARNING
You do not use **the one** in front of 'of' and a name. You do not say, for example, 'This is my mug. That's the one of Jane'. You say 'This is my mug. That's **Jane's**'.

...a northern accent like Brian's.

'one of'
You use **one of** in front of a plural noun group to talk about one member of a group of people or things.

One of my students sold me her ticket.
Graphology is one of the few subjects that you can do well by correspondence.

After the noun group you use a singular form of a verb.

One of Mirella Freni's first records was a collection of Puccini arias.
One of them was also a mountain climber.

One of is often used with superlatives.

...Mr Gordon Getty, one of the world's richest men.
It's one of the slowest cars on the market.

used as an impersonal pronoun

One is sometimes used as an impersonal pronoun to indicate that something is generally done or should generally be done. This is a fairly formal use.

I'm a socialist but one doesn't talk about politics at the club.

Occasionally, you may hear a speaker use **one** instead of 'I' or 'me' simply to refer to himself or herself. This is also a fairly formal use.

One tries to take an interest in what is going on.

The possessive determiner and reflexive pronoun corresponding to this use of 'one' are **one's** and **oneself**.

Naturally, one wanted only the best for one's children.
...the fear of making a fool of oneself.

However, when **one** has already been used as the subject of the sentence, some speakers use **his** and **himself** instead of 'one's' and 'oneself'. This use is more common in American English than British English.

In these situations, one has to do his best.

Most British and American speakers do not use **one** like this at all. Here are some other ways in which you can say that something is generally done or should be done:

'you'

You can use **you**. This is a fairly common use, especially in conversation. In this book, we usually use **you**.

There are things that have to be done and you do them and you never talk about them.
Instead of saying 'on their arrival', you can just say 'on arrival'.

'people'

You can use **people**. This is also a fairly common use.

People shouldn't leave jobs unfinished.
Do people go there on their own?

'we'

You can use **we** to say that something is generally done by a group of people that includes yourself.

If you are not known to the Bank, we usually require someone to speak for you.
We say things in the heat of an argument that we don't really mean.

'they'

They is sometimes used to refer to people in general, or to a group of people whose identity is not actually stated.

Isn't that what they call love?
They found the body in a dustbin.

Some people use **they** when they are mentioning a saying or repeating a piece of gossip.

They say that dog doesn't bite dog: whoever invented that proverb never lived under a democratic government.
He marketed some of his compounds and made a fortune, they say.

the passive	Instead of using one of these words and an active verb, you can sometimes use a passive verb. This is a fairly common use in formal writing.

If there is swelling and increasing pain, medical advice should be taken. Any claims for refund or compensation must be made in writing to our head office within 28 days of your return.

one another

See entry at **each other - one another**.

only

Only is used as an adjective or an adverb.

used as an adjective	You use **only** in front of a noun or 'one' to say that something is true about one person, thing, or group and not true about anyone or anything else. In front of **only** you put 'the' or a possessive.

Grace was the only survivor.
I was the only one smoking.
'Have you a spare one?'—'No, it's my only copy unfortunately.'

When **only** has this meaning, you must use a noun or 'one' after it. You cannot say, for example, 'He was the only to escape'. If you do not want to use a more precise noun, you can use 'person' or 'thing'. You can say, for example, 'He was **the only person** to escape'.

He was the only person authorized to issue documents of that sort.
It was the only thing they could do.

Note that if you use another adjective or a number, you put **only** in front of it.

Further expansion of the airport would be the only practicable option.
The only English city he enjoyed working in was Manchester.
At that time, they were the only two republics on earth.

Only is not normally used after 'an'. There is one common exception: if you say that someone is **an only child,** you mean that they have no brothers or sisters.

I was an only child.

used as an adverb	**Only** is used as an adverb to say that something is the one thing that is done, that happens, or that is relevant in a particular situation, in contrast to all the other things that are not done, do not happen, or are not relevant.

If **only** applies to the subject of a clause, you put it in front of the subject.

Only his close friends knew how much he idolized his daughters.
...the belief that only a completely different approach will be effective.

If the verb is 'be', you put **only** after it.

There is only one train that goes from Denmark to Sweden by night.

If the verb is not 'be' and **only** does not apply to the subject, you usually put it in front of the verb or after the first auxiliary, regardless of what it applies to. For example, instead of saying 'I see my brother only at weekends', you usually say 'I **only** see my brother at weekends'.

The motorist only encounters serious traffic jams in the city centre.
We could only choose two of them.
New technology will only be introduced by mutual agreement.

emphatic uses	However, if you want to be quite clear or emphatic, you put **only** immediately in front of the word, word group, or clause it applies to.

He played only instrumental music.
You may borrow only one item at a time.
There were other tollbooths but they were staffed only during the day.
We excavate only when something interesting is found.

For extra emphasis, you can put **only** after the word or word group that it applies to.

We insisted on being interviewed by women journalists only.
This strategy was used once only.

In writing and formal speech, you can put **only** at the beginning of a sentence, followed by the word, word group, or clause it applies to. After this word, word group, or clause, you put an auxiliary or 'be' followed by the subject of the main clause.

Only here was it safe to prepare and handle hot drinks.
Only then did Ginny realize that she still hadn't phoned her mother.
Only when the injured limb is fully mobile will the runner be encouraged to restrengthen it.

An alternative way of emphasizing is to start with 'It is only...' or 'It was only...' and the word or words that you want to emphasize. You put the rest of the sentence in a 'that'-clause.

It is only now that his virtues are beginning to be more widely appreciated.
It was only when the plans threatened middle-class areas that they ran into trouble.

'not only'	You use **not only** with 'but' or 'but also' as a way of linking words or word groups. For a full explanation, see entry at **not only**.

onto

You usually use the preposition **onto** to say where someone or something falls or is put.

He slumped down back onto his pillow.
Place the bread onto a large piece of clean white cloth.

After many verbs you can use either **onto** or **on** with the same meaning.

I fell with a crash onto a sandy bank.
He fell on the floor with a thud.

She poured some shampoo onto my hair.
Ginny poured ketchup on the beans.

Stuart put the reel of film onto the bench.
I put a hand on his shoulder.

However, after verbs meaning 'climb' or 'lift' you should use **onto**, rather than 'on'.

She climbed up onto his lap.
We stepped up onto the deck.
The little boy was hoisted onto a piano stool.

If you hold **onto** something, you put your hand round it or against it in order to prevent yourself from falling. After verbs meaning 'hold', you use **onto** as a preposition and **on** as an adverb.

She had to hold onto the edge of the table.
I couldn't put up my umbrella and hold on at the same time.

We were both hanging onto the side of the boat.
He had to hang on to avoid being washed overboard.

'on to'   **Onto** is sometimes written as two words **on to.**

She sank on to a chair.

open

Open is used as a verb or an adjective.

used as a verb   If you **open** something such as a door, you move it so that it no longer covers a hole or gap.

She opened the door with her key.
He went into his office, opened the window, and sat down at the desk.

WARNING   When you use **open** with a person as the subject, you must put an object after it. You do not say, for example, 'I went to the door and opened'. You say 'I went to the door and **opened it**'.

I went to the starboard door, opened it, and looked out.

When you are telling a story, you can use **open** as an intransitive verb, with a noun group such as 'the door' or 'the window' as the subject.

The door opened and a staff officer hurried in.
The gates opened and the procession began.

used as an   When a door or window is not covering the hole or gap it is intended to
adjective   cover, you say that it is **open.**

The door was open.
He was sitting by the open window of the office.

WARNING   When a door or window is in this position, you do not say that it is 'opened'. **Opened** is the past tense or past participle of the verb 'open'. You only use it when you are describing the action of opening a door or window.

Suddenly with a rasping sound the hatch was opened.

used after   **Open** can be used after other verbs of position besides 'be'.
other verbs
The doors of the ninth-floor rooms hung open.
The front door gaped open.

You can also use **open** after verbs of movement such as 'push'.

Buller pushed the door fully open.
He noticed the way in which the drawer slid open.

Note that **open** is one of several words that can be used after verbs of position or movement like this. Others are 'closed', 'shut', 'free', 'loose', 'straight', and 'upright'. These words are sometimes considered to be adverbs and sometimes adjectives.

WARNING   You do not use **open** as a verb or adjective to talk about electrical devices. For example, if someone causes an electrical device to work by pressing a switch or turning a knob, you do not say that they 'open' it. You say that they **put** it **on,** **switch** it **on,** or **turn** it **on.**

Do you mind if I put the light on?
I went across and switched on the TV.
I turned on the radio as I always did upon waking.

opinion

Your **opinion** of something is what you think about it.

We would like to have your opinion.
The students were eager to express their opinions.

When you want to indicate whose opinion you are giving, you can use an expression such as 'in my opinion', 'in Sarah's opinion', or 'in the opinion of the voters'.

In my opinion, there are four key problems that have to be addressed.
He is, in Bobby Robson's opinion, 'as good a player as we've ever produced'.
In the opinion of the Court of Appeal the sentence was too lenient.

In formal speech or writing, people sometimes say 'It is my opinion that...' or 'It is our opinion that...'.

It is my opinion that high school students should have the vote.

Note that you do not say 'To my opinion...' or 'According to my opinion...'. See entry at **point of view - view - opinion.**

Opinions

People often use expressions which show their attitude to what they are saying.

If you want to show how certain you are that what you are saying is true, you can use a **modal**. See entries at **can - could - be able to, might - may, must, shall - will, should,** and **should - would.**

There are many adverbials which are used to show your attitude to what you are saying. These adverbials, which are sometimes called **sentence adverbials,** are explained below. Most of them are usually put first in a clause. They can also come at the end of a clause, or within a clause.

indicating type of opinion
There are many sentence adverbials which you can use to indicate your opinion of the fact or event you are talking about, for example whether you think it is surprising or is a good thing or not. The following adverbials are commonly used in this way:

absurdly	incredibly	oddly	surprisingly
astonishingly	interestingly	of course	typically
characteristically	ironically	paradoxically	unbelievably
coincidentally	luckily	predictably	understandably
conveniently	mercifully	remarkably	unexpectedly
curiously	miraculously	sadly	unfortunately
fortunately	mysteriously	significantly	unhappily
happily	naturally	strangely	

Interestingly, the solution adopted in these two countries was the same.
Luckily, I had seen the play before so I knew what it was about.
Surprisingly, most of my help came from the technicians.
It is fortunately not a bad bump, and Henry is only slightly hurt.

A small number of adverbs are often used in front of 'enough'.

curiously	interestingly	strangely
funnily	oddly	

Funnily enough, old people seem to love bingo.
Interestingly enough, this proportion has not increased.

You can show what you think of someone's action using one of the following adverbs:

bravely	correctly	kindly	wrongly
carelessly	foolishly	rightly	
cleverly	generously	wisely	

She very kindly arranged a beautiful lunch.
Paul Gayner is rightly famed for his menu for vegetarians.
Foolishly, we had said we would do the decorating.

Note that these adverbs typically come after the subject or the first auxiliary of the clause. They can be put in other positions for emphasis.

being cautious   You can use one of the following adverbials to indicate that you are making a general, basic, or approximate statement:

all in all	by and large	on average
all things considered	essentially	on balance
altogether	for the most part	on the whole
as a rule	fundamentally	overall
at a rough estimate	generally	ultimately
basically	in essence	
broadly	in general	

Basically, the more craters a surface has, the older it is.
By and large we were free to treat this material very much as we wished.
I think on the whole we don't do too badly.

You can also use the expressions 'broadly speaking', 'generally speaking', and 'roughly speaking'.

We are all, broadly speaking, middle class.
Roughly speaking, the problem appears to be confined to the tropics.

You can use one of the following adverbials to show that your statement is not completely true, or only true in some ways:

almost	so to speak
in a manner of speaking	to all intents and purposes
in a way	to some extent
in effect	up to a point
more or less	virtually
practically	

It was almost a relief when the race was over.
In a way I liked her better than Mark.
They are, in effect, still trapped in a history which they do not understand.
Rats eat practically anything.

Note that 'almost', 'practically', and 'virtually' are not used at the beginning of a clause, unless they relate to a subject beginning with a word like 'all', 'any', or 'every'.

Practically all schools make pupils take examinations.

indicating   You can indicate how certain or definite you are about what you are saying
degree of   by using one of the following adverbials. They are arranged from 'least
certainty   certain' to 'most certain'.

▶ conceivably
▶ possibly

- perhaps, maybe
- hopefully
- probably
- presumably
- almost certainly
- no doubt, doubtless
- definitely

She is probably right.
Perhaps they looked in the wrong place.

'Maybe' is normally used at the beginning of a sentence.

Maybe you ought to try a different approach.

'Definitely' is hardly ever used at the beginning of a sentence.

You can imply that you do not have personal knowledge of something, or responsibility for it, by using 'It seems that...' or 'It appears that...'.

I'm so sorry. It seems that we're fully booked tonight.
It appears that he followed my advice.

You can also use the adverb 'apparently'.

Apparently they had a row.

indicating that something is obvious

You can use the following adverbials to indicate that you think it is obvious that what you are saying is right:

clearly	obviously	plainly
naturally	of course	

Obviously I can't do the whole lot myself.
Price, of course, is a critical factor.

You can also use expressions such as 'I need hardly say' and 'I need hardly tell you'.

I need hardly say that none of those involved saw fit to declare their latest acquisitions to the proper authorities.
I need hardly tell you what a delight it would be to serve under you again.
This, it need hardly be said, is a fantastic improvement.

emphasizing truth

You can emphasize the truth of your statement using the following adverbials:

actually	certainly	indeed	truly
believe me	honestly	really	

Sometimes we actually dared to penetrate their territory.
Believe me, if you get robbed, the best thing to do is forget about it.
I don't mind, honestly.
Eight years was indeed a short span of time.
I really am sorry.

Note that you use 'indeed' at the end of a clause only when you have used 'very' in front of an adjective or adverb.

I think she is a very stupid person indeed.

See entry at **indeed.**

You can use 'exactly', 'just', and 'precisely' to emphasize the correctness of your statement.

They'd always treated her exactly as if she were their own daughter.

I know just how you feel.
It is precisely his sensitivity to injustice which is presented as a sick deviation.

indicating personal opinion If you want to emphasize that you are expressing an opinion, you can use one of the following adverbials:

in my opinion	personally
in my view	to my mind

In my opinion it was probably a mistake.
There hasn't, in my view, been enough research done on mob violence.
Personally, I'm against capital punishment for murder.
She succeeded, to my mind, in living up to her legend.

You can also say 'As far as I'm concerned'.

As far as I'm concerned, it would be a moral duty.

indicating honesty You can indicate that you are making an honest statement using 'frankly' or 'in all honesty'.

Frankly, the more I hear about him, the less I like him.
In all honesty, I would prefer Madison.

Another way of indicating this is to use 'to be' followed by 'frank', 'honest', or 'truthful'.

I don't really know, to be honest.
To be perfectly honest, he was a tiny bit frightened of them.
'How do you rate him as a photographer?'—'Not particularly highly, to be frank.'

These types of adverbials often act as a kind of warning or apology that you are going to say something rather impolite or controversial.

indicating form of statement You can use 'to put it' followed by an adverb to draw attention to the fact that you are making your statement in a particular way.

To put it crudely, all unions have got the responsibility of looking after their members.
Other social classes, to put it simply, are either not there or are only in process of formation.

You can use 'to put it mildly' or 'to say the least' to indicate that what you are saying is an understatement.

A majority of college students have, to put it mildly, misgivings about military service.
The history of these decisions is, to say the least, disquieting.

explicitly labelling a thought You can use 'I' with a verb which refers to having an opinion or belief to indicate how strongly you hold an opinion. If you just say 'I think' or 'I reckon', this often has the effect of softening your statement and making it less definite. By using 'I suppose', you often imply that you are not really convinced about what you are saying.

The following verbs are used like this:

agree	fancy	imagine	reckon	trust
assume	guess	presume	suppose	understand
believe	hope	realize	think	

What he has been doing, I assume, is taking care of security.
A lot of that goes on, I imagine.

He was, I think, in his early sixties when I first encountered him.
I reckon you're right.
I suppose she could have shot the two of them, but I don't really see why.

You can use 'I'm' with the following adjectives in a similar way.

certain	positive
convinced	sure

I'm sure he'll win.
I'm convinced that it is a viable way of teaching.
I'm quite certain they would have made a search and found him.

explicitly labelling a statement
You can explicitly indicate what kind of thing you are saying by using 'I' and one of the following verbs:

acknowledge	confess	maintain	submit	warn
admit	contend	pledge	suggest	
assure	demand	predict	swear	
claim	deny	promise	tell	
concede	guarantee	propose	vow	

I admit there are problems about removing these safeguards.
It was all in order, I assure you.
I guarantee you'll like my work.
I warn you I am not at all a compatible person.

Note that 'I can't deny' and 'I don't deny' are used much more often than 'I deny'.

I can't deny that you're upsetting me.

'I say' is not often used. However, people often use 'say' in more complicated ways, for example with modals, to show that they are thinking carefully about what they are saying, or to show that they are only giving a personal opinion.

I must say I have a good deal of sympathy with Dr Pyke.
Well, I must say it all sounds pretty peculiar.
All I can say is that it's extraordinary how similar they are.
What I'm really saying is, I'm delighted they've got it.
I would even go so far as to say that we are on the brink of a revolution.

'Let me', 'May I', and 'I would like' are used with various verbs to introduce explicitly a point or question.

Let me give you an example.
First let me explain some of the principles involved.
May I make one other point.
I would like to ask you one question.

drawing attention to what you are about to say
You can use a structure consisting of 'the', a noun (or adjective and noun), and 'is' to classify what you are about to say, in a way that draws attention to it and shows that you think it is important. The nouns most commonly used in this structure are:

answer	point	rule	tragedy
conclusion	problem	solution	trouble
fact	question	thing	truth

The fact is they were probably right.
The point is, why should we let these people do this to us?

The only trouble is it's rather noisy.
Well, you see, the thing is she's gone away.
The crazy thing is, most of us were here with him on that day.

Note that 'that' can be used after 'is', unless the next clause is a question.

The important thing is that she's eating normally.
The problem is that the demand for health care is unlimited.

You can also use a clause beginning with 'what' as the subject.

What's particularly impressive, though, is that they use electronics so well.
What's wrong with technology is that it's not connected in any real way with matters of the spirit.
But what's happening is that each year our old machinery becomes less adequate.

opportunity

An **opportunity** is a situation in which it is possible for something to be done. You talk about an **opportunity for** something or an **opportunity to do** something.

They must regard it as an opportunity for a genuine new start.
The opportunity for constructive negotiation was not exploited.
For some, it was an opportunity to make a little money.
They don't even give them the opportunity to become better.

Note that you can use either 'the' or 'an' in front of **opportunity** in sentences like these.

You can also talk about an **opportunity for doing** something, especially if you use an adjective such as 'perfect or 'excellent' in front of **opportunity**.

This was a marvellous opportunity for exchanging gossip with the other girls.
The completeness of the fossil material offered an excellent opportunity for creating an accurate image of Neanderthal man.

You can also talk about **the opportunity of doing** something.

This gave him the opportunity of developing his talent as a teacher.

Note that you do not use 'an' in front of **opportunity** when it is followed by 'of'.

'no opportunity'   You can say there is **no opportunity to do** something.

I suppose you had no opportunity to bring it.
The public is given no opportunity to challenge official forecasts.

You do not say that there is 'no opportunity of doing' something.

'chance'   **Chance** is used in a similar way to **opportunity**. See entry at **chance**.

opposite

Opposite is used as a preposition, a noun, or an adjective.

used as a preposition   If one building or room is **opposite** another, they are separated from each other by a street or corridor.

The hotel is opposite a railway station.
The bathroom was located opposite my room.

If two people are **opposite** each other, they are facing each other, for example when they are sitting at the same table.

Lynn was sitting opposite him.
He drank off half his beer, still eyeing the Englishman opposite him.

used as a noun   If two things or people are totally different from each other in some way, you can say that one is **the opposite of** the other.

Hell is the opposite of heaven.
He was the exact opposite of Herbert, of course.

You can use **the opposite** without 'of', if it is clear what you are making a contrast with.

It isn't bad news. It's just the opposite.
They take the statement as true because the opposite is inconceivable.

WARNING   You do not express difference by saying that one thing or person is 'opposite' another.

used as an   **Opposite** can be used as an adjective either in front of a noun or after a
adjective   noun, but with different meanings.

You use **opposite** in front of a noun when you are mentioning one of two sides of something.

I was moved to a room on the opposite side of the corridor.
On the opposite side of the room a telephone rang.

You also use **opposite** in front of a noun when you are talking about something which is totally different from something else in some way.

Holmes took the opposite point of view.
Too much pressure would produce overheating, whereas too little would produce the opposite result.

You use **opposite** after a noun when you are mentioning someone or something that is on the other side of a street, corridor, room, or table from yourself.

The elderly woman opposite glanced up at the ventilation window.
In one of the smart new houses opposite, a party was in progress.

Note that the same building can be referred to as 'the house on **the opposite** side of the street' or 'the house **opposite**'. You do not refer to it as 'the opposite house'.

'opposed'   Do not confuse **opposite** with **opposed**. If someone is **opposed to** something, they disagree with it or disapprove of it.

I am opposed to capital punishment.

or

You use **or** when you are mentioning two or more alternatives or possibilities. You use **or** to link nouns, noun groups, adjectives, adverbials, verbs, or clauses.

Would you like some coffee or tea, Dr Floyd?
A bad tax or an unjust law can be changed.
It is better to defer planting if the ground is very wet or frosty.
Girls may do some work with their mothers in the fields or help in the house.

used with   You use **or** instead of 'and' after using a negative word. For example, you
negative words   say 'I do not like coffee **or** tea'. You do not say 'I do not like coffee and tea'.

The situation is just not fair on the children or their parents.
Price is not always an indicator of quality or suitability.

I am not detached or remote.
The reflectors still work because they have no batteries or circuits to wear out.

verb agreement   When you link two or more nouns using **or,** you use a plural verb after plural count nouns, and a singular verb after singular count nouns or uncount nouns.

Even minor amendments or innovations were given heavy publicity.
If your wife or husband is proficient in English there are many study courses from which they can choose.

'either ... or'   You use **either** with **or** when you are mentioning two alternatives and you want to indicate that no other alternatives are possible. **Either** goes in front of the first alternative and **or** goes in front of the second one.

Most of the fuel rods were either wholly melted down or substantially damaged.

See entry at **either ... or.**

linking more   When you are linking more than two items, you usually only put **or** in front
than two items   of the last one. After each of the others you put a comma. Often the comma is omitted in front of **or.**

Savings may come in useful for holidays, for expensive items of clothing, or perhaps for buying a car.
The costs of progress are all too often ignored, concealed or written off.

used to begin   You do not normally put **or** at the beginning of a sentence, but you can
a sentence   sometimes do so when you are reporting what someone says or thinks.

I may go home and have a steak. Or I may have some spaghetti.
Was the horror forgotten? Or buried?

used for   You can use **or** when you are correcting a mistake you have made, or when
correcting   you think of a more appropriate word or expression than the one you have just used.

They all remembered, or thought they remembered, how they had seen Smith charging ahead of them.

When you use **or** like this, you often put 'rather' after it.

One picture speaks volumes. Or rather lies volumes.

oral

See entry at **aural - oral.**

ordinary

See entry at **usual - usually.**

or else

See entry at **else.**

other

'the other'   When you are talking about two people or things and have already referred to one of them, you refer to the second one as **the other** or **the other one.**

They had two little daughters, one a baby, the other a girl of twelve.
He blew out one of his candles and moved the other one.

'the others'	When you are talking about several people or things and have already referred to one or more of them, you usually refer to the remaining ones as **the others**.

Jack and the others paid no attention.
First, concentrate only on the important tasks, then move on to the others.

'others'	When you have been talking about some people or things of a particular type, you refer to more people or things of this type as **others**.

Some writers are greater than others.
One policeman was stabbed and three others received minor injuries.

Note that you do not use 'the' with **others** in sentences like these. You do not say, for example, 'Some writers are greater than the others'.

'another'	When you have been talking about people or things of a particular type, you refer to one more person or thing of this type as **another** or **another one**.

I saw one girl whispering to another.
She had one plateful and then went back for another one.

See entry at **another**.

used in front of nouns	**The other, other,** and **another** can be used in a similar way in front of count nouns.

I was happy there, in spite of not getting on all that well with the other girls.
The roof was covered with straw and other materials.
He opened another shop last month.

otherwise

You use **otherwise** when you are mentioning an undesirable situation which would occur if something did not happen. You usually put **otherwise** at the beginning of a clause.

The defender should remember to keep a tight grip on the attacker's legs. Otherwise, his opponent will escape.
She was thankful that she'd had her baby in hospital; otherwise, she thought, she might have died.

WARNING	You do not use 'or' in front of **otherwise**.
used in relative clauses	**Otherwise** is sometimes used in a relative clause that contains a modal. You put **otherwise** after the modal or at the end of the clause.

They support services which would otherwise be uneconomic.
He was lured into a crime he would not otherwise have committed.
In doing this, we have met interesting people over the years, people we wouldn't have met otherwise.

ought to

See entry at **should - ought to**.

out

'out of'	When you go **out of** a place or get **out of** something such as a vehicle, you leave it, so that you are no longer inside it.

She rushed out of the house.
He got out of the car.
She's just got out of bed.

Note that in standard English you must use 'of' in sentences like these. You do not say, for example, 'He got out the car'. For more information about 'go out' and 'get out', see entry at **go out**.

You do not usually use 'from' after **out**. However, you use 'from' in front of another preposition such as 'behind' or 'under'.

He came out from behind the table.

'out' used as an adverb   You can use **out** as an adverb to say that someone leaves a place.

I ran out and slammed the door.
Why don't we go out into the garden?

If someone is **out,** they are not at home.

He came when I was out.

outdoors - outdoor

'outdoors'   **Outdoors** is an adverb. If something happens **outdoors,** it does not happen inside any building.

He spent a good deal of his time outdoors.
School classes were held outdoors.

When someone goes out of a building, you do not usually say that they go 'outdoors'. You say that they go **outside.** See entry at **outside.**

'outdoor'   **Outdoor** is an adjective used in front of a noun. You use it to describe things or activities that exist or take place in the open air, rather than inside a building.

...an outdoor play area.
American football is the most scientific of all outdoor games.

outside

Outside is used as a preposition or an adverb.

used as a preposition   When someone or something is close to a building but not actually inside it, you say that they are **outside** the building.

I parked outside the hotel.
There are queues for jobs outside the shipping offices.

Note that in standard English you do not say that someone is 'outside of' a building.

used as an adverb   You can also say that someone or something is **outside** or that something is happening **outside.**

There were about a dozen youths standing outside.
Patrick was cleaning out the fish tank outside.

When you go **outside,** you leave a building and go into the open air, but stay quite close to the building.

When they went outside, a light snow was falling.
Go outside and play for a bit.

If you leave a building in order to go some distance from it, you do not say that you go 'outside'. You say that you go **out.**

Towards dark he went out.
I have to go out. I'll be back late tonight.

You can also say that someone is **outside** when they are close to a room, for example in a hallway or corridor.

I'd better wait <u>outside</u> in the corridor.
Your father's lawyer is waiting <u>outside</u>.

another meaning of 'outside'

You can also talk about someone or something being **outside** a country. When **outside** is used like this, it does not have 'near' as part of its meaning. If you are **outside** a country, you can be near to the country or a long way away from it.

...if you have lived <u>outside</u> Britain.

over

Over is used as a preposition in several different ways.

position

If one thing is **over** another thing, it is directly above it.

I had reached the little bridge <u>over</u> the stream.
...the monument <u>over</u> the west door.

movement

If you go **over** something, you cross it and get to the other side.

Castle stepped <u>over</u> the dog.
...on the way back <u>over</u> the Channel.

age

If someone is **over** a particular age, they are older than that age.

She was well <u>over</u> fifty.

time

If something happens **over** a period of time, it happens during that time.

He'd had flu <u>over</u> Christmas.
...a process developed <u>over</u> many decades.

If you do something **over** a meal, you do it while you are eating the meal.

It's often easier to discuss difficult ideas <u>over</u> lunch.

overseas

Overseas is used as an adverb or an adjective.

used as an adverb

If you go **overseas**, you visit a foreign country which is separated from your own country by sea.

Roughly 4 million Americans travel <u>overseas</u> each year.

used as an adjective

Overseas is used in front of a noun to describe things relating to countries across the sea from your own country. **Overseas** has a similar meaning to 'foreign', but is more formal. You use it especially when talking about trade, finance, and travel.

...major programmes of <u>overseas</u> aid.
...on a recent <u>overseas</u> visit.

Note that you do not use **overseas** after 'be' with this meaning. If you say that someone **is overseas,** you do not mean that they are foreign; you mean that they are visiting a foreign country.

overtime

See entry at **overwork - overtime**.

overweight

See entry at **fat**.

overwork - overtime

'overwork'

If you are suffering from **overwork**, you are working too hard and exhausting yourself.

Most people believed that Stephen's illness was due to <u>overwork</u>.

'overtime'	If you do **overtime** or work **overtime,** you work for longer than your fixed working hours, often for extra pay.

I don't do <u>overtime</u> straight after a full shift.

owing to

See entry at **due to.**

own

If you want to emphasize that something belongs or relates to a particular person or thing, you use **own** after a possessive.

I took no notice till I heard <u>my own</u> name mentioned.
These people have total confidence in <u>their own</u> ability.
How far it also influenced <u>the King's own</u> beliefs, we cannot now be certain.
Now <u>the nuclear industry's own</u> experts support these claims.

'own' with a number	If you are also using a number, you put the number after **own.** You say, for example, 'She had given the same advice to her **own three** children'. You do not say 'She had given the same advice to her three own children'.

She was younger than my <u>own two</u> daughters.

'of your own'	You do not use **own** after 'an'. You do not say, for example, 'I've got an own place'. You say 'I've got **my own** place' or 'I've got a place **of my own**'.

By this time Laura had got <u>her own</u> radio.
She says we cannot have <u>our own</u> key to the apartment.
The university has a varied social and cultural life <u>of its own.</u>
I'm thinking of starting a production unit <u>of my own.</u>
...people who have no bank accounts <u>of their own.</u>

emphasizing 'own'	You can use 'very' in front of **own** for emphasis.

...the aptly-named Inside Out, the prison's <u>very own</u> pop group.
Accountants have a language of their <u>very own.</u>

'own' without a noun	You can use **own** without a noun after it, when it is clear what you are talking about. However, there must always be a possessive in front of it.

...people whose principles and values they had thought were the same as their own.
I refused to clean the cell unless I was given clothes other than <u>my own</u> to wear.

'on your own'	If you are **on your own,** you are alone.

She lived <u>on her own.</u>

If you do something **on your own,** you do it without any help from anyone else.

We can't solve this problem <u>on our own.</u>

P

pace

A **pace** is a step of normal length that you take when you walk.

The keeper took two quick paces forward.
The waiter stepped back a pace, watching his customer carefully.

'footstep' You do not use **pace** to refer to the sound made by a person's step. The word you use is **footstep.**

They heard footsteps and turned round.

'footprint' You also do not use **pace** to refer to a mark in the ground made by a person's foot. The word you use is **footprint.**

...fresh footprints in the snow.
There were no footprints or any signs of how the burglars got in.

package

See entry at **parcel.**

packet

See entry at **parcel.**

painful

You say that something is **painful** when it makes you feel pain.

My boots are still painful.
...a long and painful illness.

If a part of your body is **painful**, it hurts.

My back is so painful that I cannot stand upright.
My legs are stiff but not painful.

'in pain' When someone feels pain, you do not say that they are 'painful'. You say that they are **in pain.**

He was in pain and could not move into a comfortable position.

pair - couple

'a pair of' A **pair of** things are two things of the same size and shape that are used together, such as shoes.

...a pair of new gloves.
He bought a pair of hiking boots.

When you use **a pair of** like this, you can use either a singular or a plural form of a verb with it.

It is likely that a new pair of shoes brings more happiness to a child than a new car brings to a grown man.
He put on a pair of brown shoes which were waiting there for him.

You also use **a pair of** when you are referring to something which has two main parts of the same size and shape, such as trousers, glasses, or scissors.

She put on a pair of glasses.
There would be a razor in the bathroom or a pair of scissors.

When you use **a pair of** like this, you use a singular form of a verb with it.

On a hook behind the door was an old pair of grey trousers.
A large pair of tongs sends voltage through metal cups.

'a couple of'   **A couple of** people or things are two people or things.

They've been helped by a couple of newspaper reporters.
We'd had a couple of dances.

You use a plural form of a verb with **a couple of.**

There were a couple of tables littered with saucepans.
On the hallstand were a couple of periodicals.

Note that you do not use **a couple of** in formal writing.

referring to   Two people who do something together or are involved in a relationship
two people   together can be referred to as a **pair.** This is a slightly humorous use.
as a 'pair'
They'd always been a devoted pair.
They were a somewhat sinister pair.

When **pair** is used like this, you use a plural form of a verb with it.

The pair were wanted for the theft of certain jewellery.

referring to   You refer to two people as a **couple** when they have an intimate
two people   relationship such as that of husband and wife or boyfriend and girlfriend.
as a 'couple'
In Venice we met a South African couple.
This would raise pensions for married couples considerably.

You usually use a plural form of a verb with **couple.**

Behind me a couple were pushing a pram.

pants - shorts

In British English, **pants** are a piece of clothing worn by men, women, or children under their other clothes. Pants have two holes to put your legs through and elastic round the waist or hips to keep them up. Men's pants are sometimes referred to as **underpants.** Women's pants are sometimes referred to as **panties** or **knickers.**

In American English, men's pants are usually referred to as **shorts** or **underpants.** Women's pants are usually referred to as **panties.**

In American English, **pants** are men's or women's trousers.

In both British and American English, **shorts** are also short trousers that leave your knees and part of your thighs bare.

Both **pants** and **shorts** are plural nouns. You use a plural form of a verb with them.

The pants were big in the waist.
His grey shorts were sticking to him with sweat.

WARNING   You do not talk about 'a pants' or 'a shorts'. You say **a pair of pants** or **a pair of shorts.**

It doesn't take long to choose a pair of pants.
He wore the remains of a pair of shorts.

You usually use a singular form of a verb with **a pair of pants** or a **pair of shorts.**

I like a pair of pants that fits well.

paper

Paper is the material that you write things on or wrap things in.

The students will all be equipped with pencils and paper.

You can refer to several sheets of paper with information on them as **papers**.

He consulted the papers on his knee.

However, you do not refer to a single sheet of paper as a 'paper'. You refer to it as a **sheet of paper** or, if it is small, as a **piece of paper**.

He wrote his name at the top of a blank sheet of paper.
Rudolph picked up the piece of paper and gave it to her.

Newspapers are often referred to as **papers**.

I read about the riots in the papers.
When you get your daily paper, which page do you read first?

parcel

'parcel' and 'package'
A **parcel** or **package** is an object or group of objects wrapped in paper that can be carried somewhere or sent by post. There is very little difference in meaning between these two words. A **parcel** usually has a more regular shape than a **package**. In American English, **package** is more common than **parcel**.

International charities sent parcels of food and clothes to the refugees.
I am taking this package to the post office.

'packet'
A **packet** is a small container in which a quantity of something is sold. Packets are either small boxes made of thin cardboard, or bags or envelopes made of paper or plastic.

The room was littered with cups and cigarette packets.
Check the washing instructions on the packet.

In American English, containers like these are usually called **packages** or **packs**.

You can use **a packet of** or **a package of** to refer either to a packet or package and its contents, or to the contents only.

He took a package of cigarettes out of his pocket.
All I've had to eat today is a packet of crisps.

pardon

In old-fashioned English, if you **pardon** someone's behaviour or attitudes, you forgive them for them.

She asked him to pardon her rudeness.

apologizing
You can apologize to someone by saying '**I beg your pardon**'. Some American speakers say '**Pardon me**'. See entry at **Apologizing**.

part

Part is used as a noun or a verb.

used as a noun
Part of or **a part of** something is one of the pieces or elements that it consists of. You use **part of** or **a part of** in front of the singular form of a count noun, or in front of an uncount noun.

Economic measures must form part of any solution to this crisis.
Jailing and physical danger were a part of everyday existence.

'some of'	You do not use **part of** or **a part of** in front of a plural noun group. You do not say, for example, 'Part of the soldiers have no rifles'. You say '**Some of** the soldiers have no rifles'.

Some of the singers were having trouble getting to the theatre.
Some of them went up north.

Similarly, you do not say 'A large part of the houses have flat roofs'. You say '**Many of** the houses have flat roofs'.

Many of the old people were blind.
Many of his books are still available.

See entries at **some** and **many**.

used as a verb	When **part** is used as a verb, it is usually followed by 'from' or 'with'.

If you **part from** someone, you leave them, or you stop having a relationship with them. This is a formal or literary use.

He had parted from Gertrude.

If you **are parted from** someone or something, you cannot be with them, although you would like to be.

He had never been parted from her before.
It's perfectly natural that a mother should not wish to be parted from her children.

If you **part with** something that is valuable or that you would prefer to keep, you give it or sell it to someone else.

She didn't want to part with the money.
I took the book, thanked her, and told her I would never part with it.

partly

See section on **extent** in entry at **Adverbials**.

party

A **party** is a social event at which people enjoy themselves by eating, drinking, dancing, talking, or playing games. When someone organizes a party, you say that they **have, give,** or **throw** it. **Throw** is informal.

We are having a party on the beach.
She and Tim were giving a party.
You don't kid around when you throw a party, do you?

Note that you do not say that someone 'makes' a party.

pass

The verb **pass** is used with several different meanings.

movement	If you **pass** someone or something, you go past them.

We passed the New Hotel.
Please let us pass.

If you **pass** something to someone, you take it in your hand and give it to them.

She passed me her glass.
Pass me Philip's card, would you?

time	If you **pass** time in a particular way, you spend it that way.

We passed a pleasant afternoon together.
Am I to pass all my life abroad?

For more information about this use of **pass**, see entry at **spend - pass**.

The Passive

tests and exams If you **pass** a test or exam, you are successful in it.

> *I passed my driving test in Holland.*
> *She told me that I had passed.*

WARNING If you want to say that someone has completed a test or exam, without mentioning the result, you do not say that they have 'passed' the test or exam. You say that they have **taken** it.

> *She's not yet taken her driving test.*
> *She took her degree last year.*

GRAMMAR ## The Passive

The passive refers to verb groups whose subject is the person or thing that is affected by an action. For example, 'Our dinner's been eaten by the dog' contains a passive verb. With **active** verb groups, the subject is the person or thing doing the action, as in 'The dog's eaten our dinner'.

You use the passive when you are more interested in the person or thing affected by the action than in the person or thing doing the action, or when you do not know who performed the action. When you use the passive, you do not have to mention the performer of the action, as in 'Our dinner's been eaten'.

Passive verb groups consist of a tense of 'be', followed by the past participle of the main verb. For example, if you want to use the passive of the simple past of 'eat', you use the simple past of 'be' ('was' or 'were') and the past participle of 'eat' ('eaten'). You can have passive infinitives, such as 'to be eaten' and passive '-ing' forms, such as 'being eaten'. For full information, see entry at **Tenses**.

Nearly all transitive verbs (verbs which can have an object) can be used in the passive.

> *The room has been cleaned.*
> *Some very interesting work is being done on this.*
> *The name of the winner will be announced tomorrow.*

WARNING A few transitive verbs are rarely or never used in the passive:

elude	get	like	suit
escape	have	race	survive
flee	let	resemble	

Many phrasal verbs which consist of an intransitive verb and a preposition can also be used in the passive.

> *In some households, the man was referred to as the master.*
> *Sanders asked if such men could be relied on to keep their mouths shut.*

Note that the preposition is still put after the verb, but it is not followed by a noun group because the noun group it applies to is being used as the subject.

'by' In a passive sentence, if you want to mention the person or thing that performs an action, you use the preposition 'by'.

> *He had been poisoned by his girlfriend.*
> *He was brought up by an aunt.*

If you want to mention the thing that is used to perform an action, you use the preposition 'with'.

A circle was drawn in the dirt <u>with a stick</u>.
Moisture must be drawn out first <u>with salt</u>.

object
complements
Some verbs can have a complement after their object. The complement is an adjective or noun group which describes the object. (See section on **object complements** in entry at **Complements**.) When these verbs are used in the passive, the complement is put immediately after the verb.

In August he <u>was elected Vice President of the Senate</u>.
If a person today talks about ghosts, he <u>is considered ignorant or mad</u>.

'get'
In conversation, 'get' is sometimes used instead of 'be' to form the passive.

Our car <u>gets cleaned</u> about once every two months.
My husband <u>got fined</u> in Germany for crossing the road.

in report
structures
For information on the use of reporting verbs in the passive, see entry at **Reporting**.

past

Past is used as a noun or adjective to refer to a period of time before the present.

He never discussed his <u>past</u>.
I've spent most of the <u>past</u> eight years at sea.

telling the time
In British English, when you are telling the time, you use **past** to say how many minutes it is after a particular hour.

It's ten <u>past</u> eleven.
I went back to bed and slept until quarter <u>past</u> eight.

American speakers usually say **after**.

It's ten <u>after</u> eleven.
I arrived back in my room around a quarter <u>after</u> twelve.

For other ways of telling the time, see entry at **Time**.

going near
something
Past is also used as a preposition or adverb to say that someone goes near something when they are moving in a particular direction.

He walked <u>past</u> Lock's hat shop.
People ran <u>past</u> laughing.

'passed'
You do not use **past** as the past tense or past participle of the verb 'pass'. The word you use is **passed**.

We <u>passed</u> three cars.
The Act <u>was passed</u> at the end of last year.

GRAMMAR The Past

For the formation of past tenses, see entry at **Tenses**.

talking about
the past
The **simple past** tense is used to refer to an event in the past.

She <u>opened</u> the door.
One other factor <u>influenced</u> him.

In order to indicate exactly when something happened, or to indicate that something happened for a period of time or took place regularly, it is necessary to use additional words and expressions.

The Prime Minister flew to New York yesterday.
He thought for a few minutes.
They went for picnics most weekends.

When you want to talk about something which had been happening for some time when an event occurred, or which continued to happen after the event, you use the **past continuous** tense.

We were driving towards the racetrack when a policeman stepped in front of our car to ask for identification.
While they were approaching the convent, a couple of girls ran out of the gate.

You also use the past continuous to talk about a temporary state of affairs in the past.

Our team were losing 2-1 at the time.
We were staying with friends in Italy.

regular events 'Would' or 'used to' can be used instead of the simple past to talk about something which occurred regularly in the past.

We would normally spend the winter in Miami.
She used to get quite cross with Lally.

'Used to' is also used to talk about situations that no longer exist.

People used to believe that the earth was flat.

'Would' is not used like this.

perfect tenses When you are concerned with the present effects of something which happened at some time in the past, you use the **present perfect** tense.

I'm afraid I've forgotten my book, so I don't know.
Have you heard from Jill recently? How is she?

You also use the present perfect when you are talking about a situation which started in the past and still continues.

I have known him for years.
He has been here since six o'clock.

You use the **present perfect continuous** tense when you want to emphasize the fact that a recent event continued to happen for some time.

She's been crying.
I've been working hard all day.

When you are looking back to a point in the past, and you are concerned with the effects of something which happened at an even earlier time in the past, you use the **past perfect** tense.

I apologized because I had left my wallet at home.
…when he learned that the fence between the two properties had been removed.

You use the **past perfect continuous** tense when referring to a situation or event which started at an earlier time and continued for some time, or was still continuing.

I was about twenty. I had been studying French for a couple of years.
He hated games and had always managed to avoid children's parties.

future in the past When you want to talk about something that was in the future at a particular moment in the past, you can use 'would', 'was/were going to', or the past continuous tense.

He thought to himself how wonderful it would taste.
Her daughter was going to do the cooking.

Mike was taking his test the week after.

GRAMMAR **Past participles**

The **past participle** of a verb is used to form perfect tenses, passives, and, in some cases, adjectives. It is also called the **'-ed' form,** especially when it is used as an adjective.

Advances have continued, though actual productivity has fallen.
Jobs are still being lost.
We cannot refuse to teach children the required subjects.

See entries at **Tenses** and **'-ed' adjectives.**

The past participle is usually the same as the past form of the verb, except in the case of irregular verbs. See entry at **Irregular verbs.**

in non-finite clauses   In writing, a past participle can be used to begin a non-finite clause, with a passive meaning. For example, instead of writing 'She was saddened by their betrayal and resigned', you could write 'Saddened by their betrayal, she resigned'. The main clause can refer to a consequence of the situation mentioned in the past participle clause, or just to a related event that followed it.

Stunned by the swiftness of the assault, the enemy were overwhelmed.
Granted an amnesty and prematurely released, she rallied her followers and continued the struggle.

This structure is used especially with past participles which indicate feelings. Alternative structures are 'having been', 'after having been', or 'after being' followed by a past participle.

Having been left fatherless in early childhood he was brought up by his uncle.
...the prints of two hands pressed on the stone after having been dipped in red paint.
After being left for an hour in the shower room, we were placed in separate cells.

Past participles can be used in clauses introduced by a subordinating conjunction, with no subject or auxiliary, when the subject would be the same as the one in the main clause.

Dogs, when threatened, make themselves smaller and whimper like puppies.
Although now recognised as an important habitat for birds, the area of Dorset heathland has been cut in half since 1962.

after nouns   You can use a clause beginning with a past participle after a noun, 'those', or an indefinite pronoun to identify or describe someone by saying what happens or has happened to them.

...a successful method of bringing up children rejected by their natural parents.
Many of those questioned in the poll agreed with the party's policy on defence.
It doesn't have to be someone appointed by the government.

---

patriotic

See entry at **national - nationalist.**

pay

Pay is used as a verb or noun to talk about money. The past tense and past participle of the verb is **paid,** not 'payed'.

used as a verb

If you **pay for** something which has been done or provided, you give money to the person doing or providing it.

Pupils would be paid for any work they did.
Willie paid for the drinks.

Note that you must use 'for' after **pay** in sentences like these.

WARNING

If you pay for a drink that is drunk by someone else, you do not say that you 'pay' them the drink. You say that you **buy** them the drink.

Let me buy you a drink.
Monty bought Kaspar at least half-a-dozen whiskies.

If you pay for a meal that is eaten by someone else, you do not say that you 'pay' them the meal. You say that you **buy** them the meal or **treat** them **to** it.

I'll buy you lunch.
She offered to treat them to dinner.

used as a noun

A person's **pay** is their wages or salary.

She lost three weeks' pay.
They paid 6.5 per cent of their pay to the National Insurance Fund.

Note that you do not use 'a' with **pay.** You do not say, for example, 'It is a good pay'. You say 'The **pay** is good'.

The pay is dreadful.

other meanings

You can say that someone **pays** a call or a visit.

We went to pay a call on some people I used to know.
It would be nice if you paid me a visit.

See entries at **call** and **visit.**

You can also say that someone **pays** attention to something.

You must pay attention to his eyes.

See entry at **attention.**

people - person

'people'

People is a plural noun. You use a plural form of a verb after it.

People is most commonly used to refer to a particular group of men and women.

There were 120 people at the lecture.
We'll talk to the people concerned and see how they feel.

People can also be used to refer to a group of men, women, and children.

...the Great Fire of Chicago, when 250 people were killed.

You often use **people** to refer to all the men, women, and children of a particular country, tribe, or race.

The American people were antagonistic to his regime.

'peoples'

When you are referring to the men, women, and children of several countries, tribes, or races, you can use the plural form **peoples.**

Mediterranean peoples gesticulate more freely than northern Europeans.

<table>
<tr>
<td>**another use of 'people'**</td>
<td>**People** can also be used to say that something is generally done.</td>
</tr>
</table>

another use of 'people'   **People** can also be used to say that something is generally done.

People have an enduring tendency to protect what they have.
She could not resist being unkind to people.

Note that there are several ways of saying that something is generally done. For more information, see entry at **one.**

'person'   **Person** is a count noun. A **person** is an individual man, woman, or child.

There was far too much meat for one person.
They think you are a suitable person to join the church.

The usual plural of 'person' is **people,** but in formal English **persons** is sometimes used.

The bomb exploded killing 111 persons.

percentage - per cent

When you express an amount as a **percentage** of a whole, you say how many parts the amount would have if the whole had 100 equal parts. You write a percentage as a number followed by **per cent** or by the symbol %. So, for example, if there are 1200 people living in a village and 300 of them are children, you say that 25 per cent (25%) of the people in the village are children.

What is the percentage of nitrogen in air?
He won 28.3 per cent of the vote.
Poland is 90 per cent Roman Catholic.

Per cent is sometimes written as one word, especially in American English.

Remember that 90 percent of most food is water.

You also use **percentage** to indicate roughly how large or small an amount is as a proportion of a whole. For example, you can say that an amount is 'a large percentage' or 'a small percentage' of a whole.

It's a tiny percentage of the total income.
...areas with a very high percentage of immigrants.

When **percentage** is used like this in front of the plural form of a noun, you use a plural form of a verb after it.

A good percentage of the people were his own age.

When **percentage** is used in front of a singular form, you use a singular form of a verb after it.

A high percentage of the pet population has been adopted off the streets.

perfect

Something that is **perfect** is as good as it can possibly be.

She speaks perfect English.
I've got the perfect solution.

In conversation, some people use **perfect** to mean 'very good indeed'. It is fairly common for people to say that one thing is **more perfect** than another, or that something is the **most perfect** thing of its kind.

The resulting film is more perfect than a genuine live broadcast.
Some claim its acoustics to be the most perfect in the world.

'perfectly'   You do not use **perfect** as an adverb. You do not say, for example, 'She did it perfect'. You say 'She did it **perfectly**'.

The plan worked perfectly.
He was dressed perfectly.

perhaps

See entry at **maybe - perhaps**.

period

See entry at **full stop - period**.

permissible - permissive

'permissible'
If something is **permissible,** you are allowed to have it or do it, because it does not break any rules, laws, or conventions.

Pictures of your pets are quite permissible.
I understood that it was permissible to ask a question.

'permissive'
A **permissive** society or person tolerates things which some people disapprove of, especially freedom of sexual behaviour.

We live in a permissive age.
This opened the way for local branches of the Church to take a more permissive attitude.

permission

If someone gives you **permission** to do something, they say they will allow you to do it.

He gave me permission to go.
You can't do it without permission.

Permission is an uncount noun. You do not talk about 'permissions' or 'a permission'.

When you ask for permission to do something and are given it, you say that you **get** or **obtain** permission to do it.

I went as often as I could get permission.
Consul-General Lee obtained permission for an autopsy.

You do not say that someone 'takes' permission to do something.

When you have been given permission to do something, you say that you **have** or **have got** permission to do it.

I have permission to tell you how things went in Bonn.
We've got permission to climb the Tower.

Permission

There are several ways of asking, giving, and refusing permission.

asking permission
If you want to ask permission to do something, you can use 'Can I...?' or 'Could I...?' (You use 'we' instead of 'I' if you are speaking on behalf of a group.) 'Could I...?' is more polite.

Can I light the fire? I'm cold.
Can I have a look at the piece of paper then?
Could we put this fire on?
Could I stay at your place for a bit, Rob?

People used to be taught that, when asking for permission, it was correct to use 'may' rather than 'can', and 'might' rather than 'could'. However, 'can' and 'could' are now generally used. 'May I...?' sounds very polite and formal, and 'Might I...?' sounds even more formal.

May I look round now?
May I borrow that new lipstick you bought, Stephanie?
Might we leave our bags here for a moment?

You can add 'please' to be more polite.

David, can I look at your notes please?
Good afternoon. Could I speak to Mr Duff, please.
Could you ask for them to be taken out, please.

You can also make your request very polite by adding 'perhaps' or 'possibly' after 'Could I' or 'May I'.

Could I perhaps bring a friend with me?
May I possibly have a word with you?

You can ask permission in a stronger way by using 'can't' or 'couldn't' instead of 'can' or 'could'. You do this if you think you may not be given the permission you want.

Can't I come?
Couldn't we stay here?

Another way of requesting permission is to say 'Let me...'. However, if you use a firm tone, this can sound like an order.

Oh, let me come with you.
Please let me do it, Cyril!

Note that 'Let me...' is also used as a way of offering to do something for someone.

Anne, let me drive you home. You don't look at all well.

See entry at **Offers**.

indirect ways   There are other, more indirect, ways of asking for permission to do something. You can use expressions such as 'Would it be all right if I...?' and, more informally, 'Is it okay if I...?'

Would it be all right if I used your phone?
Is it all right if I go to the bathroom?
Is it okay if I go home now?

In very informal situations, these expressions are often shortened so that they start with the adjective. This sounds more casual, as if you are assuming the other person will give their permission.

Okay if I smoke?

An even more indirect way is to say something like 'Would it be all right to...?', using a 'to'-infinitive.

Would it be all right to take this?

A more polite way is to say 'Do you mind if I...?' or 'Would you mind if I...?'

Do you mind if we speak a bit of German?
Would you mind if I just ask you some routine questions?

Again, these expressions are shortened in very informal situations.

Mind if I bring my bike in?

You can also say 'I was wondering if I could...' or 'I wonder if I could...'.

I was wondering if I could go home now.

I wonder if I could have a few words with you.

Note that, in formal situations, you can add 'if I may' after stating your intention to do something. You do this when you do not think it is really necessary to ask permission but want to appear polite.

I'll take a seat if I may.
Switching, if I may, from the Victorian novelist to more contemporary novelists, who do you think are the good novelists of today?

giving someone permission

There are many words and expressions that you can use to give someone permission to do something when they have just asked you for it.

In informal situations, you can say 'OK' or 'All right'. 'Sure' is slightly more emphatic, and is used especially by American speakers.

'Could I have a word with him?'—'OK.'
'Can I go with you?'—'Sure.'

'Of course', 'Yes, do', and 'By all means' are more formal, and emphatic.

'Could I make a telephone call?'—'Of course.'
'Do you mind if I look in your cupboard? There are some hot water bottles somewhere.'—'Yes, do.'
'May I come too?'—'By all means.'

If you are not very certain or enthusiastic about giving permission, you can say 'I don't see why not.'

'Can I take it with me this afternoon?'—'I don't see why not.'

You can give someone permission to do something when they have not asked for it by saying 'You can...'. If you want to be more formal, you say 'You may...'.

You can go off duty now.
You may use my wardrobe.

refusing permission

The commonest way of refusing someone permission is to use an expression such as 'Sorry', 'I'm sorry', or 'I'm afraid not', and give an explanation.

'I was wondering if I could borrow a book for the evening.'—'Sorry, I haven't got any with me.'
'Could I see him – just for a few minutes?'—'No, I'm sorry, you can't. He's very ill.'
'I wonder if I might see him.'—'I'm afraid not, sir. Mr Wilt is still helping us with our enquiries.'

If you know the other person very well, you can simply say 'No' or 'No, you can't', but this is impolite. In informal situations, people sometimes use even more impolite and emphatic expressions to refuse permission, such as 'No way' and 'No chance'.

You can indicate that you do not really want someone to do something by saying 'I'd rather you didn't.' You say this when you cannot in fact prevent them from doing it.

'May I go on?'—'I'd rather you didn't.'

You can refuse someone permission to do something when they have not asked for it by saying 'You can't...' or 'You mustn't...'.

You can't go.
You mustn't open it until you have it in the right place.

You can also use 'You're not' and an '-ing' form. This is informal and emphatic.

You're not putting that thing on my boat.

permissive

See entry at **permissible - permissive**.

permit

See entry at **allow - permit - let**.

persecute - prosecute

'persecute'   To **persecute** someone means to continually treat them badly and make them suffer, for example because of their political or religious beliefs.

Members of these sects are ruthlessly persecuted.
They claim that nobody is persecuted for religious belief.

'prosecute'   To **prosecute** someone means to accuse them of a crime and bring criminal charges against them.

He was prosecuted for drunken driving.
Trespassers will be prosecuted.

person

See entry at **people - person**.

personal - personnel

'personal'   Personal /pɜːsənəl/ is an adjective. You use it to say that something belongs or relates to a particular person.

This is my personal opinion.
...a cheque drawn on his personal bank account.

'personnel'   Personnel /pɜːsənel/ is a noun. The **personnel** of a company or organization are the people who work for it.

We've advertised for extra security personnel.
...accommodation for the unmarried personnel.

Personnel is a plural noun. You do not talk about 'personnels' or 'a personnel'.

persuade

See entry at **convince**.

petrol

See entry at **gas - petrol**.

pharmacist

See entry at **chemist**.

pharmacy

See entry at **chemist's - drugstore**.

phenomenon

A **phenomenon** is something that happens or exists and that can be seen or experienced.

We are witnessing a very significant phenomenon.
Many theories have been put forward to explain this phenomenon.

The plural of 'phenomenon' is **phenomena**, not 'phenomenons'.

Constable looked at natural phenomena in a way that few painters before him had.
I had always thought those phenomena were confined to the Bahamas.

WARNING **Phenomena** is only used as a plural form. You do not talk about 'a phenomena' or 'this phenomena'.

phone

When you **phone** someone, you dial their phone number and speak to them by phone.

I went back to the motel to phone Jenny.
I phoned him and offered him a large salary.

You can also **phone** a place.

He phoned the police station and spoke to the officer in charge.
Each day we phoned Geneva Airport for a weather forecast.

Note that you do not use 'to' after **phone**.

GRAMMAR **Phrasal verbs**

A **phrasal verb** is a combination of a verb and an adverb, a verb and a preposition, or a verb, an adverb, and a preposition, which together have a single meaning. Phrasal verbs extend the usual meaning of the verb or create a new meaning.

The pain gradually wore off.
I had to look after the kids.
They broke out of prison.
Kroop tried to talk her out of it.

position of objects With phrasal verbs consisting of a transitive verb and an adverb, the object of the verb can usually be put in front of the adverb or after it.

Don't give the story away, silly!
I wouldn't want to give away any secrets.

However, when the object of the verb is a pronoun, the pronoun must go in front of the adverb.

He cleaned it up.
I answered him back and took my chances.

With phrasal verbs consisting of a transitive verb and a preposition, the object of the verb is put after the verb, and the object of the preposition is put after the preposition.

They agreed to let him into their little secret.
The farmer threatened to set his dogs on them.

With phrasal verbs consisting of a transitive verb, an adverb, and a preposition, the object of the verb is usually put in front of the adverb, not after it.

Multinational companies can play <u>individual markets</u> off against each other.
I'll take <u>you</u> up on that generous invitation.

---

physician - physicist

'physician'   A **physician** is a doctor, especially one who treats illnesses or injuries using medicine rather than surgery. **Physician** is a formal or old-fashioned word.

'physicist'   A **physicist** is a person who studies physics or does research connected with physics.

...a nuclear <u>physicist.</u>

physique

Your **physique** /fɪziːk/ is the shape and size of your body.

...a good-looking lad with a fine <u>physique.</u>

'physics'   You do not use **physique** to refer to the scientific study of such things as heat, light, sound, and electricity. The word you use is **physics** /fɪzɪks/.

...nuclear <u>physics.</u>

pick

See entry at **choose**.

picture

See entry at **film**.

Pieces and amounts

There are many words which are used in front of 'of' and an uncount noun to refer to a piece of something or a particular amount of something. The most common words are given here.

substances   Some words can be used to refer to a piece or amount of many kinds of substance:

atom	flake	mountain	scrap	stick
ball	fragment	patch	sheet	strip
bit	heap	particle	shred	trace
block	hunk	piece	slab	tuft
chunk	lump	pile	slice	wad
crumb	mass	pinch	sliver	wedge
dab	molecule	ring	speck	wodge
dollop	mound	roll	splinter	

Always kneel on a <u>bit</u> of sponge rubber.
...a big comforting soup, with <u>lumps</u> of bacon, and <u>chunks</u> of potato and cabbage stalk.
An arrow painted on a <u>strip</u> of plywood indicated a ticket office.

Pieces and amounts

liquids　Some words are used to refer to an amount of a liquid:

dash	globule	puddle	trickle
dribble	jet	splash	
drop	pool	spot	

Rub a <u>drop</u> of vinegar into the spot where you were stung.
A high pressure <u>jet</u> of water was directed onto the set of plates causing the pulley to spin.
One fireman was kneeling down in a great <u>pool</u> of oil.

food　**Helping, portion,** and **serving** are used when talking about the amount of a particular kind of food that you are given at a meal.

He had two <u>helpings</u> of ice-cream.
I chose a hefty <u>portion</u> of local salmon.

You can refer to a small piece of food as a **morsel** of food.

He had a <u>morsel</u> of food caught between one tooth and another.

typical pieces and amounts　The following table shows you which word is typically used to refer to a piece or amount of something of a particular kind.

bread	a loaf/slice of bread
butter	a knob of butter
cake	a slice/piece of cake
chocolate	a bar/piece/square of chocolate
cloth	a bolt/length/piece of cloth
coal	a lump of coal
corn	an ear/sheaf of corn
dust	a speck/particle/cloud of dust
fog	a wisp/bank/patch of fog
glass	a sliver/splinter/pane of glass
glue	a blob of glue
grass	a blade of grass
hair	a lock/strand/wisp/tuft/mop/shock of hair
hay	a bale of hay
land	a piece/area of land
light	a ray/beam/shaft of light
medicine	a dose of medicine
money	a sum of money
paper	a piece/sheet/scrap of paper
rice	a grain of rice
rope	a coil/length/piece of rope
salt	a grain/pinch of salt
sand	a grain of sand
smoke	a cloud/blanket/column/puff/wisp of smoke
snow	a flake/blanket of snow
soap	a bar/cake of soap
spirits	a measure/slug/tot of spirits
stone	a slab/block of stone
string	a ball/piece/length of string
sugar	a grain/lump of sugar
sweat	a bead/drop/trickle of sweat
tape	a reel of tape
thread	a reel/strand of thread
wax	a blob of wax
wheat	a grain/sheaf of wheat
wire	a strand/piece/length of wire
wool	a ball of wool

measurements and containers	You can also refer to an amount of something using a measurement noun such as 'pound' or 'metre', or a noun referring to a container such as 'bottle' or 'box'. See entry at **Measurements** and section on **containers** in entry at **Quantity**.

pitiful - pitiable

You say that someone is **pitiful** when they are very sad, weak, or unfortunate, and you feel great pity for them.

...a fragile and pitiful old lady.
...his thin, bony legs and his pitiful arms.

You can describe the experience of seeing a person like this as **pitiful** or **pitiable.**

It is pitiful to see old people degraded like that.
They are as pitiable a sight as you could imagine.

'sorry' However, if you feel pity for someone, you do not say that you are 'pitiful' or 'pitiable'. You say that you **are sorry** for them or **feel sorry** for them. You often use a word such as 'very' or 'deeply' in front of **sorry.**

He felt extremely sorry for the little boy.
He was truly sorry for Marcus.

place

Place is usually used as a noun.

used in descriptions You can use it after an adjective when you are describing a building, room, town, or area of land. For example, instead of saying 'Richmond is nice', you can say 'Richmond is a nice **place**'.

It's a beautiful place.
The cellar was a very dark place.
He's building himself a really comfortable place to live in.

saying where something is You can say where something is using **the place** followed by a clause beginning with 'where'. For example, you can say 'This is **the place where** I parked my car'.

He reached the place where I was standing.
He said he would walk with me to the place where I had been knocked down.

WARNING You do not use 'where' with a 'to'-infinitive after **place.** You do not say, for example, 'I'm looking for a place where to park my car'. You say 'I'm looking for **a place to park** my car' or 'I'm looking for **a place where I can park** my car'. You can also say 'I'm looking for **somewhere to park** my car'.

I always tried to find a place to hide.
It was a place where they could go swimming or surfing.
We had to find somewhere to stop for lunch.

'anywhere' You do not usually use **place** after 'any' in questions or negative statements. You do not say, for example, 'She never goes to any place without her sister'. You say 'She never goes **anywhere** without her sister'.

I changed my mind and decided not to go anywhere.
Is there an ashtray anywhere?

'there' You do not use 'that place' to refer to somewhere that has just been mentioned. You do not say, for example, 'I drove my car into a field and left it in that place'. You say 'I drove my car into a field and left it **there**'.

I decided to try Newmarket. I soon found a job there.
I must get home. Bill's there on his own.

'room'   You do not use **place** to say whether there is enough space for something. You do not say, for example, 'There was not enough place for all my things'. You say 'There was not enough **room** for all my things'.

> There wasn't enough <u>room</u> for everybody.
> Just keep the crowd back so I have <u>room</u> to move.

'place' used   **Place** is sometimes used as a verb with the same meaning as 'put'.
as a verb

> Some of the women lit candles and <u>placed</u> them carefully among the flowers.

See entry at **place - put.**

'take place'   When something **takes place,** it happens.

> The talks will <u>take place</u> in Vienna.
> ...the changes which <u>are taking place</u> at the moment.

See entry at **take place.**

place - put

The verbs **place** and **put** are often used with the same meaning. **Place** is more formal than **put,** and is mainly used in writing.

If you **place** something somewhere, you put it there. You often use **place** to say that someone puts something somewhere neatly or carefully.

> She <u>placed</u> the music on the piano and sat down.
> Each stone is firmly and correctly <u>placed</u>.

pressure   If you **place** or **put** pressure on someone, you urge them to do something.

> Renewed pressure <u>will be placed</u> on the Government this week.
> For a long time he's been trying to <u>put</u> pressure on us.

adverts   If you **place** or **put** an advert in a newspaper, you pay for the advert to be printed in the newspaper.

> We <u>placed</u> an advert in an evening paper.
> You could <u>put</u> an advert in the 'Mail'.

Places

asking about   If you want to know where someone's home is, you say 'Where do you live?'
someone's   or 'Whereabouts do you live?'
home

> 'Where do you live?'—'I have a little studio flat, in Chiswick.'
> 'Where do you live?'—'Off Frogstone Road.'—'Where's that?'

If you want to know where someone spent their early life, you can say 'What part of the country are you from?' You can also say, 'Where do you come from?' or 'Where are you from?', especially if you think they spent their early life in a different country.

'Where do you come from?'—'India.'

place names Place names such as 'Italy' and 'Amsterdam' are a type of proper noun and are spelled with a capital letter.

The table on this page and the following page shows ways of referring to different types of places. Those marked with a star are less common.

Continents	proper noun	Africa Asia
Areas and regions	'the' + proper noun adjective + proper noun 'the' + 'North', 'South', 'East', 'West'	the Arctic the Midlands Eastern Europe North London the East the South of France
Oceans, seas, deserts	'the' + modifier + 'Ocean', 'Sea', 'Desert' 'the' + proper noun	the Indian Ocean the Gobi Desert the Pacific the Sahara
Countries	proper noun *'the' + type of country	France Italy the United States the United Kingdom the Netherlands
Counties and states	proper noun *proper noun + 'County' (US)	Surrey California Butler County
Islands Groups of islands	proper noun proper noun + 'Island' 'the Isle of' + proper noun 'the' + modifier + 'Islands' 'the' + plural proper noun	Malta Easter Island the Isle of Wight the Scilly Isles the Channel Islands the Bahamas
Mountains Mountain ranges	'Mount' + proper noun proper noun *'the' + proper noun 'the' + plural proper noun 'the' + modifier + 'Mountains'	Mount Everest Everest the Matterhorn the Andes the Rocky Mountains
Rivers	'the' + 'River' + proper noun 'the' + proper noun *'the' + proper noun + 'River' (not British)	the River Thames the Thames the Colorado River

Lakes	'Lake' + proper noun	Lake Michigan
Capes	'Cape' + proper noun *'the' + 'Cape' + proper noun	Cape Horn the Cape of Good Hope
Other natural places	'the' + modifier + place noun modifier + place noun 'the' + place noun + 'of' + proper noun	the Grand Canyon the Bering Strait Sherwood Forest Beachy Head the Gulf of Mexico the Bay of Biscay
Towns	proper noun	London
Buildings and structures	proper noun + place noun 'the' + modifier + place noun 'the' + place noun + 'of' + proper noun/ noun	Durham Cathedral London Zoo the Severn Bridge the Tate Gallery the Church of St. Mary the Museum of Modern Art
Cinemas, theatres, pubs, hotels	'the' + proper noun	the Odeon the Bull
Railway stations	proper noun proper noun + 'Station'	Paddington Paddington Station
Streets	modifier + 'Road', 'Street', 'Drive', etc *'the' + proper noun *'the' + modifier + 'Street' or 'Road'	Downing Street the Strand the High Street

Most place names are used with a singular verb form. Even place names that look like plural nouns, for example 'The United States' and 'The Netherlands', are used with a singular verb form.

Canada still <u>has</u> large natural forests.
Milan <u>is</u> the most interesting city in the world.
...when the United States <u>was</u> prospering.

However, the names of groups of islands or mountains are usually used with a plural verb form.

...one of the tiny Comoro Islands that <u>lie</u> in the Indian Ocean midway between Madagascar and Tanzania.
The Andes <u>split</u> the country down the middle.

The name of a country or its capital city is often used to refer to the government of that country.

<u>Britain</u> and <u>France</u> jointly suggested a plan.
<u>Washington</u> had put a great deal of pressure on <u>Tokyo</u>.

You can also sometimes use the name of a place to refer to the people who live there. You use a singular verb form even though you are talking about a group of people.

Europe <u>was</u> sick of war.
...to pay for additional imports that Poland <u>needs</u>.

For other ways of referring to the people of a country, see entry at
Nationality words.

Place names can also be used to refer to a well-known event that occurred in that place, such as a battle or a disaster.

After Waterloo, trade and industry surged again.
...the effect of Chernobyl on British agriculture.

modifier use   You can use a place name as a modifier to indicate that something is in a particular place, or that something comes from or is characteristic of a particular place.

...a London hotel.
She has a Midlands accent.

adverbials   Many adverbials – that is, prepositional phrases and adverbs – are used to talk about place. For information on where to put these adverbials in a clause, see entry at **Adverbials.**

prepositions: The main prepositions used to indicate position are 'at', 'in', and 'on'.
position
Sometimes we went to concerts at the Albert Hall.
I am back in Rome.
We sat on the floor.

You sometimes need to be careful about choosing the right preposition. For more information, see entries at **at, in,** and **on.** See also entry at **arrive - reach.**

For the difference in use between 'by' and 'near', see entry at **by.**

Here is a full list of prepositions which are used to indicate position:

aboard	among	between	near	past
about	around	beyond	near to	through
above	astride	by	next to	throughout
across	at	close by	off	under
against	away from	close to	on	underneath
ahead of	before	down	on top of	up
all over	behind	in	opposite	upon
along	below	in between	out of	with
alongside	beneath	in front of	outside	within
amidst	beside	inside	over	

prepositions: The main preposition used to indicate a destination is 'to'.
destination and
direction   *I went to the door.*
She went to Australia in 1970.

Note that 'at' is not usually used to indicate a person's destination. It is used to indicate what someone is looking towards, or what they cause an object to move towards.

They were staring at a garage roof.
Supporters threw petals at his car.

See also entries at **into** and **onto.** See also entry at **go into** for information on how to talk about entering vehicles.

Here is a full list of prepositions which are used to indicate where something goes:

aboard	at	by	near	past
about	away from	down	near to	round
across	behind	from	off	through
ahead of	below	in	on	to
all over	beneath	in between	onto	towards
along	beside	in front of	out of	under
alongside	between	inside	outside	underneath
around	beyond	into	over	up

As you can see from the above lists, many prepositions can be used to indicate both place and direction.

The bank is just across the High Street.
I walked across the room.

We live in the house over the road.
I stole his keys and escaped over the wall.

qualifier use
Prepositional phrases are used after nouns as qualifiers to indicate the location of the thing or person referred to by the noun.

The table in the kitchen had a tablecloth over it.
The driver behind me began hooting.

prepositions
with parts
and areas
If you want to say explicitly which part of something else an object is nearest to, or exactly which part of an area it is in, you can use 'at', 'by', 'in', 'near', or 'on'. 'To' and 'towards' (which are usually used to indicate direction) are used to express position in a more approximate way.

You use 'at', 'near', and 'towards' with the following nouns:

back	centre	foot	side
base	edge	front	top
bottom	end	rear	

At the bottom of the stairs you will find a rough patch of mosaic paving.
The old building of University College is near the top of the street.
He was sitting towards the rear.

You also use 'to' with 'rear' and 'side'.

A company of infantry was swiftly redeployed in a stronger position to the rear.
There was one sprinkler in front of the statue and one to the side of it.

You use 'on' or 'to' with 'left' and 'right', and 'in' with 'middle'. You can also use 'on' instead of 'at' with 'edge'.

The church is on the left and the town hall and police station are on the right.
To the left were the kitchens and staff quarters.
My mother stood in the middle of the road, watching.
He lives on the edge of Sefton Park.

You use 'to' or 'in' with the following nouns:

east	north-east	south	south-west
north	north-west	south-east	west

To the south-west lay the city.
The National Liberation Front forces were still active in the north.

You use 'at' or 'by' with the following nouns:

bedside	graveside	poolside	riverside	waterside
dockside	kerbside	quayside	roadside	
fireside	lakeside	ringside	seaside	

...sobbing bitterly at the graveside.
We found him sitting by the fireside.

Note that you generally use 'the' with the nouns in the three previous lists.

I ran inside and bounded up the stairs. Wendy was standing <u>at the top.</u>
<u>To the north</u> are the main gardens.

However, you can also use a possessive determiner with the nouns in the first list above ('back', 'base', etc), and with 'left', 'right', and 'bedside'.

We reached another cliff face, with trees and bushes growing <u>at its base.</u>
There was a gate <u>on our left</u> leading into a field.
I was <u>at his bedside</u> at the very last.

Note that 'in front of' and 'on top of' are fixed phrases, without a determiner. They are compound prepositions.

She stood <u>in front of</u> the mirror.
I fell <u>on top of</u> him.

adverbs: There are many adverbs which indicate position. Many of these indicate
position that something is near a place, object, or person that has already been mentioned.

Seagulls were circling <u>overhead.</u>
<u>Nearby,</u> there is another restaurant.
This information is summarized <u>below.</u>

Here is a list of the main adverbs which are used to indicate position:

aboard	below	here	offshore	throughout
about	beneath	in	opposite	underfoot
above	beside	in between	out of doors	underground
abroad	beyond	indoors	outdoors	underneath
ahead	close by	inland	outside	underwater
aloft	close to	inside	over	up
alongside	down	near	overhead	upstairs
ashore	downstairs	nearby	overseas	upstream
away	downstream	next door	round	upwind
behind	downwind	off	there	

A small group of adverbs of position are used to indicate how wide an area something exists in:

globally	locally	universally	worldwide
internationally	nationally	widely	

Everything we used was bought <u>locally.</u>
Western culture was not <u>universally</u> accepted.

Unlike most other adverbs of position, these adverbs (with the exception of 'worldwide') cannot be used after 'be' to state the position of something.

The adverbs 'deep', 'far', 'high', and 'low', which indicate distance as well as position, are usually followed by another adverb or phrase indicating position, or are modified or qualified in some other way.

Many of the eggs remain buried <u>deep among the sand grains.</u>
One plane, flying <u>very low,</u> swept back and forth.

'Deep down', 'far away', 'high up', and 'low down' are often used instead of the adverbs on their own.

The window was <u>high up</u>, miles above the rocks.
Sita scraped a shallow cavity <u>low down</u> in the wall.

adverbs:
direction or
destination

There are also many adverbs which indicate direction or destination.

They went <u>downstairs</u> hand in hand.
Go <u>north</u> from Leicester Square up Wardour Street.
She walked <u>away</u>.

Here is a list of the main ones:

aboard	downtown	inwards	round
abroad	downwards	left	sideways
ahead	east	near	skyward
along	eastwards	next door	south
anti-clockwise	forwards	north	southwards
around	heavenward	northwards	there
ashore	here	on	underground
back	home	onward	up
backwards	homeward	out of doors	upstairs
clockwise	in	outdoors	uptown
close	indoors	outside	upwards
down	inland	overseas	west
downstairs	inside	right	westwards

qualifier use

Place adverbs can be used after nouns as qualifiers.

...a small stream that runs through the sand to the ocean <u>beyond</u>.
My suitcase had become damaged on the journey <u>home</u>.

modifier use

Some place adverbs can be used in front of nouns as modifiers.

Gradually the <u>underground</u> caverns fill up with deposits.
There will be some variations in your heart rate as you encounter <u>uphill</u>
stretches or increase your pace on <u>downhill</u> sections.

The following place adverbs can be used as modifiers:

anticlockwise	eastward	outside	underwater
backward	inland	overhead	uphill
clockwise	inside	overseas	upstairs
downhill	nearby	southward	westward
downstairs	northward	underground	

indefinite
place adverbs

There are four indefinite adverbs of position and direction: 'anywhere', 'everywhere', 'nowhere', and 'somewhere'.

No-one can find Howard or Barbara <u>anywhere</u>.
There were bicycles <u>everywhere</u>.
I thought I'd seen you <u>somewhere</u>.

For information on when to use 'anywhere' and when to use 'somewhere', see entry at **somewhere**.

'Nowhere' makes a clause negative.

I was to go <u>nowhere</u> without an escort.

In writing, you can put 'nowhere' at the beginning of a clause for emphasis. You put the subject of the verb after an auxiliary or a form of 'be'.

Nowhere have I seen any serious mention of this.
Nowhere are they overwhelmingly numerous.

Note that you can put a 'to'-infinitive clause after 'anywhere', 'somewhere', or 'nowhere' to indicate what you want to do in a place.

I couldn't find anywhere to put it.
We mentioned that we were looking for somewhere to live.
There was nowhere for us to go.

You can also put a relative clause after these adverbs. Note that you do not usually use a relative pronoun.

I could go anywhere I wanted.
Everywhere I went, people were angry or suspicious.

You can use 'else' after an indefinite place adverb to indicate a different or additional place.

We could hold the meeting somewhere else.
More people die in bed than anywhere else.

'Elsewhere' can be used instead of 'somewhere else' or 'in other places'.

It was obvious that he would rather be elsewhere.
Elsewhere in the tropics, rainfall is notoriously variable and unreliable.

---

plain

See entry at **homely.**

play

Play is used as a verb or a noun.

When children **play,** they spend time amusing themselves with their toys or taking part in games.

The kids went off to play on the swings.

sports and games

If you **play** a particular sport or game, you take part in it regularly.

Ray and I play squash at least three times a week.
Do you play chess?

You use **play** with 'in' to say that someone takes part in a game, match, or competition on a particular occasion.

Altogether he played in 44 Test matches.

'game'

You do not use **play** as a noun to refer to a sport or other activity in which two or more people compete against each other. The word you usually use is **game.**

You need two people to play this game.
In a game like tennis, the score is kept by the umpire.

tapes and records	If you **play** a tape, record, or compact disc, you put it in or onto a piece of equipment and listen to it.

I'll play you the tape in a minute.

However, you do not say that someone 'plays' a film or a television programme. You say that they **show** it.

One evening the school showed a cowboy film.

musical instruments	If you **play** a musical instrument, you produce music from it.

He sometimes played the organ in the cathedral.

If you want to say that someone is able to play a particular instrument, you use 'the'. For example, you say 'She **plays the piano**' or 'He **plays the flute**'.

Uncle Rudi played the cello.

However, rock and jazz musicians usually omit the 'the'. They say 'She **plays piano**' or 'He **plays guitar**'.

There was one kid who played sax.

pleased - disappointed

The following adjectives can be used to indicate how pleased or disappointed someone is. They are arranged from 'most pleased' to 'most disappointed':

► thrilled, overjoyed
► delighted
► glad, pleased
► satisfied
► resigned, philosophical
► disappointed
► upset
► shattered, devastated

pleasure

Pleasure is a feeling of happiness, satisfaction, or enjoyment.

McPherson could scarcely conceal his pleasure at my resignation.
I can't understand how people can kill for pleasure.

Pleasure is usually used as an uncount noun. You say, for example, that something gives you **pleasure**. You do not say that it gives you 'a pleasure'.

Poetry of many kinds gave me great pleasure.
The event gave enormous pleasure to a lot of people.

You can talk about the **pleasure of doing** something.

I'd travel a thousand miles just for the pleasure of meeting you.
It was not only for the pleasure of playing chess with you that I asked you to come.

You do not talk about the 'pleasure to do' something.

GRAMMAR **Plural forms of nouns**

The following table shows the basic ways of forming the plurals of count nouns.

	singular form	plural form
		add '-s' (/s/ or /z/)
regular	hat	hats
	tree	trees
		add '-s' (/ɪz/)
ending in '-se'	rose	roses
'-ze'	prize	prizes
'-ce'	service	services
'-ge'	age	ages
		add '-es' (/ɪz/)
ending in '-sh'	bush	bushes
'-ch'	speech	speeches
'-ss'	glass	glasses
'-x'	box	boxes
'-s'	bus	buses
		change '-y' to '-ies'
ending in consonant + '-y'	country	countries
	lady	ladies
		add '-s'
ending in vowel + '-y'	boy	boys
	valley	valleys

Nouns ending with a long vowel sound and the sound /θ/ have their plural forms pronounced as ending in /ðz/. For example, the plural of 'path' is pronounced /pɑːðz/ and the plural of 'mouth' is pronounced /maʊðz/.

'House' is pronounced /haʊs/, but its plural form 'houses' is pronounced /haʊzɪz/.

Note that, if the 'ch' at the end of a noun is pronounced as /k/, you add 's', not 'es', to form the plural. For example, the plural of 'stomach' /stʌmək/ is 'stomachs'.

nouns with no change in form Some nouns have the same form for both singular and plural.

...a sheep.
...nine sheep.

Many of these nouns refer to animals or fish.

bison	goldfish	moose	sheep
cod	greenfly	mullet	shellfish
deer	grouse	reindeer	trout
fish	halibut	salmon	whitebait

Note that even when a noun referring to an animal has a plural form ending in 's', it is quite common to use the form without 's' to refer to a group of the animals in the context of hunting.

Zebra are a more difficult prey.

Similarly, when you are referring to a large number of trees or plants growing together, you can use the form without 's'. However, this is used like an uncount noun, not a plural form.

...the rows of <u>willow</u> and <u>cypress</u> which lined the creek.

The following nouns also have the same form for singular and plural:

aircraft	gallows	insignia	series
crossroads	grapefruit	mews	spacecraft
dice	hovercraft	offspring	species

nouns ending in 'f' or 'fe'

There are several nouns ending in 'f' or 'fe' where you form the plural by substituting 'ves' for 'f' or 'fe'.

calf – calves	sheaf – sheaves
elf – elves	shelf – shelves
half – halves	thief – thieves
knife – knives	turf – turves
leaf – leaves	wharf – wharves
life – lives	wife – wives
loaf – loaves	wolf – wolves
scarf – scarves	

The plural of 'hoof' can be 'hoofs' or 'hooves'.

nouns ending in 'o'

With many nouns ending in 'o', you just add 's' to form the plural.

photo – photos
radio – radios

However, the following nouns have plurals ending in 'oes':

domino	embargo	negro	tomato
echo	hero	potato	veto

The following nouns ending in 'o' can have plurals ending in either 'os' or 'oes':

buffalo	ghetto	memento	stiletto
cargo	innuendo	mosquito	tornado
flamingo	mango	motto	torpedo
fresco	manifesto	salvo	volcano

irregular plurals

A few nouns have special plural forms, as shown below:

child – children	mouse – mice
foot – feet	ox – oxen
goose – geese	tooth – teeth
louse – lice	woman – women
man – men	

Note that the first syllable of 'women' /wɪmɪn/ is pronounced differently from that of 'woman' /wʊmən/.

Most nouns which refer to people and which end with 'man', 'woman', or 'child' have plural forms ending with 'men', 'women', or 'children'.

postman – postmen
Englishwoman – Englishwomen
grandchild – grandchildren

However, the plural forms of 'German', 'human', 'Norman', and 'Roman' are 'Germans', 'humans', 'Normans', and 'Romans'.

plurals of compound nouns

Most compound nouns have plurals formed by adding 's' to the end of the last word.

swimming pool — swimming pools
tape recorder — tape recorders
down-and-out — down-and-outs

However, in the case of compound nouns which consist of a noun ending in 'er' and an adverb such as 'on' or 'by' and which refer to a person, you add 's' to the first word to form the plural.

passer-by — passers-by
hanger-on — hangers-on

Compound nouns consisting of three or more words have plurals formed by adding 's' to the first word when the first word is a noun identifying the type of person or thing you are talking about.

brother-in-law — brothers-in-law
bird of prey — birds of prey

plurals of foreign words

There are words in English which are borrowed from other languages, especially Latin, and which still form their plurals according to the rules of those languages. Many of them are technical or formal, and some are also used with a regular 's' or 'es' plural ending in non-technical or informal contexts. You may need to check these in a dictionary.

Some nouns ending in 'us' have plurals ending in 'i'.

nucleus — nuclei
radius — radii
stimulus — stimuli

However, other nouns ending in 'us' have different plurals.

corpus — corpora
genus — genera

Nouns ending in 'um' often have plurals ending in 'a'.

aquarium — aquaria
memorandum — memoranda

Some nouns ending in 'a' have plurals formed by adding 'e'.

larva — larvae
vertebra — vertebrae

Nouns ending in 'is' have plurals in which the 'is' is replaced by 'es'.

analysis — analyses
crisis — crises
hypothesis — hypotheses

Some nouns ending in 'ix' or 'ex' have plurals ending in 'ices'.

appendix — appendices
index — indices
matrix — matrices

Nouns borrowed from Greek which end in 'on' have plurals in which the 'on' is replaced by 'a'.

criterion — criteria
phenomenon — phenomena

The following words borrowed from French have the same written form for the plural as for the singular. The 's' at the end is not pronounced for the singular but is pronounced /z/ for the plural.

bourgeois	corps	précis
chassis	patois	rendezvous

point

A **point** is something you say which expresses an idea, opinion, or fact.

That's a very good point.
I want to make several quick points.

A **point** is also an aspect or detail of something, or a part of a person's character.

The two books have some interesting points in common.
That's his best point, I think.

'the point'
The **point** is the most important fact in a situation.

The point was that Dick could not walk.
Philip, I may as well come straight to the point. I'm pregnant.
You've all missed the point.

The **point of doing** something is the reason for doing it.

What was the point of attempting to live together?
I didn't see the point of boring you with all this.

'no point'
If you say that **there is no point in doing** something, you mean that it has no purpose or will not achieve anything.

There's no point in talking to you.
There was not much point in thinking about it.

You do not say 'there is no point to do' something. You also do not say 'it is no point in doing' something.

'full stop'
You do not refer to the punctuation mark (.) which comes at the end of a sentence as a 'point'. In British English, it is called a **full stop**. In American English, it is called a **period**. For more information, see entry at **Punctuation**.

point of view - view - opinion

'point of view'
When you are considering one aspect of a situation, you can say that you are considering it from a particular **point of view**.

From a practical point of view it is quite irrelevant.
From the commercial point of view they have little to lose.

A person's **point of view** is their general attitude to something, or the way they feel about something that affects or concerns them.

We understand your point of view.
I tried to see things from Frank's point of view.

'view' and 'opinion'
You do not refer to what someone thinks or believes about a particular matter as their 'point of view'. You refer to it as their **view** or **opinion**.

Mr Carr's view is that the Bill is not anti-trade union.
If you want my honest opinion, I don't think it will work.

View is most commonly used in the plural.

Your views have always been respected here.
He was sent to jail for his political views.

You talk about someone's opinions or views **on** or **about** a particular matter.

He always asked for her opinions on every aspect of his work.
I have strong views about politics and the Church.

You can add expressions such as **in my opinion** or **in his view** to a statement to indicate that what you are saying is only what someone thinks, and is not necessarily a fact.

In my opinion, man is capable of reasoning but not of acting within wholly rational limits.
Such a proposal in his view would do nothing but harm.

police

The police are the official organization responsible for making sure that people obey the law. They also protect people and property and arrest criminals.

He had called the police.
Contact the police as soon as possible after a burglary.

Police is a plural noun. You use a plural form of a verb after it.

The police were called to the scene of the crime.

You do not refer to an individual member of the police force as a 'police'. You refer to him or her as a **police officer,** a **policeman,** or a **policewoman.**

You have made a very serious allegation against a police officer.
He had been a policeman for six years.
Many of the younger policewomen resented not being allowed to take part in tougher assignments.

politics

The noun **politics** is used in two ways. It is usually used to refer to the methods by which people acquire, retain, and use power in a country or society.

They are reluctant to take part in politics.
He has remained active in British politics.

When **politics** is used like this, you can use either a singular or plural form of a verb with it. Most people use a singular form.

Politics is a means for the individual to achieve fulfilment.
Politics are a subtle business.

Politics can also refer to the study of the ways in which countries are governed, and of the ways in which power is acquired and used in them. When you use **politics** like this, you must use a singular form of a verb with it.

Politics is a wide subject.

'policy' Note that there is no noun 'politic'. If you want to refer to a course of action or plan that has been agreed upon by a government or political party, the word you use is **policy.**

There is no change in our policy.
He was criticized for pursuing a policy of reconciliation.

'political' You also do not use 'politic' to mean 'relating to politics'. The word you use is **political**.

> ...*political* developments.
> ...*the major* political *parties.*
> *He was sent to jail for his* political *views.*

pollution

When there is **pollution,** the water or air in a place is dirty, impure, and dangerous, usually because poisonous chemicals have got into it.

> ...*changes in the climate due to* pollution *of the atmosphere.*

Pollution is an uncount noun. You do not talk about 'pollutions' or 'a pollution'.

pond

See entry at **lake - pool - pond.**

pool

See entry at **lake - pool - pond.**

pore - pour

These words are both pronounced /pɔː/.

'pore' A **pore** is a small hole in the skin of a person or animal.

> *There was dirt in the* pores *around his nose.*

'pore over' If you **pore over** something such as a piece of writing or a map, you examine it carefully.

> *He got out the chart and* pored over *it in a vain attempt to discover where they were.*

'pour' If you **pour** a liquid, you cause it to flow out of a container.

> *The waiter* poured *the wine into her glass.*

If it **is pouring**, it is raining very heavily.

> *It* was *absolutely* pouring.

'poor' Note that the adjective **poor** is sometimes pronounced /pɔː/.

position - post

When someone has a regular job, it is referred to in formal English as their **position** or **post.** When a job is advertised, it is often described as a **position** or **post,** and a person applying for a job usually uses one of these words.

> ...*top management* positions.
> *She is well qualified for the* post.

'job' In conversation, you do not use **position** or **post** with this meaning. You simply use **job.**

> *He's afraid of losing his* job.
> *She changed her department and got this interesting* job.

There are a number of other nouns which refer to activities which people are paid to do. For information on these words, see entry at **work.**

possess

The verb **possess** is usually used to say that someone or something has a quality, ability, or feature.

He possessed the qualities of a war leader.
For hundreds of years London possessed only one bridge.

This is a fairly formal use. In conversation, you do not use **possess**. Instead you use **have** or **have got**. See entries at **have** and **have got**.

In legal English, if you **possess** an object or substance, you own it or have it with you.

They were found guilty of possessing petrol bombs.
...the arrest of the mayor on charges of possessing cocaine.

Possession and other relationships

This entry explains how to show that something belongs to or is related to something else.

There are six basic ways of doing this:

● using a **possessive determiner** such as 'my' or 'their' in front of the main noun

● adding **apostrophe s** (**'s**) to the end of a noun and putting it in front of the main noun

● using the preposition **of** after the main noun

● using another **preposition** after the main noun

● using a **noun modifier** in front of the main noun

● using an **adjective** in front of the main noun

An apostrophe ('), not 's, is added to plural nouns ending in 's'. See entry at **'s** for more information.

A noun modifier is a noun that is used in front of another noun. It is nearly always singular. See entry at **Noun modifiers.**

something belonging to a person

If you want to indicate who something belongs to or is associated with, you can use a possessive determiner. If you are using a short noun group to refer to the person, you add 's to the noun group and put it in front of the main noun. If you are using a long noun group, you put 'of' in front of it and put it after the main noun.

...his car.
...her home.
...Hogan's car.
...a woman's voice.
...Mr Heseltine's views.
...the son of the chairman of Prudential Insurance.
...the dog of the prosperous junk dealer next door.

quality possessed by a person

If you are referring to a quality possessed by a particular person or animal, you use a possessive determiner, 's, or 'of'.

...his bravery.
...the woman's abruptness.
...the zeal and courage of the workers.

Possession and other relationships

quality possessed by a thing

If you are referring to a quality possessed by a particular thing, you use 'of' or a possessive determiner. People sometimes also use 's.

...the efficiency of the teaching processes.
...the speed of the car travelling in front.
...its speed.
...the plane's speed.

something associated with a thing

If you want to indicate that something is associated with an object or with an abstract thing, you use 'of' or a possessive determiner.

...the design of the engine.
...the impact of inflation.
...its impact.

People sometime use 's when indicating association with an object.

...the car's location.

part of a person or animal

If you are referring to part of a person or animal, you use a possessive determiner or 's with a short noun group, and 'of' with a long noun group.

...your leg.
...Laura's leg.
...the bare feet of the young girls.

In the case of an animal, you can also use 'of' with a short noun group beginning with 'a'.

...the wings of a humming-bird.

part of a thing

If you are referring to part of a thing, you generally use 'of'. You always use 'of' with words like 'top', 'middle', and 'end'.

...the top of the hill.
...the leg of the chair.

If you are referring to one of the parts that an object consists of, you can sometimes also use 's or a possessive determiner.

...the car's engine.
...its doors.

If the part is considered to be a type of thing, you use a noun modifier.

...the kitchen floor.
...a car door.

action done by a person or thing

If you are referring to an action done by a particular person or thing, you can use a possessive determiner or 's.

...her death.
...Mr Lawson's resignation.
...the Government's refusal to increase its basic 6.5 per cent pay offer.
...Ricke's acceptance of the job as chief executive.

You can also use 'of' in front of a noun group referring to the person or thing that performs an action. This is done especially when the noun group is a long one.

...the death of a prisoner last December.
...the arrival of powerful processing computers.
...the refusal of certain large grain suppliers to continue supplies until they are paid.

You can also use 'by' when mentioning an action that affects someone or something else.

...the rejection of pay offers of up to 7.8 per cent by union leaders.
...the defeat of James II by William III.

something done to a person
If you are referring to something that is done to a particular person, you use a possessive determiner or 's. You can also use 'of', especially for longer noun groups or when the agent is mentioned too.

...*his appointment as managing director.*
...*Graf's last defeat.*
...*the murder of his colleague.*
...*England's defeat of the West Indies.*

Similarly, if you are referring to someone who does something to a person, or has a particular attitude towards them, you can use a possessive determiner, 's, or 'of'.

...*their supporters.*
...*the Prime Minister's supporters.*
...*supporters of Dr Eames.*

Note that if you are referring to a type of action or person that affects people of a particular kind, you use a noun modifier.

...*staff training.*
...*child abuse.*
...*child killers.*

something done to a thing
If you are referring to something that is done to a particular thing, you use 'of'.

...*his handling of the economy.*
...*the introduction of new crops.*
...*the creation of a modern banking system.*

However, if you are referring to a person who does something to a particular thing, you can use a possessive determiner, 's, or 'of'.

...*its owner.*
...*the vessel's owner.*
...*the owner of the house rented by the bombers.*

Note that if you are referring to a type of action or person that affects things of a particular kind, you use a noun modifier.

...*crime prevention.*
...*job creation.*
...*home owners.*
...*toy manufacturers.*

However, you can also sometimes use 'of'.

...*the prevention of accidents.*
...*owners of hotels and guest houses.*
...*lovers of poetry.*

person or thing from a particular place
If you want to indicate what place a particular person or thing comes from or is associated with:

● you add 's to general nouns like 'city' and 'country'

...*the country's roads.*
...*the city's population.*
...*the world's finest wines.*

● you use an adjective indicating a particular country (or occasionally a state or city)

...*an Australian film.*
...*Swiss climbers.*
...*a strong Glaswegian accent.*

Possession and other relationships

● you use the name of a county or town (or occasionally country) as a noun modifier

...a London hotel.
...a London heart specialist.
...a Yorkshire chemist.
...the New Zealand government.

● you use a preposition such as 'in' or 'from'. 'In' is used especially after a superlative has been used.

...the largest department store in the world.
...the best goalkeeper in Britain.
...a hotel in New York.
...students from Britain.

person who controls something

If you want to indicate the country or organization that someone controls, you use 'of'.

...the President of Iceland.
...the head of the Secret Service.

Reporters and broadcasters also use an adjective or noun modifier, or 's.

...the Nicaraguan President.
...the CBI President.
...Lithuania's President.

person or thing of a particular type

If you want to indicate what a type of thing or person is suitable for or connected with, you can use a noun modifier.

...bedroom slippers.
...a milk bottle.
...gas cookers.
...chest wounds.
...car owners.
...man management.

If an appropriate adjective exists, you can use that adjective, especially in formal or technical contexts.

...industrial output.
...a political analyst.
...abdominal wounds.

You may also be able to use an appropriate preposition.

...a degree in Classics.
...a book on Chinese regional cookery.

Note that there are sometimes two ways of referring to something. For example, you can talk about 'a heart attack' (using a noun modifier) or, in formal or medical contexts, 'a cardiac arrest' (using an adjective). You can talk about 'a History degree' (using a noun modifier) or 'a degree in History' (using a preposition).

You use 's to indicate that a type of thing is suitable for or used by a type of person.

...a man's black suit.
...a knight's helmet.

When you are talking about a number of things that are suitable for a particular type of person, you usually make the noun with 's plural. For example, you talk about 'children's shoes', not 'child's shoes'.

...men's hats.

You also make the noun with 's plural when referring to a type of thing that is used by more than one person.

...a *men's* prison.
...a *children's* book.

You also use 's when referring to a type of thing that is produced by a type of animal. Note that whether you use a determiner or not depends on the main noun, not the noun with 's. For example, you do not need to use a determiner with an uncount noun such as 'milk'.

...a *hen's* egg.
...*cow's* milk.

object made of a particular material

If you want to indicate what something is made of, you usually use a noun modifier. Sometimes there is an adjective you can use.

...a *plastic* bucket.
...a *metal* box.
...*cotton* socks.
...a *wooden* spoon.

'Of' is used only in literary or old-fashioned writing.

...roofs *of iron*.

quantity of a substance

If you want to indicate how much of a substance there is, or what shape it is, you use 'of'.

...a bottle *of milk*.
...a kilo *of fruit*.
...a drop *of blood*.
...a block *of stone*.

See also entries at **Pieces and amounts** and **Quantity**.

WARNING

When you want to refer to a full container, or to its contents, you must use 'of'. For example, you would buy or eat 'a packet of cereal'. When you want to refer just to a container, especially an empty one, you use a noun modifier, as in 'a cereal packet'.

Occasionally, you can use a noun modifier with words indicating the shape of a quantity of a substance.

...a *wax* block.
...an *ice* cube.

person with a particular job

If you want to indicate what job someone does as well as the relationship they have with someone, you can use a noun modifier.

...her *soldier* husband.
...my *geologist* friend.

You can also put another noun group after the main noun and a comma.

...his friend, *a football player*.

something that lasts a particular time

If you want to indicate that something lasts a particular length of time, you use 's in front of uncount nouns and a noun modifier in front of count nouns. Note that the noun modifier is usually hyphenated.

...*two years'* imprisonment.
...a *two-year* course.

When you are talking about something that lasts one week, one month, or one year, you can use a noun modifier with 'one'. You can also use 'week-long', 'month-long', or 'year-long', which emphasizes the length of time.

...a *one-year* contract.

...a year-long experiment.

If you are talking about an amount, you use 's.

...a year's supply of cat food.
...a month's salary.

other uses   Noun modifiers, 's, and 'of' are also used to indicate the age, day, size, or time of something. See entries at **Days and dates**, **Measurements**, and **Time**. See entry at **of** for information on other uses of 'of'.

GRAMMAR   # Possessive determiners

Possessive determiners show who or what something belongs to or is connected with.

The possessive determiners are:

	singular	plural
1st person	my	our
2nd person	your	
3rd person	his her its	their

You choose a possessive determiner according to the identity of the person or thing who has the thing you are talking about. For example, if you are talking about a pen belonging to a woman, you say 'her pen', but if the pen belongs to a man, you say 'his pen'.

Soon after five that day the vicar called at my house.
Sir Thomas More built his house there.
I walked out of her house and collided with a pillar box.
Sometimes I would sleep in their house all night.

The same determiner is used whether the noun after the possessive determiner is singular or plural, or refers to a person or a thing.

I just went on writing in my notebook.
My parents don't trust me.

WARNING   You do not use another determiner with a possessive determiner. For example, you do not say 'I took off the my shoes'. You say 'I took off my shoes'.

'the' instead of   Sometimes the determiner 'the' is used when there is an obvious
possessive   possessive meaning, particularly when you are talking about someone doing something to a part of someone else's body.

They hit him over the head with a stick.
He took his daughters by the hand and led them away.

You can also use 'the' when referring to one of your possessions. For example, you can say 'I'll go and get the car' instead of 'I'll go and get my car'.

I went back to the house.
The noise from the washing-machine is getting worse.

However, you cannot use 'the' like this when referring to something that someone is wearing. For example, you say 'My watch is slow'. You do not say 'The watch is slow'.

It is not usual to use 'the' with a possessive meaning when referring to a relative such as an uncle or a sister. However, people often refer to their children as 'the children' or 'the kids'.

When the children had gone to bed I said, 'I'm going out for a while'.

Note that possessive determiners are more commonly used to indicate that something belongs to a person than to a thing. For example, it is more usual to say 'the door' than to say 'its door' when referring to the door of a room.

For more information on when to use a possessive determiner, see entry at **Possession and other relationships.**

possessive pronouns

See entry at **Pronouns.**

possibility

If there is a **possibility** of something happening or being the case, it might happen or be the case.

There was just a possibility that they had taken the wrong road.
We must accept the possibility that we might be wrong.

If there is **no possibility** of something happening or being the case, it cannot happen or be the case.

There was now no possibility of success.
There was no possibility that she hadn't heard Jane.

When people are talking or thinking about the **possibility of doing** something, they are considering whether to do it.

Senators and Congressmen were talking about the possibility of impeaching the President.

You do not say that someone talks or thinks about the 'possibility to do' something.

'opportunity' When a situation occurs in which it is possible for someone to do something, you do not say that they have the 'possibility to do' it. You say that they have the **opportunity to do** it or the **opportunity of doing** it. See entry at **opportunity.**

possible - possibly

'possible' **Possible** is an adjective. If something is **possible,** it can be done or achieved.

It is possible for us to measure his progress.
A breakthrough may be possible next year.

Possible is often used in expressions such as 'as soon as possible' and 'as much as possible'. If you do something **as soon as possible,** you do it as soon as you can.

Go as soon as possible.
I like to know as much as possible about my patients.
He sat as far away from the others as possible.

Note that you do not say that someone does something 'as soon as possibly' or 'as much as possibly'.

You also use **possible** to say that something may be true or correct.

It is possible that he said these things.
That's one possible answer.

'possibly' | **Possibly** is an adverb. You use **possibly** to indicate that you are not sure about something.

Television is possibly to blame for this.
The threat was possibly not very great.

For a graded list of words used to say how sure you are about something, see section on **probability** in entry at **Adverbials**.

You also use **possibly** when you are asking someone to do something in a very polite way. For example, you say '**Could you possibly** give me a lift to town?'

Could you possibly find a moment to tell them I'll be in on Saturday.

For more information about requests, see entry at **Requests, orders, and instructions**.

post - mail

The public service by which letters and parcels are collected and delivered is usually called the **post** in British English and the **mail** in American English. **Mail** is also sometimes used in British English, for example in the name 'Royal Mail'.

There is a cheque for you in the post.
Winners will be notified by post.
Your reply must have been lost in the mail.

British speakers usually refer to the letters and parcels delivered to them on a particular occasion as their **post**. American speakers refer to these letters and parcels as their **mail**. Some British speakers also talk about their **mail**.

They read their bosses' post.
I started to read my mail.

British speakers talk about **posting** a letter or parcel. Americans usually say that they **mail** it.

Some of the letters had been posted.
...the magazine that her friend had mailed to her.

Some words connected with the sending of letters are the same in both American and British English, for example 'post office', 'postcard', 'postmaster', 'mailbag', and 'mail order'. Otherwise, British and American speakers use different words to refer to the same person or thing. For example, a man who brings letters and parcels to your house is called a 'postman' in British English and a 'mailman' in American English.

'postage' | Note that you do not use **post** or **mail** to refer to the amount of money that you pay to send a letter or parcel. In both British and American English, this money is called **postage**.

Send 25p extra for postage and packing.

other meanings of 'post' | **Post** has several other meanings which are not connected with sending letters or parcels. For example, a person's job is sometimes referred to as his or her **post**. For more information about this meaning, see entry at **position - post**.

postgraduate

See entry at **graduate**.

postpone

See entry at **delay - cancel - postpone**.

pour

See entry at **pore - pour**.

power

If someone has **power,** they are able to control other people and their activities.

...his yearning for power.
It gave the President too much power.

'strength'   You do not use **power** to refer to someone's physical energy, or their ability to move heavy objects. The word you use is **strength.**

They were recovering their strength before setting off again.
I admired his immense physical strength.

practically

See section on **extent** in entry at **Adverbials**.

practice - practise

In British English, **practice** is a noun and **practise** is a verb.

used as an
uncount noun

Practice involves doing something regularly in order to improve your ability at it.

Skating's just a matter of practice.
I help them with their music practice.

used as a
count noun

A **practice** is something that is done regularly, for example as a custom.

Benn began the practice of holding regular meetings.
...the ancient Japanese practice of binding the feet from birth.

used as a verb   If you **practise** something, you do it or take part in it regularly.

I played the piece I had been practising for months.
They have managed to practise their religion for years.

In American English, the spelling **practise** is not normally used. The verb is spelled **practice,** like the noun.

I practiced and learned the headstand.

precaution - prevention

'precaution'   A **precaution** is something you do to try to prevent something unpleasant or undesirable from happening.

They took the necessary fire precautions.
As a precaution, I had brought an extra sweater with me.

'prevention'   **Prevention** is success in stopping something from happening.

Crime prevention is the major concern of the police force.
...research into the cause and prevention of kidney disease.

precede

See entry at **proceed - precede**.

prefer

If you **prefer** one person or thing **to** another, you like the first one better.

I prefer Barber to his deputy.
I prefer it to more expensive machines.

Note that you do not use any preposition except 'to' in sentences like these.

preferable

If one thing is **preferable to** another, it is more desirable or suitable than the other thing.

Knowledge is always preferable to ignorance.
Gradual change is preferable to sudden, large-scale change.

Note that you do not use any preposition except 'to' after **preferable**. You also do not say that one thing is 'more preferable than' another.

prepare

If you **prepare** a meal, you produce it by mixing foods together. **Prepare** is one of several verbs which can be used to say that someone produces a meal. For more information, see entry at **cook**.

GRAMMAR
Prepositions

A **preposition** is a word like 'at', 'in', 'on', or 'with' which is normally followed by a noun group, forming a **prepositional phrase**. The noun group after a preposition is sometimes called the **prepositional object**.

Prepositions are often used in phrases which indicate place and time.

She waited at the bus stop for over twenty minutes.
Tell me if you're coming to my party on Saturday.
They arrived at Scunthorpe in the morning.

See entries at **Places** and **Time**.

Prepositions are also used after nouns, adjectives, and verbs to introduce phrases which give more information about a thing, quality, or action. See entries at **Nouns, Adjectives, Verbs,** and **Qualifiers**.

without a following noun group

There are some cases where a preposition is not followed by a noun group. The noun group it relates to comes earlier in the sentence. These cases are:

● questions and reported questions

What will you talk about?
She doesn't know what we were talking about.

See entries at **Questions** and **Reporting**.

● relative clauses

...the job which I'd been training for.

See entry at **Relative clauses.**

● passive structures

Amateur theatricals have already been referred to.

See entry at **The Passive.**

● after a complement and 'to'-infinitive

She's very difficult to get on with.
The whole thing was just too awful to think about.

See entry at '**To'-infinitive clauses.**

complex prepositional object

After a preposition, you can sometimes use another prepositional phrase or a 'wh'-clause.

I had taken his drinking bowl from beneath the kitchen table.
I threw down my book and walked across the room to where she was sitting.
...the question of who should be President of the Board of Trade.

prepositions and adverbs

Some words that are used as prepositions are also used with a similar meaning as adverbs (that is, without a noun group after them).

I looked underneath the bed, but the box had gone.
Always put a sheet of paper underneath.

The door was opposite the window.
The kitchen was opposite, across a little landing.

The following words can be used as prepositions or adverbs with a similar meaning:

aboard	alongside	by	on	since
about	before	down	on board	through
above	behind	in	opposite	throughout
across	below	in between	outside	under
after	beneath	inside	over	underneath
against	beside	near	past	up
along	beyond	off	round	within

present

used as an adjective

You use **present** in front of a noun to indicate that you are talking about something which exists now, rather than about something in the past or future.

Economic planning cannot succeed in present conditions.
The present system has many failings.

You also use **present** in front of a noun to indicate that you are talking about the person who has a job, role, or title now, rather than someone who had it in the past or will have it in the future.

The present chairperson is a woman.
The author has the full support of the present Lord Montgomery.

When **present** is used after 'be', it has a different meaning. If someone is **present at** an event, they are there.

He had been present at the dance.
I was once present at a meeting in the Ministry of Education.

Note that you do not use any preposition except 'at' in sentences like these.

If it is clear what event you are talking about, you can just say that someone is **present**.

The Lord Mayor and Lady Mayoress of Westminster were present.

You can also use **present** with this meaning immediately after a noun.

There was a photographer present.
I had more to lose than any other person present.

used as a count noun **Present** is also used as a count noun. A **present** is something that someone gives you, for example on your birthday. You say that it is **a present from** them.

On the mantelpiece was a blue and gold cup, a present from Gertrude.

Note that you do not use any preposition except 'from' in a sentence like this.

GRAMMAR **The Present**

For the formation of present tenses, see entry at **Tenses**.

talking about the present The **simple present** tense is usually used for talking about long-term situations that exist at the present time, regular or habitual actions currently taking place, and general truths.

My dad works in Saudi Arabia.
I get up early and eat my breakfast in bed.
Water boils at 100 degrees centigrade.

The **present continuous** tense is used to talk about something which is regarded as temporary or something which is happening at the present moment.

I'm working as a British Council officer.
Wait a moment. I'm listening to the news.

WARNING There are a number of verbs which are not used in the present continuous tense, even when talking about the present moment. See entry at **Continuous tenses**.

Note that present tenses are sometimes used to talk about future events. See entry at **The Future**.

For the use of **present perfect** tenses, see entry at **The Past**.

presently

used to mean 'soon' If something will happen **presently**, it will happen quite soon.

He will be here presently.
I shall have more to say presently.

If you are talking about the past, you use **presently** to say that something happened quite soon after something else.

Presently all was quiet again.
Presently my sister said 'I think she was lying.'

Both these uses of **presently** are slightly old-fashioned.

<table>
<tr><td>used to mean 'now'</td><td>Some people use **presently** after 'be' to mean 'now'.</td></tr>
</table>

...the oil and gas rigs that are _presently_ in operation.
America and Japan are _presently_ working on chips which will hold a million words.

This use of **presently** is fairly new in British English, and some speakers find it unacceptable. Instead of 'presently', you can say **at present**.

He is _at present_ serving a life sentence.
The comet is _at present_ between the constellations of Pegasus and Delphinius.

You can put **at present** at the beginning or end of a clause. You cannot do this with **presently** when it means 'now'.

At present there is a world energy shortage.
We're short of staff _at present_.

present participles

See entry at '**-ing**' forms.

press

The **press** are the newspapers in a particular place, or the journalists who write them. You can use either a singular or plural form of a verb with **press**.

The press _is_ to be allowed in.
...a number of cases where the press _have_ been very aggressive.

pretty

See entry at **beautiful**.

prevent

If someone or something **prevents** you **from doing** something, they do not allow you to do it.

My only idea was to _prevent_ him _from speaking_.
Cotton mittens will _prevent_ the baby _from scratching_ his own face.

You do not say that someone 'prevents you to do' something.

'protect'   You do not use **prevent** to say that something keeps you safe from something unpleasant or harmful. The word you use is **protect**.

Babies are _protected_ against diseases like measles by their mother's milk.
She had his umbrella to _protect_ her from the rain.

prevention

See entry at **precaution - prevention**.

previous

See entry at **last - lastly**.

price - cost

The **price** or **cost** of something is the amount of money you must pay to buy it.

...the _price_ of sugar.
...an increase in the _cost_ of fertilizer.

Note that you do not use any preposition except 'of' after **price** or **cost** in sentences like these.

You can also use **cost** to refer to the amount of money needed to do or make something.

The building was recently restored at a cost of £500,000.
They are now manufactured by the billion at a cost of a few pence each.

You do not use **price** in this way.

'costs'   You use the plural noun **costs** when you are referring to the total amount of money needed to run something such as a business.

She decided she needed to cut her costs by half.
Moulton's have had to raise their prices still higher to cover increased costs.

'cost' used   You use **cost** as a verb to talk about the amount of money that you must
as a verb   pay for something.

The dress costs $200.
These four books cost £2.95 each.

You can use **cost** with two objects to say how much money someone actually pays for something on a particular occasion. Note that the past tense and past participle of 'cost' is **cost**, not 'costed'.

A two-day stay there cost me $125.

Note that you do not use 'to' after **cost** in a sentence like this.

price - prize

'price'   The **price** /praɪs/ of something is the amount of money that you must pay to buy it.

The price is still only five dollars.

See entry at **price - cost**.

'prize'   A **prize** /praɪz/ is something given to someone for winning a competition or game, or for doing good work.

He won a prize in a crossword competition.
...the Nobel Prize for Peace.

principal - principle

'principal'   **Principal** is used as an adjective or a noun.

The **principal** thing or person in a group is the most important one.

His principal interest in life was to be the richest man in Britain.
...the principal character in James Bernard Fagan's play.

The **principal** of a school or college is the person in charge of it.

Complaints from the students began arriving at the principal's office.
...Mr Patrick Miller, principal of Esher College.

'principle'   **Principle** is only used as a noun. A **principle** is a general rule that someone tries to obey in the way they behave.

...a man of high principles.
France has been dedicated for nearly two hundred years to the principle of equality.

print - publish

'print'   To **print** a book or newspaper means to produce many copies of it using machinery.

I asked him for an estimate to print a weekly paper for me.

'publish'   To **publish** a book or newspaper means to produce and distribute it for sale to the public.

Dr Johnson's dictionary was published in 1755.

prison

used as a count noun   A **prison** is a building where criminals or other people are officially kept and prevented from leaving.

Somewhere outside the prison she heard prolonged machine-gun fire.

used as an uncount noun   If you want to say that someone is in a prison without mentioning which prison they are in, you say they are **in prison**.

He died in prison.

Similarly, you say that someone is sent **to prison** or that they are released **from prison**.

He was eventually sent to prison for a very long time.

You do not use 'the' in front of **prison** unless you are referring to a particular prison.

prize

See entry at **price - prize**.

probably

You use **probably** to indicate that a statement is very likely to be true.

position in clause   If you are using a verb group consisting of an auxiliary and a main verb, you put **probably** after the auxiliary. For example, you say 'He **will probably** come soon'. You do not say 'He probably will come soon'.

He's probably telling the truth.
Chaucer was probably born in this area.

If you are using more than one auxiliary, you put **probably** after the first auxiliary.

Next year I shall probably be looking for a job.
I'll probably be sent back to London.

When there is no auxiliary, you put **probably** in front of the verb unless the verb is 'be'.

He probably misses the children.
He probably kept your examination papers.

If the verb is 'be', you put **probably** after it.

You're probably right.
The owner is probably a salesman.

In a negative sentence, if you are using a contracted form such as 'won't' or 'can't', you put **probably** in front of the contracted form.

They probably won't help.

They _probably don't want_ us to have it.

You can also put **probably** at the beginning of a clause.

Probably it can't be seen.
_400 children go to registered child-minders, and _probably_ thousands more spend their day with illegal minders._

You do not put **probably** at the end of a clause.

For a graded list of words used to say how certain someone is about something, see section on **probability** in entry at **Adverbials**.

problem

The noun **problem** has two common meanings.

an unsatisfactory situation
A **problem** is an unsatisfactory situation that needs to be dealt with.

_...the _problem_ of refugees._

You can say that someone **has a problem** or **has problems**.

_I think we may _have a problem_ here._
_They _have financial problems._

You can also say that someone **has problems doing** something.

_They _have such problems paying back_ debts that private credit is drying up._
_Already Third World countries _have desperate problems feeding, educating, and clothing_ their people._

You do not say that someone 'has problems to do' something.

'reason'
You do not use **problem** with 'why' when you are explaining why a situation has occurred. You do not say, for example, 'The problem why he couldn't come is that he is ill'. You say 'The **reason** why he couldn't come is that he is ill'.

_The _reason_ why tents were useless was that the build-up of snow simply crushed them._

For more information, see entry at **reason**.

a puzzle
A **problem** is also a puzzle that requires logical thought or mathematics to solve it.

_The next _problem_ is purely algebraic._
_What is the quickest way of doing this _problem?_

proceed - precede

'proceed'
If you **proceed** /prəsiːd/ to do something, you do it after you have finished doing something else.

_He _proceeded_ to explain._
_She _proceeded_ to hand over the key to my room._

In stories and formal English, if someone **proceeds** in a particular direction, they go in that direction.

_He _proceeded_ downstairs._
_...as we were _proceeding_ along Chiswick High Street._

'precede'
To **precede** /prɪsiːd/ an event means to happen before it. **Precede** is a formal word.

_The children's dinner _was preceded_ by party games._

produce - product

'produce' used as a verb

Produce is usually used as a verb and pronounced /prədjuːs/.

To **produce** a result or effect means to cause it to happen.

His comments produced an angry response.
All our efforts have not produced an agreement.

To **produce** goods or food means to make or grow them in large quantities.

...factories producing domestic electrical goods.
Farmers must produce a good deal more than they need.

'produce' used as a noun

Food that is grown in large quantities is called **produce** (pronounced /prɒdjuːs/).

Sugar became the chief produce of the Caribbean.

'product'

Goods that are made and sold in large quantities are called **products.**

Manufacturers spend huge sums of money advertising their products.

profession

See entry at **work.**

professor

In a British university, a **professor** is the most senior teacher in a department.

...Professor Cole.
He was Professor of English at Strathclyde University.

In an American or Canadian university or college, a **professor** is a senior teacher. He or she is not necessarily the most senior teacher in a department.

'teacher'

You do not use 'professor' to refer to a person who teaches at a school or similar institution. The word you use is **teacher.**

I'm a qualified French teacher.

programme - program

A **programme** is a plan which has been developed for a particular purpose. This word is spelled **program** in American English.

The company has major programmes of research and development.
There has been a lot of criticism of the new nuclear power program.

A television or radio **programme** is a single broadcast, for example a play, discussion, or show. This word, too, is spelled **program** in American English.

...the last programme in our series on education.
I remembered the television program I had watched in the Miami apartment.

A computer **program** is a set of instructions that a computer uses to perform a particular operation. This word is spelled **program** in both British and American English.

I decided to write a program for a microcomputer.

progress

You say that there is **progress** when something improves gradually, or when someone gets nearer to achieving or completing something.

...technological progress.
They came in from time to time to check on my progress.

Progress is an uncount noun. You do not talk about 'progresses' or 'a progress'.

You can say that someone or something **makes progress.**

She is making good progress with her German.
The offensive had got off well and was making progress.

You do not say that someone or something 'does progress'.

prohibit

To **prohibit** something means to forbid it or make it illegal.

We prohibit air guns and other weapons that might wound someone.
She believes that nuclear weapons should be totally prohibited.

You can say that someone **is prohibited from doing** something.

A professor from the University of Montana was prohibited from speaking on campus.
The country has a law prohibiting employees from striking.

You do not say that someone 'is prohibited to do' something.

promise - promising

'promise'
If you **promise** to do something, you say that you will definitely do it.

I promised to take the children to the fair.
I promised your father that you should never know that he had been in prison.

'promising'
Promising can be used as an adjective, with a different meaning. If someone or something is **promising,** they seem likely to be very good or successful.

...a promising new actress.
The menu looked promising.

GRAMMAR # Pronouns

Pronouns are words such as 'it', 'this', and 'nobody' which are used in a sentence like noun groups containing a noun. Some pronouns are used in order to avoid repeating nouns. For example, you would not say 'My mother said my mother would phone me this evening'. You would say 'My mother said she would phone me this evening'.

WARNING
You use a pronoun instead of a noun group containing a noun, not in addition to a noun group. For example, you do not say 'My mother she wants to see you'. You say either 'My mother wants to see you' or 'She wants to see you'.

In this entry, information is given on **personal pronouns, possessive pronouns, reflexive pronouns,** and **indefinite pronouns.**

For information on **demonstrative pronouns**, see entry at **this - that**. For information on **reciprocal pronouns**, see entry at **each other - one another**. Some 'wh'-words are pronouns; see entry at **'Wh'-words**.

Words such as 'many' and 'some' which are used to refer to quantities of people or things can also be used as pronouns. See section on **pronoun use** in entry at **Quantity**.

'One' can be used to replace a noun group, but can also be used to replace a noun within a noun group. See entry at **one**.

personal pronouns

Personal pronouns are used to refer to something or someone that has already been mentioned, or to the speaker or hearer. There are two sets of personal pronouns: **subject pronouns** and **object pronouns**.

Subject pronouns are used as the subject of a verb. The subject pronouns are:

	singular	plural
1st person	I	we
2nd person	you	
3rd person	he she it	they

I do the washing; he does the cooking; we share the washing-up.
My father is fat — he weighs over fifteen stone.

Object pronouns are used as the direct or indirect object of a verb, or after a preposition. The object pronouns are:

	singular	plural
1st person	me	us
2nd person	you	
3rd person	him her it	them

The nurse washed me with cold water.
I'm going to read him some of my poems.

Note that you do not use an object pronoun as the indirect object of a verb when you are referring to the same person as the subject. Instead you use a **reflexive pronoun**.

He cooked himself an omelette.

Note that 'me', not 'I', is used after 'it's' in modern English.

'Who is it?'—'It's me.'

See entry at **me**.

'We' and 'us' can be used either to include the person you are talking to or not to include the person you are talking to. For example, you can say 'We must meet more often', meaning that you and the person you are talking to must meet each other more often. You can also say 'We don't meet very often now', meaning that you and someone else do not meet very often.

'You' and 'they' can be used to refer to people in general.

You have to drive on the other side of the road on the continent.
They say she's very clever.

For more information about this, see entry at **one**.

'They' and 'them' are sometimes used to refer back to indefinite pronouns referring to people. For more information, see entry at **he - they**.

'It' is used as an impersonal pronoun in general statements about the time, the date, the weather, or a situation. See entry at **it**.

possessive pronouns

Possessive pronouns show who the person or thing you are referring to belongs to or is connected with. The possessive pronouns are:

	singular	plural
1st person	mine	ours
2nd person	yours	
3rd person	his hers	theirs

Is that coffee yours or mine?
It was his fault, not theirs.
'What's your name?'—'Frank.'—'Mine's Laura.'

WARNING

There is no possessive pronoun 'its'.

Possessive pronouns are sometimes confused with **possessive determiners,** which are quite similar in form. See entry at **Possessive determiners.**

Possessive pronouns can be used after 'of'. See entry at **of**.

He was an old friend of mine.

reflexive pronouns

Reflexive pronouns are used as the object of a verb or preposition when the person or thing affected by an action is the same as the person or thing doing it. The reflexive pronouns are:

	singular	plural
1st person	myself	ourselves
2nd person	yourself	yourselves
3rd person	himself herself itself	themselves

She stretched herself out on the sofa.
The men formed themselves into a line.

For more information about this use of reflexive pronouns, see section on **reflexive verbs** in entry at **Verbs**.

Reflexive pronouns are also used after nouns or pronouns to emphasize them.

I myself have never read the book.
The town itself was so small that it didn't have a bank.

They are also used at the end of a clause to emphasize the subject.

I find it a bit odd myself.

Reflexive pronouns are also used at the end of a clause to say that someone did something without any help from anyone else.

Did you make those yourself?

You can also indicate that someone did something without any help, or that someone was alone, by using a reflexive pronoun after 'by' at the end of a clause.

Did you put those shelves up all by yourself?
He went off to sit by himself.

indefinite
pronouns
Indefinite pronouns are used to refer to people or things without indicating exactly who or what they are.

The indefinite pronouns are:

anybody	everybody	nobody	somebody
anyone	everyone	no-one	someone
anything	everything	nothing	something

Everyone knows that.
Jane said nothing for a moment.
Is anybody there?

You always use singular verbs with indefinite pronouns.

Is anyone here?
Everything was ready.

However, the plural pronouns 'they', 'them', or 'themselves' are often used to refer back to an indefinite pronoun referring to a person. See entry at **he - they**.

You can use adjectives immediately after indefinite pronouns.

Choose someone quiet.
There is nothing extraordinary about this.

propaganda

You refer to information given by political groups as **propaganda** when you think it is distorted or biased.

It is essential to sort the truth from the propaganda.
He attacked the use of propaganda to intimidate the population.

Propaganda is an uncount noun. You use a singular form of a verb after it.

It is amusing to recall some of the propaganda that was floating around at that time.

'advertising'
You do not use **propaganda** to refer to information given by companies in order to sell their products. The word you use is **advertising.**

The tobacco industry spends 100 million pounds a year on advertising.

proper

The adjective **proper** is used with several different meanings.

used to mean
'real'
You use it in front of a noun to indicate that someone or something really is the thing referred to by the noun.

Have you been to a proper doctor?
He's never had a proper job.

used to mean
'correct'
You also use **proper** in front of a noun to say that something is correct or suitable.

Everything was in its proper place.
What's the proper word for those things?

used to mean 'acceptable'	If a way of behaving is **proper**, it is correct or acceptable. This is an old-fashioned use.

It wasn't proper for a man to show his emotions.

used to mean 'main'	**Proper** is sometimes used after a noun to refer to the main or central part of a place.

By the time I got to the village proper everyone was out to meet me.

property

If something is someone's **property**, it belongs to them.

The field is the University's property.
Eventually the piano became my property.

You can also refer to all the things that a person owns as their **property**.

Her property passes to her next of kin.
Their property was confiscated and they were driven back to the ghettos.

When **property** is used in either of these ways, it is an uncount noun. You do not talk about a person's 'properties'.

propose

suggestions	If someone **proposes** a plan or idea, they suggest it so that other people can think about it and decide on it.

Someone may propose a different solution.
This would help them to become accustomed to the methods we proposed.

You can say that someone **proposes** that something **should be done** or **proposes** that something **be done**.

They proposed that political strikes should be made illegal.
The staff association proposed that a mediator be nominated.

Note that you do not use a 'to'-infinitive in sentences like these. You do not say, for example, 'The staff association proposed a mediator to be nominated'.

intentions	However, if you intend to do something yourself, you can say that you **propose to do** it.

I propose to focus attention on one type of resource.
I propose to stay in this neighbourhood.

You can also say that you **propose doing** something.

So what do you propose doing now?

Note that you do not say that you 'propose to not do' something. You say that you **do not propose to do** it.

I do not propose to get deeply involved in it.
I do not propose to discuss this matter.

prosecute

See entry at **persecute - prosecute**.

protest

Protest is used as a verb or a noun, but with different pronunciations.

used as a verb	**Protest** /prətest/ is used as a verb to say that someone shows publicly that they do not approve of something. You can say that someone **protests about** something or **protests against** something.

He was criticized for protesting about Gerald Brooke's imprisonment.
Labour MPs took to the streets to protest against government economic policy.

Some speakers of American English use **protest** as a transitive verb. They say that someone **protests** something.

He protested the action in a telephone call to the President.

Protest is not used like this in British English.

Protest can also be used as a reporting verb. If you **protest** that something is the case, you insist that it is the case, when someone has said or suggested the opposite.

They protested that they had never heard of him.
'You're wrong,' I protested.

used as a noun	When people show publicly that they do not approve of something, you can describe their behaviour as a **protest** /prəʊtest/.

They joined in the protests against the government's proposals.
...a letter of protest.

proud

The following words can all be used to describe someone who has a high opinion of themselves:

arrogant	proud	smug
conceited	self-respecting	supercilious
haughty	self-satisfied	vain

Proud and **self-respecting** are used in a complimentary way.

...with millions of decent, proud, hard-working people.
...so that they grow into responsible and self-respecting citizens.

However, **proud** is also sometimes used to show disapproval.

She was too proud to apologize.

Arrogant, conceited, haughty, self-satisfied, smug, and **supercilious** are all used to describe someone who thinks they are better than other people. These words show disapproval.

I hope I didn't sound like a conceited know-it-all.
...his smooth, smug brother-in-law.
They were standing by themselves looking supercilious and remote.

Arrogant is used to describe people who behave in an unpleasant way towards other people.

My husband was an arrogant, bullying little drunkard.

Haughty is used in writing, not in conversation.

Without knowing it, I was acquiring that haughty bearing which is characteristic of so many eccentrics.

Vain also shows disapproval. It is used to describe someone who thinks they are very good-looking, or very clever or talented.

He was a vain, loquacious, effeminate and silly man.

<table>
<tr><td align="right">other uses of
'proud'</td><td>You can also say that someone is **proud of** something they have or something they have done. This means that they think it is good and are glad about it.</td></tr>
</table>

other uses of
'proud'   You can also say that someone is **proud of** something they have or something they have done. This means that they think it is good and are glad about it.

He was proud of his son-in-law.
We were all tired but proud of our efforts.

If someone is **proud to do** something, they feel pleased about doing it.

She's proud to work with you.

prove

If you **prove** that something is true or correct, you provide evidence which shows that it is definitely true or correct.

He was able to prove that he was an American.
The autopsy proved that she had drowned.

'test'   When you use a practical method to try to find out how good or bad someone or something is, you do not say that you 'prove' the person or thing. You say that you **test** them.

I will test you on your knowledge of French.
A number of new techniques were tested.

provide

'provide with'   To **provide** something that someone needs or wants means to give it to them or make it available to them. You can say that you **provide** someone **with** what they want.

Mrs Castle had provided her with a list.
The government cannot provide all young people with a job.

Note that you must use 'with' in sentences like these. You do not say that you 'provide someone' what they want.

'provide for'   You can also say that you **provide** something **for** someone.

Most animals provide food for their young.
It's extremely hard to provide a real home for the children.

You do not use any preposition except 'for' in sentences like these.

If you regularly give someone the things they need, such as money, food, or clothing, you say that you **provide for** them.

Parents are expected to provide for their children.
I just want to be sure you're provided for.

You must use 'for' in sentences like these. You do not say that you 'provide' someone.

pub

In Britain, a **pub** or **public house** is a building where people meet their friends and have drinks, especially alcoholic drinks. **Pub** is the word people usually use. **Public house** is only used in formal speech and writing.

He was in the pub most evenings and always offered us drinks.

'bar'   In American English, a place where you can buy and drink alcoholic drinks is usually called a **bar**. See entry at **bar**.

public

You can refer to people in general as **the public**. After **the public** you can use either a singular or plural form of a verb.

I think that the public has learnt that we have to wait for news.
The public are now involved in disputes they have never been involved in before.

public house

See entry at **pub**.

public school

In England and Wales, a **public school** is a private school that provides secondary education which parents have to pay special fees for.

In Scotland and the United States, a **public school** is a school for younger children that is supported financially by the government.

publish

See entry at **print - publish**.

Punctuation

The first section of this entry deals with the punctuation of ordinary sentences. For information on how to punctuate direct speech and how to mention titles and other words, see the sections on **direct speech** and **titles and quoted phrases** later in this entry.

full stop You start a sentence with a capital letter. You put a **full stop** (.) at the end of a sentence, unless it is a question or an exclamation.

It's not your fault.
Cook the rice in salted water until just tender.

In American English, the punctuation mark (.) is called a **period**.

question mark If a sentence is a question, you put a **question mark** (?) at the end.

Why did you do that?
Does any of this matter?
He's certain be be elected, isn't he?

Note that you put a question mark at the end of a question, even if the words in the sentence are not in the normal question order.

You know he doesn't live here any longer?

People occasionally do not put a question mark at the end of a sentence in question form if, for example, it is really a request.

Would you please call my office and ask them to collect the car.

WARNING You put a full stop, not a question mark, after a reported question.

He asked me where I was going.
I wonder what's happened.

exclamation mark If a sentence is an exclamation, that is, something said with strong emotion, you put an **exclamation mark** (!) at the end. In informal writing, people also put an exclamation mark at the end of a sentence which they feel is exciting, surprising, or very interesting.

How awful!

What an aroma! It's tremendous!
Your family and children must always come first!
We actually heard her talking to them!

In American English, the punctuation mark (!) is called an **exclamation point**.

comma   You must put a **comma** (,)

● after or in front of a vocative

Jenny, I'm sorry.
Thank you, Adam.
Look, Jenny, can we just forget it?

● between items in a list, except ones separated by 'and' or 'or'

We ate fish, steaks and fruit.
...political, social and economic equality.
The men hunted and fished, kept cattle and sheep, forged weapons and occasionally fought amongst themselves.
...educational courses in accountancy, science, maths or engineering.

● between three or more descriptive adjectives in front of a noun, without 'and'

...in a cool, light, insolent voice.
Eventually the galleries tapered to a long, narrow, twisting corridor.

● after a name or noun group, before a description or further information

...Carlos Barral, the Spanish publisher and writer.
...a broad-backed man, baldish, in a fawn coat and brown trousers.

● between the name of a place and the county, state, or country it is in. Note that a comma is usually put after the county, state, or country as well, unless it is at the end of a sentence.

She was born in Richmond, Surrey, in 1913.
There he met a young woman from Cincinnati, Ohio.

● after or in front of an adjective which is separate from the main part of the sentence, or after a separate participle

She nodded, speechless.
I left them abruptly, unwilling to let them have anything to do with my project.
Shaking, I crept downstairs.

● before a relative clause which does not specify someone or something

She wasn't like David, who cried about everything.
The only decent room is the living room, which is rather small.
He told us he was sleeping in the wood, which seemed to me a good idea.

● before a question tag

That's what you want, isn't it?
You've noticed, haven't you?

optional comma   You can put a comma, for emphasis or precision,

● after the first of two qualitative adjectives used in front of a noun

We had long, involved discussions.
...a tall, slim girl with long, straight hair.
...a lovely, sunny region.

Note that 'young', 'old', and 'little' do not usually have commas in front of them.

...a huge, silent young man.
...a sentimental old lady.
...a charming little town.

● after or in front of a word or group of words which adds something to the main part of the sentence. Note that if you put a comma in front of the word or group, you should also put one after it, unless it comes at the end of the sentence.

In 1880, John Benn founded a furniture design trades journal called 'The Cabinetmaker'.
Obviously, it is not always possible.
There are indeed stylistic links between my work and William Turnbull's, for instance.
They were, in many ways, very similar in character and outlook.
The ink, surprisingly, washed out easily.

Note that long groups of words are usually separated with commas.

He is, with the possible exception of Robert de Niro, the greatest screen actor in the world.

A comma is put after or in front of an adverbial if its meaning is otherwise likely to be misunderstood.

'No,' she said, surprisingly.
Mothers, particularly, don't like it.

● in front of 'and', 'or', 'but', or 'yet', when giving a list or adding a clause

...a dress-designer, some musicians, and half a dozen artists.
The task of changing them all seems monumental, and is probably hopeless.
...if you are prey to fear, stress, or anxiety.
This would allow the two countries to end hostilities, but neither of them seems in a mood to give way.
...remarks which shocked audiences, yet also enhanced her reputation as a woman of courage.

● after a subordinate clause

When the fish is cooked, strain off the liquid and add this to the flour and margarine.
Even if the boxer survives surgery, he may be disabled permanently.
Although the law of the land made education compulsory for all European children, François's father decided not to send him to school.

It is usually best to put a comma after a subordinate clause, although many people do not put commas after short subordinate clauses.

Note that you do not normally put a comma in front of a subordinate clause, unless it contains something such as an afterthought, contrast, or exception.

Don't be afraid of asking for simple practical help when it is needed.
Switch that thing off if it annoys you.

The poor man was no threat to her any longer, if he ever really had been.
He was discharged from hospital, although he was homeless and had nowhere to go.

If you do put a comma in front of a clause, you should also put a comma after it if it does not come at the end of the sentence.

This is obviously one further incentive, if an incentive is needed, for anybody who needs to take slimming a little more seriously.

● in front of a participle which is separate from the main part of the sentence

Maurice followed, laughing.
Marcus stood up, muttering incoherently.

● after a noun being used in front of someone's name

...that marvellous singer, Jessye Norman.
She had married the gifted composer and writer, Paul Bowles.

no comma You do not put a comma

● in front of 'and', 'or', 'but', and 'yet' when these words are being used to link just two nouns, adjectives, or verbs

Eventually they had a lunch of fruit and cheese.
...when they are tired or unhappy.

● between a qualitative adjective and a classifying adjective, or between two classifying adjectives

...a large Victorian building.
...a medieval French poet.

● after the subject of a clause, even if it is long

Few in the audience noticed the late arrival of a man in a wheelchair.
Even this part of the Government's plan for a better National Health Service has its risks and potential complications.
Indeed, the degree of backing for the principle of the community charge surprised ministers.

● in front of a 'that'-clause or a reported question

His brother complained that the office was not business-like.
Georgina said she was going to bed.
She asked why he was so silent all the time.

● in front of a relative clause which specifies someone or something

I seem to be the only one who can get close enough to him.
Happiness is all that matters.
The country can now begin to fashion a foreign policy which serves national interests.

semi-colon The **semi-colon** (;) is used in formal writing to separate clauses that are closely related and could be written as separate sentences, or that are linked by 'and', 'or, 'but', or 'yet'.

I can see no remedy for this; one can't order him to do it.
He knew everything about me; I knew nothing about his recent life.
He cannot easily reverse direction and bring interest rates down; yet a failure to do so would almost certainly push the economy into recession.

It is also sometimes used between items in a list.

...when working with the things he seemed to like: their horse, Bonnie; the cart he brought the empty bottles home in; bits of old harness; tools and things.

colon The **colon** (:) is used

● in front of a list or explanation

To be authentic these garments must be of natural materials: cotton, silk, wool and leather.
Nevertheless, the main problem remained: what should be done with the two murderers?

- between two main clauses that are connected, mainly in more formal writing

It made me feel claustrophobic: what, I wonder, would happen to someone who was really unable to tolerate being locked into such a tiny space?
Be patient: this particular cruise has not yet been advertised.

- after introductory headings

Cooking time: About 5 minutes.

- in front of the second part of a book title

...a volume entitled Farming and Wildlife: A Study in Compromise.

A colon is also sometimes used in front of quotes. See below at **direct speech.**

dash   The **dash** (–) is used

- in front of a list or explanation

The poor need simple things – building materials, clothing, household goods, and agricultural implements.
The Labour Government had just nationalised the basic industries – coal, rail and road transport.
...another of Man's most basic motives – commercialism.

- after and in front of a group of words or a clause which adds something to the main sentence but could be removed

Many species will take a wide variety of food – insects, eggs, nestlings and fruit – but others will only take the leaves of particular trees.
Number seventeen was – of all things – underground.
It is our view that very few important materials in the world – perhaps none – will become unduly scarce.

- in front of an adverbial, clause, or other group of words, for emphasis

I think Rothko was right – in theory and practice.
Let Tess help her – if she wants help.
I'm beginning to regret I ever made the offer – but I didn't seem to have much option at the time.
My family didn't even know about it – I didn't want anyone to know.
Mrs O'Shea, that's wonderful – really it is.

WARNING   Dashes are not used in very formal writing.

brackets   **Brackets** ( ), also called **parentheses,** are used after and in front of a word, group of words, or clause which adds something to the main sentence, or explains it, but could be removed.

This is a process which Hayek (a writer who came to rather different conclusions) also observed.
Normally he had the last word (at least in the early days).
A goat should give from three to six pints (1.7 to 3.4 litres) of milk a day.
This is more economical than providing heat and power separately (see section 3.2 below).

Note that full stops, question marks, exclamation marks, and commas go after the second bracket, unless they apply only to the words in the brackets.

I ordered two coffees and an ice cream (for her).
We had sandwiches (pastrami on rye and so on), salami, coleslaw, fried chicken, and potato salad.

In the face of unbelievable odds (the least being a full-time job!) Gladys took the six-hour exam – and passed.

Punctuation

square brackets **Square brackets** [ ] are used, usually in books and articles, when supplying words that make a quotation clearer or comment on it, although they were not originally said or written.

Mr Runcie concluded: 'The novel is at its strongest when describing the dignity of Cambridge [a slave] and the education of Emily [the daughter of an absentee landlord].'

apostrophe You use an **apostrophe**

- in front of an 's' added to a noun or pronoun, or after a plural noun ending in 's', to show a relationship such as possession. See entries at **'s** and **Possession and other relationships.**

...my friend's house.
...someone's house.
...friends' houses.

- in front of contracted forms of 'be', 'have', and modals, and between 'n' and 't' in contracted forms with 'not'. See entry at **Contractions.**

I'm terribly sorry.
I can't see a thing.

- in front of 's' for the plurals of letters and, sometimes, numbers

Rod asked me what grades I got. I said airily, 'All A's, of course.'
There is a time in people's lives, usually in their 40's and 50's, when they find themselves benefiting from financial windfalls.

- in front of two figures referring to a year or decade

...souvenirs from the '68 campaign.
...the grim subject that obsessed him throughout the '60s and the early '70s.

An apostrophe sometimes indicates that letters are missing from a word. Often the word is never written in full in modern English. For example, 'o'clock' has been reduced from 'of the clock', but it is never written in full.

She left here at eight o'clock this morning.
Martin had only recently recovered from a bout of 'flu.

Often people stop using an apostrophe at the beginning of a shortened word. For example, people nowadays usually write 'phone', not ' 'phone'.

WARNING You do not use an apostrophe in front of the 's' of a plural word like 'apples' or 'cars'. Also, you do not use an apostrophe in front of the 's' of the possessive pronouns 'yours', 'hers', 'ours', and 'theirs'.

hyphen When you cannot fit the whole of a word at the end of a line, you can put part of the word and a **hyphen** (-) on one line and the rest of the word on the next line.

If the word is clearly made up of two or more smaller words or elements, you put the hyphen after the first of these parts. For example, you would write 'wheel-' on one line and 'barrow' on the next, 'inter-' on one line and 'national' on the next, 'listen-' on one line and 'ing' on the next.

Otherwise, you put the hyphen at the end of a syllable. For example, you could write 'compli-' on one line and 'mentary' on the next, and 'infor-' on one line and 'mation' on the next.

WARNING It is best not to break a word if the word is a short one, or if it would mean writing just one or two letters at the end or beginning of a line. For example, it would be better to write 'unnatural' on the next line rather than writing 'un-' on one line and 'natural' on the next.

If the word already has a hyphen, because it is a compound, put the second part of the word on the next line. For example, with 'short-tempered' and 'self-control', you would put 'tempered' and 'control' on the next line.

For information on the use of the hyphen in compound words, see entry at **Spelling.**

slash or stroke A **slash, stroke,** or **oblique** (/) is used

● between two words or numbers that are alternatives

Write here, and/or on a card near your telephone, the number of the nearest hospital with a casualty ward.
...the London Hotels Information Service (telephone 629 5414/6).

● between two words describing something that is in fact two things, as in 'a washer/drier' or 'a clock/radio'

Each apartment includes a sizeable lounge/diner with colour TV.

A slash or stroke is also sometimes used to mark where a line of poetry ends when you are quoting part of a poem without putting each line on a separate line.

'Sweet and low, sweet and low,/Wind of the western sea.'

direct speech You put **inverted commas** (' ' or " "), also called **quotation marks** or **quotes,** at the beginning and end of direct speech. You start the direct speech with a capital letter.

'Thank you,' I said.
"What happened?"

Note that British writers use both single and double inverted commas (' ' and " "), but American writers tend to use double inverted commas (" ").

If you put something like **he said** after the direct speech, you put a comma in front of the second inverted comma, not a full stop. However, if the direct speech is a question or an exclamation, you put a question mark or an exclamation mark instead.

'Let's go,' I whispered.
'We have to go home,' she told him.
'What are you doing?' Sarah asked.
'Of course it's awful!' shouted Clarissa.

If you then give another piece of direct speech said by the same person, you start it with a capital letter and put inverted commas round it.

'Yes, yes,' he replied. 'He'll be all right.'

If you put something like **he said** within a sentence in direct speech, you put a comma after the first piece of direct speech and after 'he said', and you start the continuation of the direct speech with inverted commas. Note that you do not give the first word of the continuation a capital letter, unless it would have one anyway.

'Frankly darling,' he murmured, 'it's none of your business.'
'Margaret,' I said to her, 'I'm so glad you came.'

If you put something like **he said** in front of the direct speech, you put a comma in front of the direct speech and a full stop, question mark, or exclamation mark at the end of it.

She added, 'But it's totally up to you.'
He smiled and asked, 'Are you her grandson?'

People sometimes put a colon in front of the direct speech, especially to indicate that what follows is important.

I said: 'Perhaps your father was right.'

A dash is used to indicate that someone who is speaking hesitates or is interrupted.

'Why don't I — ' He paused a moment, thinking.
'It's just that — circumstances are not quite right for you to come up just now.'
'Oliver, will you stop babbling and — ' 'Jennifer,' Mr Cavilleri interrupted, 'the man is a guest!'

A line of dots (usually three) is used to show that someone hesitates or pauses.

'I think they may come soon. I...' He hesitated, reluctant to add to her trouble.
'Mother was going to join us but she left it too late...'

Note that sometimes what a person thinks is directly quoted in front of a comma or after it, rather than in inverted commas.

My goodness, I thought, Tony was right.
I thought, what an extraordinary childhood.

When you are writing a conversation, for example in a story, you start a new line for each new piece of direct speech.

WARNING   When the direct speech takes up more than one line, you do not put an opening inverted comma at the beginning of each line, only at the beginning of the direct speech. If you are giving more than one paragraph of direct speech, you put inverted commas at the beginning of each paragraph but not at the end of any paragraph except the last one.

titles and quoted phrases   When you are mentioning the title of a book, play, film, etc, you can put inverted commas round it, although people quite often do not, especially in informal writing. In books and articles, titles are often written without inverted commas, or in **italics** (sloping letters). The titles of newspapers, especially, are not usually written in inverted commas.

...Robin Cook's novel 'Coma'.
...Deighton's most recent novel, Spy Hook.

When you are mentioning a word, or quoting a few words that someone said, you put the word or words in inverted commas.

The Great Britain team manager later described the incident as 'unfortunate'.
Bragg says that all 'post-16 students' — she dislikes the term 'sixth-formers' — will follow a course of study designed to equip them with 'core skills'.
He has always claimed that the programme 'sets the agenda for the day'.

Note that you do not usually put the punctuation of your sentence within the inverted commas, in British English.

Mr Wilson described the price as 'fair'.
What do you mean by 'boyfriend'?

However, when people are quoting a whole sentence, they often put a full stop in front of the closing inverted comma, rather than after it.

You have a saying, 'Four more months and then the harvest.'

If they want to put a comma after the quote, the comma comes after the closing inverted comma.

The old saying, 'A teacher can learn from a student', happens to be literally true.

In American English, a full-stop or comma is put in front of the closing inverted comma, not after it.

The judge said the man had "richly earned a sentence of incarceration."
There was a time when people were divided roughly into children, "young persons," and adults.

If you are quoting someone who is also quoting, you need to use a second set of inverted commas. If you begin with a single inverted comma, you use double inverted commas for the second quote. If you begin with double inverted commas, you use single inverted commas for the second quote.

'What do they mean,' she demanded, 'by a "population problem"?'
"One of the reasons we wanted to make the programme," Raspiengeas explains, "is that the word 'hostage' had been used so often that it had lost any sense or meaning."

Note that people sometimes put inverted commas round a word or expression which they think is inappropriate.

The chest of one fourteen-year-old was a mass of scar tissue where a 'friend' had jokingly poured petrol over him and set fire to it.

A line of dots (usually three) is used to show that you are giving an incomplete quotation, for example from a review.

'A creation of singular beauty...magnificent.' Washington Post.

italics   You will see **italics** (sloping letters) used in printed books and articles, for example to mention titles or foreign words, and emphasize or highlight other words. Italics are not used in this way in handwriting. When mentioning titles, use inverted commas, or have no special punctuation at all. When mentioning foreign words, use inverted commas. In informal writing, you can underline words to emphasize them.

other uses of   For the use of punctuation marks in writing abbreviations, dates, numbers,
punctuation   measurements, and times, see entries at **Abbreviations, Days and dates, Numbers and fractions, Measurements,** and **Time.**

pupil

See entry at **student.**

purchase

used as a verb   In old-fashioned or formal English, to **purchase** something means to buy it.

He sold the house he had purchased only two years before.

used as a noun   The **purchase** of something is the act of buying it. This use of **purchase** is common in formal and legal English.

He advised them on the purchase of their new car.
We need to know the exact day of purchase.

Your **purchases** are things you have bought in a shop or shops.

Among his purchases were several tins of beans.

This is an old-fashioned use of **purchase.** In modern English, you talk about someone's **shopping,** not their 'purchases'.

She put her shopping away in the kitchen.

purposefully - purposely

'purposefully'　If someone does something **purposefully**, they do it in a way that suggests that they have a definite purpose and a strong desire to achieve this purpose.

A large young woman stepped purposefully towards John Franklyn.
He walked purposefully out through the secretary's office.

'purposely'　If someone does something **purposely**, they do it deliberately, rather than by accident or chance.

She purposely sat in the outside seat.
Her voice was purposely low.

purse

A **purse** is a very small bag that people, especially women, keep their money in.

In American English, a **purse** is also a woman's handbag.

put

If you **put** something in a particular place or position, you move it into that place or position. The past tense and past participle of 'put' is **put,** not 'putted'.

She put her hand on his arm
I put her suitcase on the table.

Put has several other meanings. For some of its meanings, you can use **place** instead of 'put'. For more information about this, see entry at **place - put.**

put up with

See entry at **bear.**

Q

Qualifiers

A **qualifier** is a word or group of words which comes after a noun and gives more information about the person or thing referred to. Qualifiers can be:

- **prepositional phrases**

...a girl with red hair.
...the man in the dark glasses.

- **place adverbs** or **time adverbs**

...down in the dungeon beneath.
...a reflection of life today in England.

See entries at **Places** and **Time.**

- **adjectives** followed by phrases or clauses

...machinery capable of clearing rubble off the main roads.

...the sort of weapons <u>likely to be deployed against it.</u>

● **adjectives** such as 'concerned' and 'available'

The idea needs to come from the individuals <u>concerned.</u>
...the person <u>responsible</u> for his death.

See entry at **Adjectives.**

● **relative clauses**

The man <u>who had done it</u> was arrested.
...the town <u>that John came from.</u>

● **non-finite clauses**

...two of the problems <u>mentioned above.</u>
...a simple device <u>to test lung function.</u>

See entries at **'-ing' forms, Past participles,** and **'To'-infinitive clauses.**

quality

When you are talking about things that have been made or produced, you can use **quality** to say how good or bad they are.

The <u>quality</u> of the photograph was poor.
...the high <u>quality</u> of their transmissions.

You can say that something is **of good quality** or **of poor quality.**

The dresses – all <u>of good quality</u> – had had their labels removed.
The treatment and care provided were also <u>of poor quality.</u>
Television ensures that films <u>of high quality</u> are exhibited to large audiences.

You can also use expressions such as **good quality** and **high quality** in front of nouns.

I've got some <u>good quality</u> paper.
English has one of the <u>highest quality</u> intakes.

You can also use **quality** on its own in front of a noun. When you do this, you are indicating that something is of a high standard.

...<u>quality</u> Australian fiction.
The employers don't want <u>quality</u> work any more.

GRAMMAR **Quantity**

| numbers | Quantities and amounts of things are often referred to using **numbers.** See entries at **Numbers and fractions** and **Measurements.** |
| general determiners | You can use **general determiners** such as 'some', 'any', 'all', 'every', and 'much' to talk about quantities and amounts of things. |

There is <u>some</u> chocolate cake over there.
He spoke <u>many</u> different languages.
<u>Most</u> farmers are still using the old methods.

with singular nouns: The following general determiners can only be used in front of singular count nouns:

a	another	either	neither
an	each	every	

Could I have another cup of coffee?
I agree with every word Peter says.

with plural and uncount nouns The following general determiners are used with plural forms of nouns and with uncount nouns:

all	more
enough	most

He does more hours than I do.
It had enough room to store all the information.

with plural count nouns The following general determiners are only used with plural forms of nouns:

a few	fewer	many	several
few	fewest	other	

The town has few monuments.
He wrote many novels.

with uncount nouns 'Much', 'little', and 'a little' are only used with uncount nouns.

Do you watch much television?
We've made little progress.

WARNING There are restrictions on using 'much' in positive statements. See entry at **much**.

Some people think that 'less' and 'least' should only be used with uncount nouns, not with plural forms of nouns. See entry at **less**.

with all types of noun 'Any', 'no', and 'some' are used with all types of noun.

Cars can be rented at almost any US airport.
He had no money.
They've had some experience of fighting.
This has caused some problems for foresters.

Note that 'any' is not generally used in positive statements. See entry at **any**.

words used in front of determiners A few words used to indicate amounts or quantities can come in front of specific determiners such as 'the', 'these', and 'my'.

all	double	twice
both	half	

All the boys started to giggle.
I invited both the boys.
She paid double the sum they asked for.

'Half' can also come in front of 'a' or 'an'.

I read for half an hour.

See entries at **all**, **both**, and **half - half of**.

quantifiers Quantities and amounts are also referred to using a word or phrase such as 'several', 'most', or 'a number' linked with 'of' to the following noun group. These words and phrases followed by 'of' are called **quantifiers**.

I am sure both of you agree with me.
I make a lot of mistakes.
In Tunis there are a number of art galleries.

When you use a quantifier as the subject of a verb, you use a singular verb form if the noun group after 'of' is singular or uncountable, and a plural verb form if the noun group after 'of' is plural.

Some of the information <u>has</u> already been analysed.
Some of my best friends <u>are</u> policemen.

with specific or general noun groups

Quantifiers are often used to refer to part of a particular amount, group, or thing. The noun group after 'of' begins with a specific determiner such as 'the', 'these', or 'my', or consists of a pronoun such as 'us', 'them', or 'these'.

Nearly <u>all of the increase</u> has been caused by inflation.
<u>Very few of my classes</u> were stimulating.
<u>Several of them</u> died.

Sometimes quantifiers are used to refer to part of something of a particular kind. The noun group after 'of' is a singular count noun preceded by a general determiner such as 'a', 'an', or 'another'.

It had taken him <u>the whole of an evening</u> to get her to admit that she still had a grievance.

Often quantifiers are used simply to indicate how many or how much of a type of thing you are talking about. In this case, the noun group after 'of' is a general plural or uncountable noun group, without a determiner.

I would like to ask you <u>a couple of questions</u>.
There's <u>a great deal of money</u> involved.

with specific uncount nouns

The following quantifiers are used with specific uncount noun groups, but not general ones:

all of	little of	none of	the remainder of
any of	more of	part of	the rest of
enough of	most of	some of	the whole of
less of	much of	a little of	

<u>Most of my hair</u> had to be cut off.
Ken and Tony did <u>much of the work</u>.

with specific plural noun groups

The following quantifiers are used with specific plural noun groups, but not general ones:

all of	enough of	none of	a good many of
another of	few of	one of	a great many of
any of	fewer of	several of	the remainder of
both of	many of	some of	the rest of
certain of	more of	various of	
each of	most of	a few of	
either of	neither of	a little of	

Start by looking through their papers for <u>either of the two documents</u>.
<u>Few of these organizations</u> survive for long.

with all singular noun groups

The following quantifiers are used with specific and general singular noun groups:

all of	most of	an abundance of	a lot of
any of	much of	an amount of	a quantity of
enough of	none of	a bit of	a trace of
less of	part of	a good deal of	the majority of
little of	plenty of	a great deal of	the remainder of
lots of	some of	a little bit of	the rest of
more of	traces of	a little of	the whole of

Part of the farm lay close to the river bank.
Much of the day was taken up with classes.

Meetings are quarterly and take up most of a day.
Would you know what to do if someone accidentally swallowed some of a chemical you work with?

with all uncount noun groups The following quantifiers are used with specific and general uncount noun groups:

heaps of	quantities of	a bit of	the majority of
loads of	tons of	a little bit of	a quantity of
lots of	traces of	a good deal of	a trace of
masses of	an abundance of	a great deal of	
plenty of	an amount of	a lot of	

These creatures spend a great deal of their time on the ground.
A lot of the energy that is wasted in negotiations could be directed into industry.

There had been plenty of action that day.
There was a good deal of smoke.

with all plural noun groups The following quantifiers are used with specific and general plural noun groups:

heaps of	numbers of	an abundance of	a minority of
loads of	plenty of	a couple of	the majority of
lots of	quantities of	a lot of	a number of
masses of	tons of	a majority of	a quantity of

I picked up a couple of the pamphlets.
A lot of them were middle-aged ladies.

They had loads of things to say to each other.
Very large quantities of aid were needed.

Note that 'numbers of' and 'quantities of' are very often preceded by adjectives such as 'large' and 'small'.

The report contained large numbers of inaccuracies.
Chemical batteries are used to store relatively small quantities of electricity.

WARNING 'Heaps of', 'loads of', 'lots of', 'masses of', and 'tons of' are used only in conversation. Note that when these quantifiers are used with an uncount noun or a singular noun group as the subject of a verb, the verb is singular, even though the quantifier sounds plural.

Masses of evidence has been accumulated.
Lots of it isn't relevant, of course.

pronoun use Most of the words and expressions listed so far in this entry can be used as pronouns when it is clear who or what you are referring to.

Many are themselves shareholders in companies.
A few crossed over the bridge.
I have four bins. I keep one in the kitchen and the rest in the dustbin area.

However, 'a', 'an', 'every', 'no', and 'other' are not used as pronouns.

fractions Fractions such as 'a fifth' and 'two-thirds' can be used with 'of' in the same way as quantifiers such as 'all of' and 'some of'. See entry at **Numbers and fractions.**

quantifiers used with abstract nouns	The following quantifiers are used only or mainly when referring to qualities or emotions:

> an element of   a measure of   a touch of
> a hint of   a modicum of

There was an element of danger in using the two runways together.
Women have gained a measure of independence.
I must admit to a tiny touch of envy when I heard about his success.

'A trace of' is also often used when referring to an emotion.

She spoke without a trace of embarrassment about the problems that she had had.

partitives   You can refer to a particular quantity of something using a **partitive** such as 'piece' or 'group' linked by 'of' to a noun. Partitives are all count nouns. Often a partitive indicates the shape or nature of the amount or group.

Some partitives are used with 'of' and an uncount noun.

Who owns this bit of land?
...portions of mashed potato.

Some are used with 'of' and a plural noun.

...a huge heap of stones.
It was evaluated by an independent team of inspectors.

For more information about partitives used with uncount nouns, see entry at **Pieces and amounts.** For more information about partitives used with plural nouns, see entry at **Groups of things, animals, and people.**

When you use a singular partitive as the subject, you use a singular verb form if the noun after 'of' is an uncount noun.

A piece of paper is lifeless.

If the noun after 'of' is a plural count noun, you can use a plural verb form or a singular verb form. A plural verb form is more commonly used.

The second group of animals were brought up in a stimulating environment.
Each small group of workers is responsible for their own production targets.

When you use a plural partitive, you use a plural verb form.

Two pieces of metal were being rubbed together.

measurement nouns   Nouns referring to units of measurement are often used as partitives.

He owns only five hundred square metres of land.
I drink a pint of milk a day.

See section on **measurement nouns before 'of'** in entry at **Measurements.**

containers   You can use the names of containers as partitives when you want to refer to the contents of a container, or to a container and its contents.

They drank another bottle of champagne.
I went to buy a bag of chips.

'-ful'   You can add '-ful' to partitives referring to containers.

He brought me a bagful of sweets.
Pour a bucketful of cold water on the ash.

When people want to make a noun ending in '-ful' plural, they usually add an '-s' to the end of the word, as in 'bucketfuls'. However, some people put the '-s' in front of '-ful', as in 'bucketsful'.

She ladled three spoonfuls of sugar into my tea.
…two teaspoonsful of milk.

You can also add '-ful' to some parts of the body to form partitives. The commonest partitives of this kind are 'armful', 'fistful', 'handful', and 'mouthful'.

Eleanor was holding an armful of roses.
He took another mouthful of whisky.

mass nouns   Instead of using a partitive and 'of', you can sometimes use a noun that is usually uncountable as a count noun. For example, 'two teas' means the same as 'two cups of tea', and 'two sugars' means 'two spoonfuls of sugar'.

We drank a couple of beers.
I asked for two coffees with milk.

See section on **mass nouns** in entry at **Nouns**.

quarrel

A **quarrel** is an angry argument or series of arguments between two or more people.

I don't think the office should enter into a family quarrel.
There wasn't any evidence of quarrels between them.

'fight'   You do not use **quarrel** to refer to an incident in which people try to hurt each other using their fists or weapons. The word you use is **fight**.

There would be fights sometimes between the workers.

question

'out of the question'   If you say that something is **out of the question**, you mean that it cannot be done, and is therefore not worth considering.

She knew that a holiday this year was out of the question.
It has been so cold that gardening has been out of the question.

'beyond question'   You do not use **out of the question** to say that there is no doubt about something. The expression you use is **beyond question**.

She knew beyond question that I was a person who could be trusted.
The author concentrates on the aspect which has, beyond question, the greatest human interest.

question mark

See entry at **Punctuation**.

GRAMMAR # Questions

There are two main types of question: **'yes/no'-questions** and **'wh'-questions'**.

'yes/no'-questions   Questions which can be answered by 'yes' or 'no' are called **'yes/no'-questions**.

'Are you ready?'—'Yes.'
'Have you read this magazine?'—'No.'

'Yes/no'-questions are formed by changing the order of the subject and the verb group.

If the verb group consists of more than one word, you put the first word at the beginning of the sentence, in front of the subject. You put the rest of the verb group after the subject.

Will you have finished by lunchtime?
Has he been working?

If you are using a simple tense, you use an appropriate form of the auxiliary 'do' in front of the subject. You put the base form of the main verb after the subject.

Do the British take sport seriously?
Does David do this sort of thing often?
Did you meet George in France?

'be'   However, if the main verb is 'be', you put a form of 'be' at the beginning of the clause, followed by the subject. You do not use 'do'.

Are you okay?
Was it lonely without us?

'have'   You can use a structure such as 'Have you got...?' or a structure such as 'Do you have...?' See entry at **have got**. People no longer say 'Have you...?' when using 'have' as the main verb.

WARNING   If you want to ask a 'yes/no'-question, you do not usually use the normal word order of a statement. However, you can use the normal word order of a statement if you want to express surprise, or to check that something is true.

You've flown this machine before?
You've got two thousand already?

negative 'yes/   You use a negative 'yes/no'-question when you think the answer will be, or
no'-questions   should be, 'Yes'. For example, you say 'Didn't we see Daphne last weekend?' if you think you saw Daphne last weekend. You say 'Haven't you got a pen?' if you think the person you are speaking to should have a pen.

'Can't the trade unionists do something about this?'—'Yes, but they can't solve the problem by themselves.'
'Wasn't he French?'—'Yes.'
'Didn't you say you'd done it?'—'No.'

'wh'-questions   **'Wh'-questions** are used to ask about the identity of the people or things involved in an action, or about the circumstances of an action. 'Wh'-questions begin with a **'wh'-word.** The 'wh'-words are:

● the adverbs 'how', 'when', 'where', and 'why'

● the pronouns 'who', 'whom', 'what', 'which', and 'whose'

● the determiners 'what', 'which', and 'whose'

Note that 'whom' is only used as the object of a verb or preposition, not as a subject. See entry at **who - whom.**

'wh'-word as   When a 'wh'-word is the subject of a question, the 'wh'-word comes first,
subject   followed by the verb group. The word order of the clause is the same as that of an ordinary statement.

What happened?
Who could have done it?

The form of a question is similar when the 'wh'-word is part of the subject.

Which men had been ill?

'wh'-word as object or adverb	When a 'wh'-word is the object of a verb or preposition, or when it is an adverb, the 'wh'-word comes first. The formation of the rest of the clause is the same as for 'yes/no'-questions; that is, the subject is put after the first word in the verb group, and the auxiliary 'do' is used for simple tenses.

Which do you like best?
When would you be coming down?

The form of a question is similar when the 'wh'-word is part of the object.

Which graph are you going to use?

If there is a preposition, it usually comes at the end of the clause.

What are they looking for?
Which country do you come from?

However, if a phrase such as 'at what time' or 'in what way' is being used, the preposition is put at the beginning.

In what way are they different?

If 'whom' is used, the preposition is always put first. 'Whom' is only used in formal speech and writing.

With whom were you talking?

questions in reply	When you are asking a question in reply to what someone has said, you can often just use a 'wh'-word, not a whole clause, because it is clear what you mean.

'There's someone coming.'—'Who?'
'Maria! We won't discuss that here.'—'Why not?'

indirect ways of asking questions	When you ask someone for information, it is more polite to use the expressions 'Could you tell me...?' or 'Do you know...?'

Could you tell me how far it is to the bank?
Do you know where Jane is?

Note that the second part of the question has the form of a reported question. See entry at **Reporting.**

People sometimes use expressions like 'May I ask...?' and 'Might I ask...?' to ask a question indirectly. However, it is best not to use this way of asking a question, as it can sound hostile or aggressive.

May I ask what your name is?
Might I inquire if you are the owner?

GRAMMAR **Question tags**

A **question tag** is a short phrase that you add to the end of a statement to turn it into a 'yes/no'-question. You usually do this when you expect the other person to agree with the statement. For example, if you say 'It's cold, isn't it?', you expect the other person to say 'Yes'.

You form a question tag by using the same auxiliary verb or form of 'be' as in the statement, followed by a personal pronoun. The pronoun refers to the subject of the statement.

You've never been to Benidorm, have you?
David's school is quite nice, isn't it?

If the statement does not contain an auxiliary or 'be', the verb 'do' is used in the question tag.

You like it here, don't you?
He played for Ireland, didn't he?

Note that you usually add a negative tag to a positive statement, and a positive tag to a negative statement. However, you add a positive tag to a positive statement when checking that you have guessed something correctly, or to show interest, surprise, or anger.

You've been to North America before, have you?
You fell on your back, did you?
Oh, he wants us to make films as well, does he?

If you add a tag to a statement that contains a broad negative such as 'hardly', 'rarely', or 'seldom', the tag is normally positive, as it is with other negatives.

She's hardly the right person for the job, is she?
You seldom see that sort of thing these days, do you?

If you are making a statement about yourself and you want to check if the person you are talking to has the same opinion or feeling, you can put a tag with 'you' after your statement.

I think this is the best thing, don't you?
I love tea, don't you?

For examples of the use of question tags, see entries at **Agreeing and disagreeing; Invitations; Requests, orders, and instructions;** and **Suggestions.**

quick

See entry at **fast.**

quiet

Quiet is an adjective. Someone or something that is **quiet** makes only a small amount of noise.

Bal said in a quiet voice, 'I have resigned.'
The music had gone very quiet.

If a place is **quiet,** there is very little noise there.

It was very quiet there; you could just hear the wind moving in the trees.

'quite'   Do not confuse **quiet** /kwaɪət/ with **quite** /kwaɪt/. You use **quite** to indicate that something is the case to a fairly great extent.

quite

You use **quite** in front of an adjective or adverb to indicate that something is the case to a fairly great extent but not to a very great extent.

He was quite young.
Ned was standing quite close to the cook.
The end of the story can be told quite quickly.

You can also use **quite** in front of 'a', an adjective, and a noun. For example, instead of saying 'It was quite cold', you can say 'It was **quite a cold day**'.

This might be quite a good solution.
It seemed to be quite a big fish.

Note that in sentences like these you put **quite** in front of 'a', not after it. You do not say, for example, 'It was a quite cold day'.

WARNING

You do not use **quite** in front of comparative adjectives or adverbs. You do not say, for example, 'The train is quite quicker than the bus'. Instead you use **a bit, a little,** or **slightly.**

I ought to do something a bit more ambitious.
He arrived at their bungalow a little earlier than he expected.
The risk of epidemics may be slightly higher in crowded urban areas.

Quite is one of several words and expressions which can be used to indicate degree or extent. For graded lists, see sections on **degree** and **extent** in entry at **Adverbials.**

used for emphasis

Quite can be used with a different meaning. You can use it in front of an adjective, adverb, or verb to emphasize that something is completely the case or very much the case.

You're quite right.
I saw its driver quite clearly.
I quite understand.

For a list of adverbs used to emphasize a verb, see section on **emphasis** in entry at **Adverbials.**

quotation marks

See section on **direct speech** in entry at **Punctuation.**

R

raise

See entry at **rise - raise.**

rapid

See entry at **fast.**

rarely

See section on **frequency** in entry at **Adverbials.**

rather

used as adverb of degree

Rather means 'to a small extent'. However, it is often used without any real meaning, but simply to soften the effect of the word or expression that follows it. For example, if someone asks you to do something, you might say 'I'm rather busy'. You mean that you are busy, but **rather** makes your reply seem more polite.

I'm rather puzzled by this question.

He did it rather badly.
He looked rather pathetic standing in the rain outside.

Rather usually goes in front of an adjective or an adverb, but it can also be used in front of a singular noun group.

I'm in rather a hurry.
He was rather a silent young man.

Note that you can say either 'He was **rather a** silent young man' or 'He was **a rather** silent young man'. **Rather a** is more common.

You can use **rather** in front of 'like' when you are using 'like' as a preposition.

This animal looks and behaves rather like a squirrel.
The food, rather like that provided by motorway cafes, has become a bit of a joke.

You can also use **rather** in front of verbs such as 'think' and 'hope'.

I rather think it was three hundred and fifty pounds.
I rather hoped that one day you would get married.

Note that several words and expressions can be used to say that something is the case to a smaller or greater extent. For graded lists, see section on **degree** in entry at **Adverbials** and section on **submodifiers** in entry at **Adverbs.**

used as an
emphasizer

Rather has a different meaning when you use it in front of words such as 'good' and 'well'. If you say that something is **rather** good, you are emphasizing that it is good.

There's a teashop near here that does rather good toasted muffins.
The company thought I did rather well.

'would rather'

If you say that you **would rather do** something, you mean that you would prefer to do it.

I'll order tea. Or perhaps you would rather have coffee.
'What was all that about?'—'I'm sorry, I'd rather not say.'

Note that in sentences like these you use an infinitive without 'to' after **would rather.**

You can also use **would rather** followed by a clause to say that you would prefer something to happen or be done. In the clause you use the simple past tense.

Would you rather she came to see me?
'May I go on?'—'I'd rather you didn't.'

'rather than'

Rather than is used like a conjunction to link words or expressions of the same type. You use **rather than** when you have said what is the case and you want to compare it with what is not the case.

I have used familiar English names rather than scientific Latin ones.
It made him frightened rather than angry.
He had been compelled to spend most of the time talking to Mrs Harlowe rather than to her daughter.
Gambling was a way of redistributing wealth rather than acquiring it.

correcting
a mistake

You can also use **rather** when you are correcting a mistake you have made, or when you think of a more appropriate word than the one you have just used.

Suddenly there stood before him, or rather above him, a gigantic woman.
One picture speaks volumes. Or rather lies volumes.

rational

See entry at **reasonable - rational**.

reach

See entry at **arrive - reach**.

Reactions

There are several ways of expressing your reaction to something you have been told or something you see.

exclamations You often use an **exclamation** to express your reaction to something. An exclamation may consist of a word, a group of words, or a clause.

Wonderful!
Oh dear!
That's awful!

In speech, you say an exclamation emphatically. When you write down an exclamation, you usually put an exclamation mark (!) at the end of it.

'how' 'How' and 'what' are sometimes used to begin exclamations. 'How' is normally used with an adjective and nothing else after it.

'They've got free hotels run by the state specially for tourists.'—'How marvellous!'
'There was no attempt made to set things out – they were just piled in the tomb higgledy-piggledy.'—'How strange!'

The use of 'how' to begin a clause in an exclamation, as in 'How clever he is!', is now regarded as old-fashioned. See section on **commenting on a quality** in entry at **how**.

'what' 'What' is used in front of a noun group.

'I'd have loved to have gone.'—'What a shame!'
'...and then she died in poverty.'—'Oh dear, what a tragic story.'
What a marvellous idea!
What rubbish!
What fun!

WARNING You must use 'what' and 'a' (or 'an') if you are using a singular count noun. For example, you say 'What an extraordinary experience!' You do not say 'What extraordinary experience!'

You can put a 'to'-infinitive such as 'to say' or 'to do' after the noun group, if it is appropriate.

'If music dies, we'll die.'—'What an awful thing to say!'
What a terrible thing to do!

exclamations in question form You can express a reaction by using an exclamation in the form of a question beginning with 'Isn't that'.

'University teachers seem to me far bolder here than they are over there.'—'Isn't that interesting.'
'It's one they don't make any more.'—'Oh, isn't that sad!'
'It was a big week for me. I got a letter from Paris.'—'Oh, isn't that nice!'

A few common exclamations have the same form as positive questions.

Alan! Am I glad to see you!

Well, would you believe it. They got their motor fixed.
'How much?'—'A hundred million.'—'Are you crazy?'

expressing
surprise or
interest

You can express surprise or interest by saying 'Really?' or 'What?', or by using a short fixed expression such as 'Good heavens' or 'Good grief'.

'It only takes 35 minutes from my house.'—'Really? To Oxford Street?'
'He's gone to borrow John Powell's gun.'—'What?'
Good heavens, is that the time?
'What's happened?'—'Good grief! You mean you don't know anything about it?'

'Good Lord', 'Goodness', 'My goodness', and 'Good gracious' are rather old-fashioned expressions which are still used by some people in some parts of Britain.

'You might see a boy aged four working seven or eight hours a day.'—
'Good Lord.'
My goodness, this is a difficult one.

'Good God' and 'My God' are strong expressions. You should not use them if you are with religious people who might be offended by them.

'I haven't set eyes on him for seven years.'—'Good God.'
My God, what are you doing here?

You can also express surprise or interest using a short question with the form of a question tag.

'He gets free meals.'—'Does he?'
'They're starting up a new arts centre there.'—'Are they?'
'I had a short story in Varsity last week.'—'Did you? Good for you.'

To express very great surprise, you can use a short statement that contradicts what you have just heard, although you do in fact believe it.

'I just left him there and went home.'—'You didn't!'

You can also express surprise, and perhaps annoyance, by repeating part of what has just been said, or checking that you have understood it.

'Could you please come to Ira's right now and help me out?'—'Now?
Tonight?'
'We haven't found your man.'—'You haven't?'

You can also use 'That's' or 'How' with an adjective such as 'strange' or 'interesting' to express surprise or interest.

'Is it a special sort of brain?'—'Probably.'—'Well, that's interesting.'
'He said he hated the place.'—'How strange! I wonder why.'
'They sound somehow familiar.'—'They do? How interesting.'

You can say 'Strange', 'Odd', 'Funny', 'Extraordinary', or 'Interesting' to express your reaction to something.

'You falsify your results?'—'If necessary, yes.'—'Extraordinary.'
'They both say they saw it.'—'Mmm. Interesting.'

You can also say 'What a surprise!'

Tim! Why, what a surprise!
'Flick? How are you?'—'Oh, Alan! What a surprise to hear you! Where are you?'

In informal situations, you can use expressions such as 'No!', 'You're joking!', or 'I don't believe it!' to show that you find what someone has said very surprising.

'Gertrude's got a new boyfriend!'—'No! Who is he?'—'Tim Reede!'—'You mean the little painter chap? You're joking!'

You've never sold the house? I don't believe it!

'You're kidding' is a more informal way of saying 'You're joking'.

'They'll be allowed to mess about with it.'—'You're kidding!'

Some people use expressions beginning with 'Fancy' and an '-ing' form to express surprise.

Fancy seeing you here!
Fancy choosing that!

In formal situations, you can say things like 'I find that very surprising'.

'...so these houses are designed from practice rather than theory.'—'I find that extraordinary.'

expressing pleasure

You can show that you are pleased about a situation or about what someone has said by saying something like 'That's great' or 'That's wonderful', or just using the adjective.

'I've arranged the flights.'—'Oh, that's great.'
'Today we had the final signing. We can drink champagne morning, noon, and night for the rest of our lives.'—'That's wonderful.'
'We can give you an idea of what the prices are.'—'Great.'

You can also say things like 'How marvellous' or 'How wonderful'.

'I'll be able to stay for a week.'—'How marvellous!'
'I've just spent six months in Italy.'—'How lovely!'
'She has a large flat in Rome, and a flat in London as well.'—'How nice.'
Oh, Robert, how wonderful to see you.

However, you do not say 'How great'.

You can also say things like 'Isn't that nice' or 'Isn't that wonderful'.

'The children always do the washing up. They love to.'—'Well, isn't that nice. You don't see it much any more.'
'And he can see me?'—'Perfectly.'—'Isn't that marvellous.'

In a formal situation, you can say 'I'm glad to hear it', 'I'm pleased to hear it', or 'I'm delighted to hear it' when someone tells you something.

'He saw me home, so I was well looked after.'—'I'm glad to hear it.'

Note that these expressions are often used to indicate in a humorous way that you would have been annoyed if something had not been the case.

'I have a great deal of respect for you.'—'I'm delighted to hear it!'

You can also show that you are pleased about something by saying something like 'That **is** good news' or 'That's wonderful news'.

'My contract's been extended for a year.'—'That is good news.'

expressing relief

You can express relief when you are told something by saying 'Oh good' or 'That's all right then'.

'I think he will understand.'—'Oh good.'
'They're all right?'—'They're perfect.'—'Good, that's all right then.'

You can also say 'That's a relief' or 'What a relief!'

'He didn't seem to notice much.'—'Well, that's a relief, I must say.'
'It's nothing like as bad as that.'—'What a relief!'

When you are very relieved, you can say 'Thank God', 'Thank goodness', 'Thank God for that', or 'Thank heavens for that'.

'He's arrived safely in Moscow.'—'Thank God.'

Thank God you're safe!
'You've found all my treasures?'—*'They were in the trunk.'*—*'Thank goodness.'*
'I won't bore you with my views on smoking.'—*'Thank heavens for that!'*

In formal situations, you should say something like 'I'm relieved to hear it'.

'Is that the truth?'—*'Yes.'*—*'I am relieved to hear it!'*
'I certainly did not support Captain Shays.'—*'I am relieved to hear you say that.'*

expressing annoyance
You can express annoyance by saying 'Oh no' or 'Bother'. 'Bother' is slightly old-fashioned.

'We're going to have one of those awful scrambles to get to the airport.'— *'Oh no!'*
Bother. I forgot to eat my sandwiches before I came here.

People often use swear words to express annoyance. 'Blast', 'damn', and 'hell' are mild swear words used in this way. However, you should not use even these words when you are with people you do not know well.

Damn. It's nearly ten. I have to get down to the hospital.
'It's broken.'—*'Oh, hell!'*

You can also say 'What a nuisance' or 'That's a nuisance'.

He'd just gone. What a nuisance!

Note that people often say things like 'Great' or 'Oh, that's marvellous' to express annoyance in a sarcastic way. Usually the way they say these things makes it clear that they are annoyed, not pleased.

'I phoned up about it and they said it's a mistake.'—*'Marvellous.'*

expressing disappointment or distress
You can show that you are disappointed or upset at something by saying 'Oh dear'.

'We haven't got any results for you yet.'—*'Oh dear.'*
Oh dear, I wonder what's happened.

You can also say 'That's a pity', 'That's a shame', 'What a pity,' or 'What a shame'.

'They're going to demolish it.'—*'That's a shame. It's a nice place.'*
'Perhaps we might meet tomorrow?'—*'I have to leave Copenhagen tomorrow, I'm afraid. What a pity!'*
'Why, Ginny! I haven't seen you in years.'—*'I haven't been home much lately.'*—*'What a shame.'*

People often just say 'Pity'.

'Do you play the violin by any chance?'—*'No.'*—*'Pity. We could have tried some duets.'*

You can also say 'That's too bad'.

'We don't play that kind of music any more.'—*'That's too bad. David said you were terrific.'*

You can express great disappointment or distress by saying 'Oh no!'

'Johnnie Frampton has had a nasty accident.'—*'Oh no! What happened?'*

expressing sympathy
When someone has just told you about something bad that has happened to them, you can express sympathy in several ways.

One way is to say 'Oh dear'.

'First of all, it was pouring with rain.'—*'Oh dear.'*

You can also say things like 'How awful' or 'How annoying'.

'He's ill.'—'How awful. So you aren't coming home?'
'We couldn't even see the stage.'—'Oh, how annoying.'
'We never did find the rest of it.'—'Oh, how dreadful!'

You can also say 'What a pity' or 'What a shame'.

'It took four hours, there and back.'—'Oh, what a shame.'

You can express sympathy more formally by saying 'I'm sorry to hear that'.

'I was ill on Monday.'—'Oh, I'm sorry to hear that.'
'I haven't heard from him for over a week.'—'I'm sorry to hear that. Maybe he's away from his base and out of touch.'

If what has happened is very serious, for example if a relative of the other person has died, you can express strong sympathy by saying 'I'm so sorry' or, more informally, 'That's terrible'.

'You remember Gracie, my sister? She died last autumn.'—'Oh, I'm so sorry.'
'My wife's just been sacked.'—'That's terrible.'

If someone has failed to achieve something, you can say 'Bad luck' or 'Hard luck', which implies that the failure was not their fault. If they can make a second attempt, you can say 'Better luck next time'.

'Eleanor's been appointed to the job in Cambridge.'—'Oh, bad luck.'
Well, there we are, we lost this time, but better luck next time.

---

read

reading to yourself

When you **read** /riːd/ a piece of writing, you look at it and understand what it says.

Why don't you read your letter?

The past tense and past participle of 'read' is **read** /red/, not 'readed'.

I read through the whole paper.
Have you read that article I gave you?

reading to someone else

If you **read** something such as a book to someone, you say the words aloud so that the other person can hear them. When you use **read** like this, it has two objects. If the indirect object is a pronoun, it usually goes in front of the direct object.

I'm going to read him some of my poems.
I read her the two pages dealing with Edward Aveling's desertion of Eleanor Marx.

If the indirect object is not a pronoun, it usually goes after the direct object. When this happens, you put 'to' in front of the indirect object.

One winter I read a play to the seniors.

You also put the indirect object after the direct object when the direct object is a pronoun.

You will have to read it to him.

See section on **ditransitive verbs** in entry at **Verbs**.

Note that you can also omit the direct object.

I'll go up and read to Sam for five minutes.

reading a subject

In British English, if you **read** a subject at university, you study it.

He went up to Magdalen College to read history.

Read is not used like this in American English.

readable

If you say that a book or article is **readable,** you mean that it is interesting and not boring or difficult to understand.

He has written a most readable and entertaining autobiography.

'legible' If you can recognize the letters and words that a piece of writing consists of, you do not say that the writing is 'readable'. You say that it is **legible.**

The inscription is still perfectly legible.

ready

used after a verb If you are **ready,** you have prepared yourself for something.

Are you ready now? I'll take you back to your flat.
We were getting ready for bed.

If something is **ready,** it has been prepared and you can use it.

Lunch is ready.
Go and get the boat ready.

Note that you cannot use **ready** with either of these meanings in front of a noun.

used in front of You use **ready** in front of a noun to indicate that something is available to
a noun be used very quickly and easily.

The tourists provided a ready market for Kashmir's specialities.
I have no ready explanation for this fact.

Ready money is in the form of notes and coins rather than cheques, and so can be used immediately.

...people who performed services for ready money.
...£3000 in ready cash.

real

Real is used to say that something actually exists.

...real or imagined feelings of inferiority.
Robert squealed in mock terror, then in real pain.

You also use **real** to say that a substance or object is genuine and not artificial.

The steering wheel is padded with real leather.
Rudolph couldn't tell whether the jewellery was real or not.

Some American speakers use **real** in front of an adjective or adverb for emphasis.

That suit looks real nice.
I'm being looked after real well.

This use is generally regarded as incorrect, both in British and American English. Instead of 'real', you should use **really.**

It was really good.
He did it really carefully.

See entry at **really.**

realize

See entry at **understand.**

really

You use **really** in conversation to emphasize something that you are saying.

Really usually goes in front of a verb, or in front of an adjective or adverb.

I really enjoyed that.
I really ought to go back inside.
It was really good.
He did it really carefully.

You can put **really** in front of or after an auxiliary verb. For example, you can say 'He **really is** coming' or 'He **is really** coming'. There is no difference in meaning.

That's what we really are trying to do.
Let's find out what really can be done out here.

It would really be too much trouble.
Some people thought that Dante had really been there.

When you use **really** in front of an adjective or adverb, it has a similar meaning to 'very'. Note that you can say either 'Gilbert **is really** clever' or 'Gilbert **really is** clever'. The meaning is almost the same. In both cases you are saying that Gilbert is very clever, but when you say 'Gilbert **really is** clever', you are expressing surprise that Gilbert is clever, or trying to convince someone else that he is.

This is really serious.
He really is famous.

WARNING You do not use **really** in formal writing.

reason

The **reason for** something is the fact or situation which explains why it happens, exists, or is done.

I asked the reason for the decision.
The reason for this relationship is clear.

Note that you do not use any preposition except 'for' after **reason** in sentences like these.

You can talk about a person's **reason for doing** something.

One of the reasons for coming to England is to make money.
Frank had another reason for urging caution on them both.

You can also talk about the **reason why** something happens or is done.

There are several reasons why we can't do that.

However, if you are actually stating the reason, you do not use 'why'. Instead you use a 'that'-clause.

The reason that Daniel had come under suspicion was that he'd gone to work for Bob.
The reason I'm calling you is that I know Larry talked with you earlier.

Note that the second clause in these sentences is also a 'that'-clause. Instead of a 'that'-clause, some speakers use a clause beginning with **because**.

The reason they are not like other boys is because they have been brought up differently.

This use of **because** is fairly common in spoken English. However, some people think that it is incorrect, and you should avoid it.

reasonable - rational

'reasonable'   When someone is **reasonable,** they behave in a fair and sensible way.

Our mother was always very reasonable.
I can't do that, Morris. Be reasonable.

If something such as a proposal or judgement is **reasonable,** it is acceptable because it is fair or sensible.

Rules and procedures need to be accepted as reasonable by those who operate them.
There was no reasonable explanation for her decision.

'rational'   You say that someone is **rational** when they are able to think clearly and make decisions and judgements based on reason rather than emotion.

Let's talk about this like two rational people.

You can also describe people's behaviour as **rational.**

This was a totally rational response to a set of complex problems.

receipt

A **receipt** /rɪsiːt/ is a piece of paper that confirms that money or goods have been received.

We've got receipts for each thing we've bought.

'recipe'   You do not use **receipt** to refer to a set of instructions telling you how to cook something. The word you use is **recipe** /resəpi/.

…an old Polish recipe for beetroot soup.

receive

When you **receive** something, someone gives it to you, or it arrives after it has been sent to you. **Get** is used in a similar way. You use **receive** in formal writing and **get** in conversation.

For example, in a business letter you might write 'I **received** a letter from Mr Jones', but in conversation you would say 'I **got** a letter from Mr Jones'.

He received a letter from his brother.
I got a letter from John.

The police received a call from the house at about 4.50 a.m.
I got a call from the President.

You can say that someone **receives** or **gets** a wage, salary, or pension.

His mother received a five shillings old age pension.
He was getting a very low salary.

You can also say that someone **receives** or **gets** help or advice.

She is said to have received help from Lord Cowper.
Get advice from your local health department.

recent

See entry at **new.**

recently - newly - lately

Recently and **newly** are both used to indicate that something happened only a short time ago. There is no difference in meaning, but **newly** can only be used with an '-ed' form, usually in front of a noun.

…the newly elected Labour Government.

On the newly painted white wall was a photograph of the President.

Recently can be used in several positions in a sentence.

...this recently established genre of films.
Recently a performance of Macbeth was given there.
There was recently a formal inquiry.
I have recently re-read all his books.

You can use **recently** or **lately** to say that something started happening a short time ago and is continuing to happen. You cannot use **newly** with this meaning.

They have recently been taking German lessons.
Lately he's been going around with Miranda Watkins.

recognize

If you **recognize** someone or something, you know who or what they are because you have seen them before, or because they have been described to you.

She didn't recognize me at first.
They are trained to recognize the symptoms of radiation-sickness.

If you **recognize** something such as a problem, you accept that it exists.

Governments are beginning to recognize the problem.
We recognize this as a genuine need.

'realize'   If you become aware of a fact, you do not say that you 'recognize' it. You say that you **realize** it.

I realized that this man wasn't going to hurt me.
She realized that she could not reach the shore.

recommend

If you **recommend** someone or something, you praise them and advise other people to use them or buy them.

I asked my friends to recommend a doctor who is good with children.
Margaret Drabble has just published a fine novel which I'd strongly recommend.

You can say that you **recommend** someone or something **for** a particular job or purpose.

Nell was recommended for a job as a nursery governess.
I recommend hill running for strengthening thighs.

If you **recommend** a particular action, you say that it is the best thing to do in the circumstances.

They recommended a merger of the two biggest supermarket groups.
The doctor may recommend limiting the amount of fat in your diet.

You can recommend **that someone does** something or recommend **that someone should do** something.

It is not recommended that students pay in advance.
The Committee must decide whether or not to recommend that the President should resign.

You can also recommend **someone to do** something.

Although they have eight children, they do not recommend other couples to have families of this size.

You do not say that you 'recommend someone' a particular action. You do not say, for example, 'I recommend you a visit to Stockholm'. You say 'I **recommend a visit** to Stockholm', 'I **recommend visiting** Stockholm', or 'I **recommend that you visit** Stockholm'.

recover

If you **recover,** you become well again after an illness or injury.

It was weeks before he fully recovered.

'get better' **Recover** is a fairly formal word. In conversation, you usually say that someone **gets better.**

He soon got better after a few days in bed.

You can say that someone **recovers from** an illness.

How long do people take to recover from sickness of this kind?

You do not say that someone 'gets better from' an illness.

referee

See entry at **umpire - referee.**

refuse

Refuse is used as a verb or a noun. When it is a verb, it is pronounced /rɪfjuːz/. When it is a noun, it is pronounced /refjuːs/.

used as a verb If you **refuse** to do something, you deliberately do not do it, or you say firmly that you will not do it.

He refused to accept their advice.
Three employees were dismissed for refusing to join a union.

'reject' If you do not agree with an idea or belief, you do not say that you 'refuse' it. You say that you **reject** it.

Some people reject the idea of a mixed economy.
It was hard for me to reject my family's religious beliefs.

used as a noun **Refuse** is used as a noun to refer to things that you throw away.

...a dump for refuse.
This department is also responsible for refuse collection.

Several other words are used to refer to things that are thrown away. For more information, see entry at **rubbish.**

regard

If you **regard** someone or something **as** a particular thing, you believe that they are that thing.

I regard it as one of my masterpieces.
She now regarded herself as a woman.

You can also say that someone or something **is regarded as being** a particular thing or **is regarded as having** a particular quality.

A man of sixty is regarded as being in the prime of life.
The idol was regarded as having fertility properties.

You do not say that someone or something 'is regarded to be' a particular thing or 'is regarded to have' a particular quality.

regret - be sorry

Regret and **be sorry** are both used to say that someone feels sadness or disappointment about something that has happened, or about something they have done. **Regret** is more formal than **be sorry.**

You can say that you **regret** something or **are sorry about** it.

I immediately regretted my decision.
I'm more sorry about losing Pat.

You can also say that you **regret** or **are sorry** that something has happened.

Pisarev regretted that no real changes had occurred.
He was sorry he had agreed to stay.

You can also say that you **regret doing** something.

None of the women I spoke to regretted making this change.

You do not say that you 'are sorry doing' something.

apologizing When you are apologizing to someone for something that has happened, you can say that you **are sorry about** it.

I'm sorry about last night.

You do not say that you are 'sorry for' something.

In conversation, you do not apologize by saying that you 'regret' something. **Regret** is only used in formal letters and announcements.

London Transport regrets any inconvenience caused by these delays.

For information on other ways of apologizing, see entry at **Apologizing.**

giving bad news When you are giving someone some bad news, you can begin by saying 'I**'m sorry to** tell you…'. In a formal letter, you say 'I **regret to** tell you…'.

I'm sorry to tell you this, but the Board have changed their opinion of you.
I regret to inform you that your application has not been successful.

reject

See entry at **refuse.**

related

If something is **related to** something else, the two things are connected in some way.

The musk ox is related to the antelope.
Physics is closely related to mathematics.

Note that you do not use any preposition except 'to' in sentences like these.

relation - relative - relationship

These words are used to refer to people or to connections between people.

'relation' and 'relative' Your **relations** or **relatives** are the members of your family.

I said that I was a relation of her first husband.
His wife had to visit some of her relatives.

The **relations** between people or groups are the contacts between them and the way they behave towards each other.

This fear was causing East-West relations to deteriorate.
The unions should have close relations with management.

'relationship' You can talk in a similar way about the **relationship** between two people or groups.

The old relationship between the friends was quickly re-established.
Pakistan's relationship with India has changed dramatically.

A **relationship** is also a close friendship between two people, especially one involving sexual or romantic feelings.

Do you feel you are trapped by your relationship and would like to break away?
When the relationship ended two months ago, he said he wanted to die.

GRAMMAR # Relative clauses

A **relative clause** is a subordinate clause which gives more information about someone or something mentioned in the main clause. The relative clause comes immediately after the noun which refers to the person or thing being talked about.

The man who came into the room was small and slender.
Opposite is St. Paul's Church, where you can hear some lovely music.

relative pronouns Many relative clauses begin with a **relative pronoun**. The relative pronouns are:

that	who
which	whom

The relative pronoun usually acts as the subject or object of a verb in the relative clause.

...a girl who wanted to go to college.
There was so much that she wanted to ask.

There are two kinds of relative clause: **defining relative clauses** and **non-defining relative clauses**.

defining relative clauses **Defining relative clauses** give information that helps to identify the person or thing being spoken about. For example, in the sentence 'The woman who owned the shop was away', the defining relative clause 'who owned the shop' makes it clear which particular woman is being referred to.

The man who you met yesterday was my brother.
The car which crashed into me belonged to Paul.

Defining relative clauses are sometimes called **identifying relative clauses**.

referring to people When you are referring to a person or group of people in a defining relative clause, you use 'who' or 'that' as the subject of the defining clause.

The man who employed me would transport anything anywhere.
...the people who live in the cottage.
He was the man that bought my house.

You use 'who', 'that', or 'whom' as the object of a defining clause.

...someone who I haven't seen for a long time.
...a woman that I dislike.

...distant relatives whom he had never seen.

Note that 'whom' is a formal word. See entry at **who - whom.**

referring to things When you are referring to a thing or group of things, you use 'which' or 'that' as the subject or object of a defining clause.

...pasta which came from Milan.
There are a lot of things that are wrong.

...shells which my sister has collected.
The thing that I really liked about it was its size.

not using a relative pronoun You do not have to use a relative pronoun as the object of the verb in a defining relative clause. For example, instead of saying 'a woman that I dislike', you can say 'a woman I dislike'.

The woman you met yesterday lives next door.
The car I wanted to buy was not for sale.

WARNING The relative pronoun in a relative clause acts as the subject or object of the clause. This means that you should not add another pronoun as the subject or object. For example, you say 'There are a lot of people that want to be rich'. You do not say 'There are a lot of people that they want to be rich'.

Similarly, you say 'This is the book which I bought yesterday'. You do not say 'This is the book which I bought it yesterday'. Even if you do not use a relative pronoun, as in 'This is the book I bought yesterday', you do not put in another pronoun.

non-defining relative clauses **Non-defining relative clauses** are used to give further information about someone or something, not to identify them. For example, in 'I'm writing to my mother, who's in hospital', the relative clause 'who's in hospital' gives more information about 'my mother' and is not used to indicate which mother you mean.

He was waving to the girl, who was running along the platform.
He walked down to Broadway, the main street of the town, which ran parallel to the river.

Note that you put a comma in front of a non-defining relative clause.

referring to people When a non-defining clause relates to a person or group of people, you use 'who' as the subject of the clause, or 'who' or 'whom' as the object of the clause.

Heath Robinson, who died in 1944, was a graphic artist and cartoonist.
I was in the same group as Janice, who I like a lot.
She was engaged to a sailor, whom she had met at Dartmouth.

referring to things When a non-defining clause relates to a thing or a group of things, you use 'which' as the subject or object.

I am teaching at the Selly Oak Centre, which is just over the road.
He was a man of considerable inherited wealth, which he ultimately spent on his experiments.

WARNING You cannot use 'that' to begin a non-defining relative clause. For example, you cannot say 'She sold her car, that she had bought the year before'. You must say 'She sold her car, which she had bought the year before'.

Non-defining clauses cannot be used without a relative pronoun. For example, you cannot say 'She sold her car, she had bought the year before'.

| referring to a situation | Non-defining relative clauses beginning with 'which' can be used to say something about the whole situation described in the main clause. |

I never met Brando again, which was a pity.
Small computers need only small amounts of power, which means that they will run on small batteries.

| prepositions with relative pronouns | In both types of relative clause, a relative pronoun can be the object of a preposition. In conversation, the preposition usually comes at the end of the clause, with no noun group after it. |

I wanted to do the job which I'd been trained for.
...the world that you are interacting with.

Often, in a defining relative clause, no relative pronoun is used.

...the pages she was looking at.
I'd be wary of anything Matt Davis is involved with.

In formal English, the preposition comes in front of the relative pronoun 'whom' or 'which'.

I have at last met John Parr's tenant, about whom I have heard so much.
He was asking questions to which there were no answers.

| **WARNING** | If the verb in a relative clause is a **phrasal verb** ending with a preposition, you cannot move the preposition to the beginning of the clause. For example, you cannot say 'all the things with which I have had to put up'. You have to say 'all the things I've had to put up with'. |

...the delegates she had been looking after.
Everyone I came across seemed to know about it.

Note that a non-defining relative clause can begin with a preposition, 'which', and a noun. The only common expressions of this kind are 'in which case', 'by which time', and 'at which point'.

It may be that your circumstances are different or unusual, in which case we can ensure that you have taken the right action.
Leave the whole thing to cool down for two hours, by which time the spices should have thoroughly flavoured the vinegar.

| 'of whom' and 'of which' | Words such as 'some', 'many', and 'most' can be put in front of 'of whom' or 'of which' at the beginning of a non-defining relative clause. You do this to give information about part of the group just mentioned. |

At the school we were greeted by the teachers, most of whom were middle-aged.
It is a language shared by several quite diverse cultures, each of which uses it differently.

Numbers can be put in front of 'of whom' or 'of which' or, more formally, after these phrases.

They act mostly on suggestions from present members (four of whom are women).
Altogether 1,888 people were prosecuted, of whom 1,628 were convicted.

| 'whose' in relative clauses | When you want to talk about something belonging or relating to a person, thing, or group, you use a defining or non-defining relative clause beginning with 'whose' and a noun. |

...workers whose bargaining power is weak.
According to Cook, whose book is published on Thursday, most disasters are avoidable.

Some people think it is incorrect to use 'whose' to indicate that something belongs or relates to a thing. See entry at **whose**.

<table>
<tr><td>

'when', 'where', and 'why'

</td><td>

'When', 'where', and 'why' can be used in defining relative clauses after certain nouns. 'When' is used after 'time' and other time words, 'where' is used after 'place' or place words, and 'why' is used after 'reason'.

This is one of those occasions when I regret not being able to drive.
That was the room where I did my homework.
There are several reasons why we can't do that.

'When' and 'where' can be used in non-defining relative clauses after expressions of time and place.

This happened in 1957, when I was still a baby.
She has just come back from a holiday in Crete, where Alex and I went last year.

</td></tr>
<tr><td>

referring to the future

</td><td>

In a defining relative clause, you sometimes use the simple present tense and sometimes use 'will' when referring to the future. See section on **present tenses in subordinate clauses** in entry at **The Future**.

</td></tr>
</table>

relax

When you **relax,** you make yourself calmer and less worried or tense.

Just lie back and relax.
Some people can't even relax when they are at home.

Note that **relax** is not a reflexive verb. You do not say that you 'relax yourself'.

release - let go

Release and **let go** are used in similar ways. **Release** is more formal than **let go.**

If you **release** a person or animal or **let** them **go,** you allow them to leave or escape.

They had just been released from prison.
Eventually I let the frog go.

To **release** or **let go of** something or someone also means to stop holding them.

He released her hand quickly.
Arnold didn't let go of her arm.
'Let go of me,' she said.

relieve - relief

<table>
<tr><td>

'relieve'

</td><td>

Relieve /rɪliːv/ is a verb. If something **relieves** an unpleasant feeling, it makes it less unpleasant.

Anxiety may be relieved by talking to a friend.
The passengers in the plane swallow to relieve the pressure on their eardrums.

If someone or something **relieves** you **of** an unpleasant feeling or difficulty, you no longer have it.

The news relieved him of some of his embarrassment.

</td></tr>
</table>

'relief' **Relief** /rɪliːf/ is a noun. If you feel **relief,** you feel glad because something unpleasant has stopped or has not happened.

I breathed a sigh of relief.
To my relief, he found the suggestion acceptable.

Relief is also money, food, or clothing that is provided for people who are very poor or hungry.

She outlined what was being done to provide relief.

remain - stay

Remain and **stay** are often used with the same meaning. **Remain** is more formal than **stay.**

To **remain** or **stay** in a particular state means to continue to be in that state.

Oliver remained silent.
I stayed awake.

If you **remain** or **stay** in a place, you do not leave it.

I was allowed to remain at home.
Fewer women these days stay at home to look after their children.

If something still exists, you can say that it **remains.** You do not say that it 'stays'.

Even today remnants of this practice remain.
He was cut off from what remained of his family.

If you **stay** in a town, hotel, or house, you live there for a short time.

How long can you stay in Brussels?
She was staying in the same hotel as I was.

You do not use **remain** with this meaning.

remember

If you **remember** people or events from the past, your mind still has an impression of them and you are able to think about them.

I remember Sylvia Burton's bunch of wild flowers.
He remembered the man well.

You do not usually use a continuous tense of **remember.** You do not say, for example, 'I am remembering Sylvia Burton's bunch of wild flowers'.

You can use either an '-ing' form or a 'to'-infinitive after **remember,** but with different meanings. If your mind has an impression of something you did in the past, you say that you **remember doing** it.

I remember cabling home for more money.

If you do something that you had intended to do, you can say that you **remember to do** it.

He remembered to turn the gas off.

'remind' If you mention to someone that they had intended to do something, you do not say that you 'remember' them to do it. You say that you **remind** them to do it. See entry at **remind.**

remind

If you **remind** someone **of** a fact or event that they already know about, you say something which causes them to think about it.

She reminded him of two appointments.
You do not need to remind people of their mistakes.

You can **remind** someone **that** something is the case.

She had to remind him that he had a wife.

If you **remind** someone **to do** something, you tell them again that they should do it, or you mention to them that they had intended to do it.

She reminded me to wear the visitor's badge at all times.
Remind me to speak to you about Davis.

You do not say that you remind someone 'of doing' something.

If someone or something **reminds** you **of** another person or thing, they are similar to that other person or thing and make you think about them.

Your son reminds me of you at his age.

Note that you must use 'of' in a sentence like this.

remove

If you **remove** something, you take it away.

The tea-ladies came in to remove the cups.
He removed his hand from the man's collar.

'move'   If you go to live in a different house taking your possessions with you, you do not say that you 'remove'. You say that you **move**.

Send me your new address if you move.
Last year my parents moved from Hyde to Stepney.

You can also say that you **move house**.

Cats sometimes get lost when families move house.

rent

See entry at **hire - rent - let**.

repair

See entry at **restore - repair**.

Replies

This entry explains how to reply to 'yes/no'-questions and 'wh'-questions which are being used to ask for information.

Other ways of replying to things that people say are explained in the entries at **Agreeing and disagreeing; Apologizing; Complimenting and congratulating someone; Greetings and goodbyes; Invitations; Offers; Requests, orders, and instructions; Suggestions;** and **Thanking someone**.

replying to   When you reply to a positive 'yes/no'-question, you say 'Yes' if the situation
'yes/no'-   referred to exists and 'No' if the situation does not exist.
questions

'Did you enjoy it?'—'Yes, it was very good.'
'Have you tried Woolworth's?'—'Yes, I think we've tried them all.'
'Have you decided what to do?'—'Not yet, no.'
'Did he lose his job?'—'No. They sent him home.'

You can add an appropriate tag such as 'I have' or 'it isn't'. Sometimes the tag is said first.

'Are they very complicated?'—*'Yes, they are. They have quite a number of elements.'*
'Have you ever been hypnotised by anyone?'—*'No, no I haven't.'*
'Did you have a look at the shop when you were there?'—*'I didn't, no.'*

Some people say 'Yeah' /jeə/ instead of 'Yes' when speaking informally.

'Have you got one?'—*'Yeah.'*

People sometimes make the sound 'Mm' instead of saying 'Yes'.

'Is it very expensive?'—*'Mm, it's quite pricey.'*

Sometimes you can answer a question with an adverb of degree.

'Did she like it?'—*'Oh, very much, said it was marvellous.'*
'Has he talked to you?'—*'A little. Not much.'*

If you feel a 'No' answer is not quite accurate, you can say 'Not really' or 'Not exactly' instead or as well.

'Right, is that any clearer now?'—*'Not really, no.'*
'Have you thought at all about what you might do?'—*'No, not really.'*
'Has Davis suggested that?'—*'Not exactly, but I think he'd be glad to get away.'*

If the question has 'or' in it, you reply with a word or group of words that indicates what the situation is. You only use a whole clause for emphasis or if you want to make your answer really clear.

'Do you want traveller's cheques or currency?'—*'Traveller's cheques.'*
'Are they undergraduate courses or postgraduate courses?'—*'Mainly postgraduate.'*
'Are cultured pearls synthetic or are they real pearls?'—*'They are real pearls, but a tiny piece of mother-of-pearl has been inserted in each oyster.'*

Often when people ask a question, they do not want just a 'Yes' or 'No' answer; they want detailed information of some kind. In reply to questions like this, people sometimes do not say 'Yes' or 'No' but just give the information, often after 'Well'.

'Do you have any plans yourself for any more research in this area?'—*'Well, I hope to look more at mixed ability teaching.'*
'Did you find any difficulties when you were interviewing people from the University?'—*'Well, most of them are very articulate, and in fact the problem on occasions was actually shutting them up!'*

replying to negative 'yes/no'-questions
Negative 'yes/no'-questions are usually used when the speaker thinks the answer will be, or should be, 'Yes'.

You should reply to questions of this kind with 'Yes' if the situation does exist and 'No' if the situation does not exist, just as you would reply to a positive question. For example, if someone says 'Hasn't James phoned?', you reply 'No' if he hasn't phoned.

'Haven't they just had a conference or something?'—*'Yes.'*
'Haven't you any socks or anything with you?'—*'Well – oh, yes – in that suitcase.'*
'Didn't he comment on your research, or your style, or anything?'—*'No. He just called it good.'*
'Didn't you like it, then?'—*'Not much.'*

If you are replying to a negative statement which is said as a question, you reply 'No' if the statement is true.

'So you've never been guilty of physical violence?'—*'No.'*

'You didn't mind me coming in?'—'*No*, don't be daft.'

If you are replying to a positive statement said as a question, you reply 'Yes' if the statement is true.

'He liked it?'—'*Yes, he did.*'
'You've heard me speak of Angela?'—'*Oh, yes.*'

replying when uncertain

If you do not know the answer to a 'yes/no'-question, you say 'I don't know' or 'I'm not sure'.

'Did they print the list?'—'*I don't know.*'
'Is there any chance of you getting away this summer?'—'*I'm not sure.*'

You can also sometimes use 'could', 'might', or 'may'.

'Is it yours?'—'It *could* be.'
'Is there a file on me somewhere?'—'Well, there *might* be.'
'Did you drive down that road towards Egletons on Friday morning?'—'I *might* have done.'

If you think the situation probably exists, you say 'I think so'.

'Do you understand?'—'*I think so.*'
'Will he be all right?'—'Yes, *I think so.*'

American speakers often say 'I guess so'.

'Can we go inside?'—'*I guess so.*'

If you are making a guess, you can also say 'I should think so', 'I would think so', 'I expect so', or 'I imagine so'.

'Will Sarah be going?'—'*I would think so, yes.*'
'Did you say anything when I first came up to you?'—'Well, *I expect so,* but how on earth can I remember now?'

If you are rather unenthusiastic or unhappy about the situation, you say 'I suppose so'.

'Are you on speaking terms with them now?'—'*I suppose so.*'

If you think the situation probably does not exist, you say 'I don't think so'.

'Was there any paper in the safe?'—'*I don't think so.*'
'Did you ever meet Mr Innes?'—'No, *I don't think so.*'

If you are making a guess, you can also say 'I shouldn't think so', 'I wouldn't think so', or 'I don't expect so'.

'Would Nick mind, do you think?'—'No, *I shouldn't think so.*'
'Is my skull fractured?'—'*I shouldn't think so.*'

replying to 'wh'-questions

In replying to 'wh'-questions, people usually use one word or a group of words instead of a full sentence.

'How old are you?'—'*Thirteen.*'
'How do you feel?'—'*Strange.*'
'What sort of iron did she get?'—'*A steam iron.*'
'Where are we going?'—'*Up the coast.*'
'Why did you run away?'—'*Because Michael lied to me.*'

Sometimes, however, a full sentence is used, for example when giving the reason for something.

'Why did you quarrel with your wife?'—'*She disapproved of what I'm doing.*'

If you do not know the answer, you say 'I don't know' or 'I'm not sure'.

'What shall we do?'—'*I don't know.*'

'How old were you then?'—*'I'm not sure.'*

GRAMMAR **Reporting**

quote structures

One way of reporting what someone has said is to repeat their actual words. When you do this, you use a **reporting verb** such as 'say'.

I said, 'Where are we?'
'I don't know much about music,' Judy said.

Sentences like these are called **quote structures** or **direct speech**. Quote structures are used more in stories than in conversation. See entry at **Punctuation** for information on how to punctuate them.

In stories, you can put the reporting verb after the quote. The subject is often put after the verb.

'I see', said John.

WARNING

However, when the subject is a pronoun, it must go in front of the verb.

'Hi there!' he said.

The only reporting verb you use in conversation is 'say'. However, in stories you can indicate what kind of statement someone made using reporting verbs such as 'ask', 'explain', or 'suggest'.

'What have you been up to?' he asked.
'It's a disease of the blood,' explained Kowalski.
'Perhaps,' he suggested, 'it was just an impulse.'

You can also use verbs such as 'add', 'begin', 'continue', and 'reply' to show when one statement occurred in relation to another.

'I want it to be a surprise,' I added.
'Anyway,' she continued, 'it's quite out of the question.'
She replied, 'My first thought was to protect him.

In a story, if you want to indicate the way in which something was said, you can use a reporting verb such as 'shout', 'wail', or 'scream'.

'Jump!' shouted the oldest woman.
'Oh, poor little thing,' she wailed.
'Get out of there,' I screamed.

The following verbs indicate the way in which something is said:

call	mumble	scream	storm	whisper
chorus	murmur	shout	thunder	yell
cry	mutter	shriek	wail	

You can use a verb such as 'smile', 'grin', or 'frown' to indicate the expression on someone's face while they are speaking.

'I'm awfully sorry.'—'Not at all,' I smiled.
'Hardly worth turning up for,' he grinned.

Reporting

<table>
<tr><td>report structures</td><td>

In conversation, you normally give an idea of what someone said using your own words in a **report structure**, rather than quoting them directly. You also use report structures to report people's thoughts.

She said it was quite an expensive one.
They thought that he should have been locked up.

Report structures are also often used in writing.

A report structure consists of two parts: a **reporting clause** and a **reported clause**.
</td></tr>
<tr><td>reporting verbs</td><td>

The **reporting clause** contains the **reporting verb** and usually comes first.

I told him that nothing was going to happen to me.
I asked what was going on.

The reporting verb with the widest meaning and use is 'say'. You use 'say' when you are simply reporting what someone said and do not want to imply anything about their statement.

He said that you knew his family.
They said the prison was surrounded by police.

See entry at **say** for more information on its use, and the difference between it and other verbs referring to speaking.

You can use a reporting verb such as 'answer', 'explain', and 'suggest' to indicate what kind of statement you think the person was making.

She explained that a friend of her husband's had been arrested.
I suggested that it was time to leave.

You can also indicate your own personal opinion of what someone said by using a reporting verb such as 'admit' or 'claim'. For example, if you say that someone 'claimed' that they did something, you are implying that you think they may not be telling the truth.

She admitted she was very much in love with you once.
He claims he knows more about the business now.
</td></tr>
<tr><td>reporting verbs with a negative</td><td>

With a small number of reporting verbs, you usually make the reporting clause negative rather than the reported clause. For example, you would usually say 'I don't think Mary is at home' rather than 'I think Mary is not at home'.

I don't think I will be able to afford it.
I don't believe we can enforce a total ban.
I didn't want to disappoint her.

The following reporting verbs are often used with a negative in this way:
</td></tr>
</table>

believe	feel	propose	think
expect	imagine	suppose	

<table>
<tr><td>reported clauses</td><td>

The second part of a report structure is the **reported clause**.

She said that she had been to Belgium.
The man in the shop told me how much it would cost.

There are several types of reported clause. The type used depends on whether a statement, order, suggestion, or question is being reported.
</td></tr>
</table>

| 'that'-clauses | A report clause beginning with the conjunction 'that' is used after a reporting verb to report a statement or someone's thoughts. |

He said that the police had directed him to the wrong room.
He thought that Vita needed a holiday.

Some common reporting verbs used in front of a 'that'-clause are:

accept	claim	feel	notice	report
admit	complain	hint	predict	reveal
agree	confess	hope	promise	say
announce	decide	imagine	realize	suggest
answer	deny	imply	recommend	swear
argue	discover	insist	remark	think
assume	expect	know	remember	warn
believe	explain	mention	reply	

'That' is often omitted from a 'that'-clause.

They said I had to see a doctor first.
I think there's something wrong.

However, 'that' is nearly always used after the verbs 'answer', 'argue', 'complain', 'explain', 'recommend,' and 'reply'.

He answered that the price would be three pounds.

A 'that'-clause can contain a modal, especially when someone makes a suggestion about what someone else should do.

He proposes that the Government should hold an enquiry.

| mentioning the hearer | After some reporting verbs that refer to speech, the hearer must be mentioned as the direct object. 'Tell' is the most common of these verbs. |

He told me that he was a farmer.
I informed her that I could not come.

The following verbs must have the hearer as direct object:

assure	inform	persuade	remind
convince	notify	reassure	tell

You can also choose to mention the hearer as object with 'promise' and 'warn'.

I promised that I would try to phone her.
I promised Myra I'd be home at seven.

With many other reporting verbs, if you want to mention the hearer, you do so in a prepositional phrase beginning with 'to'.

I explained to her that I had to go home.
I mentioned to Tom that I was thinking of working for George McGovern.

The following verbs need the preposition 'to' if you mention the hearer:

admit	confess	mention	suggest
announce	explain	report	swear
complain	hint	reveal	

| use of the passive | Verbs such as 'tell' and 'inform' can be used in the passive, with the hearer as the subject. |

She was told that there were no tickets left.

A passive form of other reporting verbs is sometimes used to avoid saying whose opinion or statement is being reported, or to imply that it is an opinion that is generally held. This use of the passive is formal. You can use 'it' as the subject with a 'that'-clause, or you can use an ordinary subject with a 'to'-infinitive clause.

It is now believed that foreign languages are most easily taught to young children.
He is said to have died a natural death.

'to'-infinitive clauses

You use a **'to'-infinitive clause** after a reporting verb such as 'tell', 'ask', or 'advise' to report an order, a request, or a piece of advice. The person being addressed, who is going to perform the action, is mentioned as the object of the reporting verb.

Johnson told her to wake him up.
He ordered me to fetch the books.
He asked her to marry him.

Some common reporting verbs used in front of a 'to'-infinitive clause are:

advise	command	instruct	persuade	urge
ask	encourage	invite	remind	warn
beg	forbid	order	tell	

The following verbs referring to saying, thinking, or discovering are always or usually used in the passive when followed by a 'to'-infinitive.

allege	consider	find	reckon	see
assume	discover	know	report	think
believe	estimate	learn	rumour	understand
claim	feel	prove	say	

The 'to'-infinitive that follows them is most commonly 'be' or 'have'.

The house was believed to be haunted.
Over a third of the population was estimated to have no access to the health service.
...the primitive molecules which are believed to have given rise to life on Earth.

You can also use a 'to'-infinitive after some reporting verbs which are not used with an object. The person who speaks is also the person who will perform the action.

agree	offer	refuse	threaten
demand	promise	swear	vow

They offered to show me the way.
He threatened to arrest me.

Note that when you are reporting an action that the speaker intends to perform, you can sometimes use either a 'to'-infinitive or a 'that'-clause.

I promised to come back.
She promised that she would not leave hospital until she was better.

You do not use a 'to'-infinitive if the hearer is being mentioned.

I promised her I would send her the money.
I swore to him that I would not publish the pamphlet.

'Claim' and 'pretend' can also be used with these two structures. For example, 'He claimed to be a genius' has the same meaning as 'He claimed **that** he was a genius'.

He claimed <u>to have witnessed the accident</u>.
He claimed <u>that he had found the money in the forest</u>.

Several verbs which indicate someone's intentions, wishes, or decisions, such as 'intend', 'want', and 'decide', are used with a 'to'-infinitive clause. See entry at **'To'-infinitive clauses.**

'-ing' clauses When reporting a suggestion about doing something, it is possible to use one of the reporting verbs 'suggest', 'advise', 'propose', or 'recommend' followed by an **'-ing' clause.**

Barbara <u>suggested going to another coffee house</u>.
The committee <u>recommended abandoning the original plan</u>.

Note that you only 'propose doing' actions that you yourself will be involved in.

Daisy <u>proposed moving to New York</u>.

reported questions You use the reporting verb 'ask' when reporting a question. You can mention the hearer as the direct object if you need to or want to.

He <u>asked</u> if I had a message for Cartwright.
I <u>asked her</u> if she wanted them.

'Inquire' and 'enquire' also mean 'ask', but these are fairly formal words. You cannot mention the hearer as the object of these verbs.

An **'if'-clause** or a **'whether'-clause** is used when reporting **'yes/no'** **questions**. 'Whether' is used especially if there is a choice of possibilities.

She asked him <u>if his parents spoke French</u>.
I was asked <u>whether I wanted to stay at a hotel or at his home</u>.

A reported clause beginning with a **'wh'-word** is used to report a **'wh'-question**.

He asked <u>where I was going</u>.
She enquired <u>why I was so late</u>.

WARNING The word order in a reported question is the same as that of a statement, not that of a question. For example, you say 'She asked me what I had been doing'. You do not say 'She asked me what had I been doing'.

You do not use a question mark when you write reported questions.

If the 'wh'-word in a reported question is the object of a preposition, the preposition comes at the end of the clause, with no noun after it.

She asked <u>what</u> they were looking <u>for</u>.
He asked <u>what</u> we lived <u>on</u>.

Other verbs which refer to speech or thought about uncertain things can be used in front of clauses beginning with 'wh'-words or with 'if' or 'whether'.

She doesn't <u>know</u> what we were talking about.
They couldn't <u>see</u> how they would manage without her.

A 'to'-infinitive clause beginning with a 'wh'-word or 'whether' can be used to refer to an action that someone is uncertain about doing.

I asked him <u>what to do</u>.
I've been wondering <u>whether to retire</u>.

tense of reporting verb You usually use a past tense of the reporting verb when you are reporting something said in the past.

She <u>said</u> you threw away her sweets.
Brody <u>asked</u> what happened.

However, you can use a present tense of the reporting verb, especially if you are reporting something that is still true.

She says she wants to see you this afternoon.
My doctor says it's nothing to worry about.

tense of verb in
reported clause

If you are using a present tense of the reporting verb, you use the same tense in the reported clause as you would use for an ordinary, direct statement. For example, if a woman says 'He hasn't arrived yet', you could report this by saying 'She says he hasn't arrived yet'.

He knows he's being watched.
He says he has never seen a live shark in his life.
He says he was very worried.

with past
reporting verb

If you are using a past tense of the reporting verb, you usually put the verb in the reported clause into a tense that is appropriate at the time that you are speaking.

If the event or situation described in the reported clause was in the past when the statement was made, you use the past perfect tense. You can sometimes use the simple past tense instead when you do not need to relate the event to the time that the statement was made.

Minnie said she had given it to Ben.
A Western diplomat said he saw about 250 foreigners at the airport trying to get on flights out of the country.

You can also use the present perfect tense if the event or situation is recent or relevant to the present situation.

He said there has been a 56 per cent rise in bankruptcies in the past 12 months.

When reporting a habitual past action or a situation that no longer exists, you can use 'used to'.

He said he used to go canoeing on rivers and lakes.

If the event or situation described in the reported clause was happening at the time when it was mentioned, you use the simple past tense or the past continuous tense.

Dad explained that he had no money.
She added that she was smoking too much.

Note that a past tense is usually used for the verb in the reported clause even if the reported situation still exists. For example, you say 'I told him I was eighteen' even if you are still eighteen. You are concentrating on the situation at the past time that you are talking about.

He said he was English.
I said I liked sleeping on the ground.

A present tense is sometimes used, however, to emphasize that the situation still exists or to mention a situation that often occurs among a group of people.

I told him that I don't drink more than anyone else.
A social worker at the Society explained that some children live in three or four different foster homes in one year.

referring to
the future

If the event or situation was in the future at the time of the statement or is still in the future, you usually use a **modal**. See the section below on **modals in reported clauses**.

However, you use a present tense in reported questions and similar 'wh'-clauses referring to a future event when the event will happen at about the same time as the statement or thought.

I'll telephone you. If I say it's Hugh, you'll know who it is.

If the future event will happen after the statement, you use 'will' in the reported question.

I'll tell you what I will do.

modals in reported clauses If the verb in the reporting clause is in a present tense, you use modals as you would use them in an ordinary, direct statement.

Helen says I can share her flat.
I think some of the sheep may die this year.
I don't believe he will come.
I believe that I could live very comfortably here.

See the individual entries for modals for information on their uses.

with past reporting verb If the verb in the reporting clause is in a past tense or has 'could' or 'would' as an auxiliary, you usually use 'could', 'might', or 'would' in the reported clause, rather than 'can', 'may', or 'will', in the ways explained below.

ability When you want to report a statement (or question) about someone's ability to do something, you normally use 'could'.

They believed that war could be avoided.
Nell would not admit that she could not cope.

possibility When you want to report a statement about possibility, you normally use 'might'.

They told me it might flood here.
He said you might need money.

If the possibility is a strong one, you use 'must'.

I told her she must be out of her mind.

permission When you want to report a statement giving permission or a request for permission, you normally use 'could'. 'Might' is used in more formal English.

I told him he couldn't have it.
Madeleine asked if she might borrow a pen and some paper.

the future When you want to report a prediction, promise, or expectation, or a question about the future, you normally use 'would'.

She said they would all miss us.
He insisted that reforms would save the system, not destroy it.

'can', 'may', 'will' Note that you can use 'can', 'may', 'will', and 'shall' when you are using a past tense of the reporting verb, if you want to emphasize that the situation still exists or is still in the future.

He claimed that a child's early experiences of being separated from his mother may cause psychological distress in later life.
A spokesman said that the board will meet tomorrow.

obligation When you want to report a statement in the past about obligation, it is possible to use 'must', but the expression 'had to' is more common.

He said he really had to go back inside.
Sita told him that he must be especially kind to the little girl.

You use 'have to', 'has to', or 'must' if the reported situation still exists or is in the future.

He said the Government must come clean on the issue.
A spokesman said that all bomb threats have to be taken seriously.

When you want to report a statement or thought about what is morally right, you can use 'ought to' or 'should'.

He knew he <u>ought to</u> be helping Harold.
I felt I <u>should</u> consult my family.

prohibiting

When you want to report a statement prohibiting something, you normally use 'mustn't'.

He said they <u>mustn't</u> get us into trouble.

using reporting verbs for politeness

Reporting verbs are often used to say something in a polite way. For example, if you want to contradict someone or to say something which might be unwelcome to them, you can avoid sounding rude by using a reporting verb such as 'think' or 'believe'.

I <u>think</u> it's time we stopped.
I don't <u>think</u> that will be necessary.
I <u>believe</u> you ought to leave now.

---

request

Request is used as a noun or a verb.

used as a noun

When someone asks for something to be done or provided, you can say that they make a **request**.

My friend made a polite <u>request</u>.
The Minister had granted the <u>request</u>.

You say that someone makes a **request for** something.

...a <u>request for</u> the return of important documents.
He agreed to my <u>request for</u> psychiatric help.

used as a verb

When someone **requests** something, they ask for it.

The President <u>requested</u> an emergency session of the United Nations.
The provisional government <u>requested</u> his appointment as the first Governor-General.

Note that when **request** is used as a verb, you do not use 'for' after it.

Requests, orders, and instructions

When you make a **request**, you ask someone for something or ask them to do something. If you have authority over someone or know them well, you give them an **order** or an **instruction**, that is you tell them to do something rather than asking them to do something. You can also give someone **instructions** on how to do something or what to do in a particular situation.

For information on how to request permission to do something, see entry at **Permission**.

Information on how to reply to a request or order is given at the end of this entry.

asking for something

The simplest way to ask for something is to say 'Can I have...?' (You use 'we' instead of 'I' if you are speaking on behalf of a group.) You can add 'please' in order to be more polite.

Can I have a light?
Can I have some tomatoes?
Can I have my hat back, please?

Can we have something to wipe our hands on, please?

It is more polite to use 'could'.

Could I have another cup of coffee?

People used to be taught that, when asking for something, it was correct to use 'may' rather than 'can', and 'might' rather than 'could'. However, 'can' and 'could' are now generally used. Requests with 'may' sound very polite and formal, and requests with 'might' sound old-fashioned.

May we have something to eat?

You use 'can't' or 'couldn't' instead of 'can' or 'could' to make a request sound more persuasive, if you think you may not get what you are asking for.

Can't we have some music?

You can use 'Have you got...?', or 'You haven't got...' and a question tag, to ask for something in an informal, indirect way.

Have you got a piece of paper or something I could write it on?
Have you got a match?
You haven't got that 20 pence, have you?
Oh hell, I've completely finished off this handkerchief. You haven't got a Kleenex or anything, have you?

An indirect way of asking for something you think you might not get is to say 'Any chance of...?' This is very informal and casual.

Any chance of a bit more cash in the New Year?

asking as a customer

If you want to ask for something in a shop, bar, café, or hotel, you can simply use a noun group followed by 'please'.

A packet of crisps, please.
Scotch and water, please.

You can also say 'I'd like...'.

As I'm here, doctor, I'd like a prescription for some aspirins.
I'd like a room, please. For one night.

If you are not sure whether a particular thing is available, you say 'Have you got...?'

Have you got any brochures on Holland?

When you are in a restaurant or bar, you can say 'I'll have...'. You can also say this when you are offered something to eat or drink in someone's house.

The waitress brought their drinks and said, 'Ready?' 'Yes,' said Ellen. 'I'll have the shrimp cocktail and the chicken.'
'Well, here at last, Mr Adamson! Now what'll you have?'—'I'll have a glass of beer, thanks, Mr Crike.'

You can also say 'I'd like...'.

I'd like some tea.
I think I'd like some lemonade.

asking someone to do something

You can ask someone to do something by saying 'Could you...?' or 'Would you...?' This is fairly polite. You can add 'please' to be more polite.

Could you just switch the projector on behind you?
Could you make out our bill, please?
Could you tell me, please, what time the flight arrives?

Would you tell her that Adrian phoned?
Would you take the call for him, please?

You can make a request even more polite by adding 'perhaps' or 'possibly' after 'Could you'.

Morris, could you possibly take me to the railroad station on your way to work this morning?

If you want to be very polite, you can say 'Do you think you could...?' or 'I wonder if you could...?'

Do you think you could help me?
I wonder if you could look after my cat for me while I'm away?

You can also use 'Would you mind...?' and an '-ing' form.

Would you mind doing the washing up?
Would you mind waiting a moment?

In formal letters and speech, you use very polite expressions such as 'I would be grateful if...', 'I would appreciate it if...', or 'Would you kindly...'.

I would be grateful if you could let me know.
I would appreciate it if you could do anything to bring all that happened into the open.
Would you kindly call to see us next Tuesday at eleven o'clock?

Note that these very polite expressions are in fact sometimes used as indirect ways of telling someone to do something.

In informal situations, you can say 'Can you...?' or 'Will you...?'

Can you give us a hand?
Can you make me a copy of that?
Will you post this for me on your way to work?
Will you turn on the light, please, Henry?

If you think it is unlikely that the person you are asking will agree to your request, you use 'You wouldn't...' and the tag 'would you?', or 'You couldn't...' and the tag 'could you?' You also use these structures when you realize that you are asking them to do something which is difficult or will involve a lot of work.

You wouldn't sell it to me, would you?
You wouldn't lend me a bit of your greeny eyeshadow too, would you?
You couldn't give me a lift, could you?

You can also use 'I suppose you couldn't...' or 'I don't suppose you would...'.

I suppose you couldn't just stay an hour or two longer?
I don't suppose you'd be prepared to stay in Edinburgh?

People sometimes use expressions such as 'Would you do me a favour?' and 'I wonder if you could do me a favour' to indicate that they are about to ask you to do something for them.

'Oh, Bill, I wonder if you could do me a favour.'—'Depends what it is.'—
'Could you ring me at this number about eleven on Sunday morning?'
'I wonder if you'd do me a favour.'—'Of course.'—'In that bag there's something I'd like your opinion on.'
'Will you do me a favour?'—'Depends.'—'Be nice to him.'
'Do me a favour, Grace. Don't say anything about a shark to Sally.'—'All right, Martin.'

orders and instructions People often ask someone to do something, rather than telling them to do it, even when they have authority over them, because this is more polite. More direct ways of telling someone to do something are explained below.

In an informal situation, you can use an imperative clause. This is a direct and forceful way of giving an order.

Pass the salt.
Let me see it.
Don't touch that!
Hurry up!
Look out! There's a car coming.

Note that it is not very polite to use imperative clauses like this in speech and you only commonly use them when talking to people you know well, or in situations of danger or urgency.

However, imperative forms are quite often used to invite someone to do something, in phrases such as 'Come in' and 'Take a seat'. See entry at **Invitations.**

You can use 'please' to make orders more polite.

Go and get the file, please.
Wear rubber gloves, please.

You can use the question tag 'will you?' to make an order sound less forceful and more like a request.

Come into the kitchen, will you?
Don't mention them, will you?

Note that people also use 'will you?' to make an order more forceful when they are angry. See section below on **emphatic orders.**

You can also use the tag 'won't you?' to make an order more like a request, unless you are giving a negative order.

See that she gets safely back, won't you?

You can say 'I would like you to...' or 'I'd like you to...' as an indirect, polite way of telling someone to do something, especially someone you have authority over.

John, I would like you to get us the files.
I'd like you to read this.
I shall be away tomorrow, so I'd like you to chair the weekly meeting.

emphatic orders You use 'do' in front of an imperative form to add emphasis when you are telling someone to do something that will be for their own benefit, or when you are friendly with them.

Do be careful.
Do remember to tell William about the change of plan.

You use 'You must...' to emphasize the importance and necessity of the action.

You must come at once.
You must tell no one.

You can also add emphasis to an order by putting 'you' in front of an imperative form. However, this is very informal and sometimes shows impatience.

You take it.
You get in the car.

You use 'Will you...?' to give an order in a forceful and direct way, either to someone you have authority over or when you are angry or impatient.

Will you pack everything, please, Maria.
Will you stop yelling!

People also add the tag 'will you?' to an imperative clause when they are angry.

Just listen to me a minute, will you?

People say 'Can't you...?' when they are very angry. This is very impolite.

Really, can't you show a bit more consideration?
Look, can't you shut up about it?
For God's sake, can't you leave me alone?

Adding the question tag 'can't you?' to an imperative clause is also impolite and shows annoyance.

Do it quietly, can't you?

People use 'You will...' to emphasize the fact that the other person has no choice but to carry out the order. This is a very strong form of order.

You will go and get one of your parents immediately.
You will give me those now.

signs and notices
On signs and notices, negative orders are sometimes expressed by 'no' and an '-ing' form.

No Smoking.

'Must be' is sometimes used for positive orders.

Dogs must be kept on a lead at all times.

instructions on how to do something
You can use an imperative clause to give instructions on how to do something. This is not impolite.

Turn right off Broadway into Caxton Street.
In emergency, dial 999 for police, fire or ambulance.
Fry the chopped onion and pepper in the oil.

Imperative clauses are especially common in written instructions. Note that verbs which usually have an object are often not given an object in instructions, when it is clear what the instructions refer to. For example, you might see 'Store in a dry place' on a packet of food, rather than 'Store this food in a dry place'. Similarly, determiners are often left out. You might read in a recipe 'Peel and core apples' rather than 'Peel and core the apples'.

'Must be' is used to indicate what you should do with something. 'Should be' is used in a similar way, but is less strong.

Mussels must be bought fresh and cooked on the same day.
No cake should be stored before it is quite cold.

See entry at **Advising someone**.

In conversation and informal writing, you can also use 'you' and the simple present tense to give instructions. We use 'you' like this in this book.

First you take a few raisins and soak them overnight in water.
You take an underblanket and put it on the bed, and you tuck in the four corners. And then you take the sheet and lay it in the centre of the bed.
Note that in sentences like these you use an infinitive without 'to' after 'would rather'.

replying to a request or order
You can agree to someone's request informally by saying 'OK', 'All right', or 'Sure'.

'Do them as fast as you can.'—'Yes, OK.'
'Don't do that.'—'All right, I won't.'
'Could you give me lift?'—'Sure.'

If you want to be more polite, you can say 'Certainly'.

'Could you make out my bill, please?'—'Certainly, sir.'

You can refuse someone's request by saying something like 'I'm sorry, I'm afraid I can't' or by giving the reason why you are unable to do what they want.

'Put it on the bill.'—'I'm afraid I can't do that.'
'Do me this favour. This once.'—'I'm sorry, Larry, I can't.'
'Could you phone me back later?'—'No, I'm going out in five minutes.'
'Could you do me a taxi from 1 Updale Close to the station?'—'I'm afraid there's nothing available at the moment.'

It is impolite just to say 'No'.

require

If you **require** something, you need it or want it.

Is there anything you require?
We cannot guarantee that any particular item will be available when you require it.

Require is a formal word. You do not usually use it in conversation. Instead, you use **need** or **want**.

I won't need that book any more.
All they want is a holiday.

If something **is required**, it must be obtained in order that something else can be done.

Parliamentary approval would be required for any scheme.
An increase in funds might well be required.

If you **are required to** do something, you have to do it, for example because of a rule or law.

All the boys were required to study religion.

research

Research is work that involves studying something and trying to discover facts about it. You say that someone **does research.**

I had come to India to do some research into Anglo-Indian literature.

You can refer to the research that someone is doing as their **research** or their **researches.** You normally only use **researches** after a possessive form such as 'my', 'his', or 'Gordon's'.

Soon after, Faraday began his researches into electricity.
…Professor Ornstein's research on the left and right halves of the brain.

'search'   You do not use **research** to refer to an attempt to find something by looking for it carefully. The word you use is **search.**

A huge search for the missing documents was mounted.
A quick search of the boat revealed nothing.

resist

If you **resist** something such as a change, you refuse to accept it and try to prevent it from happening.

Our trade union has resisted the introduction of automation.
He resisted demands for a public inquiry.

If you **resist** an attack by someone, you fight against them to avoid being defeated.

Any attack will be resisted with force.

If you are unable to accept something unpleasant or disagreeable, you do not say that you 'can't resist' it. You say that you **can't bear** it, **can't tolerate** it, or **can't stand** it.

Stop keeping me in suspense! I can't bear it.
They couldn't tolerate the noise.
He kept on nagging until I couldn't stand it any longer.

respectable - respectful

'respectable' Someone or something that is **respectable** is approved of by people and considered to be morally correct.

The teacher was a respectable woman who did her best.
They were young people from respectable homes.

'respectful' If your behaviour is **respectful,** you show respect for someone or something.

The woman kept a respectful silence.
The Security Officer was standing at a respectful distance holding a plastic cup of coffee.

responsible

'responsible for' If you are **responsible for doing** something, it is your job or duty to do it.

The children were responsible for cleaning their own rooms.

You do not say that someone is 'responsible to do' something.

If you are **responsible for** something bad that has happened, it is your fault.

They were charged with being responsible for the death of two policemen.

Note that you do not use any preposition except 'for' after **responsible** in a sentence like this.

used after **Responsible** can also be used after a noun. If you talk about 'the person
a noun responsible', you mean 'the person who is responsible for what has happened'.

I hope they get the man responsible.
The company responsible refused to say what happened.

used in front of However, if you use **responsible** in front of a noun, it has a completely
a noun different meaning. A **responsible** person is someone who can be relied on to behave properly and sensibly without needing to be controlled by anyone else.

...responsible members of the local community.

Responsible behaviour is sensible and correct.

I thought it was a very responsible decision.

restful - restless

'restful' Something that is **restful** helps you to feel calm and relaxed.

The lighting is restful.

'restless'   A **restless** child cannot keep still or quiet.

Some babies are tense and restless during the early weeks.

You also say that someone is **restless** when they are bored with what they are doing and want to do something else.

I knew within a fortnight I should feel restless again.

restore - repair

'restore'   To **restore** an old building, painting, or piece of furniture means to repair and clean it, so that it returns to its original condition.

Several million pounds will be required to restore the theatre.
I asked whether the pictures could be restored.

'repair'   To **repair** something that has been damaged or that is not working properly means to mend it.

No one knew how to repair the engine.

result

A **result** of something is an event or situation that happens or exists because of it.

The result of all this is that the snake moves rapidly forward.
I nearly missed the flight as a result of going to Havana.
Twice he followed his own advice, with disastrous results.

'effect'   When something produces a change in a thing or person, you do not refer to this change as a 'result' on the thing or person. The word you use is **effect**.

Improvement in water supply has had a dramatic effect on health.
Road transport has a considerable effect on our daily lives.

retarded

In the past, when a child had a mental condition that made learning difficult, people used to say that he or she was **retarded, backward, simple,** or **educationally subnormal.** Nowadays these words are avoided because they are thought to be offensive.

The adjective **mentally handicapped** is sometimes used to describe children who have a mental condition of this kind. However, the most sensitive ways of referring to such children are to call them **children with special needs** or **children with learning difficulties.**

Note that children with physical handicaps are also called **children with special needs.** See entry at **crippled.**

retire - retiring

'retire'   When someone **retires,** they leave their job and stop working, usually because they have reached the age when they can get a pension.

Gladys retired at the age of sixty-eight.
They had decided to retire from farming.

'retiring'   The adjective **retiring** has two meanings.

You use it in front of a noun such as 'MP' or 'chairman' to indicate that someone will soon give up their present job and be replaced by someone else.

...Jim Dacre, the retiring Labour MP.

...the retiring President of the Methodist Conference.

You also use it to describe someone who is very quiet and avoids meeting other people.

She was a shy, retiring girl.

return

going back   When someone **returns** to a place, they go back there after they have been somewhere else.

I returned to my hotel.
I returned from the Middle East in 1956.

WARNING   You do not say that someone 'returns back' to a place.

Return is a fairly formal word. In conversation, you usually use **go back, come back,** or **get back.**

I went back to the kitchen and poured my coffee.
He came back from the war.
I've got to get back to London.

Return is also used as a noun. When someone goes back to a place, you can refer to their arrival there as their **return.**

It was published only after his return to Russia in 1917.

In writing, if you want to say that something happens immediately after someone returns to a place, you can use a phrase beginning with 'on'. For example, you can say '**On his return** to London, he was offered a post at the Foreign Office'.

On his return to Paris he painted a series of portraits.
On her return she wrote the last paragraph of her autobiography.

giving or putting something back   When someone **returns** something they have taken or borrowed, they give it back or put it back.

He borrowed my best suit and didn't return it.
We returned the books to the shelf.

Note that you do not say that someone 'returns something back'.

'bring back'   When people start using a practice or method that was used in the past, you do not say that they 'return' the practice or method. You say that they **bring** it **back or reintroduce** it.

He was all for bringing back the cane as a punishment in schools.
They reintroduced a scheme to provide housing for refugees.

review

See entry at **critic - critical - critique.**

reward - award

Both these nouns are used to refer to something you receive because you have done something useful or good.

'reward'   A **reward** is usually something valuable, such as money.

Hearst announced a reward of £ 50,000 for information.

'award'   An **award** is something such as a prize, certificate, or medal.

The only award he had ever won was the Toplady Prize for Divinity.

rid

'get rid of'
Rid is usually used in the expression **get rid of**. If you **get rid of** something or someone that you do not want, you take action so that you no longer have them.

She bathed thoroughly to get rid of the last traces of make-up.
We had to get rid of the director.

'rid' used as a verb
You can also use **rid** as a verb. If you **rid** a place or yourself of something unpleasant or annoying, you take action so that it no longer exists or no longer affects you. Note that the past tense and past participle of 'rid' is **rid,** not 'ridded'.

We must rid the country of this wickedness.
He had rid himself of his illusions.

ride

When you **ride** an animal, bicycle, or motorcycle, you control it and travel on it.

Every morning he used to ride his mare across the fields.
They overcome their fears and learn to swim or ride a bike.

The past tense of 'ride' is **rode,** not 'rided'. The past participle is **ridden.**

Niall MacKenzie rode a Suzuki, ahead of Sito Pons, who rode a Honda.
He was the best horse I have ever ridden.

'ride on'
You can also say that someone **rides on** an animal, bicycle, or motorcycle.

At the end of the film Gregory Peck rode off with Ingrid Bergman on a horse.
He rode around the campus on a bicycle.

'drive'
When someone controls a car, lorry, or train, you do not say that they 'ride' it. You say that they **drive** it.

It was her turn to drive the car.
Two of them have never learned to drive.

However, if you are a passenger in a vehicle, you can say that you **ride in** it.

We rode back in a taxi.

right

If you say that something is **right,** you mean that it is correct or appropriate.

You've got the pronunciation right.
You must do things in the right order.

In conversation, **right** is sometimes used as an adverb. For example, someone might say 'He did it right'. In writing, it is better to avoid this use. You should say 'He did it **the right way**' or 'He did it **in the right way**'.

I assured him that he was playing exactly the right way.
The reduction of slums can obviously make a contribution, provided of course that we do it in the right way.

ring

When you **ring** someone, you dial their phone number and speak to them by phone. The past tense of 'ring' is **rang,** not 'ringed' or 'rung'.

I rang Aunt Jane this evening.

The past participle is **rung.**

Mr Carlin said he had rung Mr Macalister at Glasgow CID.

You can say that someone **rings** a place.

You must ring the hospital at once.

In conversation, people often use **ring up**, instead of 'ring'. There is no difference in meaning.

He had rung up Emily and told her all about it.

Note that you do not use 'to' after **ring** or **ring up**.

'call'
: American speakers do not say that one person 'rings' another. The word they use is **call**. Some British speakers also say **call**.

He promised to call me soon.
He called Colonel Ocker at regimental headquarters.

rise - raise

used as verbs
: **Rise** and **raise** are usually used as verbs.

'rise'
: **Rise** is an intransitive verb. If something **rises**, it moves upwards.

In a moment the moon would rise.

The other forms of **rise** are **rises, rising, rose, risen.**

The birds rose screaming around them.
The sun had risen behind them.

If an amount **rises**, it increases.

Commission rates are expected to rise.
Prices rose by more than 10% per annum.

When someone who is sitting **rises**, they raise their body until they are standing. This use of **rise** occurs mainly in stories.

Dr Willoughby rose to greet them.

In conversation, you do not usually say that someone 'rises'. You say that they **stand up**.

I put down my glass and stood up.

You can also use **rise** to say that someone gets out of bed in the morning. This use of **rise** also occurs mainly in stories, especially when the author is mentioning the time at which someone gets out of bed.

They had risen at dawn.

In conversation, you do not usually use **rise** to say that someone gets out of bed. You say that they **get up**.

Mike decided it was time to get up.

Note that you never say that someone 'gets up out of bed'.

'raise'
: **Raise** is a transitive verb. If you **raise** something, you move it to a higher position.

He tried to raise the window, but the sash cord was broken.
She raised her eyebrows in surprise.

For another meaning of **raise**, see entry at **bring up**.

used as nouns
: **Rise** and **raise** can also be used as nouns. A **rise** is an increase in an amount or quantity.

...price rises.
...the rise in crime.

In British English, a **rise** is also an increase in someone's wages or salary.

He went to ask for a rise.

In American English, this is called a **raise.**

He thought about asking his boss for a raise.

risk

Risk is used as a noun or a verb.

used as a noun   If there is a **risk** of something unpleasant, there is a possibility that it will happen.

There is very little risk of infection.
...the risk that their men might disappear without trace.

used as a verb   If someone **risks doing** something, it may happen as a result of some other action they take.

They were unwilling to risk bombing their own troops.

You can also say that someone **risks doing** something when they do it even though they know it might have unpleasant consequences.

If you have an expensive rug, don't risk washing it yourself.

You do not say that someone 'risks to do' something.

rob

The verb **rob** is not usually used in conversation, but it is often used in stories and newspaper reports.

If someone takes something that belongs to you without intending to return it, you can say that they **rob you of** it.

Pirates boarded the vessels and robbed the crew of money and valuables.
The two men were robbed of more than £700.

If something that belongs to you has been stolen, you can say that you have **been robbed.**

...increasing public alarm at the prospect of being robbed.

If someone takes several things from a building without intending to return them, you say that they **rob** the building.

The only way I can get money is to rob a few banks.

'steal'   When someone takes something without intending to return it, you do not say that they 'rob' it. You say that they **steal** it.

My first offence was stealing a pair of binoculars.

See entry at **steal.**

rock

See entry at **stone.**

role - roll

These words are both pronounced /rəʊl/.

'role'   Your **role** is your position and function in a situation or society.

What is the role of the University in modern society?
He had played a major role in the formation of the United Nations.

A **role** is also one of the characters that an actor or singer plays in a film, play, opera, or musical.

She played the leading role in The Winter's Tale.

'roll' A **roll** is a very small loaf.

...*a roll and butter.*

A **roll** of something such as cloth or paper is a long piece of it wrapped many times around itself or around a tube.

He produced several rolls of hessian sacking.

rotary

See entry at **roundabout**.

round

See entry at **around**.

roundabout

In British English, a **roundabout** or **merry-go-round** is a large mechanical device which rotates horizontally. It has plastic or wooden cars or animals on it which children sit in or on. In American English, a device like this is usually called a **carousel**.

In British English, a **roundabout** is also a circular area at a place where several roads meet. You drive round it until you come to the road you want. In American English, an area like this is called a **traffic circle** or a **rotary**.

rubbish

In British English, waste food and other unwanted things that you throw away are called **rubbish**.

In American English, waste food is called **garbage** and other things that are thrown away are called **trash**.

A more formal word for all things that you throw away is **refuse** /rɛfjuːs/. **Refuse** is used in both British and American English.

rude

If someone is **rude to** you, their behaviour towards you is not polite.

Gertrude felt she had been rude to Sylvia.
I was rather rude to a young nurse.

Note that you do not use any preposition except 'to' after **rude**.

run

When you **run**, you move in a similar way to walking, but faster and taking longer strides. The past tense of 'run' is **ran**, not 'runned' or 'run'.

Karl ran over to see if he could help.

The past participle is **run**.

Two men had run out of the wood.

For another meaning of **run**, see entry at **stand**.

S

's

used to form possessives

When a singular noun refers to a person or animal, you form the possessive by adding **'s**.

...*Ralph's voice*.
...*the President's conduct*.
...*the princess's aides*.
...*the horse's eyes*.

When a plural noun ends in 's', you form the possessive by adding an apostrophe (').

...*my colleagues' offices*.
...*their parents' activities*.

When a plural noun does not end in 's', you form the possessive by adding **'s**.

...*women's rights*.
...*children's games*.

When a name ends in 's', you usually form the possessive by adding **'s**.

...*Charles's Christmas present*.
...*Mrs Jones's dressing-table*.

In formal writing, the possessive of a name ending in 's' is sometimes formed by adding an apostrophe (').

...*a statue of Prince Charles' grandfather King George VI*.

You do not usually add **'s** to nouns that refer to things. For example, you do not say 'the building's front'; you say 'the front **of the building**'. Similarly, you do not say 'my bicycle's bell'; you say 'the bell **on my bicycle**'.

...*the bottom of the hill*.
...*the end of August*.

pronouns

You can add **'s** to the following pronouns:

another	everybody	no-one	somebody
anybody	everyone	one	someone
anyone	nobody	other	

...*one's self-esteem*.
...*the idea that one person's mind is accessible to another's*.
One side gives in too easily and accepts the other's demands.

The possessive forms of other pronouns are called **possessive determiners**. For more information about these, see entry at **Possessive determiners**.

other uses of possessives

In British English, you can add **'s** to a person's name to refer to the house where they live. For example, 'I met him at **Gwyneth's**' means 'I met him at Gwyneth's house'.

I'll just nip round to Winnie's and see if she's got any sugar.

British speakers also use words ending in **'s** to refer to shops. For example, they talk about a 'chemist's', a 'tobacconist's', or a 'greengrocer's'.

I found her buying bottles of vitamin tablets at the chemist's.
I went over the cobbled road to the grocer's.

You can use 'be' and a short noun group ending in 's to say who something belongs to. For example, if someone says 'Whose is this coat?', you might say 'It's **my mother's**'.

One of the cars was his wife's.

You do not use this construction in formal writing. Instead you use **belong to**. You also use **belong to** when you are using several words to refer to someone. For example, you say 'It **belongs to** the man next door'. You do not say 'It is the man next door's'.

The painting belongs to a man living in Norfolk.

other uses of 's Apart from its use in possessives, **'s** has three other uses:

It is used as a shortened form of 'is', especially after pronouns.

He's a novelist.
It's fantastic.
There's no hurry.

It is used as a shortened form of 'has' when 'has' is an auxiliary verb.

He's got a problem.
She's gone home.

It is used as a shortened form of 'us' after 'let'.

Let's go outside.

For more information about this use, see entry at **let's - let us**.

sack

A **sack** is a large container made of rough woven material. Sacks are used to carry and store things such as potatoes and coal.

'bag' You do not use **sack** to refer to a small container made of paper, or to a container with handles for putting shopping or personal possessions in. Containers like these are called **bags**. See entry at **bag**.

'pocket' You also do not use **sack** to refer to the parts of your clothes in which you carry money and other small articles. These parts are called **pockets**.

sad

See entry at **happy - sad**.

safe

See entry at **save - safe**.

salad - lettuce

'salad' A **salad** is a mixture of uncooked vegetables. You can eat it on its own or with other foods.

'lettuce' A salad usually includes the large green leaves of a vegetable called a **lettuce** /letɪs/. Note that you do not refer to this vegetable as a 'salad'.

salary - wages

Salary and **wages** are both used to refer to the money paid to someone regularly for the work they do.

'salary'   Professional people such as teachers are usually paid a **salary.** Their **salary** is the amount of money which they are paid each year, although they actually get a certain amount each month.

She earns a high salary as an accountant.

'wages'   If someone gets money each week for the work they do, you refer to this money as their **wages.**

His wages had been reduced to seventy pounds a week.

'wage'   You can refer in a general way to the amount that someone earns as a **wage.**

...the problems of bringing up children on a low wage.
They're campaigning for a legal minimum wage.

sale

The **sale** of something is the act of selling it, or the occasion on which it is sold.

One such measure was stricter control of the sale of dynamite.
...the sale of the Elliotdale property.

A **sale** is an event in which a shop sells things at a reduced price.

Debenhams are having a sale.

'for sale'   If something is **for sale** or **up for sale,** its owner is trying to sell it.

I enquired if the horse was for sale.
Their house is up for sale.

'on sale'   A product that is **on sale** is available for people to buy.

The only English newspaper on sale was the Morning Star.
Colonel Crockett's new book will be on sale this summer.

In American English, if you buy something **on sale,** you buy it at a reduced price, for example in a sale.

On sale. Slacks marked down from $39.95 to $20.00.

salute

When members of the armed forces **salute** someone, they raise their right hand as a formal sign of greeting or respect.

'greet'   Note that this is the only way in which the verb **salute** is used in modern English. You do not use **salute** to say that someone expresses friendliness or pleasure when they meet someone else. The word you use is **greet.**

He greeted his mother with a hug.
He hurried to greet his guests.

same - similar

Same is almost always used with 'the'.

'the same'   If two things are **the same,** they are exactly alike.

Both categories may be present and both may look the same.
The distances aren't necessarily the same.

'the same as'   You say that one thing is **the same as** another thing.

It is really just the same as any other police work.
24 Springburn Terrace was the same as its neighbours.

Note that you do not use any preposition except 'as' after **the same** in sentences like these.

You can put a noun between **the same** and **as**. You can say, for example, 'She works in **the same office as** her sister'.

It was the same colour as the wall.
They're not in the same position as the other universities.

You can also use **the same as** to compare actions. For example, you can say 'She did **the same as** her sister did', or just 'She did **the same as** her sister'.

He did exactly the same as John did.
They've got to do their housekeeping the same as anybody else.

'the same...that'
You can also use a 'that'-clause after **the same** and a noun.

He had the same stare that the rest of the marines had.
After the news they heard the same voice that Rodin had heard in 1940.

modifiers used
with 'the same'
You can use words like 'exactly' and 'nearly' in front of **the same.**

I had the impression that on the far side the view would be exactly the same.
This is practically the same as on the previous sheet.

'similar'
If two people or things are **similar,** each one has some features which the other one has.

The two men were remarkably similar.
The letters are basically very similar.

You say that one thing is **similar to** another thing.

It is similar to the rest of the field.
Do you run programmes similar to that overseas?

You can use **similar** in front of a noun when you are comparing a person or thing to someone or something else that has just been mentioned.

Many of today's adults have had a similar experience.

modifiers used
with 'similar'
You can use words like 'rather' and 'very' with **similar.**

His own background was rather similar to my own.
My problems are very similar to yours.

satisfactory

You say that something is **satisfactory** when it is acceptable or fulfils a particular need or purpose.

His doctor described his state of health as fairly satisfactory.
It's not a satisfactory system.

'satisfying'
You do not use **satisfactory** to describe something that gives you a feeling of pleasure and fulfilment. The word you use is **satisfying.**

There's nothing more satisfying than doing the work you love.
It's wonderful to have a satisfying hobby.

satisfied

If you are **satisfied with** something, you are pleased with it, because it is what you wanted.

Children at this age are satisfied with simple answers.
Are you satisfied with the pay structure in your company?

You do not use any preposition except 'with' in sentences like these.

You can use adverbs such as 'well' and 'completely' in front of **satisfied**.

He was well satisfied with the success of the aircraft.
They seemed quite satisfied with their machines.

Several other words can be used to show how pleased or disappointed someone is with something. For a graded list, see entry at **pleased - disappointed.**

save - safe

'save' **Save** /seɪv/ is a verb. If you **save** someone, you rescue them from danger or death.

He risked death to save his small daughter from a fire.

If you **save** money, you gradually collect it by not spending it.

They had managed to save enough to buy a house.

'safe' **Safe** /seɪf/ is an adjective. If you are **safe** from something, you cannot be harmed by it.

We're safe now. They've gone.

Note that when **safe** is used to describe people, you do not use it in front of a noun.

savings

See entry at **economics.**

say

When you **say** something, you use your voice to produce words. The past tense and past participle of 'say' is **said** /sed/, not 'sayed'.

You use **say** when you are quoting directly the words that someone has spoken.

'I've never felt so relaxed,' she said.
'Listen, Rudy,' he said, 'I'm not getting any younger.'
He said, 'Gertrude, I'm an awful liar.'

In writing, you can use many other verbs instead of **say** when you are quoting someone's words (see entry at **Reporting**). However, in speech you always use **say**. In speech, you mention the person whose words you are quoting first.

I said, 'Can I speak to Anna?'
She said, 'Just drop me a postcard when you're coming.'

You can use 'it' after **said** to refer to the words a person used when they said something. For example, you can say 'Jane said, "I'm going now." She **said it** very quietly'.

He hadn't said it very nicely.
I just said it for something to say.

However, if you are referring to what someone has expressed rather than their actual words, you use **so**, not 'it'. For example, you say 'I didn't agree with him and I **said so**'. You do not say 'I didn't agree with him and I said it'.

It is all quite unnecessary, but nobody dare say so, of course.
Why didn't you say so earlier?

If you say so, I suppose I'll have to accept it.

You can report what someone has said without mentioning their exact words using **say** and a 'that'-clause.

Officials said that at least one soldier had been killed.
The woman said Mr Calthrop had left some days before.

'tell'   If you are mentioning the hearer as well as the speaker, you usually use **tell**, rather than 'say'. The past tense and past participle of 'tell' is **told**.

So, for example, instead of saying 'I said to him that his mother had arrived', you say 'I **told** him that his mother had arrived'.

He told me that he had once studied chemistry.
'He has the ability to run a business,' one financial analyst told me.

Similarly, if you want to mention who an order or instruction was given to, you use **tell**, not 'say'.

She told me to be careful.
I was told to sit on the front bench.

You say that someone **tells** a story, lie, or joke.

You're telling lies now.
Mr Crosby, the organist, told jokes and stories.

Note that you can also say that someone **makes** or **cracks** a joke. However, the meaning is not the same. See entry at **joke**.

You do not say that someone 'says' a story, lie, or joke.

'ask'   You do not say that someone 'says' a question. You say that they **ask** a question.

Jill began to ask Fred a lot of questions about his childhood.

'give'   You do not say that someone 'says' an order or instruction. You say that they **give** an order or instruction.

He gave an order for special food to be brought to Harold.
The Duke had given instructions that everything possible should be done to help them.

'call'   If you want to say that someone describes someone else in a particular way, you can use **say** followed by a 'that'-clause. For example, you can say 'He **said** that I was a liar'. A simpler way is to use **call**. You say 'He **called** me a liar'.

President Nixon called his opponents traitors.

'talk about'   You do not use **say** to mention what someone is discussing. You do not say, for example, 'He said about the customs of the Incas'. You say 'He **talked about** the customs of the Incas'.

He talked about the pleasures and problems of adopting children.

scarce - scarcely

'scarce'   **Scarce** is an adjective. If something that people use is **scarce**, very little of it is available.

Good quality land is scarce.
...a place where water is scarce.

'rare'   You do not use **scarce** to say that something is not common, and is therefore interesting. The adjective you use is **rare**.

...a flower so rare that few botanists have ever seen it.
Diane's hobby is collecting rare books.

'scarcely'   **Scarcely** is an adverb. It has a totally different meaning from **scarce.** You use **scarcely** to say that something is only just the case. **Scarcely** is a fairly formal word.

...side-alleys scarcely wide enough for a cat to turn round.
It was a very young man who had said this, scarcely more than a boy.

    You do not use 'not' with **scarcely.** You do not say, for example, 'I am not scarcely able to earn a living'. You say 'I am **scarcely** able to earn a living'.

If you use an auxiliary or modal with **scarcely,** you put the auxiliary or modal first. You say, for example, 'I **could scarcely** stand'. You do not say 'I scarcely could stand'.

I can scarcely remember what we ate.
There could scarcely be a less promising environment.

Scarcely is sometimes used in longer structures to say that one thing happened immediately after another.

The noise had scarcely died away when someone started to laugh again.

Note that you use **when,** not 'than', in sentences like these. You do not say, for example, 'The noise had scarcely died away than someone started to laugh again'.

In stories, **scarcely** is sometimes put at the beginning of a sentence, followed by 'had' and the subject.

Scarcely had the car drawn to a halt when armed police surrounded it.

scene - sight

'scene'   The noun **scene** has several meanings.

It can refer to a part of a play, film, or novel.

...the balcony scene from 'Romeo and Juliet'.
It was like some scene from a Victorian novel.

The **scene** of an accident or crime is the place where it happened.

They were only a few miles from the scene of the crime.

You can indicate your impression of the things that are happening in a place at a particular time by referring to them as a **scene** of a particular kind.

...a scene of domestic tranquillity.
The moon rose over a scene of extraordinary destruction.

'sight'   If you want to indicate your impression of the appearance of a particular thing or person, you use **sight.**

The room was a remarkable sight.
He was an awful sight.

Here are some other nouns that are commonly used to refer to things that people see:

'view'   If you want to refer to what you can see from a window or high place, the word you use is **view.**

The window of her flat looked out on to a superb view of London.
From the top there is a fine view.

'landscape'   If you want to describe what you can see around you when you are travelling through an area of land, the word you use is **landscape.** You can use this word whether the area is attractive or not.

The landscape seemed desolate.
...the industrial landscape of eastern Massachusetts.

'scenery' If you want to refer to what you see around you in an attractive part of the countryside, the word you use is **scenery.**

We had time to admire the scenery.

Note that **scenery** is an uncount noun. You do not talk about 'sceneries' or 'a scenery'.

sceptic - sceptical

'sceptic' **Sceptic** is a noun. A **sceptic** is someone who has doubts about things that other people believe.

The sceptic may argue that there are no grounds for such optimism.
Benn confounded the sceptics by winning thirty-seven votes in the leadership ballot.

'sceptical' **Sceptical** is an adjective. If you are **sceptical** about something, you have doubts about it.

Robert's father was sceptical about hypnotism.
At first Meyer had been sceptical.

The usual American spellings of 'sceptic' and 'sceptical' are **skeptic** and **skeptical.**

scheme - schedule

'scheme' A **scheme** is a plan, usually invented by one person, for achieving something.

…some scheme for perfecting the world.
He had a crazy scheme to corner the champagne market.

In British English, a **scheme** is also a large-scale plan produced by a government or other organization.

…the State pension scheme.
…training schemes.

'schedule' A **schedule** is a plan that gives a list of events and indicates when and in what order they will take place. **Schedule** is pronounced /ʃedjuːl/ or /skedjuːl/ in British English, but only /skedjuːl/ in American English.

…the next place on his busy schedule.
…the launch schedules for the space shuttle.

'timetable' In American English, a **schedule** is also a list of the times when trains, buses, or boats depart or arrive. In British English, a list like this is called a **timetable.**

scholar

A **scholar** is a child or student who has obtained a **scholarship,** by which they obtain money for their studies from their school or university, or from some other organization.

…a Rhodes scholar.

A person who studies an academic subject and knows a lot about it is sometimes referred to as a **scholar.** This is a rather old-fashioned use.

…Benjamin Jowett, the theologian and Greek scholar.

In former times, any child attending a school could be referred to as a scholar, but the word is no longer used in this way. For a discussion of the words used in modern English, see entry at **student**.

school - university

used as count nouns In both British and American English, a **school** is a place where children are educated, and a **university** is a place where students study for degrees.

used as uncount nouns In American English, **school** (without 'a' or 'the') is used to refer to both schools and universities. If someone is attending a school or university, Americans say that they are **in school**.

All the children were in school.
She is doing well in school.

In British English, **school** refers only to schools. If someone is attending a school, British speakers say they are **at school**. If they are attending a university, British speakers say they are **at university**.

I was at school with her.
What do you want to do when you leave school?
Her one aim in life is to go to university.

See also entry at **student**.

scissors

Scissors are a small tool consisting of two sharp blades joined together. You use **scissors** for cutting things such as paper, cloth, or hair.

Scissors is a plural noun. You do not talk about 'a scissors'. Instead you talk about **some scissors** or **a pair of scissors**.

I wish I'd brought some scissors.
Have you got any scissors?
She took a pair of scissors and cut his hair.

search

Search is used as a verb or a noun.

used as a verb If you **search** a place or person, you examine them thoroughly because you are trying to find something.

Soldiers searched all houses near the embassy.
He stood with his arms outstretched while Fassler searched him.

You do not say that you 'search' the thing you are trying to find. You can say that you **search for** it, but you usually say that you **look for** it.

I was looking for a book.

used as a noun A **search** is an attempt to find something by looking for it carefully.

I found the keys after a long search.
...the search for oil.

seat

See entry at **sit**.

see

The verb **see** is used with several different meanings. Its past tense is **saw**, not 'seed'. Its past participle is **seen**.

<table>
<tr><td>using your eyes</td><td>If you **can see** something, you are aware of it through your eyes.</td></tr>
</table>

We can see the horizon now.

Note that you usually use **can** in sentences like these. You say, for example, 'I **can see** the sea'. You do not say 'I see the sea'. You also do not use a continuous tense. You do not say 'I am seeing the sea'.

If you want to say that someone was aware of something in this way in the past, you usually use **could see.**

He could see Wilson's face in the mirror.

If you want to say that someone became aware of something, you use **saw.**

We suddenly saw a vessel through a gap in the fog.

You can use an '-ing' form after **saw** or **could see** to indicate that someone was aware of something that was continuing to take place.

I saw Benjamin standing there patiently.
They could see the planes coming in over the fields.

You can use an infinitive without 'to' after **saw** to indicate that someone was aware of a complete event or action.

He saw the tears come to her eyes.
I saw Bogeslavski get to his feet.

WARNING	You do not use a 'to'-infinitive with an active form of **see.** You do not say, for example, 'I saw him to take the book'.

passive use	You can use a passive form of **see,** followed by either a 'to'-infinitive or an '-ing' form.

You use a 'to'-infinitive after a passive form when you are talking about a complete event or action.

One pilot was seen to bail out.

You use an '-ing' form when you are talking about an event or action that was continuing to take place.

Mr Humbert was seen eating his steak.

WARNING	Do not confuse **see** with **look at** or **watch.** For an explanation of the differences, see entry at **see - look at - watch.**

meeting someone	**See** is often used to mean 'visit' or 'meet by arrangement'.

It would be a good idea for you to see a doctor.

If two people are meeting each other regularly, for example because they are in love, you can say that they **are seeing** each other. When **see** has this meaning, it is usually used in a continuous tense.

Does he know we are seeing each other?

understanding	**See** is very commonly used to mean 'understand'.

I don't quite see how they can argue that.
He didn't seem to notice much, if you see what I mean.

People often say '**I see**' to show that they have understood something.

'Humbert is Dolly's real father.'—'I see.'

When **see** means 'understand', you can use 'can' or 'could' with it.

I can see why Mr Smith is worried.
I can't see how it can carry on at the same rate.

I could see his point.

You do not use a continuous tense when **see** means 'understand'. You do not say, for example, 'I am seeing what you mean'.

attending to something

If you **see** that something is done or **see to it** that it is done, you make sure that it is done, by getting someone else to do it or by doing it yourself.

See that everything is marked with your initials.
I'll see to it that there is some action.

When someone attends to something that needs attention, you can say that they **see to** it or **see about** it.

A man was there to see to our luggage.
Rudolph went into the station to see about Thomas's ticket.

see - look at - watch

'see'

When you **see** something, you are aware of it through your eyes, or you notice it.

We saw the black smoke rising over the barbed wire.
We suddenly saw a boat.

See entry at **see**.

'look at'

When you **look at** something, you direct your eyes towards it.

He looked at the food on his plate.
People looked at her in astonishment.

See entry at **look**.

'watch'

When you **watch** something, you pay attention to it using your eyes, because you are interested in what it is doing, or in what may happen.

He watched the newt with interest.

After **watch** you can use an infinitive without 'to' or you can use an '-ing' form. You use an infinitive without 'to' when you are referring to a complete event or action.

He watched her climb into a compartment.

You use an '-ing' form when you are referring to an action that was continuing to take place.

They watched Sheila driving around in her yellow car.

sightseeing

If you go somewhere in order to look at something or watch something, you can say that you go to **see** it.

He went to India to see the Taj Mahal.
We went to the zoo to see the giant pandas.

entertainment and sport

Both **see** and **watch** are used when you are talking about entertainment or sport.

When you go to the theatre or cinema, you say that you **see** a play or film.

I saw 'Dear Brutus' on its first night in 1917.
We saw Greta Garbo in 'Queen Christina'.

You do not say that someone 'looks at' or 'watches' a play or film.

You say that someone **watches** television. However, you can say that someone **watches** or **sees** a particular programme.

He spends several hours watching television.
...a rugby match he watched on television.
I saw it on television after the news.

Similarly you say that someone **watches** a sport such as football, but that they **watch** or **see** a particular match.

More people are watching cricket than ever before.
I'd sooner go out with a gun than watch a football match.
...those of us who saw England's defeat at Wrexham.

seek

If you **seek** something such as help, advice, or the solution to a problem, you try to obtain it.

I was seeking the help of someone who spoke French.
Thousands of people were seeking food and shelter.
The answers they seek are not forthcoming.

Note that you do not say that someone 'seeks for' something.

The past tense and past participle of 'seek' is **sought,** not 'seeked'.

Some units and formations sought the earliest opportunity to surrender.
His views on the war were sought by the American press.

Seek is often used in writing, but you do not normally use it in conversation. Instead of saying that someone 'seeks' something, you usually say that they **try to get** it or **try to find** it.

I tried to get their support for a trade union.
They tried to find other work.

In modern English, you never say that someone **seeks** a person or an object. You say that they **look for** the person or object.

I've been looking for you all over.
I looked for it for ages before I found it.

seem

You use **seem** to say that someone or something gives a particular impression.

used with adjectives

Seem is usually followed by an adjective. If someone gives the impression of being happy, you can say that they **seem** happy. You can also say that they **seem to be** happy. There is no difference in meaning.

Even minor problems seem important.
It seemed very unusual.

You seem to be very interested.
They seemed to be very good at reading.

However, if the adjective is a classifying adjective, you usually use **seem to be.** For example, you say 'He **seemed to be** alone'. You do not say 'He seemed alone'.

She seemed to be asleep.
The policemen seemed to be lost.

For an explanation of classifying adjectives, see entry at **Adjectives.**

If you want to indicate who has an impression of someone or something, you use **seem** followed by an adjective and the preposition 'to'.

He always seemed old to me.

Crook thought the proposition over; it seemed fair to him.
This attitude seemed nonsensical to the general public.

used with
noun groups

Instead of an adjective, you can use a noun group after **seem** or **seem to be**. For example, instead of saying 'She seemed nice', you can say 'She **seemed a nice person**' or 'She **seemed to be a nice person**'. In conversation, people often say 'She **seemed like a nice person**'.

It seemed a long time before the food came.
She seems to be a very nice girl.
It seemed like a good idea.

Note that you do not use 'as' after **seem**. You do not say, for example, 'It seemed as a good idea'.

If the noun group contains a determiner but not an adjective, you must use **seemed to be**. For example, you say 'He **seemed to be the owner** of the car'. You do not say 'He seemed the owner of the car'.

The parcel seemed to be a gift for our children.
What seems to be the trouble?

used with verbs

You can use other 'to'-infinitives besides 'to be' after **seem**. For example, you can say 'He **seemed to need** help'. You can also say '**It seemed that he needed** help' or '**It seemed as though he needed** help'.

The experiments seem to prove that sugar is not very good for you.
It did seem to me that she was far too romantic.
It seemed as though the war had ended.

seldom

Seldom is a formal or literary word. It is used to say that something happens only occasionally.

position in
clause

If there is no auxiliary, **seldom** usually goes in front of the verb, unless the verb is 'be'.

He seldom bathed.
It seldom rains there.

Seldom goes after 'be'.

The waiting time was seldom less than four hours.

If there are auxiliaries, **seldom** goes after the first one.

Students are seldom encouraged to analyze their own values.
The public can seldom distinguish between one actor and another.

Seldom is sometimes put at the beginning of a sentence, followed by an auxiliary and the subject.

Seldom did a week pass without a request for information.
Seldom can there have been such a happy meeting.

'hardly ever'

Seldom is not normally used in conversation. Instead people say **hardly ever**.

People are hardly ever fooled by that.
I must confess that I've hardly ever been to the British Museum.

For a graded list of words and expressions which are used to say how often something happens, see section on **frequency** in entry at **Adverbials**.

select

See entry at **choose**.

self-conscious

Someone who is **self-conscious** is easily embarrassed and worries about what other people think of them.

I stood there, feeling self-conscious.
Patrick is self-conscious about his thinness.

If someone is sure of their own abilities, qualities, or ideas, you do not say that they are 'self-conscious'. You say that they are **confident, self-confident,** or **self-assured.**

...a witty, young and confident lawyer.
She was remarkably self-confident for her age.
His comments were firm and self-assured.

semester

See entry at **term - semester.**

send - sent

Send and **sent** are different forms of the same verb. Because they sound similar, they are sometimes confused.

Send /send/ is the base form. If you **send** something to someone, you arrange for it to be taken and delivered to them, for example by post.

The children used to send me a card at Christmas.
Please send me the money.

Sent /sent/ is the past tense and past participle of **send.**

I drafted a letter and sent it to the President.
He had sent Axel a telegram.

sensible - sensitive

'sensible' A **sensible** person makes good decisions and judgements based on reason rather than emotion.

She considered they were sufficiently sensible and trustworthy to go into the village.

'sensitive' **Sensitive** has two meanings.

A **sensitive** person is easily upset or offended by other people's remarks or behaviour.

You really must stop being sensitive about your accent.
This may make a sensitive child tense and apprehensive.

However, if you say that someone is **sensitive to** other people's problems or feelings, you mean that they show understanding and awareness of them.

We're trying to make people more sensitive to the difficulties faced by working mothers.
He must have been extremely sensitive to the feelings of depression and futility that these men felt.

GRAMMAR # Sentences

A **sentence** is a group of words which expresses a statement, question, or order. A sentence usually has a verb and a subject. A **simple sentence** has one clause. A **compound sentence** or **complex sentence** has two or more clauses. See entry at **Clauses.**

Did you believe him?
I packed my gear and walked outside.
If it's four o'clock in the morning, don't expect them to be pleased to see you.

In writing, a sentence has a capital letter at the beginning and a full stop, question mark, or exclamation mark at the end. For more information, see entry at **Punctuation**.

incomplete sentences

In speech, it is possible to say something using a subordinate clause on its own, or a group of words which does not contain a verb. For example, if someone asks you when you are going home, you can say 'When I've finished' or 'This afternoon'.

Subordinate clauses and verbless groups of words are sometimes written as if they were sentences in informal letters, novels, and advertisements.

However, in any other kind of writing you should avoid writing these clauses and groups of words as if they were sentences.

serial

See entry at **cereal - serial**.

serious

You say that a problem or situation is **serious** when it is bad enough to make people worried or afraid.

Bad housing is one of the most serious problems in the inner cities.
...a serious illness.

Serious matters are important and deserve careful consideration.

It's time to get down to the serious business of the meeting.
I think this is a serious point.

People who are **serious** are thoughtful and quiet and do not often make jokes.

...a rather serious girl.

You can also describe someone's expression as **serious**.

She had a serious, thoughtful face.
Don't look so serious!

'serious about'

If someone is **serious about** doing something that they have talked about doing, they really intend to do it.

This would prove that we were serious about overcoming the obstacles.
They maintained that the West was not serious about achieving disarmament.

Note that you do not use any preposition except 'about' in sentences like these.

sew

See entry at **sow - sew**.

shadow - shade

'shadow' A **shadow** is a dark shape made on a surface when something stands between a light and the surface.

My shadow looked very long and thin.

If a place is dark because something prevents light from reaching it, you can say that it is **in shadow**.

The whole canyon is in shadow.

'shade' You refer to an area which is dark and cool because the sun cannot reach it as **the shade**.

They sat in the shade between the palms.
I moved my chair into the shade.

shall - will

Shall and **will** are used to make statements and ask questions about the future.

Shall and **will** are not usually pronounced in full when they come after a pronoun. When you write down what someone says, you usually represent **shall** or **will** as 'll and add it to the end of the pronoun.

He'll come back.
They'll spoil our picnic.
That'll be all right.

Shall and **will** have the negative forms **shall not** and **will not**. In speech, these are usually shortened to **shan't** /ʃɑːnt/ and **won't** /wəʊnt/.

I shan't ever do it again.
You won't hear much about it.
Won't you come back?

It used to be considered correct to write **shall** after 'I' or 'we', and **will** after any other pronoun or noun group. However, most people now write **will** after 'I' and 'we', and this is not regarded as incorrect.

I'm afraid I will laugh.
We will be able to defend them.

You do not use **shall** after any pronoun except 'I' or 'we'. You also do not use **shall** after a noun group. It used to be considered correct to use **shall** to express an intention or promise. For example, people used to say 'I'm sorry I haven't returned the book you lent me. You **shall** have it back tomorrow'. However, this use now sounds old-fashioned. In modern English, people say 'You **will** have it back tomorrow'.

You will have no further trouble.
You will hear nothing from me again.

There are a few special cases in which you use **shall**, rather than 'will':

suggestions You can make a suggestion about what you and someone else should do by asking a question beginning with '**Shall we…**'.

Shall we go and see a film?
Shall we talk about something different?

You can also suggest what you and someone else should do by using a sentence which begins with '**Let's…**' and ends with '**…shall we?**'

Let's try out one for size, shall we?

asking for advice	You can use **shall I** or **shall we** when you are asking for suggestions or advice.

What shall I give them for dinner?
Where shall we go for our drink?

offering You can say '**Shall I...**' when you are offering to do something.

Shall I shut the door?
Shall I tell them to send the bill to you up here?

Will also has some special uses:

requests You can use **will you** to make a request.

Will you please let me know which pair of shoes this bitumen was found on?
Don't let this out, will you, Dixon?

See entry at **Requests, orders, and instructions**.

invitations You can also use **will you** or the negative form **won't you** to make an invitation. **Won't you** is very polite.

Will you stay to lunch?
Won't you sit down, Inspector?
Glad to meet you, Mrs Swallow. Won't you take off your coat?

See entry at **Invitations**.

ability **Will** is sometimes used to say that someone or something is able to do something.

This will cure anything.
The car won't go.

WARNING You do not normally use **shall** or **will** in clauses beginning with words and expressions such as 'when', 'before', or 'as soon as'. You do not say, for example, 'I'll ring as soon as I shall get home'. Instead you use the simple present tense. You say 'I'll ring as soon as I **get** home'.

shave

When a man **shaves,** he cuts hair from his face using a razor.

When he had shaved and dressed, he went down to the kitchen.

Shave is not usually used as a reflexive verb. You do not normally say that a man 'shaves himself'.

In conversation, you usually say that a man **has a shave,** rather than that he 'shaves'.

I can't remember when I last had a shave.

she

She is used as the subject of a verb. You use **she** to refer to a woman, girl, or female animal that has already been mentioned, or whose identity is known.

'So long,' Mary said as she passed Miss Saunders.
The eggs of the female mosquito can only mature if she has a meal of human blood.

When the subject of a sentence is followed by a relative clause, you do not use **she** in front of the main verb. You do not say, for example, 'The woman who lives next door, she is a doctor'. You say 'The woman who lives next door is a doctor'.

The woman who owns this cabin will come back in the autumn.

used to refer to things She is sometimes used instead of 'it' to refer to a country, ship, or car.

Acheson had said, in the course of a friendly appraisal of Britain, that <u>she</u> 'had lost an Empire and not yet found a role'.
When the repairs had been done <u>she</u> was a fine and beautiful ship.

sheep

A **sheep** is a farm animal with a thick woolly coat. The plural of 'sheep' is **sheep,** not 'sheeps'.

...six hundred <u>sheep</u>.
...a flock of <u>sheep</u>.

'lamb' The meat of a sheep is called **lamb.** The meat of an adult sheep used to be called **mutton,** but this word is no longer used.

ship

See entry at **boat - ship.**

shooting

See entry at **hunting - shooting.**

shop - store

In British English, a building or part of a building where goods are sold is usually called a **shop.** In American English, it is called a **store,** unless it is very small and has just one type of goods, in which case it is called a **shop.**

In British English, very large shops are sometimes called **stores.**

In both British and American English, a large shop which has separate departments selling different types of goods is called a **department store.**

'shop' used as a verb **Shop** can also be used as a verb. When people **shop,** they go to shops and buy things.

I usually <u>shop</u> on Saturdays.

However, you usually say that someone **goes shopping,** rather than that they 'shop'.

They <u>went shopping</u> after lunch.

'shopping' **Shopping** is often used as a noun. It has two meanings. It can refer to the activity of buying things from shops.

I don't like <u>shopping</u>.

It can also refer to the things that someone has just bought from a shop or shops.

She put her <u>shopping</u> away in the kitchen.

Shopping is an uncount noun. You do not talk about 'a shopping' or someone's 'shoppings'.

When someone goes to the shops to buy things that they need regularly such as food, you say that they **do the shopping** or **do their shopping.**

Who's going to <u>do the shopping</u>?
She went to the next town to <u>do her shopping</u>.

shore

See entry at **beach - shore - coast.**

short - shortly

'short' **Short** is an adjective. You usually use it to indicate that something does not last for a long time.

...a short holiday.
He uttered a short cry of surprise.

'shortly' **Shortly** is an adverb. If something is going to happen **shortly**, it is going to happen soon. This is a slightly old-fashioned use.

She's going to London shortly.
They should be returning shortly.

If something happened **shortly** after something else, it happened soon after it.

She died shortly afterwards.
Very shortly after I joined the church, I became a preacher.

'briefly' You do not use **shortly** to say that something lasts or is done for a short time. You do not say, for example, 'She told them shortly what had happened'. The word you use is **briefly.**

She told them briefly what had happened.

shorts

See entry at **pants - shorts.**

should

Should is sometimes used with a similar meaning to 'ought to' and sometimes with a similar meaning to 'would'. See separate entries at **should - ought to** and **should - would.**

The following are some less common uses of **should.** When **should** is used in any of these ways, you pronounce it in full and you do not write it as **'d.** (See entry at **should - would.**)

'should' in subordinate clauses **Should** is sometimes used in subordinate clauses, especially in writing. You use it in 'that'-clauses after verbs like 'propose' and 'suggest'.

He proposes that the Government should hold an inquiry.
It was definite enough for a doctor to advise that she should have treatment.

Note that you can omit **should** and use the base form of the verb on its own. This is a rather formal use.

Someone suggested that they break into small groups.

In formal English, **should** is sometimes used in conditional clauses.

If anyone should come this way, we would be caught like rats in a trap.

In a sentence like this, **should** can be put at the beginning of the clause, followed by the subject.

Should ministers decide to instigate an inquiry, we would welcome it.

In conversation and most kinds of writing, it is not necessary to use **should** in this kind of clause. You just use the simple present tense. For example, instead of saying 'If he should come, we will talk to him', you say 'If he **comes,** we will talk to him'.

requests and offers When you are making a formal request or offer, you can use **should** in a conditional sentence.

I should be obliged if you would send them to me.
If you know of a better method, I should be delighted to try it.

should - ought to

announcements You can use **should** with 'like' when you are formally announcing that you are going to do something.

I should like to quote a few instructions from this manual.
We should like to make the following proposals.

should - ought to

Should and **ought to** are sometimes used with similar meanings. When **should** has a similar meaning to **ought to,** you pronounce it in full and you do not write it as 'd. (See entry at **should - would**.)

Should and **ought to** have the negative forms **should not** and **ought not to**. The 'not' is not usually pronounced in full. When you write down what someone says, you write **shouldn't** or **oughtn't to**.

expectation You use **should** or **ought to** to say that you expect something to happen.

We should be there by dinner time.
It ought to get better as it goes along.

You use **should** or **ought to** with 'have' to say that you expect something to have happened already.

Dear Mom, you should have heard by now that I'm O.K.

You also use **should** or **ought to** with 'have' to say that something was expected to happen, but did not happen.

Two bags which should have gone to Rome were at this moment being loaded aboard a flight to Milwaukee.
The brandy I'd swallowed ought to have knocked me silly.

Note that you must use 'have' and a past participle in sentences like these. You do not say, for example, 'The brandy I'd swallowed ought to knock me silly'.

moral rightness You use **should** or **ought to** to say that something is morally right.

Crimes should be punished.
Aid should not be tied to the purchase of goods from the donor country.

I ought to call the police.
We ought to be doing something about it.

giving advice You can say **you should** or **you ought to** when you are giving someone advice.

I think you should get in touch with your solicitor.
You shouldn't keep eggs in the refrigerator.
I think you ought to try a different approach.

should - would

Should and **would** are often used with similar meanings.

When **would** comes after a pronoun, it is not usually pronounced in full. When **should** has a similar meaning to **would**, it, too, is not usually pronounced in full after a pronoun. When you write down what someone says, you represent **should** or **would** as 'd and add it to the end of the pronoun.

Should and **would** have the negative forms **should not** and **would not**. The 'not' is not usually pronounced in full. When you write down what someone says, you write **shouldn't** or **wouldn't**.

626

possible situations You use **should** or **would** to say that something is certain to happen in particular circumstances.

After 'I' or 'we' you can use either **should** or **would**.

I should be very unhappy on the continent.
We would be glad to have money of our own.
If I were Tim, I'd be a bit uneasy.

After any other pronoun or noun, you use **would**. You do not use **should**.

Few people would agree with this as a general principle.
He would be disappointed, but he would understand.

wishes and requests You can express a wish by using **I should like** or **I would like**.

I should like to live in the country.
...a course of action I would like to follow.
I'd like to be able to help in some way.

You can say what you do not want by using **I shouldn't like** or **I wouldn't like.**

I shouldn't like Amanda to see more of him than is absolutely unavoidable.
I wouldn't like to see that banned.

You can state a preference by using **I would rather** or **I would sooner.**

I would rather stay at home.
I'd rather work in a department store.
I'd sooner walk than do any of these things.

Note that you do not say 'I should rather' or 'I should sooner'.

You can make a request by using **I should like** or **I would like.**

I should like a large cutlet, please.
I would like to ask you one question.
I'd like to have a little talk with you.

You can mention other people's wishes or requests by using **would like.**

They would like to interview both ladies.
Is there anything special you would like for dinner?

You do not use 'should like' when you are mentioning other people's wishes or requests. You do not say, for example, 'He should like to see you'.

purpose clauses **Should** and **would** are sometimes used in purpose clauses. **Should** is only used after 'I' or 'we'.

I bought six cows so that we should have some milk to sell.

shout

When you **shout,** you speak as loudly as you can.

The children on the sand were shouting with excitement.
'Stop it!' he shouted.

'shout to' If you **shout to** someone who is a long way away, you speak very loudly so that they can hear you.

'What are you doing down there?' he shouted to Robin.
Our sergeant shouted to a battalion of soldiers carrying guns: 'The war's over!'

'shout at' If you speak very loudly to someone who is near to you, for example because you are angry with them, you do not say that you 'shout to' them. You say that you **shout at** them.

Jefferson shouted at him, 'Get in! Get in!'
She shouted at us for spoiling her lovely evening.

You can use a 'to'-infinitive with **shout to** or **shout at**. If you **shout to** someone **to do** something, or **shout at** them **to do** it, you tell them to do it by shouting at them.

An officer shouted to us to stop all the noise.
She shouted at him to speak up.

show

See entry at **indicate - show**.

shrink

If something **shrinks,** it becomes smaller.

Sometimes the rains fail and the rivers shrink or dry up.
I wondered if people really did shrink with age.

'shrank'   The past tense of 'shrink' is **shrank,** not 'shrinked' or 'shrunk'.

Several other East African lakes shrank dramatically at about the same time.
If demand for a commodity increased, or the supply shrank, then the price went up.

'shrunk'   The past participle is **shrunk.**

Their workforce of 25,000 has shrunk to 8,000.

'shrunken'   **Shrunken** is an adjective, used in front of a noun. A **shrunken** thing or person has become smaller.

...old women selling shrunken baboon heads.
...a shrunken old man.

shut

See entry at **close - closed - shut**.

sick

A **sick** person has an illness or some other problem with their health.

...a sick baby.
He still looked sick.

See entry at **ill - sick**.

'be sick'   To **be sick** means to bring up food through your mouth from your stomach.

I think I'm going to be sick.
He was kneeling by the lavatory being violently sick.

Note that 'George is being sick' means 'George is bringing up food from his stomach'; 'George is sick' means 'George is ill'. However, 'George was sick' can mean either 'George brought up food from his stomach' or 'George was ill'.

'vomit'   **Vomit** has the same meaning as 'be sick'. **Vomit** is a fairly formal word.

She was stricken with pain and began to vomit.

'throw up'   In conversation, some people say **throw up** instead of 'be sick'.

I think I'm going to throw up.

'feel sick'   To **feel sick** means to feel that you want to be sick.

Flying always makes me feel sick.

sight

See entry at **scene - sight**.

sightseeing

Sightseeing is the activity of travelling around a city or region to see the interesting places that tourists usually visit.

...a two-week tour, allowing some time in all the major cities for sightseeing.

Sightseeing is an uncount noun. You do not talk about 'sightseeings' or 'a sightseeing'. However, you can talk about a **sightseeing trip**.

I took a sightseeing trip on one of those tourist buses.

You can also say that someone **goes sightseeing** or **does some sightseeing**.

Vita and Violet went sightseeing.
I decided to do some sightseeing.

sign

When you **sign** a document, you write your name on it. You do this to show, for example, that you have written the document or that you agree with what it says.

I was in the act of signing a traveller's cheque.
...an order signed by the Home Secretary.

You can also say that someone **signs** their name.

Sign your name in the book each time you use the photocopier.

'signature'   However, when you write your name, you do not refer to what you write as your 'sign'. You call it your **signature**.

Nino scrawled his signature on the bottom of the slip.
Petitions bearing nearly a half-million signatures were sent to the White House.

silken - silky

Silken and **silky** are both used to say that something is smooth and soft like silk. **Silken** is a literary word.

...silken hair.
...fine silky skin.

'silk'   If you want to say that something is made out of silk, you use **silk** in front of a noun. You do not use 'silken' or 'silky'.

...a white silk scarf.

similar

See entry at **same - similar**.

since

You use **since** to say that something has been the case from a particular time in the past until now.

It's been on my desk since 1959.
I've been wearing glasses since I was three.

Note that in these sentences you use a perfect tense with **since.** You do not say 'It is on my desk since 1959' or 'I am wearing glasses since I was three'.

You can also use **since** to say how long ago something happened. When you use **since** like this, you use a simple tense. For example, instead of saying 'I last saw him five years ago', you can say 'It's five years **since** I last saw him'.

It's three months since you were here last.
It's years since I saw a photo of him.

'for'   However, if you want to say how long something has been the case, you use **for,** not 'since'.

We've been married for seven years.

See entry at **for.**

'during'   If you want to mention how long something has been happening, you use
and 'over'   **during** or **over.**

A considerable amount of rain has fallen during the past two years.
Things have become noticeably worse over the past two or three months.

See entries at **during** and **over.**

'from ... to'   If you want to mention when something began and finished, you use **from** and **to.**

...Thomas Jefferson, the President of the United States from 1801 to 1809.

Instead of 'to', you can use **till** or **until.**

...from nine in the morning till 5 p.m.

Note that you do not use **since** and **to.** You do not say, for example, 'the President of the United States since 1801 to 1809'.

used to mean   **Since** can also be used to mean 'because'.
'because'
Aircraft noise is a particular problem here since we're close to Heathrow Airport.

See entry at **because.**

GRAMMAR   # Singular and plural

The **singular** is the form of a count noun or a verb which you use when referring to one person or thing. The **plural** is the form which you use when referring to more than one person or thing. For details of these forms, see entries at **Plural forms of nouns** and **Verbs.** There are also singular and plural pronouns: see entry at **Pronouns.**

agreement   A possessive determiner or an adjective in a noun group has the same
within   form whether the noun is singular or plural. However, the determiner 'this'
noun group   has the plural form 'these' and the determiner 'that' has the plural form
'those'.

Some progress has already been made toward alleviating this problem.
I thought about these problems all the way home.

That person has been following us all day.
For those people, however, there was no going back.

Some general determiners, such as 'each', are only used with singular count nouns; some, such as 'all', are only used with uncount nouns or plural forms of nouns; and some, such as 'several', are only used with plural forms of nouns. See entry at **Quantity**.

agreement of verb with noun group

When you use a verb in a statement or question, you must choose a singular verb form or a plural verb form to agree with the subject.

My mother hates her.
They hate each other.

However, with all verbs except 'be', only one form is used for the simple past tense, and modals only have one form, so in these cases no choice needs to be made.

Rudolph walked slowly back towards the store.
They walked towards the gate.

Power must be shared.
All these questions must be given answers.

You also have to choose an appropriate verb form when using 'there' followed by 'be'. The verb form agrees with the noun group after 'be'.

There was a car parked there.
There were no cars outside.

use of singular verb form

The singular form of a verb is used with:

- the singular form of count nouns

- uncount nouns

- 'he', 'she', and 'it'

- 'this' and 'that'

- indefinite pronouns such as 'anybody', 'no-one', and 'something'

- noun groups referring to a single quantity of something, such as 'a lump of sugar' or 'a kilo of coffee'

Note that when you are referring to a period of time or an amount of something, you use a singular verb, even though you are using the plural form of a noun.

Twenty years is a long time.
Three hundred pounds is missing from club funds.

use of plural verb form

The plural form of a verb is used with:

- the plural form of count nouns

- plural nouns such as 'clothes' and 'goods'

- 'we' and 'they'

- 'you', even when referring to just one person

- 'these' and 'those'

- pronouns such as 'several' and 'many'

- quantifiers such as 'a couple of' and 'few of'

See entry at **Quantity** for information on quantifiers and other words indicating quantity.

Note that the form of a verb used with 'I' is usually the same as the plural form. However, if the verb is 'be', you use 'am' for the simple present tense and 'was' for the simple past tense.

I like working.
I have a lot of sympathy for them.

I am not ashamed of that.
I was so cold.

Some plural forms of count nouns do not look plural because they do not end in 's'. However, they are still used with a plural verb form. See entry at **Plural forms of nouns.**

All men are equal.

On the other hand, some nouns that end in 's' and look plural are uncount nouns and are used with a singular verb form. See section on **uncount nouns** in entry at **Nouns.**

Mathematics is too difficult for me.

A small group of plural nouns refer to single items that have two linked parts, such as 'jeans', 'trousers', and 'scissors'. They are used with the plural form of a verb. See section on **plural nouns** in entry at **Nouns.**

These scissors are sharp.

However, when you want to refer to one of these items using 'a pair of' you can use a singular or plural verb form. See entry at **pair - couple.**

In the case of **collective nouns** such as 'family' and 'government', you can use a singular or a plural verb form after the singular form of the noun. See section on **collective nouns** in entry at **Nouns.**

sink

If something **sinks**, it moves slowly downwards. **Sink** is especially used to say that something moves downwards below the surface of water.

The boat was sinking.

To **sink** a ship means to cause it to sink.

The submarine was ordered to intercept the damaged ship and sink her by torpedo.

'sank' The past tense of 'sink' is **sank,** not 'sunk' or 'sinked'.

The aircraft carrier blew up and sank at once.
The boat sank to the bottom of the lake.

'sunk' The past participle is **sunk.**

The leading craft was sunk almost immediately by the artillery.

'sunken' **Sunken** is an adjective, used in front of a noun. You use it to describe things which have sunk to the bottom of the sea or a lake.

...the remains of a sunken battleship.

sit

describing a movement When you **sit** or **sit down,** you lower your body until your bottom is resting on something. The past tense and past participle of 'sit' is **sat,** not 'sitted'.

You usually use **sit** rather than 'sit down' when you mention the place where someone gets into this position.

A strange woman came and sat next to her.
She lurched into the room and sat heavily on the settee.

Sit on this chair, please.

If you are not mentioning the place, you use sit **down**.

She sat down and poured herself a cup of tea.
She placed the music on the piano and sat down.

saying where
someone is

If you **are sitting** somewhere, your bottom is resting on something such as a chair. Note that in standard English you do not say that someone 'is sat' somewhere.

They are sitting at their desks.
She was sitting on the edge of the bed.

prepositions
used with 'sit'

You usually say that someone **sits on** something.

Jack and Frances are sitting on the steps.
We were sitting on hard little chairs.

However, you say that someone **sits in** an armchair.

He was sitting quietly in his armchair, smoking a pipe.

When someone is sitting close to a desk or table, for example because they are writing or eating, you say that they are **sitting at** the desk or table.

I was sitting at my desk reading.
We don't like them sitting at the tables in their pyjamas.

another
meaning
of 'sit'

If you **sit** an exam, you take part in it.

All of them will eventually sit an exam involving knowledge of Shakespeare's works.

See entry at **exam - examination**.

'seat'

Do not confuse **sit** /sɪt/ with **seat** /siːt/. A **seat** is an object that you can sit on.

The girl in the next seat was watching him.
I had a reserved seat from Holland to Denmark.

In stories, **seat** is sometimes used as a reflexive verb. If you **seat yourself** somewhere, you sit down.

'Thank you,' she said, seating herself on the sofa.

If you **are seated** somewhere, you are sitting there.

General Tomkins was seated behind his desk.

size

For information on how to state the **size** of something, see entry at **Measurements**.

skeptic - skeptical

See entry at **sceptic - sceptical**.

skid

See entry at **slide**.

skilful - skilled - talented

'skilful'

Someone who is **skilful** at something does it very well.

...a skilful hunter.
The girl had grown more skilful with the sewing-machine.

Skilful is spelled **skillful** in American English.

'skilled' You use **skilled** in front of a noun to describe someone who has been trained to do a particular kind of work and does it very well.

A skilled engineer takes four years to train.
...hand-made items produced by skilled craftsmen.

You also use **skilled** in front of a noun to describe work that can only be done by a skilled person.

Wood turning is skilled work.
The safe removal of asbestos is a highly skilled job.

'talented' You use **talented** to describe someone who has a natural ability to do something.

...a talented writer.
...a beautiful and talented actress.

You can also use **talented** to describe someone who is naturally good at doing several things.

...talented children.
The whole family was so talented.

skinny

See entry at **thin**.

sleep - asleep

'sleep' **Sleep** is used as a noun or a verb. The past tense and past participle of the verb is **slept**, not 'sleeped'.

Sleep is the natural state of rest in which you are unconscious with your eyes closed.

I need a lot of sleep.
I haven't been getting enough sleep recently.

To **sleep** means to be in this state of rest.

He was so excited he could hardly sleep.
I had not slept or eaten for three days.

'asleep' You do not usually use the verb **sleep** simply to say that someone is in this state. You do not say, for example, 'Gordon sleeps' or 'Gordon is sleeping'. You say 'Gordon **is asleep**'.

He hoped she was asleep.
All the other men were asleep.

You use **sleep** in more complex statements, for example to say how long someone was in this state, or to talk about a regular occurrence.

She slept till ten in the morning.
He slept on the kitchen floor.

WARNING **Asleep** is only used after a verb. You do not use it in front of a noun. You do not, for example, talk about an 'asleep child'. Instead you use **sleeping**.

I glanced down at the sleeping figure.

You do not say that someone is 'very asleep' or 'completely asleep'. Instead you say that they are **sound asleep**, **fast asleep**, or **deeply asleep**.

Chris is still sound asleep in the other bed.
Colette had been fast asleep when he left her.
Miss Haynes was very deeply asleep.

'go to sleep'	When someone changes from being awake to being asleep, you say that they **go to sleep**.

They had both gone to sleep.
Now go to sleep and stop worrying about it.

'fall asleep'	When someone goes to sleep suddenly or unexpectedly, you say that they **fall asleep**.

The moment my head touched the pillow I fell asleep.

'get to sleep'	When someone goes to sleep with difficulty, for example because they are in a noisy place or because they are worried about something, you say that they **get to sleep**.

Could you turn that radio down – I'm trying to get to sleep.
I couldn't get to sleep until six in the morning.

'go back to sleep'	When someone goes to sleep again after being woken up, you say that they **go back to sleep**.

Frank said 'Yes', and went back to sleep.

'send...to sleep'	If something causes you to sleep, you say that it **sends** you **to sleep**.

I brought him a hot drink, hoping it would send him to sleep.

slide

When something **slides,** it moves smoothly over a surface.

Susan stared at the drops sliding down the glass.

The past tense and past participle of 'slide' is **slid,** not 'slided'.

The gate slid open at the push of a button.

'skid'	You do not use **slide** to describe the movement of a vehicle when its wheels move sideways on a wet or icy road. The word you use is **skid**.

The car moved forward, skidding on the loose snow.
We skidded into the ditch.

slightly

See section on **degree** in entry at **Adverbials,** and section on **submodifiers** in entry at **Adverbs.**

slim

See entry at **thin.**

small - large

The following adjectives are used to indicate how small or large something is. They are arranged from 'smallest' to 'largest'.

- ▶ microscopic, infinitesimal
- ▶ tiny, minute, miniature, diminutive, minuscule
- ▶ small, little
- ▶ medium-sized, average-sized
- ▶ large, big, great
- ▶ huge, enormous, massive
- ▶ vast, immense, gigantic, colossal

Note that the adjective **minute** is pronounced /maɪnjuːt/.

See also entries at **small - little** and **big - large - great.**

small - little

Small and **little** are both used to say that someone or something is not large. There are some important differences in the ways these words are used.

position in clause

Small can be used in front of a noun, or after a verb such as 'be'.

They escaped in small boats.
Portable computers need to be small.

Little is normally used only in front of nouns. You can talk about 'a **little** town', but you do not say 'The town is little'.

...a little table with a glass top.
...a little piece of rock.

used with submodifiers

You can use words like 'quite' and 'rather' in front of **small**.

...quite small incidents.
...a rather small paper knife.
...fairly small groups of people.

You do not use these words in front of **little**.

You can use 'very' and 'too' in front of **small**.

The trees are full of very small birds.
...houses which are too small.

You do not use 'very' or 'too' in front of **little** when you use it as an adjective. You do not say, for example, 'I have a very little car' or 'Our house is very little'.

comparatives and superlatives

Small has the comparative and superlative forms **smaller** and **smallest**.

They are smaller, darker birds.
...the smallest yachts in the fleet.

You do not use a comparative or superlative form of **little**.

used with other adjectives

You can use other adjectives in front of **little**.

...a nice little man.
...a historic little ship.

You do not normally use other adjectives in front of **small**.

For a graded list of adjectives which are used to describe how small or large something is, see entry at **small - large**.

See also entry at **little - a little**.

smell

Smell is used as a noun or a verb. The past tense and past participle of the verb is either **smelled** or **smelt**.

used as a noun

The **smell** of something is a quality it has which you are aware of through your nose.

...the smell of fresh bread.
What's that smell?

used as an intransitive verb

If you say that something **smells**, you mean that people are aware of it because of its unpleasant smell.

The fridge is beginning to smell.

You can say that a place or object **smells of** a particular thing.

The room smelled of cigars.

Everything smelt of cats and cooked cabbage.

Note that you must use 'of' in sentences like these. You do not say 'The room smelled cigars'.

You can say that one place or thing **smells like** another.

Our kitchen smelt like a rubber factory.
The tutor's breath smelled like a full ashtray.

You can also use **smell** with an adjective to say that something has a pleasant or unpleasant smell.

What is it? It smells delicious.
The papers smelt musty and stale.

Note that you do not use an adverb after **smell**. You do not say, for example, that something 'smells deliciously'.

used as a transitive verb   If you **can smell** something, you are aware of it through your nose.

I can smell the aroma from the frying trout in the kitchen.
He could smell the rich fragrance of bamboo freshly chopped.

Note that you usually use 'can' or 'could' in sentences like these. You say, for example, 'I **can smell** gas'. You do not say 'I smell gas'. Note also that you do not use a continuous tense. You do not say 'I am smelling gas'.

If you want to say that someone became aware of a smell on a particular occasion in the past, you use the simple past tense, **smelled** or **smelt**.

He smelled the smell of burning fat.
I smelt smoke, so I got up and came out.

smile

Smile is used as a verb or a noun.

used as a verb   When you **smile**, the corners of your mouth curve outwards and slightly upwards, for example because you are pleased or amused.

She smiled and waved her hand.

If someone looks at you and smiles, for example to show kindness or friendliness, you say that they **smile at** you.

The girl was smiling at me.

Note that you do not use any preposition except 'at' in a sentence like this.

used as a noun   A **smile** is the expression that you have on your face when you smile.

Barber welcomed me with a smile.
He's got a nice smile, hasn't he?

You can say that someone **gives** you **a smile**.

'How nice to see you.' He gave me a smile.

so

So is used in several different ways.

referring back   You can use **so** after 'do' to refer back to an action that has just been mentioned. For example, instead of saying 'He crossed the street. As he crossed the street, he hummed a tune', you say 'He crossed the street. As he **did so,** he hummed a tune'.

He went to close the door, tripping as he did so over a pair of boots.

A signal which should have turned red failed to <u>do so.</u>

You can use **so** after 'if' to form a conditional clause. For example, instead of saying 'Have you been to Chesterfield? If you have been to Chesterfield, you will remember the twisted spire on the church', you say 'Have you been to Chesterfield? **If so,** you will remember the twisted spire on the church'.

Do you enjoy romantic films? <u>If so,</u> you should watch the film on ITV tonight.
Will that be enough? <u>If so,</u> do not ask for more.

You often use **so** after a reporting verb, especially when you are replying to what someone has said. For example, if someone says 'Is Alice at home?', you can say '**I think so**', meaning 'I think Alice is at home'.

'Are you all right?'—'<u>I think so.</u>'
'Is there anything else you want to tell me?'—'<u>I don't think so.</u>'
'Is it to rent?'—'<u>I believe so.</u>'
'They're shut now, aren't they?'—'Oh gosh, are they?'—'<u>I expect so,</u> at this time.'

The reporting verbs most commonly used with **so** are 'believe', 'expect', 'hope', 'say', 'suppose', 'tell', and 'think'. See separate entries at these words.

So is also used in a similar way after 'I'm afraid'.

'So you think you could lose?'—'<u>I'm afraid so.</u>'

You can also use **so** to say that something which has just been said about one person or thing is true about another. You put **so** at the beginning of a clause, followed by 'be', 'have', an auxiliary, or a modal, and then the subject of the clause.

His shoes are brightly polished; <u>so is his briefcase.</u>
Etta laughed heartily, and <u>so did he.</u>
'He looks very hot and dry.'—'<u>So would you</u> if you had a temperature of 103.'

used for emphasis

You can use **so** to emphasize an adjective. For example, you can say 'It's **so cold** today'.

I was <u>so busy.</u>
These games are <u>so boring.</u>

However, if the adjective is in front of a noun, you use **such,** not 'so'. You say, for example, 'It's **such a cold day** today'.

She was <u>so nice.</u>
She was <u>such a nice girl.</u>

The children seemed <u>so happy.</u>
She seemed <u>such a happy woman.</u>

See entry at **such.**

If the adjective comes after 'the', 'this', 'that', 'these', 'those', or a possessive, you do not use **so** or **such.** You do not say, for example 'It was our first visit to this so old town'. You say 'It was our first visit to **this very old town**'.

He had recovered from <u>his very low state</u> of the previous evening.
I sincerely hope that <u>these very unfortunate people</u> will not be forgotten.

You can also use **so** to emphasize an adverb.

I sleep <u>so soundly.</u>
Time seems to have passed <u>so quickly.</u>

'ever so'	In conversation, you can use **ever so** as an emphatic form of 'so'.

I am ever so grateful to you for talking to me.
She's ever so serious.

'so ... that': **mentioning** **a result**	You use **so** in front of an adjective when you are saying that something happens because someone or something has a quality to an unusually large extent. After the adjective, you use a 'that'-clause.

The crowd was so large that it overflowed the auditorium.
We were so angry we asked to see the manager.

Note that you do not use 'so' in the second clause. You do not say, for example, 'We were so angry so we asked to see the manager'.

You can use **so** in a similar way in front of an adverb.

He dressed so quickly that he put his boots on the wrong feet.
She had fallen down so often that she was covered in mud.

Instead of using **so** in front of an adjective, you can use **such** in front of a noun group containing the adjective. For example, instead of saying 'The house was **so big** that we decided to sell it', you can say 'It was **such a big house** that we decided to sell it'.

The change was so gradual that it escaped the tourists' notice.
This can be such a gradual process that you are not aware of it happening.

When you use **so** with 'that', you can change the order of the words in the first clause for greater emphasis. You put **so** and the adjective at the beginning of the clause, followed by 'be', an auxiliary, or a modal, and then the subject.

So rapid is the rate of progress that advance seems to be following advance on almost a monthly basis.
So successful have they been that they are moving to Bond Street.

This kind of construction is only used in writing and broadcasts. You do not use it in conversation.

You can use **so, and so,** or **so that** to introduce the result of a situation that you have just mentioned.

He speaks very little English, so I talked to him through an interpreter.
She was having great difficulty getting her car out, and so I had to move my car to let her out.
My suitcase had become damaged on the journey home, so that the lid would not stay closed.

'so that' in **purpose clauses**	You also use **so that** to say that something is done for a particular purpose.

He has to earn lots of money so that he can buy his children nice food and clothes.

soccer

See entry at **football**.

social

The adjective **social** is used in front of a noun. Its usual meaning is 'relating to society'.

...social change.
...the government's social and economic policy.

You can also use **social** to indicate that something relates to a leisure activity which involves people meeting each other.

We've met at social and business functions.
...their social contacts.

'sociable' You do not use **social** to describe people who are friendly and enjoy talking to other people. The word you use is **sociable.**

Adler was an outgoing, sociable kind of man.

You also use **sociable** to describe someone's behaviour on a particular occasion. If someone is **sociable** at an event such as a party, they talk to a lot of people in a friendly way.

Kitty had tried to be sociable to everyone.

'socialist' You do not use **social** to mean 'relating to socialism' or to describe people who believe in socialism. The word you use is **socialist.**

...socialist policies.
...the socialist leader, Felipe Gonzalez.

society

used as an
uncount noun
You refer to people in general as **society** when you are thinking of them as belonging to a large organized group.

Women must have equal status in society.
We are going to have to change the whole structure of society.

When **society** has this meaning, you do not use 'a' or 'the' in front of it.

used as a
count noun
You refer to the people of a particular country as a **society** when you are thinking of them as an organized group.

We live in a multi-racial society.
...the increasing complexity of industrial societies.

A **society** is also an organization for people who have the same interest or aim.

...the Royal Horticultural Society.
...the Society of African Culture.

soft

Soft is an adjective. You can use it to describe something which is very gentle and not forceful.

...a soft breeze.
A moment later, there was the softest of bumps.

A **soft** sound or voice is quiet and not harsh.

She had a soft South German accent.
Her voice grew softer.

'softly' You do not use **soft** as an adverb. If someone does something in a gentle way, you do not say that they do it 'soft'. You say that they do it **softly.** Similarly, if someone speaks in a quiet way, you can say that they speak **softly.**

Mike softly placed his hand on her shoulder.
'Listen,' she said softly.

solicitor

See entry at **lawyer.**

some

<table>
<tr>
<td>used as a determiner</td>
<td>You use some in front of the plural form of a noun to talk about a number of people or things, without saying who or what they are, or how many of them there are.</td>
</tr>
</table>

I've got some friends coming over.
I have some important things to tell them.

You can also use **some** in front of an uncount noun to talk about a quantity of something, without saying how much of it there is.

She had a piece of pie and some coffee.
My brother got some more good news this week.

When you use **some** in front of the plural form of a noun, you use a plural form of a verb with it.

Some hunting lodges were also manor houses.
If you are doing it yourself, here are some suggestions.

When you use **some** in front of an uncount noun, you use a singular form of a verb with it.

Some action is necessary.
There's some pizza left from dinner.

used as a quantifier

You use **some of** in front of a plural noun group beginning with 'the', 'these', 'those', or a possessive. You do this to talk about a number of people or things belonging to a particular group.

...some of the large airlines.
...some of those ideas we'd talked about.
...some of Edgar Allen Poe's stories.

Similarly, you use **some of** in front of a singular noun group beginning with 'the', 'this', 'that', or a possessive to talk about a part of something.

We did some of the journey by night.
She took some of the meat from her bag.
Somebody might take some of his money away.

You can use **some of** like this in front of plural or singular pronouns.

Some of these are included in this leaflet.
Some of it is very beautiful.

You do not use 'we' or 'they' after **some of**. Instead you use **us** or **them.**

I think some of us find it a bit intrusive.
They spread out and some of them went up north.

used as a pronoun

Some can itself be used as a plural or singular pronoun.

Some activities are very dangerous and some are not so dangerous.
'You'll need some graph paper.'—'Yeah, I've got some at home.'

WARNING

You do not use **some** as part of the object of a negative sentence. You do not say, for example, 'I don't have some money'. You say 'I don't have **any** money'.

I hadn't had any breakfast.
It won't do any good.
I don't like any of this.

used in questions

In questions, you can use either **some** or **any** as part of an object. You use **some** when you are asking someone to confirm that something is true. For example, if you think someone wants to ask you some questions, you might say to them 'Do you have **some** questions?' or 'You have **some** questions?' But if you do not know whether they want to ask you any questions or not, you would say 'Do you have **any** questions?'

Sorry – have I missed out some questions?
There's some hurry?

Were you in any danger?
Did any of you see that play on television?

duration   You use **some** with 'time' or with a word such as 'hours' or 'months' to indicate that something lasts for a fairly long time.

You will be unable to restart the car for some time.
I did not meet her again for some years.

If you want to indicate that a period of time is fairly short, you do not use **some**. You talk about **a short time** or you use **a few** in front of a word such as 'hours' or 'months'.

The chiefs would be there in a short time.
Patey and I were due to arrive only a few days before the transmission.

someone - somebody

You use **someone** or **somebody** to refer to a person without saying who you mean. There is no difference in meaning between **someone** and **somebody**.

Carson sent someone to see me.
There was an accident and somebody got killed.

WARNING   You do not usually use **someone** or **somebody** as part of the object of a negative sentence. You do not say, for example, 'I don't know someone who lives in Nottingham'. You say 'I don't know **anyone** who lives in Nottingham'.

There wasn't anyone there.
There wasn't much room for anybody else.

used in questions   In questions, you can use **someone, somebody, anyone,** or **anybody** as part of the object.

You use **someone** or **somebody** when you are asking someone to confirm that something is true. For example, if you think I met someone in the park, you might say to me 'Did you meet **someone** in the park?' If you do not know whether I met someone in the park or not, you would say 'Did you meet **anyone** in the park?'

Is there someone from Plymouth who knows you?
Was there anyone behind you?
Would anybody like some wine?

WARNING   You do not use **someone** or **somebody** with 'of' in front of the plural form of a noun. You do not say, for example, 'Someone of my friends is a sculptor'. You say '**One of** my friends is a sculptor'.

One of his friends made a radio from spare parts.
'Where have you been?' one of them asked.

'some people'   **Someone** and **somebody** do not have plural forms. If you want to refer to a group of people without saying who you mean, you say **some people**.

Some people attempted to dash across the bridge.
The law may be held to be unsatisfactory by some people.

someplace

See entry at **somewhere**.

something

You use **something** to refer to an object, situation, etc without saying exactly what it is.

Hendricks saw something ahead of him.
We have something rather strange to show you.
It's something that has often puzzled me.

WARNING You do not usually use **something** as part of the object of a negative sentence. You do not say, for example, 'We haven't had something to eat'. You say 'We haven't had **anything** to eat'.

I did not say anything.
He never seemed to do anything at all.

used in questions In questions, you can use **something** or **anything** as part of the object.

If you are asking for confirmation that something is true, you use **something**. For example, if you think I found something in the cupboard, you might say 'Did you find **something** in the cupboard?' If you do not know whether I found something in the cupboard or not, you would say 'Did you find **anything** in the cupboard?'

Has something happened?
Did she take anything?
Is there anything you need?

sometimes

You use **sometimes** to say that something happens on certain occasions, rather than all the time.

Queues were sometimes a quarter of a mile long.
Sometimes I wish I was back in Africa.

Many other words and expressions can be used to say how often something happens. For a graded list, see section on **frequency** in entry at **Adverbials**.

'sometime' Do not confuse **sometimes** with **sometime**. **Sometime** means 'at a time in the past or future that is unknown or has not yet been fixed'.

He saw Frieda Maloney sometime last week.
Can I come and see you sometime?

Sometime is often written as **some time**.

He died some time last year.

somewhat

See entry at **fair - fairly**.

somewhere

You use **somewhere** to talk about a place without saying exactly where you mean.

I was somewhere in Greenwich Village.
They lived somewhere near Bournemouth.
He had to go off somewhere else for an appointment.

WARNING You do not usually use **somewhere** in negative sentences. You do not say, for example, 'I can't find my hat somewhere'. You say 'I can't find my hat **anywhere**'.

I changed my mind and decided not to go anywhere.
There is not a sound anywhere.

In questions, you can use **somewhere** or **anywhere**. If you are expecting the answer 'yes', you usually use **somewhere**. If you do not know whether the answer will be 'yes' or 'no', you can use either **somewhere** or **anywhere**.

Are you taking a trip somewhere?
Would there be a file on me somewhere?
Is there an ashtray anywhere?

'someplace'
Some American speakers say **someplace** instead of 'somewhere'.

She had seen it someplace before.
Why don't you boys sit someplace else?

Someplace is sometimes written as **some place**.

Why don't we go some place where it's quieter?

soon

talking about the future
You use **soon** to say that something will happen in a short time from now.

We should be getting some orders through to you soon.
We may very soon reach the limit of what we can cram on to a silicon chip.

talking about the past
When you are talking about the past, you use **soon** to say that something happened a short time after something else.

The mistake was very soon spotted.
The glum faces soon changed to smiles.

position in sentence
Soon is often put at the beginning or end of a sentence.

Soon unemployment will start rising.
Soon she would have to retire.

I will see you soon.
Most firms will raise prices very soon.

You can also put **soon** after the first auxiliary in a verb group. For example, you can say 'We **will soon** be home'. You do not say 'We soon will be home'.

It will soon be Christmas.
Herbert was soon taking part in numerous plays.

If there is no auxiliary, you put **soon** in front of the verb, unless the verb is 'be'.

I soon forgot about our conversation.

If the verb is 'be', you put **soon** after it.

She was soon asleep.

'how soon'
You use **how soon** when you are asking how long it will be before something happens.

How soon do I have to make a decision?
How soon are you returning to Paris?

'as soon as'
You use **as soon as** to say that one event happens immediately after another.

As soon as she got out of bed, the telephone stopped ringing.
As soon as we get the tickets, we'll send them to you.

'no sooner' **No sooner** is also used, especially in writing, to say that one event happens immediately after another. **No sooner** usually goes in front of the main verb in the first clause. The second clause begins with 'than'.

You _no sooner_ pour your aperitif _than_ the bell goes.

In stories, **no sooner** is sometimes put at the beginning of a sentence, followed by an auxiliary and the subject.

No sooner did I reach the surface than I was pulled back again.

sorry

You say '**Sorry**' or '**I'm sorry**' as a way of apologizing for something you have done.

'You're giving me a headache with all that noise.'—'_Sorry._'
I'm sorry I'm so late.

Note that **sorry** is an adjective, not a verb. You do not say 'I sorry'.

For more information about apologies, see entry at **Apologizing**. See also entry at **regret - be sorry**.

sort

Sort is used as a noun to talk about a class of people or things. **Sort** is a count noun. After words like 'all' and 'several', you use **sorts,** not 'sort'.

There are all _sorts_ of reasons why this is true.
There are several _sorts_ of stitching.

After **sorts of** you can use either the plural or singular form of a noun. For example, you can say 'They sell most sorts of **shoes**' or 'They sell most sorts of **shoe**'. The singular form is more formal.

There were five different sorts of _biscuits._
There are two sorts of _field bean._

After **sort of** you use the singular form of a noun.

I know you're interested in this sort of _thing._
'What sort of _iron_ did she get?'—'A steam iron.'

In conversation, 'these' and 'those' are often used with **sort**. For example, people say 'I don't like these sort of jobs' or 'I don't like those sort of jobs'. This use is generally thought to be incorrect, and it is best to avoid it. Instead, you should say 'I don't like **this sort of job**' or 'I don't like **that sort of job**'.

They never fly in _this sort of weather._
I've had _that sort of experience_ with other photographers.

You can also say 'I don't like jobs **of this sort**'.

A device _of this sort_ costs a good deal of money.

In conversation, people often say **like this, like that,** or **like these.**

I want to know what evidence people are using when they make statements _like this._
I haven't studied any subjects _like that._
...words _like these_ which are irregularly spelt.

sort of - kind of

In conversation, people use **sort of** or **kind of** in front of a noun to indicate that something has some of the features of a particular kind of thing.

There's a _sort of_ ridge. Do you see?
I'm a _kind of_ anarchist, I suppose.

Some people also use **sort of** in front of adjectives, verbs, and other types of word. When **sort of** is used like this, it has very little meaning.

I'm sort of fond of him.
I've sort of heard of him, but I don't know who he is.
He was sort of banging his head against a window.

Some American speakers use **kind of** in a similar way, especially in front of adjectives.

I felt kind of sorry for him.

sound

Sound is used as a noun, a verb, or an adjective.

used as a noun   A **sound** is a particular thing that you hear.

He heard the sound of footsteps in the hall.
He opened the door without a sound.

Sound is everything that can be heard.

Sound travels better in water than in air.

WARNING   Do not confuse **sound** with **noise**. For an explanation of the difference, see entry at **sound - noise**.

used as a verb   You use **sound** as a verb in front of an adjective group when you are describing something that you hear.

The stiff rustling of the woman's dress sounded alarmingly loud.

You can also use **sound** in front of an adjective group to describe the impression you have of someone when they speak.

'Ah,' Piper said. He sounded a little discouraged.

You also use **sound** to describe the impression you have of someone or something that you have just heard about or read about.

'They've got a small farm down in Devon.'—'That sounds nice.'
That sounds a bit complicated.

Note that you do not use a continuous tense. You do not say, for example, 'That is sounding nice'.

Note also that **sound** is followed by an adjective, not an adverb. You do not say 'That sounds nicely'.

'sound like'   You can use the verb **sound** in front of 'like' and a noun group in the following ways:

You can use it to say that something has a similar sound to something else.

One of this animal's commonest calls sounds like the miaow of a cat.
Her footsteps sounded like pistol shots.

You can use it to say that someone is talking the way someone else usually talks.

He sounded like a small boy boasting.
You sound just like an insurance salesman.

You can use it to say that you think you can recognize what something is, because of its sound.

They were playing a symphony that sounded like Haydn or Mozart.

You can also use it to express an opinion about something which someone has just described to you.

That sounds like a good idea.
It sounded like a serious illness.

'sound' used as
an adjective
When **sound** is used as an adjective, it has a completely different meaning. If something is **sound**, it is healthy or in good condition.

My heart is basically sound.

If something such as an argument or piece of advice is **sound,** it is sensible and based on reason.

Cook met every objection with sound arguments.

'sound asleep' If someone is **sound asleep,** they are sleeping deeply and peacefully.

Chris is still sound asleep in the other bed.

sound - noise

used as
count nouns
A **sound** is something that you can hear. If it is unpleasant or unexpected, you refer to it as a **noise.** You say that machinery makes a **noise.** People and animals can also make **noises.**

A sudden noise made Brody jump.
Dolphins produce a great variety of noises.

used as
uncount nouns
Sound and **noise** can both be used as uncount nouns.

Sound is the general term for what you hear as a result of vibrations travelling through the air, water, etc.

...the speed of sound.

Note that when you use **sound** with this meaning, you do not talk about 'the sound'.

You do not use expressions such as 'much' or 'a lot of' with **sound.** You do not say, for example, 'There was a lot of sound'. You say 'There was **a lot of noise**'.

Is that the wind making all that noise?
Try not to make so much noise.

south

The **south** /saʊθ/ is the direction which is on your right when you are looking towards the direction where the sun rises.

...the Provinces to the south.
The moon will be to the south on the 25th.

A **south** wind blows from the south.

The bigger islands gave some shelter from the south wind.

The **south** of a place is the part that is towards the south.

...urban and rural land in the south of England.
He died at his home in Antibes in the south of France.

South occurs in the names of some countries, states, and regions.

...the Republic of South Korea.
...a senator from South Carolina.
...the rivers of South America.

'southern' However, you do not usually talk about a 'south' part of a country or region. You talk about a **southern** /sʌðən/ part.

> ...the southern tip of South America.
> ...the southern half of England.

Similarly, you do not talk about 'south England' or 'south Europe'. You say **southern** England or **southern** Europe.

> ...the cities of southern Spain.

southerly

If something moves in a **southerly** /sʌðəli/ direction, it moves towards the south.

> Peter headed in a southerly direction.

However, a **southerly** wind blows **from** the south.

> The dunes afford the house some shelter from the southerly gales.

The most **southerly** of a group of things is the one that is furthest to the south.

> ...the most southerly tip of Bear Island.

southwards

If you move or look **southwards,** you move or look towards the south.

> He took the road southwards into the hills.
> You can glance southwards down Newman Street.

Southwards is only used as an adverb.

'southward' In American English and old-fashioned British English, **southward** is often used instead of 'southwards'.

> We headed southward on Route 95.

In both British and American English, **southward** is sometimes used as an adjective in front of a noun.

> You are stopped in your southward course by the traffic in the High Street.

souvenir

See entry at **memory.**

sow - sew

The verbs **sow** and **sew** are both pronounced /səʊ/.

'sow' If you **sow** seeds, you plant them in the ground. The past tense of 'sow' is **sowed**. The past participle can be either **sown** or **sowed. Sown** is more common.

> An enemy came and sowed weeds among the wheat.
> Spring wheat should be sown as early as you can get the land ready.

'sew' If you **sew,** you join pieces of cloth together by passing thread through them with a needle. The past tense of 'sew' is **sewed**. The past participle can be either **sewn** or **sewed. Sewn** is more common.

> She sewed all her own dresses.
> Before I went to Alice Springs I had never sewn a dress or mended a sock.

spare

If you can **spare** something, you can give it to someone or make it available without causing difficulties for yourself.

We have too many possessions. We can spare a few of them.
I was pleased that she could spare the time to act as one of the invigilators.

'save'   You do not use **spare** to say that someone gradually collects money by not spending it. The word you use is **save.**

They had managed to save enough to buy a house.

speak

When you **speak,** you use your voice to produce words. The past tense of 'speak' is **spoke,** not 'speaked'.

Both leaders spoke warmly of the frankness of their discussions.

The past participle is **spoken.**

A lot of women I've spoken to agree with me.

'say'   You do not use **speak** to report what someone says. You do not say, for example, 'He spoke that the doctor had arrived'. You say 'He **said** that the doctor had arrived'.

I said that I would like to teach English.
He said it was an accident.

'tell'   If you mention the person who is being spoken to, you use **tell.**

He told me that he was a farmer.
I told her what the doctor had said.

See entries at **say** and **tell.**

'talk'   Do not confuse **speak** with **talk.** For an explanation of the differences, see entry at **speak - talk.**

speak - talk

Speak and **talk** have very similar meanings, but there are some differences in the ways in which they are used.

When you mention that someone is using his or her voice to produce words, you usually say that they **are speaking.**

He hadn't looked at me once when I was speaking.
'So we won't waste any time,' he said, speaking rapidly.

However, if two or more people are having a conversation, you usually say that they **are talking.** You do not say that they 'are speaking'.

The old man was sitting near us as we were talking.
They sat in the kitchen drinking and talking.

used with 'to'   If you **speak to** someone or **talk to** them, you have a conversation with
and 'with'   them.

I saw you speaking to him just now.
I enjoyed talking to Anne.

Some American speakers say **speak with** or **talk with.**

When he spoke with his friends, he told them what had happened.
Mr Bush confirmed that he had talked with Mr Gorbachov.

When you make a telephone call, you ask if you can **speak to** someone. You do not ask if you can 'talk to' them.

Hello. Could I speak to Sue, please?

used with 'about' If you **speak about** something, you describe it to a group of people, for example in a lecture.

I spoke about my experiences at University.

In conversation, you can refer to the thing someone is discussing as the thing they **are talking about.**

You know the book I'm talking about.

You can refer in a general way to what someone is saying as **what** they **are talking about.**

What are you talking about?

If two or more people are discussing something, you say they **are talking about** it. You do not say they 'are speaking about' it.

The men were talking about some medical problem.
Was it my sister they were talking about?

languages You say that someone **speaks** or **can speak** a foreign language.

They spoke fluent English.
He does not speak English very well.
How many languages can you speak?

You do not say that someone 'talks' a foreign language.

WARNING You do not use 'in' when you are talking about someone's ability to speak a foreign language, and you do not use a continuous tense. For example, if someone is able to speak Dutch, you do not say 'She speaks in Dutch' or 'She is speaking Dutch'.

However, if you hear some people talking, you can say 'Those people **are speaking in** Dutch' or 'Those people **are talking in** Dutch'.

She heard two voices talking in French.
Boshoff and Beukes were now speaking in Afrikaans.

other transitive uses **Speak** and **talk** have some other transitive uses.

You can **speak** particular words.

He spoke the words firmly and clearly.

You cannot 'talk' words.

You can say that someone **talks** sense or **talks** nonsense. Similarly, a group of people can **talk** politics or **talk** sport.

He was talking sense for once.
Don't talk nonsense.
We used to sit down and talk politics all evening.

You cannot use **speak** in any of these ways.

reflexive use You can say that a person **is talking to** himself or herself.

She seemed to be talking to herself.

You do not say that someone 'is speaking to' himself or herself.

specially

See entry at **especially - specially.**

spectacle - spectacles

'spectacle'   A **spectacle** is a sight or view which is remarkable or impressive.

I was confronted with an appalling spectacle.
She stood at the head of the stairs and surveyed the spectacle.

'spectacles'   A person's **spectacles** are their glasses. **Spectacles** is a formal or old-fashioned word.

...a schoolteacher in horn-rimmed spectacles.

speech - talk

If you make a **speech** or give a **talk,** you speak for a period of time to an audience, usually saying things which you have prepared in advance.

'speech'   A **speech** is made on a formal occasion, for example at a dinner, wedding, or public meeting.

We listened to an excellent speech by the President.
Mr Macmillan presented the prizes and made a speech on the importance of education.

'talk'   A **talk** is more informal, and is intended to give information.

Angus Wilson came here and gave a talk last week.
That's what you said in your talk this lunchtime.

speed

Speed is used as a noun or a verb.

used as a noun   The **speed** of someone or something is the rate at which they move.

Ralph increased his speed.
...the speed of light.

Speed is often used in prepositional phrases beginning with **at** or **with.**

You can say that someone or something moves **at** a particular **speed.**

He goes on driving at the same speed.
A point on Jupiter's equator moves at a speed of 12.7 kilometres per second.

If you want to emphasize how fast something is moving, you can use **at** and an adjective in front of **speed.**

I drove at great speed to West Bank.
A plane flew low over the ship at lightning speed.

If you want to emphasize how quickly something happens or is done, you use **with** and an adjective in front of **speed.**

The shape of their bodies changes with astonishing speed.
They have succeeded in expanding their industries with remarkable speed.

used as a verb   In stories, if someone **speeds** somewhere, they move or travel there quickly. When **speed** has this meaning, its past tense and past participle is **sped.**

They sped along Main Street towards the highway.
They drove through Port Philip and sped on down south.

'speed up'   If something **speeds up** or if you **speed** it **up,** it moves, happens, or is done more quickly.

They're way ahead of us. Speed up!

The past tense and past participle of 'speed up' is **speeded up.**

Tom speeded up and overtook them.
The process is now being speeded up.

Spelling

This entry gives general information on how words are spelled, information on differences between British and American spellings, and information on the use of hyphens.

Some spellings are explained in more detail at other entries in this book: see entries at **Abbreviations, Capital letters, Comparative and superlative adjectives, Contractions, Irregular verbs, '-ly' words, Names and titles, Plural forms of nouns,** and **Verbs.** See also entries at **Words with alternative spellings** and **Words with the same pronunciation.**

spelling of consonant sounds

Many sounds can be spelled in different ways. This is how the consonant sounds can be spelled:

- The sound /b/ is usually spelled 'b' as in 'bed' but can be spelled 'bb', usually in the middle of a word, as in 'flabby'.

- The sound /d/ is usually spelled 'd' as in 'done' but can be spelled 'dd', as in 'odd' or 'ladder'. It can be spelled 'ed' at the end of a word, as in 'joined'.

- The sound /f/ is usually spelled 'f' as in 'fit' but can be spelled 'ff' as in 'stiff', 'off', and 'coffee'. It is sometimes spelled 'gh' as in 'rough' and 'ph' as in 'photograph'.

- The sound /g/ is usually spelled 'g' as in 'good' but can be spelled 'gg' as in 'egg' or 'soggy'. It is occasionally spelled 'gh' as in 'ghost'.

- The sound /h/ is usually spelled 'h' as in 'hat' but is occasionally spelled 'wh' as in 'whole'.

- The sound /j/ is usually spelled 'y' as in 'yellow'. Note that /ju:/ is sometimes spelled 'u' as in 'uniform', 'eu' as in 'euphemism', or 'ue' as in 'due'.

- The sound /k/ can be spelled 'k' as in 'king' or 'c' as in 'close'. It can also be spelled 'ck' as in 'rock' or 'ch' as in 'school'. It can be spelled 'que' at the end of a word, as in 'cheque'. It is occasionally spelled 'cc' as in 'tobacco'. Note that /kw/ is usually spelled 'qu' as in 'queen'.

- The sound /l/ is usually spelled 'l' as in 'lip' but can be spelled 'll' as in 'still' or 'fuller'.

- The sound /m/ is usually spelled 'm' as in 'mat' but can be spelled 'mm' in the middle of a word, as in 'summer'. See section on **silent consonants.**

- The sound /n/ is usually spelled 'n' as in 'nine' but can be spelled 'nn', usually in the middle of a word, as in 'dinner'.

- The sound /p/ is usually spelled 'p' as in 'pay' but can be spelled 'pp' in the middle of a word, as in 'happy'.

- The sound /r/ is usually spelled 'r' as in 'run' but can be spelled 'rr', usually in the middle of a word, as in 'furry'.

- The sound /s/ can be spelled 's' as in 'soon' or 'c' as in 'city'. It can also be spelled 'ss' as in 'fuss' or 'sc' as in 'science'.

- The sound /t/ is usually spelled 't' as in 'talk' but can be spelled 'tt' as in 'pretty'. It can be spelled 'ed' at the end of a word, as in 'walked'.

- The sound /v/ is usually spelled 'v' as in 'van'. Note that it is spelled 'f' in the word 'of'.

- The sound /w/ is usually spelled 'w' as in 'win' but can be spelled 'wh' as in 'why'.

- The sound /z/ is usually spelled 's' as in 'was' and 'busy'. It can also be spelled 'z' as in 'zoo' or 'zz' as in 'fizzy'.

- The sound /ʃ/ can be spelled 'sh' as in 'ship' or 'ch' as in 'chef'. In the middle of a word, it can be spelled 'ti' as in 'mention', 'si' as in 'tension', 'ci' as in 'efficient', or 'sci' as in 'conscience'. It is occasionally spelled 's' in front of 'u' as in 'sure' and 'sugar'.

- The sound /ʒ/ can be spelled 's' as in 'measure', 'z' as in 'azure', or 'si' as in 'television'.

- The sound /ŋ/ is usually spelled 'ng' but can be spelled 'n' in front of 'k', 'c', or 'q' as in 'ink', 'uncle', or 'inquire'.

- The sound /tʃ/ is spelled 'ch' at the beginning of a word, as in 'cheap' and 'tch' at the end of a word, as in 'watch'.

- The sound /θ/ is spelled 'th' as in 'thin'.

- The sound /ð/ is spelled 'th' as in 'the'.

- The sound /dʒ/ can be spelled 'j' or 'g' at the beginning of a word, as in 'joy' or 'gem', and 'ge' or 'dge' at the end of a word, as in 'age' or 'manage'. It can be spelled 'g', 'ge', or 'dge' in the middle of a word, as in 'managing', 'ageing', or 'hedgehog'.

spelling of vowel sounds

This is how the vowel sounds can be spelled:

- The sound /ɑ:/ can be spelled 'a' as in 'calm' or 'ar' as in 'start'. It is spelled 'ear' in 'heart', 'au' in 'laugh', and 'ah' in 'hurrah'.

- The sound /æ/ is usually spelled 'a' as in 'act'.

- The sound /aɪ/ can be spelled 'i' as in 'dive', 'ie' as in 'die', 'y' as in 'cry', 'igh' as in 'high', or 'ye' as in 'dye'. It is spelled 'uy' in 'buy'.

- The sound /aɪə/ is usually spelled 'ire' as in 'fire'. It can be spelled 'uyer' as in 'buyer', 'ier' as in 'drier', 'yer' as in 'flyer', or 'yre' as in 'tyre'.

- The sound /aʊ/ can be spelled 'ou' as in 'out' or 'ow' as in 'down'. It is sometimes spelled 'ough' as in 'plough'.

- The sound /aʊə/ can be spelled 'our' as in 'flour' or 'ower' as in 'flower'.

- The sound /e/ is usually spelled 'e' as 'met'. It is sometimes spelled 'ea' as in 'head' and 'bread'. It is spelled 'a' in 'many', 'u' in 'bury', 'ie' in 'friend', and 'ai' in 'said'.

- The sound /eɪ/ can be spelled 'a' as in 'date' or 'ai' as in 'main'. It is sometimes spelled 'ei' as in 'rein', 'eigh' as in 'weight', 'ea' as in 'break', 'ay' as in 'day', and 'ey' as in 'they'. It is spelled 'au' in 'gauge' and 'aigh' in 'straight'.

- The sound /eə/ can be spelled 'air' as in 'fair' or 'are' as in 'care'. It is occasionally spelled 'ear' as in 'bear'. It is spelled 'ere' in 'there', 'eir' in 'their', 'ayor' in 'mayor' and 'ayer' in 'prayer'.

- The sound /ɪ/ is usually spelled 'i' as in 'fit'. It is sometimes spelled 'a' as in 'manage', 'y' as in 'physics', and in many other ways.

- The sound /i:/ can be spelled 'e' as in 'me', 'ee' as in 'feed', 'ea' as in 'beat', 'ey' as in 'key', 'ie' as in 'piece', or 'ei' as in 'receive'. (See section below on 'ie' or 'ei'.)

- The sound /ɪə/ can be spelled 'ear' as in 'near', 'eer' as in 'deer', 'ier' as in 'fierce', or 'ere' as in 'here'. It is spelled 'eir' in 'weird'.

- The sound /ɒ/ is usually spelled 'o' as in 'lot'. It is sometimes spelled 'a' as in 'watch' or 'ou' as in 'cough'.

- The sound /əʊ/ can be spelled 'o' as in 'note', 'oa' as in 'coat', or 'ow' as in 'grow'. It is sometimes spelled 'ou' as in 'mould' or 'oe' as in 'toe'. It is spelled 'ew' in 'sew'.

- The sound /ɔː/ can be spelled 'a' as in 'call', 'ore' as in 'more', 'or' as in 'cord', 'oor' as in 'floor', 'oar' as in 'board', 'au' as in 'taut', or 'aw' as in 'claw'. It is sometimes spelled 'augh' as in 'caught', 'ough' as in 'ought', or 'our' as in 'four'.

- The sound /ʊ/ can be spelled 'oo' as in 'stood' or 'ou' as in 'could'. It is sometimes spelled 'u' as in 'put'.

- The sound /uː/ can be spelled 'ou' as in 'you', 'u' as in 'truth', 'oo' as in 'choose', or 'ew' as in 'grew'. It is sometimes spelled 'o' as in 'who' or 'ue' as in 'true'. It is spelled 'oe' in 'shoe' and 'ough' in 'through'.

- The sound /ɜː/ can be spelled 'ur' as in 'turn', 'ir' as in 'third', or 'er' as in 'herd'. It is sometimes spelled 'or' as in 'worm', 'our' as in 'journey', and 'ear' as in 'learn'.

- The sound /ʌ/ is usually spelled 'u' as in 'but'. It is sometimes spelled 'oo' as in 'flood', 'ou' as in 'touch' and 'o' as in 'some'. It is spelled 'oe' in 'does'.

- The sound /ə/ can be spelled 'e' as in 'silent', 'a' as in 'about', 'er' as in 'butter', 'or' as in 'forgotten', 'our' as in 'colour', 'o' as in 'station', and in many other ways.

silent consonants Many words are spelled with consonants that are not pronounced. Here are the main rules about silent consonants.

There is a silent 'b' in words like 'debt' /det/, 'doubt' /daʊt/, and 'subtle' /sʌtl/, where 'b' is followed by 't' in the same syllable. Note that 'b' is not silent in 'obtain' /əbteɪn/, because the 't' is part of the second syllable. There is also a silent 'b' in words like 'bomb' /bɒm/, 'climb' /klaɪm/, 'lamb' /læm/, and 'thumb' /θʌm/, where 'b' comes after 'm' at the end of a syllable.

There is a silent 'd' in 'sandwich' /sænwɪdʒ/ and 'Wednesday' /wenzdeɪ/.

There is a silent 'g' in 'foreign' /fɒrɪn/, 'gnat' /næt/, 'phlegm' /flem/, and 'sign' /saɪn/, where it comes in front of 'm' or 'n' at the beginning or end of a syllable.

There is a silent 'h' at the beginning of words like 'heir' /eə/, 'honest' /ɒnɪst/, 'honour' /ɒnə/, and 'hour' /aʊə/. There is a list of these words in the entry at **a - an**. There is also a silent 'h' after a vowel at the end of words such as 'hurrah' /hərɑː/ and 'oh' /əʊ/, and between vowels in words like 'annihilate' /ənaɪəleɪt/ and 'vehicle' /viːɪkl/.

There is also a silent 'h' after 'r' in words like 'rhythm' /rɪðəm/ and 'rhubarb' /ruːbɑːb/.

There is a silent 'k' at the beginning of words like 'knee' /niː/ and 'know' /nəʊ/, where it is followed by 'n'.

There is a silent 'l' in words such as 'half' /hɑːf/, 'talk' /tɔːk/, and 'palm' /pɑːm/, where it comes between 'a' and 'f', 'k', or 'm'. There is also a silent 'l' in 'could' /kʊd/, 'should' /ʃʊd/, and 'would' /wʊd/ where it comes between 'ou' and 'd'.

There is a silent 'n' at the end of words such as 'column' /kɒləm/ and 'hymn' /hɪm/, where it comes after 'm'.

There is a silent 'p' at the beginning of words of Greek origin such as 'pneumatic' /njuːmætɪk/, 'psychology' /saɪkɒlədʒi/, and 'pterodactyl' /terədæktɪl/, where it comes in front of 'n', 's', or 't'.

In standard British English, 'r' is silent when it is followed by a consonant or a silent 'e', or is at the end of a word, for example in 'farm' /fɑːm/, 'more' /mɔː/, and 'stir' /stɜː/. Note also the pronunciation of 'iron' /aɪən/.

There is a silent 's' in 'island' /aɪlənd/ and in many words of French origin such as 'debris' /debri/ and 'viscount' /vaɪkaʊnt/.

There is a silent 't' in words such as 'listen' /lɪsn/ and 'thistle' /θɪsl/, and at the end of words of French origin such as 'buffet' /bʊfeɪ/ and 'chalet' /ʃæleɪ/.

There is a silent 'w' at the beginning of words such as 'wreck' /rek/ and 'write' /raɪt/, where it comes in front of 'r', and also in the words 'answer' /ɑːnsə/, 'sword' /sɔːd/, and 'two' /tuː/.

general rules The following are some general rules that you can use if you are not sure how to spell a word.

short vowel or long vowel If a one-syllable word has a short vowel, it usually does not have 'e' at the end. If it has a long vowel represented by a single letter, the word usually does have an 'e' at the end. For example:

- /fæt/ is spelled 'fat' and /feɪt/ is spelled 'fate'

- /bɪt/ is spelled 'bit' and /baɪt/ is spelled 'bite'

- /rɒd/ is spelled 'rod' and /rəʊd/ is spelled 'rode'

doubling final consonants If a one-syllable word ends in a single vowel and consonant, you double the final consonant before adding a suffix that begins with a vowel.

run – runner
set – setting
stop – stopped
wet – wettest

If the word has more than one syllable, you usually only double the final consonant if the final syllable is stressed.

admit – admitted
begin – beginner
refer – referring

motor – motoring
open – opener
suffer – suffered

However, in British English, you double the final 'l' of verbs like 'travel' and 'quarrel', even though the last syllable is not stressed.

travel – travelling
quarrel – quarrelled

In British English, and sometimes in American English, the final consonant of the following verbs is doubled, even though the last syllable is not stressed.

hiccup	program
kidnap	worship

Note that the final 'p' of 'handicap' is also doubled.

omitting final 'e' If a final 'e' is silent, you omit it before adding a suffix beginning with a vowel.

bake – baked
blame – blaming
fame – famous
late – later
nice – nicest
secure – security

You do not omit the final 'e' of words like 'courage' or 'notice' when forming words like 'courageous' /kəreɪdʒəs/ and 'noticeable' /nəʊtɪsəbl/, because the 'e' indicates that the preceding 'g' is pronounced /dʒ/ and the preceding 'c' is pronounced /s/. Compare 'analogous' /ənæləgəs/ and 'practicable' /præktɪkəbl/.

You sometimes omit the silent final 'e' in front of suffixes that begin with a consonant. For example 'awful' is formed from 'awe', and 'truly' is formed from 'true'. However, you do not always omit the 'e': 'useful' is formed from 'use', and 'surely' is formed from 'sure'.

changing final 'y' to 'i' If a word ends in a consonant and 'y', you usually change 'y' to 'i' before adding a suffix.

carry – carries
early – earlier
lovely – loveliest
try – tried

However, you do not change 'y' to 'i' when adding 'ing'.

carry – carrying
try – trying

You do not usually change the final 'y' of one-syllable adjectives like 'dry' and 'shy'.

dry – dryness
shy – shyly

'ie' or 'ei' When the sound is /iː/, the spelling is often 'ie'. Here is a list of the commonest words in which /iː/ is spelled 'ie':

achieve	chief	niece	relieve	siege
belief	field	piece	reprieve	thief
believe	grief	priest	retrieve	wield
brief	grieve	relief	shield	yield

Note that in 'mischief' and 'sieve' the 'ie' is pronounced /ɪ/.

After 'c', when the sound is /s/, the spelling is usually 'ei'.

ceiling	conceive	deceive	receipt
conceit	deceit	perceive	receive

In some words, 'c' is followed by 'ie', but the sound of 'ie' is not /iː/: for example, 'efficient' /ɪfɪʃnt/, 'science' /saɪəns/, and 'financier' /fɪnænsɪə/.

In the following words 'ei' is pronounced /eɪ/:

beige	feign	reign	veil	weight
deign	freight	rein	vein	
eight	neighbour	sleigh	weigh	

The 'ei' in 'either' and 'neither' can be pronounced /aɪ/ or /iː/. Note also the pronunciation of 'ei' in 'height' /haɪt/, 'foreign' /fɒrɪn/, and 'sovereign' /sɒvrɪn/.

'-ically' With adjectives ending in 'ic', you add 'ally' to form adverbs, for example, 'artistically', 'automatically', 'democratically', 'specifically', and 'sympathetically'. You do not add 'ly', although the 'ally' ending is often pronounced like 'ly'. However, 'publicly' is an exception. See entry at '**-ly' words** for full information on forming adverbs.

'-ful' You form some adjectives by adding 'ful' to a noun, for example, 'careful', 'harmful', 'useful', and 'wonderful'. You do not add 'full'.

'-ible' Many adjectives end in 'ible', but there is a fixed set of them, and new words are not formed by adding 'ible'. Here is a list of the most common adjectives ending in 'ible':

accessible	edible	indivisible	plausible
audible	eligible	inexhaustible	possible
collapsible	fallible	inexpressible	reducible
combustible	feasible	intelligible	reprehensible
compatible	flexible	invincible	responsible
comprehensible	forcible	irascible	reversible
contemptible	gullible	irrepressible	sensible
convertible	horrible	irresistible	susceptible
credible	inadmissible	legible	tangible
crucible	incorrigible	negligible	terrible
defensible	incorruptible	ostensible	visible
digestible	indelible	perceptible	
discernible	indestructible	permissible	

Negative forms are only included in the above list if the positive form is rarely used. You can add a negative prefix to many of the positive forms in the list, for example, 'illegible', 'impossible', 'invisible', 'irresponsible', and 'unintelligible'.

'-able' Many adjectives end in 'able'. There is no fixed set of them, and new words are often formed by adding 'able' to verbs. Here is a list of the most common adjectives ending in 'able':

acceptable	considerable	invaluable	reasonable	valuable
available	desirable	liable	reliable	
capable	fashionable	miserable	remarkable	
comfortable	formidable	probable	respectable	
comparable	inevitable	profitable	suitable	

You can add a negative prefix to most of the positive forms in the list, for example, 'incapable' and 'uncomfortable'.

'-ent' and '-ant' You cannot usually tell from the sound of a word whether it ends in 'ent' or 'ant'. These are the commonest adjectives ending in 'ent':

absent	decent	independent	permanent	urgent
confident	different	innocent	present	violent
consistent	efficient	intelligent	prominent	
convenient	evident	magnificent	silent	
current	frequent	patient	sufficient	

These are the commonest adjectives ending in 'ant':

abundant	elegant	important	redundant	tolerant
arrogant	expectant	intolerant	relevant	vacant
brilliant	extravagant	militant	reluctant	vigilant
buoyant	exuberant	poignant	resistant	
defiant	fragrant	predominant	resonant	
distant	hesitant	pregnant	self-reliant	
dominant	ignorant	radiant	significant	

These are the commonest nouns ending in 'ent':

accident	development	government	present
achievement	element	investment	president
agent	employment	management	punishment
agreement	environment	moment	statement
apartment	equipment	movement	student
argument	establishment	parent	treatment
department	excitement	parliament	unemployment

Note that nouns referring to actions and processes, such as 'assessment' and 'improvement', end in 'ment', not 'mant'.

These are the commonest nouns ending in 'ant'. Note that many of them refer to people.

accountant	defendant	instant	participant	tenant
applicant	descendant	lieutenant	peasant	tyrant
attendant	giant	merchant	pheasant	
commandant	immigrant	migrant	protestant	
confidant	infant	occupant	sergeant	
consultant	informant	pageant	servant	

See also entry at **currant - current**.

Adjectives ending in 'ent' have related nouns ending in 'ence' or 'ency'. Here are some other common nouns ending in 'ence' or 'ency':

agency	currency	influence	sentence
audience	deterrence	licence	sequence
coincidence	emergency	preference	subsistence
conference	essence	presidency	tendency
conscience	existence	reference	
consequence	experience	residence	
constituency	incidence	science	

Adjectives ending in 'ant' have related nouns ending in 'ance' or 'ancy'. Here are some other common nouns ending in 'ance' or 'ancy':

acceptance	assurance	inheritance	resemblance
acquaintance	balance	instance	substance
alliance	disturbance	insurance	tenancy
allowance	entrance	maintenance	
appearance	guidance	nuisance	
assistance	infancy	performance	

difficult words

Many people find some words especially hard to spell. Here is a list of some common problem words (with the spellings in British English):

accommodation	exceed	occasion	secretary
acknowledge	February	occurred	separate
across	fluorescent	parallel	skilful
address	foreign	parliament	succeed
allege	gauge	precede	supersede
argument	government	privilege	surprise
awkward	harass	proceed	suspicious
beautiful	inoculate	professor	threshold
bureau	instalment	pronunciation	tomorrow
bureaucracy	language	psychiatrist	vegetable
calendar	library	pursue	vehicle
cemetery	manoeuvre	recommend	Wednesday
committee	mathematics	reference	withhold
conscience	medicine	referred	
embarrass	necessary	science	

British and American spellings

The regular differences in spelling between British English and American English are given below. In some cases, both spellings can be used in British English and in American English.

doubling consonants

In American English, when you add a suffix to a two-syllable word whose final syllable is not stressed, you do not double the 'l'. For example, American English uses the spellings 'traveling' and 'traveled', whereas British English uses the spellings 'travelling' and 'travelled'.

If the final syllable is stressed, the final consonant is doubled in both British and American English. For example, both use the spellings 'admitting' and 'admitted'.

A few verbs have a single consonant in the base form and '-s' form in British English, but a double consonant in American English. For example, British English uses the spellings 'appal' and 'appals', but American English uses 'appall' and 'appalls'. Both British and American English use the spellings 'appalling' and 'appalled'.

appal	enrol	instal
distil	fulfil	

Note also the British spelling 'skilful' and the American spelling 'skillful'.

Note that a few words have a double consonant in British English, and a single consonant in American English.

carburettor — carburetor
jeweller — jeweler
jewellery — jewelry

programme – program
tranquillize – tranquilize
woollen – woolen

'-our' and '-or' Many words, mostly abstract nouns of Latin origin, have their ending spelled 'our' in British English, but 'or' in American English.

behaviour – behavior
colour – color
flavour – flavor
humour – humor
neighbour – neighbor

'-oul' and '-ol' Note that some words spelled with 'oul' in British English are spelled with 'ol' in American English.

mould – mold
moult – molt
smoulder – smolder

'-re' and '-er' Many words, mostly of French origin, have their ending spelled 're' in British English and 'er' in American English.

centre – center
fibre – fibre
reconnoitre – reconnoiter
sombre – somber
theatre – theater

See also entry at **metre - meter.**

'ae' or 'oe' and 'e' Many words, mostly of Greek or Latin origin, are spelled with 'ae' or 'oe' in British English, but 'e' in American English. However, the American spellings are now sometimes used in British English as well.

aesthetic – esthetic
amoeba – ameba
diarrhoea – diarrhea
gynaecology – gynecology
mediaeval – medieval

Note that 'manoeuvre' is spelled 'maneuver' in American English.

'-ise' and '-ize' Many verbs can end in either 'ise' or 'ize'. For example, 'authorise' and 'authorize' are alternative spellings of the same verb. The 'ise' ending is more common in British English than American English, but British people are increasingly using the 'ize' ending. In this book, we use the 'ize' ending.

Note that for the following verbs you can only use the 'ise' ending:

advertise	circumcise	excise	revise
advise	compromise	exercise	supervise
arise	despise	improvise	surmise
chastise	devise	promise	surprise

small groups Note also the following small groups of words that are spelled differently in British and American English. The British spelling is given first.

analyse – analyze
breathalyse – breathalyze
paralyse – paralyze

analogue – analog
catalogue – catalog

dialogue — dialog

defence — defense
offence — offense
pretence — pretense

'Vice' is spelled 'vise' in American English when it refers to the tool used to hold a piece of wood or metal firmly. See also entries at **licence - license** and **practice - practise.**

individual words Some individual words are spelled differently in British English and American English. In the list below, the British spelling is given first.

axe - ax	nought - naught
chequer - checker	plough - plow
dependence - dependance	pyjamas - pajamas
distension - distention	sceptic - skeptic
glycerine - glycerin	tyre - tire
grey - gray	

See also entries at **assure - ensure - insure, cheque - check, curb - kerb, dependent - dependant, disc - disk, draught - draft,** and **story - storey.**

With the following pairs there is also a slight change of pronunciation:

aluminium — aluminum
behove — behoove
furore — furor
speciality — specialty

two words or one word In British English, some items are usually written as two words, but in American English they can be written as one word.

any more — anymore
de luxe — deluxe
per cent — percent

hyphens: compound nouns Compound nouns can often be written as two separate words or with a hyphen.

At seven he was woken by the alarm clock.
She's the kind of sleeper that even the alarm-clock doesn't always wake.

Note that you must always use a hyphen in words referring to relatives, for example 'great-grandmother' and 'mother-in-law'.

You usually use a hyphen in compound nouns such as 'T-shirt', 'U-turn', and 'X-ray' where the first part consists of only one letter.

Words used together as compound nouns are often hyphenated when they are used to modify another noun, in order to make the meaning clearer. For example, you would refer to the 'sixth form' in a school, but use a hyphen for a 'sixth-form class'.

The stained glass above the door cast lozenges of yellow, green and blue upon the floor.
...a stained-glass window.

I did a lot of drawing in my spare time.
'Volunteering' for things was an accepted spare-time occupation for their particular social group.

compound adjectives Compound adjectives can usually be written with a hyphen or as one word.

...any anti-social behaviour such as continuous lateness.
...the activities of antisocial groups.

Some adjectives are generally written with a hyphen in front of a noun and as two words after 'be'.

He was wearing a brand-new uniform.
His uniform was brand new.

Prefixes that are used in front of a word beginning with a capital letter always have a hyphen after them.

...a wave of anti-British feeling.
...from the steps of the neo-Byzantine cathedral.

When you are describing something that is two colours, you use 'and' between two adjectives, with or without hyphens.

...an ugly black and white swimming suit.
...a black-and-white calf.

If you are talking about a group of things, it is best to use hyphens if each thing is two colours.

...fifteen black-and-white police cars.

If each thing is only one colour, you cannot use hyphens.

...black and white dots.

A hyphen is used between two adjectives or noun modifiers that indicate that two countries or groups are involved in something.

Swedish-Norwegian relations improved.
...the United States-Canada free trade pact.

A hyphen is also used to indicate that something goes between two places.

If it was close to 6:27, they would amble to the train track and wait for the New York-Montreal train to roar through.

compound verbs   Compound verbs are usually written with a hyphen or as one word.

Take the baby along if you can't find anyone to baby-sit.
I can't come to London, because Mum'll need me to babysit that night.

phrasal verbs   Phrasal verbs are written as two (or three) words, without a hyphen.

She turned off the radio.
They broke out of prison on Thursday night.

However, nouns and adjectives that are related to phrasal verbs are written with a hyphen, if the first part ends in 'ing', 'er', 'ed', or 'en'.

Finally, he monitors the working-out of the plan.
One of the boys had stopped a passer-by and asked him to phone an ambulance.
Gold was occasionally found in the dried-up banks and beds of the rivers.
...selling broken-down second-hand cars at exorbitant prices.

Other nouns and adjectives related to phrasal verbs are written with a hyphen or as one word, or can be written in either way. For example, 'break-in' is always written with a hyphen, 'breakthrough' is always written as one word, and 'takeover' can also be written as 'take-over'.

numbers   Numbers between twenty and a hundred are usually written with a hyphen, as in 'twenty-four' and 'eighty-seven'. Fractions are also often written with a hyphen, as in 'one-third' and 'two-fifths'. However, when you use 'a' instead of 'one' you do not use a hyphen: 'a third'.

other points   If a word has two clear parts and the first letter of the second part is the same as the last letter of the first part, it is best to use a hyphen, especially if the letter is a vowel. For example, it is best to write 'pre-eminent' and 'co-operate', not 'preeminent' and 'cooperate'.

When people are using a pair of hyphenated words which have the same second part, they sometimes just write the first part of the first word. However, it is clearer to write each word in full.

...the militants whose careers bridged the pre- and post-war eras.
...long- and short-term economic planning.
...commodity speculators with their six- and seven-digit incomes.

See a Cobuild dictionary for information on the usual way to write a particular compound word.

For the use of the hyphen to break a word at the end of a line, see entry at **Punctuation.**

spend

You usually use the verb **spend** when you are talking about money or time. The past tense and past participle of 'spend' is **spent,** not 'spended'.

money   When you **spend** money, you use it to pay for things.

I had no very clear idea how much I had spent.
Her husband had spent all her money.

You say that someone spends money **on** something.

We always spend a lot of money on parties.
The buildings need a lot of money spent on them.

Note that you do not use any preposition except 'on' in sentences like these.

time   If you **spend** a period of time doing something, you do it from the beginning to the end of that time.

He spent all day planning the election campaign.

For more information about this use, see entry at **spend - pass.**

spend - pass

These verbs are used in a similar way to talk about time.

If someone does something from the beginning to the end of a period of time, you say that they **spend** the time doing it.

Deery spent the evening reading Symonds's Life of Michelangelo.
She woke early, meaning to spend all day writing.

You do not say that someone spends a period of time 'in doing', 'on doing', or 'to do' something.

If someone is in a place from the beginning to the end of a period of time, you can say that they **spend** the time there.

He spent most of his time in the library.
I have spent all my life in this town.
We found a hotel where we could spend the night.

You can say that someone **spends** or **passes** a period of time in another person's company. This use of **pass** is rather old-fashioned.

I spent an evening with Davis.
We passed a pleasant afternoon together.

'to pass   If you do something to occupy yourself while you are waiting for
the time'   something, you say that you do it **to pass the time.**

He had brought a book along to pass the time.
To pass the time they played Scrabble.

'have'   If you enjoy yourself while you are doing something, you do not say that you 'pass' or 'spend' a good time. You say that you **have** a good time.

The customers were having a good time drinking and eating and shouting jokes at each other.
A lot of my friends had a marvellous time over New Year.

spite

See entry at **in spite of - despite**.

GRAMMAR   # Split infinitives

A **split infinitive** is a 'to'-infinitive which has the 'to' separated from the base form by an adverbial.

There are enough nuclear arms to utterly destroy all civilization.

Some people think this structure is not acceptable and believe that the adverbial should be put elsewhere in the clause.

However, when an adverbial can be put in front of a verb in an ordinary clause, it sometimes seems natural to put the same adverbial in front of the base form in a 'to'-infinitive clause. For example, you say 'You must really make an effort', so it seems natural to say 'I told them to really make an effort'.

Use that opening to really establish contact with the other actors.
The directors of companies in this position often own some of the shares, but rarely enough to actually control a majority.
Then in front of me I saw two cars placing themselves in such a manner as to completely block my way.

It usually sounds unnatural to put an adverbial in front of a 'to'-infinitive when the adverbial relates to the event described in the 'to'-infinitive clause. With an intransitive 'to'-infinitive, you can put the adverbial after the 'to'-infinitive or at the end of the clause.

They seemed to have disappeared completely.
Do you think it is right for you and your family to rely completely on the State?
Nancy wanted to go back to China immediately.

With transitive 'to'-infinitives, it is often possible to put an adverbial after the object or at the end of the clause.

The treatment is to remove these foods completely from the diet.
Uncle Nick was tactful enough not to shatter this illusion immediately.
It's better to introduce him to school gradually.

However, if the clause is very long, it is better to put the adverbial after the 'to' (if it is not possible to rephrase the sentence).

...an incomes policy which aimed to gradually reduce wage settlements in the public sector.
When several injections are given they stimulate the body to slowly build its own, long-lasting protection against tetanus.

spoil

See entry at **destroy**.

spokesman

A **spokesman** is someone who is asked to speak as the representative of an organization or group of people.

A spokesman for the charity said the labels were referring to indirect rather than direct support.
'We regret the heavy loss of life and call upon all involved to show respect for the rule of law,' a White House spokesman said.

'spokeswoman'

In the past, **spokesman** was used to refer to both men and women, but it is now hardly ever used to refer to women. A female representative is now usually referred to as a **spokeswoman.**

A spokeswoman said official grant figures might need to be revised.
A police spokeswoman said 'This man is extremely dangerous.'

'spokesperson'

Spokesperson is a fairly new word which can refer to either a man or a woman.

A spokesperson confirmed that M. Attali would meet Mrs Thatcher the following day.

spring

Spring is used as a noun or a verb.

used as a noun

Spring is the season between winter and summer.

If you want to say that something happens every year during this season, you say that it happens **in spring** or **in the spring.**

In spring birds nest there.
...a huge flower bed which is full of tulips in the spring.

Note that you do not say that something happens 'in the springs'.

used as a verb

When a person or animal **springs,** they suddenly move upwards or forwards. The past tense of 'spring' is **sprang,** not 'springed'.

She sprang to her feet.

The past participle is **sprung.**

The lions had sprung out to kill passing antelope.

In American English, **sprung** is sometimes used as the past tense.

She sprung at him, and aimed a wild blow at his face.

staff

The people who work for an organization can be referred to as its **staff.**

She was invited to join the staff of the BBC.
The police questioned me and all the staff.

You can use a plural or singular form of a verb after **staff.** The plural form is more common.

The staff are very helpful.
The FI staff is concerned with intelligence collection operations.

WARNING

You do not refer to an individual person who works for an organization as a 'staff'. You refer to him or her as a **member of staff.**

There are two students to every member of staff.
At times members of HQ staff adopted a secretive attitude.

stair

See entry at **step - stairs.**

stand

Stand is usually used as a verb. Its past tense and past participle is **stood**, not 'standed'.

saying where someone is

When you **are standing** somewhere, your body is upright, your legs are straight, and your weight is supported by your feet. Note that in standard English you do not say that someone 'is stood' somewhere.

He is standing in the middle of the road.
She was standing at the bus stop.

saying where someone goes

Stand is also used to say that someone moves to a different place and remains standing there.

She told the girls to stand aside and let her pass.
She came and stood close to him.

'stand up'

Stand is sometimes used to say that someone raises their body to a standing position when they have been sitting.

The children stood and applauded.

However, you normally say that someone **stands up.**

Lewis Jones refused to stand up when I came into the room.
I put down my glass and stood up.

other meanings of 'stand'

If you **cannot stand** someone or something, you do not like them at all.

She can't stand children.

In British English, if you **stand** in an election, you are a candidate in it.

She was invited to stand as the Liberal candidate.
He has stood for Parliament 21 times.

American speakers say **run,** not 'stand'.

He then ran for Governor of New York.

start - begin - commence

If you **start, begin,** or **commence** something, you do it from a particular time.

My father started work when he was ten.
The prisoners plan to begin a hunger strike today.
I commenced a round of visits.

There is no difference in meaning between these words, but **commence** is a formal word. You do not use it in conversation.

The past tense of 'begin' is **began,** not 'beginned' or 'begun'.

Botanists everywhere began a dramatic revision of their ideas.

The past participle is **begun.**

The company has begun a programme of rationalization.

used with other verbs

You can use a 'to'-infinitive or an '-ing' form after **start** and **begin.**

Ralph started to run.
He started laughing.

I was beginning to feel better.
We began chattering and laughing together.

Note that you do not use an '-ing' form after **starting** or **beginning.** You do not say, for example, 'Now that I feel better, I'm beginning eating more'. You must say 'Now that I feel better, I'm beginning to eat more'.

After **commence**, you use an '-ing' form. You do not use a 'to'-infinitive.

He let his oars sink into the water and commenced pulling with long strokes.

used as intransitive verbs

Start, begin, and **commence** can all be used as intransitive verbs to say that something happens from a particular time.

His meeting starts at 7.
My career as a journalist was about to begin.
He had been held for 9 months when his trial commenced.

special uses of 'start'

Start has some special meanings. You do not use **begin** or **commence** with any of these meanings.

You use **start** to say that someone makes a machine or engine start to work.

He couldn't get his engine started.
He started the car and drove off.

You use **start** to say that someone creates a business or other organization.

He scraped up the money to start a restaurant.

In stories, **start** is used to say that someone starts to move in a particular direction.

Ralph started back to the shelters.
They started down the street together.

stationary - stationery

These words look similar and are both pronounced /steɪʃənəri/. However, their meanings are completely different.

'stationary'

Stationary is an adjective. If a vehicle is **stationary**, it is not moving.

...a stationary car.
Only use the handbrake when your vehicle is stationary.

'stationery'

Stationery is a noun. It refers to paper, envelopes, pens, and other equipment used for writing.

We buy things like stationery and toilet rolls in bulk.
...the office stationery cupboard.

'stationer'

A shop where you buy these things is called a **stationer** or a **stationer's**. It is not called a 'stationery'.

...a high street stationer.
...a stationer's in Islington.

Stationer's is not normally used in American English.

statistics

Statistics are numerical facts obtained from analysing information.

I happen to have the official statistics with me.
...accident statistics.

When **statistics** is used with this meaning, it is a plural noun. You use the plural form of a verb with it.

The same statistics are fed into the computer.
Statistics never prove anything.

Statistics is also the branch of mathematics dealing with these facts.

...a Professor of Statistics.

When you use **statistics** with this meaning, it is an uncount noun. You use a singular form of a verb with it.

Statistics has never been taught here before.

'statistical'   You do not use **statistic** as an adjective to mean 'relating to statistics'. The word you use is **statistical**.

Statistical techniques are regularly employed.
...the Central Statistical Office.

stay

See entry at **remain - stay**.

steal

When someone **steals** something, they take it without permission and without intending to return it.

He tried to steal a caravan from a caravan site.
My first offence was stealing a pair of binoculars.

The past tense of 'steal' is **stole**, not 'stealed'.

Armed raiders disguised as postmen stole 50 bags of mail.

The past participle is **stolen**.

My car was stolen on Friday evening.
He was sentenced to probation for receiving stolen property.

WARNING   If someone takes something from you without your permission, you do not say that they 'steal' you. You can say that they **rob** you, but it is more usual to use **steal** or **take** and mention the thing that has been stolen.

I had stolen my father's money.
I know you've taken my stamps.

'break into'   If someone steals things from a building, you do not say that they 'steal' the building. If they use force to get into the building, you say that they **break into** it.

He broke into the temporary premises of the Commercial Bank at Beauly.
The house next door was broken into.

step - stairs

'step'   A **step** is a raised flat surface which you put your feet on to move to a different level.

Mind the step.
She was sitting on the top step.

A series of steps, for example on a steep slope or on the outside of a building, is called a **flight** of steps.

...a flight of concrete steps.

'stairs'   A series of steps inside a building which you use to get from one floor to another is called **stairs** or a **staircase**.

I was running up and down the stairs.
There was a large hall with a big staircase winding up from it.

still

Still is most commonly used to say that a situation continues to exist.

position in sentence

You usually put **still** after the first auxiliary in a verb group. For example, you say 'He **was still** waiting'. You do not say 'He still was waiting'.

He could still get into serious trouble.
I've still got three left.

If there is no auxiliary, you put **still** in front of the verb, unless the verb is 'be'.

She still lives in London.

If the verb is 'be', you put **still** after it.

She was still beautiful.
There is still a chance that a few might survive.

In conversation, **still** is sometimes put at the end of a sentence.

We have a lot to do still.

However, you do not use **still** with this meaning at the beginning of a sentence.

used with 'even if'

Still is often used in sentences which begin with **even if** or **even though**.

But even if they do change the system, they've still got an economic crisis on their hands.

For more information about this use, see entry at **even**.

used in negative clauses

You can use **still** in a negative clause for emphasis. **Still** goes in front of the first auxiliary in the clause.

I still don't understand.
That still did not make it good enough for her.

However, you do not use **still** in a negative clause simply to say that something has not happened up to the present time. The word you use is **yet**. **Yet** goes after 'not' or at the end of the clause.

I haven't yet met Davis.
It isn't dark yet.

See entry at **yet**.

sting

Sting is usually used as a verb. Its past tense and past participle is **stung**, not 'stang' or 'stinged'.

If a creature such as a bee, wasp, or scorpion **stings** you, it pricks your skin and pushes poison into your body.

Bees do not normally sting without being provoked.
Perry was taken to hospital, stung by a wasp inside the mouth.

'bite'

You do not say that a mosquito or ant 'stings' you. You say that it **bites** you. The past tense and past participle of 'bite' are **bit** and **bitten**.

The mosquitoes always made her swell up when they bit her.
A mosquito had bitten her on the wrist.

You also say that a snake **bites** you.

In Britain you are more likely to be struck by lightning than bitten by a snake.

stone

Stone is the hard, solid substance which is found in the ground and is often used for building.

The bits of stone are joined together with cement.
...a stone wall.

'stone' and 'rock'   In British English, a **stone** is a small piece of stone which you can pick up in your hand.

Roger picked up a stone and threw it.

In American English, a small piece of stone like this is called a **rock**.

Rocks are thrown and the police come running.

In both British and American English, a **rock** is also a large piece of stone that sticks up out of the ground or the sea, or that has broken away from a mountain.

'stone' and 'pit'   In British English, the large, hard seed in a fruit such as a cherry, date, or apricot is called the **stone**.

...a cherry stone.

In American English, this seed is called the **pit**.

stop

You usually use the verb **stop** to say that someone no longer does something. After **stop,** you can use either an '-ing' form or a 'to'-infinitive, but with different meanings.

If you **stop doing** something at a particular time, you no longer do it after that time.

We all stopped talking.
He couldn't stop crying.

If you **stop to do** something, you interrupt what you are doing in order to do something else. For example, if you are talking about someone who is walking somewhere, you can say 'She **stopped to admire** the view'; this means that she stopped walking and admired the view before starting to walk again.

I was driving near Toulon and stopped to walk in a pine wood.
I stopped to tie my shoelace.

If you are prevented from doing something, you can say that something **stops you doing** it or **stops you from doing** it.

Did any of them try to stop you coming?
How do you stop a tap dripping?
Nothing was going to stop Sandy from being a writer.

You do not say that something 'stops you to do' something.

'stop' and 'stay'   In conversation, you can use **stop** to say that someone is staying somewhere for a short time.

They're stopping a couple of nights.
I can go and stop with my brother for a couple of days.

In writing, you use **stay,** not 'stop'.

The children were staying with Betty's stepmother in Glasgow.

store

See entry at **shop - store**.

storey - floor

'storey'   You refer to the different levels in a building as its **storeys** or **floors.** If you are saying how many levels a building has, you usually use **storeys.** For example, you say 'The new hospital is **five storeys** high' or 'I work in a **six-storey** building'.

...a house with four storeys.
...a single-storey building.

Storey is spelled **story** in American English. The plural of 'story' is **stories.**

...a four-story building.
...three hotel towers, each 30 stories high.

'floor'   If you are talking about a particular level in a building, you usually use **floor,** not 'storey'. You do not say that something is on a particular 'storey'. You say that it is on a particular **floor.**

My office is on the second floor.
...a ground floor flat.

story - storey

'story'   A **story** is a description of imaginary people and events, written or told in order to entertain people. The plural of 'story' is **stories.**

Tell me a story.
Kunta remembered the stories he had heard so many times.

Note that a description of a series of real events can also be called a **story.**

We had succeeded in selling the story of the expedition to the Daily Express.

In American English, a **story** is also one of the floors or levels in a building.

The house was four stories high.

'storey'   In British English, one of these floors is called a **storey.**

The house was three storeys high.

See entry at **storey - floor.**

strange

You use **strange** to say that something is unfamiliar or unexpected in a way that makes you puzzled, uneasy, or afraid.

The strange thing was that this teacher didn't even know us.
It was strange to hear her voice again.
I had a strange dream last night.

'unusual'   If you just want to say that something is not common, you use **unusual,** not 'strange'.

He had an unusual name.
The California race is over the unusual distance of one mile and a half.

For a list of words which can be used to describe someone who is unusual, see entry at **unusual.**

stranger

A **stranger** is someone who you have never met before.

A stranger appeared.
Antonio was a stranger to all of us.

WARNING

You do not use **stranger** to talk about someone who comes from a country which is not your own. You can refer to him or her as a **foreigner,** but this word can sound rather impolite. It is better to talk, for example, about 'someone **from abroad**' or 'a person **from overseas**'.

...visitors from abroad.
...when speaking to this man from overseas.

street

A **street** is a road in a town or large village, usually with houses or other buildings built alongside it.

The two men walked slowly down the street.
They went into the café across the street.

You do not use **street** to refer to a road in the countryside.

strike

If you **strike** someone or something, you hit them with your hand, a stick, or something else. This is a formal use.

He was striking his dog with his whip.

The past tense and past participle of 'strike' is **struck,** not 'striked'.

The young man struck his father.
He had struck her only in self-defence.

Strike is also used in the following ways to describe the effect something has on a person's mind:

If an idea or thought **strikes** you, it comes into your mind suddenly.

It struck him how foolish his behaviour had been.

If something **strikes** you in a particular way, it gives you a particular impression.

Gertie strikes me as a very silly girl.
How did London strike you?

If you **are struck by** something, you are very impressed with it.

I was struck by his good manners.

strong

The adjective **strong** is used in a number of different ways to describe people.

When you say that someone is **strong,** you usually mean that they have powerful muscles and the ability to lift or carry heavy objects.

Claudia was young, strong, and healthy.
The little boy has grown into a tall, strong man.

A **strong** personality is someone who is very confident and not easily influenced by other people.

He is a strong personality known for his enthusiasm for modernizing the government structure.

A **strong** believer in something is convinced that it is very good or desirable.

The Secretary of State is a strong believer in parental involvement in classrooms.

A **strong** supporter of a person or organization supports them in an enthusiastic way.

An old lady, a strong Labour supporter, grabbed me by the arm.

If someone smokes a lot or drinks a lot of alcohol, you do not say that they are a 'strong smoker' or a 'strong drinker'. You say that they are a **heavy smoker** or a **heavy drinker.**

strongly

You use **strongly** when you are talking about people's feelings or attitudes. For example, if you are **strongly** in favour of something, you are very much in favour of it.

I feel this very strongly.
He remains strongly opposed to commercial radio.

If you are urging someone to do something that will be to their advantage, you can say that you **strongly advise** them to do it.

I strongly advise you to get someone to help you.

You do not use **strongly** to describe the way someone holds something. Instead, you use **tightly** or **firmly.**

...the rifle which he gripped tightly in his right hand.
He held her arm firmly.

You do not say that a person works 'strongly'. You say that they work **hard.**

He had worked hard all his life.

stubborn

The following words can all be used to describe someone who is determined to do what they want to do, and refuses to change their mind:

firm	obstinate	rigid	stubborn
intransigent	pig-headed	steadfast	

You use **firm** or **steadfast** to show that you approve of someone's behaviour. **Steadfast** is a rather literary word.

If parents are firm, children accept discipline.
He relied on the calm and steadfast Kathy.

Stubborn, obstinate, pig-headed, rigid, and **intransigent** are all used to show disapproval. **Intransigent** is a formal word.

He and his officials remained as stubborn as ever.
...an obstinate and rebellious child.
They can be stupid and pig-headed.
They have a reputation for being rigid, distant and unloving.
He told them how intransigent the racists in his country had been.

student

In British English, a **student** is someone who is studying or training at a university or college.

...medical students.
...the students of Edinburgh University.

In American English, anyone who studies at a school, college, or university can be referred to as a **student**.

...high school students.

'schoolchildren' In British English, children attending schools are referred to generally as **schoolchildren**, **schoolboys**, or **schoolgirls**.

Each year the sanctuary is visited by thousands of schoolchildren.
...when I was still a schoolboy.
...the number of schoolgirls attracted to engineering.

'pupils' In Britain, the children attending a particular school are officially referred to as its **pupils**.

...a school with more than 1300 pupils.

'children' However, in conversation you talk about the **children** at a school, not its 'pupils'.

We have forty-three children in Fairacre School.

subconscious

used as a noun Your **subconscious** is the part of your mind that can influence you or affect your behaviour without your being aware of it.

They forget to take precautions because their subconscious deliberately makes them fail to do so.

used as an adjective You can also use **subconscious** as an adjective in front of a noun.

...the dark stirrings of a subconscious mind.
He was urged on by some subconscious desire to punish himself.

'unconscious' You do not say that a person is 'subconscious'. If someone is not conscious, you say that they are **unconscious**.

The blow knocked him unconscious.

subject

The **subject** of something such as a book or talk is the thing that is discussed in it.

He knew what the subject of the meeting was.
What was the subject of the opera you planned to write?

You do not say that the subject of a book or talk 'is about' something.

GRAMMAR # Subjects

In an active clause, the **subject** is the part of the clause that refers to the person or thing that does the action indicated by the verb, or that is in the state indicated by the verb. The subject is usually a noun group.

Our computers can give you all the relevant details.
They need help badly.

In a passive clause, the subject refers to the person or thing that is affected by an action or involved in someone's thoughts.

She had been taught logic by an uncle.
The examination is regarded as an arbitrary, unnecessary barrier.

You do not add a pronoun after the subject in a clause. For example, you do not say 'My sister she came to see me yesterday'. You say 'My sister came to see me yesterday'.

You can also use an '-ing' clause, a clause beginning with 'what', a 'wh'-clause, or a 'to'-infinitive clause as the subject of a verb.

Measuring the water correctly is most important.
What I saw was unforgettably horrifying.
Whether they believed me or not didn't matter.
To generalize would be wrong.

See entries at '**-ing forms, what, 'Wh'-clauses**, and **'To'-infinitive clauses**.

agreement The verb in a clause should agree with the subject. This means it should have an appropriate form depending on whether the subject is singular, uncountable, or plural.

He wears striped shirts.
People wear woollen clothing here even on hot days.

For detailed information, see entry at **Singular and plural**.

position In a statement, the subject usually comes in front of the verb.

I want to talk to Mr Castle.
Gertrude looked at Ann.

See entry at **Inversion** for information on when the subject comes after all or part of a verb group.

In questions, the subject comes after an auxiliary verb or after the verb 'be', unless the subject is a 'wh'-word or begins with a 'wh'-word.

Did you give him my letter?
Where is my father?

Who taught you to read?
Which library has the book?

In an imperative clause, there is usually no subject.

Give him a good book.
Show me the complete manuscript.

GRAMMAR # The Subjunctive

The **subjunctive** is a structure which is not very common in English and which is usually regarded as formal or old-fashioned. Using the subjunctive involves using the base form of a verb instead of a present or past tense, or instead of 'should' and a base form.

'whether' and The subjunctive can be used instead of a present tense in a conditional
'though' clause beginning with 'whether' or a clause containing 'though'.

The new world must be welcomed, if only because it will come whether it be welcomed or not.
The church absorbs these monuments, large though they be, in its own immense scope.

'that' The subjunctive can be used in a 'that'-clause when making a suggestion.

Someone suggested that they break into small groups.
It was his doctor who suggested that he change his job.

'lest'	'Lest' is sometimes used with a subjunctive verb form in a purpose clause to say what an action is intended to prevent.

He was put in a cell with no clothes and shoes <u>lest he injure</u> himself.

subjunctive use of 'were'	In writing and sometimes in conversation, 'were' is used instead of 'was' in conditional clauses referring to a situation that does not exist or that is unlikely. This use of 'were' is also a type of subjunctive use.

He would be persecuted <u>if he were</u> sent back.
<u>If I were</u> asked to define my condition, I'd say 'bored'.

'Were' is also often used instead of 'was' in clauses beginning with 'as though' and 'as if'.

You talk <u>as though he were</u> already condemned.
Margaret looked at me <u>as if I were</u> crazy.

GRAMMAR Subordinate clauses

A **subordinate clause** is a clause which adds to or completes the information given in a main clause. Most subordinate clauses begin with a **subordinating conjunction** such as 'because', 'if', or 'that'.

Many subordinate clauses are **adverbial clauses**. These clauses give information about the circumstances of an event. The different types of adverbial clause are described in detail below.

For information about other kinds of subordinate clause, see entry at **Relative clauses** and section on **report structures** in entry at **Reporting**. See also entries at **'-ing' forms**, **Past participles**, and **'To'-infinitive clauses**.

position of adverbial clauses	The usual position for an adverbial clause is just after the main clause.

Her father died <u>when she was young</u>.
They were going by car <u>because it was more comfortable</u>.

However, most types of adverbial clause can be put in front of the main clause when you want to draw attention to the adverbial clause.

<u>When the city is dark</u>, we can move around easily.
<u>Although crocodiles are inactive for long periods</u>, on occasion they can run very fast indeed.

Occasionally, an adverbial clause is put in the middle of another clause, especially a relative clause.

They make allegations which, <u>when you analyse them</u>, do not have too many facts behind them.

concessive clauses	**Concessive clauses** contain a fact that contrasts with the main clause. These are the main conjunctions used to introduce concessive clauses:

although	though	while
even though	whereas	whilst

I used to read a lot <u>although I don't get much time for books now</u>.
<u>While I did well in class</u>, I was a poor performer at games.

'Whilst' is a formal word.

omitting the subject The subject of a concessive clause beginning with 'although', 'though', 'while', or 'whilst' is sometimes omitted when it is the same as the main subject, and a participle is used as the verb. For example, instead of saying 'Whilst he liked cats, he never let them come into his house', you might say 'Whilst liking cats, he never let them come into his house'. This is a rather formal use.

...some of my colleagues who, whilst not voting for the Tories, had abstained.
Both the journalists, though greeted as heroes on their return from prison, not long afterwards quietly disappeared from their newspapers.

These four conjunctions can also be used in front of a noun group, an adjective group, or an adverbial.

It was an unequal marriage, although a stable and long-lasting one.
Though not very attractive physically, she possessed a sense of humour.

words in front of 'though' You can put a complement in front of 'though' for emphasis in formal English. For example, instead of saying 'Though he was ill, he insisted on coming to the meeting', you can say 'Ill though he was, he insisted on coming to the meeting'.

Astute businessman though he was, Philip was capable at times of extreme recklessness.
I had to accept the fact, improbable though it was.
Tempting though it may be to follow this point through, it is not really relevant and we had better move on.

When the complement is an adjective, you can use 'as' instead of 'though'.

Stupid as it sounds, I was so in love with her that I believed her.

Similarly, you can put an adverb such as 'hard', 'bravely', or 'valiantly' in front of 'though'.

Some members of the staff couldn't handle Murray's condition, hard though they tried.

'much as' When you are talking about a strong feeling or desire, you can use 'much as' instead of using 'although' and 'very much'. For example, instead of saying 'Although I like Venice very much, I couldn't live there', you can say 'Much as I like Venice, I couldn't live there'.

Much as they admired her looks and her manners, they had no wish to marry her.

'despite' and 'in spite of' 'Despite' and 'in spite of' are also used to introduce a contrast, but they are used as prepositions in front of noun groups or '-ing' clauses, not as conjunctions.

These mothers still play a big part in their children's lives, despite working and having a full-time nanny.
In spite of his mildness he was tremendously enthusiastic about his subject.

However, you can say 'despite the fact that...' or 'in spite of the fact that...'.

Despite the fact that it sounds like science fiction, most of it is technically realizable at this moment.

See also entry at **in spite of - despite**.

conditional clauses **Conditional clauses** are used to talk about possible situations. The event described in the main clause depends on the condition described in the subordinate clause. Conditional clauses usually begin with 'if' or 'unless'. See entries at **if** and **unless**.

When using a conditional clause, you often use a **modal** in the main clause. You always use a modal in the main clause when talking about a situation which does not exist.

If you weren't here, she would get rid of me in no time.
If anybody had asked me, I could have told them what happened.

inversion
Instead of using 'if' or 'unless', you can use **inversion** in formal speech and writing. For example, instead of saying 'If I'd been there, I would have stopped them', you can say 'Had I been there, I would have stopped them'.

Had I been found innocent, I would have been accepted as innocent by society.

imperatives
People sometimes use an imperative clause followed by 'and' or 'or' instead of a conditional clause. For example, instead of saying 'If you keep quiet, you won't get hurt', they say 'Keep quiet and you won't get hurt'. See entries at **Advising someone** and **Warning someone**.

less common conjunctions
You use 'provided', 'providing', 'as long as', or 'only if' to begin a conditional clause referring to a situation that is a necessary condition for the situation referred to in the main clause.

A child will learn what is right and what is wrong in good time provided he is not pressured.
As long as you print fairly clearly you don't have to learn any new typing skills.
Only if oil is very scarce is it likely that there will be a major use of coal to make oil.

Note that you use inversion in the main clause when you have used 'only if'.

To indicate that a situation is not affected by another possible situation, you use 'even if'.

Even if you've never been taught to mend a fuse, you don't have to sit in the dark.
I would have married her even if she had been penniless.

To indicate that a situation is not affected by any of several possibilities, you use 'whether' and 'or'.

If the lawyer made a long, oratorical speech, the client was happy whether he won or lost.
Some children start with a huge appetite at birth and never lose it afterwards, whether they're well or sick, calm or worried.

To indicate that a situation is not affected by either of two opposite possibilities, you use 'whether or not'.

A parent shouldn't hesitate to talk over the child's problems with the teacher, whether or not they are connected with school.
He will have to foot at least part of the bill whether he likes it or not.

manner clauses
Manner clauses describe someone's behaviour or the way that something is done. The following conjunctions are used to introduce manner clauses:

as	as though	the way
as if	like	

I don't understand why he behaves as he does.
Is she often rude and cross like she's been this last month?
Joyce looked at her the way a lot of girls did.

See entry at **like - as - the way**.

'As if' and 'as though' are used to say that something is done as it would be done if something else were the case. Note that a past tense is used in the subordinate clause.

Presidents can't dispose of companies as if people didn't exist.
She treats him as though he was her own son.

The subjunctive form 'were' is often used instead of 'was'.

He swallowed a little of his whisky as if it were nasty medicine.

place clauses **Place clauses** indicate the location or position of something. Place clauses usually begin with 'where'.

He said he was happy where he was.
He left it where it lay.

You use 'wherever' to say that something happens in every place where something else happens.

Soft-stemmed herbs and ferns spread across the ground wherever there was enough light.
Wherever I looked, I found patterns.

'Everywhere' can be used instead of 'wherever'.

Everywhere I went, people were angry or suspicious.

purpose clauses **Purpose clauses** indicate the intention someone has when they do something. The most common type of purpose clause is a 'to'-infinitive clause.

All information in this brochure has been checked as carefully as possible to ensure that it is accurate.
Carol had brought the subject up simply to annoy Sandra.

In formal writing and speech, 'in order' followed by a 'to'-infinitive clause is often used instead of a simple 'to'-infinitive clause.

They had to take some of his land in order to extend the church.

You can also use 'so as' followed by a 'to'-infinitive clause.

The best thing to do is to fix up a screen so as to let in the fresh air and keep out the flies.

WARNING You cannot use 'not' with a simple 'to'-infinitive clause when indicating a negative purpose. For example, you cannot say 'He slammed on his brakes to not hit it'. Instead, you must use 'to avoid' followed by an '-ing' form, or 'in order' or 'so as' followed by 'not' and a 'to'-infinitive.

He had to hang on to avoid being washed overboard.
I would have to give myself something to do in order not to be bored.
They went on foot, so as not to be heard.

Other purpose clauses are introduced by 'so', 'so that', or 'in order that'.

She said she wanted to be ready at six so she could be out by eight.
I have drawn a diagram so that my explanation will be clearer.
...people who are learning English in order that they can study a particular subject.

Note that you usually use a modal in these purpose clauses.

reason clauses **Reason clauses** explain why something happens or is done. They are usually introduced by 'because', 'since', or 'as'.

I couldn't feel anger against him because I liked him too much.
I didn't know that she had been married, since she seldom talked about herself.

Subordinate clauses

You use 'in case' or 'just in case' when you are mentioning a possible future situation which is someone's reason for doing something. In the reason clause, you use the simple present tense.

Mr Woods, I am here just in case anything out of the ordinary happens.

When you are talking about someone's reason for doing something in the past, you use the simple past tense in the reason clause.

Sam had consented to take an overcoat in case the wind rose.

People used to use reason clauses beginning with 'for', but this use is now old-fashioned.

We never see Henry these days, for Henry has grown fat and lazy.

result clauses **Result clauses** indicate the result of an event or situation. Result clauses are introduced by the conjunctions 'so that' or 'so'. They always come after the main clause.

A great storm had brought the sea right into the house, so that they had been forced to make their escape by a window at the back.
The young do not have the money to save and the old are consuming their savings, so it is mainly the middle-aged who are saving.

'That'-clauses (with or without 'that') can also be used as result clauses when 'so' or 'such' has been used in the main clause.

They were so surprised they didn't try to stop him.
These birds have such small wings that they cannot get into the air even if they try.

See entry at **so**.

time clauses **Time clauses** indicate the time of an event. The following conjunctions are used to introduce time clauses:

after	before	the minute	until	whilst
as	once	the moment	when	
as soon as	since	till	while	

We arrived as they were leaving.
When the jar was full, he turned the water off.

More information on the uses of the words listed above can be found in the entry for each word.

tenses in When talking about the past or the present, the verb in a time clause has
time clauses the same tense that it would have in a main clause or a simple sentence. However, if the time clause refers to the future, you use the simple present tense. You do not use 'will'.

As soon as I get back, I'm going to call my lawyer.
He wants to see you before he dies.

When mentioning an event in a time clause which will happen before an event referred to in the main clause, you use the present perfect tense in the time clause. You do not use 'will have'.

We won't be getting married until we've saved enough money.
Tell the DHSS as soon as you have retired.

When reporting a statement or thought about such an event, you use the simple past tense or the past perfect tense in the time clause.

I knew he would come back as soon as I was gone.
He constantly emphasised that violence would continue until political oppression had ended.

For information on the use of tenses with 'since' in a time clause, see entry at **since**.

omitting the subject If the subject of the main clause and the time clause are the same, the subject in the time clause is sometimes omitted and a participle is used as the verb. This is done especially in formal English.

I read the book before going to see the film.
The car was stolen while parked in a London street.

'When', 'while', 'once', 'until', or 'till' can be used in front of a noun group, an adjective group, or an adverbial.

He had read of her elopement while at Oxford.
Steam or boil them until just tender.

regular occurrences If you want to say that something always happens or happened in particular circumstances, you use a clause beginning with 'when' or, more emphatically, 'whenever', 'every time', or 'each time'.

When he talks about the Church, he does sound like an outsider.
Whenever she had a cold, she ate only fruit.
Every time I go to that class I panic.
He flinched each time she spoke to him.

---

subway

In some American cities, the **subway** is a railway system in which electric trains travel below the ground in tunnels.

'Underground' In Britain, a railway system like this is not called the 'subway'. The London and Glasgow systems are both called the **Underground.** The London system is also called the **tube.**

In both British and American English, the **subway** is also a path for pedestrians under a busy road.

succeed

If you **succeed in doing** something that involves difficulty or effort, you do it.

I succeeded in getting the job.
She had succeeded in deceiving Michael.

You do not say that you 'succeed to do' something,

successful

If something is **successful,** it achieves what it was intended to achieve.

...a successful attempt to land on the moon.
If this method is not successful, consult your health visitor or doctor.

You can also say that a person **is successful in doing** something.

On finishing his training, he was successful in obtaining a post at Halifax.

You do not say that someone 'is successful to do' something.

such

referring back **Such** a thing or person means a thing or person like the one that has just been described, mentioned, or experienced.

Do you welcome the emergence of such a form?

When **such** is used like this in front of a noun group, 'as this' or 'as these' is sometimes added after the noun group. This is a fairly formal use.

They were not sharp enough to see through such a mask as this.
It's the only way to behave at such times as these.

In sentences like these, the word order is often changed. For example, instead of saying 'such times as these', people say **times such as these.** You can also say **times like these.**

They were not involved in issues such as this.
It is their job to establish broad principles such as these.
There is nothing wrong in having thoughts like these.

<table>
<tr><td>**WARNING**</td><td>You do not use **such** when you are talking about something that is present, or about the place where you are. For example, if you are admiring someone's watch, you do not say 'I'd like such a watch'. You say 'I'd like a watch **like that**'. Similarly, you do not say about the town where you are living 'There's not much to do in such a town'. You say 'There's not much to do in a town **like this**'.</td></tr>
</table>

I would have thought I was free in a place like this.
I'm sure they don't have chairs like these.

'such as' You use **such as** between two noun groups when you are giving an example of something.

...a game of chance such as roulette.

The first noun group is sometimes put between **such** and **as.**

We talked about such subjects as the weather.

'such' used **Such** is sometimes used to emphasize the adjective in a noun group. For
for emphasis example, instead of saying 'He's a nice man', you can say 'He's **such a nice man**'.

She was such a nice girl.
She seemed such a happy woman.

Note that you must use 'a' when the noun group is singular. You do not say, for example, 'She was such nice girl'. You also do not say 'She was a such nice girl'.

For greater emphasis, some people say **ever such** instead of 'such'.

There's ever such a nice helper who comes in every day to see if you're all right.

You do not use **ever such** in writing.

You can use **such** to refer to something or someone that has just been described or mentioned and to emphasize some quality that they have. For example, instead of saying 'It was a very dull place. I was surprised to see her there', you can say 'I was surprised to see her in **such a dull place**'.

I was, of course, impressed to meet such a famous actress.
I wondered how he'd react to such a blunt question.
You really shouldn't tell such obvious lies.

'such ... that': You can also use **such** in front of a noun group when you are saying that
mentioning something happens because someone or something has a quality to an
a result unusually large extent. After the noun group, you use a 'that'-clause.

A few boas grow to such a length that they can tackle creatures as big as goats.
This can be such a gradual process that you are not aware of it happening.

suffer

You can say that someone **suffers** pain or an unpleasant experience.

He suffered a lot of discomfort.
Young suffered imprisonment and intimidation.

'put up with'   You do not use **suffer** to say that someone tolerates an unpleasant person. You say that they **put up with** the person.

The local people have to put up with gaping tourists.

'stand' and 'bear'   If you do not like someone at all, you do not say that you 'can't suffer' them. You say that you **can't stand** them or **can't bear** them.

She said she couldn't stand him.
I can't bear kids.

suggest

When you **suggest** something, you mention it as a plan or idea for someone to consider.

Your bank manager will probably suggest a personal loan.
We have to suggest a list of possible topics for next term's seminars.

You can use a 'that'-clause after **suggest**.

I suggest that we let them do this.
Perhaps you could suggest that he talks the matter over with his solicitor.

In sentences like these, you usually use a simple tense in the 'that'-clause. However, it is possible to use an infinitive without 'to'. This is a formal use.

The committee suggest that even greater emphasis be placed upon this effort.

The modals 'might' and 'should' are also sometimes used. This is also a formal use.

Sometimes he would suggest that the destitute might turn to their own families for support.
I suggest that he should discover the diversity of the material that is now available.

Suggestions

There are many ways of suggesting a course of action to someone.

You can say 'You could...'.

You could make a raft or something.
You could phone her and ask.
'Well, what shall we do?'—'You could try Ebury Street.'

You can also use 'How about...?' or 'What about...?', followed by an '-ing' form.

How about taking him outside to have a game?
What about becoming an actor?

Note that you can also use 'How about...?' or 'What about...?' with a noun group, to suggest that someone has a drink or some food, usually with you, or to suggest an arrangement.

How about a steak and a couple of pints?
What about a drink?
'I'll explain when I see you.'—'When will that be?'—'How about late tonight?'

Suggestions

A more indirect way of suggesting a course of action is to use 'Have you thought of...?', followed by an '-ing' form.

Have you thought of asking what's wrong with Henry?

firm suggestions
A firmer way of making a suggestion is to say 'Couldn't you...?', 'Can't you...?', or 'Why not...?'

Couldn't you get a job in one of the smaller colleges around here?
Can't you just tell him?
Why not write to her?

You can also use 'Try...', followed by an '-ing' form or a noun group.

Try advertising in the local papers.
Try a little methylated spirit.

A very firm way of making a suggestion is to say 'I suggest you...'.

I suggest you leave this to me.

If you want to suggest persuasively but gently that someone does something, you can say 'Why don't you...?'

Why don't you go out and have a stroll along the towpath for half an hour?
Why don't you think about it and decide later?
Why don't you go to bed?

For other ways of saying firmly what course of action someone should take, see entry at **Advising someone.**

less firm suggestions
If you do not feel strongly about what you are suggesting, but cannot think of anything better that the other person might do, you can say 'You might as well...' or 'You may as well...'.

You might as well drive on back to Famagusta by yourself.
You may as well go home and come back in the morning.

suggestions in writing and broadcasting
People who are writing or broadcasting make suggestions using expressions like 'You might like to...' and 'It might be a good idea to...'.

Alternatively, you might like to consider discussing your insurance problems with your bank manager.
You might consider moving to a smaller house.
You might want to have a separate heading for each point.
It might be a good idea to rest on alternate days between running.

suggesting doing something together
There are several ways of making a suggestion about what you and someone else might do.

If you want to make a firm suggestion which you think the other person will agree with, you say 'Let's...'.

Come on, let's go.
Let's meet at my office at noon. All right?
Come on now. Let's be practical. How can we help?

You can make the suggestion seem persuasive rather than firm and forceful by adding the tag 'shall we?'

I tell you what, let's slip back to the hotel and have a drink, shall we?
Let's do some of these letters, Mrs Taswell, shall we?

For a negative suggestion, you say 'Let's not...'.

Let's not talk here.
We have twenty-four hours. Let's not panic.
Let's not go jumping to conclusions.

Another way of making a firm suggestion is to say 'We'll...'.

We'll talk later, Percival.
'What do you want to do with Ben's boat?'—'We'll leave it here till tomorrow.'

Again, you can make the suggestion persuasive rather than forceful by adding the tag 'shall we?'

We'll leave somebody else to clear up the mess, shall we?
All right, we'll change things around a bit now, shall we?

Another firm way of suggesting is to say 'I suggest we…'.

I suggest we discuss this elsewhere.
I suggest we go to the hospital in St Johnsbury right away.

Another way of making a suggestion is to say 'Shall we…?' You can make a suggestion like this sound firm or less firm by altering your tone of voice.

Shall we go and see a film?
Shall we make a start?
Shall we sit down?

less firm suggestions
When you want to make a suggestion without being too forceful, you use 'We could…'. You use this form of suggestion when the issue of what to do has already been raised.

I did ask you to have dinner with me. We could discuss it then.
We could tow one of them in.
'I'm tired.'—'Too tired for a walk, even? We could go to the Cave of Shulamit.'

You can also make a non-forceful suggestion in an indirect way, using 'I thought we…' or 'I wonder if we…' and a modal.

I thought we might have some lunch.
In the meantime, I wonder if we can just turn our attention to something you mentioned a little earlier.
I wonder whether we could have a little talk, after the meeting.

If you are unenthusiastic about your own suggestion, but cannot think of a better course of action, you say 'We might as well…'.

We might as well go in.
We might as well go home.

very firm suggestions
If you want to make a very firm and forceful suggestion, which you feel is very important, you say 'We must…'.

We must be careful.
We must hurry.
We must look to the future. We must plan.

suggestions about what would be best
When you are suggesting doing something which you think is the sensible thing to do, you say 'We ought to…' or 'We'd better…'. People often soften this form of suggestion by saying 'I think' or 'I suppose' first, or adding the tag 'oughtn't we?' or 'hadn't we?'

We ought to give the alarm.
Come on, we'd better try and find somebody.
' think we'd better leave.
I suppose we'd better take a look through the bushes.
We ought to order, oughtn't we?

'I think we should…' is also used.

I think we should go back.
I think we should change the subject.

If you are not sure that your suggestion will be accepted without argument, you say 'Shouldn't we...?' or 'Oughtn't we to...?'

Shouldn't we have supper first?
Shouldn't we be on our way?
Oughtn't we to phone for the police?

You can also say 'Don't you think we should...?' or 'Don't you think we'd better...?'

Don't you think we'd better wait and see whether or not the charges stand up?

replying to a suggestion

The usual way of replying to a suggestion that you agree with is to say 'All right' or 'OK'. You can also say something like 'Good idea' or 'That's a good idea'.

'Let's dance now.'—'All right then.'
'Let's not do that. Let's play cards instead.'—'That's all right with me.'
'Try up there.'—'OK.'
'What am I going to do?'—'Lock him in a closet in his office is what I would do.'—'That's a good idea.'

You can reply 'Yes, I could' to a suggestion starting with 'You could'.

'You could get a job over there.'—'Oh yes, I could do that, couldn't I?'

A more casual way of replying is to say 'Why not?'

'Shall we take a walk?'—'Why not?'

People also sometimes say 'Fine' or 'That's fine by me' when replying to a suggestion about doing something together. If they are very enthusiastic, they say 'Great'.

'What about Tuesday?'—'Fine.'

If you do not agree with the suggestion, you can say 'I don't think that's a good idea', 'No, I can't', or 'No, I couldn't'.

'You could ask her.'—'I don't think that's a very good idea.'
'Well, can you not make synthetic ones?'—'We can't, no.'

You can also give a reason for not accepting the suggestion.

'I'll ring her up when I go out to lunch.'—'Why not do it here and save money?'—'I like my calls private.'

---

suit - suite

'suit'

Suit /suːt/ is used as a verb or a noun.

If something **suits** you, it is convenient, acceptable, or appropriate for you.

Would Monday suit you?
A job where I was indoors all day wouldn't suit me.

You do not say that something 'suits to' you.

A **suit** is a set of clothes made from the same material.

He arrived at the office in a suit and tie.

'suite'

Suite /swiːt/ is a noun.

A **suite** is a set of rooms in a hotel.

They always stayed in a suite at the Ritz.

A **suite** is also a set of matching furniture for a sitting room or bathroom.

I need a three-piece suite for the lounge.

suitable

Someone or something that is **suitable for** a particular person or purpose is right or acceptable for them.

These flats are not really suitable for families with children.
Farm tractors are not suitable for small plots of land.

Note that you do not use any preposition except 'for' in sentences like these.

suitcase

See entry at **bag**.

summer

Summer is the season between spring and autumn.

If you want to say that something happens every year during this season, you say that it happens **in summer** or **in the summer.**

In summer trees grow quickly and produce large wood cells.
In the summer there is no more than a foot of water among the stones.

You do not say that something happens 'in the summers'.

sunk - sunken

See entry at **sink**.

superior

If one person or thing is **superior to** another, they are better than the other person or thing.

I secretly felt superior to him.
The film is vastly superior to the book.

You do not use any preposition except 'to' after **superior.** You also do not say that one person or thing is 'more superior to' another.

supper

Some people call a large meal they eat in the early part of the evening their **supper.** Other people use **supper** to refer to a small meal eaten just before going to bed at night. For more information, see entry at **Meals.**

supply

If you **supply** someone **with** something, you provide them with it.

I can supply you with food and drink.
They are negotiating to buy a replacement reactor from the French, who supplied them with the last one.

Note that you must use 'with' in sentences like these. You do not say, for example, 'I can supply you food and drink'.

You can also say that something **is supplied to** someone.

This system ensures that heat is supplied to all customers at an adequate temperature.
Much of the material supplied to the army was faulty.

support

If you **support** someone or **support** their aims, you agree with their aims and try to help them to succeed.

We supported the nurses by taking industrial action.
A lot of building workers supported the campaign.

If you **support** a sports team, you want them to win.

He has supported Oldham Athletic all his life.

If you **support** someone, you provide them with money or the things they need.

He has a wife and three children to support.

WARNING

You do not use **support** in any of the following ways:

You do not use **support** to say that someone accepts pain or an unpleasant situation. You say that they **bear** it, **put up with** it, or **tolerate** it.

It was painful of course but I bore it.
You have to put up with these inconveniences.
I was wondering how much longer I could tolerate isolation.

You do not use **support** to say that someone allows something that they do not approve of. You say that they **put up with** it or **tolerate** it. If they do not allow it, you can say that they **won't stand for** it.

I've put up with more than enough from you already.
...the tendency to tolerate the extremes of human behaviour.
I won't stand for any more of your disobedience.

If you do not like something at all, you do not say that you 'can't support' it. You say that you **can't bear** it or **can't stand** it.

I can't bear weddings.
She can't stand children.

suppose - assume

'suppose'

If you **suppose** that something is the case, you think it is probably the case.

I suppose it was bound to happen.
I suppose he left fairly recently.

'assume'

If you **assume** that something is the case, you are fairly sure that it is the case, and act as if it were the case.

I assumed that he had started working as soon as he left.
When you have a language degree, people assume that you speak the language fluently.

You do not say that someone supposes or assumes 'something to be' the case.

'don't suppose'

Instead of saying that you **suppose** something is **not** the case, you usually say that you **don't suppose that it is** the case.

I don't suppose you would be prepared to stay in Edinburgh?

'I suppose so'

If someone says that something is the case, or asks you whether something is the case, you can say '**I suppose so**' as a way of agreeing with them or saying 'yes'. When you say '**I suppose so**', you are indicating that you are uncertain or unenthusiastic about something.

'So it was worth doing?'—'I suppose so.'

Note that you do not say 'I suppose it'.

'I suppose not'	Similarly, you can agree with a negative statement or question by saying **'I suppose not'**.

'It doesn't often happen.'—'No, I suppose not.'

'suppose' used as a conjunction	You can use **suppose** as a conjunction when you are considering a possible situation or action and trying to think what effects it would have.

Suppose we don't say a word, and somebody else finds out about it.

Supposing can be used in a similar way.

Supposing something should go wrong, what would you do then?

'be supposed to'	If something **is supposed to** be done, it should be done because of a rule, instruction, or custom.

You are supposed to report it to the police as soon as possible.
I'm not supposed to talk to you about this.

If something **is supposed to** be true, people generally think that it is true.

The hill was supposed to be haunted by a ghost.
She was supposed to be very good as an actress.

Note that you do not say that something 'is suppose to' be done or be true.

sure

See entry at **certain - sure**.

surely

You use **surely** for emphasis when you are objecting to something that has been said or done.

Academics tend to use journalism as a dirty word, but surely some of the best writers have been journalists.
Too many plays have been spoiled in this way. What many of us surely want are more productions like Trevor Nunn's 'Othello'.

'definitely' and 'certainly'	You do not use **surely** simply to give strong emphasis to a statement. The word you use is **definitely**.

They were definitely not for sale.
The call definitely came from your phone.

You also do not use **surely** when you are agreeing with something that has been said, or confirming that something is true. The word you use is **certainly**.

Ellie was certainly a student at the university but I'm not sure about her brother.

You do not use **surely** to say emphatically that something will happen in the future. Instead you use **definitely** or **certainly**.

The Conference will definitely be postponed.
If nothing is done, there will certainly be an economic crisis.

'naturally'	You do not use **surely** to emphasize that someone is behaving in the way you would expect in particular circumstances. The word you use is **naturally**.

Dina was crying, so naturally Hannah was upset.

surgery

used as an uncount noun	In both British and American English, **surgery** is medical treatment in which a person's body is cut open so that a surgeon can deal with a diseased or damaged part.

He underwent surgery at Queen's Medical Centre.

used as a count noun	In British English, a doctor's or dentist's **surgery** is the building or room where he or she works and where people go to receive advice and minor treatment.

His surgery was rebuilt three years ago.

'office'	In American English, a building or room like this is called the doctor's or dentist's **office.**

Dr Peabody's office was just across the street.

In American English, a **surgery** or **operating room** is a room in a hospital where surgeons carry out medical operations. In British English, a room like this is called an **operating theatre.**

surprise

Surprise is used as a verb or a noun.

used as a verb	If something **surprises** you, you did not expect it.

Dad's reply surprised me.
Her sudden death had surprised everybody.

You do not use a continuous form of **surprise.** You do not say, for example, 'What you say is surprising me'.

used as a noun	If something is a **surprise,** it surprises someone.

The ruling came as a surprise to everyone.
It was a great surprise to find that this is a most friendly university.

In stories, expressions such as **to my surprise** and **to her surprise** are sometimes used. They indicate that someone is surprised at something that happens.

To her surprise he sat down.

You do not use any preposition except 'to' in expressions like these.

'surprised'	**Surprised** is an adjective. If you are **surprised to see** something or **surprised to hear** something, you did not expect to see it or hear it.

I was surprised to see Judith Haynes there.
You'll be surprised to learn that Charles Boon is living here.

WARNING	You do not say that someone is 'surprised at seeing' or 'surprised at hearing' something. You also do not say that someone is 'surprise to' see or hear something.

swamp

See entry at **marsh - bog - swamp.**

sweetcorn

See entry at **corn.**

sweets - candy

'sweets'	In British English, small, sweet things that you eat, such as toffees and chocolates, are called **sweets.**

She urged her children not to eat too many sweets.

'candy'	In American English, sweet things like these are called **candy. Candy** is an uncount noun.

You eat too much candy. It's bad for your teeth.

swift

See entry at **fast**.

sympathetic

You say that someone is being **sympathetic** when they are kind to someone who has problems, and show that they understand their feelings.

My boyfriend was very sympathetic and it did make me feel better.

'nice' and 'likeable'

You do not say that someone is 'sympathetic' when they are very pleasant and easy to like. The word you use is **nice** or **likeable**.

He was a terribly nice man.
...a very likeable and attractive young man.

See entry at **nice**.

T

---

take

Take is one of the commonest verbs in English. It is used in many different ways. Its other forms are **takes, taking, took, taken**.

actions and activities

Take is most commonly used with a noun referring to an action to say that someone performs that action.

She took a shower.
He formed the habit of taking long, solitary walks.

For more information about this use, see entry at **have - take**.

moving things

If you **take** something from one place to another, you carry it there.

Don't forget to take your umbrella.
He has to take the boxes to the office every morning.

For more information about this use, see entry at **carry - take**.

WARNING

Do not confuse **take** with **bring** or **fetch**. For an explanation of some of the differences, see entry at **bring - take - fetch**.

exams and tests

When someone completes an exam or test, you say that they **take** the exam or test.

She's not yet taken her driving test.
She took her degree last year.

time

If something **takes** a certain amount of time, you need that amount of time in order to do it.

How long will it take?
It may take them several weeks to get back.

take place

You say that an event **takes place**.

The first meeting of this committee took place on 9 January.
A second revolution in fashion took place just after World War I.

Happen and **occur** have a similar meaning, but they can only be used to talk about events which were not planned. You can use **take place** to talk about either planned or unplanned events.

The talks will take place in Vienna.
The pressure becomes so great that an explosion takes place.

Note that **take place** is intransitive. You do not say that something 'was taken place'.

take up

If you **take up** an activity, you become interested in it and start doing it.

I thought I'd take up fishing.
He took up gymnastics at the age of nine.

Take up has another meaning. If an activity **takes up** a lot of your time, you spend a lot of time doing it.

...the cumbersome administrative work that took up staff time.
At the moment 'Oliver' is taking a lot of my time up.

Similarly, if something **takes up** an amount of space, it occupies all of it.

Dresses don't take up much space.
They don't take up any more room than a passport.

'take off' When a plane leaves the ground and starts flying, you do not say that it 'takes up'. You say that it **takes off**.

...small planes standing ready to take off.
Journalists gathered at the airport to watch us take off.

talented

See entry at **skilful - skilled - talented.**

talk

Talk is used as a verb or a noun.

used as a verb When you **talk**, you say things.

Nancy's throat was so sore that she could not talk.

You do not use **talk** to report what someone says. You do not say, for example, 'He talked that the taxi had arrived'. You say 'He **said** that the taxi had arrived'.

I said that I would like to teach English.

If you mention the person who is being spoken to, you use **tell**.

He told me that Sheldon would be over to see me in a few days.

See entries at **say** and **tell.**

Do not confuse **talk** with **speak**. For an explanation of the differences, see entry at **speak - talk.**

used as a noun If you give a **talk,** you speak for a period of time to an audience.

Colin Blakemore came here and gave a talk a couple of years ago.

For more information about this use, see entry at **speech - talk.**

tall

See entry at **high - tall.**

tasteful - tasty

'tasteful' Something that is **tasteful** is attractive and elegant. You can use **tasteful** to talk about things such as furniture, ornaments, and clothes.

The bedroom was simple but tasteful.
He always sent the most tasteful Christmas cards.

'tasty' Food that is **tasty** has a pleasant flavour.

He cooked some tasty food and took it to his father.
The seeds, when toasted, are tasty and nutritious.

'delicious' Note that you do not usually describe sweet foods as 'tasty'. Instead, you can say that they are **delicious.**

Martha makes the most delicious chocolate pudding.

tasteless - distasteful

'tasteless' Something that is **tasteless** is vulgar and unattractive.

...tasteless ornaments.
Apart from a few tasteless remarks, he was reasonably well-behaved.

Tasteless food has very little flavour.

...cold, tasteless pizzas.

'distasteful' If something is **distasteful** to you, you dislike it or disapprove of it.

Unnecessary slaughter of animals is distasteful to most people.

Note that **distasteful** is not the opposite of 'tasteful'.

tasty

See entry at **tasteful - tasty**.

taxi - cab

A **taxi** or **cab** is a car driven by a person whose job is to take people where they want to go, in return for money.

There is no difference in meaning between **taxi** and **cab.** Both words are used in British and American English. However, **taxi** is more common in British English and **cab** is more common in American English.

tea

the drink **Tea** is a drink made by pouring boiling water onto the dried leaves of the tea bush. In Britain, **tea** is usually drunk with milk.

She poured herself another cup of tea.
She went into the kitchen to make a fresh pot of tea.

meals **Tea** is also used to refer to two different types of meal.

Some people use it to refer to a light meal eaten in the afternoon. This meal usually consists of sandwiches and cakes, with tea to drink. It is sometimes called **afternoon tea.**

Other people use **tea** to refer to a main meal eaten in the early evening. For more information, see entry at **Meals.**

teach

<table>
<tr><td>teaching a subject</td><td>If you **teach** a subject, you explain it to people so that they know about it or understand it. The past tense and past participle of 'teach' is **taught,** not 'teached'.</td></tr>
</table>

I taught history for many years.
English will be taught in primary schools.

When **teach** has this meaning, it often has an indirect object. The indirect object can go either in front of the direct object or after it. If it goes after the direct object, you put 'to' in front of it.

...the guy that taught us English at school.
I found a job teaching English to a group of adults in Paris.

<table>
<tr><td>teaching a skill</td><td>If you **teach** someone **to do** something, you give them instructions so that they know how to do it.</td></tr>
</table>

He taught me to sing a song.
Boylan had taught him to drive.

When **teach** is used with a 'to'-infinitive like this, it must have a direct object. You do not say, for example, 'Boylan had taught to drive'.

Instead of using a 'to'-infinitive, you can sometimes use an '-ing' form. For example, instead of saying 'I taught them to ski', you can say 'I taught them **skiing**'. You can also say 'I taught them **how to ski**'.

She taught them singing because she enjoyed it herself.
My mother taught me how to cook.

team

A **team** is a group of people who play against another group in a game.

He got into the New Zealand rugby team in 1978.

After **team** you can use either a singular or plural form of a verb.

The team has qualified again for Italy next summer.
Graham Gooch estimates that his team have missed twenty chances in their last three games.

technique - technology

<table>
<tr><td>'technique'</td><td>A **technique** is a method of doing something.</td></tr>
</table>

...the techniques of film-making.
...modern management techniques.

Technique is skill and ability which you develop through training and practice.

He could not possibly have had any film technique.

<table>
<tr><td>'technology'</td><td>**Technology** is the use of scientific knowledge for practical purposes, for example in industry.</td></tr>
</table>

...our belief in the power of modern technology.
Computer technology can be expected to change.

telegram

See entry at **wire**.

Telephoning

In the examples in this entry, A is the person answering the phone, and B is the person who is making the phone call.

answering the phone

There are several ways of answering the telephone when someone phones you. You can just say 'Hello', or you can give your telephone number.

A: *Hello.*
B: *Hello. It's me.*

A: *76459.*
B: *Hello. Is that Carol?*

Note that you say each digit of the telephone number. For example, you would say 435 1916 as 'four three five one nine one six'. British speakers usually say 0 as 'oh'. American speakers usually say 'zero'. When a number is repeated, British speakers use the word 'double'. For example, they say 4335 as 'four double three five'.

If you are at work, you can give the name of your organization or department, or your own name. You can say 'Good morning' or 'Good afternoon' instead of 'Hello'.

A: *Parkfield Medical Centre.*
B: *Hello. I'd like to make an appointment to see one of the doctors this morning please.*

A: *Hello. Tony Parsons speaking.*
B: *Oh, hello. It's Tom Roberts here.*

A: *Good morning.*
B: *Good morning. Who am I speaking to?*
A: *Er, my name is Alan Fentiman.*

Some people say 'Yes?' when answering a phone call, especially one within an organization, but this can sound abrupt and rude.

If you recognize the person's voice when they say 'Hello', you can say 'Hello' followed by their name.

A: *Hello.*
B: *Hello, Jim.*
A: *Hello, Alex, how are you?*

If you don't recognize the caller's voice, you can ask who it is. If you are at home, you say 'Sorry, who is it?' or 'Who is this?' Some people say 'Who's that?', but this can sound rude.

A: *Hello.*
B: *Hello.*
A: *Sorry, who is it?*
B: *It's me, Terry.*

If you think you know who the caller is, you say, for example, 'Is that James?' or 'That's James, isn't it?'

A: *Hello.*
B: *Hello. Can I speak to John?*
A: *I'm afraid he's just gone out. Is that Sarah?*
B: *Yes.*

If you are at work, and the caller wants to speak to someone else, you say 'Who's calling?' or 'Who's speaking?'

B: *Hello, could I speak to Mrs George, please?*

A: *Who's calling?*
B: *The name is Pearce.*
A: *Hold on a minute, please.*

If the caller has got through to the wrong number, you say something like 'I think you've got the wrong number' or 'Sorry, wrong number'.

A: *Hello.*
B: *Mrs Clough?*
A: *No, you've got the wrong number.*
B: *I'm sorry.*

telephoning someone When you are phoning a friend or relative, you can just say 'Hello' when they answer the phone, if you think they will recognize your voice. You can add their name.

A: *Hello.*
B: *Hello! I just thought I'd better ring to let you know what time I'll be arriving.*

A: *Hello.*
B: *Hello, Alan.*
A: *Hello, Mark, how are you?*
B: *Well, not so good.*

Note that after saying 'Hello' friends and relatives normally ask each other how they are.

If you need to make it clear who you are when you phone someone, you say 'It's' or 'This is' and your name.

A: *Hello.*
B: *Hello. It's Jenny.*

A: *Hello.*
B: *Hello, Alan. This is Eila.*

You can also say 'It's ... here'.

A: *Hello.*
B: *It's Maggie Turner here.*

Sometimes you do not need to give your name, for example when you are asking for general information.

A: *Citizen's Advice Bureau.*
B: *Hello. I'd like some advice about a dispute with my neighbours.*

If you are not sure who has answered the phone, you say 'Who am I speaking to?' or, informally, 'Who's that?'

A: *Hello.*
B: *Hello. Who am I speaking to, please?*

A: *Yes?*
B: *I want to speak to Mr Taylor.*
A: *I'm afraid Mr Taylor's not in the office right now.*
B: *Who's that?*

You can check that you have the right person, organization, or number by saying 'Is that...?, or by just saying the name or number like a question.

A: *Hello.*
B: *Is that Mrs Thompson?*
A: *Er, yes it is.*
B: *This is Kaj Mintti from Finland.*

A: *Hello.*

B: Hello? <u>435 1916?</u>
A: Yes?

Note that American speakers usually say 'Is this...?' instead of 'Is that...?'

A: Hello.
B: Hello. <u>Is this the Casa Bianca restaurant?</u> I want to speak with Anna. Anna di Pietro.

asking to speak to someone If the person who answers the phone is not the person you want to speak to, you say, for example, 'Can I speak to Paul, please?' or 'Is Paul there?'

A: Hello.
B: <u>Can I speak to Sue, please?</u>
A: Hang on – I'm sorry, but she's not in at the moment.
B: Can I leave a message?
A: Yes.
B: Would you tell her that Adrian phoned?

If you are making a business call, you say, for example, 'Could I speak to Mr Green, please?' or just say the name of the person or department you want, followed by 'please'.

A: William Foux and Company.
B: Er, good afternoon. <u>Could I speak to Mr Duff, please?</u>
A: Oh, I'm sorry, he's on another line at the moment. Will you hang on?
B: No, it's all right. I'll ring later.

A: British Steel Corporation.
B: <u>Data room, please.</u>
A: I'll put you through.

If the person you are speaking to is in fact the person you want, they sometimes say 'Speaking'.

A: Personnel.
B: Could I speak to Mr Wilson, please.
A: <u>Speaking.</u>
B: Oh, right. I wanted to ask you a question about sick pay.

ending a phone call When you end a phone call, you say 'Goodbye' or, informally, 'Bye'.

A: I'm afraid I can't talk to you now.
B: OK, I'll phone back after lunch.
A: OK. <u>Goodbye.</u>
B: <u>Goodbye.</u>

A: I'll just check. Yes, it's here.
B: Oh, OK. Thanks. <u>Bye.</u>

People sometimes also say 'Speak to you soon' or 'Thanks for ringing'.

---

tell

Tell is a common verb which is used in several different ways. Its past tense and past participle is **told**, not 'telled'.

information If someone **tells** you something, they give you some information. You usually refer to this information by using a 'that'-clause or a 'wh'-clause.

Tell Father <u>the carpenter has come.</u>
I told her <u>what the doctor had said.</u>

You can sometimes refer to the information that is given by using a noun group as the direct object of **tell**. When the direct object is not a pronoun, you put the indirect object first.

She told him the news.
They immediately told him the answer.
I never told her a thing.

When the direct object is a pronoun, you usually put it first. You put 'to' in front of the indirect object.

I've never told this to anyone else in my whole life.

When you are referring back to information that has already been mentioned, you use **so** after **tell**. For example, you say 'I didn't agree with him and I **told him so**'. You do not say 'I didn't agree with him and I told him it'.

She knows that you and I adore each other. I have told her so.
'Then how do you know she's well?'—'She told me so.'

stories,
jokes, lies

You say that someone **tells** a story or a joke.

She told me the story of her life.
He has a way of screwing up his face when he is telling a joke.

You can also say that someone 'makes' or 'cracks' a joke. For more information, see entry at **joke**.

You say that someone **tells** a lie.

We told a lot of lies.

If someone is not lying, you say that they are **telling the truth.**

We knew that he was telling the truth.
I wondered why I hadn't told Mary the truth.

When you use **tell** to talk about stories, jokes, or lies, the indirect object can go either after the direct object or in front of it.

His friend told me this story.
Many hours had passed when Karen finished telling her story to Kitty.

He thinks he knows why his mother told him a lie.
She would never tell a lie to anyone.

orders

If you **tell** someone **to do** something, you order or instruct them to do it. When **tell** has this meaning, it is followed by an object and a 'to'-infinitive.

Tell Martha to build a fire.
They told us to put on our seat-belts.

WARNING

You do not use **tell** like this without an object. You do not say, for example, 'They told to put on our seat-belts'.

recognizing
the truth

If you **can tell** what is happening or what is true, you are able to judge correctly what is happening or what is true.

I can usually tell when I'm being lied to.
I couldn't tell what they were thinking.
If you look into the bag, you will be able to tell which pebble I took by the colour of the one that is left.

Note that when **tell** has this meaning, you usually use 'can', 'could', or 'be able to' with it.

temperature

For information on stating **temperatures**, see section on **temperature** in entry at **Measurements**.

tendency

See entry at **trend - tendency**.

GRAMMAR Tenses

Tenses are the different verb forms and verb groups that indicate roughly what time you are referring to.

Simple tenses are used to refer to situations, habitual actions, and single completed actions.

I like him very much.
He always gives both points of view.
He walked out of the kitchen.

Continuous tenses are used when talking about temporary situations at a particular point in time.

Inflation is rising.
We believed we were fighting for a good cause.

Some verbs are not used in continuous tenses. For information about this, see section on **stative verbs** in entry at **Continuous tenses**.

Perfect tenses are used when relating an action or situation to the present or to a moment in the past.

Football has become international.
She did not know how long she had been lying there.

Passive tenses are used when the subject of a clause is the person or thing affected by an action. Passive tenses are formed by using an appropriate tense of 'be' and the past participle of the main verb.

The earth is baked by the sun into a hard, brittle layer.
They had been taught to be critical.

For more information on the uses of tenses, see entries at **The Future, The Past,** and **The Present.** Sometimes the tense used in a subordinate clause is not what you would expect: see entries at **The Future, Reporting,** and **Subordinate clauses.**

present and past tenses

The following table shows how to form present and past tenses.

Active	Passive
simple present	
base form *I want a breath of air.* (3rd person singular) '-s' form *Flora laughs again.*	simple present of 'be' + past participle *It is boiled before use.*
present continuous	
simple present of 'be' + '-ing' form *Things are changing.*	present continuous of 'be' + past participle *My advice is being ignored.*
present perfect	
simple present of 'have' + past participle *I have seen this before.*	present perfect of 'be' + past participle *You have been warned.*

Tenses

present perfect continuous	
present perfect of 'be' + '-ing' form *Howard has been working hard.*	present perfect continuous of 'be' + past participle (Not common)
simple past	
past form *I resented his attitude.*	simple past of 'be' + past participle *He was murdered.*
past continuous	
simple past of 'be' + '-ing' form *I was sitting on the rug.*	past continuous of 'be' + past participle *We were being watched.*
past perfect	
'had' + past participle *Everyone had liked her.*	past perfect of 'be' + past participle *Raymond had been rejected.*
past perfect continuous	
'had been' + '-ing' form *Miss Gulliver had been lying.*	past perfect continuous of 'be' + past participle (Not common)

future tenses There are several ways of referring to the future in English. The commonest way is to use the modal 'will' or 'shall'. See entry at **shall - will**. Verb groups in which 'will' and 'shall' are used to talk about the future are sometimes called **future tenses**.

The following table shows future tenses.

Active	**Passive**
future	
'will' or 'shall' + base form *They will arrive tomorrow.*	'will be' or 'shall be' + past participle *More land will be destroyed.*
future continuous	
'will be' or 'shall be' + '-ing' form *I shall be leaving soon.*	'will be being' or 'shall be being' + past participle (Not common)
future perfect	
'will have' or 'shall have' + past participle *They will have forgotten you.*	'will have been' or 'shall have been' + past participle *By the end of the year, ten projects will have been approved.*
future perfect continuous	
'will have been' or 'shall have been' + '-ing' form *By March, I will have been doing this job for six years.*	'will have been being' or 'shall have been being' + past participle (Very rare)

For other ways of referring to the future, see entry at **The Future.**

term - semester

'term' At a British school, each year is divided into three **terms.** At an American school, it is divided into four **terms.**

'semester' At a British college or university, each year is also divided into three **terms.** At an American college or university, it is divided into two **semesters** or three **trimesters.**

terrible - terribly

'terrible' The adjective **terrible** is used in two ways.

In conversation, you use it to say that something is very unpleasant or of very poor quality.

I know this has been a terrible shock to you.
His eyesight was terrible.

In writing or conversation, you use **terrible** to say that something is very shocking or distressing.

That was a terrible air crash last week.

'terribly' The adverb **terribly** is sometimes used to emphasize how shocking or distressing something is.

The gang beat up Mahesh terribly.
The wound bled terribly.

However, **terribly** is much more commonly used to emphasize that someone or something has a feeling or quality to a great extent.

I'm terribly sorry.
I've always been terribly fond of you.
She had missed him terribly.
It's a terribly dull place.

You do not use **terribly** like this in formal writing.

test

A **test** is a series of questions which you answer to show how much you know about a subject. You say that someone **takes** or **does** a test of this kind.

All candidates will be required to take an English language test.
We did another test.

A **test** is also a series of actions which you do to show how well you are able to do something. You say that someone **takes** a test of this kind.

She's not yet taken her driving test.

Note that you never say that someone 'makes' a test.

If someone is successful in a test of either kind, you say that they **pass** it.

I passed my driving test in Holland.

WARNING To **pass** a test always means to succeed in it. It does not have the same meaning as 'take' or 'do'.

If someone is unsuccessful in a test, you say that they **fail** it.

I told her I thought I'd failed the test.

text

The **text** of a book or magazine is the main written part of it, rather than the introduction, pictures, or index.

The illustrations and text were beautifully produced.

You do not refer to a piece of writing written for a newspaper or magazine as a 'text'. You call it an **article**.

Four years ago Clive Norling wrote an article in the Times.

than

Than is mainly used after comparative adjectives and adverbs. After **than** you use a noun group, a clause, or an adverbial.

The cataloguing is more difficult than the other part of the work.
I am happier than I have ever been.
They had to work harder than expected.
Last year, terrorist activities were worse than in any of the previous twelve years.

If you use a personal pronoun on its own after **than,** it must be an object pronoun such as 'me' or 'him'. It used to be considered correct to use a subject pronoun such as 'I' or 'he', but this now sounds very old-fashioned.

My brother is younger than me.
Lamin was shorter than her.

However, if the pronoun is the subject of a clause, you use a subject pronoun.

They knew my past much better than she did.
He's taller than I am.

You can use **than** after a noun group which contains a comparative adjective. For example, instead of saying 'Suzanne was more contented than her brother', you can say 'Suzanne was **a more contented baby than** her brother'.

Kairi was a more satisfactory pet than Tuku had been.
Willy owned a larger collection of books than anyone else I have ever met.

You can also use a comparative adjective immediately after a noun, followed by **than.** For example, instead of saying 'I wouldn't like to live in a town which is larger than Lichfield', you can say 'I wouldn't like to live in a town **larger than** Lichfield'.

We've got a rat bigger than a cat living in our roof.
...packs of cards larger than he was used to.

You can use an infinitive with or without 'to' after **than.**

He is more likely to continue his crimes than to stop.
The number of seats is more likely to rise to 151 than fall to 149.

You can also use an '-ing' form after **than.**

Turbocharging an engine involves more than bolting on a unit.

You can also use 'ever' or 'ever before' after **than.** For example, if you say that something is 'bigger **than ever**' or 'bigger **than ever before**', you are emphasizing that it has never been as big as it is now, although it has always been big.

Bill worked harder than ever.
The baby will get fatter than ever if he is kept too much in his cot.
He was now farming a bigger area than ever before.

WARNING	You do not use **than** when you are making comparisons using 'not as' or 'not so'. You do not say, for example, 'He is not as tall than his sister'. You say 'He is not as tall **as** his sister'. See entry at **as … as**.

For more information about comparatives, see entries at **Comparative and superlative adjectives** and **Comparative and superlative adverbs**.

'more than'   You use **more than** to say that the number of people or things in a group is greater than a particular number.

…in a city of more than a million people.
There are more than two hundred and fifty species of shark.

For more information about this use, see entry at **more**.

You can also use **more than** in front of some adjectives as a way of emphasizing them. For example, instead of saying 'If you can come, I shall be very pleased', you can say 'If you can come, I shall be **more than** pleased'. This is a fairly formal use.

Their life may be horribly dull, but they are more than satisfied.
You would be more than welcome.

'more...than'   You can use **more** and **than** to say that something is one type of thing rather than another. You put **more** in front of the first of two noun groups and **than** in front of the second one.

Music is more a way of life than an interest.
This is more a war movie than a western.

'less than' and 'fewer than'   You use **less than** to say that an amount or measurement is below a particular level.

Half of all working women earned less than twenty pounds a week.

You use **fewer than** to say that the number of people or things in a group is smaller than a particular number.

In 1900 there were fewer than one thousand university teachers in the United Kingdom.

For more information about these uses, see entry at **less**.

'rather than'   You use **rather than** when you have said what is the case and you want to compare it with what is not the case.

Its interests lay in London rather than in Nottingham.
She was angry rather than afraid.

See entry at **rather**.

'no sooner... than'   In stories, **than** is often used after 'no sooner'. If you say **no sooner** did one thing happen **than** another thing happened, you mean that the second thing happened immediately after the first.

No sooner had he closed his eyes than he fell asleep.

For more information about this use, see entry at **soon**.

WARNING	You do not use **than** after 'barely', 'hardly', or 'scarcely'. You do not say, for example, 'He had barely got in than the telephone rang'. You say 'He had barely got in **when** the telephone rang'. See entries at **bare - barely, hard - hardly,** and **scarce - scarcely**.

'different than'   Some American speakers use **than** after 'different'.

I love the English style of football. It's so different than ours.

See entry at **different**.

thank

<table>
<tr>
<td>'thank you'</td>
<td>Thank is mainly used in the expressions 'Thank you' and 'Thanks'. For an explanation of these uses, see entry at Thanking someone.</td>
</tr>
</table>

'thank you'
    Thank is mainly used in the expressions 'Thank you' and 'Thanks'. For an explanation of these uses, see entry at **Thanking someone.**

'thank' used
as a verb
    Thank is also used as a verb. If you **thank** someone, you express gratitude for something they have done or something they have given you.

She smiled at him, thanked him, and drove off.

You say that you **thank** someone **for** something.

I thanked him for his thoughtful gesture.
He thanked me for what I had done.

You can also **thank** someone **for doing** something.

He thanked the miners for coming.
He thanked me for bringing the beer.

You do not say that you thank someone 'to do' something.

Thanking someone

You thank someone when they have just done something for you or given you something. You say 'Thank you' or, more casually, 'Thanks'.

'I'll take over here.'—'Thank you.'
'Don't worry, Caroline. I've given you a marvellous reference.'—'Thank you, Mr Dillon.'
'There's your receipt.'—'Thanks.'
'Would you tell her that Adrian phoned and that I'll phone at eight?'—'OK.'—'Thanks.'

Some speakers of British and Australian English say 'Cheers' to thank someone in a casual way. See entry at **cheers - cheerio.** Some British speakers also say 'Ta' /tɑː/.

If you need to indicate why you are thanking the other person, you say 'Thank you for...' or 'Thanks for...'.

Thank you for the earrings, Whitey.
Thank you for a delicious lunch.
Well, then, good-night, and thanks for the lift.
Thanks for helping out.

emphatic ways
of thanking
    People often add 'very much' or 'very much indeed' to be more emphatic.

'Here you are.'—'Thank you very much.'
'I'll ring you tomorrow morning.'—'OK. Thanks very much indeed.'

Note that you can say 'Thanks a lot', but you cannot say 'Thank you a lot' or 'Thanks lots'.

'All right, then?'—'Yes, thanks a lot.'

If you want to show that you are very grateful, you can say something like 'That's very kind of you' or 'That's very good of you'.

'Any night when you feel a need to talk, you will find me here.'—'That's very kind of you.'
'Would you give this to her?'—'Sure. When I happen to see her.'—'That's very good of you, Rudolph.'

You can also say something like 'That's wonderful' or 'Great'.

'I'll see if she can be with you on Monday.'—*'That's wonderful!'*
'Do them as fast as you can.'—*'Yes. OK.'*—*'Great.'*

Even more emphatic ways of thanking are shown below.

'All right, Sandra?'—*'Thank you so much, Mr Atkinson; you've been wonderful. I just can't thank you enough.'*
'She's safe.'—*'I don't know how to thank you.'*
I can't tell you how grateful I am to you for having listened to me.

more formal ways of thanking

People sometimes thank someone more formally by saying 'I wanted to thank you for...' or 'I'd like to thank you for...', especially when expressing thanks for something that was done or given a little while ago.

I wanted to thank you for the beautiful necklace.
I want to thank you all for coming.
We learned what you did for Ari and I want to tell you how grateful I am.
I'd like to thank you for your patience and your hard work.

You can also express thanks more formally by saying things like 'I'm very grateful to you' or 'I really appreciate it'.

I'm grateful for the information you've given me on Mark Edwards.
I'm extremely grateful to you for rescuing me.
Thank you for coming to hear me play. I do appreciate it.

thanking someone for an offer

You can say 'Thank you' or 'Thanks' when accepting something that is offered.

'Have a cake.'—*'Thank you.'*

You say 'No, thank you' or 'No, thanks' when refusing something that is offered.

'There's one biscuit left. Do you want it?'—*'No, thanks.'*

Note that you do not refuse something by just saying 'Thank you'.

See entry at **Offers.**

thanking someone for a present

When you have been given a present, you say 'Thank you', or something like 'It's lovely'.

'It's lovely. What is it?'—*'It's a shark tooth. The casing's silver.'*

People sometimes say 'You shouldn't have' as a polite way of indicating that they are very grateful.

'Here. This is for you.'—*'Joyce, you shouldn't have.'*

thanking someone for an enquiry

You also say 'Thank you' or 'Thanks' when replying to someone who has asked how you are or how a member of your family is, or if you have had a nice weekend or holiday.

'How are you?'—*'Fine, thank you.'*
'How is Andrew today?'—*'Oh, Andrew's very well, thank you.'*
'Did you have a nice weekend?'—*'Lovely, thank you.'*

thanking someone in a letter

When thanking someone in a letter, you most commonly say 'Thank you for...'. In a formal business letter, you can say 'I am grateful for...'.

Dear Madam, Thank you for your letter replying to our advertisement for an assistant cashier.
I am grateful for your prompt reply to my request.

If the letter is to a friend, you can say 'Thanks for...'.

Thanks for writing.

| replying to thanks | When someone thanks you for handing them something or doing a small service for them, it is acceptable not to say anything in reply in Britain. |

However, people in the United States, especially employees in shops, often say 'You're welcome'.

When someone thanks you for helping them or doing them a favour, you reply 'That's all right' or 'That's OK'.

'Thank you, Charles.'—'That's all right, David.'
'Thanks. I really appreciate it.'—'That's okay.'

If you want to be both polite and friendly, you can say 'It's a pleasure' or 'Pleasure'.

'Thank you very much for talking to us about your research.'—'It's a pleasure.'
'Thank you for the walk and the conversation.'—'Pleasure.'

'Any time' is more casual.

'Thanks for your help.'—'Any time.'

If someone thanks you in a very emphatic way, you can reply using the expressions below.

'He's immensely grateful for what you did for him.'—'It was no trouble.'
'Thanks, Johnny. Thanks for your trouble.'—'It was nothing.'
'I'm enormously grateful to you for telling me.'—'Not at all.'

'Don't mention it' is old-fashioned.

'Thanks. This really kind of you.'—'Don't mention it.'

---

that

That has three main uses:

| used to refer back | You use it in various ways to refer to something which has already been mentioned or which is already known about. When **that** is used like this, it is always pronounced /ðæt/. |

That old woman saved my life.
How about natural gas? Is that an alternative?

For more information about this use, see entry at **that - those**.

| used in 'that'-clauses | **That** is used at the beginning of a special type of clause called a **'that'-clause**. In 'that'-clauses, **that** is usually pronounced /ðət/. |

He said that the police had directed him to the wrong room.
Mrs Kaul announced that the lecture would now begin.

For more information about this use, see entries at **'That'-clauses** and **Reporting**.

| used in relative clauses | **That** is also used at the beginning of another type of clause called a **defining relative clause**. In defining relative clauses, **that** is usually pronounced /ðət/. |

I reached the gate that opened onto the lake.

See entry at **Relative clauses**.

| WARNING | You do not use **that** to introduce a **reason clause**. You do not say, for example, 'Jane was worried because Tom was late, especially that it was snowing so heavily'. You say '...especially **as** it was snowing so heavily' or '...especially **since** it was snowing so heavily'. |

I do feel isolated, especially <u>as</u> we're not active in our community.
The easiest way to provide children with protein is to give them milk,
particularly <u>since</u> this supplies calcium to their bones as well.

For more information about these uses, see section on **'as' and 'since'** in
entry at **because**.

that - those

That and **those** are used in a number of different ways when you are
referring to people, things, events, or periods of time. They can both be
used as determiners or pronouns. **Those** is the plural form of **that**.

referring back You can use **that** or **those** to refer to people, things, or events which have
already been mentioned or which are already known about.

I knew <u>that</u> meeting would be difficult.
'Did you see him?'—'No.'—'<u>That's</u> a pity.'

Not all crimes are committed for <u>those</u> reasons.
One problem is you're going to get oxides of nitrogen, but one can remove
<u>those,</u> I think.

things you can see You can also use **that** or **those** to refer to people or things that you can see
but that are not close to you.

Look at <u>that</u> bird!
<u>That's</u> a strong piece of furniture.

Don't be afraid of <u>those</u> people.
I'll put <u>those</u> in the cupboard.

'that' used to refer to a person However, you do not usually use **that** as a pronoun to refer to a person.
You only use it when you are identifying someone or asking about their
identity.

'Who's the woman with the handkerchief?'—'<u>That's</u> my wife.'
Who's <u>that</u>?

For information on the way people use **that** when telephoning, see entry at
Telephoning.

saying when something happened When you have been describing an event, you can use **that** with a word like
'day', 'morning', or 'afternoon' to indicate that something else happened
during the same day.

There were no services <u>that day,</u> and the church was empty.
Paula had been shopping in Sapele <u>that morning</u>.

You can also use **that** with 'week', 'month', or 'year' to indicate that
something happened during the same week, month, or year.

There was a lot of extra work to do <u>that week</u>.
Later <u>that month</u> 11,000 attended another party at Maidenhead.

talking about a part of something When you are talking about a particular part of a place or thing, you can
use **that** instead of 'the' in front of words like 'part'. This is a rather formal
use.

...<u>that part of the world</u> which forms the immediate environment.

Similarly, you can use **those** instead of 'the' in front of a plural noun to talk
about a group of people or things which is part of a larger group.

Students should write off to <u>those</u> bodies which provide awards.
...<u>those</u> firms with the most progressive policies.

Those can be used in a similar way as a pronoun.

Many were finding it difficult to make ends meet, especially <u>those</u> with young children.

'this' and 'these' **This** and **these** are used in some similar ways to **that** and **those**. For an explanation of the differences, see entry at **this - that**.

GRAMMAR # 'That'-clauses

A **'that'-clause** is a clause beginning with 'that' which is used to refer to a fact or idea.

reporting 'That'-clauses are commonly used to report something that is said.

She said <u>that she'd been married for about two months</u>.
Sir Peter recently announced <u>that he is to retire at the end of the year</u>.

See entry at **Reporting**.

after adjectives You can use a 'that'-clause after adjectives which indicate someone's feelings or beliefs to say what fact those feelings or beliefs relate to.

She was <u>sure that he meant it</u>.
He was <u>frightened that something terrible might be said</u>.

The following adjectives often have a 'that'-clause after them:

afraid	certain	frightened	relieved	upset
amazed	concerned	glad	sad	worried
angry	confident	happy	sorry	
anxious	conscious	pleased	sure	
astonished	convinced	positive	surprised	
aware	disappointed	proud	unaware	

You can use a 'that'-clause after 'it is' and an adjective to comment on a situation or fact.

It is <u>extraordinary that we should ever have met</u>.

See entry at **it**.

after nouns Nouns such as 'assumption', 'feeling', and 'rumour', which refer to what someone says or thinks, can be followed by a 'that'-clause.

Our strategy has been based on <u>the assumption that our adversary is just one man</u>.
I had a <u>feeling that no-one thought I was good enough</u>.
There is no truth in the <u>rumour that the delay was due to a judge falling asleep</u>.

The following nouns are often followed by a 'that'-clause:

admission	claim	news	thought
advice	decision	promise	threat
agreement	expectation	report	view
announcement	feeling	rule	warning
argument	hope	rumour	wish
assertion	idea	saying	
assumption	impression	sense	
belief	information	statement	

after 'be' A 'that'-clause can be used as a complement after 'be'.

Our hope is <u>that this time all parties will co-operate</u>.
The important thing is <u>that we love each other</u>.

omitting 'that'	'That' is sometimes omitted in all of the above cases, especially in spoken English.

He knew the attempt was hopeless.
She is sure Harold doesn't mind.
I'd just walk in and have the feeling I'd seen some of it before.
All I hope is I can hang back when we have to attack.

'the fact that'	In very formal English, a 'that'-clause is sometimes used as the subject of a sentence.

That man can aspire to and achieve goodness is evident through all of history.

However, if the main verb is a reporting verb or 'be', it is much more usual to have 'it' as the subject, with the 'that'-clause coming later.

It cannot be denied that this view is abundantly justified by history.

In other cases, it is more usual to use a structure consisting of 'the fact' and a 'that'-clause as the subject.

The fact that your boss is actually offering to do your job for you should certainly prompt you to question his motives.

Structures beginning with 'the fact that' are also used as the object of prepositions and of verbs which cannot be followed by a simple 'that'-clause.

...acknowledgement of the fact that we have no intrinsic right to receive answers to all our questions.
We overlooked the fact that the children's emotional development had been retarded.

the

The is called the **definite article.** You use **the** at the beginning of a noun group to refer to someone or something that has already been mentioned or that is already known to the hearer or reader.

A man and a woman were struggling up the dune. The man wore shorts, a T-shirt, and basketball sneakers. The woman wore a print dress.

You add a qualifier, such as a prepositional phrase or a relative clause, when you need to indicate which person or thing you are talking about.

I've no idea about the geography of Scotland.
The book that I recommended now costs over three pounds.

You use **the** with a singular noun to refer to something of which there is only one.

They all sat in the sun.
The sky was a brilliant blue.
The air was warm.

types of thing or person	You can use **the** with the singular form of a count noun when you want to make a general statement about all things of a particular type.

The computer allows us to deal with a lot of data very quickly.
My father's favourite flower is the rose.

Note that you can make a similar statement using a plural form. If you do this, you do not use **the**.

It is then that computers will have their most important social effects.

If you like roses, go out in the garden.

Similarly, you do not use **the** with an uncount noun when it is used with a general meaning. For example, if you are talking about pollution in general, you say '**Pollution** is a serious problem'. You do not say 'The pollution is a serious problem'.

...victims of crime.
Alcoholism causes disease and death.

You can use **the** with words such as 'rich', 'poor', 'young', 'old', or 'unemployed' to refer to all people of a particular type.

Only the rich could afford his firm's products.
They were discussing the problem of the unemployed.

Note that when you use one of these words like this, you do not add '-s' or '-es' to it. You do not talk, for example, about 'the unemployeds'.

nationalities You can use **the** with some nationality adjectives to refer to the people who live in a particular country, or to a group of people who come from that country.

They will be increasingly dependent on the support of the French.
The Spanish claimed that the money had not been paid.

For more information about this use, see entry at **Nationality words**.

systems and services You use **the** with a singular count noun to refer to a system or service.

I don't like using the phone.
How long does it take on the train?

musical instruments You usually use **the** with the name of a musical instrument when you are talking about someone's ability to play it.

You play the guitar, I see.

However, rock and jazz musicians omit the **the**.

...the night spot where John played guitar.

professions **The** is sometimes used at the beginning of a noun group in which you mention a well-known person's profession as well as their name. For example, you can talk about '**the singer** Jill Gomez'.

...the Russian poet Yevtushenko.

If the person has two professions, you can mention both of them. For example, you can talk about '**the pianist and conductor** Daniel Barenboim'. Note that you only use **the** once; you do not say 'the pianist and the conductor Daniel Barenboim'.

...the Irish writer and critic Maeve Binchy.

Journalists and broadcasters sometimes omit the **the**.

...writer and critic William Gass.

institutions You do not usually use **the** between a preposition and a word like 'church', 'college', 'home', 'hospital', 'prison', 'school', or 'university'.

Will we see you in church tomorrow?
I was at school with her.

For more information about this use, see separate entries at these words.

meals You do not usually use **the** in front of the names of meals.

I open the mail immediately after breakfast.
I haven't had dinner yet.

See entry at **Meals**.

used instead of a possessive	You sometimes use **the** instead of a possessive determiner, particularly when you are talking about something being done to a part of a person's body.

She hit him smartly and swiftly on the head.
He took her by the arm and began drawing her firmly but gently away.

For more information about this use, see entry at **Possessive determiners**.

used with superlatives and comparatives	You usually use **the** in front of superlative adjectives.

...the smallest church in England.

You do not usually use **the** in front of superlative adverbs.

...the language they know best.

You do not usually use **the** in front of comparative adjectives or adverbs.

The model will probably be smaller.
I wish we could get it done quicker.

However, there are a few exceptions to this. For more information, see entries at **Comparative and superlative adjectives** and **Comparative and superlative adverbs**.

their

See entry at **there**.

them

Them is used as the object of a verb or preposition. You use **them** to refer to people or things that have just been mentioned or whose identity is known.

I think some of them may attempt to take an overdose.
She gathered the last few apples and stuffed them into a bag.

WARNING	You do not use **them** as the object of a clause when you are referring to the same people as the subject. Instead you use **themselves**.

The age at which babies feed themselves depends largely on the adults' attitude.

used to mean 'him or her'	You can use **them** instead of 'him or her' to refer to a person whose sex is not known or not stated. Some people consider this use to be incorrect.

If anyone phones, tell them I'm out.

For more information, see entry at **he - they**.

there

There has two main uses. You use it in front of a verb such as 'be', or you use it as an adverb to refer to a place.

used in front of 'be'	You use **there** in front of 'be' to say that something exists or happens, or that something is in a particular place. When **there** is used like this, it is usually pronounced /ðe/ or /ðə/. In slow or careful speech, it is pronounced /ðeə/.

There must be a reason.
There was an accident and somebody got killed.
There was a new cushion on one of the settees.

After **there,** you use a singular form of 'be' in front of a singular noun group, and a plural form in front of a plural noun group.

There is a fire on the fourth floor.
There are big women and small men.

In conversation, some people use 'there's' in front of a plural noun group. For example, they say 'If it's foggy, there's more collisions'. This use is generally regarded as incorrect.

You do not use **there is** or **there are** with 'since' to say how long ago something happened. You do not say, for example, 'There are four days since she arrived in London'. You say '**It's** four days since she arrived in London' or 'She arrived in London four days **ago**'.

It's three months since you were here last.
Her husband died four years ago.

'there seems to be...'

You can use **there** in front of 'seems to be' to say that you have the impression that something exists, or that something is in a particular place. For example, you can say '**There seems to be** a misunderstanding'. You do not say 'There seems a misunderstanding'.

There seems to be a problem.
I'm sorry, there seems to be a dirty mark on it.

'there happens to be...'

You can also use **there** in front of 'happens to be' to say that something is in a particular place by chance. For example, you can say 'There happened to be a post office in the next street'. You do not say 'There happened a post office in the next street'.

There happened to be a roll of thin nylon tubing lying on the desk.

used with other verbs

In formal English, **there** is sometimes used with other verbs to say that something exists or is in a particular place.

There still remains the point about creativity.
There follow below guidelines on two aspects of terminal connection.

In stories, **there** is sometimes used with 'was' or 'came' to say that something happened suddenly.

There was a tremendous explosion and the boat disintegrated.
There came the crack of a shot.

used as an adverb

In its other main use, **there** is used to refer to a place which has just been mentioned. When **there** is used like this, it is always pronounced /ðeə/.

I must get home. Bill's there on his own.
Come into the kitchen. I spend most of my time there now.

You do not use 'to' in front of **there**. You do not say, for example, 'I like going to there'. You say 'I like going **there**'.

My family live in India. I still go there often.

You do not use **there** to introduce a subordinate clause. You do not say, for example, 'I went back to the park, there my sister was waiting'. You say 'I went back to the park, **where** my sister was waiting'.

There was still fear in closed communities, where everyone knew everyone else's business.

'their'

Do not confuse **there** with **their**, which is also pronounced /ðeə/. You use **their** to show that something belongs or relates to particular people, animals, or things.

I looked at their faces.
What would they do when they lost their jobs?

these

See entry at **this - these**.

they

They is used as the subject of a verb. You use **they** to refer to people or things that have just been mentioned or whose identity is known.

All universities have chancellors. They are always rather senior people.
The women had not expected a visitor and they were in their everyday clothes.

Note that when the subject of a sentence is followed by a relative clause, you do not use **they** in front of the main verb. You do not say, for example, 'The people who live next door, they keep pigs'. You say 'The people who live next door keep pigs'.

Two children who were rescued by their father from a fire are in a critical condition in hospital.
Behind him two girls who had been following him came to a halt.

They is sometimes used to refer to people in general, or to a group of people whose identity is not actually stated.

Isn't that what they call love?
In Bradford, they put special teachers in areas with a high percentage of immigrants.

For more information about this use, see entry at **one.**

You can also use **they** instead of 'he or she' to refer to an individual person whose sex is not known or not stated.

I was going to stay with a friend, but they were ill.

For more information about this use, see entry at **he - they.**

WARNING

You do not use **they** with 'are' to say that a number of things exist or are in a particular place. You do not say, for example, 'They are two bottles of wine in the fridge'. You say '**There are** two bottles of wine in the fridge'.

There are always plenty of jobs to be done.
There are about 80 books in the library.

See entry at **there.**

thin

The following words can all be used to describe someone who has very little flesh on their body:

bony	lean	slender	spare	underweight
emaciated	scrawny	slight	thin	willowy
lanky	skinny	slim	trim	

Thin is used to describe someone's appearance in a neutral way.

She was tall and thin, with fairish hair.

Lean, slender, slim, slight, spare, and **trim** are all used to show approval of someone's appearance. **Slim** is the commonest of these words. The others are used mainly in stories.

She used to be pretty and slim.
The door sprang open and a lean, well-tailored man stepped out.
...a beautiful slender girl with a strong American accent.

Bony, scrawny, and **skinny** are used to show disapproval.

She was rather ugly and skinny.

...Ernie Timson, a <u>scrawny</u> youth with glasses.

If you say that someone is **underweight,** you mean that they are too thin, because they have not eaten enough or are ill. When they are very thin indeed, you can say that they are **emaciated.**

Many people who are <u>underweight</u> are happy with their size.
...<u>emaciated</u> kids begging for milk.

Lanky and **willowy** are used to say that someone is tall and thin. **Lanky** is a slightly humorous word. **Willowy** is used to show approval.

Quentin was a <u>lanky</u> boy with long skinny legs.
...looking so much more slender and <u>willowy</u> than in her photo.

think

The verb **think** is used in several different ways. Its past tense and past participle is **thought**, not 'thinked'.

You can use **think** with a 'that'-clause when you are giving your opinion about something or mentioning a decision that you have made.

I <u>think</u> you should go.
I <u>thought</u> I'd wait.

When you use **think** like this, you do not use a continuous tense. You do not say, for example, 'I am thinking you should go'.

Instead of saying that you think something is not the case, you usually say that you **don't think** it **is** the case.

I <u>don't think</u> they really represent the people.
I <u>don't think</u> there is any doubt about that.

'I think so'   If someone asks you whether something is the case, you can express your opinion that it is probably the case by saying **'I think so'**. You do not say 'I think it'.

'Do you think my mother will be all right?'—'I <u>think so.</u>'
'Will she get social security?'—'I <u>think so.</u>'

If you want to reply that something is probably not the case, you usually say **'I don't think so'**. You can also say **'I think not'**, but this is rather formal.

'I have another friend, Barbara Robson. Do you know her?'—'I <u>don't think so.</u>'
'Are you going to be sick?'—'I <u>don't think so.</u>'
'She doesn't want a real investigation, does she?'—'I <u>think not.</u>'

using a   When someone **is thinking**, they are considering something. When you use
continuous   **think** with this meaning, you often use a continuous tense.
tense

I'll fix us both a gin-and-tonic while I'm <u>thinking</u>.
You <u>have been thinking</u>, haven't you?

You also use a continuous tense when you are talking about what is in someone's mind at a particular time.

That's what I <u>was thinking</u>.
It's very difficult to determine what the other people <u>are thinking</u>.

You can say that someone **is thinking about** something or someone, or **is thinking of** something or someone.

I spent hours in the warmth of the bathtub <u>thinking about</u> China.
She <u>was thinking of</u> her husband.

If you are considering doing something, you can say that you **are thinking of doing** it.

Who is she thinking of marrying?
That's why I was thinking of getting out.

You do not say that you 'are thinking to do' something.

this - that

This and **that** are used as determiners or pronouns. The plural form of 'this' is **these**. The plural form of 'that' is **those**. See entries at **this - these** and **that - those**.

This entry deals with the similarities and differences between the ways in which these words are used.

referring back **This**, **these**, **that**, and **those** are all used to refer to people, things, events, etc that have already been mentioned. It is more common to use **this** and **these** than **that** and **those**.

New machines are of course more expensive and this is something one has to consider.
So, for all these reasons, my advice is to be very, very careful.

You use **that** or **those** when you are referring to something for the second time in a sentence, using the same noun.

You haven't shown any interest in the identity of the person who's been poisoned or how ill that person is.
Students and staff suggest books for the library, and normally we're quite happy to get those books.

You usually use **that,** rather than 'this', to refer to a statement that someone has just made.

'She was terribly afraid of offending anyone.'—'That's right.'
'The cold kills off lots of pests and next summer your crops will be very much better.'—'Yes, that's a good point.'

present and past You can use **this** or **that** to talk about events or situations.

You use **this** to refer to a situation that is continuing to exist, or to an event that is continuing to take place.

'My God,' I said, 'This is awful.'
I'm sorry to barge in on you like this.
This whole business has gone on too long.

You use **that** to refer to an event or situation that has taken place recently.

I knew that meeting would be difficult.
That was a terrible air crash last week.

closeness You use **this** or **these** to refer to people or things that are very near to you. For example, you use **this** to refer to an object when you are holding it in your hand, or when it is on a desk or table in front of you.

'What is this?' said a policeman, holding up a canister of shaving cream.
This coffee tastes like tea.
Wait a minute. I just have to sort these books out.

You use **that** or **those** to refer to people or things that you can see or hear, but that are not very near to you, so that, for example, you cannot put out your hand and touch them.

Look at that bird!

Can you move those books off there?

When you are comparing two things and one of them is nearer to you than the other, you can use **this** to refer to the one which is nearer and **that** to refer to the one which is further away.

This one's nice but I don't like that one much.
This side of the street doesn't get the sun in the afternoon.

this - these

This and **these** are used in a number of different ways when you are referring to people, things, situations, events, or periods of time. They can both be used as determiners or pronouns. **These** is the plural form of **this**.

referring back You can use **this** or **these** to refer to people, things, or events that have just been mentioned.

He's from the Institute of English Language in Bangkok. This institute has been set up to serve language teachers in the area.
Tax increases may be needed next year to do this.

These particular students are extremely bright.
The Treasurer went on to talk about the door-to-door and street collections. These had raised slightly less than last year.

You do not use **this** as a pronoun to refer to a person who has just been mentioned. Instead you use **he** or **she**.

He was known to all as Eddie.
'So long,' Mary said as she passed Miss Saunders.

In conversation, many people use **this** and **these** as determiners even when they are mentioning people or things for the first time.

And then this woman came up to me and she said, 'I believe you have a goddaughter called Celia Ravenscroft.'
At school we had to wear these awful white cotton hats.

closeness You can use **this** or **these** to refer to people or things that are very near to you. For example, if you are holding a book, you refer to it as '**this** book'.

This book is sensational.
The colonel handed him the bag. 'This is for you,' he said.

Get these kids out of here.
I'm sure they don't have chairs like these.

This is not usually used as a pronoun to refer to a person. You only use it when you are identifying someone or asking them about their identity. For example, you use **this** when you are introducing someone. Note that when you are introducing more than one person, you use **this**, not 'these'.

This is Bernadette, Mr Zapp.
This is my brother Andrew and his wife Claire.

You also use **this** to say who you are when you phone someone.

Sally? This is Martin Brody.

present situations You can use **this** to refer to a situation that exists at present or to an event that is happening now.

You know a lot about this situation.
This is an opportunity to put into practice thoughts I have had for some time.

This is used in the following ways in time expressions:

You use it with 'morning', 'afternoon', or 'evening' to refer to the morning, afternoon, or evening of the present day.

I've got to go to the University this morning.
I was here this afternoon. Have you forgotten?
Come and have a drink with me this evening.

However, you do not say 'this day'. You say **today**.

I had a letter today from my solicitor.

You also do not say 'this night'. You refer to the previous night as **last night**. You refer to the night of the present day as **tonight**.

We left our bedroom window open last night.
I think I'll go to bed early tonight.

This week, month, or year means the present week, month, or year.

They're talking about going on strike this week.
The Congress was held in Portoviejo earlier this month.

You usually use **this** with 'weekend' or with the name of a day, month, or season to refer to the next weekend or to the next day, month, or season with that name.

Come down there with me this weekend.
Let's fix a time. This Sunday. Four o'clock.
Any chance of you getting away this summer?

However, you can also use **this** with one of these words to refer to the previous weekend, or the previous day, month, or season with that name.

His presence this weekend was especially ominous.
This summer he also authorised £15 million to provide emergency shelters for the homeless.

These days means 'at the present time'. You usually use **these days** as an adverbial, but it can also be qualified and used as an ordinary noun group.

The prices these days are absolutely astronomical.
In these days of airline strikes and extreme weather conditions, it sometimes happens that the boss is unexpectedly marooned abroad.

'that' and 'those'

That and **those** are used in some similar ways to **this** and **these**. For an explanation of the differences, see entry at **this - that**.

those

See entry at **that - those**.

though

See entry at **although - though**.

thousand

A **thousand** or **one thousand** is the number 1,000.

You can say that there are **a thousand** things or **one thousand** things.

We'll give you a thousand dollars for the story.
...a ship about one thousand yards off shore.

You do not say that there are 'thousand' things.

You do not change the word **thousand** when you put another number in front of it. You do not say, for example, 'five thousands'. You say 'five **thousand**'.

...seven thousand dollars.

threaten

If you **threaten to do** something that will harm or upset someone, you warn them that you may do it.

The police threatened to imprison me.
He threatened to resign.

You do not say that you 'threaten doing' something.

You can threaten someone **with** an action that will harm them.

The group's members were threatened with imprisonment.
He was threatened with assault in the street.

You do not use any preposition except 'with' in sentences like these.

till

See entry at **until - till**.

time

This entry deals with uses of the word **time**. For information on telling the time, and on prepositions and adverbs used to talk about time, see entry at **Time**.

Time is what we measure in hours, days, years, etc.

...a period of time.
More time passed.

You do not usually use **time** when you are saying how long something takes or lasts. You do not say, for example, 'The course took two years' time' or 'Each song lasts ten minutes' time'. You say 'The course took **two years**' or 'Each song lasts **ten minutes**'.

The whole process probably takes twenty-five years.
The run lasts two hours.

You can, however, use **time** when you are saying how long it will be before something happens. For example, you can say 'We are getting married **in two years' time**'.

The exchange ends officially in a month's time.
In a few days' time, she may change her mind.

Time is usually used as an uncount noun, so you do not use 'a' with it. You do not say, for example, 'I haven't got a time to go shopping'. You say 'I haven't got **time** to go shopping'.

I didn't know if we'd have time for tea.

'a...time' However, you can use 'a' with an adjective and **time** when you are indicating how long something takes or lasts. You can say, for example, that something takes 'a long time' or takes 'a short time'.

The proposal would take quite a long time to discuss in detail.
After a short time one of them said 'It's all right, we're all friends here.'

You can also use expressions like these, with or without 'for', as adverbials.

They had been camped there for a long time.
He's going to have to wait a very long time.

They worked together for a short time.
You've only been in the firm quite a short time.

If you are enjoying yourself while you are doing something, you can say, for example, that you **are having a good time.**

Downstairs, Eva was having a wonderful time.
Did you have a good time up in Edinburgh?

Note that you must use 'a' in sentences like these. You do not say, for example, 'Eva was having wonderful time'.

'a time' You use **a time** after 'for' or 'after' to mean 'a fairly long time'.

She sat down for a time on a rush-seated chair.
After a time Welch began pulling.

You also use **a time** with a qualifier to refer to a period of time when something was or will be the case.

He retains some recollection of a time before these ills had become common.
I cannot remember a time when a Prime Minister allowed so much freedom for the expression of dissent.

used to mean **Time** is used with 'the' or 'that' and a qualifier to refer to the occasion
'occasion' when something happened or will happen.

By the time the waiter brought their coffee, she was drunk.
Do you remember that time when Adrian phoned up?

When **time** has this meaning, you can use words like 'first' or 'last' in front of it.

It was the first time she spoke.
When was the last time I saw you?

Expressions such as **the first time** and **the next time** are often used as adverbials.

The next time he would offer to fight.
The second time I hired a specialist firm.

Next time (without 'the') is also used as an adverbial.

You'll see a difference next time.
Next time you will do everything right.

'on time' If something happens **on time,** it happens at the right time or punctually.

He turned up regularly on time for guard duty.
He might play poker until dawn but he was always on time.

'in time' Do not confuse **on time** with **in time.** If you are **in time** for a particular event, you are not late for it.

We're just in time.
I thought I'd get here in time.
He returned to his hotel in time for a late supper.

If something such as a job or task is finished **in time,** it is finished at or before the time when it should be finished.

I can't do it in time.

In time has another meaning. You use it to say that something happens eventually, after a lot of time has passed.

In time the costs will decrease.
In time I came to see how important this was.

Time

This entry deals with clock times and periods of the day, and prepositions and adverbs used to indicate time. For information on referring to days and longer periods of time, see entry at **Days and dates.** For information on time clauses, see entry at **Subordinate clauses.**

clock times   When you want to know the time at the moment you are speaking, you say 'What time is it?' or 'What's the time?'

'What time is it?'—*'Three minutes past five.'*
'What's the time now?'—*'Twenty past.'*

When asking about the time of an event, you usually use 'when'.

'When did you come?'—*'Just after lunch.'*

You can also use 'what time'.

'What time did you get back to London?'—*'Ten o'clock.'*
'What time do they shut?'—*'Half past five.'*

When you tell someone the time, you say 'It's...'.

It's ten to eleven now. You'd better be off.

The table opposite shows different ways of referring to times.

Note the following points:

● The twenty-four hour clock is used on some digital clocks and on timetables. In this system, five o'clock in the afternoon, for example, is expressed as 17.00.

● You can use 'o'clock' only when saying exact hours, not times between hours. For example, you can say 'five o'clock', but you do not say 'ten past five o'clock' or 'a quarter past five o'clock'.

Come round at five o'clock.
I must leave by eight o'clock.

Note that when using 'o'clock', people usually write the number as a word (for example 'five'), not a figure ('5').

You do not have to use 'o'clock' when referring to an exact hour. People often just use a number.

I used to get up every morning at six.

● When saying times between hours, you can use 'past' and 'to'. You use 'past' and a number when referring to a time thirty minutes or less after a particular hour. You use 'to' and a number when referring to a time less than thirty minutes before a particular hour.

It's twenty past seven.
He returned to the house at half past four.
He got to the station at five to eleven.

Note that you do not normally use the word 'minutes' in these expressions.

Speakers of American English often use 'after' instead of 'past', and 'of' instead of 'to'.

	four o'clock four 4.00	four in the morning 4 a.m.	`04:00`
		four in the afternoon 4 p.m.	`16:00`
	nine o'clock nine 9.00	nine in the morning 9 a.m.	`09:00`
		nine in the evening nine at night 9 p.m.	`21:00`
	twelve o'clock twelve 12.00	twelve in the morning 12 a.m. midday noon	`12:00`
		twelve at night 12 p.m. midnight	`00:00`
		a quarter past twelve quarter past twelve twelve fifteen 12.15	`12:15` `00:15`
		twenty-five past two twenty-five minutes past two two twenty-five 2.25	`02:25` `14:25`
		half past eleven half eleven eleven-thirty 11.30	`11:30` `23:30`
		a quarter to one quarter to one twelve forty-five 12.45	`12:45` `00:45`
		ten to eight ten minutes to eight seven-fifty 7.50	`07:50` `19:50`

It was twenty after eight.
At a quarter of eight, he called Mrs Curry.

● You only use the word 'minutes' when you are talking about times between sets of five minutes, or when you want to show that you are being accurate and precise.

It was twenty-four minutes past ten.
We left Grosvenor Crescent at five minutes to ten.

● If it is clear what hour you are talking about, you do not need to add the hour after 'past' or 'to'.

'What time is it?'—'It's eighteen minutes past.'
It's quarter past.
'What time's break?'—'Twenty-five to.'

● You can also express a time by saying the hour first and then the number of minutes past the hour. For example, you can say 7.35 as 'seven thirty-five'. Note that if the number of minutes is less than 10, many people say '0' as 'oh' before the number of minutes. For example, 7.05 can be said as 'seven oh five' or 'seven five'.

Note that you put a full stop after the hour when writing a time like this. Some people, especially Americans, use a colon instead.

At 6.30 each morning, the partners meet to review the situation.
The door closes at 11.15.
By 3:34 p.m. the first thread had been removed and labelled.

• You can make it clear when a time occurs, if necessary, by adding a prepositional phrase. Note that you say 'in the morning', 'in the afternoon', and 'in the evening', but you say 'at night', not 'in the night'.

It was about four o'clock in the afternoon.
They worked from seven in the morning until five at night.

See sections on **exact times** in entries at **afternoon, evening, morning,** and **night.**

You can also add 'a.m.' to indicate a time between midnight and midday, or 'p.m.' to indicate a time between midday and midnight. These abbreviations are not generally used in conversation.

The doors will be opened at 10 a.m.
We will be arriving back in London at 10.30 p.m.

WARNING	You do not use 'a.m.' or 'p.m.' with 'o'clock'.
prepositions indicating time	The commonest preposition used to indicate the time when something happens is 'at'.

The taxi arrived at 7.30.
They'd arranged to leave at four o'clock in Welch's car.
I'll be back at four.

Other prepositions are used in the following ways to indicate when something happens:

• If something happens 'after' a particular time, it happens during the period that follows that time.

She complained that Hamilton was a very quiet place with little to do after ten at night.

• If something happens 'before' a particular time, it happens earlier than that time.

I was woken before six by the rain hammering against my bedroom window.

• If something happens 'by' a particular time, it happens at or before that time.

I have to get back to town by four o'clock.

• If something happens 'until' a particular time, it stops at that time. 'Till' is often used instead of 'until' in conversation.

I work until three.
I didn't get home till five.

• If something has been happening 'since' a particular time, it started at that time and it is still happening.

He had been up since 4 a.m.

For information on other uses of these words, see separate entries at each word.

approximate times   You can indicate that a time is approximate by using 'about' or 'around' in front of the time.

At about four o'clock in the morning, we were ambushed.
The device, which exploded at around midnight on Wednesday, severely damaged the fourth-floor bar.

'At' is sometimes left out.

He left about ten o'clock.

In conversation, people sometimes indicate an approximate time by adding '-ish' to the time.

Shall I ring you about nine-ish?

You can say that something happens 'just after' or 'just before' a particular time. You can also use 'shortly after' or 'shortly before'.

We drove into Jerusalem just after nine o'clock.
He had come home just before six o'clock and lain down for a nap.
Shortly after nine, her husband appeared.

When saying what the time is or was, you can also use 'just gone'.

It was just gone half past twelve.

periods of the day The main periods of the day are:

morning	evening
afternoon	night

You can use the prepositions 'in' or 'on' with words referring to periods of the day. You can also use 'last', 'next', 'this', 'tomorrow', and 'yesterday' in front of these words to form adverbials.

I'll ring the agent in the morning.
On Saturday morning all flights were cancelled to and from Glasgow.
I spoke to him this morning.
He is going to fly to Amiens tomorrow morning.

For detailed information on how to use these words and which prepositions to use with them, see entry at each word. See also entries at **last - lastly, next,** and **this - that.**

There are also several words which refer to the short period when the sun rises or sets:

dawn	first light	dusk	sunset
daybreak	sunrise	nightfall	twilight

You use 'at' with these words when indicating that something happens during the period they refer to.

At dawn we landed for refuelling in Tunisia.
Draw the curtains at sunset.

adverbs indicating time The adverbs and adverbial expressions in the two lists below are used to indicate that something happened in the past. Note that all these adverbials can be put after the first auxiliary in a verb group.

The following adverbials can be used with past tenses and with the present perfect:

in the past	lately	recently
just	previously	

It wasn't all that successful as a deterrent in the past.
Her husband had recently died in an accident.
He's had a tough time lately.

The following adverbials can be used with past tenses but not normally with the present perfect:

at one time	earlier on	once	sometime
earlier	formerly	originally	then

The cardboard folder had been blue underlinedoriginally but now the colour had faded to a light grey.
The world was different then.

'Before' is not used with the present perfect when simply indicating that a situation existed in the past. However, it is used with the present perfect to indicate that this is not the first time that something has happened.

I'm sure I've read that before.

The tenses used with 'already' are different in American English and British English. See entry at **already.**

You use the following adverbials when referring to the future:

afterwards	in a minute	later on	sometime
at once	in a moment	one day	soon
before long	in future	one of these days	sooner or later
eventually	in the future	shortly	within minutes
immediately	later	some day	within the hour

We'll be free soon.
I'll remember in a minute.
In future when you visit us you must let us know in advance.

These adverbials are usually put at the end or beginning of the clause.

'Momentarily' is used when referring to the future in American English, but not in British English. See entry at **momentarily.**

You use the following adverbials to contrast the present with the past or the future, or to indicate that you are talking about a temporary situation in the present:

at the moment	just now	presently
at present	now	right now
currently	nowadays	these days

Biology is their great passion at the moment.
Well, we must be going now.

These adverbials are usually put at the end or beginning of the clause.

Note that 'today' is used, mainly in newspapers and broadcasting, to refer to the present time in history as well as to the day on which you are speaking.

...the kind of open society which most of us in the Western world enjoy today.

See also entries at **now** and **presently.**

Note that 'already' is used when referring to a present situation, as well as when referring to the past.

I'm already late.

See entry at **already.**

times as modifiers	Clock times and periods of the day can be used as modifiers.

Every morning he would set off right after the eight o'clock news.
Castle was usually able to catch the six thirty-five train from Euston.
But now the sun was already dispersing the morning mists.

Note that people often refer to a train or bus by the time it leaves a particular place. They talk, for example, about 'the six-eighteen', meaning 'the train that leaves at six-eighteen'.

We caught the eight-five.

Possessive forms of periods of the day can also be used as modifiers, when talking about a particular day.

It was Jim Griffiths, who knew nothing of the morning's happenings.

Note that they are also used when saying how long an activity lasts.

...the turpentine they had used to get paint off themselves after an afternoon's work on the house.

times as qualifiers You can use time adverbials as qualifiers to specify events or periods of time.

I'm afraid the meeting this afternoon tired me badly.
No admissions are permitted in the hour before closing time.

timetable

See entry at **scheme - schedule**.

tiny

See entry at **small - large**.

tiresome - tiring

'tiresome' You say that someone or something is **tiresome** when they make you feel annoyed, irritated, or bored.

She can be a very tiresome child at times.
I really came to ask you some rather tiresome questions.

'tiring' Something which is **tiring** makes you feel tired.

We should have an early night after such a tiring day.

title

The **title** of a book, play, painting, or piece of music is its name.

He wrote a book with the title 'The Castle'.
'Walk under Ladders' is the title of her new play.

'headline' You do not refer to the words printed in large letters at the top of a newspaper report as a 'title'. You call them a **headline.**

The headlines that day were full of the news of the kidnapping.

to

To is used in several different ways as a preposition. Its usual pronunciation is /tə/. However, when it is followed by a word beginning with a vowel sound, it is pronounced /tu/ and when it comes at the end of a clause, it is pronounced /tuː/.

destination	You use **to** when you mention the place where someone goes.

I'm going with her to Australia.
The children have gone to school.
I made my way back to my seat.

You do not use **to** in front of 'here' or 'there'. You do not say, for example, 'We go to there every year'. You say 'We go **there** every year'.

I don't know what idea you had of the English before you came here.
Sir Geoffrey Howe went there in 1986.

You also do not use **to** in front of 'home'.

I want to go home.
I'll pick the parcels up on my way home.

direction	You can use **to** to indicate the place that a person is intending to arrive at.

We're sailing to Europe.
We used to go through Yugoslavia on our way to Greece.

However, you do not use **to** to indicate the general direction in which someone or something is moving. You do not say, for example, 'The boat was drifting to the shore'. You say 'The boat was drifting **towards** the shore'.

He saw his mother running towards him.
We started to walk back towards Heathrow.

Toward is sometimes used instead of **towards**.

They walked along the pathway toward the house.

You also say that someone looks **towards** or **toward** something.

She glanced towards the mirror.
He stood looking toward the rear of the restaurant.

You can use **to, towards,** or **toward** to indicate what someone or something is pointing at or facing.

He was pointing to an oil tanker somewhere on the horizon.
The window faced towards Paris.
'Turn in here,' he said, pointing toward a footpath.

position	You can use **to** to indicate the position of something. For example, if something is **to** your left, it is nearer your left side than your right side.

My father was in the middle, with me to his left carrying the umbrella.
To the west lies Gloucester.

You can also use **to** to indicate where something is tied or attached, or what it is touching.

I was planning to tie him to a tree.
He clutched the parcel to his chest.

time	**To** is sometimes used with a similar meaning to 'until'.

Breakfast was from 9 to 10.
Only ten shopping days to Christmas.

indirect objects	You put **to** in front of the indirect object of some verbs when the indirect object comes after the direct object.

He showed the letter to Barbara.
She had given German lessons to a leading industrialist.

See section on **ditransitive verbs** in entry at **Verbs**.

used in infinitives	**To** is used to introduce a special kind of clause called a 'to'-infinitive clause.

They could use these bombs to destroy airfields and oil depots.
The rocket soon begins to accelerate upwards.

See entry at '**To**'-infinitive clauses.

WARNING	Do not confuse **to** with **too** or **two**, both of which are pronounced /tuː/.

You use **too** to indicate that what has just been said applies to someone or something else.

I'm on your side. Seibert is too.

You also use **too** when you want to say that an amount or degree of something is more than is desirable or acceptable.

Do not be too proud to ask for help.

See entry at **too**.

Two is the number 2.

The two boys glanced at each other.

today

Today means the day on which you are speaking or writing.

I had a letter today from my solicitor.
Today is Thursday.

You do not use **today** in front of 'morning', 'afternoon', or 'evening'. Instead, you use **this**.

His plane left this morning.
Can I take it with me this afternoon?
Come and have a drink with me this evening.

toilet

A **toilet** is a large bowl connected to the plumbing and used by people to get rid of waste from their bodies.

British speakers also use **toilet** to refer to a room containing a toilet. When this room is in a house, they might also refer to it as the **lavatory**, the **loo**, the **cloakroom**, or the **WC**. **Lavatory** and **WC** are rather old-fashioned words. **Loo** is only used in conversation.

In American English, the room in a house containing a toilet is called the **bathroom**. **Washroom** and **john** are also used. **John** is only used in conversation.

'conveniences'	In British English, a group of toilets in a public place can be referred to as **conveniences** or **public conveniences**. They can also be referred to as **the ladies** and **the gents**.

In American English, a group of toilets in a public place can be referred to as a **rest room**, a **comfort station**, or a **washroom**. They can also be referred to as **the ladies' room** and **the mens' room**.

GRAMMAR	# 'To'-infinitive clauses

A '**to**'-**infinitive clause** is a subordinate clause beginning with a 'to'-infinitive — that is, 'to' and the base form of a verb.

She began to laugh.
Christopher and I went to see him.

I wanted <u>to be popular.</u>

A 'to'-infinitive clause can include auxiliaries.

Only two are known <u>to have defected.</u>
I seem <u>to have been eating</u> all evening.
I didn't want <u>to be caught</u> off guard.

negative
'to'-infinitives

When you use 'not' with a 'to'-infinitive, you put 'not' in front of the 'to'.

I told him <u>not to be late.</u>

For information on the position of adverbs in relation to 'to'-infinitives, see entry at **Split infinitives.**

linking
'to'-infinitive
clauses

When two infinitives are linked by 'and', 'or', 'rather than', or 'than', the second infinitive can be used without 'to'.

I told Dave to wait and <u>watch.</u>
I'd far prefer to drive than <u>go</u> by train.

after verbs

When a verb is followed by a 'to'-infinitive clause, the subject of the verb is also the subject of the 'to'-infinitive clause. The following verbs are often followed by a 'to'-infinitive clause:

aim	endeavour	learn	opt	seek
appear	expect	long	plan	seem
arrange	fail	manage	prepare	tend
attempt	forget	mean	pretend	venture
choose	happen	need	prove	want
decide	hope	neglect	resolve	wish

They <u>decided to wait.</u>
England <u>failed to win</u> a place in the finals.
She <u>seemed to like</u> me.

Some verbs, such as 'begin', 'continue', and 'prefer' can be followed by a 'to'-infinitive or an '-ing' form.

Marcus <u>began to scream.</u>
They all <u>began screaming.</u>

See entry at **'-ing' forms** for a list of these verbs.

Sometimes you use a 'to'-infinitive clause after the object of a verb. The object is the subject of the 'to'-infinitive clause. The following verbs are often used with an object and a 'to'-infinitive:

allow	defy	inspire	pay	train
cause	enable	intend	permit	want
challenge	expect	lead	prefer	will
choose	force	like	programme	
compel	get	mean	prompt	
dare	induce	oblige	teach	

Higher productivity <u>has enabled companies to earn</u> higher profits.
...until ill health <u>forced him to retire.</u>

Note that 'help' can be followed by a 'to'-infinitive or an infinitive without 'to'. See entry at **help.**

A 'to'-infinitive clause is used after reporting verbs such as 'advise', 'persuade', and 'promise'. See entry at **Reporting.**

after 'be' In formal English, newspapers, and broadcasting, 'to'-infinitive clauses are used after 'be' to indicate that something is planned to happen.

After dinner they were to go to a movie.
A clean coal-fired power plant is to be built at Bilsthorpe Colliery.

You can also use a 'to'-infinitive clause after 'be' when specifying something such as a task, aim, or method.

Our job is to work out what the rules are.
Their aim is to help countries achieve an independent judiciary.
The simplest way is to smuggle the cash out of the country and invest it in tax havens.

You can also say that it is someone's job 'to do something'.

It is my job to keep the players confident.

after 'be' in questions A 'to'-infinitive clause can be used in questions after 'who' or 'what' and 'be' to ask what should happen or be done in a particular situation.

Who is to question him?
What is to be done with the wastelands of old industry?

For information on the use of 'to'-infinitives in reported questions, see entry at **Reporting.**

as purpose clauses People often use 'to'-infinitive clauses to show the purpose of an action.

They locked the door to stop us from getting in.
He patted his breast pocket to make sure his wallet was in place.

For other ways of indicating purpose, see section on **purpose clauses** in entry at **Subordinate clauses.**

after adjectives Some adjectives need to be followed by a 'to'-infinitive clause to complete their meaning. For example, you cannot say 'He is unable'. You have to say 'He is unable to come', 'He is unable to cope', etc.

They were unable to help her.
I am willing to try.

The following adjectives are usually or always followed by a 'to'-infinitive clause:

able	due	inclined	loath	unwilling
bound	fated	liable	prepared	willing
doomed	fit	likely	unable	

You can put a 'to'-infinitive clause after other adjectives when you want to give information about the action that a feeling relates to.

afraid	disappointed	happy	sad
anxious	frightened	pleased	surprised
ashamed	glad	proud	unhappy

I was afraid to go home.
He was anxious to leave before it got dark.
They were terribly pleased to see you.

You use a 'to'-infinitive clause after adjectives such as 'easy' or 'nice' when you want to say how easy, difficult, or pleasant it is to do something to a person or thing.

She had been easy to deceive.
The windows will be almost impossible to open.

They're quite nice to look at.

Note that you use a transitive verb or a verb followed by a preposition in this structure. The subject of the main clause is the object of the 'to'-infinitive clause.

You can also use this structure with a complement consisting of a noun group.

They're a pleasure to have in the class.

You can use a 'to'-infinitive clause after the following adjectives which describe someone, as a way of commenting on how sensible or right an action is.

crazy	mad	silly	wrong
foolish	right	stupid	

Am I wrong to stay here?
I have been extremely stupid and foolish to leave it there tonight.

You can use 'it' with a link verb and an adjective followed by a 'to'-infinitive clause as a way of describing an experience or action.

It's nice to be made a fuss of!
It would be interesting to hear the Government explain this.

See also entry at **it**.

with 'too' and 'enough'
When you are using 'too', you can use a 'to'-infinitive clause to indicate the action that is not possible. Similarly, you can use a 'to'-infinitive clause after 'enough' to indicate the action that is possible.

He was too proud to apologise.
She spoke too quickly for me to understand.
He was old enough to understand.
I could see well enough to know we were losing.

after a noun group
You can use a 'to'-infinitive clause after a noun group to indicate the aim or purpose of something.

We arranged a meeting to discuss the new rules.

You can also use a 'to'-infinitive clause after a noun group to indicate that something needs to have something done to it, or can have something done to it.

I gave him several things to mend.
I have work to do.
He now had plenty to eat and clean clothes to wear.

You can also use a 'to'-infinitive clause after a noun group that includes an ordinal number, a superlative, or a word like 'next', 'last', or 'only'.

She was the first woman to be elected to the council.
Mr Holmes was the oldest person to be chosen.
The only person to speak was James.

A 'to'-infinitive clause is used after some abstract nouns to indicate the action that they relate to.

All it takes is a willingness to learn.
He'd lost the ability to communicate with people.

The following abstract nouns are often followed by a 'to'-infinitive clause:

ability	desire	need	willingness
attempt	failure	opportunity	
chance	inability	unwillingness	

used as subject	In formal writing and speech, a 'to'-infinitive clause is sometimes used as the subject of a clause.

To impose these reforms on the trade union movement would be folly.
To enjoy mischief is surely a long way from being wicked. |

tolerate

See entry at **bear**.

too

Too is used as an adverb or a submodifier.

used as an adverb	You use **too** as an adverb to indicate that what has just been said applies to or includes someone or something else.

Of course, you know Africa too, don't you?
I wondered whether I too would become one of its victims.
Hey, where are you from? Brooklyn? Me too!
Physically, too, the peoples of the world are incredibly mixed.

For more information about this use of **too**, see entry at **also - too - as well**. |
| **used as a submodifier** | You use **too** in front of an adjective or adverb to say that an amount or degree of a quality is more than is desirable or acceptable.

...a pair of rubber boots, bought second-hand and too big for him.
Do not be too proud to ask for help.
I realized my mistake too late.

You do not use 'very' in front of **too**. You do not say, for example, 'The slipper was very too small for her'. You say 'The slipper was **much** too small for her' or 'The slipper was **far** too small for her'.

That may well seem much too dramatic.
The eyes were far too deeply set.

You can use **rather, slightly,** or **a bit** in front of **too**.

The dress was rather too small for her.
They sat round a table that was slightly too long and shiny for the simple meal it carried.
My sister's boots were a bit too small for her long feet.

You do not use 'fairly', 'quite', or 'pretty' in front of **too**.

You do not normally use **too** with an adjective in front of a noun. You do not say, for example, 'These are too big boots'. You say 'These boots **are too big**'.

However, **too** is sometimes used with an adjective in front of a noun in formal or literary English. 'A' or 'an' is put after the adjective. For example, you can say 'This is **too complex a problem** to be dealt with here'. You do not say 'This is a too complex problem to be dealt with here'.

That's too easy an answer.
His statements were of too assertive a character to require comment. |
| **used as an intensifier** | Some people use **too** in front of words like 'kind' to express their gratitude for something that someone has done.

You're too kind.

However, you do not usually use **too** in front of an adjective or adverb simply to emphasize it. You do not say, for example, 'I am too pleased with my new car'. The word you use is **very**. |

She was upset and very angry.
Think very carefully.

See entry at **very**.

'too much' and If there is more of something than is necessary or desirable, you can say
'too many' that there is **too much** of it.

There is too much chance of error.
…the danger of too much money.

You can also say that there is **too little** of something.

Too little money was made available.
There would be too little moisture for plants to get started again.

If there are more people or things than are necessary or desirable, you can
say that there are **too many** of them.

I was making too many mistakes.
You ask too many questions, Sam.

You can also say that there are **too few** people or things.

Too few people nowadays are interested in literature.

If there is very much more of something than is necessary or desirable,
you can say that there is **much too much** of it or **far too much** of it.

This would leave much too much power in the hands of the judges.
There's far too much attention being paid to these people.

If there is a very much larger number of people or things than is necessary
or desirable, you say that there are **far too many** of them. You do not say
that there are 'much too many' of them.

Every middle-class child gets far too many toys.

You can also say that there are **far too few** people or things.

There are far too few cars to cause any serious traffic problems.

WARNING You do not use **too much** or **much too much** in front of an adjective which
is not followed by a noun. You do not say, for example, 'It's too much hot
to play football'. You say 'It's **too hot** to play football' or 'It's **much too hot**
to play football'.

tools

The following are general words used to refer to objects or pieces of
equipment that you use to help you to do a particular kind of job:

appliance	gadget	instrument	tool
device	implement	machine	utensil

'tool' A **tool** is usually a simple object that you use to make, shape, or mend
something, for example a hammer, saw, spade, or spanner.

Remember to put all your tools away safely.
…a glass-cutting tool.

Tools that operate by electricity are called **power tools.**

Keep power tools out of children's reach.

Other things which are used to achieve something can also be referred to
as **tools.** This is a fairly formal use.

Textbooks became the essential tools of the teacher.

'implement'   An **implement** is a simple tool used for digging or cooking. **Implement** is a formal word.

Lava was the most common rock used to manufacture simple stone implements.
Don't use metal implements such as spoons when using non-stick pans.

'instrument'   An **instrument** is an object used for a scientific or medical purpose, or for measuring something.

...surgical and dental instruments.

A **musical instrument** is an object from which music is produced, for example a violin, a drum, or a flute.

'utensil'   A **utensil** is usually a container or small object used for cooking, such as a saucepan or a spoon. **Utensil** is a formal word.

Students usually provide their own crockery, cutlery, cooking utensils and bedding.

'device' and   A **device** or **gadget** is usually a fairly small object, often a complicated or
'gadget'   unusual one. Some devices and gadgets are powered by electricity. **Gadget** is an informal word, and is often used showing disapproval.

...a tiny 'pacemaker' – a device that sends pulses of electricity to activate the heart.
These gadgets are costly, ugly, and extraordinarily wasteful of water and electricity.

'machine'   A **machine** is a piece of equipment which uses electricity or some other form of power to perform a task. It can be quite large.

...when Walter Hunt and Elias Howe invented the sewing machine.
Employers have to provide workplaces, machines and methods of work that are safe.

'appliance'   An **appliance** is usually a machine that is used in people's homes, such as a washing machine or cooker. **Appliance** is a formal word.

...household appliances.

touch

If you **touch** something, you gently put your fingers or hand on it.

The metal is so hot I can't touch it.
Madeleine stretched out her hand to touch his.

If you **are touched** by something, it makes you feel sad, sympathetic, or grateful.

I was touched that he should remember the party where he had kissed me for the first time.
I was touched by his thoughtfulness.

'affect'   You do not use **touch** to say that something changes or influences a person or thing. You do not say, for example, 'We wanted to know how these proposals would touch our town'. The word you use is **affect**.

...the ways in which computers can affect our lives.
The disease affected Jane's lungs.

toward - towards

See section on **direction** in entry at **to**.

traffic

You use **traffic** to refer to all the vehicles moving along a road.

...rush-hour traffic.

Traffic is an uncount noun. You do not talk about 'traffics' or 'a traffic'.

traffic circle

See entry at **roundabout**.

translate

If you **translate** something that has been said or written, you say or write it in a different language.

These jokes would be far too difficult to translate.

You say that someone translates something from one language **into** another.

An interpreter was going to translate his words into English.
My books have been translated into many languages.

You do not use any preposition except 'into' in sentences like these.

Transport

prepositions   You can use **by** with most forms of transport when you are talking about travel using that form of transport.

Most visitors to these parts choose to travel by bicycle.
I never go by car.
It is cheaper to travel to London by coach.

WARNING   You do not use a determiner after **by**. For example, you do not say 'I never go by a car'. Note also that you cannot use **by** when you are giving more detail about the vehicle. For example, you do not say 'I came by Tom's car'. You say 'I came **in** Tom's car'.

If you want to emphasize that someone walks somewhere, you say that they go **on foot**. You do not say 'by foot'.

They'd have to go on foot.

You can also use **in** when you are talking about travel using a car, taxi, ambulance, lorry, small boat, or small plane. Similarly, you can use **in** or **into** when talking about entering one of these vehicles and **out of** when talking about leaving one of them.

I always go back in a taxi.
She and Oliver were put into a lorry.
I saw that he was already out of the car.

However, you usually use **on, onto,** and **off** when you are talking about other forms of transport, such as buses, coaches, planes, trains, and ships.

...your trip on planes, ships and cross-channel ferries.
He got onto the bus and we waved until it drove out of sight.
Sheila looked very pretty as she stepped off the train.

Note that **in, into,** and **out of** are sometimes used with these other forms of transport too.

He could hear the people in the plane screaming.
Just before I got into the bus, I went over to him.
We jumped out of the bus and ran into the nearest shop.

You can also say that someone is **aboard** or **on board** these other forms of transport, especially planes and ships.

He fled the country aboard a US Air Force plane.
...before the fish could be hauled on board his boat.

verbs You usually use the verb **get** followed by a preposition to say that someone enters or leaves a vehicle.

Then I stood up to get off the bus.
They got on the wrong train.

The verbs **board, embark,** and **disembark** are used in formal English.

You use **board** to talk about getting on a bus, train, large plane, or ship.

...so that he could be the first to board the plane.

You can also use **embark on** to talk about getting on a ship and **disembark from** to talk about getting off a ship.

Even before they embarked on the ferry at Southampton she was bored.
...as they disembarked from the QE2 after their trip.

When you are talking about travel by public transport, you can use **take** instead of 'go by'. For example, instead of saying that you will 'go by' bus, you can say that you will **take** a bus.

We then took a boat downriver.
'I could take a taxi,' I said.

transport - transportation

'transport' In British English, vehicles that you travel in are referred to generally as **transport.**

It's easier to travel if you have your own transport.
...free public transport in Inner London.

Transport is an uncount noun. You do not refer to a single vehicle as 'a transport'.

British speakers also use **transport** to refer to the moving of goods or people from one place to another.

The goods were ready for transport and distribution.
High transport costs make foreign goods too expensive.

'transportation' American speakers usually use **transportation** to refer both to vehicles and to the moving of goods or people.

Do you two children have transportation home?
...long-distance transportation.

trash

See entry at **rubbish.**

travel

Travel is used as a verb or a noun. The other forms of the verb are **travels, travelling, travelled** in British English, and **travels, traveling, traveled** in American English.

used as a verb	If you make a journey to a place, you can say that you **travel** there.

I travelled to work by train.

When you **travel,** you go to several places, especially in foreign countries.

They brought news from faraway places in which they travelled.
You have to have a passport to travel abroad.

used as a noun	**Travel** is the act of travelling. When **travel** has this meaning, it is an uncount noun.

They arrived after four days of hard travel.
...air travel.
...space travel.

'travels'	When someone has made several journeys to different places, especially places a long way from their home, you can refer to these journeys as their **travels.**

Marsha told us all about her travels.
...rare plants and trees collected during lengthy travels in the Far East.

You do not talk about 'a travel'. Instead you talk about a **journey,** a **trip,** or a **voyage.** See entry at **journey.**

trend - tendency

Both these words are used to refer to a change towards something different involving a large number of things or people.

There is a trend towards equal opportunities for men and women.
Interest rates could resume their downward trend.

There is a fairly even spread of population and no tendency towards the formation of excessive concentrations.
Surprisingly, this tendency has declined in the mid-1970s.

You can talk about the tendency **for** a group of people or things **to do** something.

The tendency for motorists to buy in August seems to be increasing.
There is no visible tendency for interest rates to decline.

You cannot use **trend** with 'for' and a 'to'-infinitive like this.

You can also use **tendency** to refer to the behaviour of an individual person or thing.

She has a tendency to be a worrier.

You cannot use **trend** to refer to the behaviour of individuals.

trip

See entry at **journey.**

trouble

used as an uncount noun	**Trouble** is most commonly used as an uncount noun. If something causes you **trouble,** you have difficulty dealing with it.

The obstacles were causing more trouble than the enemy.
This would save everyone a lot of trouble.

You can say that someone **has trouble doing** something.

Did you have any trouble finding your way here?

You do not say that someone 'has trouble to do' something.

'troubles' Your **troubles** are the problems in your life.

These roads are the cause of all our troubles.
Egotism may have been the beginning of all his troubles.

You do not usually refer to a single problem as 'a trouble'.

'the trouble' If a particular aspect of something is causing problems, you can refer to this aspect as **the trouble.**

It's getting a bit expensive now, that's the trouble.
The trouble is, wars are not the product of rational thought.

trousers

Trousers are a piece of clothing that covers your body from the waist downwards, and covers each leg separately. **Trousers** is a plural noun. You use a plural form of a verb with it.

His trousers were covered in mud.

You do not talk about 'a trousers'. You say **some trousers** or **a pair of trousers.**

It's time I bought myself some new trousers.
Claud was dressed in a pair of black trousers.

You usually use a singular form of a verb with **a pair of trousers.**

There was a pair of trousers in his carrier-bag.

The form **trouser** is often used in front of another noun.

The waiter took a handkerchief from his trouser pocket.
Hamo was rolling up his trouser leg.

truck

See entries at **carriage** and **lorry - truck.**

true

A **true** story or statement is based on facts, and is not invented or imagined.

The story about the murder is true.
Unfortunately it was true about Sylvie.

'come true' If a dream, wish, or prediction **comes true,** it actually happens.

Remember that some dreams come true.
The worst of the predictions might come true.

You do not say that something 'becomes true'.

trunk

See entry at **boot - trunk.**

try - attempt

Both these words are used as verbs or nouns. The other forms of 'try' are **tries, trying, tried.**

'try' used If you **try to do** something, you make an effort to do it.
as a verb
My sister tried to cheer me up.
He was trying his best to understand.

You can also **try and do** something. There is no difference in meaning.

Try and see how many of these questions you can answer.

Angelica started to try and help her up.
We must try and understand.

Note that you can only use 'and' after the base form of **try** — that is, when you are using it as an imperative or infinitive, or after a modal. You cannot say, for example, 'I was trying and help her' or 'I was trying and helping her'.

If you **try doing** something, you do it in order to find out how useful, effective, or enjoyable it is.

He tried changing the subject.
Have you ever tried painting, Humbert?

'attempt' used as a verb

If you **attempt to do** something, you try to do it. **Attempt** is a more formal word than **try**.

Some of the crowd attempted to break through police cordons.
Rescue workers attempted to cut him from the wreckage.

You do not say that you 'attempt and do' something or 'attempt doing' something.

'try' and 'attempt' used as nouns

When someone tries to do something, you can refer to what they do as a **try** or an **attempt**. **Try** is normally used only in conversation. In writing, you usually talk about an **attempt**.

After a few tries they gave up.
The young birds manage to fly several kilometres at their first attempt.

You say that someone **has a try** at something or **gives** something **a try**.

You've had a good try at it.
'I'll go and see him in the morning.'—'Yes, give it a try.'

You say that someone **makes an attempt to do** something.

Wilt made an attempt to conciliate the man.
Two recent reports made an attempt to assess the success rate of the project.

'trying'

The adjective **trying** is not related to the verb 'try'. You say that someone or something is **trying** when they make you feel impatient or annoyed.

I find him very trying.
It had been a most trying experience for them.

type

Type is used as a noun to talk about a class of people or things. **Type** is a count noun. After words like 'all' and 'many', you use **types**, not 'type'.

...hundreds of ships of every size and type.
...in hospitals of all types.
...many types of public service.

After **types of** you can use either the plural or singular form of a noun. You can say 'He eats most types of **vegetables**' or 'He eats most types of **vegetable**'. The singular form is more formal.

How many types of people live in these households?
This only happens with certain types of school.

If you use a number in front of **types of**, you should use a singular form after it.

There are three types of muscle in the body.
...two types of playgroup.

After **type of** you use the singular form of a noun.

He was an unusual type of actor.
...the commonest type of car number.

In conversation, 'these' and 'those' are often used with **type**. For example, people say 'These type of books are boring' or 'Those type of books are boring'. This use is generally thought to be incorrect, and it is best to avoid it. Instead you should say **'This type of book** is boring' or **'That type of book** is boring'.

This type of person has very little happiness.
I could not be happy in that type of household.

You can also say **'Books of this type** are boring'.

Conferences of this type have already been held.

U

ultimately

You use **ultimately** to indicate that something is the final result of a series of events.

Elections might ultimately produce a Communist victory.
The rebels hoped to create bad feeling and ultimately war between Spain and the United States.

You also use **ultimately** when you are drawing attention to a basic fact about a situation.

Ultimately, the problems are not scientific but moral.
It is ultimately the fault of the universities.

'lately'   You do not use **ultimately** to say that something has been happening since a short time ago. You do not say, for example, 'Ultimately I have been feeling rather unwell'. You say 'I have been feeling rather unwell **lately**'. For more information, see entry at **recently - newly - lately**.

umpire - referee

An **umpire** or **referee** is an official whose job is to make sure that a game is played fairly and that the rules are not broken.

'umpire'   These games have an umpire or umpires:

badminton	cricket	tennis
baseball	table tennis	volleyball

'referee'   These games have a referee:

basketball	boxing	rugby football	wrestling
billiards	football	snooker	

The official in charge of a hockey match is sometimes called an **umpire** and sometimes a **referee**.

unconscious

See entry at **subconscious**.

under - below - beneath

'under'
Under is almost always used as a preposition. You use **under** to say that one thing is at a lower level than another, and that the other thing is directly above it. For example, you might say that an object on the floor is **under** a table or chair.

There was a cask of beer under the bench.

'underneath'
Underneath is used as a preposition or adverb with a similar meaning to **under**.

The tortoise was underneath the table.
There was a portrait with an inscription underneath.

'below'
Below is usually used as an adverb. You normally use it to say that one thing is at a much lower level than another. For example, if you are at the top of a mountain, you can talk about a valley **below**.

You can see the town spread out below.
Down below in the valley the chimneys were smoking.

'beneath'
Beneath is used as a preposition or an adverb. It has a similar meaning to **under** or **below**. **Beneath** is a rather formal word.

...the feel of the soft ground beneath his feet.
The Minister stared out of the window into the circular courtyard beneath.

understand

If you can **understand** someone or can **understand** what they are saying, you know what they mean.

She had a heavy Italian accent. Sara could hardly understand her.
...listening to stories that are hard to understand.

If you say that you **understand** that something is the case, you mean that you have been told that it is the case.

I understand he's had several wives.
There was no definite evidence, I understand, which could be brought against her.

'realize'
You do not use **understand** to say that someone becomes aware of something. You do not say, for example, 'Until he stopped working he hadn't understood how late it was'. You say 'Until he stopped working he **hadn't realized** how late it was'.

As soon as I saw him, I realized that I'd seen him before.
She had realized that she was pregnant again.

understanding

See entry at **comprehension - understanding**.

underweight

See entry at **thin**.

unhappy

See entry at **happy - sad**.

uninterested

See entry at **disinterested**.

unique

If something is **unique**, it is the only thing of its kind.

It was a unique experience.
Humans are unique because they have the capacity to choose what they do.

For emphasis, you can use words such as 'totally' or 'absolutely' in front of **unique**.

By the late 1930's the country had full employment – an absolutely unique achievement.

You can say that something is **almost unique**.

The opportunity for change is almost unique.

used to mean 'unusual'
Some people use **unique** to mean 'unusual'. They say, for example, that something is 'very unique' or 'rather unique'.

Oh, I say, that's rather unique, isn't it?
I realized I had hit on something pretty unique.
His most unique ability was as a song writer.

These uses of **unique** are generally thought to be incorrect.

university

See entry at **school - university**.

unless

You usually use **unless** to say that something can only happen or be true in particular circumstances. For example, instead of saying 'I will go to France only if the firm pays my expenses', you can say 'I will **not** go to France **unless** the firm pays my expenses'.

In Scotland you have no right to keep people off your land unless they are doing damage.

Note that in the subordinate clause you use the simple present tense. You do not say, for example, 'I will not go to France unless the firm will pay my expenses'.

When you are talking about a situation in the past, you use the simple past tense after **unless**.

She wouldn't go with him unless I came too.

You also use **unless** to mention the only circumstances in which something will not happen or be true. For example, instead of saying 'If we are not told to stop, we will carry on selling the furniture', you can say 'We will carry on selling the furniture **unless** we are told to stop'.

The mail will go by air unless it is quicker by other means.
We might as well stop unless you've got something else you want to talk about.

WARNING
You do not use **unless** to say that something would happen or be true if particular circumstances did not exist. For example, if you have a cold, you do not say 'I would go to the party unless I had this cold'. You say 'I would go to the party **if I didn't have** this cold'.

She'd be pretty if she didn't wear so much make-up.

unqualified - disqualified

'unqualified' Unqualified people have not passed or taken the exams which relate to their work.

> ...some unqualified member of the teaching staff.
> ...highly paid but unqualified clerical staff.

'disqualified' When someone **is disqualified,** they are officially told they cannot do something, because they have broken a law or rule.

> They were disqualified from driving.
> If the complaint is upheld, he could be disqualified from election for three years.

unsatisfied - dissatisfied

'unsatisfied' If something such as a demand is **unsatisfied,** there is not enough of what is wanted.

> There is already an unsatisfied demand for timber products.

'dissatisfied' If a person is **dissatisfied,** they are not contented and want changes in a situation or in their lives.

> People are utterly dissatisfied with the economic situation.
> The universities produced a number of dissatisfied idealists.

unsociable

See entry at **anti-social.**

until - till

Until and till are common words which are used as prepositions or conjunctions. There is no difference in meaning between **until** and **till. Till** is more common in conversation, and is not used in formal writing.

used as prepositions If you do something **until** or **till** a particular time, you stop doing it at that time.

> He continued to practise as a vet until 1960.
> She would have to wait until Wednesday.

> We had to wait till the end of the war.
> I said I'd work till 4 p.m.

If you want to emphasize that something does not stop before the time you mention, you can use **up until, up till,** or **up to.**

> Up until 1950 coal provided over 90% of our energy needs.
> Etta had not up till then taken a very active part in the discussion.
> Up to now they've had very little say.

If something does not happen **until** or **till** a particular time, it does not happen before that time.

> Details will not be available until January.
> We didn't get back till two.

used with 'after' You can use **until** or **till** with phrases beginning with 'after'.

> The Count had resolved to wait until after Christmas to propose to Gertrude.
> They have to wait till after school.

WARNING You do not use **until** or **till** to say that something will have happened before a particular time. You do not say, for example, 'The work will be finished until four o'clock'. You say 'The work will be finished **by** four o'clock'.

By 8.05 the groups were ready.
Total sales in these countries reached 1 million by 1980.

used with 'from' **From** is often used with **until** or **till** to say when something finishes and ends.

The ticket office will be open from 10.00am until 1.00pm.
They seem to be working from dawn till dusk.

In sentences like these, you can use **to** instead of 'until' or 'till'. Some American speakers also use **through**.

The Blitz on London began with nightly bombings from 7 September to 2 November.
I was in college from 1927 through 1932.

saying how much time there is If you want to say how much time there is before a particular event, you usually use **to**, rather than 'until' or 'till'.

Only ten shopping days to Christmas.

WARNING You only use **until** or **till** when you are talking about time. You do not use these words to talk about position. You do not say, for example, 'She walked until the post office'. You say 'She walked **as far as** the post office'.

I walked as far as her office.
They have gone as far as the Cantabrian mountains.

used as conjunctions Instead of a noun group, you can use a subordinate clause after **until** or **till**.

Stay here with me until help comes.
Hold these for me until I ask for them.
They concentrate on one language till they go to university.

Note that you use the simple present tense in the subordinate clause. You do not say, for example 'Hold these for me until I will ask for them'.

You can also use the present perfect tense in the subordinate clause. For example, you can say 'I'll wait here until you **have had** your breakfast'. You do not say 'I'll wait here until you will have had your breakfast'.

Tell him I won't discuss anything until I've spoken to my wife.

When you are talking about events in the past, you use the simple past tense or the past perfect tense after **until** or **till**.

Dr Owen remained Foreign Secretary until Labour lost office in 1979.
He continued watching until I had driven off in my car.

unused

See entry at **disused - unused - misused**.

unusual

The following words can all be used to describe someone whose character or appearance is different from that of most other people:

bizarre	funny	peculiar	striking
curious	interesting	queer	unusual
extraordinary	odd	strange	weird

If you say, for example, 'She's odd' or 'She's an odd woman', you are talking about someone's character. If you say 'She looks odd' or 'She has an odd face', you are describing her appearance.

'unusual' **Unusual** is a neutral word which does not show approval or disapproval.

I was not prepared for this unusual man.
He noted the boy's expensive unusual clothes.

'interesting' and **Interesting** and **striking** are used to indicate approval. **Striking** is only used
'striking' to describe someone's appearance, not their character.

...filling your life up with interesting new acquaintances.
You've got a very interesting face. Striking.

'extraordinary' When **extraordinary** is used to describe someone's character, it usually indicates approval.

She was an extraordinary, fascinating woman.

other words **Bizarre, curious, funny, odd, peculiar, queer, strange,** and **weird** indicate amusement or disapproval when they are used to describe people.

His old school tie and blazer looked distinctly bizarre.
There was something a bit odd about this woman.
The girl was wearing a very peculiar trouser suit.

up

Up is used as a preposition or an adverb. You usually use it to indicate that someone or something moves towards a higher place or position.

I carried my suitcase up the stairs behind her.
The coffee was sent up from the kitchen below.
Bill put up his hand.

You also use **up** as an adverb to indicate that someone or something is in a high place.

He was up in his bedroom.
...comfortable houses up in the hills.

'up to' You can say that someone goes **up to** a higher place.

We went up to Arthur's Seat just recently.

You also say that someone goes **up to** a place when it is further north than the place they started from.

I thought of going up to Yorkshire.
Why did you come up to Edinburgh?

British speakers sometimes use **up to** instead of 'to' for no special reason.

The other day I went up to the supermarket.
We all went up to the pub.

upset

See entry at **pleased - disappointed**.

upstairs

If you go **upstairs** in a building, you go up a staircase towards a higher floor.

He went upstairs and pulled down the blind.

If you say that someone or something is **upstairs,** you mean that they are on a higher floor than the one you are on.

...the student who lived upstairs.
He had a revolver upstairs in a drawer beside his bed.

You do not use 'to', 'at', or 'in' in front of **upstairs.**

upwards

In British English, if you move or look **upwards,** you move or look towards a place that is higher than the place where you are.

She stretched upwards to the curtain pole.
He had happened to look upwards.

Upwards is only used as an adverb.

'upward' Speakers of American English usually say **upward** instead of 'upwards'.

I began to climb upward over the steepest ground.

In both British and American English, **upward** is used as an adjective. An **upward** movement or look is one in which someone or something moves or looks upwards.

...a quick upward flick of the arm.
He would steal upward glances at the clock.

When **upward** is an adjective, you can only use it in front of a noun.

urban - urbane

'urban' **Urban** /ɜːbən/ means 'belonging or relating to cities or towns'.

...urban unemployment.
More and more people are moving to urban areas.

Urban is only used in front of a noun. You do not say that an area 'is urban'.

'urbane' Someone who is **urbane** /ɜːbeɪn/ is well-mannered and relaxed, and appears comfortable in social situations.

...a moderate, urbane Dallas lawyer.

urge

If you **urge** someone **to do** something, you try hard to persuade them to do it.

I urged him to take a year off to study drawing.
Father Swiebel urged him to talk.

Note that **urge** must be followed by an object when you use it with a 'to'-infinitive. You say, for example, 'He **urged them to stay**'. You do not say 'He urged to stay'.

In writing, you can use a 'that'-clause after **urge.** In the 'that'-clause, you use 'should' or the base form of a verb.

The Press Commission urged that the ownership of the press and broadcasting should be kept separate.
Sir Fred urged that Britain join the European Monetary System.

In writing, **urge** can also be used with an object referring to a course of action.

US officials urged restraint.
The report urged a more positive role for local government.

us

Us is used as the object of a verb or preposition. You use **us** to refer to yourself and one or more other people.

Why didn't you tell us?
There wasn't room for us all.

WARNING
In standard English, you do not use **us** as the object of a sentence when 'we' is the subject. You do not say, for example, 'We bought us some drinks'. You say 'We bought **ourselves** some drinks'.

After the meeting we introduced ourselves.

use - used - used to

'use'
If you **use** /juːz/ something, you do something with it in order to achieve a particular result.

They used the money to buy foreign technology.
You can use a cheque.
It is better not to use a knife.

The **use** /juːs/ of something is the act of using it.

…the dangers of the large-scale use of fertilisers and insecticides.

'used'
Used /juːzd/ can be used as an adjective in front of a noun. You use it to indicate that something has been owned by someone else, or is dirty as a result of being used before.

…a used glass on the coffee table.
…a used napkin.

'used to'
If something **used to** /juːs tuː, juːs tə/ happen, it happened regularly in the past. Similarly, if something **used to** be the case, it was the case in the past.

She used to tell me stories about people in India and Egypt.
I used to be told I looked quite handsome.
I used to be frightened sometimes.

'used to' in negative structures
Used to is not common in negative structures.

In conversation, you can say that something **didn't used to** happen or **didn't used to** be the case.

They didn't used to mind what we did.

You can also say that something **never used to** happen or be the case.

Where I was before, we never used to have posters on the walls.
Snooker and darts never used to be televised sports.

You can also say that something **used not to** happen or be the case. This is a fairly formal use.

It used not to be taxable, but now it will be subject to tax.

Note that in standard English you do not say that something 'usedn't to' happen or be the case.

'used to' in questions
You form 'yes/no'-questions with **used to** by putting 'did' in front of the subject, followed by **used to**.

Did you used to play with your trains?
Didn't they used to mind?

Used to can also be used in 'wh'-questions. If the 'wh'-word is the subject of the clause, or part of the subject, you put **used to** after it, without an auxiliary.

What used to annoy you most about him?

If the 'wh'-word is the object of the clause, or part of the object, you use the auxiliary 'do' after it, followed by the subject and **used to**.

What did you used to do on Sundays?

familiarity **Used to** has another meaning. If you are **used to** something, you have become familiar with it and you accept it.

Pilots are used to the mid-afternoon switch from one runway to another.
They are used to thinking of education as something in itself.

For more information about this use, see entry at **accustomed to.**

usual - usually

'usual' **Usual** is used to describe the thing that happens most often, or that is done or used most often, in a particular situation.

They are not taking the usual amount of exercise.
He sat in his usual chair.
The machine started with its usual clatter.

Usual normally comes after 'the' or a possessive. You do not use it after 'a'.

You can say that it is **usual for** a person or animal **to do** something.

It is usual for union representatives to meet regularly.
It was quite usual for the ponies to wander short distances.

You do not say that it is 'usual that' a person or animal 'does' something.

'ordinary' You do not use **usual** to say something is not of a special kind. You do not say, for example, 'I haven't got any chocolate biscuits, only usual ones'. You say 'I haven't got any chocolate biscuits, only **ordinary** ones'.

These children should be educated in an ordinary school.
It was furnished with ordinary office furniture.

'usually' You use the adverb **usually** when you are mentioning the thing that most often happens in a particular situation.

She usually found it easy to go to sleep at night.
He realized he was talking more freely than he usually did with strangers.

'as usual' When something happens on a particular occasion and it is the thing that most often happens in that situation, you can say that it happens **as usual.**

Nino sounded a little drunk, as usual.
She wore, as usual, her black dress.

You do not say that something happens 'as usually'.

V

vacation

See entry at **holiday - vacation**.

variety

'a variety of' If there are **a variety of** things or people, there are several different kinds of them.

We have learned to use a variety of cameras.
These were not easy aims to achieve, for a variety of reasons.

After **a variety of** you use a plural form of a verb.

A variety of treatment methods exist.

If you want to emphasize how many different kinds of people or things there are, you can use 'great' or 'wide' in front of **variety.**

A great variety of animals survive there.
The college library had a wide variety of books.

used as   You can refer to a type of plant or animal as a **variety of** that plant or
a count noun animal.

The courgettes were from Spain, as was one variety of lettuce.
There are numerous varieties of fish to choose from.

After **varieties of** you can use either the plural or singular form of a noun. The singular form is more formal.

Dozens of varieties of roses are carefully cultivated.
There are many varieties of water turbine on the market.

After **variety of** you use a singular form.

Each variety of tree has its own name.

GRAMMAR ## Verbless clauses

Most clauses contain a verb. However, some groups of words have the same function as a main clause or a subordinate clause, but do not contain a verb. These groups of words are called **verbless clauses.**

The following examples show verbless clauses used as exclamations and questions.

What a pleasant surprise!
What about your breakfast?
Well, professor?
Drink, Ted?

In writing, verbless subordinate clauses are sometimes used. These clauses can be based on an adjective, or on a subordinating conjunction and an adjective.

Surprised at my reaction, she tried to console me.
Weak with laughter, they lumbered off.

Though not very attractive physically, she possessed a good sense of humour.
Fry the fritters on both sides until golden brown.

For information on the conjunctions that can be used in this way with an adjective and no verb, see entry at **Subordinate clauses.**

Other verbless subordinate clauses are based on a noun group and an adjective or adverbial describing a state. These clauses are used to describe people in stories.

'What do you mean by that?' said Hugh, his face pale.
I became aware that Otto was standing close by, his eyes wide, his mouth slightly open.
Marie Pennington sat in her study, her head in her hands.

Note that 'with' is often used in front of groups of words like these.

She walked on, with her eyes straight ahead.

GRAMMAR **Verbs**

A **verb** is a word which is used with a subject to say what someone or something does, what they are, or what happens to them. This entry explains the different verb forms and then gives information about different types of verbs.

verb forms **Regular verbs** have the following forms:

- a base form, for example 'walk'

- an '-s' form, for example 'walks'

- an '-ing' form or present participle, for example 'walking'

- a past form, for example 'walked'

In the case of regular verbs, the past form is used for the past tense and is also used as the past participle. However, with many **irregular verbs** there are two past forms:

- a past tense form, for example 'stole'

- a past participle form, for example 'stolen'

See entry at **Irregular verbs.** The forms of the common irregular verbs 'be', 'have', and 'do' are given in the entry at **Auxiliaries.**

Sometimes there is a spelling change when the '-s', '-ing', and '-ed' endings are added, as shown in the table on the next page.

Verbs

	base form	'-s' form	'-ing' form or present participle	past form and past participle
		add '-s'	add '-ing'	add '-ed'
	join	joins	joining	joined
ending in '-sh' '-ch' '-ss' '-x' '-z' '-o'	finish reach pass mix buzz echo	add '-es' finishes reaches passes mixes buzzes echoes	finishing reaching passing mixing buzzing echoing	finished reached passed mixed buzzed echoed
ending in '-e'	dance	dances	omit '-e' before adding '-ing' or '-ed' dancing	danced
ending in '-ie'	tie	ties	change '-ie' to '-y' before adding '-ing' tying	omit '-e' before adding '-ed' tied
ending in consonant + '-y'	cry	change '-y' to '-ies' cries	crying	change '-y' to '-ied' cried
one syllable ending in single vowel + consonant	dip	dips	double final consonant before adding '-ing' or '-ed' dipping	dipped
last syllable stressed	refer	refers	double final consonant before adding '-ing' or '-ed' referring	referred
ending in '-ic'	panic	panics	add '-k' before adding '-ing' or '-ed' panicking	panicked

Note that:

● In the case of the following verbs ending in 'e', you just add '-ing' in the normal way to form the '-ing' form. For example, the '-ing' form of 'age' is 'ageing'.

age	dye	hoe	singe
agree	eye	knee	tiptoe
disagree	free	referee	

● You do not double the final consonant of verbs ending in 'w', 'x', or 'y' when forming the '-ing' form or past form.

row – rowing – rowed
box – boxing – boxed
play – playing – played

● In British English, you double the final 'l' of verbs like 'travel' and 'quarrel', even though the last syllable is not stressed.

travel – travelling – travelled
quarrel – quarrelling – quarrelled

You do not double the final 'l' in American English.

● In British English, and sometimes in American English, the final consonant of the following verbs is doubled, even though the last syllable is not stressed.

hiccup	program
kidnap	worship

Note that the final 'p' of 'handicap' is also doubled.

**uses of
verb forms**

The base form is used for the simple present tense, the imperative, and the infinitive, and is used after modals.

I hate him.
Go away.
He asked me to send it to him.
He asked if he could take a picture.

The '-s' form is used for the third person singular of the simple present.

She likes you.

The '-ing' form or present participle is used for continuous tenses, '-ing' adjectives, verbal nouns, and some non-finite clauses. See entries at '**-ing' adjectives** and '**-ing' forms.**

The attacks are getting worse.
...the increasing complexity of industrial societies.
She preferred swimming to tennis.
'So you're quite recovered now?' she said, smiling at me.

The past form is used for the simple past tense, and for the past participle of regular verbs.

I walked down the garden with him.
She had walked out without speaking.

The past participle is used for perfect tenses, passive tenses, '-ed' adjectives, and some non-finite clauses. See entries at '**-ed' adjectives** and **Past participles.**

Two countries have refused to sign the document.
It was stolen weeks ago.
He became quite annoyed.
The cargo, purchased all over Europe, included ten thousand rifles.

See also entry at **Tenses.**

intransitive verbs

Some verbs do not take an object. These verbs are called **intransitive verbs**. Intransitive verbs often describe actions or events which do not involve anyone or anything other than the subject.

Her whole body ached.
The gate squeaked.

Some intransitive verbs always or typically have a preposition after them.

I'm relying on Bill.
The land belongs to a rich family.

These are some of the commonest:

amount to	depend on	object to	resort to
apologize for	hint at	pay for	sympathize with
aspire to	hope for	qualify for	wait for
believe in	insist on	refer to	
belong to	lead to	relate to	
consist of	listen to	rely on	

You will find information on what preposition to use after a particular verb in many of the entries for individual words in this book.

transitive verbs   Some verbs describe events that must, in addition to the subject, involve someone or something else. These verbs are called **transitive verbs.** They take an **object,** that is, a noun group which is put after the verb.

He closed the door.
Some of the women noticed me.

Some transitive verbs always or typically have a particular preposition after their object.

The police accused him of murder.
The judge based his decision on constitutional rights.
He just prevented the bottle from toppling.

These are some of the commonest:

accuse of	deprive of	pelt with	return to	trust with
attribute to	entitle to	prevent from	rob of	view as
base on	mistake for	regard as	subject to	
dedicate to	owe to	remind of	swap for	

Some transitive verbs have a complement after their object when used with a particular meaning, as in 'They make me angry'. See section on **object complements** in entry at **Complements.**

Most transitive verbs can be used in the passive. However, a few, such as 'have', 'get', and 'let', are rarely or never used in the passive. See entry at **The Passive.**

reflexive verbs   A **reflexive verb** is a transitive verb which is normally or often used with a **reflexive pronoun** such as 'myself', 'himself', or 'themselves' as its object. The following verbs are reflexive verbs:

amuse	cut	excel	hurt	restrict
apply	distance	exert	introduce	strain
blame	dry	express	kill	teach
compose	enjoy	help	prepare	

Sam amused himself by throwing branches into the fire.
'Can I borrow a pencil?'—'Yes, help yourself.'

The verbs 'busy', 'content', and 'pride' must be used with a reflexive pronoun.

He had busied himself in the laboratory.
He prides himself on his tidiness.

WARNING   Reflexive pronouns are not used as much in English as in some other languages when talking about actions that you normally do to yourself. You only use a reflexive pronoun to emphasize that a person is doing the action himself or herself.

She washed very quickly and rushed downstairs.
Children were encouraged to wash themselves.

delexical verbs   A number of very common verbs can be used with an object referring to an action simply to indicate that the action takes place. They are called **delexical verbs.** The verbs most commonly used in this way are:

do	have	take
give	make	

The noun which is the object of the delexical verb is usually countable and singular, although it can sometimes be plural.

We were having a joke.
She gave an amused laugh.
They took regular walks along cart-tracks.

In a few cases, an uncount noun is used after a delexical verb.

We have made progress in both science and art.
A nurse is taking care of him.

For information on the nouns used with delexical verbs, see entries at **do, give, have - take,** and **make.**

transitive or intransitive

Many verbs are transitive when used with one meaning and intransitive when used with another meaning.

She runs a hotel.
The hare runs at enormous speed.

It is often possible to use a verb intransitively because the object is known or has already been mentioned.

I don't own a car. I can't drive.
Both dresses are beautiful. I can't choose.

Note that even verbs which are almost always followed by a direct object can occasionally be used intransitively, when you are making a very general statement.

Some people build while others destroy.
She was anxious to please.

ergative verbs

An **ergative verb** can be used either transitively to focus on the person who performs an action, or intransitively to focus on the thing affected by an action.

When I opened the door, there was Laverne.
Suddenly the door opened.

The driver stopped the car.
The big car stopped.

Many ergative verbs refer to change or movement:

age	crack	fade	shake	stick
balance	darken	finish	shatter	stop
begin	decrease	grow	shrink	stretch
bend	diminish	improve	shut	swing
bleach	disperse	increase	slow	tear
break	double	move	spin	thicken
burn	drop	open	split	turn
burst	drown	quicken	spread	widen
change	dry	rest	stand	worsen
close	empty	rock	start	
continue	end	rot	steady	

I shattered the glass.
Wine bottles had shattered all over the pavement.

Jefferson spun the globe slowly on its axis.
The wheels of the car spun furiously.

Verbs which refer to cooking are usually ergative verbs.

She made some soup and roasted a chicken.

The stake burnt more quickly than the pig roasted.

So are verbs which refer to driving or controlling vehicles.

The boys reversed their car and set off down the road we had just climbed.
The jeep reversed at full speed.

The following verbs are used ergatively with one or two nouns only:

catch (an article of clothing)
fire (a gun, rifle, pistol)
play (music)
ring (a bell, the alarm)
show (an emotion such as fear, anger)
sound (a horn, the alarm)

He had caught his sleeve on a splinter of wood.
The hat caught on a bolt and tore.

I rang the bell.
The bell rang.

The following ergative verbs usually have an adverbial after them when they are used intransitively:

clean	handle	polish	stain
freeze	mark	sell	wash

I like the new Range Rover. It handles beautifully.
Wool washes well if you treat it carefully.

reciprocal verbs A **reciprocal verb** describes an action which involves two or more people doing the same thing to each other. The people are referred to together using a plural subject and the verb is used intransitively.

Their children are always fighting.
He came out and we hugged.

To emphasize that the participants are equally involved in the action, 'each other' or 'one another' can be put after the verb group.

We embraced each other.
It was the first time they had touched one another.

The following reciprocal verbs can be followed by 'each other' or 'one another':

cuddle	fight	marry	touch
embrace	hug	match	
engage	kiss	meet	

With some verbs it is necessary to use a preposition, usually 'with', in front of 'each other' and 'one another'.

You've got to be able to communicate with each other.
Third World countries are competing with one another for a restricted market.

The following reciprocal verbs can be followed by 'with':

agree	communicate	correspond	mix
alternate	compete	disagree	quarrel
argue	conflict	engage	struggle
clash	contend	fight	talk
coincide	contrast	integrate	
collide	converse	mate	
combine	co-operate	merge	

You can also use 'against' after 'compete' and 'fight', and 'to' after 'correspond' and 'talk'. You use 'from' after 'part' and 'separate'. You use 'to' after 'relate'.

Note that 'engage' and 'fight' can be used either transitively or with a preposition.

<table>
<tr><td>**verbs with object
or prepositional
phrase**</td></tr>
</table>

A small group of verbs can be followed by either an object or a prepositional phrase. For example, you can say either 'He tugged her sleeve' or 'He tugged at her sleeve'. There is usually little difference in meaning between using the verb on its own and using a preposition after it.

Her arm brushed my cheek.
Something brushed against the back of the shelter.

We climbed the mountain.
I climbed up the tree.

The following verbs can be used with an object or a prepositional phrase:

boo (at)	gnaw (at)	play (against)
brush (against)	hiss (at)	rule (over)
check (on)	infiltrate (into)	sip (at)
distinguish (between)	jeer (at)	sniff (at)
enter (for)	juggle (with)	tug (at)
fight (against)	mock (at)	twiddle (with)
fight (with)	mourn (for)	
gain (in)	nibble (at)	

ditransitive verbs

Some verbs can have two objects: a **direct object** and an **indirect object**. These verbs are called **ditransitive verbs.** The indirect object usually refers to the person who benefits from the action or receives something as a result.

When the indirect object is a short noun group such as a pronoun, or 'the' and a noun, you often put it in front of the direct object.

I gave him the money.
Sheila showed the boy her new bike.
I taught myself French.

Note that you do not usually put a preposition in front of the indirect object when it is in this position. For example, you do not say 'I gave to him the money'.

Instead of putting the indirect object in front of the direct object, it is possible to put it in a prepositional phrase that comes after the direct object. It is normal to use this prepositional structure when the indirect object is long, or when you want to emphasize it.

He handed his driving licence to the policeman.
I've given the key to the woman who lives in the house next door to the garage.
I bought that for you.

You must use a preposition when the direct object is a personal pronoun and the indirect object is not.

He got a glass from the cupboard, filled it and gave it to Atkinson.
Then Stephen Jumel bought it for his wife.

If both the direct object and the indirect object are personal pronouns, you should use a preposition in writing. A preposition is also often used in conversation.

He gave it to me.
Save it for me.

However, some people do not use a preposition in conversation. Sometimes the direct object follows the indirect object, and sometimes the indirect object follows the direct object. For example, someone might say either 'My mother bought me it' or 'My mother bought it me'.

With the following verbs, you use 'to' to introduce the indirect object.

accord	give	mail	quote	serve
advance	grant	offer	read	show
award	hand	owe	rent	teach
deal	lease	pass	repay	
feed	lend	pay	sell	
forward	loan	post	send	

He lent my apartment to a friend for the weekend.
We picked up shells and showed them to each other.

You can sometimes use 'to' to introduce the indirect object of 'tell'. See entry at **tell.**

With the following verbs, you use 'for' to introduce the indirect object.

book	design	keep	pour	spare
build	fetch	make	prepare	win
buy	find	mix	reserve	
cash	fix	order	save	
cook	get	paint	secure	
cut	guarantee	pick	set	

They booked a place for me.
She painted a picture for her father.

With the following verbs, you can use either 'to' or 'for' to introduce the indirect object, depending on the meaning you want to express.

bring	play	take
leave	sing	write

Mr Schell wrote a letter the other day to the New York Times.
Once, I wrote a play for the children.

With a few ditransitive verbs, the indirect object almost always comes in front of the direct object rather than being introduced by 'to' or 'for'.

allow	bet	cost	envy	promise
ask	cause	deny	forgive	refuse
begrudge	charge	draw	grudge	

The radio cost me three quid.
It was time for one of them to go and meet a man who had promised him a job.

Note that in passive sentences either the direct object or the indirect object can become the subject. For example, you can say either 'The books will be sent to you next week' or 'You will be sent the books next week'.

A seat had been booked for him on the 6 o'clock flight.
I was given two free tickets.

Most of the verbs listed above as ditransitive verbs can be used with the same meaning with just a direct object.

He left a note.
She fetched a jug from the kitchen.

A few verbs can be used with a direct object referring to the person who benefits from the action, or receives something.

ask	feed	pay
envy	forgive	teach

I fed the baby when she awoke.
I forgive you.

link verbs A **link verb** is a verb that is followed by a **complement** rather than an object. The complement gives more information about the subject, and can be an adjective or a noun group.

The link verbs are:

appear	feel	keep	remain	stay
be	get	look	seem	taste
become	go	pass	smell	turn
come	grow	prove	sound	

I am proud of these people.
She was getting too old to play tennis.

For information on which link verbs are used with which kind of complement, see entry at **Complements**.

Some link verbs, such as 'appear', 'prove', and 'seem', are often followed by 'to be' and an adjective, instead of immediately by an adjective.

Mary was breathing quietly and seemed to be asleep.
The task of inspecting it proved to be exacting and interesting.

compound verbs **Compound verbs** consist of two words which are normally linked by a hyphen.

It may soon become economically attractive to mass-produce hepatitis vaccines.
Somebody had short-changed him.
Send it to the laundry. Don't dry-clean it.
He chain-smoked cheap cigars.

Only the second part of a compound verb changes to show tense and number.

dry-clean – dry-cleans – dry-cleaning – dry-cleaned
force-feed – force-feeds – force-feeding – force-fed

other verbs For information on verbs followed by a reported clause, see section on **report structures** in entry at **Reporting**. For information on verbs followed by an '-ing' form or an infinitive, see entries at **'-ing' forms, Infinitives,** and **'To'-infinitive clauses**. See also entry at **Phrasal verbs**.

---

very

You use **very** to emphasize an adjective or adverb.

...a very small child.
That's very nice of you.
Think very carefully.

<table>
<tr><td>

**used with
'-ed' words**

</td><td>

You can use **very** to emphasize adjectives ending in '-ed', especially when they refer to a state of mind or emotional condition. For example, you can say 'I was **very bored**' or 'She was **very frightened**'.

</td></tr>
</table>

He seemed very interested in everything.
Joe must have been very worried about her.

However, you do not use **very** to emphasize '-ed' words when they are part of a passive construction. You do not say, for example, 'He was very liked'. You say 'He was **well liked**'. Similarly, you do not say 'She was very admired'. You say 'She was **much admired**', 'She was **very much admired**', or 'She was **greatly admired**'.

Argentina were well beaten by Italy in the first round.
I was much influenced by many writers.
He is very much resented by the unions.
She was greatly changed in appearance.

WARNING

You do not say that someone is 'very awake'. You say that they are **wide awake** or **fully awake**.

He was wide awake by the time we reached my flat.
He was not fully awake.

You do not say that someone is 'very asleep'. You say that they are **sound asleep**, **fast asleep**, or **deeply asleep**.

Chris is still sound asleep in the other bed.
Charlotte had been fast asleep when he left her.
Miss Haynes was very deeply asleep.

You do not say that two things are 'very apart'. You say that they are **far apart**.

His two hands were far apart.

You also do not use **very** with adjectives which already describe an extreme quality. You do not say, for example, that something is 'very enormous'. Here is a list of adjectives of this kind:

absurd	delighted	excellent	massive	terrible
awful	enormous	furious	perfect	wonderful
brilliant	essential	huge	splendid	

**comparatives
and superlatives**

You do not use **very** with comparatives. You do not say, for example, 'Tom was very quicker than I was'. You say 'Tom was **much quicker** than I was' or 'Tom was **far quicker** than I was'.

It was much colder than before.
It is a far better picture than the other one.

You can use **very** in front of 'best', 'worst', or any superlative which ends in '-est'.

It's one of Shaw's very best plays.
...the very worst suspicions.
...the very latest photographs.

However, you do not use **very** with superlatives that begin with 'the most'. Instead you use **much, by far,** or **far and away**.

Music may have been much the most respectable of his tastes.
He insists that, of all his novels, 'The Hammer of God' was by far the most difficult to write.
This is far and away the most important point.

used with 'first', 'next', and 'last'	You can use **very** in front of 'first', 'next', or 'last' to emphasize that something is the first, next, or last thing of its kind.

...the very first light of day.
The very next day we held a jumble sale in the village hall.
Those were his very last words.

You do not use **very** to say that something happens because someone or something has a quality to an unusually large extent. You do not say, for example, 'He looked very funny that we couldn't help laughing'. You say 'He looked **so** funny that we couldn't help laughing'.

He found the girl so attractive that he fell in love.
He had shouted so hard that he had no voice left.

See entry at **so**.

prepositions You do not use **very** in front of prepositions such as 'ahead of' or 'behind'. Instead you use **well** or **far**.

Applications are well ahead of last year's.
Clark was not far behind him in agility.

prepositional phrases You also do not use **very** in front of prepositional phrases. You do not say, for example, 'He was very in love with Kate'. Instead, you use **very much** or **greatly**.

The findings were very much in line with previous medical thinking.
I was greatly in awe of Jane at first.

very much

See entry at **much**.

vest

In British English, a **vest** is a piece of clothing which you wear on the top half of your body underneath a shirt, blouse, or dress in order to keep warm. In American English, a piece of clothing like this is called an **undershirt**.

In American English, a **vest** is a piece of clothing with buttons and no sleeves, which a man wears over his shirt and under his jacket. In British English, a piece of clothing like this is called a **waistcoat**.

victim

You refer to someone as a **victim** when they have suffered as the result of a crime, natural disaster, or serious illness.

...a rape victim.
We have been the victims of a monumental swindle.
After about two weeks, the victim's hair starts to fall out.

'casualty' You do not usually use **victim** to refer to someone who has been injured or killed in a war or accident. The word you use is **casualty**.

There were heavy casualties on both sides.
The casualty figure has increased.
The casualties were taken to the nearest hospital.

Casualty or **the casualty ward** is the part of a hospital where people are taken for emergency treatment when they have been hurt in an accident or have suddenly become ill.

view

A **view** is a belief or opinion that you have on a particular subject.

He was sent to jail for his political views.
I have strong views about politics and the Church.

See entry at **point of view - view - opinion.**

You also use **view** to refer to what you can see from a window or high place.

From the top there is a fine view.
The window of her flat looked out on to a superb view of London.

'in view of'   You use **in view of** when you are mentioning a reason why something has been done or should be done.

The folder was marked 'Very Secret', not surprisingly, in view of the contents.
In view of the fact that all the other members of the group are going, I think you should go too.

'with a view to'   If you do something **with a view to** doing something else, you do it with the aim of eventually doing the second thing.

We have exchanged letters with a view to meeting to discuss these problems.
They entered into talks with a view to amalgamation.

visit

used as a verb   If you **visit** a place, you go to see it because you are interested in it.

He had arranged to visit a number of museums in Paris.
I could visit Blackpool next.

If you **visit** someone, you go to see them at their home, or you stay with them there for a short time.

I visited the newly-married couple.
She visited some of her relatives for a few days.

You can also **visit** a professional person such as a doctor or lawyer, in order to get treatment or advice.

He persuaded me to visit a doctor.
You might need to visit a solicitor before thinking seriously about divorce.

Some American speakers use **visit with** instead of 'visit'.

She wanted to visit with her family for a few weeks.

However, in American English, to **visit with** someone usually means to chat to them.

You and I could visit with each other undisturbed.

used as a noun   **Visit** is also used as a noun. You can **make** or **pay** a visit to someone.

He was supposed to make his visit to the club.
It was after nine o'clock, too late to pay a visit to Sally.

You do not say that someone 'does' a visit.

visual - visible

'visual'   **Visual** means 'relating to sight'.

...visual jokes.
...exhibitions of the visual arts.

'visible' Something that is **visible** is large enough to be seen, or is in a position where it can be seen.

These tiny creatures are hardly <u>visible</u> to the naked eye.
It was just <u>visible</u> from the beach.

voyage

See entry at **journey**.

W

wages

See entry at **salary - wages**.

wagon

See entry at **carriage**.

waist - waste

These words are both pronounced /weɪst/.

'waist' **Waist** is a noun. Your **waist** is the middle part of your body, above your hips.

She tied an apron around her <u>waist.</u>
He was naked from the <u>waist</u> up.

'waste' used **Waste** is most commonly used as a verb. If you **waste** time, money, or
as a verb energy, you use it on something that is unimportant or unnecessary.

You're <u>wasting</u> your time.
...fear of <u>wasting</u> money on a new idea.

'waste' used You can also say that something is **a waste of** time, money, or energy.
as a noun
I'll never do that again. It's <u>a waste of</u> time.
It's <u>a waste of</u> money hiring skis.

Waste has another meaning. You use it to refer to material which has been used and is no longer wanted, for example because the useful part of it has been removed.

The river was thick with industrial <u>waste.</u>

waistcoat

See entry at **vest**.

wait

You use the verb **wait** to say that someone remains in the same place, or avoids doing something, until something happens or someone arrives.

I <u>waited</u> in a reception room until a secretary came for me.
She had been <u>waiting</u> in the queue to buy some stamps.
The man <u>waited</u>, and said nothing.

'wait for'   You can say that someone **waits for** something or someone.

He waited for an answer.
He drew my picture while I waited for his mother.

You can also say that someone **waits for** a person or thing **to do** something.

She waited for me to say something.
I waited for Donald to come home.

Wait is never used as a transitive verb. You do not say that someone 'waits' someone or something. You must use **wait for.**

See also entry at **await.**

wake - waken

See entry at **awake.**

wallet

A **wallet** is a small, flat case made of leather or plastic, in which someone, especially a man, keeps banknotes and other small things such as credit cards.

In American English, a man's wallet is sometimes called a **billfold,** and a woman's wallet is sometimes called a **pocketbook.**

want

If you **want** something, you feel a need for it or a desire to have it.

Do you want a cup of coffee?
All they want is a holiday.

You do not normally use a continuous tense of **want.** You do not say, for example, 'All they are wanting is a holiday'.

used with   You can say that someone **wants to do** something.
a 'to'-infinitive
They wanted to go shopping.
I want to ask a favour of you, Anna.

You do not say that someone 'wants to not do' something or 'wants not to do' something. You say that they **don't want to do** it.

I don't want to discuss this.
He didn't want to come.

Instead of using a 'to'-infinitive clause, you can sometimes use 'to' on its own after **don't want.** For example, instead of saying 'I was invited to go, but I didn't want to go', you would normally say 'I was invited to go, but I **didn't want to**'. Note that you do not say 'I was invited to go, but I didn't want it'.

I could finish it by October, but I just don't want to.
I think that it is very wrong to force people to work if they don't want to.

You can say that you **want** someone else **to do** something.

I want him to learn to read.
The little girl wanted me to come and play with her.

You do not use a 'that'-clause after **want.** You do not say, for example, 'I want that he should learn to read'.

requests	You do not normally use **want** when you are making a request. It is not polite, for example, to walk into a shop and say 'I want a box of matches, please'. You should say 'Could I have a box of matches, please?' or just 'A box of matches, please.'

For more information about requests, see entry at **Requests, orders, and instructions.**

another meaning of 'want'	**Want** has another meaning. If something **wants doing,** there is a need for it to be done.

We've got a couple of jobs that want doing in the garden.
The fields were full of weeds and the buildings wanted roofing.

Note that you do not use a 'to'-infinitive in sentences like these. You do not say, for example, 'We've got a couple of jobs that want to be done in the garden'.

'be about to'	You do not use **want to** to say that someone is going to do something very soon. You do not say, for example, 'I had put on my coat, and was just wanting to leave when the telephone rang'. The expression you use is **be about to.**

Her father is about to retire soon.
He was just about to go on stage again.

wardrobe

See entry at **cupboard.**

Warning someone

There are several ways of warning someone not to do something.

In conversation, you can say 'I wouldn't ... if I were you'.

I wouldn't drink that if I were you.

A weaker way of warning is to say 'I don't think you should...' or 'I don't think you ought to...'.

I don't think you should go in there. There's no telling what he might try to do.
I don't think you ought to turn me down quite so quickly, before you know a bit more about it.
I don't think you should try to make a decision when you are so tired.

You can also warn someone indirectly not to do something by saying what will happen if they do it.

You'll fall down and hurt yourself if you insist on wearing that old gown.

You can warn someone not to do something by accident or because of carelessness by saying 'Be careful not to...' or 'Take care not to...'.

Be careful not to keep the flame in one place too long, or the metal will be distorted.
Well, take care not to get arrested.

strong warnings	'Don't' is used in strong warnings.

Don't put more things in the washing machine than it will wash.
Don't turn the gas on again until the gasman tells you it's safe to do so.
Don't open the door for anyone.

You can emphasize 'don't' with 'whatever you do'.

Whatever you do don't overcrowd your greenhouse.
Don't get in touch with your wife, whatever you do.

You can mention the consequences of not doing what you say by adding 'or' and another clause.

Don't drink so much or you'll die.

explicit warnings People sometimes say 'I warn you' or 'I'm warning you' when warning someone, especially when preparing them for something they are going to experience.

I warn you it's going to be expensive.
I must warn you that I have advised my client not to say another word.
It'll be very hot, I'm warning you.

Note that these expressions are also used as threats.

Much as I like you, I warn you I'll murder you if you tell anyone.
I'm warning you, if you do that again there'll be trouble.

warnings in writing and broadcasting 'Never' is used with an imperative as a warning in writing and broadcasting.

Never put antique china into a dishwasher.
If you have children, never keep a pet if you intend eventually to eat it.

'Beware of…' is used to warn against doing something, or to warn about something that might be dangerous or unsatisfactory.

Beware of becoming too complacent.
I would beware of companies which depend on one product and one man.

The expression 'A word of warning' is sometimes used to introduce a warning. So are 'Warning' and 'Caution', in books and articles.

A word of warning: Don't have your appliances connected by anyone who is not a specialist.
Warning! Keep all these liquids away from children.
Caution. Keep the shoulders well down when doing this exercise.

warnings on products and notices 'Warning' and 'Caution' are also used on products and notices. 'Danger' and 'Beware of…' are used on notices.

Warning: Smoking can seriously damage your health.
CAUTION: This helmet provides limited protection.
DANGER – RIVER.
Beware of Falling Tiles.

immediate warnings When you want to warn someone about something that they might be just about to do, you say 'Careful' or 'Be careful', or, more informally, 'Watch it'.

Careful! You'll break it.
He sat down on the bridge and dangled his legs. 'Be careful, Tim.'
Watch it! There's a rotten floorboard somewhere just here.
I should watch it, Neil, you're putting this on record.

You can also use 'Mind', followed by a noun referring to something the other person might hit, fall into, or harm, or a clause referring to something they must be careful about.

Mind the pond.
Mind your head.
Mind you don't slip.

'Watch' is sometimes used in a similar way, especially with a clause.

Watch where you're putting your feet.

Other warning expressions are 'Look out' and 'Watch out'. 'Look out' is used only in urgent situations of danger. 'Watch out' is used for urgent situations and for situations that are going to arise or might arise.

Look out. There's someone coming.
Watch out for that beast there.
'I think I'll just go for a little walk.'—'Watch out – it's a very large city to take a little walk in.'

---

wash

used as a
transitive verb

If you **wash** something, you clean it with water and usually with soap or detergent.

...the clatter of the dishes being washed and put away.
She washes and irons his clothes.

You can **wash** a part of your body.

First wash your hands.
She combed her hair and washed her face.

used as an
intransitive verb

If someone **washes,** they wash parts of their body, especially their hands and face. **Wash** is used like this mainly in stories.

She got up and washed.
She had not washed, yet her mouth was freshly painted.

'have a wash'

In conversation, you usually say that someone **has a wash.**

He was having a wash.
They look as if they haven't had a wash.

'wash up'

In American English, if someone **washes up,** they wash parts of their body, especially their hands and face.

He always asks permission before he washes up in the bathroom.

Wash up is not used with this meaning in British English. In British English, if you **wash up,** you wash the pans, plates, cups, and cutlery which have been used in cooking and eating a meal.

We washed up in the kitchen while the coffee heated on the stove.

'wash your
hands'

In British English, if someone asks where they can **wash their hands,** they may be asking politely where the toilet is.

washroom

See entry at **toilet.**

waste

See entry at **waist - waste.**

way

You use **way** to refer to the thing or series of things that someone does in order to achieve a particular result. You can talk about a **way of doing** something or a **way to do** it. There is no difference in meaning.

...the most effective way of helping the unemployed.
...the best way to help a fourteen-year-old with reading problems.

There are other ways of achieving the same ends.
There may be far better ways to achieve the desired ends.

Note that if you use a possessive with **way**, you must use 'of' and an '-ing' form after it. You do not use a 'to'-infinitive.

...a nurse who is willing to fit in with your way of doing things.
They are part of the author's way of telling his story.

'means'
You do not usually use a noun after **way of** when you are saying how something is done or achieved. For example, you do not refer to an animal or vehicle as a 'way of transport'. The word you use is **means**.

The essential means of transport for the islanders was the donkey.
...the use of drums as a means of communication.

used in adverbials of manner
You can say that something is done **in** a particular **way**.

It was done in a very civilized way.
...how to behave in an aristocratic way.
We have to describe this in some other way.

When you use 'this' or 'that' with **way**, you usually omit the 'in'.

I can do it this way.
It might be done that way.

You can also omit 'in' when you are using 'the' or a possessive.

We don't look at things the same way.
I'm going to handle this my way.

used with relative clauses
When **the way** is followed by a defining relative clause, this clause can be either a 'that'-clause or a clause beginning with 'in which'. For example, you can say **'the way** she told the story', **'the way that** she told the story', or **'the way in which** she told the story'. There is no difference in meaning.

It's the way they used to do it.
...the way that they would behave.
...the way in which we treat our juveniles.

'in the way'
If someone or something is **in the way** or **in your way,** they are preventing you from moving freely or from seeing clearly.

A large tree was in the way.
Why did you stand in the way?
Get out of my way.

'on the way'
If something happens to you during a journey, you do not say that it happens to you 'in the way' or 'in your way'. You say that it happens **on the way** or **on your way.**

On the way she went into the sweet shop.
Lynn was on her way home.

we

You use **we** to refer to yourself together with one or more other people. **We** is used as the subject of a verb.

We could hear the birds singing.
We both sat down.

You can use **we** to include the person or people you are speaking or writing to.

If you had to stay in town we might have dinner together.

Note that you never say 'you and we' or 'we and you'. Instead of saying 'You and we must go and see John', you say **'We** must go and see John'.

wear

When you **wear** something, you have it on your body. You can **wear** clothes, shoes, a hat, gloves, jewellery, make-up, or a pair of glasses. The past tense of 'wear' is **wore**, not 'weared'. The past participle is **worn**.

...a girl who wore spectacles.
I've worn the same suit for five years.

'dressed in' You can also say that someone is **dressed in** particular clothes.

...a handsome African dressed in a Western business suit.

However, you do not say that someone is 'dressed in' a hat, shoes, gloves, jewellery, make-up, or glasses.

See also entry at **dress.**

'in' You can also use **in** to mention the clothes, shoes, hat, or gloves someone is wearing. **In** usually goes immediately after a noun group.

...a small girl in a blue dress watching a cricket match.
The bar was full of men in cloth caps.

You can use **in** as part of an adverbial.

...when I see you walking along in your light-blue suit.
I stood all alone in my Sunday dress.

You do not usually use **in** after 'be' when you are mentioning what someone is wearing. You do not say, for example, 'Mary was in a red dress'. You say 'Mary **was wearing** a red dress'.

However, you can use **in** after 'be' when you are using a possessive determiner such as 'his' or 'my'. You can say, for example, 'Mary was **in her red dress**'.

I was in my dark suit and my university tie.
Hilary was in her nightdress and dressing gown.

In is sometimes used to mean 'wearing only'. For example, 'George was **in** his underpants' means 'George was wearing only his underpants'.

He was standing in the hall in his underpants.
...a girl lying on a bed in her bra and panties.

If you say that a man is **in shirtsleeves** or **in his shirtsleeves,** you mean that he is wearing a shirt but not a jacket, usually because it is hot or he is working hard.

I started coming to work in shirtsleeves.
I lay on the bed in my shirtsleeves.

If you say that someone is **in their stockinged feet,** you mean that they are wearing socks, stockings, or tights, but no shoes.

I stood five-and-a-half feet tall in my stockinged feet.

weather

If you are talking about the **weather,** you are saying, for example, that it is raining, cloudy, sunny, hot, or cold.

The weather was good for the time of year.
...bad weather conditions.

Weather is an uncount noun. You do not use 'a' with it. You do not say, for example, 'We can expect a bad weather in the next few days'. You say 'We can expect **bad weather** in the next few days'.

They remained on the move for seventeen days, in <u>appalling weather.</u>
The journey to Fyn, in <u>perfect May weather,</u> was beautiful.

You do not tell someone what the weather is like by saying, for example, 'It's lovely weather'. You say 'The weather **is lovely**'.

The weather <u>is horrid.</u>

'whether' Do not confuse **weather** with **whether**. You use **whether** when you are talking about two or more alternatives. You say, for example, 'I don't know **whether** to go out or stay at home'. See entry at **whether.**

weave

When people **weave** cloth, they make it by crossing threads over and under each other using a machine called a loom. When you use **weave** with this meaning, its past tense is **wove**, not 'weaved'. Its past participle is **woven.**

They were famous for the brilliant patterns of cloth they <u>wove.</u>
'Broadloom' just means that the cloth <u>was woven</u> on a loom over 6 feet wide.

Weave has another meaning. If you **weave your way** somewhere, you keep changing direction while you go there, in order to avoid hitting things. When you use **weave** with this meaning, its past tense and past participle is **weaved**, not 'wove'.

A stout woman <u>weaved her way</u> along the edge of the pool.

wedding

See entry at **marriage.**

week

A **week** is a period of seven days. A week is sometimes regarded as beginning on a Sunday, and sometimes on a Monday.

That was a terrible air crash last <u>week.</u>
She won't be back till next <u>week.</u>

If something happens **in the week** or **during the week**, it happens on weekdays, rather than at the weekend.

<u>In the week</u>, we get up at seven.
I can never be bothered to cook much <u>during the week.</u>

For more information about the word **week**, see entries at **last, next,** and **this.** See also entry at **Days and dates.**

weekday

A **weekday** is any of the days of the week except Saturday or Sunday.

She spent every <u>weekday</u> at meetings.
...an ordinary working <u>weekday.</u>

Saturday is also sometimes considered to be a weekday.

The Tower is open 9.30 to 6.30 on <u>weekdays</u> and 2.00 to 6.00 on Sundays.

You can say that something happens **on weekdays.**

I visited them <u>on weekdays</u> for lunch.
Commercials are limited to 12 minutes per hour <u>on weekdays.</u>

American speakers sometimes omit the 'on'.

Weekdays after six, I'd go fetch him for dinner.

weekend

A **weekend** consists of a Saturday and the Sunday that comes after it. Sometimes Friday evening is also considered to be part of the weekend. The weekend is the time when most people in Europe, North America, and Australia do not go to work or school.

I spent the weekend at home.
Traffic was normal for an August weekend.

regular events British speakers say that something takes place **at weekends.**

The tower is often open to the public at weekends.

American and Australian speakers usually say that something takes place **on weekends.**

On weekends we would sit in St Philip's graveyard with our sketchbooks on our knees.

single events You can say that an event takes place **during** a particular weekend.

50,000 people turned out during the bank holiday weekend to watch the aircraft make its first stop at Newcastle Airport.

On a weekday, **the weekend** or **this weekend** can refer either to the previous weekend or the following weekend. You can use 'at', 'during', or 'over' in front of **the weekend.** You do not use any preposition in front of **this weekend.**

Nine people were killed in road accidents at the weekend.
I may well call you over the weekend.

His first film, The Producers, was shown on television this weekend.
We might be able to go skiing this weekend.

weep

See entry at **cry.**

welcome

Welcome is used as a verb, a noun, or an adjective. It can also be used as a greeting.

used as a verb If you **welcome** someone, you greet them in a friendly way when they arrive at the place where you are.

He moved eagerly towards the door to welcome his visitor.

used as a noun If you want to describe the way in which someone is welcomed to a place, you can use **welcome** as a noun. For example, you can say that someone is given 'a warm welcome'.

He was given a warm welcome by the President of Harvard himself.
...the tumultuous welcome he received there.

used as an adjective If you are **welcome** in a place, the people there are glad that you have come.

All members of the public are welcome.
I was a welcome visitor in both camps.

Note that the adjective is **welcome,** not 'welcomed'. You do not say, for example, 'I was a welcomed visitor in both camps'.

If something is **welcome,** people are pleased to get it, or pleased that it happens.

The money was welcome, of course.
...a welcome cup of cocoa.
This is a welcome development.

used as a greeting

When someone arrives at the place where you are, you can greet them in a rather formal way by saying '**Welcome**' to them.

Welcome to Peking
Welcome home, Marsha.
Welcome back.

well

People sometimes say **well** when they are about to make a statement. There is often no special reason for this, but sometimes **well** can indicate hesitation or uncertainty.

'Is that right?'—'Well, I think so.'

People also use **well** when they are correcting something they have just said.

We walked along in silence for a bit; well, not really silence, because she was humming.
It took me years, well months at least, to realise that he'd lied to me.

used as an adverb

Well is very commonly used as an adverb.

You use **well** to say that something is done to a high standard or to a great extent.

He handled it well.
The strategy has worked very well in the past.
They did not look after my family very well.

You use **well** to emphasize some past participles when they are part of a passive construction.

You seem to be well liked everywhere.
Argentina were well beaten by Italy in the first round.

You also use **well** in front of some prepositions such as 'ahead of' and 'behind'.

Applications are well ahead of last year's.
I did manage to get my foot well behind the line.

When **well** is an adverb, its comparative and superlative forms are **better** and **best.**

People are better housed than ever before.
Whatever works best is what she should adopt.

used as an adjective

Well is also used as an adjective. If you are **well,** you are healthy and not ill.

She looked well.
I am very well, thank you.

Note that most British speakers do not use **well** in front of a noun. They do not say, for example, 'He's a well man'. They say 'He's **well**'. However, American and Scottish speakers sometimes use **well** in front of a noun.

When **well** is an adjective, it does not have a comparative form. However, you can use **better** to say that the health of a sick person has improved. When **better** is used like this, it means 'less ill'.

He seems better today.

Better is more commonly used to say that someone has completely recovered from an illness or injury.

I hope you'll be better soon.
Her cold was better.

'as well'   You use **as well** when you are giving more information about something.

Filter coffee is definitely better for your health than boiled coffee. And it tastes nicer as well.
They will have a difficult year next year as well.

For more information about this use, see entry at **also - too - as well**.

well-known

See entry at **famous**.

were

Were is the plural form and the second person singular form of the past tense of 'be'.

They were only fifty miles from the coast.
We were quite busy that week.
You were only twelve at the time.

used in
conditional
clauses

Were has a special use in conditional clauses when these clauses are used to mention situations that do not exist, or events that are unlikely to happen. When the subject of the clause is 'I', 'he', 'she', 'it', 'there', or a singular noun, it is generally considered correct to use **were** instead of 'was'.

If I were in his circumstances, I would go his way too.
It would be a disaster if he were not re-elected.
If education were even better organized, there would be no complaint about the content or level of work required.

However, in conversation people usually use **was** (except in the expression 'If I were you').

If I was an architect, I'd re-design this house.
This would still be true if Britain was out of the Community.

You can use **was** or **were** in conversation, but you should use **were** in formal writing.

WARNING   Do not confuse **were** /wə, wɜː/ with **where** /weə/. You use **where** to make statements or ask questions about place or position.

Where can I get my book published?

See entry at **where**.

west

The **west** is the direction which you look towards in order to see the sun set.

The next settlement is two hundred miles to the west.
The hills behind Agadir in the west are built of blue limestone.

A **west** wind blows from the west.

A warm west wind rushed to us across the downs.

The **west** of a place is the part that is towards the west.

...in remote rural areas of the west of Ireland.

West occurs in the names of some states and regions.

...West Virginia.
...a town in West Sumatra.

'western' You do not usually talk about a 'west' part of a country or region. You talk about a **western** part.

...the northern and western parts of the United Kingdom.

Similarly, you do not talk about 'west Europe' or 'west France'. You say **western** Europe or **western** France.

...the peoples of western Europe.
...western Nigeria.

You can use **Western** to describe people and things connected with the United States, Canada, the countries of western Europe, and sometimes other industrialized countries.

...the gullibility of some Western politicians.
...the defects of Western society.

westerly

If something moves in a **westerly** direction, it moves towards the west.

...a westerly journey.

However, a **westerly** wind blows **from** the west.

The ship was driven by the incessant westerly gales.

westwards

If you move or look **westwards**, you move or look towards the west.

The reef stretches westwards from the tip of Florida.
Ten minutes later we were flying westwards over the great marshes.

Westwards is only used as an adverb.

'westward' In American English and old-fashioned British English, **westward** is often used instead of 'westwards'.

General Sherman was travelling westward with a new peace council.

In both British and American English, **westward** is sometimes used as an adjective in front of a noun.

...the westward expansion of the city.

what

asking for
information
You use **what** when you are asking for information about something. You can use **what** as a pronoun or a determiner.

When you use **what** as a pronoun, it can be the subject, object, or complement of a verb. It can also be the object of a preposition.

What happened to the crew?
What did she say then?
What is your name?
What did he die of?

Note that when **what** is the object of a verb, it is followed by an auxiliary verb, the subject, and then the main verb. Note also that when **what** is the object of a preposition, the preposition usually goes at the end of the question.

used as a determiner

When you use **what** as a determiner, it usually forms part of the object of a verb.

What books can I read on the subject?
What qualifications do you have?
What church did you say you attend?

WARNING

You do not use **what** when your question involves a choice from a limited number of people or things. For example, if someone has hurt their finger, you do not say to them 'What finger have you hurt?' You say '**Which** finger have you hurt?'

When you get your daily paper, which page do you read first?
Which department do you want?

You use **what** when you are asking about the time.

What time is it?
What time does the coach get in?

used in reported clauses

What is often used in reported clauses.

I asked her what had happened.
I don't know what to do.
I find it difficult to understand what people are saying.

For more information about this use, see entry at **Reporting**.

'what...for'

You use **what** with 'for' when you are asking about the purpose of something. You put **what** at the beginning of the question and 'for' at the end of it. For example, '**What** is this handle **for**?' means 'What is the purpose of this handle?'

What are those lights for?

Some people use **what** with 'for' when they are asking about the reason for something. They say, for example, '**What** are you staring **for**?' This means 'Why are you staring?'

What are you going for?

'what if'

You use **what if** to ask what should be done if a particular difficulty occurs. For example, '**What if** the bus doesn't come?' means 'What shall we do if the bus doesn't come?'

What if it's really bad weather?
What if they don't want to part with it, what would you do then?

'what about'

You use **what about** to remind someone of something, or to draw their attention to something. **What about** is followed by a noun group.

What about the others on the list?
What about your breakfast?

Note that when you ask someone a question beginning with **what about** you are often expecting them to do something, rather than answer your question.

used in relative clauses

What is sometimes used at the beginning of a special kind of relative clause called a **nominal relative clause**. This kind of clause functions like a noun group; it can be used as the subject, object, or complement of a verb, or the object of a preposition. In a nominal relative clause, **what** means 'the thing which' or 'the things which'.

What he said was perfectly true.
They did not like what he wrote.
I'm what's generally called a traitor.
That is a very good account of what happened.

People often use a nominal relative clause in front of 'is' or 'was' to focus attention on the thing they are about to mention.

What I need is a lawyer.
What we as a nation want is not words but deeds.
What impressed me most was their sincerity.

A similar type of clause consists of **what** followed by the subject and 'do'. After a clause like this, you use 'be' and an infinitive structure with or without 'to'. For example, instead of saying 'I wrote to George immediately', you can say '**What I did** was to write to George immediately'.

What Stephen did was to interview a lot of old people.
What he did was get Christopher followed by a private detective.
What you need to do is to choose five companies to invest in.

WARNING

You do not use **what** in defining or non-defining relative clauses. You do not say, for example, 'The man what you met is my brother' or 'The book what you lent me is very good'. In sentences like these, you use **who, which,** or **that,** or you do not use a relative pronoun at all. For more information, see entry at **Relative clauses.**

used to mean 'whatever'

What can be used with the same meaning as 'whatever', both as a pronoun and a determiner.

Do what you like.
People survived by sharing out what money they could get from cattle work.

See entry at **whatever.**

used in exclamations

What is often used in exclamations.

What a marvellous idea!
What fun!

For more information about this use, see entry at **Reactions.**

whatever

Whatever is used as a pronoun, a determiner, or an adverb.

used as a pronoun or determiner

You use **whatever** as a pronoun or determiner to refer to anything or everything of a particular kind.

I went to the library and read whatever I could find about Robert Owen.
He volunteered to do whatever he could.
She had to rely on whatever books were lying around.

You can also use **whatever** to say that something is the case in all possible circumstances.

I have to bring my family back whatever happens.
Whatever brand you use, you will need four times as many teaspoonfuls as before.

used as an adverb

You use **whatever** after 'nothing' or after a noun group beginning with 'no' to emphasize that there is nothing of a particular kind.

He knew nothing whatever about it.
There is no scientific evidence whatever to support such a view.

used in
questions
When you are asking a question, you can use 'ever' after 'what' to express surprise.

What ever does it mean?

What ever is sometimes written **whatever**.

Whatever is the matter?
Whatever do you want to go up there for?

However, many people consider this form to be incorrect, and it is better to write **what ever** as two separate words.

GRAMMAR **'Wh'-clauses**

A **'wh'-clause** is a clause beginning with a **'wh'-word** such as 'who' or 'what', or with 'whether'. 'Wh'-clauses are used to refer to matters that are uncertain or about which a choice has to be made.

'Wh'-clauses are used after some verbs referring to speaking and thinking, for example in reported questions.

She wanted to know where you were.
She asked whether my baby had recovered.

See section on **reported questions** in entry at **Reporting**.

You can also use 'wh'-clauses after prepositions, and as the subject of verbs such as 'be', 'depend', and 'matter'.

The State is desperately uncertain about what it wants artists to do.
What you get depends on how badly you were injured.
Whether I went twice or not doesn't matter.

Structures consisting of a 'wh'-word plus a 'to'-infinitive clause, which refer to a possible course of action, are used after verbs and prepositions. However, they are not usually used as subjects.

He couldn't decide what to do.
They do not know how to make them.
...the problem of where to eat dinner.
The attendant on duty has instructions on how to act in these circumstances.

'Why' is not usually used in this kind of structure.

WARNING Note that 'if'-clauses, which are used for reported questions, cannot be used after prepositions or as the subject of a verb. For example, you can say 'Whether she likes it or not is irrelevant', but you cannot say 'If she likes it is irrelevant'.

---

when

used in
questions
You use **when** to ask about the time that something happened or will happen.

When did you arrive?
When are you getting married?
'I have to go to Germany.'—'When?'—'Now.'

used in time clauses	You use **when** in time clauses to say that something happened, happens, or will happen at a particular time.

He left school when he was eleven.
When I have free time, I always spend it fishing.

If you are talking about the future, you use the simple present tense in the time clause, not a future tense.

When you arrive in Britain, you will have to pass through immigration control.
Stop when you feel that your muscles have had enough.

'when' and 'if'	Do not confuse **when** with **if**. You use **if** to mention an event or situation that might happen. You use **when** to mention something that you expect to happen.

For example, if you say '**When** we buy a new car, you must come for a drive', you have decided that you are going to buy a new car. If you say '**If** we buy a new car, you must come for a drive', you are still undecided about whether or not to buy a car.

'when', 'as', and 'while'	If you want to say what was happening at the time that an event occurred, you can begin by saying what was happening, then add a clause beginning with **when**.

I was just going out when there was a knock at the door.
I was watching him go when Joey Morphy came into the alley.

You can also use **as** or **while** to say what was happening when an event occurred. However, when you use one of these words, you describe the event in the main clause and say what was happening in the clause beginning with **as** or **while**.

As I was walking one day in Hyde Park, I noticed two elderly ladies.
While I was standing outside Woolworth's, I saw Jeremy.

If you want to say that two events are continuing to happen at the same time, you usually use **while**.

What were you thinking about while I was getting the drinks?
I disliked the noise of football while I was working.

used in non-finite clauses	**When** is sometimes used in non-finite clauses – that is, in clauses containing an infinitive or participle, rather than a finite verb.

You can use a clause containing **when** and a 'to'-infinitive to report an order or instruction.

We are now being told much more specifically when not to enter a horse for a race.

In writing, people often use a clause containing **when** and a participle. For example, instead of writing 'I often read a book when I am travelling by train', they write 'I often read a book **when travelling by train**'.

Adults sometimes do not realize their own strength when dealing with children.
Two other important matters must be considered by anglers when deciding where to fish.

Similarly, instead of writing 'When he is interrupted, he gets very angry', someone might write '**When interrupted,** he gets very angry'.

Michael used to look hurt and surprised when scolded.

used with prepositional phrases and adjectives	In writing, **when** is sometimes not followed by a clause at all, but by a prepositional phrase or an adjective such as 'necessary' or 'possible'. For example, instead of writing 'When you are in Paris, you should visit the Louvre', you might write '**When in Paris,** you should visit the Louvre'.

When under threat, man reverts with terrifying ease to his primitive past.
She had spoken only when necessary.
Fresh yeast can be used when available.

used in relative clauses	**When** is often used in non-defining relative clauses.

I want to see you at 12 o'clock, when you go to lunch.
The Fleishers arrived on a Wednesday, when I was alone.

When can also be used in defining relative clauses after 'time' or after a word such as 'day' or 'year'.

There had been a time when she thought they were wonderful.
This is the year when the profits should start.

For information about defining and non-defining clauses, see entry at **Relative clauses.**

used with 'why'	**When** has a special use which is not related to time. You can add a clause beginning with **when** to a question which begins with 'why'. You do this as a way of expressing surprise or disagreement at something that someone has said. The 'when'-clause indicates the reason for your surprise or disagreement.

Why should he do me an injury when he has already saved my life?
Why worry her when it's all over?

whenever

used in time clauses	You use **whenever** in time clauses to say that something always happens or is always the case when something else happens or is the case.

Whenever she had a cold, she only ate fruit.
The pike will take any small fish whenever it is on the hunt.

If you are talking about the future, you use the simple present tense in the time clause, not a future tense.

Come and see me whenever you feel depressed.

Every time and **each time** can be used in a similar way to 'whenever'.

Every time I go to that class I panic.
He flinched each time she spoke.

used with 'possible'	You can use **whenever** with 'possible' instead of using a time clause. For example, instead of saying 'She met him whenever it was possible for her to meet him', you simply say 'She met him **whenever possible**'.

I avoided conflict whenever possible.
It paid to speak the truth whenever possible.

where

used in questions	You use **where** to ask questions about place or position.

Where's Jane?
Where does she live?
Where is the station?

You also use **where** to ask about the place that someone or something is coming from or going to.

Where does all this energy come from?
Where are you going?
Where do you want to fly to?

used in
place clauses

You use **where** in place clauses when you are talking about the place or position in which someone or something is.

He said he was happy where he was.
He left it where it lay.
...an official policy which encouraged people to stay where they were.

A place clause usually goes after the main clause. However, in stories, the place clause can be put first.

Where Kate had stood last night, Maureen now stood.
Where the pink cliffs rose out of the ground there were often narrow tracks winding upwards.

used in
reported
clauses

Where is often used in reported clauses.

I think I know where we are.
I asked someone where the cheapest accommodation was.

After some reporting verbs, **where** can be used in a non-finite clause containing a 'to'-infinitive.

How did you know where to find me?

For more information about this use, see entry at **Reporting**.

used in
relative clauses

Where is often used in non-defining relative clauses.

He came from Herne Bay, where Lally had once spent a holiday.
She carried them upstairs to the art room, where the brushes and paint had been set out.

Where can also be used in defining relative clauses after 'place' or after a word such as 'room' or 'street'.

...the place where they work.
...the room where I did my homework.
...the street where my grandmother had lived.

Where can also be used in defining clauses after words such as 'situation' and 'stage'.

Increasing poverty has led to a situation where the poor openly admit that they cannot afford to have children.
In time we reached a stage where we had more black readers than white ones.
I've reached the point where I'm about ready to retire.

For more information about defining and non-defining clauses, see entry at **Relative clauses**.

used with
'possible' and
'necessary'

Where is sometimes used in front of adjectives such as 'possible' and 'necessary'. When it is used like this, it has a similar meaning to 'when' or 'whenever'.

Where possible, prisoners with long sentences were put in the same blocks.
Help must be given where necessary.

wherever

used in
place clauses

You use **wherever** in place clauses to say that something happens or is the case in every place where something else happens or is the case.

Soft-stemmed herbs and ferns spread across the ground wherever there was enough light.
In Bali, wherever you go, you come across ceremonies.

Wherever I looked, I found patterns.

You can also use **wherever** to say that something is the case and that it does not matter what place is involved.

Wherever it is, you aren't going.

used with 'possible'

Wherever is sometimes used in front of adjectives such as 'possible' and 'practicable'. When it is used like this, it has a similar meaning to 'when' or 'whenever'.

All experts agree that, wherever possible, children should learn to read in their own way.

used in questions

When you are asking a question, you can use 'ever' after 'where' to express surprise.

Where ever did you get that hat?

Where ever is sometimes written **wherever**.

Wherever did you get this?
Wherever have you been?

However, many people consider this form to be incorrect, and it is better to write **where ever** as two separate words.

whether

Whether is used in reported clauses and conditional clauses.

used in reported clauses

You can use a clause beginning with **whether** after a reporting verb such as 'know', 'ask', or 'wonder'. You use **whether** when you are mentioning two or more alternatives. You put **whether** in front of the first alternative, and **or** in front of the second one.

I don't know whether he's in or out.
I was asked whether I wanted to stay at a hotel or at his home.

When the two alternatives are opposites, you do not need to mention both of them. For example, instead of saying 'I don't know whether he's in or out', you can simply say 'I don't know whether he's in'.

Lucy wondered whether Rita had been happy.
She didn't say whether he was still alive.
I asked Professor Fred Bailey whether he agreed.

'whether...or not'

You can also mention the second alternative using **or not**. You put **or not** either at the end of the sentence or immediately after **whether**.

I didn't know whether to believe him or not.
The barman didn't ask whether or not they were over eighteen.

'if'

If can be used instead of 'whether', especially when the second alternative is not mentioned.

I asked her if I could help her.
I rang up to see if I could get seats.

reporting uncertainty

If someone is uncertain about taking a particular course of action, or uncertain how to respond to a situation, you can report this using a clause consisting of **whether** and a 'to'-infinitive.

I've been wondering whether to retire.
He didn't know whether to feel glad or sorry at his dismissal.

used in conditional clauses

You can add a clause containing **whether** and **or not** to a sentence to indicate that something is true in any of the circumstances you mention.

He's going to buy a house whether he gets married or not.

Do not confuse **whether** with **weather,** which is pronounced the same way. If you say that it is raining, windy, hot, or cold, you are talking about the **weather.**

...the wet <u>weather</u> which persisted through the holiday.

See entry at **weather.**

which

Which is used as a determiner or a pronoun.

asking for information
You use **which** when you are asking for information about one of a limited number of things or people. A noun group beginning with **which** or consisting of the pronoun **which** can be the subject, object, or complement of a verb. It can also be the object of a preposition.

<u>Which mattress</u> is best?
<u>Which</u> came first?

<u>Which hotel</u> did you want?
<u>Which</u> do you fancy?

<u>Which one</u> is Brian Clough?
<u>Which</u> is her room?

<u>Which station</u> did you come from?
<u>Which</u> did you take it from?

Note that when the noun group is the object of a verb or preposition, you put an auxiliary verb after the object, followed by the subject and the main verb. Note also that when the noun group is the object of a preposition, the preposition usually goes at the end of the clause.

used in reported clauses
Which is often used in reported clauses.

Do you know <u>which country he played for?</u>
I don't know <u>which to believe.</u>

For more information about this use, see entry at **Reporting.**

used in relative clauses
Which is used as a relative pronoun in both defining and non-defining relative clauses. In relative clauses, **which** always refers to things, never to people.

Last week we heard about the awful conditions <u>which exist in British prisons.</u>
I'm teaching at the Selly Oak Centre, <u>which is just over the road.</u>

In relative clauses, you can use either **which** or **who** after a collective noun such as 'family', 'committee', or 'group'. After **which** you use a singular verb.

He is chairing a scientific group <u>which has</u> set itself the task of preventing liver cancer.

After **who** you use a plural verb.

There are a large group of people <u>who qualify</u> by reason of income and social habits.

WARNING
When **which** is the subject of a non-defining clause, you do not use another pronoun after it. You do not say, for example, 'He stared at the painting, which it was completely ruined'. You say 'He stared at the painting, **which** was completely ruined'.

For more information about relative clauses, see entry at **Relative clauses.**

whichever

Whichever is used as a determiner or a pronoun. It is used in two different ways.

You can use it to say that it does not matter which of a range of alternatives happens or is chosen.

The United States would be safe whichever side won.
Whichever way you look at it, neutrality is folly.
Then they have lunch, have a chat, have a sleep, whichever they like, up in the lounge.

You can also use **whichever** when you are indicating which of a range of things is the right one or the one you mean.

Use whichever soap powder is recommended by the manufacturer.
Use whichever of the forms is appropriate.

while

used in time clauses

If one thing happens **while** another thing is happening, the two things happen at the same time.

He stayed with me while Dad talked with Dr Leon.
While I was overseas she was in Maritzburg studying.

used in non-finite clauses

In writing, people often use a non-finite clause beginning with **while**. For example, instead of writing 'I often knit while I am watching television', they write 'I often knit **while watching** television'.

Mark watched us while pretending not to.
While crouched on the edge of the sofa, he had put his hands over his face.

used with prepositional phrases

In writing, **while** is sometimes not followed by a clause at all, but by a prepositional phrase. For example, instead of writing 'I heard the news while I was on holiday', you might write 'I heard the news **while on holiday**'.

He had read of her elopement while at Oxford.
They wanted a place to stay while in Paris.

'while' in concessive clauses

While has a special use which is not related to time. You use it to introduce a clause that contrasts with something else that you are saying.

Fred gambled his money away while Julia spent all hers on dresses.
While I have some sympathy for these fellows, I think they went too far.

'a while'

A while is a period of time.

After a while, my eyes became accustomed to the darkness.

See entry at **awhile - a while**.

whilst

Whilst is a formal word which has the same meaning as 'while'. It is used in both time clauses and concessive clauses.

Her sister had fallen whilst walking in her sleep at night.
Raspberries have a matt, spongy surface whilst blackberries have a taut, shiny skin.

You do not use **whilst** in conversation.

who - whom

Who and **whom** are pronouns.

<table>
<tr><td>asking for
information</td><td>You use **who** when you are asking about someone's identity. **Who** can be the subject, object, or complement of a verb. It can also be the object of a preposition.</td></tr>
</table>

asking for
information

You use **who** when you are asking about someone's identity. **Who** can be the subject, object, or complement of a verb. It can also be the object of a preposition.

Who invited you?
Who are you going to invite?
Who are you?
Who did you dance with?

Note that when **who** is the object of a verb or preposition, it is followed by an auxiliary verb, the subject, and then the main verb. Note also that when **who** is the object of a preposition, the preposition must go at the end of the clause. You do not use it in front of **who.**

Whom is a formal word which is sometimes used instead of 'who'. **Whom** can only be used as the object of a verb or preposition.

Whom shall we call?
By whom are they elected?

Note that when **whom** is the object of a preposition, the preposition must go in front of **whom.** You do not use it at the end of a clause.

used in
reported
clauses

Who is often used in reported clauses.

She didn't know who I was.
Have you found out who Hegel is yet?

For more information, see entry at **Reporting.**

used in
relative clauses

Who and **whom** are used in both defining and non-defining relative clauses.

He's the man who I saw last night.
Joe, who was always early, was there already.

...two girls whom I met in Edinburgh.
...Lord Scarman, for whom I have immense respect.

In relative clauses, you can use either **who** or **which** after a collective noun such as 'family', 'committee', or 'group'. After **who** you use a plural verb.

There are a large group of people who qualify by reason of income and social habits.

After **which** you use a singular verb.

He is chairing a scientific group which has set itself the task of preventing liver cancer.

WARNING

When **who** is the subject of a non-defining clause, you do not use another pronoun after it. You do not say, for example, 'He told his mother, who she was very shocked'. You say 'He told his mother, **who** was very shocked'.

whoever

You use **whoever** to refer to any person involved in the kind of situation you are describing.

If death occurs at home, whoever discovers the body should contact the family doctor.
...a person with written authority from whoever is dealing with the will.

You also use **whoever** to refer to someone whose identity you do not know.

Whoever answered the telephone was a very charming woman.

You also use **whoever** to say that the identity of someone will not affect a situation.

Whoever wins this civil war, there will be little rejoicing at the victory.
Whoever you vote for, prices will go on rising.

used in
questions
When you are asking a question, you can use 'ever' after 'who' to express surprise.

Who ever told you that?

Who ever is sometimes written **whoever.**

Whoever could that be at this time of night?

However, many people consider this form to be incorrect, and it is better to write **who ever** as two separate words.

whole

When you talk about **the whole of** something, you mean all of it.

...the whole of July.
...the whole of Europe.
The whole of the eyeball was visible.

Instead of using **the whole of** in front of a noun group beginning with 'the', you can simply use **whole** after 'the'. For example, instead of saying 'The whole of the house was on fire', you can say '**The whole house** was on fire'.

I spent the whole day in the Prado.
They're the best in the whole world.

You can use **whole** in a similar way after 'this', 'that', or a possessive.

I just want to say how sorry I am about this whole business.
I've never told this to anyone else in my whole life.

You use **whole** after 'a' to emphasize that you mean all of something of a particular kind.

I played Macbeth for a whole year.
You can easily devote a whole morning to it.

You can also use **whole** like this in front of the plural form of a noun.

There were whole speeches I did not understand.

Note that in front of plurals **whole** does not have the same meaning as **all.** If you say '**All** the buildings have been destroyed', you mean that every building has been destroyed. If you say '**Whole** buildings have been destroyed', you mean that some buildings have been destroyed completely.

'as a whole'
You use **as a whole** after a noun to emphasize that you are talking about all of something and regarding it as a single unit.

Is this true just in India, or in the world as a whole?
Roads are essential to a country as a whole.

'on the whole'
You add **on the whole** to a statement to indicate that what you are saying is only true in general and may not be true in every case.

One or two were all right, but on the whole I used to hate going to lectures.
I don't pretend that housework is fun because on the whole it isn't.

whom

See entry at **who - whom.**

whose

used in relative clauses

You use a noun group containing **whose** /huːz/ at the beginning of a relative clause to show who or what something belongs to or is connected with. **Whose** is used in both defining and non-defining clauses.

A noun group containing **whose** can be the subject or object of a verb, or the object of a preposition. When it is the object of a preposition, the preposition can come at the beginning or end of the clause.

...a woman whose husband had deserted her.
...Martin Browne, whose autobiography I have been reading.
...the governments in whose territories they operate.
...some strange fragment of thought whose origin I have no idea of.

It used to be considered incorrect to use **whose** to refer back to things rather than people. Learners used to be taught that you should use **of which** to refer to a thing, not 'whose'. For example, instead of saying 'a house whose windows were broken', learners were taught to say 'a house **the windows of which** were broken'.

I travelled in a lorry the back of which the owner had loaded with yams.

However, in modern English, it is acceptable to use either **whose** or **of which** to refer back to things.

used in questions

You use **whose** in questions when you are asking who something belongs to or is connected with. **Whose** can be used as a determiner or a pronoun.

Whose fault is it?
Whose babies do you think they were?
Whose is this?

used in reported clauses

Whose is also used in reported clauses.

It would be interesting to know whose idea it was.
Do you know whose fault it is?
The forecasts will not say whose house is about to be broken into.

For more information about reported clauses, see entry at **Reporting.**

WARNING

Note that 'who is' and 'who has' are also sometimes pronounced /huːz/. When you write down what someone says, you can write 'who is' or 'who has' as **who's.** You do not write them as 'whose'.

'Edward drove me here.'—'Who's Edward?'
...an American author who's settled in London.

GRAMMAR ## 'Wh'-words

'Wh'-words are a set of adverbs, pronouns, and determiners which all, with the exception of 'how', begin with 'wh'. They are:

- the adverbs 'how', 'when', 'where', and 'why'
- the pronouns 'who', 'whom', 'what', 'which', and 'whose'
- the determiners 'what', 'which', and 'whose'

'Wh'-words are used in questions.

Why are you smiling?

See entry at **Questions.**

They are also used in reported questions.

He asked me where I was going.

See entry at **Reporting**.

With the exception of 'how' and 'what', 'wh'-words can be used to begin relative clauses.

...nurses who have trained for two years.

'That' is also used to begin relative clauses, although it is not used for questions and reported questions. See entry at **Relative clauses**.

See entry at **'Wh'-clauses** for information on the use of 'wh'-words to begin clauses used as subjects and prepositional objects.

You will find information on how to use each 'wh'-word in the entry for that word.

why

used in questions

You use **why** when you are asking a question about the reason for something.

'I had to say no.'—'Why?'
Why did you do it, Martin?

used when no answer is expected

You sometimes use **why** in questions without expecting an answer. For example, you can make a suggestion by asking a question beginning with 'Why don't'.

Why don't we all go?
Why don't you write to her yourself?

You can emphasize that there is no reason for something to be done by asking a question beginning with 'Why should'.

Why should I be angry with you?
'Will you come?'—'No, why should I?'

You can emphasize that there is no reason why something should not be done by asking a question beginning with 'Why shouldn't'.

Why shouldn't he go to college?

You can suggest that an action is pointless by using **why** followed by an infinitive without 'to'.

Why ring the police? It wouldn't do any good.

used in reported clauses

Why is often used in reported clauses.

I knew why Solly had been killed.
He wondered why she had come.
Trevor Aldridge, an expert in housing law, told me why the clause was there.

Why can be used on its own instead of a reported clause, if it is clear what you mean. For example, instead of saying 'She doesn't like him. I don't know why she doesn't like him', you can say 'She doesn't like him, I don't know why'.

They won't call me David — I don't know why.
He's certainly cheerful, though I can't think why.

used in relative clauses

Why is used in defining relative clauses after the word 'reason'.

That is a major reason why they were such poor countries.
There are several good reasons why I have a freezer.

When you use 'the' in front of 'reason', you can use 'that' instead of **why** in the defining clause, or you can use no pronoun at all. For example, instead of saying 'the reason why I came', you can say 'the reason that I came' or 'the reason I came'.

...the reason that non-violence is considered to be a virtue.
That's the reason I'm checking it now.

wide - broad

Something that is **wide** or **broad** measures a large distance from one side to the other. You can say that something such as a street or river is **wide** or **broad**. **Wide** is more common in conversation.

There were no shops on this wide street.
The streets of this town are broad.

In front of them was a long, wide river.
He thought of the prisoners peering out at the broad river.

When you are talking about objects, you usually say that they are **wide**, rather than 'broad'.

...a wide bed.
Six men came stumbling out through a wide doorway.

When you are talking about people's physical characteristics, you usually use **broad,** rather than 'wide'.

He was tall, with broad shoulders.
...a broad, hefty Irish nurse.

widow - widower

'widow' You say that a woman is a **widow** when her husband has died and she has not married again.

I had been a widow for five years.

When a man has died, you can refer to his wife as **his widow.**

His savings had been left to his widow.
...Coretta Scott King, widow of Martin Luther King.

'widower' You say that a man is a **widower** when his wife has died and he has not married again.

Mr Starke, a widower, owned the practice.

However, when a woman has died, you do not refer to her husband as 'her widower'.

will

See entry at **shall - will.**

win

If you **win** a war, fight, game, or contest, you defeat your opponent. The past tense and past participle of 'win' is **won** /wʌn/, not 'winned'.

The Party won a convincing victory at the polls.
They had won a great victory.

'defeat' and   You do not say that someone 'wins' an enemy or opponent. In a war or
'beat' battle, you say that one side **defeats** the other.

The French defeated the English troops.

In a game or contest, you say that one person or side **defeats** or **beats** the other.

Hampstead defeated Bath 18-9.
They were playing draughts and she beat him.

wind

Wind is used as a noun or a verb.

used as a noun   The **wind** /wɪnd/ is a current of air moving across the earth's surface.

...an icy wind blowing clouds of snow.
...a leaf blown on the wind.

used as a verb   The verb **wind** /wɪnd/ is usually used in the passive. If you **are winded** by something such as a blow, the air is suddenly forced out of your lungs so that you have difficulty in breathing for a short time. The past tense and past participle of this verb is **winded.**

If you go too fast, you get winded.
I fell with a crash onto a sandy bank, winded but not hurt.

The verb **wind** /waɪnd/ has a completely different meaning. If a road or river **winds** in a particular direction, it goes in that direction with a lot of bends.

...the river winding between the mountains.

The past tense and past participle of this verb is **wound,** pronounced /waʊnd/.

The road wound through the desolate salt ranges.

You can also **wind** /waɪnd/ something round something else. For example, you can **wind** a wire round a stick. This means that you wrap the wire round the stick several times.

She started to wind the bandages around her arm.
He had a long green woollen scarf wound about his neck.

When you **wind** /waɪnd/ a watch or a clock, you turn a knob or handle several times in order to make the watch or clock operate.

Wound can also be pronounced /wuːnd/. When it is pronounced like this, it is a noun or a verb, and it has a completely different meaning. See entry at **wound.**

winter

Winter is the season between autumn and spring. In winter, the weather is cold.

It was a terrible winter.
...a dark winter's night.

If you want to say that something happens every year during this season, you say that it happens **in winter** or **in the winter.**

In winter, the Tower closes an hour earlier.
In the winter the pleasure boats cease.

You do not say that something happens 'in the winters'.

wire

A **wire** is a long, thin piece of metal used for fastening things, or for carrying electricity or electrical signals.

In American English, a **wire** is also a message sent by telegraph and then printed and delivered to your house or office.

'telegram' In British English, a message like this is usually called a **telegram**.

wish

Wish is used as a noun or a verb.

used as a noun A **wish** is a longing or desire for something, often something that is difficult to obtain or achieve.

She told me of her wish to leave the convent.
The wish for excitement led them to undertake a long and dangerous journey over mountains and deserts.

used as a verb When **wish** is used as a verb, it is usually followed by a 'that'-clause. If you **wish** that something was the case, you would like it to be the case, although you know it is unlikely or impossible.

I wish I lived nearer London.
They never have enough resources and they wish they had more.

Note that you use a past tense in the 'that'-clause, not a present tense. You do not say, for example, 'I wish I have more friends'. You say 'I wish **had** more friends'. Similarly, you do not say 'I wish I have sold my car'. You say 'I wish I **had sold** my car'.

I wish I had more time for it.
I wish I had asked her more about her stage career.
I envy you. I wish I was going away too.

When you are talking about the past, you use the same tense in the 'that'-clause that you would use if you were talking about the present. For example, you say 'She wished she **lived** in Tuscany' as well as 'She wishes she **lived** in Tuscany'.

The inspector wished he carried a gun.
He wished he had phoned for a cab.
There were some days when Johnnie wished that he was working for the Americans.

When the subject of the 'that'-clause is a singular pronoun such as 'I' or 'he' or a singular noun group, you can use either 'was' or 'were' after it. This use of 'were' is rather formal, especially in British English.

Sometimes, I wish I was back in Africa.
I often wish I were really wealthy.

He wished it was time for Lamin to return.
My sister occasionally wished that she were a boy.

You can also use 'could' in the 'that'-clause.

I wish I could mimic.
He wished he could believe her.

You can also use 'would' in the 'that'-clause. If you **wish** that something **would** happen, you want it to happen, and you are angry, worried, or frustrated because it has not happened already.

I wish he would come!
I wish she would explain it to me.

If you say to someone that you **wish** they **would** do something, you are indicating that you want them to do it, and you are annoyed or disappointed because they have not done it already.

I wish you would try to understand.
I wish you would get your facts right before you get into such a state.

You can also use a 'to'-infinitive after **wish**. If you **wish to do** something, you want to do it.

They are in love and wish to marry.
We do not wish to waste our money.

However, this is a formal use. The word you normally use is **want**.

I want to be an actress.
He doesn't want to get up.

You do not use **wish** with a 'that'-clause simply to express a wish for the future. You do not say, for example, 'I wish you'll have a nice time in Finland'. You say 'I **hope you'll have** a nice time in Finland' or 'I **hope you have** a nice time in Finland'.

I hope I'll see you before you go.
I hope you like this village.

However, you can sometimes express a wish for the future using **wish** as a transitive verb with two objects.

May I wish you luck in writing your book.
I wish you every possible happiness.
She shook hands with Alix and wished her a happy vacation.

with

If one person or thing is **with** another, they are together in one place.

I stayed with her until dusk.
He spent several seasons there with a man called Cartwright.
Put the knives with the other cutlery.

If you do something **with** a tool or object, you do it using that tool or object.

Clean mirrors with a mop.
He brushed back his hair with his hand.

used to mention an opponent
You use **with** after verbs like 'fight' or 'quarrel'. For example, if two people are fighting, you can say that one person is fighting **with** the other.

He was always fighting with his brother.
Judy was quarrelling with Bal.

Similarly, you can use **with** after nouns like 'fight' or 'quarrel'.

...my quarrel with Greenberg.
...a naval war with France.

used in descriptions
You can use **with** immediately after a noun group to mention a physical feature that someone or something has.

...an old man with a beard.
...an old house with steep stairs and dark corridors.

Note that you can use **with** like this to identify someone or something. For example, you can refer to someone as 'the tall man **with** red hair'.

...the man with the wart.
...that lovely cool bungalow with the purple creeper.

You do not usually use **with** to mention something that someone is wearing. Instead you use **in**.

...an old peasant woman in a black dress.
The bar was full of men in cloth caps.

For more information about this use, see entry at **wear**.

within

location   If you are **within** something, you are inside it or surrounded by it.

The prisoners demanded the freedom to congregate within the prison.
The central shrine was a huge copper dome within a railing.

This is a fairly formal use. Instead of 'within', you usually use **inside**.

Ibrahim waited inside the house for a few moments.
They've been sitting inside that green car ever since we came back from the restaurant.

See entry at **inside**.

limits   If something is **within** a particular limit, it does not go beyond that limit, or is not more than what is allowed.

Within these limitations there were a number of options open to me.
We must ask the schools to keep within their budget.

time   If something happens **within** a particular length of time, it happens before that length of time has passed.

Within six years a fifty-mile canal was cut.
The population doubled within a few hundred years.

'by'   Do not confuse **within** with **by**. If you do something **by** a particular time, you have done it at or before that time.

By two in the morning I had come to a conclusion.
By 8.05 the group were in position.

See entry at **by**.

without

If someone or something is **without** something, they do not have it.

She was without an ambition in the world.
...city slums without lights, roads or water.

If you do one thing **without** doing another thing, you do not do the second thing.

I could go out at night without disturbing anyone.
They drove into town without talking to each other.
'Goodbye, dear,' Mrs Saunders said, without looking up.

Note that in sentences like these you use an '-ing' form after **without**, not an infinitive. You do not say, for example, 'I could go out at night without to disturb anyone'.

woman - lady

You usually refer to an adult female person as a **woman** /wʊmən/.

...a tall, dark-eyed woman in a simple brown dress.

The plural of 'woman' is **women** /wɪmɪn/, not 'womans' or 'womens'.

There were men and women working in the fields.

You can use **lady** as a polite way of referring to a woman, especially if the woman is present.

...a rich American lady.
There is a Japanese lady here, looking for someone who looks like you.

Note that it is almost always better to refer to someone as an **old lady** or an **elderly lady,** rather than an 'old woman'.

There's an old lady who lives in Cameron Road just round the corner and I go and help her.
...elderly ladies living on their own.

If you are addressing a group of women, you call them **ladies,** not 'women'.

Ladies, could I have your attention, please?
Good evening, ladies and gentlemen.

used as modifiers

Woman and **lady** are sometimes used in front of other nouns.

...a woman politician.
...a lady novelist.

You use **women** in front of plural nouns, not 'woman'.

...women drivers.
...women candidates.

However, you use **lady** in front of plural nouns, not 'ladies'.

...lady traffic wardens.
The two most important lady guests were Karen Blixen and Edith Sitwell.

WARNING

Many women object to being referred to as 'lady doctors', 'lady teachers', etc. They prefer being referred to just as 'doctors' or 'teachers', but if it is necessary to indicate their sex, they usually prefer to be called **women doctors, women teachers,** and so on.

another use of 'lady'

In the past, a **lady** was a woman from the upper classes.

The lords and ladies are all gathered at the palace.
I rode in her carriage like a lady.

Lady is now hardly ever used with this meaning.

See also entries at **female - feminine - effeminate, girl,** and **Male and female.**

wonder

The verb **wonder** is usually used to say that someone thinks about something and tries to guess or understand more about it.

I keep wondering and worrying about what you said.

used with 'wh'-clauses

Wonder is often used with 'wh'-clauses.

I wonder what she'll look like.
I wonder which hotel it was.

used with 'if' and 'whether'

Wonder is also used with 'if' or 'whether'. If you **wonder if** something is the case, you think about it and try to decide whether it is the case.

He wondered if Dominic was going to give him a signal.
He was beginning to wonder whether Gertrude was there at all.

Note that you do not use a 'that'-clause in sentences like these. You do not say, for example, 'He wondered that Dominic was going to give him a signal'.

Wonder is sometimes used with 'if' to make an invitation. See section on **casual invitations** in entry at **Invitations.**

<table>
<tr><td>another
meaning
of 'wonder'</td><td>**Wonder** has another meaning. If you **wonder at** something, you are surprised and amazed about it. This use of **wonder** occurs mainly in writing.</td></tr>
</table>

I used to wonder at their slowness.

When **wonder** has this meaning, you can use a 'that'-clause after it.

I wondered that the porpoises had not long since gone away.

wood

used as an uncount noun	**Wood** is the material which forms the trunks and branches of trees, and which is used to make things such as furniture.

...a piece of wood.
The screws are very fine and won't split the wood.

Note that you do not refer to a piece of wood as 'a wood'.

'wooden'	You do not usually use 'wood' in front of a noun to say that something is made of wood. The word you use is **wooden.**

...a wooden box with instructions on the lid.
They were all sitting at a long wooden table.

'wood' used as a count noun	A **wood** is a large area of trees growing close to each other.

...the big wood where the pheasants lived.

People sometimes refer to a very large wood as **the woods**.

They walked through the woods towards the main house.

'forest'	An extremely large area of trees is called a **forest**.

They had their picnic in a clearing in the forest.
...Sherwood Forest.

wool - woollen - woolly

'wool'	**Wool** is the hair that grows on sheep and some other animals.

Wool is also the material made from weaving or knitting wool. It is used to make clothes, blankets, and carpets.

'woollen' and 'woolly'	**Wool, woollen,** and **woolly** can all be used in front of a noun to indicate that something is made from wool. Note that this use of **wool** is not common, and that **woolly** is not used in formal writing.

...a lovely light wool dress with a pattern of leaves.
...a simple blue woollen dress.
...long woollen socks.
...a woolly cap.

Woolly can also be used as a noun. A **woolly** is a jumper or cardigan.

She wore a long droopy woolly.
They sat round the fire muffled in their woollies.

In American English, **woollen** and **woolly** are spelled **woolen** and **wooly**.

She wore a heavy <u>woolen</u> shawl and a large bonnet.
...<u>wooly</u> underwear.

Words with alternative spellings

The following words can be spelled in two ways. The commonest spelling is given first.

acknowledgement - acknowledgment	granny - grannie
adrenalin - adrenaline	guerrilla - guerilla
adviser - advisor	gypsy - gipsy
ambience - ambiance	hiccup - hiccough
annex - annexe	hippie - hippy
artefact - artifact	hooray - hurray
balk - baulk	icon - ikon
banister - bannister	impostor - imposter
by-law - bye-law	inflection - inflexion
caffeine - caffein	jibe - gibe
carcass - carcase	judgement - judgment
castor - caster	kilogram - kilogramme
caviar - caviare	likeable - likable
chaperone - chaperon	liquorice - licorice
chilli - chili	mackintosh - macintosh
cipher - cypher	mantelpiece - mantlepiece
conjurer - conjuror	milligram - milligramme
connection - connexion	movable - moveable
curtsy - curtsey	Muslim - Moslem
dexterous - dextrous	nosy - nosey
dispatch - despatch	OK - okay
douse - dowse	phoney - phony
duffel coat - duffle coat	saccharine - saccharin
dyke - dike	sheikh - sheik
forego - forgo	siphon - syphon
gram - gramme	swap - swop
grandad - granddad	veranda - verandah

'Racket' can be spelled 'racquet' when used to refer to a bat with strings which is used for playing a game such as tennis or squash.

Two words have alternative spellings in British English only:

jail — gaol
wagon — waggon

In American English, the spellings 'jail' and 'wagon' are used.

Two words have three possible spellings:

hello — hallo — hullo
yoghurt — yoghourt — yogurt

'-ise' and '-ize'   Many verbs can end in either '-ise' or '-ize'. For information on this, see section on '-ise' and '-ize' in entry at **Spelling**.

For information on differences between British and American spellings, see entry at **Spelling**.

Words with the same pronunciation

There are many words in English that are pronounced the same but spelled differently. The following pairs of words are explained at separate entries in this book because they are often confused:

bass - base	draught - draft
bear - bare	fair - fare
born - borne	here - hear
break - brake	pore - pour
cereal - serial	principal - principle
chord - cord	role - roll
complement - compliment	sow - sew
council - counsel	stationary - stationery
curb - kerb	there - their
currant - current	waist - waste
die - dye	whether - weather

The entries are usually at the pairs of words given above, but see entries at **there** and **whether** for information about words pronounced like these words.

Note that 'paw' is pronounced the same as 'pore' and 'pour', and 'poor' is also often pronounced the same. 'So' is pronounced the same as 'sew' and 'sow'.

There are many other pairs of words with the same pronunciation. Some of the commonest ones are listed below.

altar - alter	hair - hare	none - nun
berry - bury	hangar - hanger	one - won
blew - blue	heal - heel	packed - pact
boar - bore	heard - herd	pain - pane
bough - bow	heroin - heroine	peace - piece
bread - bred	hoarse - horse	peal - peel
bridal - bridle	hole - whole	pedal - peddle
caught - court	key - quay	peer - pier
cell - sell	knead - need	place - plaice
coarse - course	knew - new	plain - plane
core - corps	knight - night	pole - poll
creak - creek	knot - not	pray - prey
cue - queue	know - no	profit - prophet
cymbal - symbol	lain - lane	raise - raze
dear - deer	leak - leek	rap - wrap
dew - due	lessen - lesson	raw - roar
earn - urn	loan - lone	retch - wretch
feat - feet	made - maid	ring - wring
fir - fur	mail - male	road - rode
flaw - floor	main - mane	root - route
flea - flee	maize - maze	sail - sale
flour - flower	medal - meddle	sauce - source
fort - fought	miner - minor	scene - seen
foul - fowl	moan - mown	sea - see
gorilla - guerrilla	morning - mourning	seam - seem
grate - great	naval - navel	shear - sheer

sole - soul	tail - tale	wait - weight
some - sum	tear - tier	war - wore
son - sun	threw - through	warn - worn
stair - stare	throne - thrown	way - weigh
stake - steak	toe - tow	weak - week
stalk - stork	too - two	which - witch
steal - steel	vain - vein	whine - wine
storey - story	wail - whale	

Note that the verb 'read' has the same pronunciation as 'reed', but its past form, also spelled 'read', has the same pronunciation as 'red'.

The noun 'lead' has the same pronunciation as 'led', the past form of the verb 'lead'.

There are also the following groups of words which are pronounced the same:

awe - oar - ore	flew - flu - flue	rain - reign - rein
buy - by - bye	meat - meet - mete	rite - right - write
cent - scent - sent	pair - pare - pear	saw - soar - sore
cite - sight - site	peak - peek - pique	ware - wear - where

Words with two pronunciations

different meanings

Several words have different pronunciations when they are used with different meanings or in different ways.

Some of these words are explained in other entries. See entries at **lead, read, use - used - used to, wind,** and **wound.** See entry at **old** for a note on the pronunciation of 'aged'.

The following words also have different pronunciations for different meanings:

● 'Bow' is pronounced /baʊ/ when it is used as a verb or a noun to refer to the act of bending your body. It is also pronounced /baʊ/ when it refers to the front of a boat.

We bowed to one another across the room.
He made a little bow and closed the door.
Soon the canoe was cutting through the water with froth curling at her bow.

'Bow' is pronounced /bəʊ/ when it refers to a looped knot, a weapon, or the object drawn across the strings of a musical instrument.

He tied a neat bow.
Then she picked up her bow and positioned her cello.

● 'Buffet' is pronounced /bʊfeɪ/ or /bʌfeɪ/ when it refers to a meal.

Ruth's got a cold buffet for us later.

It is pronounced /bʌfɪt/ when it means 'to push something violently'.

We splashed back to the jeep, buffeted by the wind.

● 'Contract' is pronounced /kɒntrækt/ when it is used to refer to a legal agreement.

795

I did not sign a contract with them.

It is pronounced /kəntrækt/ when it means 'to become smaller'.

Metals expand with heat and contract with cold.

● 'Recess' is pronounced /rɪses/ when it refers to a break from working.

The judge announced a five-minute recess.

It is pronounced /riːses/ when it refers to an area in a room that is set back or hidden.

The bed is in a recess.

● 'Relay' is pronounced /riːleɪ/ when it refers to a race or when it means 'to send on television or radio signals'.

They came second in the 4x100 metres relay.
The dense cloud prevented the BBC from using a helicopter to relay pictures of the event.

It is pronounced /rɪleɪ/ when it means 'to pass on something that was said'.

I have been asked to relay to you a number of messages.

● 'Row' is pronounced /rəʊ/ when it refers to a group of things in a line, or when it means 'to move a boat using oars'.

...a row of parked cars.
He began to row steadily out towards the middle of the river.

It is pronounced /raʊ/ when it refers to a quarrel or a great deal of noise.

She took an overdose after a row with her mother.

● 'Second' is pronounced /sekənd/ when it refers to part of a minute, when it is used as an ordinal, or when it means 'to formally support a proposal'.

Could I see your book for a second?
...at the top of the second flight of stairs.
I'll second that proposal.

It is pronounced /sɪkɒnd/ when it means 'to move someone temporarily to perform special duties'.

I am being seconded abroad for two years.

● 'Sow' is pronounced /səʊ/ when it means 'to plant seeds'.

You can sow winter wheat in October.

It is pronounced /saʊ/ when it refers to a female pig.

● 'Tear' is pronounced /tɪə/ when it refers to a drop of liquid produced when you cry.

A single tear rolls slowly down his cheek.

It is pronounced /teə/ when used with other meanings, for example when it means 'to pull cloth or paper apart' or 'to run somewhere very fast'.

She folded the letter, meaning to tear it up.
I used to tear up the ladder onto the stage with only seconds to spare.

different word classes Many words have different pronunciations for different word classes – for example they are always pronounced in one way when they are used as a noun and always pronounced in a different way when they are used as a verb. Various groups of words which have different pronunciations for different word classes are explained below.

different stress A number of words have stress on the first syllable when they are used as a noun or adjective and stress on the second syllable when they are used as a verb. For example, 'record' is pronounced /rekɔːd/ when used as a noun or adjective and /rɪkɔːd/ when used as a verb. 'Contest' is pronounced /kɒntest/ when used as a noun and /kəntest/ when used as a verb.

The following words have this pronunciation pattern:

abstract	converse	extract	perfect	redress
accent	convert	ferment	permit	refund
ally	convict	fragment	pervert	reject
combine	defect	frequent	present	relapse
compound	desert	implant	produce	reprint
conduct	dictate	import	progress	subject
conflict	discharge	imprint	project	survey
conscript	discount	incense	prospect	suspect
console	dispute	incline	prostrate	torment
consort	entrance	increase	protest	transfer
construct	escort	insult	rebel	transplant
contest	exploit	intrigue	record	transport
contrast	export	object	recount	

Similarly, the verb 'confine' is pronounced /kənfaɪn/ and the noun 'confines' is pronounced /kɒnfaɪnz/. The verb 'proceed' is pronounced /prəsiːd/ and the noun 'proceeds' is pronounced /prəusiːdz/. 'Compact' is pronounced /kəmpækt/ when used as a verb and /kɒmpækt/ or /kəmpækt/ when used as an adjective.

'-ate' A number of words have their last syllable pronounced /ət/ when they are used as an adjective or a noun and /eɪt/ when they are used as a verb. For example, 'delegate' is pronounced /delɪgət/ when used as a noun and /delɪgeɪt/ when used as a verb.

The following words have this pronunciation pattern:

advocate	associate	deliberate	estimate	moderate
appropriate	consummate	designate	graduate	separate
approximate	degenerate	duplicate	initiate	subordinate
articulate	delegate	elaborate	intimate	

Note that in the case of 'alternate', there is a stress change too: it is pronounced /ɒltɜːnət/ when used as an adjective and /ɒltəneɪt/ when used as a verb.

'-se' 'Use' is pronounced /juːz/ when used as a verb and /juːs/ when used as a noun. The same applies to the last syllable of 'abuse', 'excuse', and 'misuse'. Similarly, 'diffuse' is pronounced /dɪfjuːz/ when used as a verb and /dɪfjuːs/ when used as an adjective.

Note that 'refuse' is pronounced /rɪfjuːz/ when used as a verb and /refjuːs/ when used as a noun.

'Close' is pronounced /kləuz/ when used as a verb and /kləus/ when used as an adjective or adverb.

'House' is pronounced /haus/ when used as a singular noun and /hauz/ when used as a verb. The plural of the noun is pronounced /hauzɪz/.

<table>
<tr><td>

other pronunciations

</td><td>

'Attribute' is pronounced /ətrɪbju:t/ when used as a verb and /ætrɪbju:t/ when used as a noun.

'Content' is pronounced /kɒntent/ when used as a noun and /kəntent/ when used as an adjective or verb.

'Excess' is pronounced /ekses/ when used as an adjective and /ɪkses/ or /ekses/ when used as a noun.

'Implement' is pronounced /ɪmplɪment/ when used as a verb and /ɪmplɪmənt/ when used as a noun.

'Invalid' is pronounced /ɪnvəli:d/ when used as a noun or modifier and /ɪnvælɪd/ when used as an adjective.

'Live' is pronounced /lɪv/ when used as a verb and /laɪv/ when used as an adjective or adverb. 'Lives' is pronounced /laɪvz/ when used as the plural of the noun 'life' and /lɪvz/ when used as the '-s' form of the verb 'live'.

'Minute' is pronounced /mɪnɪt/ when used as a noun and /maɪnju:t/ when used as an adjective.

'Mouth' is pronounced /maʊθ/ when used as a singular noun and /maʊð/ when used as a verb. The plural of the noun is pronounced /maʊðz/.

'Overall' is pronounced /əʊvərɔ:l/ when used as an adjective or adverb and /əʊvərɔ:l/ when used as a noun.

'Overflow' is pronounced /əʊvəfləʊ/ when used as a verb and /əʊvəfləʊ/ when used as a noun. Similarly, 'overlap' is pronounced /əʊvəlæp/ when used as a verb and /əʊvəlæp/ when used as a noun, and 'overthrow' is pronounced /əʊvəθrəʊ/ when used as a verb and /əʊvəθrəʊ/ when used as a noun.

'Overhead' is pronounced /əʊvəhed/ when used as an adjective and /əʊvəhed/ when used as an adverb. The noun 'overheads' is pronounced /əʊvəhedz/.

'Underground' is pronounced /ʌndəɡraʊnd/ when used as an adverb and /ʌndəɡraʊnd/ when used as an adjective or noun.

'Upset' is pronounced /ʌpset/ when used as a verb or as an adjective after a verb. It is pronounced /ʌpset/ when used as a noun or as an adjective in front of a noun.

</td></tr>
</table>

work

Work is used as a verb or a noun.

<table>
<tr><td>

used as a verb

</td><td>

People who **work** have a job which they are paid to do.

I'm not working any more.
I used to work in a hotel.

You can use 'as' with **work** to say what a person's job is.

Pam works as a careers officer.

</td></tr>
<tr><td>

used as an uncount noun

</td><td>

If you have **work**, you have a job which you are paid to do.

...people who can't find work.
...different types of work.

When someone has a job, you can say that they are **in work**.

...ways of allowing people to remain in work.

When someone does not have a job, you can say that they are **out of work**.

</td></tr>
</table>

There are one and a half million people <u>out of work</u> in this country.

Work is also used to talk about the place where someone works. When **work** has this meaning, you do not use a determiner in front of it.

He too drives to <u>work</u> by car.
I can't leave <u>work</u> till five.

'works'
A place where things are made is sometimes called a **works.** For more information, see entry at **factory.**

nouns with a
similar meaning
The following nouns all refer generally to activities which people are paid to do:

business	job	position	profession
employment	occupation	post	trade

'employment'
Employment is a formal word with a similar meaning to 'work'. Like 'work', it is an uncount noun.

Of those who had paid jobs, perhaps only half were in full-time <u>employment</u>.
There is no hope of regular <u>employment</u> as an agricultural labourer.

Employment is also used to talk about the number of people in a country or area who have jobs.

...the government's commitment to full <u>employment</u>.
Only 18 per cent thought <u>employment</u> would rise over the next year.

'job'
A person's **job** is a particular set of duties which they are paid to do. **Job** is a count noun.

Her mother had a cleaning <u>job</u>.
When you are settled in your new <u>job</u>, invite some of your old friends out to lunch.

For another meaning of **job,** see below.

'position'
and 'post'
In formal English, **position** and **post** are used instead of 'job'. When a job is advertised, it is often described as a **position** or **post.** A person applying for a job usually uses one of these words.

He had left Birmingham suddenly to fly back to London, having resigned his <u>position</u>.
Today the Foreign Ministry announced that the Ambassador to Cuba is retiring from his <u>post</u>.

'occupation'
Your **occupation** is your job. **Occupation** is often used on official forms.

The Judge asked his <u>occupation</u>. 'Security consultant,' he replied.
...men preparing to switch to a new <u>occupation</u>.

Note that if you are asked to write your occupation on a form, you can put 'student', 'housewife', 'unemployed', or 'retired' if you do not have a paid job.

'profession'
and 'trade'
Profession and **trade** are both used to refer to types of job which require special training.

A **profession** is a type of job which requires formal training and which has fairly high status, for example the job of a doctor, teacher, or lawyer.

Both her parents had been school teachers and after college she entered the same <u>profession</u>.

You can also use **profession** to refer to all the people in a particular profession. For example, you can talk about 'the teaching **profession**' or 'the medical **profession**'.

There would be an outcry from the legal profession if these proposals were seriously put forward.

A **trade** is a type of skilled job, usually one which involves making or repairing something.

I learned a trade, began to work, worked hard and earned money.
He was the son of a newspaperman and he never thought there was any other trade to follow.

You also use **trade** to refer to work that involves buying and selling things, or catering for tourists.

...the effect such an arrangement would have on Britain's hugely successful art trade.
The absence of a tourist trade will bring more economic hardships.

'business'   **Business** is used to refer to work that involves making, buying, or selling things.

You were in the film business?
You'd better go into the oil business or become a banker.

another meaning of 'job'   **Job** has another meaning. You can use it to refer to one particular thing that needs to be done.

It will be a long job, I'm afraid.
It's always better to concentrate on the job in hand.

'piece of work' and 'task'   You can also call this a **piece of work**. If it is difficult or unpleasant, you can call it a **task**. **Task** is a fairly formal word.

...a means of doing an essential piece of work.
The first task is to raise educational levels.

worse

Worse is the comparative form of 'bad' and the usual comparative form of 'badly'. See entry at **bad - badly**.

worst

Worst is the superlative form of 'bad' and the usual superlative form of 'badly'. See entry at **bad - badly**.

worth

Worth is used as a preposition or a noun.

used as a preposition   If something is **worth** an amount of money, that is the amount you would get for it if you sold it.

His yacht is worth $1.7 million.
...a two-bedroom house worth $550,000.

Note that **worth** is not a verb. You do not say 'His yacht worths $1.7 million'.

used as a noun   You use **worth** as a noun after words like 'pounds' or 'dollars' to indicate how much money you would get for an amount of something if you sold it.

...about fifty pence worth of chocolate.
...12 million pounds worth of gold and jewels.

You do not talk about the 'worth' of something that someone owns. You do not say, for example, 'The worth of his house has greatly increased'. You say 'The **value** of his house has greatly increased'.

What will happen to the value of my property?
The value of the horse is now in excess of £500,000.

worthless

See entry at **invaluable**.

would

Would is a modal. It is used in a number of different ways.

When **would** comes after a pronoun, it is not usually pronounced in full. When you write down what someone says, you represent 'would' as **'d** and add it to the end of the pronoun.

Would has the negative form **would not**. The 'not' is not usually pronounced in full. When you write down what someone says, you usually write **wouldn't**.

'should' **Would** is sometimes used with a similar meaning to 'should'. For an explanation of this use, see entry at **should - would**.

The following are some other ways in which you can use **would**. You cannot use 'should' in any of these ways.

talking about You can use **would** to talk about something which happened regularly in
the past the past but which no longer happens.

We would normally spend the winter in Miami.
She would often hear him grumbling.

Note that **used to** is used in a similar way.

She used to get quite cross with Lally.
In the afternoons, I used to hide and read.

However, **used to** can also be used to talk about states and situations that existed in the past but no longer exist. You cannot use **would** like this.

I'm not quite as sure as I used to be.

You use **would have** to talk about actions and events that were possible in the past, although they did not in fact happen.

Denial would have been useless.
I would have said yes, but Julie talked us into staying at home.

When **would not** is used to talk about something that happened in the past, it has a special meaning. It is used to say that someone was unwilling to do something, or refused to do something.

They just would not believe what we told them.

Would is sometimes used in stories to talk about someone's thoughts about the future.

He thought to himself how wonderful it would taste.
They would reach the castle some time.

used in You use **would** in a conditional sentence when you are talking about a
conditional situation which you know does not exist. You use **would** in the main
sentences clause; in the conditional clause, you use the simple past tense, the past
continuous tense, or 'could'.

If I had enough money, I would buy the car.

If he was coming, he would ring.
If I could afford it, I would buy a boat.

You do not use **would** in the conditional clause in sentences like these. You do not say, for example, 'If I would have enough money, I would buy the car'.

When you are talking about the past, you use **would have** in a conditional sentence to mention an event that might have happened but did not in fact happen. In this kind of sentence, you use the past perfect tense in the conditional clause and **would have** in the main clause.

Perhaps if he had realized, he would have run away while there was still time.
If she had not married, she would probably have become something special in her field.

used in reported clauses

Would is also used in reported clauses.

He asked if I would answer some questions.
He made me promise that I would never break the law.
I felt confident that everything would be all right.

For more information about this use, see entry at **Reporting**.

requests, orders, and instructions

You can use **would** to make a request.

Would you do me a favour?

You can also use **would** to give an order or instruction.

Put the light on, Bryan, would you?
Would you ask them to leave, please?

For more information about these uses, see entry at **Requests, orders, and instructions**.

offers and invitations

You can say '**Would you...?**' when you are offering something to someone, or making an invitation.

Would you like a drink?
Would you care to stay with us?

For more information about these uses, see entries at **Offers** and **Invitations**.

wound

Wound is pronounced /waʊnd/ or /wuːnd/.

When it is pronounced /waʊnd/, it is a past tense and past participle of the verb 'wind'. See entry at **wind**.

When **wound** is pronounced /wuːnd/, it is a noun or a verb.

used as a noun

A **wound** is damage to part of your body, caused by a gun, knife, or other weapon.

...a soldier with a leg wound.
Raising the gun, as if oblivious of his wound, he fired twice.

used as a verb

If someone **wounds** you, they damage your body using a weapon.

He had been badly wounded in the fighting.
He was wounded in the leg.

'injury' Note that when someone is hurt in an accident, such as a car crash or a natural disaster, you do not say that they receive a 'wound' or that they 'are wounded'. You say that they receive an **injury** or **are injured.**

A fall on the head is a common injury for a baby.
A 74-year-old man was killed and five other people were injured when three cars crashed on the A21 near Tonbridge.

See entry at **injure.**

write

When you **write** something or **write** it **down,** you use a pen or pencil to make words, letters, or numbers on a surface. The past tense of 'write' is **wrote.** The past participle is **written.**

I wrote down what the boy said.
...the page on which the words are written.

writing a letter When you **write** a letter to someone, you write information or other things in a letter and send it to the person. When you use **write** like this, it has two objects. If the indirect object is a pronoun, it usually goes in front of the direct object.

We wrote them a threatening letter.
I wrote him a very nice letter.

If the indirect object is not a pronoun, it usually goes after the direct object. When this happens, you put 'to' in front of the indirect object.

He wrote a letter to his brother in England.
Once a week, on Tuesdays, she wrote a letter to her husband.

You can also omit the direct object. If you **write to** someone, you write a letter to them.

She wrote to me last summer.
I wrote to Kettles and we arranged a number of successful meetings.

American speakers often omit the 'to'.

If there is anything you want, write me.
I had a letter from a friend. He wrote me I'd better be careful in Russia.

You can write '**I am writing...**' at the beginning of a letter to introduce the topic you are writing about.

Dear Morris, I am writing to ask whether you would care to come and visit us during the Easter vacation.

Note that you do not write 'I write to ask...'.

Y

yard

The noun **yard** has two main meanings.

measurement   A **yard** is a unit of length in the imperial system of measurement. It is equal to thirty-six inches, or approximately 91.4 centimetres.

Jack was standing under a tree abut ten yards away.

Note that in Britain it is becoming more common to give measurements in metres, rather than yards.

See also entry at **Measurements.**

area behind a house   In both British and American English, a **yard** or **back yard** is an area of ground behind a house. In British English, it is a small area with a hard surface and usually a wall round it. In American English, it is a fairly large area, usually with grass growing on it. In British English, a fairly large area like this is called a **garden** or **back garden.**

year

A **year** is a period of 365 or 366 days, especially one beginning on the first day of January and ending on the last day of December.

...at the end of next year.
...in the year 2000.

You can use **year** when you are mentioning the age of a person or thing.

She is now seventy-four years old.
A friend of mine has just bought a house which is about 300 years old.

When you use **year** to talk about age, you must use 'old' after it. You do not say, for example, 'She is now seventy-four years'.

See also entries at **Age** and **old.**

yes

You use **yes** to agree with someone, to say that something is true, or to accept something.

'They are more likely to be swayed by eloquent arguments than the judge is.'—'Yes, of course they are.'
'Is that true?'—'Yes.'
'Tea?'—'Yes, thanks.'

WARNING   When someone asks a negative question, you must say **yes** if you want to give a positive answer. For example, if someone says 'Aren't you going out this evening?', you say '**Yes**, I am'. You do not say 'No, I am'. Similarly, if someone says 'Haven't you met John?', you say, '**Yes**, I have'. You do not say 'No, I have'.

'Haven't you any socks or anything with you?'—'Yes, in that suitcase.'
'Didn't you get a dictionary from him?'—'Yes, I did.'

Similarly, you say **yes** if you want to disagree with a negative statement. For example, if someone says 'He doesn't want to come', you can say '**Yes**, he does'. You do not say 'No, he does'.

'That isn't true.'—'Oh yes, it is.'

yesterday

Yesterday means the day before today.

It was hot yesterday.
We spent yesterday in Glasgow.

You refer to the morning and afternoon of the day before today as **yesterday morning** and **yesterday afternoon.**

Yesterday morning there were more than 1500 boats waiting in the harbour for the weather to improve.
We circulated printed copies to other London newspapers yesterday afternoon.

You can also talk about **yesterday evening,** but it is more common to refer to the previous evening as **last night.**

I met your husband last night.
I've been thinking about what we said last night.

You can also use **last night** to refer to the previous night.

We left our bedroom window open last night.

You do not talk about 'yesterday night'.

another meaning   In writing, **yesterday** is sometimes used to refer to the past, especially the recent past.

The worker of today is different from the worker of yesterday.

yet

used in negative sentences   You use **yet** in negative sentences to say that something has not happened up to the present time. In conversation, you usually put **yet** at the end of a clause.

It isn't dark yet.
I haven't decided yet.

In writing, you can put **yet** immediately after 'not'.

Computer technology has not yet reached its peak.
The city had not yet been bombed.

'have yet to'   Instead of saying that something 'has not yet happened', you can say that it **has yet to happen.** People often use this structure to indicate that they do not expect something to happen.

I have yet to meet a man I can trust.
A just, ordered society without a bureaucracy has yet to be established.

used in questions   You often use **yet** in questions when you are asking if something has happened. You put **yet** at the end of the clause.

Have you done that yet?
Have you had your lunch yet?

Note that some American speakers use the simple past tense in questions like these. They say, for example, '**Did** you **have** your lunch yet?'

'already'   Do not confuse **yet** with **already.** You use **already** at the end of a question to express surprise that something has happened sooner than expected.

Is he down there already?
You mean you've been there already?

See entry at **already.**

'still' You do not use **yet** to say that something is continuing to happen. You do not say, for example, 'I am yet waiting for my luggage'. The word you use is **still**.

He still doesn't understand.
Her body was still curled up.

See entry at **still**.

'just yet' If you do not intend to do something **just yet,** you do not intend to do it immediately.

It is too risky to announce an increase in our charges just yet.
There may be other reasons not to panic just yet.

you

You use **you** to refer to the person or people that you are speaking or writing to. **You** can be the subject or object of a verb, or the object of a preposition.

Have you got any money?
I have nothing to give you.
I want to come with you.

You can also be used to refer to people in general, rather than to a particular person or group. **You** is often used like this in this book. For more information, see entry at **one**.

your

You use **your** /jə/ or /jɔː/ to indicate that something belongs or relates to the person or people that you are speaking to.

…your books.
Where's your father?

'you're' Note that 'you are' is also sometimes pronounced /jɔː/. When you write down what someone says, you write this as **you're**. You do not write it as 'your'.

You're quite right.
You're not an expert.

yourself - yourselves

When 'you' is the subject of a verb and refers to one person, you use **yourself** as the object of the verb or of a preposition in the clause to refer to the same person.

Are you feeding yourself properly?
You might be making a fool of yourself.

When 'you' refers to more than one person, you use **yourselves** as the object of the verb or preposition.

I hope you both behaved yourselves.
Don't you boys ever think for yourselves?

Yourself and **yourselves** are often used in imperative structures.

Control yourself.
Please help yourselves to another drink.

<table>
<tr><td>used for
emphasis</td><td>**Yourself** and **yourselves** can also be used to emphasize the subject of a clause.</td></tr>
</table>

You don't even know it yourself.
Racialism is what you yourselves are causing and promoting.

If you do something **yourself,** you do it without any help from anyone else.

You didn't do this yourself, did you?

youth

<table>
<tr><td>used as an
uncount noun</td><td>Someone's **youth** is the period of their life when they are a child or an adolescent.</td></tr>
</table>

We change and learn from youth to old age.

When **youth** has this meaning, it is an uncount noun. You use a singular form of verb with it.

Youth has always been the time for rebellion.

<table>
<tr><td>used as a
count noun</td><td>A **youth** is a boy or a young man, especially a teenager. This use occurs mainly in writing.</td></tr>
</table>

The road was occupied by a long line of youths and young girls carrying black flags.

<table>
<tr><td>used as a
plural noun</td><td>**The youth of** a place or country are the young people there. This is a formal use.</td></tr>
</table>

...the youth of America.

You can also talk about **the youth of** a particular period.

...the youth of today.

When **youth** has either of these meanings, it is a plural noun. You use a plural form of a verb with it.

The youth of the country are too often uncouth, unfit, and uncivilised.
The youth of the Nineties are seeing splits and social divisions opening up before them.

Z

z

The letter 'z' is called **zed** /zed/ in British English and **zee** /ziː/ in American English.

zero

Zero is the number 0. American speakers use **zero** in both conversation and writing.

Why are we so crazy about getting the thing down to zero?
There we stood, five men holding infants between zero and three.

In British English, **zero** is normally used only in scientific writing.

The path coefficient is now greater than zero.

The gravitational pull would grow weaker until we reached the very centre of the planet, when it would be zero.

In conversation, British speakers usually say **nought** or **oh**.

...nought point nine.
...linguistic development between the ages of nought and one.
You arrive at Palma at oh two thirty-five.

For more information about these uses, see section on **zero** in entry at **Numbers and fractions**.